Fodor's

MAINE, VERMONT & NEW HAMPSHIRE

Excerpted from Fodor's New England.

WELCOME TO MAINE, VERMONT, AND NEW HAMPSHIRE

Maine, Vermont, and New Hampshire are iconic New England, with the quaint towns, brilliant fall foliage, and picturesque landscapes the region is famous for. It's easy to enjoy the outdoors by hiking a section of the Appalachian Trail, skiing the Green Mountains, or taking a scenic drive in Acadia National Park. Shopping for antiques or browsing at a farmers' market are equally inviting pastimes. Smaller cities offer their own pleasures: boutiques and galleries, dockside lobster shacks, and Colonial architecture. All these charms keep visitors coming back.

TOP REASONS TO GO

★ **Fall Foliage:** Leaf peepers gather for the country's best festival of colors.

★ **Regional Food:** Vermont maple syrup and cheese, Maine lobster and blueberries.

★ **Outdoor Fun:** Hiking, boating, biking, or simply taking in a magnificent view.

★ **Small Towns:** A perfect day includes strolling a town green and locavore dining.

★ **Fantastic Skiing:** All three states have wonderful winter retreats with superb slopes.

★ **The Coast:** Iconic lighthouses and harbors, plus whale-watching and sailing.

Fodor's MAINE, VERMONT & NEW HAMPSHIRE

Design: Tina Malaney, *Associate Art Director*; Erica Cuoco, *Production Designer*

Photography: Jennifer Arnow, *Senior Photo Editor*

Maps: Rebecca Baer, *Senior Map Editor*; Mark Stroud (Moon Street Cartography) and David Lindroth, *Cartographers*

Production: Angela L. McLean, *Senior Production Manager*; Jennifer DePrima, *Editorial Production Manager*

Sales: Jacqueline Lebow, *Sales Director*

Business & Operations: Chuck Hoover, *Chief Marketing Officer*; Joy Lai, *Vice President and General Manager*; Stephen Horowitz, *Head of Business Development and Partnerships*

Writers: Grace-Yvette Gemmell, Debbie Hagan, Kim MacKinnon, Mary Ruoff, Aaron Starmer

Editor: Salwa Jabado; Danny Mangin (editorial contributor)

Production Editor: Jennifer DePrima

15th edition

ISBN 978-1-101-87997-9

ISSN 1073–6581

All details in this book are based on information supplied to us at press time. Always confirm information when it matters, especially if you're making a detour to visit a specific place. Fodor's expressly disclaims any liability, loss, or risk, personal or otherwise, that is incurred as a consequence of the use of any of the contents of this book.

SPECIAL SALES

This book is available at special discounts for bulk purchases for sales promotions or premiums. For more information, e-mail specialmarkets@penguinrandomhouse.com.

PRINTED IN THE UNITED STATES OF AMERICA

10 9 8 7 6 5 4 3 2 1

CONTENTS

Fodor's Features

MAPS

ABOUT THIS GUIDE

Fodor's Recommendations

Everything in this guide is worth doing—we don't cover what isn't—but exceptional sights, hotels, and restaurants are recognized with additional accolades. Fodor'sChoice★ indicates our top recommendations. Care to nominate a new place? Visit Fodors.com/contact-us.

Trip Costs

We list prices wherever possible to help you budget well. Hotel and restaurant price categories from $ to $$$$ are noted alongside each recommendation. For hotels, we include the lowest cost of a standard double room in high season. For restaurants, we cite the average price of a main course at dinner or, if dinner isn't served, at lunch. For attractions, we always list adult admission fees; discounts are usually available for children, students, and senior citizens.

Hotels

Our local writers vet every hotel to recommend the best overnights in each price category, from budget to expensive. Unless otherwise specified, you can expect private bath, phone, and TV in your room. For expanded hotel reviews, facilities, and deals, visit Fodors.com.

Top Picks	Hotels &
★ Fodor'sChoice	Restaurants
	☒ Hotel
Listings	↩ Number of
☒ Address	rooms
☒ Branch address	⛱ Meal plans
☎ Telephone	✗ Restaurant
🖷 Fax	⌚ Reservations
⊕ Website	⌂ Dress code
✉ E-mail	▬ No credit cards
🎫 Admission fee	Ⓢ Price
⊙ Open/closed times	
Ⓜ Subway	**Other**
⊹ Directions or	⇨ See also
Map coordinates	☞ Take note
	🏌 Golf facilities

Restaurants

Unless we state otherwise, restaurants are open for lunch and dinner daily. We mention dress code only when there's a specific requirement and reservations only when they're essential or not accepted.

Credit Cards

The hotels and restaurants in this guide typically accept credit cards. If not, we'll say so.

EUGENE FODOR

Hungarian-born Eugene Fodor (1905–91) began his travel career as an interpreter on a French cruise ship. The experience inspired him to write *On the Continent* (1936), the first guidebook to receive annual updates and discuss a country's way of life as well as its sights. Fodor later joined the U.S. Army and worked for the OSS in World War II. After the war, he kept up his intelligence work while expanding his guidebook series. During the Cold War, many guides were written by fellow agents who understood the value of insider information. Today's guides continue Fodor's legacy by providing travelers with timely coverage, insider tips, and cultural context.

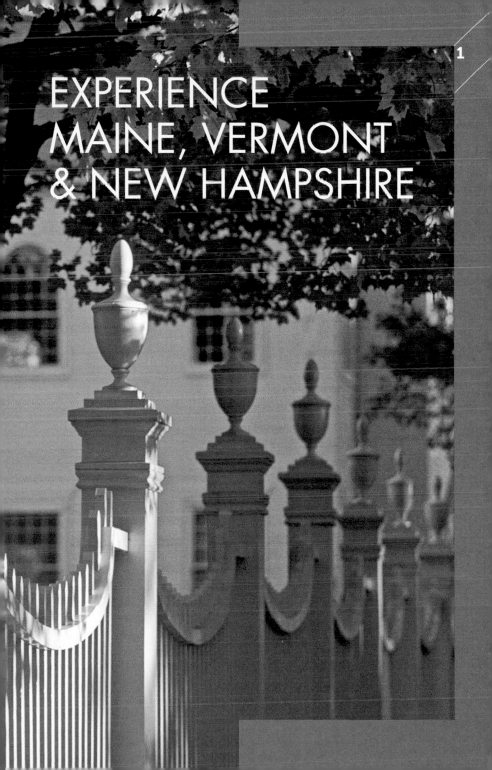

EXPERIENCE MAINE, VERMONT & NEW HAMPSHIRE

WHAT'S WHERE

The following numbers refer to chapters.

3 Vermont. Southern Vermont has farms, freshly starched New England towns, quiet back roads, and bustling ski resorts. Central Vermont's trademarks include marble quarries, dairies, and pastures that create the quilted patchwork of the Champlain Valley. The heart of the area is the wilderness of the Green Mountain National Forest. But the state's largest city (Burlington) and the nation's smallest state capital (Montpelier) are in northern Vermont, as are some of the most rural and remote areas of New England. The Green Mountain State is synonymous with cheese and maple syrup, and its billboard-free back roads may be the most scenic in the region.

4 New Hampshire. Portsmouth is the star of the state's 18-mile coastline, has great shopping, restaurants, music, and theater, as well as one of the best historic districts in the nation. The Lakes Region is a popular summertime escape, rich in historic landmarks, good restaurants, golf courses, and antiques shops. People come to the White Mountains to hike and climb, to photograph the dramatic vistas and the vibrant foliage, and to ski. The lures in western and central New Hampshire include Lake

1

NORTH
WOODS

MAINE

5

WESTERN
LAKES

Skowhegan ○

Waterville ○

Beltast ○

AUGUSTA ★

○ Gardiner

Auburn ○

Lewiston ○

Bath

95

○ Portland

○ South Portland

Biddeford

○ Kennebunk

○ Kennebunkport

○ Old Town

○ Bangor

○ Ellsworth

○ Bar Harbor

MT. DESERT
ISLAND

Penobscot
Bay

Acadia
National Park

○ Rockland

Gulf of Maine

Atlantic Ocean

CAPE ANN

○ Gloucester

Massachusetts Bay

CAPE COD

Plymouth ○

○ Provincetown

Cape Cod Bay

Cape Cod
National Seashore

○ Hyannis

○ Oak Bluffs

MARTHA'S
VINEYARD

NANTUCKET

○ Nantucket

| 0 | | 50 mi |
| 0 | 50 km | |

Sunapee, the charming college town of Hanover, and Mt. Monadnock, the second-most-climbed mountain in the world.

5 **Inland Maine.** Maine is by far the largest state in New England. At its extremes it measures 300 miles by 200 miles; all the other New England states could fit within its perimeter. The Western Lakes and vast North Woods regions attract skiers, hikers, campers, anglers, and other outdoors enthusiasts.

6 **Coastal Maine.** Classic villages, rocky shorelines, punctuated by sandy beaches, and picturesque Main Streets draw scores of vacationers to Maine. Maine's southern-most coastal towns are too overdeveloped to give you the rugged, Down East experience, but the Kennebunks will. Purists hold that the Maine Coast begins at Penobscot Bay, where the vistas over the water are wider and bluer, the shore a jumble of granite boulders. East of the bay is Acadia National Park, where majestic mountains meet the coast; Bar Harbor is the park's gateway town.

MAINE, VERMONT & NEW HAMPSHIRE PLANNER

When to Go

All three New England states are year-round destinations. Winter is popular with skiers, summer draws beach lovers, and fall delights those who love the bursts of autumnal color. Spring can also be a great time, with sugar shacks transforming maple sap into all sorts of tasty things. ■TIP→ You'll probably want to avoid rural areas during mud season (April) and black fly season (mid-May to mid-June).

Memorial Day sets off the great migration to the beaches and the mountains, and summer begins in earnest on July 4. Those who want to drive to the Maine Coast in July or August, beware: on Friday and Sunday, weekenders clog Interstate 95 and U.S. 1.

In the fall, a rainbow of reds, oranges, yellows, purples, and other vibrant hues emerges. The first scarlet and gold colors appear in mid-September in northern areas; "peak" color occurs at different times from year to year. Generally, it's best to visit the northern reaches in late September and early October and move south as October progresses.

CLIMATE

In winter, coastal New England is cold and damp; inland temperatures may be lower, but generally drier conditions make them easier to bear. Snowfall is heaviest in the interior mountains and can range up to several hundred inches per year in northern Maine, New Hampshire, and Vermont. Spring is often windy and rainy; in some years it feels as if winter tumbles directly into summer. Coastal areas can be quite humid in summer, while inland, particularly at higher elevations, there's a prevalence of cool summer nights. Autumn temperatures can be mild even into October.

Getting Here and Around

Air Travel: The main gateway to New England is Boston's Logan International Airport (BOS). Other New England airports include Manchester Boston Regional Airport (MHT, in New Hampshire), Portland International Jetport (PWM, in Maine), and Burlington International Airport (BTV, in Vermont).

Car Travel: New England is best explored by car. Areas in the interior are largely free of heavy traffic and congestion, and parking is consistently easy to find. Coastal New England is considerably more congested. Still, a car is typically the best way to get around, even on the coast—though once you arrive, you may want to explore on foot, on a bike, or by public transportation. In New England's interior, public transportation options are more limited and a car is practically essential.

Train Travel: Amtrak offers frequent daily service to several New England destinations, including Boston; Portland, Maine; coastal New Hampshire; and several points in Vermont.

Visitor Information

Each New England state provides a helpful free information kit, including a guidebook, a map, and listings of attractions and events; all kits include listings and advertisements for lodging and dining.

Contacts Maine Office of Tourism. ☎ 888/624–6345 ⊕ www.visitmaine.com. **New Hampshire Division of Travel and Tourism Development.** ☎ 800/386–4664 ⊕ www.visitnh.gov. **Vermont Department of Tourism and Marketing.** ☎ 800/837–6668, 802/828–3237 ⊕ www.vermontvacation.com.

MAINE, VERMONT & NEW HAMPSHIRE TODAY

1

The People

The idea of the self-reliant, thrifty, and often stoic New England Yankee has taken on almost mythic proportions in American folklore, but in some parts of New England—especially in rural Maine, New Hampshire, and Vermont—there still is some truth to this image, which shouldn't come as a surprise. You need to be independent if you farm an isolated field, live in the middle of a vast forest, or work a fishing boat miles off the coast. As in any part of the country, there are stark differences between the city mice and the country mice of New England. Both, however, are usually well educated and fiercely proud of the region, its rugged beauty, and its contributions to the nation.

The Politics

Though they're often portrayed as liberal states, the political makeup of New England is actually more complex. The region's representation in both the U. S. Senate and in the House of Representatives skews heavily Democratic. That said, there is also a conservative tendency of a distinctly libertarian character among rural New Englanders and in New Hampshire, which hosts the nation's first primary each presidential election season.

The Economy

Long gone are the days when New England's shoe and textile industries sailed overseas, when many a mill town suffered blows to employment and self-image. In recent years the unemployment rate has fallen below the national average.

Exports are a major part of the modern New England economy, consisting heavily of computers and other electronics, chemicals, and specialized machinery. The service industries are also strong, especially in the insurance and financial sectors. Some towns are known for a particular export: Bath, Maine, has naval shipyards supplying the military with high-tech ships and submarines and Barre, Vermont, quarries granite. Assorted foods produced include maple syrup, blueberries, cranberries, lobster, and other seafood.

The Language

As people move around, local accents have begun to blend together, creating a broader New England accent. In some urban areas, you may not in fact detect any accent, but linguistic differences are still evident in some places, especially close to the coast.

Maine has a Boston-like accent with nuanced differences. True Mainers drop or soften their R's—making their favorite dish "lobstah"; they also often accentuate the vowel, so a one-word syllable can be pronounced like two, meaning "here" may become "hee-yuh." In New Hampshire, the accent is not nearly as strong, but it comes out in certain words, like how locals pronounce Concord ("Cahn-cuhd").

MAINE, VERMONT & NEW HAMPSHIRE TOP ATTRACTIONS

Acadia National Park

(A) This wonder of the Maine Coast was the first national park established east of the Mississippi River. In the warmer months, take a drive around Mount Desert Island's 27-mile Park Loop Road to acquaint yourself with the area while indulging in spectacular views of the mountains and the sea. Head to the top of Cadillac Mountain for amazing 360-degree views or bike the scenic 45-mile carriage-road system. Adorable Bar Harbor is the park's gateway town.

Appalachian Trail

(B) The 2,180-mile Appalachian Trail, running from Springer Mountain, Georgia, to Mt. Katahdin, Maine, cuts through five New England states. The trail is best known as a weeks-long endurance test for expert hikers, but many stretches can be walked in a few hours. "AT" terrain in New Hampshire and Maine can be quite challenging.

Baxter State Park

(C) Baxter State Park's more than 200,000 acres with countless lakes and streams, plus Mt. Katahdin, Maine's tallest peak and the northern terminus of the Appalachian Trail. Offering frequent sightings of moose, white-tailed deer, and black bear, and attracting only 60,000 visitors a year, Baxter State Park provides a wilderness experience unparalleled in New England.

Green Mountains

(D) Vermont takes both its nickname (the Green Mountain State) and its actual name (*verts monts*, or "green mountains" in French) from this 250-mile-long mountain range that forms the spine of the state. Part of the Appalachian Mountain system, the Green Mountains are a wild paradise filled with rugged hiking trails (most notably the Long Trail and the Appalachian Trail), unspoiled forests, quaint towns, and some of the East Coast's best ski resorts.

1

Lake Winnipesaukee

(E)As fun to fish as it is to pronounce, the largest and longest lake in New Hampshire is home to three species of trout, small- and largemouth bass, bluegill, and more. The 72-square-mile lake and its more than 250 islands also contain beaches, arcades, water parks, and countless other fun family diversions.

Maine Coast

(F)Counting all its nooks, crannies, and crags, Maine's coast would stretch for thousands of miles if you could pull it straight. The Southern Coast is the most visited section, stretching north from Kittery to just outside Portland, but don't let that stop you from heading farther "Down East" (Maine-speak for "up the coast"). Beachgoers enjoy miles of sandy—or, more frequently, rocky—beaches, with sweeping views of lighthouses, forested islands, and the wide-open sea.

Mt. Washington

(G)New England's highest mountain, this New Hampshire peak has been scaled by many a car. You can also take a cog railway to the top or, if you're an intrepid hiker, navigate a maze of trails. Bundle up if you make the trek: the average temperature at the summit is below freezing.

Portland Head Light

(H)One of the most photographed lighthouses in the nation, the historic white-stone Portland Head Light features an informative museum in the Victorian-style innkeeper's cottage. The lighthouse is located in Fort Williams Park, about 2 miles from the town center of Cape Elizabeth.

TOP EXPERIENCES

Peep a Leaf

Tourist season in most of New England is concentrated in late spring and summer, with a reprise in September and October, especially in the northern states, when leaf peepers from all over descend by the car- and busload to see the leaves turn red, yellow, orange, and all shades in between. Foliage season can be fragile and unpredictable—temperature, winds, and rain all influence when the leaves turn and how long they remain on the trees—but that makes the season even more precious. Apple picking at a local orchard and searching for the perfect pumpkin for a jack-o'-lantern amid the falling leaves are quintessential New England experiences.

Comb a Beach

Whether sandy or rocky, New England beaches can be filled with flotsam and jetsam. Anything from crab traps unmoored by heavy waves to colored sea glass worn smooth by the water to lost watches, jewelry, and the like can appear at your feet. Also common are the shells of sea urchins, clams, and other bivalves. During certain times of the year sand dollars of all sizes and colors are plentiful—you may even find one still whole.

Hit the Slopes

The mountain snow in New England may not be as legendarily fine as the powder out west—in fact, it can be downright unpleasant when packed snow becomes crusty ice—but skiing is quite popular here. Vermont has several ski areas, with Killington ranking among the largest resorts in the Northeast: its nearly 200 trails span seven mountains. New Hampshire's White Mountains also cater to snow-sports lovers, while Sunday River and Sugarloaf in Maine are perennial favorites with advanced-intermediate and expert skiers. Beginners (and lift-ticket bargain hunters) can choose from a number of small but fun hills throughout northern New England.

Eat a Maine Lobster

Maine lobsters are world renowned, and lobstermen and fish markets all along the coast will pack a live lobster in seaweed for overnight shipment to almost anywhere nationwide. These delectable crustaceans are available throughout New England, but without a doubt the best place to eat them is near their waters of origin. Lobster meat is sweet (especially the claws), and most agree that a simple preparation is the best way to go: steamed and eaten with drawn butter, or pulled into chunks and placed in a toasted split-top bun—the famous New England lobster roll. There are two types of lobster rolls to try: traditional Maine-style features a cold lobster salad with a leaf of lettuce and the barest amount of mayonnaise, while the Connecticut lobster roll is served warm with drawn butter (no mayo). Don't forget to save room for New England's other culinary treasure: *chowdah*. No two clam chowders taste the same, but they're all delicious.

Rise and Shine at a B&B

New England's distinctive architecture, much of it originating in the 18th and 19th centuries, has resulted in beautiful buildings of all shapes and sizes, many of which have been restored as bed-and-breakfasts. These inns typify the cozy, down-home, historical feel of New England, and are an ideal lodging choice. This is especially true when the weather is cold, and the warm ambience of many of these inns more than justifies their slightly steeper rates.

Watch a Whale

The deep, cold waters of the North Atlantic serve as feeding grounds and migration routes for a variety of whales, including fin and humpback whales, the occasional blue whale, and the rare, endangered white whale. Maine's Southern Coast and Mid-Coast regions are the best places to hop aboard a whale-watching boat. Boats head to whale feeding grounds about 20 miles offshore, where the majestic animals are numerous. Some captains go so far as to guarantee at least a single sighting or they'll give you a ticket for a second tour. Whale-watching season varies by tour skipper, but generally runs April–October.

Fair Thee Well

New Englanders love their fairs and festivals. "Maine-iacs" celebrate the moose, clam, lobster, and blueberry. Maple sugar and maple syrup are feted in Vermont, while "live free or die" New Hampshire honors American independence. Many rural communities throughout New England hold agricultural fairs in late August and September.

Get Up Close and Personal with Nature

New England may be known for its flashy foliage in the fall and spectacular slopes in the winter, but the outdoors in spring and summer delights all the senses as well. Breathe in the ocean air as you drive along the Maine Coast. Revel in the fragrance of the mountains and forests in Vermont's Green Mountains and New Hampshire's White Mountains while hiking the Appalachian Trail. Observe moose and bear in their natural habitat, or spot birds, seals, dolphins, and whales in theirs.

Savor Sweet Stuff

Summer vacations in New England go hand in hand with sweet treats; it's difficult to visit without sampling homemade fudge at an old-fashioned candy store, buying an ice cream for your sweetie, or bringing some saltwater taffy to share with the folks back home. Be sure to try one Maine specialty: the whoopie pie. Made from two chocolate circles of cake with vanilla-cream filling in between, it's a delectable Maine tradition. If you are visiting Maine when the tiny wild blueberry is in season, take every opportunity to savor this flavorful fruit—in pie, muffin, or pancake form—and you'll understand its legendary culinary status. In Vermont, go on a factory tour at Ben & Jerry's, and have a delicious cone afterward. You can even have dessert for breakfast when you top your pancakes with Vermont's maple syrup.

Check Out Lighthouses

Maine's long and jagged coastline is home to more than 60 lighthouses, perched high on rocky ledges or on the tips of wayward islands. Though modern navigational technology has made many of the lights obsolete, various preservation groups restore and maintain them, often making them accessible to the public. Some of the state's more famous include the Portland Head Light, commissioned by President George Washington in 1787 and immortalized in one of Edward Hopper's paintings; Two Lights, a few miles down the coast in Cape Elizabeth; and West Quoddy Head, on the easternmost tip of land in the United States. Some lighthouses are privately owned and others accessible only by boat, but plenty are within easy reach and open to the public, some with museums and tours. At the Maine Lighthouse Museum in Rockland, visitors can view a collection of Fresnel lenses and Coast Guard artifacts.

Sail the Coast

The coastline of northern New England is a sailor's paradise, with its hidden coves, windswept islands, and picture-perfect harbors where you can pick up a mooring for the night. With nearly 3,500 miles of undulating, rocky shoreline, you could spend a lifetime of summers sailing the waters off the Maine Coast and never see it all. If you're not one of the lucky few with a sailboat to call your own, there are many companies that offer sailboat charters, whether for day trips or weeklong excursions. It might sound like an expensive getaway, but as meals and drinks are usually included, an overnight sailing charter might not cost any more than a seaside hotel room—plus you'll be accompanied by an experienced captain to provide history and insight along the voyage.

Get the First Sight of First Light

At 1,530 feet, Cadillac Mountain, in Maine's Acadia National Park, is the highest mountain on the New England coast: what better place to view the sunrise? Drive the narrow, winding, 3½-mile road to the summit before dawn (not accessible when the Loop Road is closed in the winter), and you could be the first person in the United States to see the summer sun's rays. (Depending on the time of year: sometimes the first sunrise is at West Quoddy Head Lighthouse in Lubec, Maine.)

FLAVORS OF MAINE, VERMONT & NEW HAMPSHIRE

FOOD FESTIVALS

New England has a plethora of food festivals that celebrate local offerings ranging from blueberries to cheese. The following is a small sample of the celebrations honoring regional cuisine.

Maine Lobster Festival, Rockland, Maine. Stuff your face with lobster tails and claws during this "lobstravaganza" (⊕ *www. mainelobsterfestival.com*) in late July and early August.

New Hampshire Pumpkin Festival, Laconia, New Hampshire. Formerly located in Keene, the newly renamed and relocated festival (as of 2015) tries to outdo itself each October for most lighted pumpkins (⊕ *www.pumpkinfestival2015.org*). Enjoy hayrides and contests ranging from pie eating to pumpkin-seed spitting.

Vermont Cheesemakers Festival, Shelburne, Vermont. Artisanal cheeses and local beer and wine highlight this daylong festival (⊕ *www.vtcheesefest.com*) in late July. Sample more than 200 cheese varieties from 40 local cheese makers in the Coach Barn of Shelburne Farms.

Wilton Blueberry Festival, Wilton, Maine. You can pick your own wild blueberries and sample baked goods from pancakes to pies at the annual Wilton Blueberry Festival (⊕ *www.wiltonbbf.com*), which takes place in early August.

SPECIALTIES BY STATE

Vermont

Vermonters are big on **maple syrup** straight-up and in candy, but dairy products take top billing in this state. Milk and cream from the region's dairy farms are used in cheeses, like the famous **cheddar;** and in **ice cream,** from the likes of Ben & Jerry's. Willow Hill Farm in Milton, Vermont, is famous for its sheep's milk cheeses; try the savory Vaquero Blue, a blue cheese made from both sheep and cow's milk. For a family-friendly stop, check out Shelburne Farms' children's farmyard. Located on the shore of Lake Champlain, Shelburne Farms uses only Brown Swiss cows to make its famous cheddar. In addition to the Vermont Cheesemakers Festival, Shelburne attracts visitors year-round to taste cheeses and explore walking trails.

New Hampshire

Northern New Hampshire's cuisine carries a heavy French Canadian influence; try the *poutine* (french fries covered with cheese curds and gravy). The local **corn chowder** substitutes corn for clams and bacon, putting a twist on a Northeastern classic. The Smuttynose Brewing Company, a craft brewery in Portsmouth, offers tours and tastings.

Maine

Lobster classics include **boiled lobster**—a staple at picnic-bench-and-paper-plate spots along the Maine Coast—and **lobster rolls,** a lobster meat and mayo (or melted butter) preparation served in a toasted hot dog bun. **Blueberries, strawberries, raspberries,** and **blackberries** grow wild (and on farms) all over the Northeast in the summer. Blueberry pancakes with maple syrup, blueberry muffins, and blueberry pies are popular, especially along the coast. Mainers also love **whoopie pies,** cake-like cookies sandwiched together with frosting.

Portland's waterfront Commercial Street is bookended by two typical Maine diners, Gilbert's Chowderhouse and Becky's Diner. The former has one of the state's finest lobster rolls and homemade clam cakes; the latter opens for breakfast at 4 am.

OUTDOOR ADVENTURES

BEACHCOMBING AND SWIMMING

Long, wide beaches line the Northern New England coast from New Hampshire to Maine. Many beaches have lifeguards on duty in season; some have picnic facilities, restrooms, changing facilities, and concession stands. Depending on the locale, you may need a parking sticker to use the lot.

When to Go

The waters are at their warmest in August, though they're cold even at the height of summer along much of Maine and New Hampshire. Inland, small lake beaches abound, most notably in New Hampshire and Vermont. The best time to beachcomb is after the tide has gone out, when the retreating water has left behind its treasures. Early spring is an especially good time to see sand dollars washed up on beaches.

What to Look For

The best part of beachcombing is that you never quite know what you'll find at your feet. Sea glass—nothing more than man-made glass worn smooth from its seaward journeys—is common and most prized in rare shades of blue. You'll also find shells in abundance: blue mussels, tiny periwinkles, razor (or "jackknife") clams, ridged scallops, and briny oysters, with their rough outside shell and lovely mother-of-pearl interiors.

Best Beaches

Ellacoya State Beach, New Hampshire. On the southwestern shore of bustling Lake Winnipesaukee, Ellacoya has mountain views, a sandy beach, and shallow water ideal for small children.

Hampton Beach State Park, New Hampshire. The Granite State's ocean shore is short, but this state park along historic Route 1 takes full advantage of the space it has. In addition to swimming and fishing, there are campsites with full hookups for RVs, as well as an amphitheater with a bandshell for outdoor concerts.

Popham Beach State Park, Maine. At low tide, you can explore the tidal flats and tide pools at this state park. There are also lifeguards and bathhouses.

BICYCLING

Biking on a road through New England's countryside is an idyllic way to spend a day. Many ski resorts accommodate mountain bikes in summer.

Bike Tours

There are a multitude of tour operators and magnificent trails throughout New England, and many bike shops rent and repair bicycles. Bike New England offers cycling routes and maps throughout the Northeast.

Safety

On the road, watch for trucks and stay as close as possible to the side of the road, in single file. On the trail, ride within your limits and keep your eyes peeled for hikers and horses (both have the right of way), as well as dogs. Always wear a helmet and carry plenty of water.

Best Rides

Acadia National Park, Maine. At the heart of this popular park is the 45-mile network of historic carriage roads covered in crushed rock that cyclists share with equestrians and hikers. Mountain bikes (or hybrids) are the way to go here, so leave your road bike at home. Fit and experienced riders can ascend the road to the top of Cadillac Mountain, but take caution: heavy traffic in high season can make this a dangerous proposition.

All Along the Coast. U.S. 1, Maine. The major road that travels along the Maine Coast is just a narrow two-lane highway most of the way, but it is still one of the country's most historic highways. As a result, it's very popular in spring, summer, and fall with serious long-distance cyclists.

Killington Resort, Vermont. Following the lead of many ski resorts in the western United States, Killington allows fat-tire riders on many of its ski trails after the snow has melted. Stunt riders can enjoy the jumps and bumps of the mountain-bike park.

Portland, Maine. The paved Eastern Prom Trail extends from the edge of the Old Port to East End Beach, then to Back Bay for a 6-mile loop, before returning.

BOATING

Along many of New England's larger lakes, sailboats, rowboats, canoes, kayaks, and outboards are available for rent at local marinas. Rentals are available at a number of seacoast locations, but you may be required to prove your own seaworthiness before setting sail. Lessons are commonly available.

What to Wear

It can get cold on the water, especially while sailing, so dress in layers and bring along a windbreaker and fleece even if it's warm on land. Don't wear cotton or jeans: once they get wet, they stay wet and will leave you chilled. Sunscreen, sunglasses (with Croakies so they don't fall overboard), and a hat are also musts, as are water and high-energy snacks, especially for canoe and kayak expeditions.

Best Boating

Allagash Wilderness Waterway, Maine. This scenic and remote waterway (92 miles of lakes, ponds, rivers, and streams) is part of the 740-mile Northern Forest Canoe Trail, which also floats through New York, Vermont, and New Hampshire.

Lake Champlain, Vermont. Called by some the sixth Great Lake, 435-square-mile Lake Champlain is bordered by Vermont's Green Mountains to the east and the Adirondacks of New York to the west. Burlington, Vermont, is the largest lakeside city and a good bet for boat rentals—be it a canoe, kayak, rowboat, skiff, or motorboat. Attractions include numerous islands and deep-blue water often brushed by pleasant New England breezes.

Lakes Region, New Hampshire. Lake Winnipesaukee is the largest lake in New Hampshire, but there are plenty of other puddles, both large and small, worth dipping a paddle into. Squam Lake is a tranquil area made famous by *On Golden Pond*, and Lake Wentworth has a state park with a boat launch, bathhouse, and picnic tables.

Rockland, Maine. For a guided trip on the water, consider a windjammer excursion out of Rockland, Camden, or Rockport. From day sails to multiday cruises, trips run $50–$1,000 and include meals. Check The Maine Windjammer Association (⊕ *www.sailmainecoast.com*) or Windjammer Cruises (⊕ *www.mainewindjammercruises.com*) for more information.

HIKING

Probably the most famous trails in the region are the 270-mile Long Trail, which runs north–south through the center of Vermont, and the Maine-to-Georgia

Appalachian Trail, which runs through New England on private and public land. The Appalachian Mountain Club (AMC) maintains a system of staffed huts in New Hampshire's Presidential Range, with bunk space and meals available by reservation. There's plenty of good hiking at state parks throughout the region.

Safety

There are few real hazards to hiking, but a little preparedness goes a long way. Know your limits, and make sure the terrain you are about to embark on doesn't exceed your abilities. Check the trail map carefully and pay attention to elevation changes, which make a huge difference in the difficulty of a hike: a steep mile is much tougher to negotiate and takes longer than a flat 2- or even 3-mile stretch. Bring layers of clothing to accommodate changes in weather, and always carry enough drinking water. Before you go, be sure to tell someone where you're going and how long you expect to be gone.

Best Hikes

Acadia National Park, Maine. Acadia's network of old carriage roads make for great, relatively flat hiking through the woods where you can often spot wildlife. If you're up for a challenge, hike up Cadillac Mountain or Acadia Mountain; both provide steep climbs and breathtaking views. The Ocean Path Trail has spectacular seaside views and leads to not-to-be-missed Thunder Hole, where waves crash spectacularly.

Appalachian Trail, Vermont, New Hampshire, Maine. The Northern New England section of the trail, which reaches south to Georgia, provides the opportunity for a great day hike or for the start of a challenging six-month endurance test. The popular trail is marked by rectangular white blazes which are well maintained and relatively easy to follow.

Mt. Washington, New Hampshire. The cog railroad and the auto road to the summit are both popular routes up New England's highest mountain, but for those with stamina and legs of steel, it's one heck of a hike. Of the handful of trails to the top, the most popular begins at the Pinkham Notch Visitor Center. Be sure to dress in layers and pack warm clothing for the frequent winds toward the peak.

The Long Trail, Vermont. Following the main ridge of the Green Mountains from one end of Vermont to the other, this is the nation's oldest long-distance trail. In fact, some say it was the inspiration for the Appalachian Trail. Hardy backpackers make a go of its full 270 miles, but day hikers can drop in and out at many places along the way.

1

MAINE, VERMONT & NEW HAMPSHIRE WITH KIDS

From the great outdoors to fantastic children's museums, there's no end of activities and attractions for kids and families all over New England.

Vermont

ECHO Leahy Center for Lake Champlain, Burlington. Lots of activities and hands-on exhibits make learning about the geology and ecology of Lake Champlain an engaging experience.

Montshire Museum of Science, Norwich. This interactive museum uses more than 60 hands-on exhibits to explore nature and technology. The building sits amid 110 acres of nature trails and woodlands, where animals roam freely.

Shelburne Farms, Shelburne. This working dairy farm is also an educational and cultural resource center. Visitors can watch artisans make the farm's famous cheddar cheese from the milk of more than 100 purebred and registered Brown Swiss cows. A children's farmyard and walking trails round out the experience.

New Hampshire

Hampton Beach. This seaside diversion draws families to its almost Coney Island–like fun. Along the boardwalk, kids enjoy arcade games, parasailing, live music, and an annual children's festival. They can even learn how saltwater taffy is made.

Lake Winnipesaukee, Weirs Beach. The largest lake in the state, Lake Winnipesaukee provides plenty of family-friendly fun. Base yourself in Weirs Beach and the kids can swim, play arcade games, cruise the lake, take a scenic railroad along the shoreline, and even see a drive-in movie.

SEE Science Center, Manchester. For kids who love LEGO, the models of old Manchester and the millyard are sure to impress.

There are also rotating exhibits and science demonstrations.

Maine

Acadia National Park, Mount Desert Island. Head out on a whale- and puffin-watching trip from Bar Harbor, drive up scenic Cadillac Mountain, swim at Echo Lake Beach, hike one of the many easy trails, and don't forget to sample some wild blueberry pie.

Maine Discovery Museum, Bangor. There are three floors of fun, educational activities at the Maine Discovery Museum. Exhibits include Nature Trails; Booktown; Sounds Abound; Artscape; and Body Journey.

Maine Narrow Gauge Railroad Museum, Portland. For train fans, check out the scenic rides on these narrow-gauge trains. In the winter, they have *Polar Express*–themed trips.

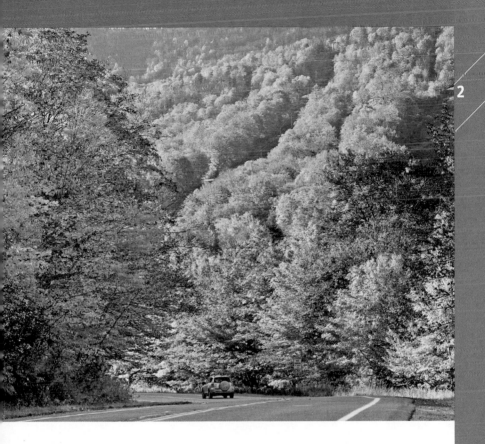

BEST FALL FOLIAGE
DRIVES & ROAD TRIPS

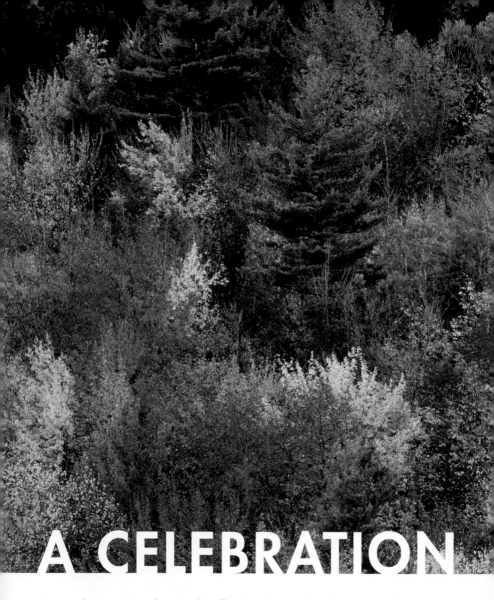

A CELEBRATION

Picture this: one scarlet maple offset by the stark white spire of a country church, a whole hillside of brilliant foliage foregrounded by a vintage barn or perhaps a covered bridge that straddles a cobalt river. Such iconic scenes have launched a thousand postcards and turned New England into the ultimate fall destination for leaf peepers.

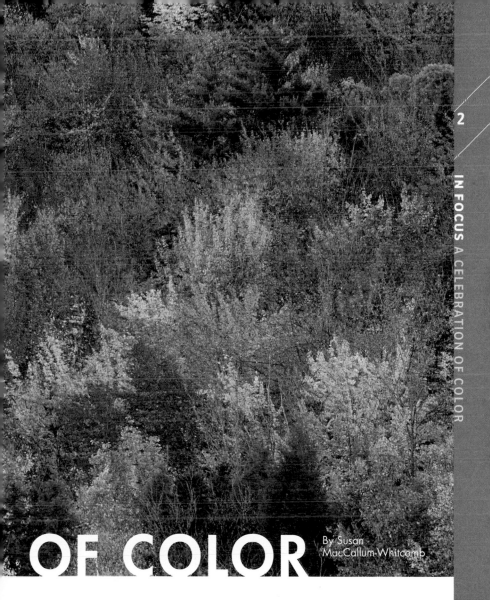

2

IN FOCUS A CELEBRATION OF COLOR

OF COLOR

By Susan
MacCallum-Whitcomb

Mother Nature, of course, puts on an annual autumn performance elsewhere, but this one is a showstopper. Like the landscape, the mix of deciduous (leaf-shedding) trees is remarkably varied here and creates a broader than usual palette. New England's abundant evergreens lend contrast, making the display even more vivid. Every September and October, leaf peepers arrive to cruise along country lanes, join outdoor adventures, or simply stroll on town greens.

Did you know the brilliant shades actually lurk in the leaves all year long? Leaves contain three pigments. The green chlorophyll, so dominant in summer that it obscures the red anthocyanins and orangey-yellow carotenoids, decreases in fall and reveals a crayon box of color.

Above, Vermont's Green Mountains are multicolored in the fall (and often white in winter).

PREDICTING THE PEAK

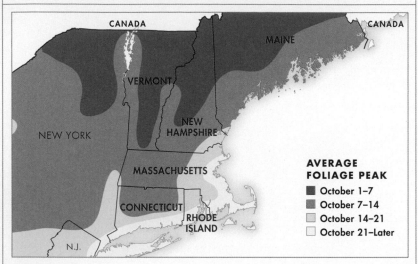

AVERAGE
FOLIAGE PEAK
■ October 1–7
■ October 7–14
□ October 14–21
□ October 21–Later

LOCATION

Pinning down precisely when colors will appear remains an inexact science, although location plays a major role. Typically, the transformation begins in the highest and northernmost parts of New England in mid-September, then moves steadily into lower altitudes and southern sectors throughout October.

For trip planning, think in terms of regions rather than states. In Maine (a huge state that runs north–south) leaf color can peak anytime from the fourth week of September to the third week of October, depending on the locale.

WEATHER

Early September weather is another deciding factor. From the foliage aficionado's perspective, the ideal scenario is calm, temperate days capped by nights that are cool but still above freezing. If the weather is too warm, it delays the onset of the season. If it's too dry or windy, the leaves shrivel up or blow off.

COLOR CHECK RESOURCES

Curious about current conditions? In season, each state maintains a dedicated website reporting on foliage conditions. Weather Channel has peak viewing maps and Foliage Network uses a network of spotters to chart changes.

■ **Connecticut:** ☎ 800/282-6863 ⊕ www.ct.gov/dep
■ **Foliage Network:** ⊕ www.foliagenetwork.com
■ **Maine:** ☎ 888/624-6345 ⊕ www.mainefoliage.com
■ **Massachusetts:** ☎ 800/227-6277 ⊕ www.massvacation.com

■ **New Hampshire:** ☎ 800/258-3608 ⊕ www.visitnh.gov
■ **Rhode Island:** ☎ 800/556-2484 ⊕ www.visitrhodeisland.com
■ **Vermont:** ☎ 800/837-6668 ⊕ www.vermontvacation.com
■ **Weather Channel:** ⊕ www.weather.com

TOP TREES FOR COLOR

A AMERICAN BEECH. This tree's smooth, steel-gray trunk is crowned with gold, copper, and bronze tinted leaves in autumn, giving it a metallic sheen. Though the elliptical leaves sometimes hang on all winter, its "fruit" goes fast because beechnuts are a popular snack for birds, squirrels, and even bears.

B NORTHERN RED OAK. The upside of oaks is that they retain their fall shading until late in the season—the downside is that, for most species, that color is a boring brown. Happily, the northern red isn't like other members of the oak family. Its elongated, flame-shaped leaves turn fiery crimson and incandescent orange.

C QUAKING ASPEN. Eyes and ears both prove useful when identifying this aspen. Look for small, ovate leaves that usually become almost flaxen. Or listen for the leaves' quake: a sound, audible in even a gentle breeze, which the U.S. Forest Service likens to that made by "thousands of fluttering butterfly wings."

D SUGAR MAPLE. The leaf of the largest North American maple species is so lovely that Canada put it on its national flag. Each generally has five multipointed lobes—plus enough anthocyanin to produce a deep red color. The tree itself produces plentiful sap and is the cornerstone of New England's syrup industry.

E WHITE ASH. This tall tree typically grows to between 65 to 100 feet. Baseball enthusiasts admire the wood (which is used to craft bats); while foliage fans admire the compound leaves, each consisting of five to nine slightly serrated, tapering leaflets. They range in hue from burgundy and purple to amber.

F WHITE BIRCH. A papery, light, bright bark makes this slender hardwood easily recognizable. Centuries ago, Native Americans used birch wood to make everything from canoes to medicinal teas. Today's photographers know the bark also makes great pictures since it provides a sharp contrast to the tree's vibrant yellow leaves.

FANTASTIC FALL ITINERARY

The Berkshires

Fall is the perfect time to visit New England—country roads wind through dense forests exploding into reds, oranges, yellows, and purples. For inspiration, here is an itinerary for the truly ambitious that links the most stunning foliage areas; choose a section to explore more closely. Like autumn itself, this route works its way south from northern Vermont into Connecticut, with one or two days in each area.

VERMONT

NORTHWEST VERMONT

In Burlington, the elms will be turning colors on the University of Vermont campus. You can ride the ferry across Lake Champlain for great views of Vermont's Green Mountains and New York's Adirondacks. After visiting the resort town of Stowe, detour off Route 100 beneath the cliffs of Smugglers' Notch. The north country's palette unfolds in Newport, where the blue waters of Lake Memphremagog reflect the foliage.

NORTHEAST KINGDOM

After a side trip along Lake Willoughby, explore St. Johnsbury, where the Fairbanks Museum and St. Johnsbury Athenaeum reveal Victorian tastes in art and natural-history collecting. In Peacham, stock up for a picnic at the Peacham Store.

NEW HAMPSHIRE

WHITE MOUNTAINS AND LAKES REGION

In New Hampshire, Interstate 93 narrows as it winds through craggy Franconia Notch. Get off the interstate for the sinuous Kancamagus Highway portion of Route 112 that passes through the mountains to Conway. In Center Harbor, in the Lakes Region, you can ride the MS *Mount Washington* for views of the Lake Winnipesaukee shoreline, or ascend to Moultonborough's Castle in the Clouds for a falcon's-eye look at the colors.

MT. MONADNOCK

In Concord, stop at the Museum of New Hampshire History and the State House. Several trails climb Mt. Monadnock, near Jaffrey Center, and colorful vistas extend as far as Boston.

⇨ For local drives perfect for an afternoon, also see our Fall Foliage Drive Spotlights on Vermont, New Hampshire, and Inland Maine.

THE MOOSE IS LOOSE!

Take "Moose Crossing" signs seriously because things won't end well if you hit an animal that stands six feet tall and weighs 1,200 pounds. Some 40,000 reside in northern New England. To search out these ungainly creatures in the wild, consider an organized moose safari in northern New Hampshire or Maine.

MASSACHUSETTS

THE MOHAWK TRAIL

In Shelburne Falls, Massachusetts, the Bridge of Flowers displays the last of autumn's blossoms. Follow the Mohawk Trail section of Route 2 as it ascends into the Berkshire Hills—and stop to take in the view at the hairpin turn just east of North Adams (or drive up Mt. Greylock, the tallest peak in New England, for more stunning vistas). In Williamstown, the Clark Art Institute houses a collection of impressionist works.

THE BERKSHIRES

The scenery around Lenox, Stockbridge, and Great Barrington has long attracted the talented and the wealthy. Near U.S. 7, you can visit the homes of novelist Edith Wharton (the Mount, in Lenox), sculptor Daniel Chester French (Chesterwood, in Stockbridge), and diplomat Joseph Choate (Naumkeag, in Stockbridge).

CONNECTICUT

THE LITCHFIELD HILLS

This area of Connecticut combines the feel of upcountry New England with exclusive urban polish. The wooded shores of Lake Waramaug are home to country inns and wineries in pretty towns. Litchfield has a perfect village green—an idealized New England town center.

FOLIAGE PHOTO HINT

Don't just snap the big panoramic views. Look for single, brilliantly colored trees with interesting elements nearby, like a weathered gray stone wall or a freshly painted white church. These images are often more evocative than big blobs of color or panoramic shots.

LEAF PEEPER PLANNER

Hot-air balloons and ski-lift rides give a different perspective on fall's color.

Enjoying fall doesn't necessarily require a multistate road trip. If you are short on time (or energy), a simple autumnal stroll might be just the ticket: many state parks even offer free short ranger-led rambles.

HIKE AND BIKE ON A TOUR
You can sign on for foliage-focused hiking holidays with **Country Walkers** (☎ *800/234–6900* ⊕ *www.countrywalkers.com*) and **Boundless Journeys** (☎ *800/941–8010* ⊕ *www.boundlessjourneys.com*); or cycling ones with **Discovery Bike Tours** (☎ *800/257–2226* ⊕ *www.discoverybiketours.com*) and **VBT Bicycling Vacations** (☎ *800/245–3868,* ⊕ *www.vbt.com*). Individual state tourism boards list similar operators elsewhere.

SOAR ABOVE THE CROWDS
New Hampshire's **Cannon Mountain** (☎ *603/823–8800* ⊕ *www.cannonmt.com*) is only one of several New England ski resorts that provides gondola or aerial tram rides during foliage season. Area hot-air balloon operators, like **Balloons of Vermont, LLC** (☎ *802/369–0213* ⊕ *www.balloonsofvermont.com*), help you take it in from the top.

ROOM AT THE INN?

Accommodations fill quickly in autumn. Vermont's top lodgings sell out months in advance for the first two weeks in October. So book early and expect a two-night minimum stay requirement. If you can't find a quaint inn, try basing yourself at a B&B or off-season ski resort. Also, be prepared for some sticker shock; if you can travel midweek, you'll often save quite a bit.

RIDE THE RAILS OR THE CURRENT
Board the **Essex Steam Train** for a ride through the Connecticut countryside (☎ *800/377–3987* ⊕ *www.essexsteamtrain.com*) or float through northern Rhode Island on the **Blackstone Valley Explorer** riverboat (☎ *401/724–2200* ⊕ *www.rivertourblackstone.com*).

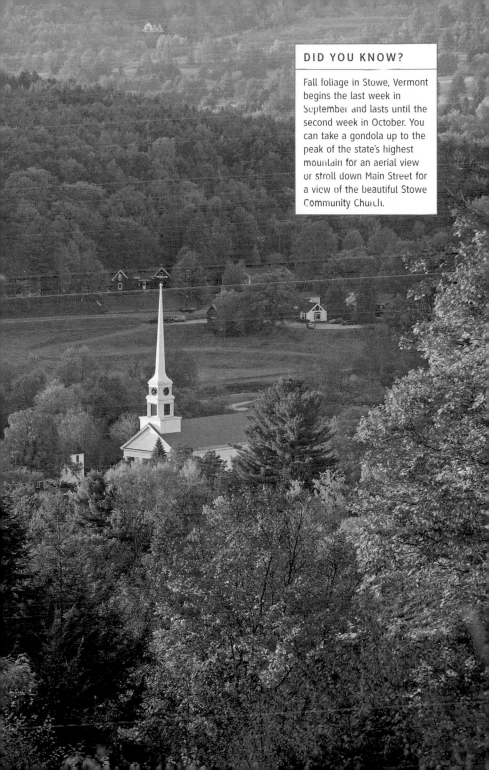

VERMONT FALL FOLIAGE DRIVE

Nearly 80% of Vermont is forested, with cities few and far between. The state's interior is a rural playground for leaf peepers, and it's widely considered to exhibit the most intense range of colors anywhere on the continent. Its tiny towns and hamlets—the few distractions from the dark reds, yellows, oranges, and russets—are as pristine as nature itself.

Begin this drive in Manchester Village, along the old-fashioned, well-to-do homes lining Main Street, and continue south to Arlington, North Bennington, and Old Bennington. Stop just a mile south along Route 7A at **Hildene.** The 412 acres of explorable grounds at the estate of Abraham Lincoln's son are ablaze with color, and the views over the Battenkill Valley are as good as any you can find. Drive south another mile along 7A to the **Equinox Valley Nursery,** where you can sample delicious apple cider and doughnuts amid views of the arresting countryside. A few more miles south along 7A is the small town of Arlington.

BEST TIME TO GO

Late September and early October are the times to go, with the southern area peaking about a week later than the north. Remember to book hotels in advance. The state has a Fall Foliage Hotline and an online interactive map (☎ *802/828–3239* ⊕ *www.foliage-vermont. com*). The drive from Manchester to Bennington outlined here takes just 30 minutes, but a relaxed pace is best suited to taking in all the sights.

From 7A in Arlington you can take two adventurous and stunning detours. One is pure foliage: follow 313 west a few miles to the New York State border for more beautiful views. Or head east a mile to East Arlington where delightful stores await you, including a chocolate emporium. (You can continue even farther east from this spot to Kelly Stand Road leading into the Green Mountains; this is a little-known route that can't be beat.) Back on 7A South in Arlington, stop at the **Cheese House**, the delightfully cheesy roadside attraction.

Farther south into Shaftsbury is **Clear Brook Farm**, a brilliant place for cider and fresh produce and pumpkins. Robert Frost spent much of his life in South Shaftsbury, and you can learn about his life at his former home, the **Stone House**. From South Shaftsbury take Route 67 through North Bennington and continue on to Route 67A in Old Bennington. Go up the 306-foot-high **Bennington Battle Monument** to survey the seasonal views across four states. Back down from the clouds, walk a few serene blocks to the cemetery of the **Old First Church**, where Robert Frost is buried, and contemplate his autumnal poem, "Nothing Gold Can Stay."

NEED A BREAK?

Equinox Valley Nursery. This nursery carries fresh produce, seasonal snacks, and is full of family-friendly fall activities—a corn maze, pumpkin golf (mini golf played with small pumpkins), hay rides, and pumpkin carving. ⊠ *1158 Main St., Manchester* ☎ *802/362-2610* ⊕ *www.equinoxvalleynursery.com* 🎫 *Free.*

Clear Brook Farm. Set on more than 25 acres, Clear Brook Farm sells its own organic produce, in addition to baked goods and other seasonal treats. ⊠ *47 Hidden Valley Rd., Manchester* ☎ *802/442-4273* ⊕ *www.clearbrookfarm.com.*

The Cheese House. Get your Vermont cheddar fix at the The Cheese House, which also sells maple syrup and other local products and gifts. ⊠ *5187 Vermont Rte. 7A, Arlington* ☎ *802/375-9033* ⊕ *www.thevermontcheesehouse.com* 🎫 *Free* ☉ *Closed Tues.*

NEW HAMPSHIRE FALL FOLIAGE DRIVE

Quaint villages graced with green commons, white town halls, and covered bridges: southwestern New Hampshire is dominated by the imposing rocky summit of Mt. Monadnock and the brilliant colors of autumn. Kancamagus Highway is another classic foliage route, but for more solitude and less traffic, try this more accessible route that peaks a few weeks later than the state's far north.

The Granite State is the second-most-forested state in the nation; by Columbus Day the colors of the leaves of its maple, birch, elm, oak, beech, and ash trees range from green to gold, purple to red, and orange to auburn. Routes 12, 101, 202, and 124 compose a loop around **Mt. Monadnock**. Start in Keene with a cup of coffee at Prime Roast; for New Hampshire–made products, take a walk on Main Street or detour west on Route 9 to reach **Stonewall Farm** for something more country.

BEST TIME TO GO

The best time to view foliage in southern New Hampshire is generally early October, but it can vary by up to four weeks. For updates about leaf changes, visit the Foliage Tracker page on the website of **Visit New Hampshire** (☎ *800/258–3608* ⊕ *www.visitnh.gov*).

PLANNING YOUR TIME

Expect to travel about 55 miles. The journey can take up to a full day if you stop to explore along the way.

From Keene, travel east on Route 101 through Dublin and over Pack Monadnock, a 2,290-foot peak (not to be confused with the 3,165-foot Grand, or Mt. Monadnock). In quaint **Peterborough**, browse the local stores, whose attitude and selection mirror the state's independent spirit.

Then turn south on Route 202 toward Jaffrey Village. Just west on Route 124, in historic Jaffrey Center, be sure to visit the **Meeting House Cemetery,** where author Willa Cather is buried. A side trip, 4 miles south on Route 202, leads to the majestic **Cathedral of the Pines** in Rindge, one of the best places in the region for foliage viewing because the evergreens offset the brilliant shades of red.

Heading west on Route 124, you can take Dublin Road to the main entrance of **Monadnock State Park** or continue along to the Old Toll Road parking area for one of the most popular routes up the mountain, the **Halfway House Trail.** All the hiking trails have great views, including the area's many lakes. Continuing on Route 124, you come to Fitzwilliam and Route 12; turn north back to Keene.

NEED A BREAK?

Stonewall Farm. This nonprofit working farm teaches about the importance of agriculture. The farm offers an active schedule of events, including maple sugaring and seasonal horse-drawn hayrides. Walking trails wind throughout the farm—in winter you can borrow snowshoes for free. Young children love the discovery room, and the interactive greenhouse is geared for all ages. ⊠ *242 Chesterfield Rd., Keene* ☎ *603/357-7278* ⊕ *www.stonewallfarm.org* ⊙ *Weekdays 9–4:30.*

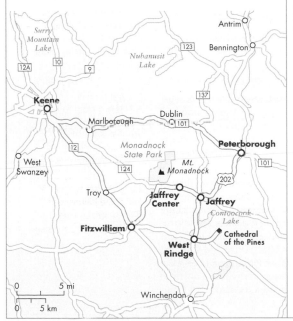

INLAND MAINE FALL FOLIAGE DRIVE

Swaths of pine, spruce, and fir trees offset the red, orange, and yellow of maples and birches along this popular foliage drive through western Maine's mountains, but hardwoods largely dominate the landscape.

Wending its way to the four-season resort town of Rangeley, near its northern terminus, the route passes stunning overlooks, forest-lined lakes, waterfalls, hiking trails, and a state park. Mountain vistas are reflected in the many (often connected) lakes, ponds, rivers, and streams.

From U.S. 2 in Mexico, Route 17 heads north past old homesteads and fields along the Swift River Valley before making a mountainous switchback ascent to **Height of Land,** the drive's literal pinnacle. The must-stop overlook here has off-road parking, interpretive panels, stone seating, and a short path to the **Appalachian Trail.** On a clear day, you can look west to New Hampshire and Canada. **Mooselookmeguntic Lake** and **Upper Richardson Lake** seem to float amid the forestland below. A few miles north of here is an overlook for Rangeley Lake, also with interpretive panels.

BEST TIME TO GO

Fall color usually peaks in the Rangeley area in the first or second week of October. Get fall foliage updates at ⊕ *www.maine-foliage.com*

PLANNING YOUR TIME

The Rangeley Lakes National Scenic Byway (⊕ *www.byways.org*) makes up much of this 59-mile drive (1½ hours without stops), but plan for a relaxed full day of exploring.

2

In tiny, welcoming Oquossoc, where Routes 17 and 4 meet, **The Farmer's Daughter** welcomes passersby with displays of pumpkins and mums during autumn. Inside the seasonal specialty foods store you can pick up apple cider and picnic items. Or stop at the **Gingerbread House Restaurant** for a meal, or just ice cream or baked goods. The hamlet is also home to the **Rangeley Outdoor Sporting Heritage Museum**, where you can learn why visitors have come here to fish, hunt, and enjoy the outdoors since the mid-1800s.

Rangeley, 7 miles east on Route 4, has restaurants, inns, waterfront parks, and outdoorsy shops. The countryside sweeps into view along public hiking trails at both **Saddleback Maine** ski resort and the 175-acre **Wilhelm Reich Museum**.

The road to **Rangeley Lake State Park** is accessible from both Routes 4 and 17, as is the **Appalachian Trail**. Overhanging foliage frames waterfalls at the scenic rest areas at or near each end of the drive: Smalls Falls on Route 4, the byway's eastern terminus, and Coos Canyon on Route 17 en route to Height of Land. Both spots have several falls, swimming holes, and paths with views of the drops. Coos Canyon is along the Swift River, a destination for recreational gold panning. You can rent or buy panning equipment at **Coos Canyon Rock and Gift**, across from its namesake. It also sells sandwiches and snacks.

NEED A BREAK?

The Farmer's Daughter. At The Farmer's Daughter, much of the produce—including pumpkins and gourds come fall—is from the family farm. At the bakery counter you can buy a cup of coffee or apple cider in season. ⊠ *13 Rumford Rd., Oquossoc* ☏ *207/864-2492.*

Wilhelm Reich Museum. This museum showcases the life and work of controversial physician-scientist Wilhelm Reich (1897–1957). There are magnificent views from the observatory and the many trails on the 175-acre grounds. ⊠ *19 Orgonon Circle, off Rte. 4, Rangeley* ☏ *207/864-3443* ⊕ *www. wilhelmreichtrust.org* 🎟 *Museum $6, grounds free* ⊙ *Museum July and Aug., Wed.–Sun. 1–5; Sept., Sat. 1–5. Grounds daily 9–5.*

Rangeley Lakes Heritage Trust. This trust protects 13,000 acres of area land. It has trail maps and information about outdoor activities in the area. ⊠ *52 Carry Rd., Oquossoc* ☏ *207/864-7311* ⊕ *www. rlht.org.*

GREAT ITINERARIES

NEW HAMPSHIRE AND MAINE, 7 DAYS

Revel in the coastlines of two New England states—New Hampshire and Maine—on the path from the region's smallest shoreline, to the its highest peak, Mt. Washington. An assortment of New England's coastal treasures are at your fingertips as you pilot the ins and outs of the jagged northeastern coastline, before ascending the heights of the White Mountains. Plenty of fascinating towns and villages will vie for your attention with charming shops, seafood restaurants and picture-perfect views.

Fly in: Manchester-Boston Regional Airport (MHT), Manchester

Fly out: Manchester-Boston Regional Airport (MHT), Manchester

DAY 1: NEW HAMPSHIRE COAST

Kick off your trek in the southeastern corner of the Granite State. New Hampshire fronts the Atlantic for a scant 18 miles, but its coastal landmarks range from honky-tonk **Hampton Beach** to quiet **Odiorne Point State Park** in Rye and pretty Portsmouth, where the cream of pre-Revolutionary society built Georgian- and Federal-style mansions—visit a few at the **Strawbery Banke Museum.** Stay the night in **Portsmouth** at the centrally located **Ale House Inn.**

DAY 2: THE YORKS

Much of the appeal of the Maine Coast lies in its geographical contrasts, from its long stretches of swimming and walking beaches in the south to the cliff-edged, rugged, rocky coasts in the north. And not unlike the physical differences of the shoreline, each town along the way reveals a slightly different character, starting with **York.**

In **York Village** take a leisurely stroll through the seven buildings of the **Old York Historical Society,** getting a glimpse of 18th-century life in this gentrified town. Spend time wandering amid the shops or walking the nature trails and beaches around York Harbor. There are several grand lodging options here, most with views of the harbor. If you prefer a livelier pace, continue on to **York Beach,** a haven for families with plenty of entertainment venues. Stop at **Fox's Lobster House** after visiting **Nubble Light** for a seaside lunch or dinner.

Logistics: 10 miles; via I-95 N; 15 minutes, starting in Portsmouth

DAYS 3: OGUNQUIT AND THE KENNEBUNKS

For well over a century, **Ogunquit** has been a favorite vacation spot for those looking to combine the natural beauty of the ocean with a sophisticated environment. Take a morning walk along the **Marginal Way** to see the waves crashing on the rocks. In **Perkins Cove,** have lunch, stroll the shopping areas, or sign on with a lobster-boat cruise to learn about Maine's most important fishery—the state's lobster industry supplies more than 90% of the world's lobster intake. See the extraordinary collection at the **Ogunquit Museum of American Art,** take in a performance at one of the several theater venues, or just spend time on the beach.

Head north to the Kennebunks, allowing at least two hours to wander through the shops and historic homes of **Dock Square** in **Kennebunkport.** This is an ideal place to rent a bike and amble around the backstreets, head out on Ocean Avenue to view the large mansions, or ride to one of the several beaches to relax awhile. Spend your third night in Kennebunkport.

Logistics: 22 miles; via I-95 N; 30 minutes, starting in York

DAYS 4 AND 5: PORTLAND

If you have time, you can easily spend several days in Maine's largest city, exploring its historic neighborhoods, shopping and eating in the **Old Port**, or visiting one of several excellent museums. A brief side trip to **Cape Elizabeth** takes you to **Portland Head Light**, Maine's first lighthouse, which was commissioned by George Washington in 1787. The lighthouse is on the grounds of **Fort Williams Park** and is an excellent place to bring a picnic. Be sure to spend some time wandering the ample grounds. There are also excellent walking trails (and views) at nearby **Two Lights State Park.** If you want to take a boat tour while in Portland, get a ticket for Casco Bay Lines and see some of the islands that dot the bay. Spend two nights in Portland.

Logistics: 28 miles; via I-95 N; 40 minutes, staring in Kennebunkport

DAY 6: BRETTON WOODS

Wake up early and drive to Bretton Woods, where you will spend nights six and seven. The driving time from Portland to Bretton Woods is approximately three hours, due to two-lane, steep mountain roads. ■TIP→ Be sure to drive a four-wheel-drive vehicle in winter. Drive northwest along U.S. 302 toward **Sebago Lake,** a popular water-sports area in the summer, and continue on toward the time-honored New England towns of Naples and Bridgton. Just 15 miles from the border of New Hampshire, and nearing Crawford Notch, U.S. 302 begins to thread through New Hampshire's **White Mountains,** passing beneath brooding **Mt. Washington** before arriving in Bretton Woods.

Logistics: 98 miles; via ME 113 N and U.S. 302 W; 3 hours, starting in Portland

DAY 7: THE WHITE MOUNTAINS

In Bretton Woods, the **Mt. Washington Cog Railway** still chugs to the summit, and the **Omni Mount Washington Resort** recalls the glory days of White Mountain resorts. Beloved winter activities here include snowshoeing and skiing on the grounds of the Mount Washington Resort. You can even zip-line here in winter. Afterward, defrost with a cup of steaming hot cider while checking out vintage photos of the International Monetary Conference, held here in 1944, or head to the Cave, a prohibition-era speakeasy, for a drink.

MAINE'S NORTHERN COAST: PORTLAND TO ACADIA NATIONAL PARK, 6 DAYS

Lighthouses, beaches, lobster rolls, and water sports—Maine's northern coast has something for everyone. Quaint seaside villages and towns line the shore as U.S. 1 winds its way toward the easternmost swath of land in the United States at Quoddy Head State Park. Antiquing is a major draw, so keep an eye out for roadside shops crammed with gems. Maine's only national park, Acadia, is a highlight of the tour, drawing more than 2 million visitors per year.

Fly in: Portland International Jetport (PWM), Portland

Fly out: Bangor International Airport, (BGR), Bangor

DAY 1: PORTLAND TO BRUNSWICK

Use Maine's maritime capital as your jumping-off point to head farther up the Maine Coast, or, as Mainers call it, "Down East." Plan to spend half of your first day in Portland, then head to Brunswick for the night.

Portland shows off its restored waterfront at the **Old Port.** From there, before you

depart, you can grab a bite at either of two classic Maine eateries: **Gilbert's Chowder House** or **Becky's Diner,** or check out what's new in the buzzy restaurant scene here. For a peek at the freshest catch of the day, wander over to the **Harbor Fish Market,** a Portland institution since 1968, and gaze upon Maine lobsters and other delectable seafood. Two lighthouses on nearby **Cape Elizabeth, Two Lights** and **Portland Head,** still stand vigil.

Following U.S. 1, travel northeast along the ragged, island-strewn coast of Down East Maine and make your first stop at the retail outlets of **Freeport,** home of **L.L. Bean.** Almost 3 million people visit the massive flagship store every year, where you can find everything from outerwear to camping equipment. Just 10 miles north of Freeport on U.S. 1, **Brunswick** is home to the campus of **Bowdoin College** and also features a superb coastline for kayaking. Spend the night in Brunswick at one of the many inns that line U.S. 1.

Logistics: 30 miles; via U.S. 1 N; 30 minutes from Portland airport.

DAY 2: BATH

From Brunswick, head to **Bath,** Maine's shipbuilding capital, and tour the **Maine Maritime Museum,** stopping for lunch on the waterfront. Check out the boutiques

2

and antiques shops, or take in the plenitude of beautiful homes. From here it's a 30-minute detour down Route 127 to Georgetown Island and Reid State Park, where you will find a quiet beach lining Sheepscot Bay—and maybe even a sand dollar or two to take home, if you arrive at low tide. For a stunning vista, make your way to Griffith Head.

Drive north and reconnect with U.S. 1. Continue through the towns of **Wiscasset** and **Damariscotta**, where you may find yourself pulling over to stop at the outdoor flea markets and intriguing antiques shops that line the road. Another hour from here is **Rockland**, where you'll spend your second night.

Logistics: 52 miles; via U.S. 1 N; 1 hour 15 minutes, starting in Brunswick.

DAY 3: ROCKLAND, CAMDEN, AND CASTINE
From Rockland, spend the day cruising on a majestic schooner or reserve a tee time at Somerset Resorts' 18-hole championship course that overlooks the Rockland Harbor. If you're an art lover, save some time for Rockland's **Farnsworth Art Museum** and the **Wyeth Center.**

In **Camden** and **Castine**, exquisite inns occupy homes built from inland Maine's gold and timber. Camden is an ideal place to stay overnight as you make your way closer to Acadia National Park; it is a beautiful seaside town with hundreds of boats bobbing in the harbor, immaculately kept antique homes, streets lined with boutiques and specialty stores, and restaurants serving lobster at every turn. The modest hills (by Maine standards, anyway) of nearby Mt. Battie offer good hiking and a great spot from which to picnic and view the surrounding area. It is also one of the hubs for the beloved

and historic windjammer fleet—there is no better way to see the area than from the deck of one of these graceful beauties.

Logistics: 62 miles; via U.S. 1 N and Rte. 166 S; 1½ hours, starting in Rockland.

DAYS 4 AND 5: MOUNT DESERT ISLAND AND ACADIA NATIONAL PARK
On Day 4, head out early for **Bar Harbor** and plan to spend two nights here, using the bustling village as jumping off point for the park—Bar Harbor is less than 5 miles from the entrance to **Mount Desert Island**'s 27-mile Park Loop Road. Spend at least a day exploring **Acadia National Park**, Maine's only national park and its most popular tourist destination. Enjoy the island's natural beauty by kayaking its coast, biking the 45-mile, historic, unpaved, carriage-road system, and driving to the summit of **Cadillac Mountain** for a stunning panorama.

Logistics: 52 miles; via Rte. 166 N, U.S. 1 N and Rte. 3 E; 1¼ hours, starting in Castine.

DAY 6: BAR HARBOR TO QUODDY HEAD STATE PARK
About 100 miles farther along U.S. 1 and "Way Down East" is Quoddy Head State Park in Lubec, Maine. Here, on the easternmost tip of land in the United States, sits the **West Quoddy Head Light**, one of 60 lighthouses that dot Maine's rugged coastline. Depending on the time of year (and your willingness to get up very early), you may be lucky enough to catch the East Coast's first sunrise here.

Logistics: 103 miles; via U.S. 1 N; 2½ hours, starting in Bar Harbor. From the park, it is 119 miles (2½ hours) to the Bangor airport via Rte. 9 W.

BEST OF VERMONT, 7 DAYS

Following roads that weave through the Green Mountains and charming towns, this 200-mile journey is ideal at any time of year and covers Vermont from top to bottom.

Fly in: Bradley International Airport (BDL), Hartford

Fly out: Burlington International Airport (BTV), Burlington

DAY 1: BRATTLEBORO

Artsy **Brattleboro** is the perfect place to begin a tour of Vermont, and it's worth taking a day to do some shopping and exploring. Catch a movie at the art deco **Latchis Theatre,** browse in a bookstore, or simply grab a cup of joe and people-watch. For dinner, make a reservation well in advance at tiny **T.J. Buckley's,** one of the best restaurants in the state. Spend your first night in Brattleboro.

Logistics: 78 miles; via I–91 N; 1 hour and 15 minutes from Bradley airport.

DAYS 2-4: KILLINGTON

Depart Brattleboro heading west on Route 9 and link up with Route 100 in Wilmington. As you travel north along the eastern edge of **Green Mountain National Forest,** you'll pass a plethora of panoramic overlooks and delightful ski towns. Stop to snap a photo, or take a moment to peruse the selection at a funky general store, as you make your way toward gigantic Killington Peak. Spend the next three nights in **Killington,** the largest ski resort in Vermont, and an outdoor playground year-round. A tip for skiers: one of the closest places to the slopes to stay is **The Mountain Top Inn & Resort.**

Wake up early to carve the mountain's fresh powder in winter. Nonskiers can still enjoy the snow, whether at the tubing park, on a snowmobile adventure, or in snowshoes on one of several trails. In summer, long after the ground has thawed, those trails are opened to mountain bikers and hikers. For a more leisurely activity, try your hand at the 18-hole disc-golf course. The excellent Grand Spa is also a lovely way to spend the day.

Logistics: 94 miles; via Rte. 9 W, Rte. 100 N, 2½ hours, starting in Brattleboro.

DAY 5: KILLINGTON TO BURLINGTON

Continue on Route 100 north until you reach Hancock, then head west on Route 125. Welcome to the land of poet Robert Frost, who spent almost 40 years living in Vermont, summering in the nearby tiny mountain town of Ripton, where he wrote numerous poems. Plaques along the 1.2-mile **Robert Frost Interpretive Trail,** a quiet

2

woodland walk that takes about 30 minutes, display commemorative quotes from his poems, including his classic, "The Road Not Taken." After your stroll, head north on U.S. 7 until you hit Burlington.

Burlington, Vermont's largest city and home to the **University of Vermont,** is located on the eastern shore of Lake Champlain. Bustling in the summer and fall, the **Burlington Farmers' Market** is filled with everything from organic meats and cheeses to freshly cut flowers and maple syrup. Spend the night in Burlington. In the evening, check out **Nectar's,** where the band Phish played their first bar gig, or wander into any of the many other pubs and cafés that attract local musicians.

Logistics: 84 miles; via Rte. 100 N, Rte. 125 W, and U.S. 7 N; 2½ hours, starting in Killington.

DAY 6: SHELBURNE AND LAKE CHAMPLAIN

On your second day in Burlington, you can take a day trip south to the **Magic Hat Brewing Company;** established in 1994, it was at the forefront of Vermont's microbrewery explosion. Take a free half-hour guided or self-guided tour of the Artifactory (even dogs are welcome), and fill a growler from one of the 48 taps pumping out year-round, seasonal, and experimental brews. A stone's throw down U.S. 7, in **Shelburne,** is family-friendly **Shelburne Farms.** Watch the process of making cheese from start to finish, or wander the gorgeous 1,400-acre estate designed by Frederick Law Olmsted, co-designer of New York's Central Park. The grounds overlook beautiful **Lake Champlain** and make the perfect setting for a picnic. In winter Shelburne Farms offers sleigh rides and other themed activities; if you're visiting in late July, don't miss the **Vermont Cheesemakers Festival,** showcasing more than 200 varieties of cheese crafted by 40 local purveyors. If you can't get enough, you can opt to spend the night here.

Logistics: 3.6 miles, via U.S. 7 to Magic Hat; another 3.4 miles to Shelburne Farms; 40 minutes round-trip altogether.

DAY 7: STOWE

A 30-minute drive down Interstate 89 from Burlington reunites you with Route 100 in the small town of Waterbury. Head north in the direction of Stowe, and in under 2 miles you can make the obligatory pit stop at **Ben & Jerry's Ice Cream Factory.** The factory tour offers a lively behind-the-scenes look at how their ice cream is made; at the end of the tour, you get to taste limited-release creations only available at the factory before voting on your favorites.

Next, set out for the village of **Stowe.** Its proximity to Mt. Mansfield (Vermont's highest peak at 4,395 feet) has made Stowe a popular ski destination since the 1930s. If there's snow on the ground, hit the slopes, hitch a ride on a one-horse open sleigh, or simply put your feet up by the fire and enjoy a Heady Topper (an unfiltered, hoppy, American Double IPA beloved by Vermonters). In warmer weather, pop into the cute shops and art galleries that line the town's main street and sample some of the finest cheddar cheese and maple syrup that Vermont has to offer. Rejuvenate yourself at **Topnotch Resort,** which offers more than 100 different treatments. Spend your final night here.

Logistics: 36 miles; via I–89 S and Rte. 100 N; 45 minutes, starting in Burlington. From Stowe to the Burlington airport: 33 miles; via Rte. 100 and I–89 N; 41 minutes.

VERMONT

WELCOME TO VERMONT

TOP REASONS TO GO

★ **Small-Town Charm:** Vermont rolls out a seemingly never-ending supply of tiny towns replete with white-steepled churches, town greens, red barns, general stores, and bed-and-breakfasts.

★ **Ski Resorts:** The East's best skiing can be found in well-managed, modern facilities with great views and lots and lots of fresh snow.

★ **Fall Foliage:** Perhaps the most vivid colors in North America wave from the trees in September and October, when the whole state is ablaze.

★ **Gorgeous Landscapes:** This sparsely populated, heavily forested state is an ideal place to find peace and quiet amid the mountains, valleys, and lakes.

★ **Tasty and Healthy Eats:** The rich soil and an emphasis on using local ingredients has led to great dairies, orchards, vineyards, specialty stores, and farm-to-table restaurants.

1 Southern Vermont. Most people's introduction to the state is southern Vermont, a relatively short drive from New York and Boston. As elsewhere across the state, you'll find unspoiled towns, romantic bed-and-breakfasts, lush farms, and pristine forests. There are two notable exceptions: sophisticated Manchester has upscale shopping, and independent Brattleboro remains a hippie enclave with an environmentally conscious disposition.

2 Central Vermont. Similar to southern Vermont in character and geography, central Vermont stretches from workaday Rutland in the south to the picturesque Mad River Valley in the north. Woodstock, Waitsfield, and Middlebury number among its inviting small towns.

3 Northern Vermont. The state's northernmost part is a place of contrasts. Burlington, with dramatic views of Lake Champlain and the Adirondacks, is Vermont's most populous city, with around 60,000 residents; an arts-loving, laid-back college town, it has a sophisticated food scene. On the other side of Mount Mansfield is Stowe, the quintessential eastern ski town, beyond which the landscape becomes increasingly rural. Stupendous natural beauty and a sparse population make the Northeast Kingdom a refuge for nature lovers and for those who love getting away from it all.

GETTING ORIENTED

Vermont can be divided into three regions. The southern part of the state, flanked by Bennington on the west and Brattleboro on the east, played an important role in Vermont's Revolutionary War—era drive for independence—yes, there was once a Republic of Vermont—and eventual statehood. The central part is characterized by rugged mountains and the gently rolling dairy lands east of Lake Champlain's southern sliver. And northern Vermont is home to the state's capital, Montpelier, and its largest city, Burlington, as well as its most rural area, the Northeast Kingdom. The Green Mountains run north–south through the center of the state, covered in protected national forest.

CANADA
QUÉBEC

Lake Carmi

Lake Champlain

Lake Willoughby

MAD RIVER VALLEY

GREEN MOUNTAINS

NEW
HAMPSHIRE

NEW
YORK

MASSACHUSETTS

Alburg
North Troy
Derby Line
Derby Center
Norton
Beecher Falls

Swanton
Richford
Jay
Newport

Enosburg Falls
105
114

North Hero
Saint Albans
Lowell
Orleans
Island Pond
3

Grand Isle
Fairfax
Jeffersonville
Barton
Albany
West Burke
105

South Hero
2
Milton
Johnson
Wolcott
16
91
Guildhall

Mt. Mansfield 2,360 ft
Morrisville
15
Lyndonville
Lyndon

Burlington
Essex Junction
Hardwick
Saint Johnsbury
Concord
2

Richmond
Stowe
Danville
93

Shelburne
116
Waterbury
MONTPELIER
Marshfield
Barnet

Vergennes
Waitsfield
Plainfield
Wells River
302

Middlebury
Warren
Barre
Newbury
25

Bristol
West Topsham
Bradford

East Middlebury
Chelsea
Fairlee

Shoreham
Hancock
East Randolph
Randolph

Brandon
Bethel

Proctor
Killington
Wilder

Castleton
Rutland
Woodstock
White River Junction

Poultney
West Rutland
Hartland

Granville
Wallingford
Windsor

West Pawlet
Ludlow
Ascutney

Darset
Perkinsville

Manchester
Springfield
Chester

Arlington
Grafton
Bellows Falls

Shaftsbury
Jamaica
Westminster

Newfane
Putney

West Dover

Bennington
Wilmington
Brattleboro

Pownal
Jacksonville

Readsboro

87
89
22

0   10 mi
0   10 km

Updated by
Aaron Starmer

Vermont is a land of hidden treasures and unspoiled scenery. Wander anywhere in the state—nearly 80% is forest—and you'll find pristine countryside dotted with farms and framed by mountains. Tiny towns with picturesque church steeples, village greens, and clapboard Colonial-era houses are perfect for exploring.

Sprawl has no place here. Highways are devoid of billboards by law, and on some roads cows still stop traffic twice a day en route to and from pasture. In spring, sap boils in sugarhouses, some built generations ago, while up the road a chef trained at the New England Culinary Institute in Montpelier might use the syrup to glaze a pork tenderloin.

It's the landscape, for the most part, that attracts people to Vermont. Rolling hills belie rugged terrain underneath the green canopy of forest growth. In summer, clear lakes and streams provide ample opportunities for swimming, boating, and fishing; hills attract hikers and mountain bikers. The more than 14,000 miles of roads, many of them only intermittently traveled by cars, are great for biking. In fall the leaves have their last hurrah, painting the mountainsides in yellow, gold, red, and orange. Vermont has the best ski resorts in the eastern United States, centered along the spine of the Green Mountains running north to south; and the traditional heart of skiing here is the town of Stowe. Almost anywhere you go, no matter what time of year, the Vermont countryside will make you reach for your camera.

Although Vermont may seem locked in time, technological sophistication appears where you least expect it: wireless Internet access in a 19th-century farmhouse-turned-inn and cell phone coverage from the state's highest peaks. Like an old farmhouse under renovation, though, the state's historic exterior is still the main attraction.

PLANNING

WHEN TO GO

In summer Vermont is lush and green, and in winter the hills and towns are blanketed white with snow, inspiring skiers to challenge the peaks at Stowe and elsewhere. Fall, however, is always the most amazing time to come. If you have never seen the state's kaleidoscope of autumn colors, it's well worth braving the slow-moving traffic and shelling out a few extra bucks for lodging. The only time things really slow down is during "mud season" in late spring, when even innkeepers counsel guests to come another time. Activities in the Champlain Islands essentially come to a halt in the winter, except for ice fishing and snowmobiling, and two of the biggest attractions, Shelburne Farms and the Shelburne Museum, are closed mid-October–April. Otherwise, Vermont is open for business year-round.

PLANNING YOUR TIME

There are many ways to take advantage of Vermont's beauty: skiing or hiking its mountains, biking or driving its back roads, fishing or sailing its waters, shopping for local products, visiting museums and sights, or simply finding the perfect inn and never leaving the front porch.

Distances are relatively short, yet the mountains and back roads will slow a traveler's pace. You can see a representative north–south cross-section of Vermont in a few days; if you have up to a week, you can really hit the highlights.

AIR TRAVEL

Allegiant, American, Delta, JetBlue, Porter, and United fly into Burlington International Airport. Rutland State Airport has daily service to and from Boston on Cape Air.

BOAT TRAVEL

Lake Champlain Ferries. This company operates ferries on three routes between Vermont and New York: from Grand Isle to Plattsburgh, New York; Burlington to Port Kent; and Charlotte to Essex. ☎ *802/864–9804* ⊕ *www.ferries.com* ⊙ *No Burlington–Port Kent service early Sept.–early June.*

CAR TRAVEL

Vermont is divided by a mountainous north–south middle, with a main highway on either side: scenic U.S. 7 on the western side and Interstate 91 (which begins in New Haven and runs through Hartford, central Massachusetts, and along the Connecticut River in Vermont to the Canadian border) on the east. Interstate 89 runs from New Hampshire across central Vermont from White River Junction to Burlington and up to the Canadian border. For current road conditions, check ⊕ *www.511vt.com* or call ☎ *511* in Vermont and ☎ *800/429–7623* from other states.

TRAIN TRAVEL

Amtrak. Amtrak has daytime service on the *Vermonter,* linking Washington, D.C., and New York City with Brattleboro, Bellows Falls, Windsor, White River Junction, Randolph, Montpelier, Waterbury,

Essex Junction, and St. Albans. Amtrak's *Ethan Allen Express* connects New York City with Castleton and Rutland. ☎ *800/872–7245* ⊕ *www.amtrak.com.*

RESTAURANTS

Everything that makes Vermont good and wholesome is distilled in its restaurants. Many of them belong to the **Vermont Fresh Network** (⊕ *www. vermontfresh.net*), a partnership that encourages chefs to create menus emphasizing Vermont's wonderful bounty; especially in summer and early fall, the produce and meats are impeccable. The resulting Vermont cuisine is accordingly better defined than that found in neighboring states.

Great chefs come to Vermont for the quality of life, and the Montpelier-based New England Culinary Institute is a recruiting ground for new talent. Seasonal menus use local fresh herbs and vegetables along with native game. Look for imaginative approaches to native New England foods like maple syrup (Vermont is the largest U.S. producer), dairy products (cheese in particular), native fruits and berries, "new Vermont" products such as salsa and salad dressings, and venison, quail, pheasant, and other game.

Your chances of finding a table for dinner vary with the season: lengthy waits are common in tourist centers at peak times—a reservation is always advisable. Some of the best dining is at country inns. *Prices in the reviews are the average cost of a main course at dinner or, if dinner is not served, at lunch.*

HOTELS

Vermont's only large chain hotels are in Burlington and Rutland; elsewhere it's just inns, bed-and-breakfasts, and small motels. The inns and B&Bs, some of them quite luxurious, provide what many visitors consider the quintessential Vermont lodging experience. Most areas have traditional ski-base condos; at these you sacrifice charm for ski-and-stay deals and proximity to the lifts. Lodging rates are highest during foliage season, late September–mid-October, and lowest in late spring and November, although many properties close during these times. Winter is high season at ski resorts. *Prices in the reviews are the lowest cost of a standard double room in high season. Hotel reviews have been shortened. For full reviews visit Fodors.com.*

WHAT IT COSTS			
$	**$$**	**$$$**	**$$$$**
Restaurants	under $18	$18–$24	$25–$35	over $35
Hotels	under $200	$200–$299	$300–$399	over $399

TOURS

Country Inns Along the Trail. This company arranges guided and self-guided hiking, skiing, and biking trips from inn to inn in Vermont. ⊠ *52 Park St., Brandon* ☎ *802/247–3300, 800/838–3301* ⊕ *www.inntoinn. com* ☎ *From $545.*

P.O.M.G. Bike Tours of Vermont. The initials in this outfitter's name are short for "Peace Of Mind Guaranteed." The company leads weekend and multiday bike tours around the state. ☎ *802/434–2270, 888/635–2453* ⊕ *www.pomgbike.com* ✉ *From $1,750.*

Vermont Bicycle Touring. This guide company leads bike tours across the state. ☎ *802/453–4811, 800/245–3868* ⊕ *www.vbt.com* ✉ *From $1,895.*

VISITOR INFORMATION

Statewide Ski Vermont/Vermont Ski Areas Association. ⊠ *26 State St., Montpelier* ☎ *802/223-2439* ⊕ *www.skivermont.com.* **Vermont Department of Tourism and Marketing.** ⊠ *1 National Life Dr., 6th fl., Montpelier* ☎ *802/828-3237, 800/837-6668* ⊕ *www.vermontvacation.com.* **Vermont Seasonal Hotline.** ☎ *802/828-3239 for foliage information, snow conditions, and events.*

Regional Northeast Kingdom Travel and Tourism Association. ☎ *802/626-8511* ⊕ *www.travelthekingdom.com.*

SOUTHERN VERMONT

Cross into the Green Mountain State from Massachusetts on Interstate 91, and you might feel as if you've entered another country. There isn't a town in sight: what you see are forested hills punctuated by rolling pastures. When you reach Brattleboro, no strip malls line the exits to signal your arrival at southeastern Vermont's gateway city, and en route downtown, you pass Victorian-era homes on tree-lined streets. From here, you can cross over the spine of the Green Mountains toward Bennington and Manchester.

The state's southwest corner is the southern terminus of the Green Mountain National Forest, dotted with lakes, threaded with trails and old forest roads, and home to three big ski resorts: Bromley, Stratton, and Mount Snow.

BRATTLEBORO

60 miles south of White River Junction.

Brattleboro has drawn political activists and earnest counterculturists since the 1960s. The arts-oriented town and environs (population 12,000) remains politically and culturally active; after Burlington, this is Vermont's most offbeat locale.

GETTING HERE AND AROUND

Brattleboro is near the intersection of Route 9, the principal east–west highway also known as the Molly Stark Byway, and Interstate 91. For downtown, take Exit 2 from Interstate 91.

ESSENTIALS

Visitor Information Brattleboro Area Chamber of Commerce. ⊠ *180 Main St.* ☎ *802/254-4565, 877/254-4565* ⊕ *www.brattleborochamber.org.*

EXPLORING

Brattleboro Museum and Art Center. Downtown is the hub of Brattleboro's art scene, at the forefront of which is this museum in historic Union Station. It presents changing exhibitions of works by local, national, and international artists, and hosts lectures, readings, and musical performances. ⊠ *10 Vernon St.* ☎ *802/257–0124* ⊕ *www.brattleboromuseum.org* ✉ *$8.*

NEED A BREAK

✕ **Mocha Joe's Cafe.** The team at this spot for coffee and conversation takes great pride in sourcing direct-trade beans from places like Kenya, Ethiopia, and Guatemala. Ground zero for Brattleboro's bohemian contingent and fellow travelers, the café is open until 9 on Friday and Saturday, closing at 8 the rest of the week. ⊠ *82 Main St., at Elliot St.* ☎ *802/257–5637* ⊕ *www.mochajoes.com.*

OFF THE BEATEN PATH

Putney. Nine miles upriver, this town of fewer than 3,000 residents—the country cousin of bustling Brattleboro—is a haven for writers and fine-craft artists. There are many pottery studios to visit, the requisite general store, and a few orchards. Each November during the Putney Craft Tour, dozens of artisans open their studios and homes for live demonstrations and plenty of fun. ⊠ *Putney* ⊕ *www.discoverputney.com.*

OUTDOOR ACTIVITIES

Biking: Vermont, especially the often-deserted roads of the Northeast Kingdom, is great bicycle-touring country. Many companies lead weekend tours and weeklong trips throughout the state. If you'd like to go it on your own, most chambers of commerce have brochures highlighting the best cycling routes in their areas.

Canoeing and Kayaking: Getting on Vermont's many rivers and lakes is a great way to experience nature. Outfitters can be found almost anywhere there's water.

Fishing: Central Vermont is the heart of the state's warm-water lake and pond fishing area. Lake Champlain, stocked annually with salmon and lake trout, has become the state's ice-fishing capital.

Hiking: Vermont is an ideal state for hiking: nearly 80% of the state is forest, and trails are everywhere. The Long Trail runs the length of the state. It includes the first portion of the Appalachian Trail to be completed, an achievement that inspired the development of the rest of that trail. Many bookstores carry guides about local hiking.

Skiing: The Green Mountains run through the middle of Vermont like a bumpy spine, visible from almost every point in the state; generous accumulations of snow make them ideal for skiing. Route 100, also known as Skier's Highway, paves the way to 13 ski areas.

WHERE TO EAT

$ — AMERICAN — ✕**Brattleboro Food Co-op.** Pick up a plate of chicken or beef *satay* (skewered grilled meat) at the deli counter of this hot spot for local and organic groceries, then find a seat in the glassed-in café area or out on the river-view patio. The deli also serves fabulous sandwiches, and there's a good beer and wine selection. The many fine products for sale in the store include a self-serve selection of varying grades of maple syrup. ⑤ *Average main: $8* ✉ *2 Main St.* ☎ *802/257–0236* ⊕ *www.brattleborofoodcoop.com.*

$$ — MODERN AMERICAN — ✕**Duo.** A corner location in the historic Brooks House and huge, inviting windows make this stylish farm-to-table restaurant impossible to miss. The locally sourced fare changes with the season, but the menu always includes an innovative take on fritters and a winning pork dish. Brunch is a great way to sample what the owner calls "food you're familiar with, done better." ⑤ *Average main: $22* ✉ *136 Main St.* ☎ *802/254–4141* ⊕ *www.duorestaurants.com* ⊗ *No lunch weekdays* ⚑ *Reservations essential.*

$$ — ITALIAN — ✕**Fireworks.** The airy and colorful Fireworks serves salads, pastas, and flatbread pizzas. Daily specials, often variations on the usual pizzas or pastas, are always worth considering, and cocktails are creatively mixed. In nice weather, check out the back patio. ⑤ *Average main: $18* ✉ *69–73 Main St.* ☎ *802/254–2073* ⊕ *www.fireworksrestaurant.net/brattleboro* ⊗ *Closed Mon. No lunch.*

$$$ — AMERICAN — **Fodor's**Choice ★ — ✕**Peter Havens.** A longtime Brattleboro favorite helmed since 2012 by chef Zachary Corbin, this chic little bistro is known for impeccably presented cuisine that draws heavily on local sources. One room is painted a warm red, another in sage, and a changing lineup of contemporary

paintings adorns the walls of both rooms. Whatever your main dish, start off with the heavenly tuna tartare and a seasonal cocktail or glass of wine from a list that hits all the right notes. ⑤ *Average main: $30* ✉ *32 Elliot St.* ☎ *802/257-3333* ⊕ *www.peterhavens.com* ⊙ *Closed Mon. and Tues. No lunch Nov.–May.*

$$$$
AMERICAN
Fodor'sChoice
★

✕ **T.J. Buckley's.** It's easy to pass by this small place housed inside a converted 1925 lunch car (diner) built in Worcester, Massachusetts, but it's one of Vermont's most romantic restaurants. The sleek red and black space amounts to an intimate, candlelit theater with just 18 seats—its stage an open kitchen whose flames flare mere feet from enraptured patrons. Performing with aplomb under the whisper of jazz is the star of the show: Michael Fuller, the dashing owner and sole chef for more than three decades. The contemporary menu, conveyed verbally each day, is based on locally available ingredients. ⑤ *Average main: $40* ✉ *132 Elliot St.* ☎ *802/257-4922* ⊕ *www.tjbuckleysuptowndining.com* ⊙ *Closed Mon., Tues., and most Wed. No lunch* ⌲ *Reservations essential.*

$
BARBECUE
FAMILY

✕ **Top of the Hill Grill.** Don't let the diminutive size of this roadside smokehouse deceive you. The place produces big flavors locals line up for: hickory-smoked ribs, apple-smoked turkey, beef brisket, and pulled pork, to name a few. Homemade pecan pie is the dessert of choice. The restaurant probably has the best view in town, with outdoor picnic tables and an enclosed area overlooking the West River. ⑤ *Average main: $15* ✉ *632 Putney Rd.* ☎ *802/258-9178* ⊕ *www.topofthehillgrill. com* ⊟ *No credit cards* ⊙ *Closed Nov.–Mar.*

$
CAFÉ

✕ **The Works Bakery Cafe.** Natural light fills this spot in the center of town, whose patrons work on laptops at long wooden tables or sit with a book and some coffee in one of the comfortable armchairs. Fresh-fruit smoothies, panini, wraps, and salads are among the menu highlights. This is a perfect breakfast or lunch stop, or just a great place to catch up on email. ⑤ *Average main: $7* ✉ *118 Main St.* ☎ *802/579-1851* ⊕ *www.worksbakerycafe.com.*

WHERE TO STAY

$$
B&B/INN
Fodor'sChoice
★

🛏 **Forty Putney Road.** Realizing her dream to run an inn, Rhonda Calhoun took over this 1931 French-style manse and has added her own colorful touches to the original features. **Pros:** caring host makes you feel like a guest, not a customer; comforting details; fabulous breakfast. **Cons:** tight parking. ⑤ *Rooms from: $219* ✉ *192 Putney Rd.* ☎ *802/254-6268, 800/941-2413* ⊕ *www.fortyputneyroad.com* ⇆ *5 rooms, 1 suite* |⊙| *Breakfast.*

$
B&B/INN
Fodor'sChoice
★

🛏 **Hickory Ridge House.** If you're looking for a relaxing country getaway, this 1808 Federal-style mansion on the wide meadow of a former sheep farm is a good bet. **Pros:** peaceful property; great breakfast; quintessential bed-and-breakfast experience. **Cons:** not within walking distance of town. ⑤ *Rooms from: $175* ✉ *53 Hickory Ridge Rd., 11 miles north of Brattleboro, Putney* ☎ *802/387-5709, 800/380-9218* ⊕ *www.hickoryridgehouse.com* ⇆ *6 rooms, 1 cottage* |⊙| *Breakfast.*

$
HOTEL

🛏 **Latchis Hotel.** To stay in the heart of town, you won't find a more economical option than this art-deco hotel. **Pros:** heart-of-town location; lots of personality; reasonable rates. **Cons:** limited breakfast. ⑤ *Rooms from: $100* ✉ *50 Main St.* ☎ *802/254-6300, 800/798-6301* ⊕ *www. latchis.com* ⇆ *30 rooms, 3 suites* |⊙| *Breakfast.*

The rolling green hills of Putney are home to many organic farm operations.

PERFORMING ARTS

Latchis Theatre. This movie theater's architecture represents a singular blending of art deco and Greek Revival style, complete with statues, columns, and 1938 murals by Louis Jambor (1884–1955), a noted artist and children's book illustrator. The Latchis hosts art exhibits, streams live events, and has four screening rooms. For a sense of the theater's original grandeur, buy a ticket for whatever is showing on the big screen. Though the space may lack state-of-the-art technology, watching a film here is far more memorable than at any multiplex. ✉ *50 Main St.* ☎ *802/254–6300, 800/798–6301* ⊕ *www.latchis.com.*

SPORTS AND THE OUTDOORS

BICYCLING

Brattleboro Bicycle Shop. This shop rents hybrid bikes (call ahead to reserve one), does repair work, and sells maps and equipment. ✉ *165 Main St.* ☎ *802/254–8644, 800/272–8245* ⊕ *www.bratbike.com.*

CANOEING

Vermont Canoe Touring Center. Canoes and kayaks are available for rent here. Payment is by cash or check only. ✉ *451 Putney Rd.* ☎ *802/257–5008* ⊕ *www.vermontcanoetouringcenter.com.*

HIKING

Fort Dummer State Park. You can hike and camp within the 217 acres of forest at this state park, the location of the first permanent white settlement in Vermont. That site is now submerged beneath the Connecticut River, but it is viewable from the northernmost scenic vista on Sunrise Trail. ✉ *517 Old Guilford Rd.* ☎ *802/254–2610* ⊕ *www.vtstateparks. com/htm/fortdummer.htm* ⊠ *$4* ☉ *Facilities closed early Sept.–late May.*

MULTISPORTS OUTFITTERS

Sam's Outdoor Outfitters. At this labyrinthine two-story sports emporium you can find outerwear, shoes, and gear for all seasons and activities. Grab a bag of free popcorn while you're shopping. ⊠ *74 Main St.* ☎ *802/254–2933* ⊕ *www.samsoutfitters.com.*

SHOPPING

ART GALLERIES

Gallery in the Woods. This funky trilevel store sells art, jewelry, and light fixtures from around the world. Rotating shows take place in the upstairs and downstairs galleries. ⊠ *145 Main St.* ☎ *802/257–4777* ⊕ *www.galleryinthewoods.com.*

Gallery Walk. On this walk, you'll pass more than 30 galleries and other venues downtown and nearby that exhibit art; it takes place 5:30–8:30 on the first Friday evening of the month. ☎ *802/257–2616* ⊕ *www. gallerywalk.org.*

Vermont Artisan Designs. Artworks and functional items in ceramics, glass, wood, fiber, and other media created by more than 300 artists are on display at this gallery. ⊠ *106 Main St.* ☎ *802/257–7044* ⊕ *www. vtart.com.*

BOOKS

Everyone's Books. The literary (and literal) center of a bookish town, this is the place to pick up a best seller, a local classic, or a book on progressive politics or the environment. The shop hosts readings and author events. ⊠ *25 Elliot St.* ☎ *802/254–8160* ⊕ *www.everyonesbks.com.*

FOOD

Serenity Herbs and Teas. Even if you're not an avid tea drinker, it's hard not to admire the passion and expertise of the proprietors of this elegant shop; ask what makes a true Earl Grey and you'll learn more than you ever thought possible. All teas are hand blended in the back. ⊠ *60 Elliot St.* ☎ *802/246–1310* ⊕ *www.serenityherbsandteas.com* ⊙ *Closed Sun.–Tues.*

WILMINGTON

18 miles west of Brattleboro.

The village of Wilmington, with its classic Main Street lined with 18th- and 19th-century buildings, anchors the Mount Snow Valley. Most of the valley's lodging and dining establishments, however, can be found along Route 100, which travels 5 miles north to West Dover and Mount Snow, where skiers flock on winter weekends. The area abounds with cultural activity from concerts to art exhibits year-round.

GETTING HERE AND AROUND

Wilmington is at the junction of Route 9 and Route 100. West Dover and Mount Snow are a few miles to the north along Route 100.

ESSENTIALS

Visitor Information Southern Vermont Deerfield Valley Chamber of Commerce. ⊠ *21 W. Main St.* ☎ *802/464–8092, 877/887–6884* ⊕ *www.visitvermont.com.*

EXPLORING

FAMILY **Adams Family Farm.** At this working farm you can collect fresh eggs from the chicken coop, feed a rabbit, milk a goat, ride a tractor or a pony, catch a fish in the pond, or take a sleigh ride in winter. A livestock barn is open November–mid-June; the animals roam free the rest of the year. ⊠ *15 Higley Hill Rd., off Rte. 100* ☎ *802/464-3762* ⊕ *www.adamsfamilyfarm.com* ⊠ *$6.95.*

> ## BILLBOARDLESS VERMONT
>
> Did you know that there are no billboards in Vermont? The state banned them in 1967 (similar laws exist in Maine, Alaska, and Hawaii), and the last one came down in 1975, so when you look out your window, you see trees and other scenery—not advertisements.

3

FAMILY **Southern Vermont Natural History Museum.** This museum 5 miles east of Wilmington houses one of New England's largest collections of mounted birds, including three extinct species and a complete collection of mammals native to the Northeast. The museum also has exhibits with live hawks, owls, and reptiles, and there's an adjacent 600-acre nature preserve. ⊠ *7599 Rte. 9, West Marlboro* ☎ *802/464-0048* ⊕ *www.vermontmuseum.org* ⊠ *$5.*

WHERE TO EAT

$ ✕ **Dot's Restaurant.** Look for the classic red neon sign (one of only a
DINER handful still permitted in Vermont) at the main corner in downtown
FAMILY Wilmington: Dot's is a local landmark. After Hurricane Irene ravaged the building in 2011, the community rallied to save its traditional country diner. Donations poured in, the structure was entirely renovated and fortified against future flooding, and by 2013 Dot's was back in business. It remains a friendly place where locals and skiers pack the tables and counter to order favorites like chicken *cordon bleu* (stuffed with ham and cheese, then breaded and fried), barbecue ribs, and home-style roast beef. The Berry-Berry pancakes with four kinds of berries are de rigueur for breakfast, which starts at 5:30 am. A bowl of chili is perfect for lunch. ⑤ *Average main: $10* ⊠ *3 W. Main St.* ☎ *802/464-7284* ⊕ *www.dotsofvermont.com.*

$$$ ✕ **Nonna's.** Terrance Brannan, a James Beard–nominated consultant,
ITALIAN crafted the menu at the haute-cuisine restaurant at Sawmill Farm. The focus is on traditional Italian dishes such as tuna carpaccio, fettuccine carbonara, lobster risotto, and saltimbocca. You can order à la carte, though the restaurant recommends the four-course prix-fixe presentation. ⑤ *Average main: $30* ⊠ *Inn at Sawmill Farm, 7 Crosstown Rd., at Rte. 100, West Dover* ☎ *802/464-8131* ⊕ *www.theinnatsawmillfarm.com* ⊗ *Closed Tues. and Wed. No lunch.*

WHERE TO STAY

$ ▦ **Deerhill Inn.** The restaurant at this quintessential New England inn
B&B/INN is among the best in town. **Pros:** special place; great restaurant. **Cons:** must drive to town and resort. ⑤ *Rooms from: $185* ⊠ *14 Valley View Rd., West Dover* ☎ *802/464-3100, 800/993-3379* ⊕ *www.deerhill.com* ⟿ *10 rooms, 3 suites* ☒ *Breakfast.*

$$$ ▦ **Grand Summit Hotel.** Mount Snow's comfortable main hotel is an easy
RESORT choice for skiers whose main priority is getting on the slopes as quickly
FAMILY as possible. **Pros:** easy ski access; modern property. **Cons:** somewhat

CLOSE UP

Vermont Maple Syrup

Vermont is the country's largest producer of maple syrup. A visit to a maple farm is a great way to learn all about sugaring, the process of extracting maple tree sap and making syrup. Sap is stored in a sugar maple tree's roots in the winter, and in the spring when conditions are just right, the sap runs up and can be tapped. Sugaring season runs March–April, which is when all maple syrup in the state is produced.

One of the best parts of visiting a maple farm is getting to taste and compare the four grades of syrup. As the sugaring season goes on and days become warmer, the sap becomes progressively darker and stronger in flavor. Grades are defined by color, clarity, and flavor. Is one grade better than another? Nope, it's just a question of taste. Sap drawn early in the season produces the lightest color, and has the most delicate flavor: this

is called Vermont Fancy. Vermont Grade A Medium Amber has a mellow flavor. Vermont Grade A Dark Amber is much more robust, and Vermont Grade B is the most flavorful, making it often the favorite of first-time tasters.

When visiting a maple farm, make sure they make their own syrup, as opposed to just bottling or selling someone else's. You'll learn more about the entire process that way. **Vermont Maple Syrup** (☏ 802/858–9444 ⊕ www.vermontmaple.org), a great resource, has a map of maple farms that host tours, a directory of producers open year-round, and a list of places from which you can order maple syrup by mail. You can also get the lowdown on events such as the annual Maple Open House Weekend, when sugarhouses throughout the state open their doors to visitors.

bland decor. ⑤ *Rooms from: $380* ⊠ *89 Grand Summit Way, West Dover* ☏ *800/498–0479* ⊕ *www.mountsnow.com* ⤳ *196 rooms, suites, and studios* �’⊘*No meals.*

SPORTS AND THE OUTDOORS
BOATING
Green Mountain Flagship Company. Canoes and kayaks are available for rent May–mid-October on Lake Whitingham. ⊠ *389 Rte. 9, 2 miles west of Wilmington* ☏ *802/464–2975.*

SKI AREAS
Mount Snow. The closest major ski area to all of the Northeast's big cities, Mount Snow prides itself on its hundreds of snowmaking fan guns—more than any other resort in North America. There are four major downhill areas. The main mountain comprises mostly intermediate runs, while the north face has the majority of expert runs. The south face, Sunbrook, has wide, sunny trails. It connects to Carinthia, which is dedicated to terrain parks and glade skiing. In summer, the 800-acre resort has an 18-hole golf course, 45 miles of mountain-biking trails, and an extensive network of hiking trails. **Facilities:** 80 trails; 588 acres; 1,700-foot vertical drop; 30 lifts. ⊠ *39 Mount Snow Rd., West Dover* ☏ *802/464–3333, 802/464–2151 for snow conditions* ⊕ *www.mountsnow.com* ▱ *Lift ticket: $90.*

Timber Creek. North of Mount Snow, this appealingly small cross-country skiing and snowshoeing center has 4½ miles of groomed loops. You can rent equipment and take lessons here. ⊠ *13 Tanglewood La., at Rte. 100, West Dover* ☎ *802/464–0999* ⊕ *www.timbercreekxc.com* ⊠ *$20.*

SNOWSHOE TRAIL

FAMILY **Molly Stark State Park.** This park is home to some of the state's most popular snowshoe trails. Mount Olga Trail is a relatively easy 1.7-mile loop culminating in a 360-degree view of southern Vermont and northern Massachusetts. ⊠ *705 Rte. 9 E* ☎ *802/464–5460* ⊕ *www.vtstateparks.com/htm/mollystark.htm.*

SHOPPING

Quaigh Design Centre. For half a century, this store has sold great pottery and artworks from Britain and New England, including woodcuts by Mary Azarian, a Vermont-based artist. Scottish woolens are also on offer. ⊠ *11 W. Main St.* ☎ *802/464–2780* ⊘ *Closed Wed. July–Sept., and Mon.–Thurs. Oct.–June.*

> ## WHO WAS MOLLY STARK?
>
> In the heart of Wilmington beside the Crafts Inn stands a sculpture in honor of Molly Stark, the wife of the Revolutionary War general John Stark. The general was said to have roused his troops in the Battle of Bennington, vowing victory over the British: "They are ours, or this night Molly Stark sleeps a widow!" He lived, and hence the victory path across Vermont (now Route 9) is called the Molly Stark Trail (or Byway).

BENNINGTON

21 miles west of Wilmington.

Bennington is the commercial focus of Vermont's southwest corner and home to Bennington College. It's really three towns in one: Downtown Bennington, Old Bennington, and North Bennington. Downtown has retained much of the industrial character it developed in the 19th century, when paper mills, gristmills, and potteries formed the city's economic base. The outskirts of town are commercial and not worth a stop, so make your way right into Downtown and Old Bennington to appreciate the area's true charm.

GETTING HERE AND AROUND

The heart of modern Bennington is the intersection of U.S. 7 and Route 9. Old Bennington is a couple of miles west on Route 9, at Monument Avenue. North Bennington is a few miles north on Route 67A.

ESSENTIALS

Visitor Information Bennington Area Chamber of Commerce. ⊠ *100 Veterans Memorial Dr.* ☎ *802/447–3311* ⊕ *www.bennington.com.*

EXPLORING

TOP ATTRACTIONS

FAMILY **Bennington Battle Monument.** This 306-foot stone obelisk with an elevator to the top commemorates General John Stark's Revolutionary War victory over the British, who attempted to capture Bennington's stockpile of supplies. Inside the monument you can learn all about the battle, which took place near Walloomsac Heights in New York State on August 16, 1777, and helped bring about the surrender of British commander "Gentleman Johnny" Burgoyne two months later. The top of the tower affords commanding views of the Massachusetts Berkshires, the New York Adirondacks, and the Vermont Green Mountains. ⊠ *15 Monument Circle, Old Bennington* ☎ *802/447–0550* ⊕ *www.benningtonbattlemonument.com* ✉ *$5.*

Bennington Center for the Arts. The center mounts exhibitions by local and national artists in its galleries, and sculptures often dot the lawns. Permanent-collection highlights include wildlife paintings and Native American art and artifacts. ⊠ *44 Gypsy La.* ☎ *802/442–7158* ⊕ *www. thebennington.org* ✉ *$9.*

Bennington Museum. The rich collections here feature military artifacts, early tools, dolls, and the Bennington Flag, one of the oldest of the Stars and Stripes in existence. Other areas of interest include early Bennington pottery, the Gilded Age in Vermont, mid-20th-century modernist painters who worked in or near Bennington, glass and metalwork by Lewis Comfort Tiffany, and photography, watercolors, and other works on paper. The highlight for many visitors, though, is the largest public collection of works by Grandma Moses (1860–1961), the popular self-taught artist who lived and painted in the area. ⊠ *75 Main St., Old Bennington* ☎ *802/447–1571* ⊕ *www.benningtonmuseum.com* ✉ *$10.*

Park-McCullough House. The architecturally significant Park-McCullough House is a 35-room classic French Empire–style mansion, built in 1865 and furnished with period pieces. Several restored flower gardens grace the landscaped grounds, and a stable holds some antique carriages. House tours are given on Friday in summer. The grounds are open daily year-round. ⊠ *1 Park St., at West St., North Bennington* ☎ *802/442– 5441* ⊕ *www.parkmccullough.org* ✉ *$10.*

Robert Frost Stone House Museum. Robert Frost came to Shaftsbury in 1920, he wrote, "to plant a new Garden of Eden with a thousand apple trees of some unforbidden variety." The museum tells the story of the poet's life and highlights the nine years (1920–29) he spent living in the house with his wife and four children. It was here that he penned "Stopping by Woods on a Snowy Evening" and published two books of poetry. You can wander 7 of the Frost family's original 80 acres. Among the apple boughs you just might find inspiration of your own. ⊠ *121 Historic Rte. 7A, Shaftsbury* ☎ *802/447–6200* ⊕ *www. frostfriends.org* ✉ *$6.*

WORTH NOTING

Bennington College. Contemporary stone sculpture and white-frame neo-Colonial dorms surrounded by acres of cornfields punctuate the green meadows of the placid campus of Bennington College. ⊠ *1 College Dr., off U.S. 7, North Bennington* ☎ *802/442–5401* ⊕ *www.bennington.edu.*

Old Bennington. West of downtown, this National Register Historic District is well endowed with stately Colonial and Victorian mansions. The Catamount Tavern, where Ethan Allen organized the Green Mountain Boys to capture Fort Ticonderoga in 1775, contains a bronze statue of Vermont's indigenous mountain lion, now extinct. ✉ *Monument Ave., Old Bennington.*

The Old First Church. In the graveyard of this church, the tombstone of the poet Robert Frost proclaims, "I had a lover's quarrel with the world." ✉ *1 Monument Circle, at Monument Ave., Old Bennington* ☎ *802/447–1223* ⊕ *www.oldfirstchurchbenn.org* ⊠ *Free.*

WHERE TO EAT

$
DINER

✗ Blue Benn Diner. Breakfast is served all day in this authentic diner whose menu includes turkey hash and breakfast burritos with scrambled eggs, sausage, and chilies, plus pancakes of all imaginable varieties, and there are many vegetarian selections. The line may be long, especially on weekends: locals and tourists can't stay away. $ *Average main: $10* ✉ *314 North St.* ☎ *802/442–5140* ▭ *No credit cards* ♺ *Reservations not accepted.*

$
ECLECTIC

✗ Pangaea Lounge. Locals head here for affordable comfort food and excellent cocktails. The regionally sourced fare includes pulled-pork tacos, Cobb salad with Danish blue cheese, salmon burgers, and pork tenderloin with sweet potatoes and maple syrup. On warm-weather weekends, follow the crowd out back to the deck. Next door is the restaurant's fancier, fine-dining twin, which is overpriced and not as intimate. $ *Average main: $17* ✉ *3 Prospect St., 3 miles north of Bennington, North Bennington* ☎ *802/442–7171* ⊕ *www.vermontfinedining.com* ◷ *No lunch.*

WHERE TO STAY

$
B&B/INN

☖ The Eddington House Inn. A stay in this impeccably maintained, historic three-bedroom house is a great value. **Pros:** budget prices for a great bed-and-breakfast; privacy and gentle service; spotless and nicely updated. **Cons:** slightly off usual tourist track; only three rooms so it fills up fast. $ *Rooms from: $159* ✉ *21 Main St., North Bennington* ☎ *802/442–1511* ⊕ *www.eddingtonhouseinn.com* ⇆ *3 suites* ⑩ *Breakfast.*

$
B&B/INN
Fodor's Choice
★

☖ Four Chimneys Inn. One of the best inns in Vermont, this three story 1915 neo-Georgian looks out over a substantial lawn and a wonderful old stone wall. **Pros:** stately mansion; nicely renovated rooms; extremely well kept. **Cons:** dinner only offered for special events. $ *Rooms from: $159* ✉ *21 West Rd., Old Bennington* ☎ *802/447–3500* ⊕ *www.fourchimneys.com* ⇆ *9 rooms, 2 suites* ⑩ *Breakfast.*

PERFORMING ARTS

Basement Music Series. The Vermont Arts Exchange sponsors this fun and funky contemporary music series at the downtown Masonic Lodge. Some performances sell out, so it's wise to purchase tickets in advance. ✉ *504 Main St.* ☎ *800/838–3006 for ticket hotline* ⊕ *www.vtartxchange.org/music.*

Oldcastle Theatre Company. This fine regional theater company focuses on American classics and crowd-pleasing musicals. The group's venue also hosts occasional concerts. ✉ *331 Main St.* ☎ *802/447–0564* ⊕ *www.oldcastletheatre.org* ◷ *Closed Dec.–Mar.*

SPORTS AND THE OUTDOORS

FAMILY **Lake Shaftsbury State Park.** You'll find a swimming beach, nature trails, boat and canoe rentals, and a snack bar at this pretty park. ⊠ *262 Shaftsbury State Park Rd., 10½ miles north of Bennington* ☎ *802/375–9978* ⊕ *www.vtstateparks.com/htm/shaftsbury.htm* ☉ *Facilities closed early Sept.–mid-May.*

Long Trail. Four miles east of Bennington, the Long Trail crosses Route 9 and runs south to the top of Harmon Hill. Allot two or three hours for this steep hike. ⊠ *Bennington.*

FAMILY **Woodford State Park.** This park has an activities center on Adams Reservoir, a playground, boat and canoe rentals, and nature trails. ⊠ *142 State Park Rd., 10 miles east of Bennington* ☎ *802/447–7169* ⊕ *www.vtstateparks.com/htm/woodford.htm* ☉ *Facilities closed mid-Oct.–mid-May.*

SHOPPING

FAMILY **The Apple Barn & Country Bake Shop.** Homemade baked goods, fresh cider, Vermont cheeses, maple syrup, and 30 varieties of apples are among the treats for sale here. There's berry picking in season, for a fun family stop, and on weekends you can watch the bakers make cider doughnuts. ⊠ *604 Rte. 7S, 1½ miles south of downtown Bennington* ☎ *802/447–7780, 888/827–7537* ⊕ *www.theapplebarn.com.*

The Bennington Bookshop. The state's oldest independent bookstore sells the latest new releases and hosts weekly readings, signings, and lectures. ⊠ *467 Main St.* ☎ *802/442–5059* ⊕ *www.benningtonbookshop.com.*

Bennington Potters Yard. The yard's showroom stocks goods from the famed Bennington Potters. On a self-guided tour you can see the potters at work (except Sunday). ⊠ *324 County St.* ☎ *802/447–7531, 800/205–8033* ⊕ *www.benningtonpotters.com.*

Now & Then Books. This great second-story bookstore stocks nearly 45,000 secondhand volumes. ⊠ *439 Main St.* ☎ *802/442–5566* ⊕ *www.nowandthenbooksvt.com.*

ARLINGTON

15 miles north of Bennington.

Smaller than Bennington and more down-to-earth than upper-crust Manchester to the north, Arlington exudes a certain Rockwellian folksiness, and it should: the illustrator Norman Rockwell lived here from 1939 to 1953, and many neighbors served as models for his portraits of small-town life.

GETTING HERE AND AROUND

Arlington is at the intersection of Route 313 and Route 7A. Take Route 313 West to reach West Arlington.

EXPLORING

West Arlington. Norman Rockwell once lived in this place with a quaint town green. If you follow Route 313 west from Arlington, you'll pass by the Wayside Country Store, a slightly rickety charmer where you can pick up sandwiches and chat with locals. The store carries everything from ammo and sporting goods to toys, teas, and maple syrup.

Continue on, and cross West Arlington's red covered bridge, which leads to the town green. To loop back to Route 7A, take River Road along the south side of the Battenkill River, a scenic drive. ⊠ *West Arlington.*

WHERE TO STAY

$ **The Arlington Inn.** The Greek Revival columns of this 1847 home lend
B&B/INN it an imposing presence in the middle of town, but the atmosphere within is friendly and old-fashioned. **Pros:** heart-of-town location; friendly atmosphere. **Cons:** expensive dining. ⑤ *Rooms from: $199* ⊠ *3904 VT Rte. 7A* ☎ *802/375-6532* ⊕ *www.arlingtoninn.com* ⇆ *13 rooms, 3 suites* ⏀ *Breakfast.*

$$ **Hill Farm Inn.** Simple cottages and the best views in the Manchester
B&B/INN area make this former dairy farm a winner. **Pros:** glorious open meadow
FAMILY setting; innkeeper is a former private chef; updated rooms and bathrooms. **Cons:** books up on weekends with weddings. ⑤ *Rooms from: $215* ⊠ *458 Hill Farm Rd., off Rte. 7A, Sunderland* ☎ *802/375-2269, 800/882-2545* ⊕ *www.hillfarminn.com* ⇆ *8 rooms, 3 suites, 1 farmhouse* ⏀ *Breakfast.*

$ **West Mountain Inn.** This 1810 farmhouse sits on 150 mountainside
B&B/INN acres with hiking trails and easy access to the Battenkill River, where
FAMILY you can canoe or go tubing. **Pros:** mountainside location; lots of activi-
Fodor's Choice ties; great views. **Cons:** dining room not ideal for kids. ⑤ *Rooms from:*
★ *$195* ⊠ *144 West Mountain Inn Rd., at Rte. 313* ☎ *802/375-6516* ⊕ *www.westmountaininn.com* ⇆ *14 rooms, 6 suites* ⏀ *Some meals.*

SPORTS AND THE OUTDOORS

BattenKill Canoe. This outfitter rents canoes for trips along the Battenkill River, which runs directly behind the shop. If you're hooked, the company also conducts more involved white-water trips as well as inn-to-inn tours. ⊠ *6328 Historic Rte. 7A* ☎ *802/362-2800, 800/421-5268* ⊕ *www.battenkill.com.*

SHOPPING

ANTIQUES

East Arlington Antiques Center. More than 70 dealers display their wares at the center, which occupies a converted 1930s movie theater. Among the finds is one of the country's best stoneware collections. ⊠ *1152 East Arlington Rd., East Arlington* ☎ *802/375-6144.*

GIFTS

FAMILY **Village Peddler.** This shop has a "chocolatorium," where you can learn all about cocoa. It sells fudge and other candies and stocks a large collection of teddy bears. ⊠ *261 Old Mill Rd., East Arlington* ☎ *802/375-6037* ⊕ *www.villagepeddlervt.com.*

MANCHESTER

9 miles northeast of Arlington.

Well-to-do Manchester has been a popular summer retreat since the mid-19th century, when city dwellers traveled north to take in the cool clean air at the base of 3,840-foot Mt. Equinox. Manchester Village's tree-shaded marble sidewalks and stately old homes—Main Street here could hardly be more picture-perfect—reflect the luxurious resort life-style of more than a century ago. A mile north on Route 7A, Manchester Center is the commercial twin to Colonial Manchester Village; it's also where you'll find the town's famed upscale factory outlets doing business in attractive faux-Colonial shops.

Manchester Village houses the world headquarters of Orvis, the outdoor-goods brand that was founded here in the 19th century and has greatly influenced the town ever since. The complex includes a fly-fishing school featuring lessons given in its casting ponds and the Battenkill River.

GETTING HERE AND AROUND
Manchester is the main town for the ski resorts of Stratton (a half-hour drive on Route 30) and Bromley (15 minutes to the northeast on Route 11). It's 15 minutes north of Arlington along scenic Route 7A.

ESSENTIALS
Visitor Information Green Mountain National Forest Visitor Center. ✉ *2538 Depot St.* ☎ *802/362–2307* ⊕ *www.fs.usda.gov/main/gmfl.* **Manchester and the Mountains Regional Chamber of Commerce.** ✉ *39 Bonnet St.* ☎ *802/362–6313* ⊕ *www.visitmanchestervt.com.*

EXPLORING
American Museum of Fly Fishing. This museum houses the world's largest collection of angling art and angling-related objects—more than 1,500 rods, 800 reels, 30,000 flies, including the tackle of Winslow Homer, Babe Ruth, Jimmy Carter, and other notables. Every August, vendors sell antique equipment at the museum's fly-fishing festival. You can also practice your casting out back. ✉ *4104 Main St.* ☎ *802/362–3300* ⊕ *www.amff.com* 🎫 *$5.*

FAMILY

Fodor's Choice

★

Hildene. A twofold treat, the summer home of Abraham Lincoln's son Robert provides insight into the lives of the Lincoln family, as well as an introduction to the lavish Manchester life of the early 1900s. The only son of the president to survive into adulthood, Robert Lincoln served as secretary of war, U.S. ambassador to Great Britain, and general counsel and later president of the Pullman Palace Car Company. In 1905, Robert built a 24-room mansion where he and his descendants lived until 1975. The sturdy Georgian Revival house, the centerpiece of a beautifully preserved 412-acre estate, holds many of the family's prized possessions, including one of three surviving stovepipe hats owned by Abraham and a Lincoln Bible. When the 1,000-pipe Aeolian organ is played, the music reverberates as though from the mansion's very bones.

Rising from a 10-acre meadow, Hildene Farm, which opened in 2008, is magnificent. The agriculture center is built in a traditional style—post-and-beam construction of timber felled and milled on the estate. Best of all, you can meet the resident goats and watch goat cheese being made.

The highlight, though, may be the elaborate formal gardens, where a thousand peonies bloom every June. To get a glimpse of luxury travel in the Gilded Age, step aboard the restored 1903 Pullman car parked in a patch of forest north of the house. There is also a teaching greenhouse, a 600-foot floating boardwalk across the Battenkill wetlands, and more than 10 miles of walking trails. When conditions permit, you can cross-country ski and snowshoe on the property.

The formal gardens and mansion at Robert Todd Lincoln's Hildene are a far cry from his father's log cabin.

In good weather, a restored 1928 Franklin car once owned by Robert's daughter Jessie is parked in front of the carriage house, now occupied by a gorgeous museum store and welcome center. Allow at least half a day for exploring Hildene. ⊠ *1005 Hildene Rd., at Rte. 7A* ☎ *802/362–1788* ⊕ *www.hildene.org* ☚ *Tour $18.*

Fodor'sChoice **Southern Vermont Arts Center.** Located at the end of a long, winding drive-
★ way, this center has a permanent collection of more than 800 19th- and 20th-century American artworks and presents temporary exhibitions. The original building, a Georgian mansion set on 100 acres, contains 10 galleries with works by more than 600 artists, many from Vermont. The building also hosts concerts, performances, and film screenings. In summer and fall, the views from the restaurant at lunchtime are magnificent. ⊠ *930 SVAC Dr., West Rd.* ☎ *802/362–1405* ⊕ *www.svac.org* ☚ *$6.*

WHERE TO EAT

$$$ ✕ **Bistro Henry.** The presence of chef-owner Henry Bronson accounts for
FRENCH the popularity of this friendly place, as does the fact that dishes cost about $5 less than at Manchester's other upscale restaurants. Bistro classics include steak au poivre and medium-rare duck breast served with a crispy leg, but Bronson mixes things up with tuna wasabi accompanied by a spicy pad thai and Sicilian salmon served with couscous. Wines are well chosen, and the desserts made by Dina Bronson, Henry's wife, are memorable. (The couple met while working in Manhattan restaurants.) Indulge in the "gooey chocolate cake," a great molten treat paired with a homemade malted ice cream. ⑤ *Average main: $25* ⊠ *1942 Depot St., 3 miles east of Manchester Center* ☎ *802/362–4982* ⊕ *www.bistrohenry.com* ☉ *Closed Mon. No lunch.*

$$$$ ✕**Chantecleer.** There is something wonderful about eating by candle-
EUROPEAN light in an old barn; and with the rooster art above their rough-hewn
wooden beams, Chantecleer's dining rooms are especially romantic. In
winter, ask to sit by the great fieldstone fireplace. The menu runs to the
Continental, with starters like escargot glazed with Pernod in a hazelnut
and parsley butter. Crowd-pleasing entrées include Colorado rack of
lamb and whole Dover sole filleted table-side. The Matterhorn chocolate sundae—vanilla ice cream covered with hazelnut nougatine and
Toblerone chocolate sauce—makes a winning winter dessert. ⑤ *Aver-*
age main: $38 ✉ 8 Reed Farm La., 3½ miles north of Manchester, East
Dorset ☎ *802/362–1616* ⊕ *www.chantecleerrestaurant.com* ⊘ *Closed*
Mon. and Tues., and Nov. and Apr. No lunch ⚘ *Reservations essential.*

$$$$ ✕**Chop House.** Walk to the very back room of the Equinox's Marsh
STEAKHOUSE Tavern, past a velvet curtain, to enter this special, very expensive steak
house. The dining room has a bit of history: the marble above the
fireplace is chiseled "L.L. ORVIS 1832," and way before he claimed
the spot, the Green Mountain Boys gathered here to plan their Revolutionary War–era resistance. Today, you'll yield to aged corn- or
grass-fed beef broiled at 1,700°F and finished with herb butter. The
New York strip, rib eye, filet mignon, milk-fed veal chops, and seafood are delicious—a must for deep-pocketed carnivores. ⑤ *Average*
main: $47 ✉ 3567 Main St. ☎ *802/362–4700* ⊕ *www.equinoxresort.*
com ⊘ *Closed Mon. and Tues. No lunch.*

$$ ✕**Depot 62 Cafe and Bistro.** The best pizzas in town are topped with ter-
PIZZA rific fresh ingredients and served in the middle of a high-end antiques
showroom, making this Turkish-Mediterranean restaurant a local secret
worth knowing about. The wood-fired oven yields masterful results—
like the arugula pizza, a beehive of fresh greens atop a thin crust. This
is a great place for lunch or an inexpensive but satisfying dinner. Sit on
your own or at the long communal table. ⑤ *Average main: $18 ✉ 515*
Depot St. ☎ *802/366–8181* ⊕ *www.depot62.us.*

$$$ ✕**Mistral's at Toll Gate.** This classic French restaurant is tucked in a grotto
FRENCH on the climb to Bromley Mountain. The two dining rooms are perched
over the Bromley Brook, and at night a small waterfall is magically
illuminated—ask for a window table. Chef Dana Markey's specialties include chateaubriand béarnaise for two and crispy sweetbreads
dijonnaise. ⑤ *Average main: $32 ✉ 10 Toll Gate Rd., off Rte. 11/30*
☎ *802/362–1779* ⊕ *www.mistralsattollgate.com* ⊘ *Closed Wed., and*
Tues. Nov.–June. No lunch.

$$$ ✕**Perfect Wife.** Owner-chef Amy Chamberlain, a Manchester native,
ECLECTIC creates a fun, free-form atmosphere with dishes like Peking duck rolled
Fodor'sChoice in Mandarin pancakes and sesame-crusted yellowfin tuna topped with
★ crispy rice sticks. Her establishment has two entrances: one to the res-
taurant on the lower level and another to the Other Woman Tavern
above. The tavern, which is open more often in winter, is among the
town's livelier spots, with Vermont microbrews on tap, live music on
weekends, and a pub menu with burgers and potpies. ⑤ *Average main:*
$27 ✉ 2594 Depot St., 2½ miles east of Manchester Center ☎ *802/362–*
2817 ⊕ *www.perfectwife.com* ⊘ *Closed Sun., and Mon.–Wed. in win-*
ter. No lunch.

$$$$ ✕ **The Reluctant Panther Inn & Restaurant.** The dining room at this luxurious
AMERICAN inn is a large, modern space where rich woods and high ceilings meld into
a kind of "nouveau Vermont" aesthetic. The contemporary American
cuisine emphasizes farm-to-table ingredients and has earned the restaurant
"Gold Barn" honors from the Vermont Fresh Network. You can pair your
meal with a bottle from the award-winning wine list. When it's warm
outside, sit on the landscaped patio, where there's a raw bar Thursday–
Saturday evenings. $ *Average main: $36* ✉ *39 West Rd.* ☎ *800/822–2331,
802/362–2568* ⊕ *www.reluctantpanther.com* ☾ *No lunch.*

$$$ ✕ **The Silver Fork.** This intimate bistro with a Caribbean flair is owned by
ECLECTIC husband-and-wife team Mark and Melody French. They spent years in
Fodor's Choice Puerto Rico, and the flavors of the island are reflected in their menu—
★ it's certainly the only one in town to feature shrimp *mofongo* (with
mashed plantains) alongside Wiener schnitzel, pulled pork empana-
das, and warm apple-cinnamon beignets. Reserve one of the six tables
ahead of time, or sit at the wine bar for a casual and romantic dinner
with a maple martini or a bottle from the impressive wine list. $ *Av-
erage main: $30* ✉ *4201 Main St., across from Orvis Flagship Store*
☎ *802/768–8444* ⊕ *www.thesilverforkvt.com* ☾ *Closed Sun. No lunch*
⬧ *Reservations essential.*

$$ ✕ **Ye Olde Tavern.** This circa-1790 Colonial inn dishes up Yankee favor-
AMERICAN ites like pot roast and cheddar-and-ale onion soup, along with plenty
of New England charm. A favorite of regulars and visitors alike, the
tavern serves excellent food in a casual, colorful setting, and the mellow
tap room is a nice stop for a drink and a taste of Vermont. $ *Average
main: $22* ✉ *5183 Main St.* ☎ *802/362–0611* ⊕ *www.yeoldetavern.net.*

WHERE TO STAY

$$$ ⛾ **Equinox.** The Equinox defines the geographic center and historic heart
RESORT of Manchester Village, and has been *the* fancy hotel in town—and in the
state—since the 18th century. **Pros:** heart-of-town location; full-service
hotel; great golf and spa. **Cons:** corporate feel; spotty service; overrun
by out-of-towners on weekends. $ *Rooms from: $365* ✉ *3567 Main
St.* ☎ *802/362–4700, 888/367–7625* ⊕ *www.equinoxresort.com* ⇨ *195
rooms and suites* ⦿ *No meals.*

$$$ ⛾ **Taconic Hotel.** A fresh-faced Kimpton boutique venture in Manchester
HOTEL Village, the Taconic, which opened in late 2015, has public areas that
include a wraparound porch and the Copper Grouse restaurant, run
by a top Burlington chef known for upscale comfort food. **Pros:** contemporary Kimpton style; village location; Frette robes, Atelier Bloom
bath products; fitness center open 24 hours; yoga mats in all rooms.
Cons: perhaps too fresh-faced to feel truly "Vermont"; only chain's
rewards members get free high-speed Internet/Wi-Fi. $ *Rooms from:
$340* ✉ *3835 Main St.* ☎ *802/362–0147* ⊕ *www.taconichotel.com*
⇨ *87 rooms, 3 cottages* ⦿ *No meals.*

$ ⛾ **Wilburton Inn.** Stepping into this hilltop 1902 Tudor-style mansion,
B&B/INN you might think you've stumbled on a lavish film set: there's a palpably
Fodor's Choice cinematic quality to the richly paneled guest rooms and the common
★ rooms containing part of the owners' vast art collection. **Pros:** beautiful

setting; easy access to Manchester; fine dining. **Cons:** limited indoor facilities; popular wedding site. ⑤ *Rooms from: $190* ✉ *257 River Rd.* ☎ *802/362–2500, 800/648–4944* ⊕ *www.wilburton.com* ⤳ *30 rooms, 4 suites* ⦿ *Breakfast.*

NIGHTLIFE

Falcon Bar. This sophisticated bar has live music on weekends. In summer, don't miss the wonderful outdoor deck. In winter, the place to be is around the giant Vermont slate fire pit. ✉ *Equinox Resort, 3567 Main St.* ☎ *800/362–4747* ⊕ *www.equinoxresort.com.*

SPORTS AND THE OUTDOORS

BIKING

Battenkill Sports Bicycle Shop. This shop rents, sells, and repairs bikes and provides maps and route suggestions. ✉ *1240 Depot St., off U.S. 7* ☎ *802/362–2734, 800/340–2734* ⊕ *www.battenkillsports.com.*

FISHING

Battenkill Anglers. Teaching the art and science of fly-fishing, Battenkill Anglers offers both private and group lessons. ✉ *6204 Main St.* ☎ *802/379–1444* ⊕ *www.battenkillangler.com.*

HIKING

There are bountiful hiking trails in the Green Mountain National Forest. Shorter hikes begin at the Equinox Resort, which owns about 1,000 acres of forest and has a great trail system open to the public.

Long Trail. One of the most popular segments of Vermont's Long Trail leads to the top of Bromley Mountain. The strenuous 5.4-mile round-trip takes about four hours. ✉ *Rte. 11/30* ⊕ *www.greenmountainclub.org.*

Lye Brook Falls. This 4.6-mile hike starts off Glen Road and ends at Vermont's most impressive cataract, Lye Brook Falls. The moderately strenuous journey takes four hours. ✉ *Off Glen Rd., south from E. Manchester Rd. just east of U.S. 7* ⊕ *www.greenmountainclub.org.*

Mountain Goat. Stop here for hiking, cross-country-skiing, and snowshoeing equipment (some of which is available to rent), as well as a good selection of warm clothing. ✉ *4886 Main St.* ☎ *802/362–5159* ⊕ *www.mountaingoat.com.*

ICE-SKATING

FAMILY **Riley Rink at Hunter Park.** This Olympic-size indoor ice rink has skate rentals and a concession stand. ✉ *410 Hunter Park Rd.* ☎ *802/362–0150* ⊕ *www.rileyrink.com.*

SHOPPING

ART AND ANTIQUES

Long Ago & Far Away. This store specializes in fine indigenous artwork, including Inuit stone sculpture. ✉ *Green Mountain Village Shops, 4963 Main St.* ☎ *802/362–3435* ⊕ *www.longagoandfaraway.com.*

Tilting at Windmills Gallery. This large gallery displays the paintings and sculptures of nationally known artists. ✉ *24 Highland Ave., Manchester Center* ☎ *802/362–3022* ⊕ *www.tilting.com.*

BOOKS

FAMILY **Northshire Bookstore.** The heart of Manchester Center, this bookstore is adored by visitors and residents alike for its ambience, selection, and service. Up the iron staircase is a second floor dedicated to children's books, toys, and clothes. Connected to the store is the Spiral Press Café, where you can sit down to a grilled pesto-chicken sandwich or a latte and scone. ⊠ *4869 Main St.* ☎ *802/362–2200, 800/437–3700* ⊕ *www. northshire.com.*

CLOTHING

Manchester Designer Outlets. This is the most upscale collection of stores in northern New England—and every store is a discount outlet. The architecture reflects the surrounding homes, so the place looks a bit like a Colonial village. The long list of famous-brand clothiers here includes Kate Spade, Yves Delorme, Michael Kors, Ann Taylor, Tumi, BCBG, Armani, Coach, Polo Ralph Lauren, Brooks Brothers, and Theory. ⊠ *97 Depot St.* ☎ *802/362–3736, 800/955–7467* ⊕ *www.manchesterdesigneroutlets.com.*

Orvis Flagship Store. The lodgelike Orvis store carries the company's latest clothing, fly-fishing gear, and pet supplies—there's even a trout pond. At this required shopping destination for many visitors—the Orvis name is pure Manchester—there are demonstrations of how fly rods are constructed and tested. You can attend fly-fishing school across the street. ⊠ *4200 Rte. 7A* ☎ *802/362–3750* ⊕ *www.orvis.com.*

SPAS

Spa at Equinox. With mahogany doors and beadboard wainscoting, this spa feels like a country estate. At one end are an indoor pool and an outdoor hot tub; at the other end are the treatment rooms. The signature 100-minute Spirit of Vermont combines Reiki, reflexology, and massage. In the co-ed relaxation room, you can nestle into overstuffed chairs next to a two-sided fireplace made of Vermont gneiss. The locker rooms, with marble accents and pottery-bowl wash basins, have steam rooms and saunas. ⊠ *Equinox Resort, 3567 Rte. 7A* ☎ *802/362–4700, 800/362–4747* ⊕ *www.equinoxresort.com.*

DORSET

7 miles north of Manchester.

Lying at the foot of many mountains and with a village green surrounded by white clapboard homes and inns, Dorset has a solid claim to the title of Vermont's most picture-perfect town. Dorset has just 2,000 residents, but two of the state's best and oldest general stores.

The country's first commercial marble quarry opened here in 1785. Dozens more opened, providing the marble for the main research branch of the New York Public Library and many Fifth Avenue mansions, among other notable landmarks, as well as the sidewalks here and in Manchester. A remarkable private home made entirely of marble can be seen on Dorset West Road, a beautiful residential road west of the town green. The marble Dorset Church on the green has two Tiffany stained-glass windows.

EXPLORING

FAMILY
Fodor's Choice
★

Dorset Quarry. On hot summer days the sight of dozens of families jumping, swimming, and basking in the sun around this massive 60-foot-deep swimming hole makes it one of the most wholesome and picturesque recreational spots in the region. First mined in 1785, the stone from the country's oldest commercial marble quarry was used to build the main branch of the New York Public Library and the Montreal Museum of Fine Arts. ⊠ *Rte. 30* ✉ *Free.*

FAMILY

Merck Forest & Farmland Center. This 3,100-acre educational center has 30 miles of nature trails for hiking, cross-country skiing, snowshoeing, and horseback riding. You can visit the 60-acre farm, which grows organic fruit and vegetables (sold at the farm stand), and check out the horses, cows, sheep, pigs, and chickens while you're there—you're even welcome to help out with the chores. ⊠ *3270 Rte. 315, Rupert* ☎ *802/394–7836* ⊕ *www.merckforest.org* ✉ *Free.*

WHERE TO EAT

$$$
AMERICAN

✕ **The Dorset Inn.** Built in 1796, this inn has been continuously operating ever since. The comfortable tavern, which serves the same menu as the more formal dining room, is popular with locals, and Patrick, the amiable veteran bartender, will make you feel at home. Recent favorites include the Dorset Inn poutine and the maple-glazed duck breast. A member of the Vermont Fresh Network, the restaurant benefits greatly from its strong connections with local farmers. $ *Average main: $25* ⊠ *Dorset Green, 8 Church St.* ☎ *802/867–5500* ⊕ *www.dorsetinn.com* ✆ *No lunch Mon. and Tues.*

$$$
ECLECTIC

✕ **Inn at West View Farm.** Chef-owner Raymond Chen was the lead line cook at New York City's Mercer Kitchen before opening this restaurant. You'll find traditional floral wallpaper and soft classical music, but that's where the similarities to Dorset's other eateries end. Chen skillfully applies French techniques to Asian dishes crafted from fresh Vermont ingredients. You could make a meal out of the many small plates—think of them as a cross between tapas and dim sum. $ *Average main: $30* ⊠ *2928 Rte. 30* ☎ *802/867–5715, 800/769–4903* ⊕ *www.innatwestviewfarm.com* ✆ *Closed Tues. and Wed.*

WHERE TO STAY

$$
HOTEL

🏨 **Barrows House.** If you've tired of the floral fabrics found in many New England inns, this renovated 19th-century manse, once the residence of the town's pastor, provides a pleasant alternative. **Pros:** good bar and restaurant; chintz-free decor. **Cons:** rooms can become drafty in cold weather. $ *Rooms from: $275* ⊠ *3156 Rte. 30* ☎ *802/867–4455* ⊕ *www.barrowshouse.com* ✆ *18 rooms, 9 suites, 3 cottages* ⏣ *Breakfast.*

$$
B&B/INN

🏨 **Squire House Bed & Breakfast.** On a wonderfully quiet road, this inn has three guest rooms that combine modern comforts and antique fixtures. **Pros:** big estate feels like your own; well-maintained rooms; quiet. **Cons:** bathrooms less exciting than rooms. $ *Rooms from: $210* ⊠ *3395 Dorset West Rd.* ☎ *802/867–0281* ⊕ *www.squirehouse.com* ✆ *2 rooms, 1 suite* ⏣ *Breakfast.*

PERFORMING ARTS

Dorset Players. The prestigious summer theater troupe presents the annual Dorset Theater Festival. Plays are staged in a wonderful converted pre-Revolutionary War barn. ⊠ *Dorset Playhouse, 104 Cheney Rd.* ☎ *802/867–5777* ⊕ *www.dorsetplayers.org.*

SPORTS AND THE OUTDOORS

Emerald Lake State Park. This park has a well-marked nature trail, a small beach, boat rentals, and a snack bar. ⊠ *65 Emerald Lake La., East Dorset* ☎ *802/362–1655* ⊕ *www.vtstateparks.com/htm/emerald. htm* ⊠ *$4* ⊙ *Facilities closed mid-Oct.–mid-May.*

SHOPPING

Dorset Union Store. Dating to 1816, this general store has good prepared dinners and a big wine selection. They also sell interesting gifts. ⊠ *Dorset Green, Church St.* ☎ *802/867–4400.*

H. N. Williams General Store. Started in 1840 by William Williams, this trilevel country store has been run by the same family for six generations. This is one of those places where you can buy maple syrup and ammo, while catching up on posted town announcements. There's a deli on-site for sandwiches; a farmers' market is held outside on Sunday in summer. ⊠ *2732 Rte. 30* ☎ *802/867–5353* ⊕ *www.hnwilliams.com.*

STRATTON

26 miles southeast of Dorset.

Stratton is really Stratton Mountain Resort, a mountaintop ski resort with a self-contained "town center" of shops, restaurants, and lodgings clustered at the base of the slopes. When the snow melts, golf, tennis, and a host of other summer activities are big attractions, but the ski village remains quiet.

GETTING HERE AND AROUND

From Manchester or U.S. 7, follow Route 11/30 east until they split. Route 11 continues past Bromley ski mountain, and Route 30 turns south 10 minutes toward Bondville, the town at the base of the mountain. At the junction of Routes 30 and 100 is the village of Jamaica, with its own cluster of inns and restaurants on the eastern side of the mountain.

WHERE TO EAT

$

AMERICAN

FAMILY

✕ **J.J. Hapgood General Store and Eatery.** You won't find a better meal at any other general store in the state. This is really more of a restaurant than a place to pick up the essentials, but like any good general store it's a friendly and relaxed gathering spot for locals. Breakfast is all about farm-fresh eggs and organic oatmeal. Lunch brings soups and sandwiches—in autumn, try a grilled cheese with local apple. After 3 pm, cooks fire up the pizza oven and crank out pies with Thai peanut sauce, pulled pork, kale, chickpeas, and other out-of-the-ordinary ingredients. ⑤ *Average main: $9* ⊠ *305 Main St., Peru* ☎ *802/824–4800* ⊕ *www. jjhapgood.com.*

$$$ ✗ **The Red Fox Inn.** This converted bi-level barn has the best nightlife in
AMERICAN   town and a fun dining room. The restaurant is on the upper level, where
you'll see wagon wheels and a carriage suspended from the A-frame
ceiling. Settle in near the huge fireplace for beef tenderloin, roasted half
duckling, or penne alla vodka. Their apple pie was served at the inaugu-
ration of President Obama. Downstairs in the tavern (open year-round)
there's Irish music, half-price Guinness, and fish 'n' chips on Wednesday.
On the premises are some relaxed, no-frills accommodations. $ *Aver-
age main: $26* ✉ *103 Winhall Hollow Rd., Bondville* ☎ *802/297–2488*
⊕ *www.redfoxinn.com* ☉ *Closed Mon.–Wed. June–Oct. No lunch.*

WHERE TO STAY

$$$ ⛾ **Long Trail House.** Directly across the street from the ski village, this
RENTAL   condo complex is one of the closest to the slopes. **Pros:** across from ski-
ing; reasonable rates for weekdays; outdoor heated pool. **Cons:** room
decor varies; two-night stay required on weekends. $ *Rooms from:*
$350 ✉ *5 Village Lodge Rd.* ☎ *802/297–4000, 800/787–2886* ⊕ *www.*
stratton.com ⋑ *100 units* ❙❀❙ *No meals.*

$$ ⛾ **Three Mountain Inn.** A 1780s tavern, this romantic inn in downtown
B&B/INN   Jamaica feels authentically Colonial, from the wide-plank paneling to
Fodor'sChoice   the low ceilings. **Pros:** romantic; well-kept rooms; great dinners. **Cons:**
★   15-minute drive to skiing. $ *Rooms from: $234* ✉ *30 Depot St., 10*
miles northeast of Stratton, Jamaica ☎ *802/874–4140* ⊕ *www.three-*
mountaininn.com ⋑ *8 rooms, 1 suite, 1 cottage* ❙❀❙ *Breakfast.*

NIGHTLIFE

Mulligans. Popular Mulligans hosts bands and DJs in the downstairs
Green Door Pub on weekends. ✉ *Village Sq., Stratton Mountain*
☎ *802/297–9293* ⊕ *www.green-door-pub.com.*

SPORTS AND THE OUTDOORS
SKI AREAS

FAMILY   **Bromley Mountain Resort.** About 20 minutes from Stratton, Bromley is
a favorite with families thanks to a child-care center for kids ages 6
weeks–6 years and programs for ages 3–17. The trails are evenly split
among beginner, intermediate, and advanced, with nothing too chal-
lenging. Beginning skiers and snowboarders have expanded access to
terrain-based training in the dedicated Learning Zone, and everyone
can unwind in the newly renovated base lodge. An added bonus: trails
face south, making for glorious spring skiing and warm winter days.
Facilities: 46 trails; 300 acres; 1,334-foot vertical drop; 9 lifts. ✉ *3984
Rte. 11, Peru* ☎ *802/824–5522, 866/856–2201 for snow conditions*
⊕ *www.bromley.com* ⛷ *Lift ticket: $71.*

Stratton Mountain. About 30 minutes from Manchester, and featuring
an entire faux Swiss village at its base, Stratton Mountain draws afflu-
ent families and young professionals. Beginners will find more than
40% of the mountain accessible to them, but that doesn't mean there
aren't some great steeps for the experts. The resort prides itself on its
immaculate grooming and excellent cruising on all trails. An on-site
day-care center takes children ages 6 weeks–5 years for indoor activities
and outdoor excursions. Children also love careening down one of four
groomed lift-serviced lanes at the resort's Coca Cola Tube Park. Stratton

has 11 miles of cross-country skiing, and in summer there are 15 outdoor clay tennis courts, 27 holes of golf, and hiking trails accessed by a gondola. The sports complex (open year-round) has a 25-meter indoor pool, a hot tub, a steam room, and a fitness center. **Facilities:** 97 trails; 670 acres; 2,003-foot vertical drop; 11 lifts. ⊠ *5 Village Lodge Rd., Bondville* 🖻 *802/297–4211 for snow conditions,* 800/787–2886 ⊕ *www.stratton.com* ⛷ *Lift ticket: $99.*

WESTON

3

17 miles north of Stratton.

Best known as the home of the Vermont Country Store, Weston was one of the first Vermont towns to discover its own intrinsic loveliness—and marketability. With its summer theater, classic town green with Victorian bandstand, and an assortment of shops, the little village really lives up to its vaunted image.

WHERE TO STAY

$

B&B/INN

🖬 **The Inn at Weston.** A short walk from the town green and a stone's throw from four ski areas, this 1848 inn is run by Bob and Linda Aldrich, whose love of plants is evident from their immaculate gardens and on-site greenhouse. **Pros:** great rooms; terrific town location. **Cons:** high-end rooms are expensive. ⑤ *Rooms from: $185* ⊠ *630 Main St.* 🖻 *802/824–6789* ⊕ *www.innweston.com* ⇆ *13 rooms* � *Breakfast.*

PERFORMING ARTS

Weston Playhouse. The oldest professional theater in Vermont produces plays, musicals, and other works. The season runs late June–early September. ⊠ *703 Main St., off Rte. 100* 🖻 *802/824–5288* ⊕ *www. westonplayhouse.org.*

SHOPPING

The Vermont Country Store. This store opened in 1946 and is still run by the Orton family, though it has become something of an empire, with a large catalog and online business. One room is set aside for Vermont Common Crackers and bins of fudge and copious candy. In others you'll find nearly forgotten items such as Lilac Vegetol aftershave, as well as practical items like sturdy outdoor clothing. Nostalgia-evoking implements dangle from the rafters. The associated Bryant House restaurant next door serves three country meals a day and if you can't get enough, there's a second store on Route 103 in Rockingham. ⊠ *657 Main St.* 🖻 *802/824–3184* ⊕ *www.vermontcountrystore.com.*

LUDLOW

9 miles northeast of Weston.

Ludlow is a largely nondescript industrial town whose major draw is Okemo, one of Vermont's largest and most popular ski resorts.

GETTING HERE AND AROUND

Routes 100 and 103 join in northern Ludlow, separating about 2 miles south in the small downtown, where Route 103 becomes Main Street.

You never know what you'll find at a rambling general store like Weston's Vermont Country Store.

WHERE TO EAT

$$
AMERICAN
✕ **Coleman Brook Tavern.** Slope-side at the Jackson Gore Inn, Coleman Brook is the fanciest and most expensive of Okemo's dozen or so places to eat, but it's not formal—you'll find diners wearing ski boots crowding the tables at lunch. Large wing chairs and big banquettes line window bays. Ask to sit in the Wine Room, a separate section where tables are surrounded by their noteworthy collection of bottles. Start with a pound of mussels steamed in butter, garlic, white wine, and fresh herbs. Then move on to the sesame seed–crusted ahi tuna served over green-tea soba noodles in a ginger-miso broth. The s'mores dessert is cooked over a tabletop "campfire." $ *Average main: $24* ✉ *Jackson Gore Inn, Okemo, 111 Jackson Gore Rd.* ☎ *802/228–1435* ⊕ *www.okemo.com/dining/coleman-brook-tavern.*

$
PIZZA
FAMILY
✕ **Goodman's American Pie.** This place has the best wood-fired pizza in town. It also has character to spare: sit in chairs from old ski lifts and order from a counter that was once a purple VW bus. Though Goodman's is on Main Street, it's set back and somewhat hidden. Locals and Okemo regulars in the know stop by to design their own pies from 27 ingredients. There are also six specials; one of these, the Rip Curl, has mozzarella, Asiago, ricotta, chicken, fresh garlic, and fresh tomatoes. Pizza is available by the slice, and there are arcade games in the back. $ *Average main: $10* ✉ *5 Lamere Sq.* ☎ *802/228–4271* ⊕ *www.goodmansamericanpie.com.*

$$
ECLECTIC
✕ **Harry's.** A local favorite across from the Jackson Gore access road, this casual restaurant has a number of international influences. Traditional contemporary entrées such as roast duck are at one end of the menu and Asian and Mexican dishes at the other. The large and tasty burrito,

made with fresh cilantro and black beans, is one of the best bargains around. Chef-owner Trip Pearce often uses ingredients from his own garden. He also owns the equally popular Little Harry's in Rutland. $ *Average main: $24* ✉ *68 Rte. 100 N, Mount Holly* ☎ *802/259–2996* ⊕ *www.harryscafe.com* ⊘ *Closed Mon. and Tues. No lunch.*

$$$

ECLECTIC

Fodor'sChoice

★

✕ **The Inn at Weathersfield.** One of Vermont's best restaurants, this culinary gem is part of an 18th-century countryside inn. A chalkboard in the foyer lists the farms that grow the food that is served to the patrons. Executive chef Jean-Luc Matecap, who has extensive experience cooking for top restaurants in France, Nantucket, and his native Vermont, is passionate about local ingredients. His farm-to-table cuisine can be enjoyed à la carte or prix fixe. Dishes on the latter menu include roasted Cavendish game birds and dry-aged Black Watch Farm sirloin. Service is excellent, and wines are reasonably priced. For a quicker bite, have a burger or some appetizers in the tavern. In summer, enjoy your meal on the patio. $ *Average main: $25* ✉ *1342 Rte. 106, 15 miles east of Ludlow, Perkinsville* ☎ *802/263–9217* ⊕ *www.weathersfieldinn.com* ⊘ *Closed Mon. and Tues., and Apr. and early Nov. No lunch.*

WHERE TO STAY

$

B&B/INN

⛺ **Inn at Water's Edge.** Former Long Islanders Bruce and Tina Verdrager converted their old ski house and barns into this comfortably refined haven, perfect for those who want to ski but not stay in town. **Pros:** bucolic setting on a lakefront; interesting house. **Cons:** ordinary rooms. $ *Rooms from: $175* ✉ *45 Kingdom Rd., 5 miles north of town* ☎ *802/228–8143, 888/706–9736* ⊕ *www.innatwatersedge.com* ☞ *9 rooms, 2 suites* ⦿ *Some meals.*

$

B&B/INN

⛺ **Inn at Weathersfield.** This is the kind of place where relaxation rules, unless you want to take advantage of seasonal activities like hiking, cross-country skiing, and apple picking. **Pros:** dynamite restaurant and tavern; laid-back inn; quiet setting. **Cons:** 15-mile drive from the Okemo slopes. $ *Rooms from: $149* ✉ *1342 Rte. 106, Perkinsville* ☎ *802/263–9217* ⊕ *www.innatweathersfield.com* ⊘ *Closed first 2 wks in Nov.* ☞ *12 rooms* ⦿ *Breakfast.*

$$$

HOTEL

FAMILY

⛺ **Jackson Gore Village.** This slope-side base lodge is the place to stay if your aim is Okemo skiing. **Pros:** ski-in, ski-out access to mountain; good for families. **Cons:** chaotic and noisy on weekends; expensive. $ *Rooms from: $355* ✉ *111 Jackson Gore Rd., off Rte. 103* ☎ *802/228–1400, 800/786–5366* ⊕ *www.okemo.com* ☞ *263 rooms and suites* ⦿ *No meals.*

SPORTS AND THE OUTDOORS

SKI AREAS

FAMILY

Okemo Mountain Resort. Family fun is the focus of southern Vermont's biggest ski resort, which has dozens of beginner trails, some wide intermediate runs, terrain parks throughout, a tubing facility, a nursery, an ice rink, indoor basketball and tennis courts, and a children's pool with slides. There's even a Kids' Night Out child-care program on Saturday evening during the regular season, so parents can have date nights. The Okemo Valley Nordic Center has miles of cross-country and snowshoeing trails. Summer diversions include golfing, mountain biking, and activities and rides in the Adventure Zone. The newer Jackson Gore

Vermont Artisanal Cheese

Vermont is the artisanal cheese capital of the country, with several dozen creameries open to the public churning out hundreds of different cheeses. Many creameries are "farmstead" operations, meaning that the animals whose milk is made into cheese are kept on-site. If you eat enough cheese during your time in the state, you may be able to differentiate between the many types of milk (cow, goat, sheep, or even water buffalo) and make associations between the geography and climate of where you are and the taste of the local cheeses.

This is one of the reasons that taking a walk around a dairy is a great idea:

you can see the process in action, from grazing to aging to eating. The **Vermont Cheese Trail map,** which you can view or download on the website of the Vermont Cheese Council (☎ *866/261–8595* ⊕ *www. vtcheese.com*), has a comprehensive list of dairies, many of which you can visit. Though hours are given for some, it's generally recommended that you still call ahead.

At the **Vermont Cheesemakers Festival** (☎ *802/261–8595* ⊕ *www. vtcheesefest.com*), which takes place in July in Shelburne, cheese makers gather to sell their various cheeses. Beer and wine are served to wash it all down.

base features the latest (and fanciest) venues the resort has to offer. **Facilities:** 121 trails; 667 acres; 2,200-foot vertical drop; 20 lifts. ⊠ *77 Okemo Ridge Rd.* ☎ *802/228–4041, 802/228–5222 for snow conditions* ⊕ *www.okemo.com* 🖃 *Lift ticket: $92.*

GRAFTON

20 miles south of Ludlow.

Out-of-the-way Grafton is as much a historical museum as a town. During its heyday, citizens grazed 10,000 sheep and spun their wool into sturdy yarn for locally woven fabric. As the wool market declined, so did Grafton. In 1963 the Windham Foundation—Vermont's second-largest private foundation—commenced the town's rehabilitation. The Old Tavern (now called The Grafton Inn) was preserved, along with many other commercial and residential structures.

GETTING HERE AND AROUND

Routes 11, 35, and 103 intersect in Grafton.

EXPLORING

Historical Society Museum. This endearingly cluttered museum documents the town's history with photographs, soapstone displays, musical instruments, furniture, tools, and other artifacts. ⊠ *147 Main St.* ☎ *802/843–2584* ⊕ *www.graftonhistoricalsociety.com* 🖃 *$3.*

WHERE TO STAY

$$

B&B/INN

🖭 **The Grafton Inn.** One of the country's oldest operating inns, this 1801 classic encourages you to linger on its wraparound porches, in its authentically Colonial common rooms, or with a book by the fire in its old-fashioned library. **Pros:** classic Vermont inn and tavern; professionally run; appealing common areas. **Cons:** rooms are attractive but not stellar. $ *Rooms from: $200* ✉ *92 Main St.* ☎ *802/234–8689, 800/843–1801* ⊕ *www.graftoninnvermont.com* ⊃ *24 rooms, 6 suites, 5 houses* ⦿ *Breakfast.*

SHOPPING

Gallery North Star. Inside this restored 1877 home, original oil paintings, watercolors, lithographs, and sculptures by more than 30 New England artists are on display. ✉ *151 Townshend Rd.* ☎ *802/843–2465* ⊕ *www.gnsgrafton.com.*

Grafton Village Cheese Company. You can sample the best of Vermont cheddar at this downtown wine and cheese shop. ✉ *56 Townshend Rd.* ☎ *802/843–1062* ⊕ *www.graftonvillagecheese.com.*

TOWNSHEND

9 miles south of Grafton.

One of a string of attractive villages along the banks of the West River, Townshend embodies the Vermont ideal of a lush town green presided over by a gracefully proportioned church spire. The spire belongs to the 1790 Congregational Meeting House, one of the state's oldest houses of worship. North on Route 30 is the Scott Bridge, the state's longest single-span covered bridge. It makes for a pretty photo, though it's in a state of disrepair and therefore closed to foot and vehicle traffic.

GETTING HERE AND AROUND

Route 35 heading south from Grafton dead-ends into Route 30 at Townshend Common. Route 30 is the town's main drag.

EXPLORING

OFF THE BEATEN PATH

Newfane. With a village green surrounded by pristine white buildings, Newfane, 6 miles southeast of Townshend, is sometimes described as the quintessential New England small town. The 1839 First Congregational Church and the Windham County Court House, with green-shuttered windows and a rounded cupola, are often open. The building with the four-pointed spire is Union Hall, built in 1832. ✉ *Newfane* ⊕ *www.newfanevt.com.*

WHERE TO EAT

$

DINER

✕ **Townshend Dam Diner.** Folks come from miles around to enjoy traditional fare such as meat loaf, roast beef, chili, and croquettes, as well as Townshend-raised bison burgers and creative daily specials. Breakfast, served all day, includes raspberry-chocolate-chip walnut pancakes and homemade French toast. You can sit at any of the 1930s enamel-top tables or in the big swivel chairs at the U-shaped counter. The diner is a few miles northwest of the village. $ *Average main: $8* ✉ *5929 Rte. 30, West Townshend* ☎ *802/874–4107* ▭ *No credit cards* ⊙ *Closed Tues.*

WHERE TO STAY

$

B&B/INN

☷ **Boardman House.** This handsome Greek Revival home on the town green combines modern comfort with the relaxed charm of a 19th-century farmhouse. **Pros:** inexpensive; perfect village green location. **Cons:**

no phone, mobile reception is bad. $ *Rooms from: $80* ⊠ *Grafton Rd.* ☎ *802/365–4086* ▭ *No credit cards* ⇆ *4 rooms, 1 suite* ⦿ *Breakfast.*

$$ 🖵 **Four Columns Inn.** Rooms and suites in this white-columned, 1834
B&B/INN   Greek Revival mansion were designed for luxurious romantic getaways. **Pros:** updated rooms; heart of town. **Cons:** little entertainment in these parts. $ *Rooms from: $225* ⊠ *21 West St., Newfane* ☎ *802/365–7713* ⊕ *www.fourcolumnsvt.com* ⇆ *15 rooms, 1 cottage* ⦿ *Breakfast.*

$$ 🖵 **Windham Hill Inn.** As there's not too much to do nearby, you might
B&B/INN   find yourself sitting by a fire or swimming in the outdoor pool at this inn, part of the Relais & Châteaux collection. **Pros:** West River Valley views; exceedingly cozy spa. **Cons:** expensive; staff not always helpful. $ *Rooms from: $259* ⊠ *311 Lawrence Dr., West Townshend* ☎ *802/874–4080, 800/944–4080* ⊕ *www.windhamhill.com* ⇆ *11 rooms, 10 suites, 1 cottage* ⦿ *Breakfast.*

SPORTS AND THE OUTDOORS

Townshend State Park. At this park you'll find a sandy beach and a trail that climbs up a ravine full of small chutes and waterfalls. The hike here leads to views at the summit of 1,680-foot Bald Mountain. ⊠ *2755 State Forest Rd.* ☎ *802/365–7500* ⊕ *www.vtstateparks.com/htm/townshend. htm* ☉ *Facilities closed early Sept.–late May.*

CENTRAL VERMONT

Central Vermont's economy once centered on marble quarrying and mills. But today, as in much of the state, tourism drives the economic engine. The center of the dynamo is Killington, the East's largest downhill ski resort, but there's more to discover in central Vermont than high-speed chairlifts and slope-side condos. The old mills of Quechee and Middlebury now house restaurants and shops, with wonderful views of the waterfalls that once powered the mill turbines. Woodstock has upscale shops and a national historic park. Away from these settlements, the protected lands (except for occasional logging) of the Green Mountain National Forest are laced with hiking trails.

NORWICH

6 miles north of White River Junction.

On the bank of the Connecticut River, Norwich is graced with beautifully maintained 18th- and 19th-century homes set about a handsome green. Norwich is the Vermont sister town to sophisticated Hanover, New Hampshire (home of Dartmouth College), across the river.

GETTING HERE AND AROUND

Most attractions are off Interstate 91; the town sits a mile to the west.

EXPLORING

FAMILY   **Montshire Museum of Science.** Numerous hands-on exhibits at this sci-
Fodor's Choice   ence museum explore nature and technology. Kids can make giant
★   bubbles, see images from NASA space telescopes, watch marine life swim in aquariums, and explore a maze of outdoor trails by the river. Adults will happily join the fun. An ideal destination for a rainy day,

Central Vermont

this is one of the finest museums in New England. ⊠ *1 Montshire Rd.* ☎ *802/649–2200* ⊕ *www.montshire.org* ⊠ *$16 mid-June–early Sept., $14 early Sept.–mid-June.*

SPORTS AND THE OUTDOORS

Lake Morey Ice Skating Trail. For the most fun you can have on skates, head to America's longest ice-skating trail. From January to March, the frozen lake is groomed for ice-skating, providing a magical 4½-mile route amid forested hillsides. Bring your own skates or rent them at the Lake Morey Resort, which maintains the trail. ⊠ *1 Clubhouse Rd., Fairlee* ☎ *800/123–1211* ⊕ *www.lakemoreyresort.com.*

SHOPPING

King Arthur Flour Baker's Store. This shop is a must-see for those who love bread. The shelves are stocked with all the ingredients and tools in the company's *Baker's Catalogue,* including flours, mixes, and local jams, and syrups. The bakery has a viewing area where you can watch the products being made, and you can learn to bake them yourself at classes conducted on-site. The store is a fine spot for a quick bite if you're driving along Interstate 91; the timber-frame café serves high-quality pizzas, sandwiches, and baked items. ⊠ *135 U.S. 5 S* ☎ *802/649–3361* ⊕ *www.kingarthurflour.com.*

QUECHEE

11 miles southwest of Norwich, 6 miles west of White River Junction.

A historic mill town, Quechee sits just upriver from its namesake gorge, an impressive 165-foot-deep canyon cut by the Ottauquechee River. Most people view the gorge from U.S. 4. To escape the crowds, hike along the gorge or scramble down one of several trails to the river.

EXPLORING

FAMILY
Fodor'sChoice
★
Simon Pearce. A restored woolen mill by a waterfall holds Quechee's main attraction: this marvelous glassblowing factory, store, and restaurant. Water power still drives the factory's furnace. Take a free self-guided tour of the downstairs factory floor, and see the amazing glassblowers at work. The store sells beautifully crafted contemporary glass and ceramic tableware. An excellent, sophisticated restaurant with outstanding views of the falls uses Simon Pearce glassware and is justifiably popular. ⊠ *The Mill, 1760 Quechee Main St.* ☎ *802/295–2711* ⊕ *www.simonpearce.com.*

FAMILY
Vermont Institute of Natural Science Nature Center. Next to Quechee Gorge, this science center has 17 raptor exhibits, including bald eagles, peregrine falcons, and owls. All caged birds had been found injured and are unable to survive in the wild. Raptors Up Close, a 30-minute live bird program, starts daily at 1:30. ⊠ *6565 Woodstock Rd.* ☎ *802/359–5000* ⊕ *www.vinsweb.org* 🎫 *$13.50.*

WHERE TO EAT AND STAY

$$$
AMERICAN
Fodor'sChoice
★
✕ **Simon Pearce.** Sparkling glassware from the studio downstairs, exposed brick, flickering candles, and large windows overlooking the falls of the roaring Ottauquechee River create an ideal setting for contemporary American cuisine. The food here is worthy of a pilgrimage: horseradish-crusted blue cod with crispy leeks, herbed mashed potatoes, and a balsamic shallot reduction is a house specialty, as is roast duck with mango chutney sauce. The wine cellar holds several hundred labels. ⑤ *Average main: $28* ⊠ *The Mill, 1760 Main St.* ☎ *802/295–1470* ⊕ *www.simonpearce.com.*

$$
B&B/INN
🛏 **The Parker House Inn.** This beautiful 1857 house on the National Historic Register once belonged to Senator Joseph Parker, who also owned the textile mill next door. **Pros:** riverfront location; spacious rooms. **Cons:** no yard. ⑤ *Rooms from: $245* ⊠ *1792 Main St.* ☎ *802/295–6077, 800/295–6077* ⊕ *www.theparkerhouseinn.com* ⇆ *7 rooms* ⋈ *Breakfast.*

$$
B&B/INN
🛏 **Quechee Inn at Marshland Farm.** Each room in this handsomely restored 1793 country home has Queen Anne–style furnishings and period antiques. **Pros:** historic house; spacious grounds. **Cons:** some bathrooms are dated; fills up with weddings. ⑤ *Rooms from: $287* ⊠ *1119 Main St.* ☎ *802/295–3133, 800/235–3133* ⊕ *www.quecheeinn.com* ⇆ *22 rooms, 3 suites* ⋈ *Breakfast.*

SPORTS AND THE OUTDOORS

Wilderness Trails and Vermont Fly Fishing School. In summer, Wilderness Trails leads fly-fishing workshops; rents bikes, canoes, kayaks, and paddleboards; and arranges guided canoe, kayaking, and hiking trips.

Simon Pearce is a glassblowing factory, store, and restaurant; the factory's furnace is still powered by hydroelectricity from Quechee Falls.

In winter, the company conducts cross-country skiing and snowshoeing treks. ✉ *1119 Quechee Main St.* ☎ *802/295–7620* ⊕ *www.wildernesstrailsvermont.com.*

SHOPPING

FAMILY **Quechee Gorge Village.** Hundreds of dealers sell their wares at this antiques-and-crafts mall in a reconstructed barn that also houses a country store and a classic diner. Outlets for Cabot and Danforth Pewter neighbor an ice-cream shop and a toy-and-train museum, where a merry-go-round and a small-scale working railroad operate when weather permits. ✉ *573 Woodstock Rd., off U.S. 4* ☎ *802/295–1550* ⊕ *www.quecheegorge.com.*

Scotland by the Yard. This store sells all things Celtic, from kilts to argyle jackets and tartan ties. ✉ *8828 Woodstock Rd.* ☎ *802/295–5351* ⊕ *www.scotlandbytheyard.com.*

WOODSTOCK

4 miles west of Quechee.

Woodstock is a Currier & Ives print come to life. Well-maintained Federal-style houses surround the tree-lined village green, which is not far from a covered bridge. The town owes much of its pristine appearance to the Rockefeller family's interest in historic preservation and land conservation and to native George Perkins Marsh, a congressman, diplomat, and conservationist who wrote the pioneering book *Man and Nature* (1864) about humanity's use and abuse of the land. Only busy U.S. 4 mars the tableau.

ESSENTIALS

Visitor Information Woodstock Vermont Area Chamber of Commerce.
⊠ *59 Central St.* ☎ *802/457–3555, 888/496–6378* ⊕ *www.woodstockvt.com.*

EXPLORING

FAMILY **Billings Farm and Museum.** Founded by Frederick H. Billings in 1871, this is one of the oldest operating dairy farms in the country. In addition to watching the herds of Jersey cows, horses, and other farm animals at work and play, you can tour the restored 1890 farmhouse, and in the adjacent barns learn about 19th-century farming and domestic life. The biggest takeaway, however, is a renewed belief in sustainable agriculture and stewardship of the land. Pick up some raw-milk cheddar while you're here. ⊠ *5302 River Rd., ½ mile north of Woodstock* ☎ *802/457–2355* ⊕ *www.billingsfarm.org* 🎟 *$14.*

Marsh-Billings-Rockefeller National Historical Park. Vermont's only national park is the nation's first to focus on conserving natural resources. The pristine 555-acre spread includes the mansion, gardens, and carriage roads of Frederick H. Billings (1823–1890), a financier and the president of the Northern Pacific Railway. The entire property was the gift of Laurance S. Rockefeller (1910–2004), who lived here with his wife, Mary (Billings's granddaughter). You can learn more at the visitor center, tour the residential complex with a guide every hour on the hour, and explore the 20 miles of trails and old carriage roads that climb Mt. Tom. ⊠ *54 Elm St.* ☎ *802/457–3368* ⊕ *www.nps.gov/mabi* 🎟 *Tour $8.*

WHERE TO EAT

$$$$ ✗ **Barnard Inn Restaurant and Max's Tavern.** The dining room in this 1796
AMERICAN   brick farmhouse exudes 18th-century charm, but the food is decidedly 21st century. Former San Francisco restaurant chef-owner Will Dodson creates inventive three-course prix-fixe menus with specialties like seafood curry and Wiener schnitzel with lemon-caper sauce. In the back is a relaxed local favorite, Max's Tavern, which serves some of the same dishes à la carte, along with upscale pub fare. ⑤ *Average main: $65* ⊠ *5518 Rte. 12, 8 miles north of Woodstock, Barnard* ☎ *802/234–9961* ⊕ *www.barnardinn.com* ⊗ *Closed Sun. and Mon. No lunch* ⚴ *Reservations essential.*

$$$$ ✗ **Cloudland Farm.** With the table literally on the farm, this restaurant
AMERICAN   delivers a unique farm-to-table experience that makes it worth the short drive from Woodstock. Prix-fixe dinners ($45) are served on Friday, Saturday, and most Thursdays. All ingredients for the seasonal menu come fresh from the farm or from other growers; Cloudland's own pork and beef figure in such main dishes as maple-glazed ham with apple-and-onion compote, and beef shank osso bucco with sautéed kale and beef bacon. The desserts—among them homemade carrot cake with red wine caramel and carrot jam—are delicious. Bring your own wine or beer, and the restaurant will provide glassware and a corkscrew for a small corkage. ⑤ *Average main: $45* ⊠ *1101 Cloudland Rd., North Pomfret* ☎ *802/457–2599* ⊕ *www.cloudlandfarm.com* ⊗ *Closed Sun.– Wed., and Mar. No lunch* ⚴ *Reservations essential.*

$$ ✗ **Keeper's Café.** Creatively prepared, moderately priced fare draws cus-
CAFÉ   tomers from all over the region to chef Chris Loucka's café. The organic

3

dishes he prepares include char-grilled kielbasa and an arugula and beet salad. Located in a former general store, the three dining rooms feel relaxed, with locals table-hopping to chat with friends. ⑤ *Average main: $22* ✉ *3685 Rte. 106, 12 miles south of Woodstock, Reading* ☎ *802/484–9090* ⊕ *www.keeperscafe.com* ⊙ *Closed Sun. and Mon. No lunch.*

$$ ✕ **Pane e Saluto.** Don't let the size fool you: meals at this little upstairs
ITALIAN restaurant are exciting and memorable, thanks to young couple Deir-
Fodor'sChoice dre Heekin and Caleb Barker. Hip decor, an intimately small space,
★ and Heekin's discreetly passionate front-of-house direction all come together to complement Barker's slow food–inspired dishes. Try *ragù d'agnello e maiale* (spaghetti with a ragù of roasted lamb and pork) followed by *cotechino e lenticchie* (garlic sausage with lentils). Reserve well in advance, as this tiny osteria fills up fast. The couple also run a farm and winery in Barnard, a consuming endeavor that often results in them closing the restaurant for weeks at a time; it's wise to call ahead before coming to make sure it's open. ⑤ *Average main: $22* ✉ *61 Central St.* ☎ *802/457–4882* ⊕ *www.osteriapaneesalute.com* ⊙ *Closed Mon.–Thurs., and Apr., Sept.–mid-Oct., and late Nov. No lunch* ⚑ *Reservations essential.*

$$ ✕ **The Prince and the Pauper.** Modern French and American fare with a
FRENCH Vermont accent is the focus of this candlelit Colonial restaurant off the town green. The grilled duck breast might have an Asian five-spice sauce, and the boneless rack of lamb is wrapped in puff pastry and splashed with bordelaise sauce. Three-course prix-fixe meals cost $51; a less expensive bistro menu is available in the lounge. If you like the artwork hanging above your table, you can purchase it. ⑤ *Average main: $21* ✉ *24 Elm St.* ☎ *802/457–1818* ⊕ *www.princeandpauper. com* ⊙ *No lunch.*

$ ✕ **Worthy Kitchen.** Be sure to consult the chalkboard near the entrance,
AMERICAN so you can place your order for small bites, sandwiches, sides, and
FAMILY perhaps a craft beer at the bar. Then, grab a seat at a booth under the lofty, wood-beam ceilings in the dining room or at a table outside on the patio. Your meal will be ready in just a few minutes. The owners describe their eatery as a "farm diner," an apt description for a place serving locally sourced comfort food that's by turns decadent, familiar, and fresh. Go with anything fried, from buttermilk chicken to dough-nuts. Up the road in South Royalton, the same people run the immensely popular Worthy Burger. ⑤ *Average main: $10* ✉ *442 Woodstock Rd.* ☎ *802/457–7281* ⊕ *www.worthyvermont.com* ⊙ *No lunch weekdays.*

WHERE TO STAY

$$ ⚏ **The Fan House Bed and Breakfast.** If you're searching for an authentic
B&B/INN inn in the heart of a textbook Vermont town, consider this Colonial
Fodor'sChoice dating to 1840. **Pros:** center of old town; plenty of creature comforts;
★ good library; real sense of home. **Cons:** upstairs rooms can be cool in winter. ⑤ *Rooms from: $200* ✉ *6297 Rte. 12 N* ☎ *802/234–6704* ⊕ *www.thefanhouse.com* ▬ *No credit cards* ⊙ *Closed Apr.* ⇄ *2 rooms, 1 suite* ⦿ *Breakfast.*

$$ ⚏ **Kedron Valley Inn.** You're likely to fall in love at first sight with the
B&B/INN main 1828 three-story brick building here, the centerpiece of a 15-acre

The upscale Woodstock area is known as Vermont's horse country.

retreat. **Pros:** good food; quiet setting; handsome main building. **Cons:** 5 miles south of Woodstock. $⑤ Rooms from: $259 ✉ 4778 South Rd., South Woodstock ☎ 802/457–1473, 800/836–1193 ⊕ www.kedronval-leyinn.com ⊗ Closed Apr. ⇄ 24 rooms, 1 suite ⦿ Breakfast.*

$　⊡ **The Shire Riverview Motel.** Many rooms in this immaculate motel have
HOTEL decks, and most have fabulous views of Ottauquechee River, which runs right along the building. **Pros:** inexpensive access to the heart of Woodstock; views. **Cons:** basic rooms; unexciting exterior. $⑤ Rooms from: $175 ✉ 46 Pleasant St. ☎ 802/457–2211 ⊕ www.shiremotel.com ⇄ 42 rooms ⦿ No meals.*

$$$$　⊡ **Twin Farms.** Let's just get it out there: Twin Farms is the best lodging
RESORT in Vermont; if you can afford it (stays begin at well more than $1,000 a
Fodor'sChoice night), you'll want to experience it. **Pros:** impeccable service; gorgeous
★ rooms; sensational meals. **Cons:** steep prices. $⑤ Rooms from: $1900 ✉ 452 Royalton Tpke., Barnard ☎ 802/234–9999 ⊕ www.twinfarms. com ⊗ Closed Apr. ⇄ 10 rooms and suites, 10 cottages ⦿ All-inclusive.*

$$$　⊡ **The Woodstock Inn and Resort.** Far from the main road but still on
RESORT Woodstock's gorgeous green, this resort has a hard-to-beat loca-
Fodor'sChoice tion. **Pros:** attractive historic property; numerous amenities; soothing
★ spa. **Cons:** can lack intimacy. $⑤ Rooms from: $315 ✉ 14 The Green ☎ 802/332–6853, 888/338–2745 ⊕ www.woodstockinn.com ⇄ 135 rooms, 7 suites ⦿ No meals.*

SPORTS AND THE OUTDOORS
GOLF
Woodstock Inn and Resort Golf Club. Robert Trent Jones Sr. designed the resort's challenging course. ⊠ *76 South St.* ☎ *802/457–6674, 888/338–2745* ⊕ *www.woodstockinn.com/golf-club* ⌚ *$59 for 9 holes, $79 for 18 holes, weekdays; $79 for 9 holes, $125 for 18 holes, weekends* ⅄. *18 holes, 6000 yards, par 70.*

3

SHOPPING
ART GALLERIES
Gallery on the Green. This corner gallery in one of Woodstock's oldest buildings showcases paintings by New England artists depicting regional landscapes. ⊠ *1 The Green* ☎ *802/457–4956* ⊕ *www.galleryonthegreen.com.*

CRAFTS
Collective. This funky and attractive shop sells local jewelry, glass, pottery, and clothing. ⊠ *47 Central St.* ☎ *802/457–1298* ⊕ *www.collectivetheartofcraft.com.*

FOOD
Sugarbush Farm. Take the Taftsville Covered Bridge to this farm, where you can learn how maple sugar is made and can sample as much maple syrup as you'd like. The farm also makes excellent cheeses. ⊠ *591 Sugarbush Farm Rd., off U.S. 4* ☎ *802/457–1757, 800/281–1757* ⊕ *www.sugarbushfarm.com.*

Taftsville Country Store. East of town, the store sells Vermont cheeses, moderately priced wines, and Vermont-made specialty foods. ⊠ *404 U.S. 4, Taftsville* ☎ *802/457–1135* ⊕ *www.taftsville.com.*

Village Butcher. This emporium of Vermont edibles has great sandwiches, cheeses, local beers, and delicious baked goods—perfect for a picnic or for lunch on the go. ⊠ *18 Elm St.* ☎ *802/457–2756* ⊕ *www.thebutcher.biz.*

Woodstock Farmers' Market. The market is a year-round buffet of local produce, fresh fish, and excellent sandwiches and pastries. The maple-walnut scones go fast, so get there early. ⊠ *468 Woodstock Rd., aka U.S. 4* ☎ *802/457–3658* ⊕ *www.woodstockfarmersmarket.com* ⊗ *Closed Mon.*

SPAS
Out of the Woods Spa at Twin Farms. A visit to Twin Farms is a trip to another world, and a spa treatment here completes the getaway. The spa at the luxury lodging expounds a philosophy of wellness that goes beyond the realm of massages and skin treatments. Employing an organic product line by Vermont-based Tata Harper and Lunaroma, the spa offers facials, polishes, aromatherapy, massages, and mud wraps that administer a heavenly reboot to your skin and muscles. ⊠ *Twin Farms, 452 Royalton Tpke., Barnard* ☎ *802/234–9999* ⊕ *www.twinfarms.com/experience/spa.*

Spa at the Woodstock Inn and Resort. A mesmerizing, 10,000-square-foot, nature-inspired facility, this LEED-certified spa has 10 treatment rooms, a full-service salon, and a sophisticated shop devoted to wellness and relaxation. Elegant, minimalist design accentuates the beautiful setting: natural light pours into sparkling dressing rooms and the firelit Great Room, and an outdoor meditation courtyard has a soaking pool and a Scandinavian-style sauna that face the sky. The mood is serene, the treatments varied: opt for The Works, and you'll receive a massage, a facial, a manicure, and a pedicure over the course of five or six hours. ⊠ *Woodstock Inn and Resort, 14 The Green* ☎ *802/457–6697, 888/338–2745* ⊕ *www.woodstockinn.com/spa.*

KILLINGTON

15 miles east of Rutland.

With only a gas station, a post office, a motel, and a few shops at the intersection of U.S. 4 and Route 100, it doesn't quite feel like the East's largest ski resort is nearby. The village of Killington has suffered from unfortunate strip development along the access road to the ski resort, but the 360-degree views atop Killington Peak, accessible via the resort's gondola, make it worth the drive.

WHERE TO STAY

$$ ⛄ **Birch Ridge Inn.** A slate-covered carriageway about a mile from
B&B/INN the Killington ski resort leads to one of the area's most popular off-mountain stays, a former executive retreat in two renovated A-frames. **Pros:** quirky design; well-maintained property; tasty cuisine. **Cons:** oddly furnished; outdated style. [$] *Rooms from: $200* ⊠ *37 Butler Rd.* ☎ *802/422–4293, 800/435–8566* ⊕ *www.birchridge.com* ⊘ *Closed May* ⇱ *10 rooms* ⦿| *Breakfast.*

$$ ⛄ **The Mountain Top Inn & Resort.** This cross-country skiing and horseback
RESORT riding haven has stunning views and laid-back yet luxurious accom-
FAMILY modations. **Pros:** family-friendly vibe; great spot for outdoor activities. **Cons:** fees for activities can add up. [$] *Rooms from: $275* ⊠ *195 Mountain Top Rd., Chittenden* ☎ *802/483–2311* ⊕ *www.mountaintopinn. com* ⇱ *32 rooms, 4 cabins, 4 cottages, 18 rental homes and condos* ⦿| *No meals.*

$$ ⛄ **The Woods Resort & Spa.** Not a traditional hotel or resort, the Woods is
RESORT a collection of upscale two- and three-bedroom town houses on wooded lots along a winding road. **Pros:** contemporary facility; spacious rooms; access to spa, pool, and tennis courts; private shuttle to ski area. **Cons:** lacks traditional Vermont feel; several management companies handle the units. [$] *Rooms from: $250* ⊠ *53 Woods La.* ☎ *802/422–3100* ⊕ *www.woodsresort.net* ⇱ *107 units* ⦿| *No meals.*

NIGHTLIFE

McGrath's Irish Pub. On weekends, listen to live Irish music and sip Guinness draft at the Inn at Long Trail's pub. ⊠ *709 U.S. 4* ☎ *802/755–7181* ⊕ *www.innatlongtrail.com.*

Pickle Barrel Night Club. During ski season, this club has live music on Friday and Saturday. After 8, the crowd moves downstairs for dancing, sometimes to big-name bands. ⊠ *1741 Killington Rd.* ☎ *802/422–3035* ⊕ *www.picklebarrelnightclub.com.*

Wobbly Barn. Twentysomethings dance at the Wobbly Barn nightclub, open during ski season, and families dig into giant steaks and graze at the salad bar in the restaurant. ⊠ *2229 Killington Rd.* ☎ *802/422–6171* ⊕ *www.wobblybarn.com.*

SPORTS AND THE OUTDOORS

BIKING

True Wheels Bike Shop. Part of the Basin Sports complex, this shop rents bicycles and has information about local routes. ⊠ *2886 Killington Rd.* ☎ *802/422–3234, 877/487–9972* ⊕ *www.basinski.com/our-stores/ true-wheels.*

CROSS-COUNTRY SKIING

The Mountain Top Inn & Resort. This resort has 37 miles of hilly trails groomed for cross-country skiing, 24 miles of which can be used for skate skiing. You can also enjoy snowshoeing, ice-skating, and snowmobile and sleigh rides. Summer activities include horseback riding, clay-bird shooting, fishing, hiking, sand volleyball, and water sports. ⊠ *195 Mountaintop Rd., Chittenden* ☎ *802/483–2311* ⊕ *www.mountaintopinn.com* ⊠ *Trail pass $18 per half day, $22 per day for guests not staying overnight.*

FISHING

Gifford Woods State Park. This state park's Kent Pond is a terrific fishing spot. ⊠ *34 Gifford Woods Rd., ½ mile north of U.S. 4* ☎ *802/775–5354* ⊕ *www.vtstateparks.com/htm/gifford.htm* ◔ *Facilities closed late Oct.–mid-May.*

GOLF

Killington Golf Course. At its namesake resort, the course has a challenging layout. ⊠ *4763 Killington Rd.* ☎ *802/422–6700* ⊕ *www.killington.com/ summer/golf_course* ⊠ *$30 for 9 holes and $50 for 18 holes, weekdays; $40 for 9 holes and $65 for 18 holes, weekends* ⅃ *18 holes, 6186 yards, par 72* ◔ *Closed mid-Oct.–mid-May.*

HIKING

Deer Leap Trail. This 3-mile round-trip hike begins near the Inn at Long Trail and leads to a great view overlooking Sherburne Gap and Pico Peak. ⊠ *Trailhead off U.S. 4, just east of Inn at Long Trail, Rutland.*

SKI AREAS

FAMILY

Fodor'sChoice

★

Killington. "Megamountain" aptly describes Killington. Thanks to its extensive snowmaking capacity, the resort typically opens in early November, and the lifts often run into late April or early May. Skiing includes everything from Outer Limits, the East's steepest and longest mogul trail, to the 6½-mile Great Eastern. The 22-foot Superpipe is one of the best rated in the East. There are also acres of glades. Après-ski activities are plentiful, and Killington ticket holders can also ski Pico Mountain—a shuttle connects the two areas. Summer activities at Killington–Pico include mountain biking, hiking, and golf. **Facilities:** 155 trails; 1,509 acres; 3,050-foot vertical drop; 22 lifts. ■TIP→ Park at the base of the Skyeship Gondola to avoid the more crowded access road. ⊠ *4763 Killington Rd.* ☎ *802/422–3261 for snow conditions, 802/621–6867* ⊕ *www.killington.com* ⊠ *Lift ticket: $96.*

Pico. When weekend hordes descend upon Killington, locals head to Pico. One of Killington's "seven peaks," Pico is physically separated from its parent resort. Trails range from elevator-shaft steep to challenging intermediate runs near the summit. Easier terrain can be found near the bottom of the mountain's nearly 2,000-foot vertical drop, and the learning slope is separated from the upper mountain, so hotshots won't bomb through it. The lower express quad can get crowded, but the upper one rarely has a line. **Facilities:** 57 trails; 468 acres; 1,967-foot vertical drop; 7 lifts. ⊠ *73 Alpine Dr., Mendon* ☎ *802/422–6200, 802/422–1200 for snow conditions* ⊕ *www.picomountain.com* ⌁ *Lift ticket: $69.*

SNOWMOBILE TOURS

Snowmobile Vermont. Blazing down forest trails on a snowmobile is one way Vermonters embrace the winter landscapes. Rentals are available through Snowmobile Vermont at several locations, including Killington and Okemo. Both have hour-long guided tours across groomed ski trails ($99). If you're feeling more adventurous, take the two-hour backcountry tour through 25 miles of Calvin Coolidge State Forest ($154). ⊠ *170 Rte. 100, Bridgewater Corners* ☎ *802/422–2121* ⊕ *www.snowmobilevermont.com.*

RUTLAND

15 miles southwest of Killington, 32 miles south of Middlebury.

The strip malls and seemingly endless row of traffic lights on and around U.S. 7 in Rutland are very un-Vermont. Two blocks west, however, stand the mansions of marble magnates. In Rutland you can grab a bite and see some interesting marble, and Depot Park hosts the county farmers' market Saturday 9–2. This isn't a place to spend too much time sightseeing, though.

ESSENTIALS

Visitor Information Rutland Region Chamber of Commerce. ⊠ *50 Merchants Row* ☎ *802/773–2747, 800/756–8880* ⊕ *www.rutlandvermont.com.*

EXPLORING

Chaffee Art Center. Housed in a beautiful mansion, the center exhibits the work of more than 200 Vermont artists. A second location is open downtown on Merchants Row. ⊠ *16 S. Main St.* ☎ *802/775–0356* ⊕ *www.chaffeeartcenter.org* ⌁ *Free.*

New England Maple Museum. Maple syrup is Vermont's signature product, and this museum north of Rutland explains the history and process of turning sap into syrup. If you don't get a chance to visit a sugarhouse, this is a fine place to sample the different grades and pick up some souvenirs. ⊠ *4578 U.S. 7, 9 miles south of Brandon, Pittsford* ☎ *802/483–9414* ⊕ *www.maplemuseum.com* ⌁ *Museum $5.*

Paramount Theatre. The highlight of downtown Rutland is this 838-seat gilded playhouse, an architectural gem dating to 1913. The gorgeous theater presents music, theater, films, and stand-up comedy. ⊠ *30 Center St.* ☎ *802/775–0570* ⊕ *www.paramountvt.org.*

Vermont Marble Museum. This monument to marble highlights one of the main industries in this region. The hall of presidents has a carved bust of each U.S. president, and in the marble chapel is a replica of Leonardo da Vinci's *Last Supper*. Elsewhere, you can watch a sculptor-in-residence at work, compare marble from around the world, learn about the geological history of the Earth, and check out the Vermont Marble Company's original "stone library." A short walk away is the original quarry, which helped finish the U.S. Supreme Court. ⊠ *52 Main St., off Rte. 3, Proctor* ☎ *800/427–1396, 802/459–2750* ⊕ *www.vermont-marble.com* ⊠ *$7.*

Wilson Castle. Completed in 1867, this 32-room mansion was built over the course of eight years by a Vermonter who married a British aristocrat. Within the opulent setting are 84 stained-glass windows (one inset with 32 Australian opals), hand-painted Italian frescoes, and 13 fireplaces. The place is magnificently furnished with European and Asian objets d'art. October evenings bring haunted castle tours. ⊠ *2708 West St., Proctor* ☎ *802/773–3284* ⊕ *www.wilsoncastle.com* ⊠ *$10.*

WHERE TO EAT

$$
ECLECTIC
✕ Little Harry's. Laminated photos of regular customers adorn the tabletops of this restaurant, which locals have packed since 1997, when chef-owners Trip Pearce and Jack Mangan brought Vermont-cheddar ravioli and lamb lo mein to downtown Rutland. If you have a big appetite on a small budget, try the signature pad thai. The place is "little" compared to the bigger Harry's, near Ludlow. ⑤ *Average main: $20* ⊠ *121 West St.* ☎ *802/747–4848* ⊕ *www.littleharrys.com* ☽ *No lunch.*

SPORTS AND THE OUTDOORS

BOATING
Woodard Marine. Rent pontoon boats, speedboats, stand-up paddleboards, and kayaks at the Lake Bomoseen Marina. ⊠ *145 Creek Rd., off Rte. 4A, Castleton* ☎ *802/265–3690* ⊕ *www.woodardmarine.com.*

HIKING
Mountain Travelers. This place sells hiking, sporting, and boating equipment; gives advice on local hikes; and rents skis. ⊠ *147 U.S. 4 E* ☎ *802/775–0814* ⊕ *www.mtntravelers.com.*

BRANDON

15 miles northwest of Rutland.

Thanks to an active group of artists, tiny Brandon is making a name for itself. In 2003 the Brandon Artists Guild, led by American folk artist Warren Kimble, auctioned off 40 life-size fiberglass pigs painted by local artists. The "Really Really Pig Show" raised money for the guild, and has since brought small-town fame to this community through its annual shows. Brandon is also home to the Basin Bluegrass Festival, held in July.

ESSENTIALS
Visitor Information Brandon Visitor Center. ⊠ *4 Grove St.* ☎ *802/247–6401* ⊕ *www.brandon.org.*

EXPLORING

Brandon Artists Guild. The guild exhibits and sells affordable paintings, sculpture, and pottery by more than 50 local member artists. ⊠ *7 Center St.* ☎ *802/247–4956* ⊕ *www.brandonartistsguild.org/the-gallery* ⛛ *Free.*

Brandon Museum at the Stephen A. Douglas Birthplace. The famous statesman was born in this house in 1813. He left 20 years later to establish himself as a lawyer, becoming a three-time U.S. senator and arguing more cases before the U.S. Supreme Court than anyone else. This museum recounts the early Douglas years, early town history, and the antislavery movement in Vermont, the first state to abolish slavery. ⊠ *4 Grove St., at U.S. 7* ☎ *802/247–6401* ⊕ *www.brandon.org* ⛛ *Free.*

WHERE TO EAT AND STAY

$$
CAFÉ
✕ **Café Provence.** Robert Barral, the former director of the New England Culinary Institute, graces Brandon with this informal eatery one story above the main street. Flowered seat cushions, dried-flower window valences, and other hints of Barral's Provençal birthplace abound. His café specializes in eclectic farm-fresh dishes: the goat-cheese cake with mesclun greens, braised veal cheeks, and caramelized endive, and the portobello pizza from the restaurant's hearth oven both count among recent favorites. Sunday brunch offerings include buttery pastries, eggs Benedict, and breakfast pizza. There's outdoor seating under large umbrellas. ⑤ *Average main: $20* ⊠ *11 Center St.* ☎ *802/247–9997* ⊕ *www.cafeprovencevt.com* ⊗ *Closed Mon. in winter.*

$$
B&B/INN
Fodor'sChoice
★
🛏 **Blueberry Hill Inn.** In the Green Mountain National Forest, 5½ miles off a mountain pass on a dirt road, you'll find this secluded inn with lush gardens and a pond with a wood-fired sauna on its bank. **Pros:** peaceful setting within the national forest; lots of activities; great food. **Cons:** fills up with wedding parties. ⑤ *Rooms from: $269* ⊠ *1245 Goshen–Ripton Rd., Goshen* ☎ *802/247–6735* ⊕ *www.blueberryhillinn. com* ⊲ *12 rooms* ⦿❘ *Some meals.*

$$
B&B/INN
🛏 **The Lilac Inn.** The best bed-and-breakfast in town has cheery, comfortable guest rooms in a central setting half a block from the heart of Brandon. **Pros:** big manor house; within walking distance of town; cheery rooms. **Cons:** busy in summer with weddings. ⑤ *Rooms from: $210* ⊠ *53 Park St.* ☎ *802/247–5463, 800/221–0720* ⊕ *www.lilacinn. com* ⊲ *8 rooms, 1 suite* ⦿❘ *Breakfast.*

SPORTS AND THE OUTDOORS

GOLF

Neshobe Golf Club. This bent-grass course has terrific views of the Green Mountains. Several local inns offer golfing packages. ⊠ *224 Town Farm Rd.* ☎ *802/247–3611* ⊕ *www.neshobe.com* ⛛ *$35 for 9 holes, $60 for 18 holes* 🎿 *18 holes, 6500 yards, par 72.*

HIKING

Branbury State Park. A large turnout on Route 53 marks the trailhead for a moderate hike to the Falls of Lana, a highlight of this park on the shores of Lake Dunmore near the Moosalamoo National Recreation Area. ⊠ *3570 Lake Dunmore Rd.* ⊕ *www.vtstateparks.com/htm/branbury.htm* ⛛ *$4* ⊗ *Facilities closed late Oct.–late May.*

Mt. Horrid, For great views from a vertigo inducing cliff, hike up the Long Trail to Mt. Horrid. The steep, hour-long hike starts at the top of Brandon Gap. ⊠ *Trailhead at Brandon Gap Rte. 73 parking lot, about 8 miles east of Brandon* ⊕ *www.fs.usda.gov/main/gmfl.*

Mt. Independence State Historic Site. West of Brandon, four trails—two short ones of less than a mile each and two longer ones—lead to some abandoned Revolutionary War fortifications. ⊠ *28 Shoales Dr., off Mt. Independence Rd. just west of Orwell, Orwell* ✢ *Parking lot is at top of hill* ☎ *802/948-2000* ⊕ *historicsites.vermont.gov/directory/ mount_independence* ⊠ *$5* ⊙ *Closed mid-Oct.–late May.*

PARKS

Moosalamoo National Recreation Area. Covering more than 15,000 acres of the Green Mountain National Forest, this area northeast of Brandon attracts hikers, mountain bikers, and cross-country skiers who enjoy the 70-plus miles of trails through wondrous terrain. If there is anywhere to stop and smell the flowers in Vermont, this is it. ⊠ *Off Rtes. 53 and 73* ⊕ *www.moosalamoo.org.*

MIDDLEBURY

17 miles north of Brandon, 34 miles south of Burlington.

In the late 1800s Middlebury was the largest Vermont community west of the Green Mountains, an industrial center of river-powered wool and grain mills. This is Robert Frost country: Vermont's late poet laureate spent 23 summers at a farm east of Middlebury. Still a cultural and economic hub amid the Champlain Valley's serene pastoral patchwork—and the home of top-notch Middlebury College—the town and rolling countryside invite a day of exploration.

EXPLORING

TOP ATTRACTIONS

Edgewater Gallery. This gallery sits alongside picturesque Otter Creek, and the paintings, jewelry, ceramics, and pieces of furniture inside are just as arresting. Exhibitions in the bright, airy space change regularly, demonstrating the owner's ambition to be more gallery than shop, though all pieces are for sale. A second gallery is across the creek in the Battell Building. ⊠ *1 Mill St.* ☎ *802/458-0098* ⊕ *www.edgewatergallery-vt.com* ⊠ *Free.*

Middlebury College. Founded in 1800, this college was conceived as a more godly alternative to the worldly University of Vermont, though it has no religious affiliation today. The postmodern architecture of the **Mahaney Center for the Arts,** which offers music, theater, and dance performances throughout the year, stands in provocative contrast to the early-19th-century stone buildings in the middle of town. ⊠ *131 College St.* ☎ *802/443-5000* ⊕ *www.middlebury.edu.*

Robert Frost Interpretive Trail. Plaques along this easy 1.2-mile wooded trail bear quotations from Frost's poems. A picnic area is located across the road from the trailhead. ⊠ *Trailhead on Rte. 125, 10 miles east of downtown* ⊕ *www.fs.usda.gov/main/gmfl.*

WORTH NOTING

FAMILY **University of Vermont Morgan Horse Farm.** The Morgan horse, Vermont's official state animal, has an even temper, high stamina, and slightly truncated legs in proportion to its body. This farm, about 2½ miles west of Middlebury, is a breeding and training center where in summer you can tour the stables and paddocks. ✉ *74 Battell Dr., off Morgan Horse Farm Rd., Weybridge* ☎ *802/388–2011* ⊕ *www.uvm.edu/morgan* ✐ *$5.*

Vermont Folklife Center. The redbrick center's exhibits include photography, antiques, folk paintings, manuscripts, and other artifacts and contemporary works that examine various facets of Vermont life. ✉ *88 Main St.* ☎ *802/388–4964* ⊕ *www.vermontfolklifecenter.org* ✐ *Donations accepted.*

WHERE TO EAT

$$ ✗ **American Flatbread Middlebury Hearth.** On weekends this is the most
PIZZA happening spot in town, and it's no wonder: the pizza is extraordinary, and the attitude is pure Vermont. Wood-fired clay domes create masterful thin crusts from organically grown wheat. If you love pizza, you're in for a treat. Besides the innovative, delicious pizzas, try an organic mesclun salad tossed in the house ginger-tamari vinaigrette. There are also locations in Waitsfield and Burlington. ⑤ *Average main: $20* ✉ *137 Maple St.* ☎ *802/388–3300* ⊕ *www.americanflatbread.com* ⊗ *Closed Sun. and Mon. No lunch Tues.–Fri.* ⚌ *Reservations not accepted.*

$$ ✗ **The Bobcat Cafe & Brewery.** Worth the drive from Middlebury to the
AMERICAN small town of Bristol, the Bobcat is fun, funky, and hip—suitable for a date but casual enough for the whole family. Comfort food served here ranges from locally sourced burgers to clever takes on fried fish, meat loaf, and tacos. Wash your meal down with excellent house-brewed beer, and save room for a rich dessert, like the peach upside-down cake. ⑤ *Average main: $20* ✉ *5 Main St., Bristol* ☎ *802/453–3311* ⊕ *www.thebobcatcafe.com* ⊗ *No lunch.*

$$ ✗ **Fire & Ice Restaurant.** It's hard not to have a good time at this restau-
AMERICAN rant constructed around a vintage boat. This self-described "museum
FAMILY of Vermont" has nine themed rooms, including a library and a college nostalgia room. Choose from prime rib, steak, fish, and a 55-item salad bar (including peel-and-eat shrimp). Families may wish to request a table next to the "children's theater," where kids can watch movies. Sunday dinner begins at 1 pm. Locals gravitate towards the Big Moose Pub section. ⑤ *Average main: $24* ✉ *26 Seymour St.* ☎ *802/388–7166, 800/367–7166* ⊕ *www.fireandicerestaurant.com* ⊗ *No lunch Mon.–Thurs.*

$$$ ✗ **Mary's at Baldwin Creek.** People drive from the far reaches of Vermont
AMERICAN to dine at this restaurant just beyond Bristol, 13 miles northeast of
Fodor's Choice Middlebury. Allow a little extra time to visit the sprawling gardens
★ around the beautiful property; they represent the slow approach to cooking that earned this restaurant its stellar reputation. Hearty fare includes the summer lasagna packed with vegetables and the near-legendary garlic soup, a creamy year-round staple that seems calculated to please. Desserts can be hit-or-miss. ⑤ *Average main: $25* ✉ *1868 N. Rte. 116, Bristol* ☎ *802/453–2432* ⊕ *www.innatbaldwincreek.com* ⊗ *Closed Mon. and Tues.*

$$ ✕ **The Storm Cafe** There's no setting in town quite like this restaurant's
MODERN deck, which overlooks Otter Creek Falls at one end of a long footbridge.
AMERICAN Even if you're not here in summer, the eclectic, ever-changing menu
makes this small café a worthy stop at any time of year. Spicy calamari
and vegetable curry are recent dinner favorites, and large salads and
diverse sandwiches make for satisfying lunches. $ *Average main: $19*
✉ *Frog Hollow Mill, 3 Mill St.* ☎ *802/388–1063* ⊕ *www.thestormcafe.*
com ☺ *Closed Mon. No dinner Tues. and Wed.*

3

WHERE TO STAY

$ 🏠 **Inn on the Green.** Listed on the National Register of Historic Places,
B&B/INN this 1803 inn and its carriage house sit in the center of bucolic Middle-
bury near the college campus. **Pros:** ideal location; great breakfast.
Cons: some rooms small and close together. $ *Rooms from: $169* ✉ *71*
S. Pleasant St. ☎ *802/388–7512, 888/244–7512* ⊕ *www.innonthegreen.*
com ⌁ *9 rooms, 2 suites* ❗ *Breakfast.*

$ 🏠 **Swift House Inn.** The 1814 Georgian home of a 19th-century gover-
B&B/INN nor has white-panel wainscoting, mahogany furnishings, and marble
fireplaces. **Pros:** attractive, spacious, well-kept rooms; professionally
run. **Cons:** not quite in the heart of town. $ *Rooms from: $179* ✉ *25*
Stewart La. ☎ *866/388–9925* ⊕ *www.swifthouseinn.com* ⌁ *20 rooms*
❗ *Breakfast.*

SHOPPING

Danforth Pewter Workshop & Store. In addition to its handcrafted pewter
vases, lamps, and jewelry, this store offers you a front-row seat to the art
of pewter spinning in the back workshop. There's also a small museum.
✉ *52 Seymour St.* ☎ *802/388–0098* ⊕ *www.danforthpewter.com.*

Historic Marble Works. This renovated marble manufacturing facility has
a collection of shops and eateries set amid quarrying equipment and
factory buildings. ✉ *2 Maple St.* ☎ *802/388–3701* ⊕ *www.thehistoric-*
marbleworks.com.

WAITSFIELD AND WARREN

32 miles northeast (Waitsfield) and 25 miles east (Warren) of Middlebury.

Skiers first discovered the high peaks overlooking the pastoral Mad
River Valley in the 1940s. Today, this valley and its two towns, Waits-
field and Warren, attract the hip, the adventurous, and the low-key.
Warren in particular is tiny and adorable, with a general store popular
with tour buses. The gently carved ridges cradling the valley and the
swell of pastures and fields lining the river seem to keep notions of
ski-resort sprawl at bay. With a map from the Sugarbush Chamber
of Commerce you can investigate back roads off Route 100 that have
exhilarating valley views.

ESSENTIALS

Visitor Information Mad River Valley Chamber of Commerce. ✉ *4061 Main*
St., Waitsfield ☎ *802/496–3409, 800/828–4748* ⊕ *www.madrivervalley.com.*

WHERE TO EAT

$$
PIZZA
Fodor's Choice
★

✕**American Flatbread Waitsfield.** Is this among the best pizza experiences in the world? It may well be. The organically grown flour and vegetables—and the wood-fired clay ovens that unite them—take the pizza here to another level. Local favorites include the maple–fennel sausage pie topped with sun-dried tomatoes, caramelized onions, cheese, and herbs—it's a dream, and so are the more traditional flavors. This is the original American Flatbread location. In summer, you can dine outside around fire pits in the beautiful valley. Seats can be hard to come by, but if you stay at the adjoining inn, they're reserved. ⑤ *Average main: $20* ✉ *46 Lareau Rd., off Rte. 100, Waitsfield* ☎ *802/496–8856* ⊕ *www. americanflatbread.com* ⊘ *Closed Mon.–Wed. No lunch* ⚑ *Reservations not accepted.*

$$$
MODERN AMERICAN

✕**Common Man.** This restaurant is situated in a big 1800s barn with hand-hewn rafters and crystal chandeliers. That's the Common Man for you: fancy and après-ski all at once. Bottles of Moët & Chandon signed by the customers who ordered them sit atop the beams. The eclectic, sophisticated new American cuisine showcases locally sourced produce and meats; the menu may include grilled octopus with sticky rice and bok choy, orecchiette with pork and fennel sausage, or roast chicken with red onion jam. Seven-course tasting menus are available by request. Dinner is served by candlelight. Couples sit by the big fireplace. ⑤ *Average main: $25* ✉ *3209 German Flats Rd., Warren* ☎ *802/583–2800* ⊕ *www.commonmanrestaurant.com* ⊘ *Closed Sun.–Wed. No lunch.*

WHERE TO STAY

$$
B&B/INN

⌂ **The Inn at Round Barn Farm.** A Shaker-style round barn—one of only five in Vermont—is the centerpiece of this bed-and-breakfast, but what you'll remember when you leave is how comfortable your stay was. **Pros:** great trails, gardens, and rooms; tasty breakfasts; unique architecture. **Cons:** no restaurant; fills up for wedding parties. ⑤ *Rooms from: $205* ✉ *1661 E. Warren Rd., Waitsfield* ☎ *802/496–2276* ⊕ *www.theroundbarn.com* ⇆ *11 rooms, 1 suite* ⦿⃝ *Breakfast.*

$$$$
B&B/INN
Fodor's Choice
★

⌂ **The Pitcher Inn.** "Sublime" is the word that comes to mind when thinking about a night at the elegant Pitcher Inn, one of Vermont's trio of Relais & Châteaux properties. **Pros:** exceptional service; fabulous restaurant; beautiful location. **Cons:** at some point, you have to go home. ⑤ *Rooms from: $450* ✉ *275 Main St., Warren* ☎ *802/496–6350* ⊕ *www.pitcherinn.com* ⇆ *9 rooms, 2 suites* ⦿⃝ *Breakfast.*

NIGHTLIFE AND PERFORMING ARTS

NIGHTLIFE

Fodor's Choice
★

Tracks. Downstairs at the Pitcher Inn, this comfortable tavern has a tasteful lodge-style setting complete with a crackling fireplace. The bar menu is terrific—featuring items like seared scallops over sweet potatoes and bacon, and skirt steak with chimichurri—and the selection of wines and beers is excellent. There are billiards tables, dartboards, and table shuffleboard. ✉ *Pitcher Inn, 275 Main St., Warren* ☎ *802/493–6350* ⊕ *www.pitcherinn.com.*

Sheep's milk cheese is just one of the many food products that contribute to great fresh local meals in Vermont.

PERFORMING ARTS

Green Mountain Cultural Center. The center hosts concerts, art exhibits, and educational workshops in the historic Round Barn. ⊠ *Inn at the Round Barn Farm, 1661 E. Warren Rd., Waitsfield* ☎ *802/496–7722* ⊕ *www.greenmountainculturalcenter.org.*

SPORTS AND THE OUTDOORS

GOLF

Sugarbush Resort Golf Club. Great views and challenging play are the hallmarks of this mountain course designed by Robert Trent Jones Sr. ⊠ *Sugarbush, 1840 Sugarbush Access Rd., Warren* ☎ *802/583–6725* ⊕ *www.sugarbush.com* ✉ *$95 for 18 holes, weekdays; $110 for 18 holes, weekends* ⚑ *18 holes, 6464 yards, par 71.*

MULTISPORT OUTFITTER

Clearwater Sports. This outfitter rents canoes and kayaks, and leads guided river trips in warmer months. When the weather turns cold, it offers snowshoeing and backcountry skiing tours. ⊠ *4147 Main St., Waitsfield* ☎ *802/496–2708* ⊕ *www.clearwatersports.com.*

SKI AREAS

Blueberry Lake Cross Country and Snowshoeing Center. This ski area has 18 miles of trails through thickly wooded glades. ⊠ *424 Plunkton Rd., East Warren* ☎ *802/496–6687* ⊕ *www.blueberrylakeskivt.com* ✉ *Trail pass: $13.*

Mad River Glen. A pristine alpine experience, Mad River attracts rugged individualists looking for less polished terrain. The area was developed in the late 1940s and has changed relatively little since then. It remains one of only three resorts in the country that ban snowboarding, and it's the only one that still has a single-chair lift. Mad River is steep, with slopes that follow the mountain's fall lines. The terrain changes constantly on the interconnected trails of mostly natural snow (expert trails are never groomed). Telemark skiing and snowshoeing are also popular. **Facilities:** 45 trails; 125 acres; 2,036-foot vertical drop; 5 lifts. ✉ *62 Mad River Resort Rd., off Rte. 17, Waitsfield* ☏ *802/496–3551* ⊕ *www.madriverglen.com* ⛷ *Lift ticket: $79.*

FAMILY   **Sugarbush.** A true skier's mountain, Sugarbush has plenty of steep, natural snow glades and fall-line drops. Not as rough around the edges as Mad River Glen, the resort has an extensive computer-controlled system for snowmaking and many groomed trails between its two mountain complexes. This a great choice for intermediate skiers, who will find top-to-bottom runs all over the resort; there are fewer options for beginners. Programs for kids include the enjoyable Sugarbear Forest, a terrain garden full of fun bumps and jumps. At the base of the mountain are condominiums, restaurants, shops, bars, and a health-and-racquet club. **Facilities:** 111 trails; 484 acres; 2,600-foot vertical drop; 16 lifts. ✉ *102 Forest Dr., Warren* ⬦ *From Rte. 17, take German Flats Rd. south; from Rte. 100, take Sugarbush Access Rd. west* ☏ *802/583–6300, 802/583–7669* ⊕ *www.sugarbush.com* ⛷ *Lift ticket: $91.*

SHOPPING

All Things Bright and Beautiful. This eccentric Victorian house is filled to the rafters with stuffed animals of all shapes, sizes, and colors, as well as folk art, European glass, and Christmas ornaments. ✉ *27 Bridge St., Waitsfield* ☏ *802/496–3997* ⊕ *www.allthingsbright.com.*

The Warren Store. This general store has everything you'd hope to find in tiny but sophisticated Vermont: a nice selection of local beer and wine, cheeses, baked goods, strong coffee, and delicious sandwiches and prepared foods. In summer, grab a quick lunch on the small deck by the water; in winter, warm up at the wood stove. Warm, woolly clothing and accessories can be found upstairs. ✉ *284 Main St., Warren* ☏ *802/496–3864* ⊕ *www.warrenstore.com.*

NORTHERN VERMONT

Vermont's northernmost region presents the state's greatest contrasts. To the west, Burlington and its suburbs have grown so rapidly that rural wags now say that Burlington's main advantage is that it's "close to Vermont." The north country also contains Vermont's tiny capital, Montpelier, and its highest mountain, Mt. Mansfield, site of the famous Stowe and Smugglers' Notch ski resorts. Northeast of Montpelier is a sparsely populated and heavily wooded territory, which former Senator George Aiken dubbed the "Northeast Kingdom"—the domain of loggers, farmers, and avid outdoors enthusiasts.

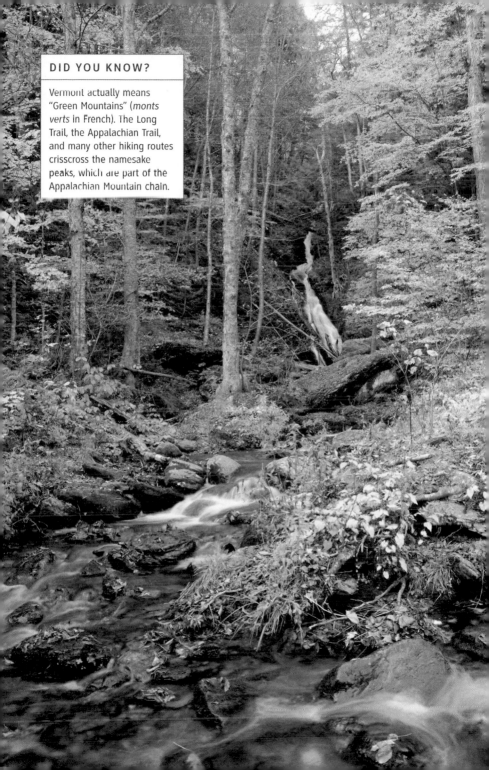

MONTPELIER

38 miles southeast of Burlington, 115 miles north of Brattleboro.

With only about 8,000 residents, little Montpelier is the country's smallest capital city, but it has a youthful energy—and certainly an independent spirit—that makes it seem almost as large as Burlington. The well-preserved downtown area bustles with state and city workers walking to meetings and restaurants, and students heading to funky coffee shops.

EXPLORING

Hope Cemetery. Barre, the "Granite Capital of the World," lies 7 miles southeast of Montpelier, and many of this cemetery's superbly crafted tombstones were carved by local stonecutters to demonstrate their skill. A few embrace the avant-garde, while others take defined shapes like a race car, a biplane, and a soccer ball. ⊠ *201 Maple Ave., Barre* ☎ *802/476-6245.*

FAMILY
Fodor'sChoice
★
Morse Farm Maple Sugarworks. With eight generations of sugaring, the Morses may be the oldest maple family in existence, so you're sure to find an authentic experience at their farm. Burr Morse heads up the operation now, along with his son Tom, but you can still see Burr's father playing the role of the curmudgeon in the dated video that screens in the Woodshed Theater. More than 5,000 trees produce the sap used for syrup (you can sample all the grades), candy, cream, and sugar—all sold in the gift shop. Grab a creemee (soft-serve ice cream), take a seat on a swing, and stay awhile. Surrounding trails offer pleasant strolls in summer and prime cross-country skiing in winter. ⊠ *1168 County Rd.* ☎ *800/242-2740* ⊕ *www.morsefarm.com* ⊠ *Free.*

OFF THE
BEATEN
PATH
Rock of Ages Granite Quarry. Attractions here range from the awe-inspiring (the quarry resembles the Grand Canyon in miniature) to the mildly ghoulish (you can consult a directory of tombstone dealers throughout the country) to the whimsical (an outdoor granite bowling alley). At the crafts center, skilled artisans sculpt monuments and blast stone, while at the quarries themselves, workers who clearly earn their pay cut 25-ton blocks of stone from the sheer 475-foot walls. (You may recognize these walls from a chase scene in the 2009 *Star Trek* movie.) ⊠ *560 Graniteville Rd., off I-89, Graniteville* ☎ *802/476-3119* ⊕ *www. rockofages.com* ⊠ *Tours $6.*

Vermont History Museum. The collection here, begun in 1838, focuses on all things Vermont—from a catamount (the now-extinct local cougar) to Ethan Allen's shoe buckles. The museum store stocks fine books, prints, and gifts. A second location in Barre, the Vermont History Center, has three rotating exhibits with notable photographs and artifacts. ⊠ *109 State St.* ☎ *802/828-2291* ⊕ *www.vermonthistory.org* ⊠ *$5.*

QUICK
BITES
La Brioche Bakery. New England Culinary Institute students are up at 5 am preparing breads for the thankful patrons of this super breakfast and lunch stop. Soups, salads, and sandwiches are all on the menu, but the pastries are the most tempting. ⊠ *89 Main St.* ☎ *802/229-0443* ⊕ *www.neci.edu/ labrioche.*

Northern Vermont

QUÉBEC

NEW HAMPSHIRE

NEW YORK

COLD HOLLOW MOUNTAINS

GREEN MOUNTAINS

Lake Champlain

Lake Champlain Islands

Burlington

Montpelier

St. Johnsbury

Stowe

Jeffersonville

Montgomery

Jay

Shelburne

Vergennes

Beecher Falls
Colebrook
North Stratford
Groveton
Guildhall
Whitefield
Norton
Island Pond
Lake Willoughby
West Burke
Burke Mountain
East Burke
Lyndonville
Elmore Mountain
Concord
Woodsville
Liston
Wells River
Derby Line
Newport
Lake Memphremagog
North Troy
Richford
Jay Peak
Enosburg Falls
Highgate Center
Swanton
Alburg
Rouses Point
St. Anne's Shrine
Chazy
Champlain
Plattsburgh
North Hero
North Hero State Park
Grand Isle
Grand Isle State Park
Sand Bar State Park
Snow Farm Vineyard and Winery
Allenholm Farm
South Hero
Saint Albans
Milton
Fairfax
Cambridge
Boyden Valley Winery & Spirits
Jericho
Essex Junction
Ethan Allen Homestead
Winooski
South Burlington
Essex
Westport
Willsboro Point
Port Kent
Shelburne Farms
Shelburne Museum
Magic Hat Brewing Company
Vermont Teddy Bear Company
Shelburne Vineyard
Richmond
Bolton Valley Resort
Green Mountain Audubon Nature Center
Waterbury
Ben & Jerry's Ice Cream Factory
Trapp Family Lodge
Stowe Mountain Resort
Smugglers' Notch Resort
Morrisville
Hyde Park
Wolcott
Hardwick
Greensboro
Hill Farmstead Brewery
Bread and Puppet Museum
Albany
Orleans
Lowell
Ricthford
Lake Carmi
Northeast Kingdom
Caspian Lake
Cabot Creamery
Marshfield
Plainfield
Danville
Peacham
Barnet
Barre
South Barre
Rock of Ages Granite Quarry
Morse Farm Maple Sugarworks
Northfield
Waitsfield
Rokeby Museum
Lake Champlain Maritime Museum
Westmore
West Burke
Lyndon
Lyndonville
Molly's Falls Pond
Lake Groton
Magog Falls Pond
Seymour Lake
Maidstone Lake
Island Pond
North Hero

10 mi

10 km

223

133

114

102

3

3

3

93

116

302

302

93

91

91

89

89

89

37

2

2

2

2

5

5

5

5A

14

14

15

15

16

12

105

105

111

100

100

100

100

100

242

108

108

108

104

36

78

78

128

9

22

22

17

116

7

7

7

15

Vermont State House. The regal capitol building surrounded by forest is emblematic of this proudly rural state. With a gleaming dome topped by the goddess of agriculture and columns of Barre granite measuring six feet in diameter, the state house is home to the country's oldest legislative chambers still in their original condition. A half-hour tour takes you through the governor's office and the house and senate chambers. Interior paintings and exhibits depict much of Vermont's sterling Civil War record. ✉ *115 State St.* ☎ *802/828–2228* ✉ *Donations accepted.*

WHERE TO EAT

$$$
ECLECTIC

✗ **Ariel's.** Well off the beaten path, this small restaurant overlooking a lake is worth the drive down a dirt road. The chef prepares small, medium, and large plates of New England–inspired cuisine based on local sources. Favorites include herb-crusted lamb loin and line-caught swordfish. Don't leave without ordering a board of Vermont cheeses, which pair especially well with the excellent wines. Ⓢ *Average main: $26* ✉ *29 Stone Rd., 18 miles south of Montpelier, Brookfield* ☎ *802/276–3939* ⊕ *www.arielsrestaurant.com* ⊘ *Closed Mon. and Tues., and Nov.–Mar. No lunch.*

$
SOUTHERN
FAMILY

✗ **Down Home Kitchen.** Barbecue isn't hard to track down in Vermont, but there aren't many places serving the down-home Southern cuisine found at this breakfast-and-lunch spot. Biscuits, gravy, and fried chicken and catfish are the specialties, but it's the atmosphere that really sells the place. Plop down at the long soda fountain and sip a float or mint julep; or pull up a blue painted chair to the communal wooden table dressed with fresh flowers in mason jars and settle in for a leisurely and social brunch. The on-site bakery cranks out muffins, cupcakes, and peach and pecan pies, so you won't lack for baked goods. The food may be locally sourced, but the attitude and flavors are all North Carolina—the owner's original home. Ⓢ *Average main: $15* ✉ *100 Main St.* ☎ *802/225–6665* ⊕ *www.downhomekitchenvt.com* ⊘ *Closed Tues. No dinner.*

$$
AMERICAN

✗ **NECI on Main.** Nearly everyone working at this restaurant is a student at the New England Culinary Institute, but the quality and inventiveness of the food is anything but beginner's luck. The menu changes seasonally, but the soups and Misty Knoll Farm free-range chicken are reliable winners. The lounge downstairs offers the same menu in a more casual atmosphere. Reservations are strongly recommended for the popular Sunday brunch. Ⓢ *Average main: $20* ✉ *118 Main St.* ☎ *802/223–3188* ⊕ *www.neci.edu* ⊘ *Closed Mon. No dinner Sun.*

$
CAFÉ

✗ **Red Hen Baking Co.** If you're a devotee of artisanal bakeries, it'd be a mistake not to trek the 7-plus miles from Montpelier (15 from Stowe) to have lunch, pick up freshly baked bread, or sample a sweet treat here. Try the ham-and-cheese croissants, sticky buns, homemade soups, and savory sandwiches. Red Hen supplies bread to some of the state's best restaurants, including Hen of the Wood, and has varied offerings every day. Ⓢ *Average main: $8* ✉ *961B U.S. 2, Middlesex* ☎ *802/223–5200* ⊕ *www.redhenbaking.com* ⊘ *No dinner* ⚏ *Reservations not accepted.*

$
ITALIAN

✗ **Sarducci's.** Legislative lunches have become a lot more leisurely since Sarducci's came along to fill the trattoria void in Vermont's capital. The bright, cheerful rooms here alongside the Winooski River are a local favorite for pizza served fresh from wood-fired ovens, wonderfully textured homemade Italian breads, and imaginative dishes like pasta *pugliese,* which marries penne with basil, black olives, roasted eggplant, portobello mushrooms, and sun-dried tomatoes. $ *Average main: $17* ⊠ *3 Main St.* ☎ *802/223–0229* ⊕ *www.sarduccis.com* ☾ *No lunch Sun.*

$

CAFÉ

✕ **The Skinny Pancake.** This dine-in creperie makes a great stop for breakfast, lunch, or an easy dinner. The Breakfast Monster, made with eggs and local Cabot cheddar, is a winner. For lunch, try the spinach and feta crêpe, the Veggie Monster (spinach, roasted red peppers, caramelized onions, and cheddar), or the Lamb Fetatastic (local lamb sausage, baby spinach, feta, and kalamata olives). If you're in the mood for dessert, sample the Nutella crêpe or the Pooh Bear, served with warm local honey and cinnamon. $ *Average main: $9* ⊠ *89 Main St.* ☎ *802/262–2253* ⊕ *www.skinnypancake.com.*

$

ECLECTIC

Fodor's Choice

★

✕ **Three Penny Taproom.** This lively taproom is quickly becoming one of the best in Vermont. The Three Penny serves many craft beers, including the justly celebrated Hill Farmstead. Now featuring a full menu and expanded seating, the pub has become a dining destination as well, sharing an award for the state's best burger. The vibe feels straight out of an artsy neighborhood in Brussels, but with the earthiness of Vermont. $ *Average main: $15* ⊠ *108 Main St.* ☎ *802/223–8277* ⊕ *www. threepennytaproom.com.*

WHERE TO STAY

$

B&B/INN

⛨ **Inn at Montpelier.** The capital's most charming lodging option, this lovingly tended inn dating to 1830 has rooms filled with antique four-poster beds and Windsor chairs—all have private (if small) baths. **Pros:** beautiful home; relaxed central setting; amazing porch. **Cons:** some rooms are small. $ *Rooms from: $170* ⊠ *147 Main St.* ☎ *802/223–2727* ⊕ *www.innatmontpelier.com* ⤵ *19 rooms* ⦿ *Breakfast.*

SHOPPING

Artisans Hand Craft Gallery. For more than 30 years, Maggie Neale has been celebrating and supporting Vermont's craft community. Her store sells jewelry, textiles, sculptures, and paintings by many local artists. ⊠ *89 Main St.* ☎ *802/229–9492* ⊕ *www.artisanshand.com.*

Vermont Creamery. A leader in the artisanal cheese movement, this creamery invites aficionados to visit its 4,000-square-foot production facility, where goat cheeses such as Bonne Bouche—a perfectly balanced, cloud-like cheese—are made on weekdays. The creamery is in Websterville, southwest of Montpelier. ⊠ *20 Pitman Rd., Websterville* ☎ *800/884–6287, 802/479–9371* ⊕ *www.vermontcreamery.com* ☾ *Closed weekends.*

Zutano. Head here for hip newborn, baby, and toddler clothing designed in Vermont. ⊠ *79 Main St.* ☎ *802/223–2229* ⊕ *www.zutano.com.*

EN ROUTE

Ben & Jerry's Ice Cream Factory. The 30-minute tours at the famous brand's factory are unabashedly corny and only skim the surface of the behind-the-scenes goings on, but this flaw is almost forgiven when the samples are dished out. To see the machines at work, visit on a weekday but call ahead to confirm if they will indeed be in operation. ⊠ *1281 Waterbury-Stowe Rd., 1 mile north of I–89, Waterbury* ☎ *802/846–1500* ⊕ *www. benjerry.com* ⛉ *Tour $4.*

Cabot Creamery. The state's biggest cheese producer has a visitor center with displays about the dairy co-op that provides milk for the creamery's famous products. The informative tour is worthwhile at any time, though it's best to arrive on a cheese-making day, so call ahead and adjust your schedule if possible. Either way, you may never leave the gift shop, where samples are diverse and plentiful. ⊠ *2878 Main St., 5 miles north of U.S. 2, Cabot* ☎ *800/837–4261* ⊕ *www.cabotcheese. coop* ⊠ *$3.*

STOWE

22 miles northwest of Montpelier, 36 miles east of Burlington.

Fodor's Choice
★

Long before skiing came to Stowe in the 1930s, the rolling hills and valleys beneath Vermont's highest peak, 4,395-foot Mt. Mansfield, attracted summer tourists looking for a reprieve from city heat. Most stayed at one of two inns in the village of Stowe. When skiing made the town a winter destination, visitors outnumbered hotel beds, so locals took them in. This spirit of hospitality continues, and many of these homes are now country inns. The village itself is tiny—just a few blocks of shops and restaurants clustered around a picture-perfect white church with a lofty steeple—but it serves as the anchor for Mountain Road, which leads north past restaurants, lodges, and shops on its way to Stowe's fabled slopes.

ESSENTIALS

Visitor Information Stowe Area Association. ⊠ *51 Main St.* ☎ *802/253–7321, 877/467–8693* ⊕ *www.gostowe.com.*

EXPLORING

Trapp Family Lodge. Built by the Von Trapp family (of *The Sound of Music* fame), this Tyrolean lodge and its grounds are the site of a popular outdoor music series in summer. You can hike the trails in warm weather, or go cross-country skiing in winter; a ski-in cabin serves homemade soups, sandwiches, and hot chocolate. There's a fine-dining restaurant, and the lodge's café serves tasty food over a breathtaking mountain vista. Finally, an on-site brewery produces Austrian lagers, a welcome change of pace from all the local craft ales. ⊠ *700 Trapp Hill Rd.* ☎ *802/253–8511, 800/826–7000* ⊕ *www.trappfamily.com.*

Vermont Ski and Snowboard Museum. The state's skiing and snowboarding history is documented here. Exhibits cover subjects such as the 10th Mountain Division of World War II, the national ski patrol, Winter Olympians, and the evolution of equipment. An early World Cup trophy is on loan, and one of the most memorable mobiles you'll ever see, made from a gondola and ski-lift chairs, hangs from the ceiling. One recent exhibit, Slope Style, focused on ski fashion from 1930 to 2014. ⊠ *1 S. Main St.* ☎ *802/253–9911* ⊕ *www.vtssm.com* ⊠ *$5.*

WHERE TO EAT

$$

AMERICAN

✕ **Harrison's Restaurant.** For an excellent dinner at a warm and unpretentious American bistro, head to Harrison's, tucked away in downtown Stowe. A lively locals' scene, booths by the fireplace, and creative cuisine paired with well-chosen wines and regional brews make this place perfect for couples and families alike. Stop in for braised short ribs in blackberry-chipotle barbecue sauce, sirloin bistro steak, or lobster mac 'n' cheese made with Cabot cheddar. The inviting bar is a good spot to dine alone or to chat with a regular. $ *Average main: $23* ✉ *25 Main St., behind TD Bank* ☎ *802/253-7773* ⊕ *www.harrisonsstowe. com* ⊗ *No lunch* ⚶ *Reservations essential.*

$$$

ECLECTIC

Fodor'sChoice

★

✕ **Hen of the Wood.** Ask Vermont's great chefs where they go for a tremendous meal, and Hen of the Wood inevitably tops the list. The setting is riveting: a converted 1835 gristmill beside a waterfall. On the mill's underground level, supported by thick wooden beams, the sunken millstone pit holds tables surrounded by uneven stone walls dotted with tiny candles—it's utterly romantic. Sophisticated dishes showcase an abundance of local produce, meat, and cheese. The daily changing menu might include goat's milk dumplings, local farm pork loin, grass-fed rib eye, or wild Alaskan halibut. When it's warm outside, angle for a coveted patio table overlooking a dramatic series of falls. The restaurant has a second location in Burlington. $ *Average main: $26* ✉ *92 Stowe St., Waterbury* ☎ *802/244-7300* ⊕ *www.henofthewood.com* ⊗ *Closed Sun. and Mon. No lunch* ⚶ *Reservations essential.*

$$$

EUROPEAN

✕ **Michael's on the Hill.** Swiss-born chef Michael Kloeti trained in Europe and New York City before opening this establishment in a 19th-century farmhouse outside Stowe. The seasonal three-course prix-fixe menus ($45 and $67) blend European cuisine with farm-to-table earthiness, exemplified by dishes such as spice-roasted duck breast and venison *navarin* (ragout). You can also order à la carte. $ *Average main: $32* ✉ *4182 Stowe-Waterbury Rd., 6 miles south of Stowe, Waterbury Center* ☎ *802/244-7476* ⊕ *www.michaelsonthehill.com* ⊗ *Closed Tues. No lunch.*

$

AMERICAN

Fodor'sChoice

★

✕ **Prohibition Pig.** This restaurant and brewery in downtown Waterbury is always packed for a reason: fabulous craft beers, sandwiches, salads, and barbecue served in an airy and friendly bar and dining room. Preparations can be decadent—case in point: the duck-fat fries—yet the flavors are more nuanced than the low prices imply. The house burger with pimento cheese and fried green tomato is a winner, as are the roasted brisket and pit-smoked chicken. If you just want a quick bite and a draft, belly up to the tasting room bar at the brewery in the back. For more suds, pop across the street to the Craft Beer Cellar, one of the state's best beer stores. $ *Average main: $12* ✉ *23 S. Main St., Waterbury* ☎ *802/244-4120* ⊕ *www.prohibitionpig.com* ⊗ *No lunch Tues.–Thurs.*

WHERE TO STAY

$

HOTEL

🛏 **Field Guide.** A new boutique enterprise just north of Stowe, Field Guide supplies a whimsically stylish alternative to the town's staid resorts and cadre of inns stuck in ski-chalet mold. **Pros:** great location; distinct style; fun attitude. **Cons:** style not for everyone; no elevator. $ *Rooms from: $199* ✉ *433 Mountain Rd.* ☎ *802/253-8088* ⊕ *www. fieldguidestowe.com* ⊶ *17 rooms, 10 suites, 3 cottages* ⦿|*Breakfast.*

$

B&B/INN

🛏 **Green Mountain Inn.** Welcoming guests since 1833, this classic redbrick inn puts you within reach of downtown buzz. **Pros:** fun location; lively tavern; lots of character. **Cons:** farther from skiing than other area hotels.

⑤ *Rooms from: $189* ⊠ *18 Main St.* ☎ *802/253–7301, 800/253–7302* ⊕ *www.greenmountaininn.com* ⤳ *103 rooms* ⫶◎⫶ *No meals.*

$$
B&B/INN
⫶⫶ **Stone Hill Inn.** A contemporary bed-and-breakfast where classical music plays in the hallways, the Stone Hill has guest rooms with two-sink vanities and two-person whirlpools in front of double-sided fireplaces. **Pros:** very comfortable rooms; convenient location. **Cons:** grounds could use grooming. ⑤ *Rooms from: $299* ⊠ *89 Houston Farm Rd.* ☎ *802/253–6282* ⊕ *www.stonehillinn.com* ⤳ *9 rooms* ⫶◎⫶ *Breakfast.*

$
HOTEL
FAMILY
⫶⫶ **Stowe Motel & Snowdrift.** The accommodations at this family-owned motel on 16 acres range from studios with small kitchenettes and modern two-bedroom suites warmed by their own fireplaces to rental houses that can sleep 10 or more people. **Pros:** inexpensive rates; complimentary bikes; friendly game room. **Cons:** motel-style accommodations. ⑤ *Rooms from: $129* ⊠ *2043 Mountain Rd.* ☎ *802/253–7629, 800/829–7629* ⊕ *www.stowemotel.com* ⤳ *52 rooms, 4 suites, 6 houses* ⫶◎⫶ *Breakfast.*

$$$
RESORT
Fodor's Choice
★
⫶⫶ **Stowe Mountain Lodge.** At the base of the ski slopes, this lodge would be king of the hill for its location alone, but a stay here also affords many perks. **Pros:** perfect setting; great concierge; activities galore. **Cons:** somewhat sterile feel; no separate kids' pool. ⑤ *Rooms from: $350* ⊠ *7412 Mountain Rd.* ☎ *802/253–3560* ⊕ *www.stowemountainlodge.com* ⤳ *312 rooms* ⫶◎⫶ *No meals.*

$$
RESORT
⫶⫶ **Stoweflake Mountain Resort and Spa.** With one of the largest spas in the area, Stoweflake lets you enjoy an herb-and-flower labyrinth, a fitness center reached via a covered bridge, and a hydrotherapy waterfall that cascades into a hot tub. **Pros:** nice spa; wide range of rooms. **Cons:** mazelike layout can make rooms a bit hard to find. ⑤ *Rooms from: $219* ⊠ *1746 Mountain Rd.* ☎ *800/253–2232* ⊕ *www.stoweflake.com* ⤳ *120 rooms, 60 town houses* ⫶◎⫶ *No meals.*

$$$
RESORT
FAMILY
Fodor's Choice
★
⫶⫶ **Topnotch Resort.** On 120 acres overlooking Mt. Mansfield, this posh property has a contemporary look and an outstanding spa. **Pros:** Mt. Mansfield views; impeccable service; family-friendly atmosphere. **Cons:** boutique style may not be for everyone. ⑤ *Rooms from: $350* ⊠ *4000 Mountain Rd.* ☎ *800/451–8686* ⊕ *www.topnotchresort.com* ⤳ *68 rooms and suites, 22 town houses* ⫶◎⫶ *No meals.*

NIGHTLIFE AND PERFORMING ARTS
NIGHTLIFE
Doc Ponds. A gastropub from the folks behind the Hen of the Wood restaurant, this place has a diverse beer list. The food's great, too. ⊠ *294 Mountain Rd.* ☎ *802/760–6066* ⊕ *www.docponds.com.*

Matterhorn. This nightspot hosts live music and dancing on weekends during the ski season. If you'd rather just watch, there's a separate martini bar. ⊠ *4969 Mountain Rd.* ☎ *802/253–8198* ⊕ *www.matterhornbar.com* ☉ *Closed Mon.*

Rusty Nail. This bar rocks to live music on weekends. ⊠ *1190 Mountain Rd.* ☎ *802/253–6245* ⊕ *www.rustynailvt.com.*

Continued on page 115

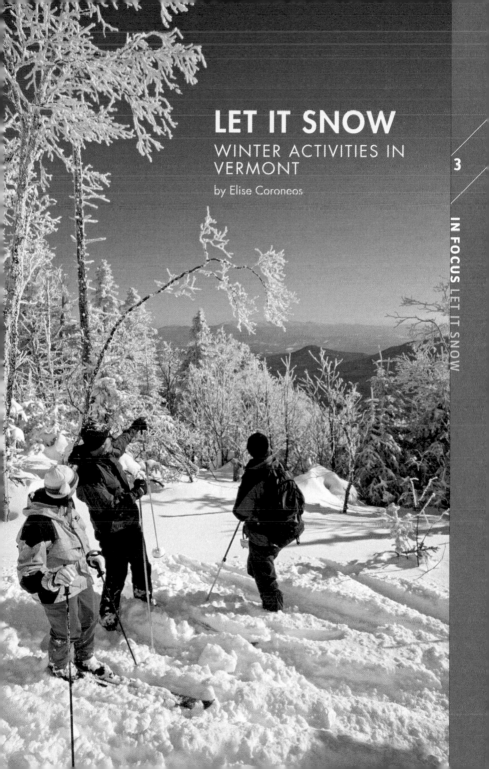

LET IT SNOW

WINTER ACTIVITIES IN VERMONT

by Elise Coroneos

SKIING AND SNOWBOARDING IN VERMONT

Less than 5 miles from the Canadian border, Jay Peak is Vermont's northernmost ski resort.

Ever since America's first ski tow opened in a farmer's pasture near Woodstock in January 1934, skiers have headed en masse to Vermont in winter. Today, 19 alpine and 30 nordic ski areas range in size and are spread across the state, from Mount Snow in the south to Jay Peak near the Canadian border. The snow-making equipment has also become more comprehensive over the years, with more than 80% of the trails in the state using man-made snow. Here are some of the best ski areas by various categories:

GREAT FOR KIDS Smugglers' Notch, Okemo, and **Bromley Mountain** all offer terrific kids' programs, with classes organized by age categories and by skill level. Kids as young as 3 (4 at some ski areas) can start learning. Child care, with activities like stories, singing, and arts and crafts, are available for those too young to ski; some ski areas, like Smuggler's Notch, offer babysitting with no minimum age daytime and evening.

BEST FOR BEGINNERS Beginner terrain makes up nearly half of the mountain at **Stratton,** where options include private and group lessons for first-timers. Also good are small but family-friendly **Bolton Valley** and **Bromley Mountains,** which both designate a third of their slopes for beginners.

EXPERT TERRAIN The slopes at **Jay Peak** and massive **Killington** are most notable for their steepness and pockets of glades. About 40% of the runs at these two resorts are advanced or expert. Due to its far north location, Jay Peak tends to get the most snow, making it ideal for powder days. Another favorite with advanced skiers is Central Vermont's **Mad River Glen,** where many slopes are ungroomed (natural) and the motto is "Ski it if you can." In addition, **Sugarbush, Stowe,** and **Smugglers' Notch** are all revered for their challenging untamed side country.

Mount Mansfield is better known as Stowe. Stratton Mountain clocktower

NIGHT SKIING Come late afternoon, **Bolton Valley** is hopping. That's because it's the only location in Vermont for night skiing. Ski and ride under the lights from 4 until 8 Wednesday through Saturday, followed by a later après-ski scene.

APRÈS-SKI The social scenes at **Killington**, **Sugarbush**, and **Stowe** are the most noteworthy (and crowded). Book a seat on the Snowcat that takes intrepid partiers to the Motor Room Bar in Killington, or stop by the always popular Wobbly Barn. For live music, try Castlerock Pub in Sugarbush or the Matterhorn Bar in Stowe.

SNOWBOARDING Boarders (and some skiers) will love the latest features for freestyle tricks in Vermont. **Stratton** has four terrain parks for all abilities, one of which features a boarder cross course. **Mount Snow's** Carinthia Peak is an all-terrain park–dedicated mountain, the only of its kind in New England. Head to **Killington** for Burton Stash, another

beautiful all-natural features terrain park. **Okemo** has a superpipe and eight terrain parks and a gladed park with all-natural features. Note that snowboarding is not allowed at skiing cooperative **Mad River Glen.**

CROSS-COUNTRY To experience the best of cross-country skiing in the state, simply follow the Catamount Trail, a 300-mile nordic route from southern Vermont to Canada. **The Trapp Family Lodge** in Stowe has 37 miles of groomed cross-country trails and 62 miles of back-country trails. Another top option is **The Mountain Top Inn & Resort,** just outside of Killington. Its Nordic Ski and Snowshoe Center provides instruction for newcomers, along with hot drinks and lunches when it is time to take a break and warm up.

TELEMARK Ungroomed snow and tree skiing are a natural fit with free-heel skiing at **Mad River Glen. Bromley** and **Jay Peak** also have telemark rentals and instruction.

MOUNTAIN-RESORT TRIP PLANNER

TIMING

■ **Snow Season.** Winter sports time is typically from Thanksgiving through April, weather permitting. Holidays are the most crowded.

■ **March Madness.** Most of the season's snow tends to come in March, so that's the time to go if you want to ski on fresh, nature-made powder. To increase your odds, choose a ski area in the northern part of the state.

■ **Summer Scene.** During summertime, many ski resorts reinvent themselves as prime destinations for golfers, zipline and canopy tours, mountain bikers, and weddings. Other summer visitors come to the mountains to enjoy hiking trails, climbing walls, aquatic centers, chairlift and horseback rides, or a variety of festivals.

■ **Avoid Long Lift Lines.** Try to hit the slopes early—many lifts start at 8 or 9 am, with ticket windows opening a half-hour earlier. Then take a mid-morning break as lines start to get longer and head out again when others come in for lunch.

SAVINGS TIPS

■ **Choose a Condo.** Especially if you're planning to stay for a week, save money on food by opting for a condominum unit with a kitchen. You can shop at the supermarket and cook breakfast and dinner.

■ **Rent Smart.** Consider ski rental options in the villages rather than those at the mountain. Renting right at the ski area may be more convenient, but it may also cost more.

■ **Discount Lift Tickets.** Online tickets are often the least expensive; multi-day discounts and and ski-and-stay packages will also lower your costs. Good for those who can plan ahead, early-bird tickets often go on sale before the ski season even starts.

■ **Hit the Peaks Off-peak.** In order to secure the best deals at the most competi-tive rates, avoid booking during school holidays. President's Week in February is the busiest, because that's when Northeastern schools have their spring break.

Top left, Killington's six mountains make up the largest ski area in Vermont. Top right, Stratton has a Snowboard-cross course.

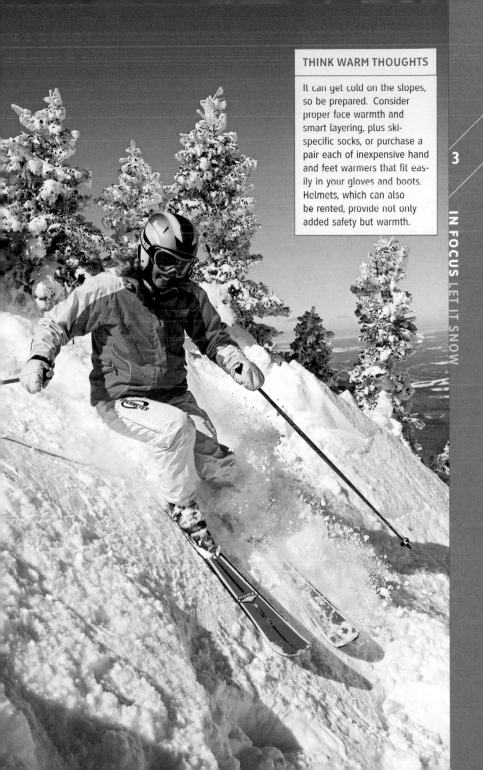

THINK WARM THOUGHTS

It can get cold on the slopes, so be prepared. Consider proper face warmth and smart layering, plus ski-specific socks, or purchase a pair each of inexpensive hand and feet warmers that fit easily in your gloves and boots. Helmets, which can also be rented, provide not only added safety but warmth.

Vermont
Ski Areas

PERFORMING ARTS

Spruce Peak Performing Arts Center. Part of the Mountain Lodge complex, this state-of-the-art space hosts theater, music, and dance performances. ⊠ *122 Hourglass Dr.* ☎ *802/760–4634* ⊕ *www.sprucepeakarts.org.*

SPORTS AND THE OUTDOORS

CANOEING AND KAYAKING

Umiak Outdoor Outfitters. This full-service outfitter rents canoes and kayaks, organizes tours, and sells equipment. It has seasonal outposts at the Waterbury Reservoir and at North Beach in Burlington. ⊠ *849 S. Main St.* ☎ *802/253–2317* ⊕ *www.umiak.com.*

FISHING

The Fly Rod Shop. This shop provides a guide service, offers introductory classes, and rents tackle and other equipment. ⊠ *2703 Waterbury Rd., 1½ miles south of Stowe* ☎ *802/253–7346* ⊕ *www.flyrodshop.com.*

GOLF

Stowe Country Club. A scenic 18-hole golf course, a driving range, and a putting green are available at this country club. ⊠ *744 Cape Cod Rd.* ☎ *802/760–4653* ⊕ *www.stowe.com/golf/club* 🏌 *$115 for 18 holes.*

HIKING

Mt. Mansfield. Ascending Mt. Mansfield makes for a challenging day hike. Trails lead from Mountain Road to the summit, where they meet the north–south Long Trail. Views encompass New Hampshire's White Mountains, New York's Adirondacks, and southern Québec. The Green Mountain Club publishes a trail guide. ⊠ *Trailheads along Mountain Rd.* ☎ *802/244–7037* ⊕ *www.greenmountainclub.org.*

Fodor's Choice
★

Stowe Recreation Path. An immaculately maintained, paved recreation path begins behind the Community Church in town and meanders about 5 miles along the river valley, with many entry points along the way. Whether you're on foot, skis, bike, or in-line skates, it's a tranquil spot to enjoy the outdoors. In autumn, there's a corn maze, and at least four shops along the path rent bikes. ⊠ *Stowe* ⊕ *www.stowerec.org.*

ICE-SKATING

Stowe Arena. Skate rentals are available at this popular rink. Public skating hours change daily, so it's wise to check before coming here. ⊠ *350 Park St.* ☎ *802/253–3054* ⊕ *www.stowerec.org/stowe-arena/ about* 🏷 *$5* ⊗ *No skating Apr. and May.*

SKI AREA

Stowe Mountain Resort. The name of the village is Stowe, and the name of the mountain is Mt. Mansfield—but to generations of skiers, it's all just plain "Stowe." The area's mystique attracts as many serious skiers as social ones. Stowe is a giant among Eastern ski mountains with intimidating expert runs, but its symmetrical shape allows skiers of all abilities to enjoy long, satisfying runs from the summit. Improved snowmaking capacity, new lifts, and free shuttle buses that gather skiers along Mountain Road have made it all much more convenient. Yet the traditions remain, like the Winter Carnival in January and the Sugar Slalom in April, to name two. Spruce Peak, where you'll find the Adventure Center and the Mountain Lodge, is separate from the main mountain; the peak has a teaching hill and offers a pleasant experience for intermediates and beginners. In the summer, there's a TreeTop Adventure course and an awe-inspiring zip line that extends from the top of the gondola to the bottom in three breathtaking runs. **Facilities:** 116 trails; 485 acres; 2,360-foot vertical drop; 13 lifts. ⊠ *5781 Mountain Rd.* ☎ *802/253–3000, 802/253–3600 for snow conditions* ⊕ *www.stowe.com* ☜ *Lift ticket: $115.*

SLEDDING

FAMILY   **Peacepups Dog Sledding.** This one-man (and multiple-dog) company offers two- and four-hour tours with a team of eight Siberian huskies. You can ride inside a padded toboggan, join in the driving using a two-person tandem sled, or learn how to mush and drive on your own. If you prefer to walk the trails yourself, snowshoe rentals are also available. Lake Elmore is a roughly 20-minute drive from Stowe. ⊠ *239 Cross Rd., Lake Elmore* ☎ *802/888–7733* ⊕ *www.peacepupsdogsledding.com* ☜ *$275 for dog sledding tours.*

SHOPPING

Cabot Cheese Annex Store. In addition to shelves of Vermont-made jams, mustards, crackers, and maple products, the store features a long central table with samples of a dozen Cabot cheeses. ⊠ *2657 Waterbury–Stowe Rd., 2½ miles north of I–89* ☎ *802/244–6334* ⊕ *www.cabotcheese.coop.*

FAMILY   **Cold Hollow Cider Mill.** You can watch apples pressed into fabulous
Fodor's Choice   cider at this working mill. Its store sells apple butter, jams and jellies,
★   Vermont-made handicrafts, and 50¢ cider doughnuts. Kids get free cider popsicles and will love watching the "doughnut robot" in action. ⊠ *3600 Waterbury–Stowe Rd., 3 miles north of I–89, Waterbury Center* ☎ *800/327–7537* ⊕ *www.coldhollow.com.*

SPAS

Spa and Wellness Center at Stowe Mountain Lodge. This 21,000-square-foot facility has 18 private treatment rooms, a fitness center, and an outdoor pool and hot tub. In addition to the usual array of facials, scrubs, and massages for adults, the spa offers a separate program for kids. ⊠ *Stowe Mountain Lodge, 7412 Mountain Rd.* ☎ *802/760–4782* ⊕ *www.stowemountainlodge.com.*

Spa at Stoweflake. One of the largest spas in New England, the Spa at Stoweflake features a massaging hydrotherapeutic waterfall, a Hungarian mineral pool, 30 treatment rooms, and 120 services like the Bingham Falls Renewal, named after a local waterfall. This treatment begins with a body scrub and a Vichy shower, followed by an aromatherapy oil massage. The spacious men's and women's sanctuaries have saunas, steam rooms, and whirlpool tubs. ⊠ *Stoweflake Mountain Resort and Spa, 1746 Mountain Rd.* ☎ *802/760–1083* ⊕ *www.stoweflake.com.*

Spa at Topnotch. An aura of calm pervades the Spa at Topnotch, with its birchwood doors and accents, natural light, and cool colors. Signature services include the Mount Mansfield Saucha, a three-stage herbal body treatment (scrub, wrap, and massage), and the Little River Stone Massage, which uses the resort's own wood-spice oil. Athletes and skiers might opt for a Thai Massage, while your canine friend will beg for Rover Reiki (really). Locker areas are spacious and spotless, with saunas, steam rooms, and whirlpool tubs. The pool has high ceilings and lots of natural light. Classes in tai chi, yoga, and Pilates are offered throughout the day in the nearby fitness center. ⊠ *Topnotch Resort and Spa, 4000 Mountain Rd.* ☎ *802/253–8585* ⊕ *www.topnotchresort.com.*

JEFFERSONVILLE

18 miles north of Stowe.

Jeffersonville is just over Smugglers' Notch from Stowe but miles away in feeling and attitude. In summer, you can drive over the notch road as it curves precipitously around boulders that have fallen from the cliffs above, then pass open meadows and old farmhouses and sugar shacks on the way down to town. Below the notch, Smugglers' Notch Ski Resort is the hub of activity year-round. Downtown Jeffersonville, once home to an artists' colony, is quiet but has excellent dining and nice art galleries.

EXPLORING

Boyden Valley Winery & Spirits. On a beautiful stretch of farmland west of Jeffersonville, this winery conducts tours and tastings and showcases an excellent selection of Vermont specialty products and local handicrafts. The winery's Big Barn Red is full-bodied, but the real fun may be in the ice wines, maple crème liqueur, and hard ice cider. ⊠ *Rte. 15 and Rte. 104, Cambridge* ☎ *802/644–8151* ⊕ *www.boydenvalley.com* ⌚ *Tasting $10.*

WHERE TO EAT AND STAY

$

AMERICAN

✗ **158 Main Restaurant and Bakery.** The best and most popular restaurant in Jeffersonville, 158 Main easily earns its accolades: portions are big, prices are not. For breakfast, locals love the Two Eggs Basic, which comes with two eggs any style, homemade toast, and home fries for $4. Menu selections for dinner range from sesame-seared yellowfin tuna with wok-seared vegetables to hanger steak with a maple-chipotle sauce. Sunday brunch is very popular. ⑤ *Average main: $17* ⊠ *158 Main St.* ☎ *802/644–8100* ⊕ *www.158Main.com* ⊘ *Closed Mon. No dinner Sun.*

$$$

RESORT

FAMILY

Fodor's Choice

★

⌂ **Smugglers' Notch Resort.** With four giant water parks for summer fun and just about every winter activity imaginable, this family resort has amenities other places only dream about. **Pros:** great place for families to learn to ski. **Cons:** not a romantic getaway for couples. ⑤ *Rooms from: $300* ⊠ *4323 Rte. 108 S* ☎ *802/332–6841, 800/419–4615* ⊕ *www.smuggs.com* ↝ *600 condominiums* ⏀ *No meals.*

SPORTS AND THE OUTDOORS

KAYAKING

Vermont Canoe and Kayak. This outfitter rents canoes and kayaks for use on the Lamoille River, and leads guided canoe trips to Boyden Valley Winery. ⊠ *4805 Rte. 15, behind the Family Table* ☎ *802/644–8336* ⊕ *www.vermontcanoeandkayak.com* ⊘ *Closed mid-Sept.–late May.*

LLAMA RIDES

Northern Vermont Llama Co. These llamas carry everything, including snacks and lunches, for half-day treks along the trails of Smugglers' Notch. Reservations are essential. ⊠ *766 Lapland Rd., Waterville* ☎ *802/644–2257* ⊕ *www.northernvermontllamaco.com* ⌚ *$60* ⊘ *Closed early Sept.–late May.*

SKI AREA

FAMILY **Smugglers' Notch.** The "granddaddy of all family resorts," Smugglers' Notch (or "Smuggs") receives consistent praise for its family programs. Its children's ski school is one of the best in the country—possibly *the* best—and there are challenges for skiers of all levels, spread over three separate areas. This was the first ski resort in the East to designate a triple–black diamond run: the Black Hole. There's ice-skating, tubing, five terrain parks, Nordic skiing, snowshoe trails, and a snowboarding area for kids ages three–six. Summer brings waterslides, treetop courses, zip lines, and crafts workshops—in other words, something for everyone. **Facilities:** 78 trails; 300 acres; 2,610-foot vertical drop; 8 lifts. ⊠ *4323 Rte. 108 S* ☎ *802/332–6841, 800/419–4615* ⊕ *www.smuggs. com* ⌦ *Lift ticket: $72.*

SHOPPING

ANTIQUES

Route 15 between Jeffersonville and Johnson is dubbed the "antiques highway."

Buggy Man. This store sells all sorts of collectibles, including horse-drawn vehicles. ⊠ *853 Rte. 15, 7 miles east of Jeffersonville* ☎ *802/635–2110.*

Smugglers' Notch Antiques. In a rambling barn, this shop sells antiques, collectibles, and custom-made furniture from 60 dealers. ⊠ *906 Rte. 108 S* ☎ *802/644–2100* ⊕ *www.smugglersnotchantiques.com* ۞ *Closed Mon.–Wed.*

CLOTHING

Fodor'sChoice **Johnson Woolen Mills.** This factory store has great deals on woolen blan-
★ kets, household goods, and the famous Johnson outerwear. ⊠ *51 Lower Main St. E, 9 miles east of Jeffersonville, Johnson* ☎ *802/635–2271* ⊕ *www.johnsonwoolenmills.com.*

BURLINGTON

31 miles southwest of Jeffersonville, 76 miles south of Montreal, 349 miles north of New York City, 223 miles northwest of Boston.

Fodor'sChoice As you drive along Main Street toward downtown Burlington, it's easy
★ to see why this four-college city is often called one of the most livable small cities in the United States. Downtown Burlington is filled with hip restaurants and bars, art galleries, and the Church Street Marketplace, a bustling pedestrian mall with trendy shops, crafts vendors, street performers, and sidewalk cafés. Just beyond, Lake Champlain shimmers beneath the towering Adirondacks on the New York shore. The revitalized Burlington waterfront teems with outdoors enthusiasts who bike or stroll along its recreation path, picnic on the grass, and ply the waters in sailboats and motor craft in summer.

EXPLORING

TOP ATTRACTIONS

Fodor'sChoice **Burlington Farmers' Market.** Burlington's Saturday farmers' market is an
★ absolute must-see when visiting in summer or fall. Set up in the center of town, the market is jam-packed with local farmers selling a colorful array of organic produce, flowers, baked goods, maple syrup, meats,

BURLINGTON'S LOCAL FOOD MOVEMENT

Burlington is exploding on the national food scene as one of the hubs of the local food movement. Known for its excellent soil and abundance of organic farms—as showcased in its huge weekly farmers' market (Saturday May–October) and popular outdoor summertime farm suppers—this health-conscious and liberal city is home to restaurants and markets with a focus on fresh, high-quality ingredients rivaling those of a much larger city. Burlington residents are likely to be seen biking to pick up their weekly CSA (Community Supported Agriculture) share at the Intervale, the city's huge web of community gardens, doing some weeding in their own urban garden plots, or stopping by one of the farms to pick berries or flowers on their way to a dinner party.

cheeses, and prepared foods. Local artisans also sell their wares. There's live music on the green, fresh cider and doughnuts in the fall, and always superb people-watching. From November to March, the market is held every other Saturday at Memorial Auditorium. ⊠ *City Hall Park, College and St. Paul Sts.* ☏ *802/310–5172* ⊕ *www.burlingtonfarmersmarket.org* ☑ *Free.*

FAMILY
Fodor's Choice
★

Church Street Marketplace. For more than 30 years, this pedestrian-only thoroughfare has served as Burlington's center of commerce and activity, with boutiques, cafés, restaurants, and street vendors the focus by day, and a lively bar and live-music scene at night. On sunny days, there are few better places to be in Burlington. ⊠ *2 Church St.* ☏ *802/863–1648* ⊕ *www.churchstmarketplace.com.*

Ethan Allen Homestead Museum. When Vermont hero Ethan Allen retired from his Revolutionary activities, he purchased 350 acres along the Winooski River and built this modest cabin in 1787. The original structure is a real slice of 18th-century life, including such frontier hallmarks as saw-cut boards and an open hearth for cooking. The kitchen garden resembles the one the Allens would have had. There's also a visitor center and miles of biking and hiking trails. In warmer months, climb Ethan Allen Tower at the west end of the property for stupendous views of Lake Champlain and the Green Mountains. Don't forget mosquito repellent. ⊠ *1 Ethan Allen Homestead, off Rte. 127* ☏ *802/865–4556* ⊕ *www.ethanallenhomestead.org* ☑ *$8.*

WORTH NOTING

FAMILY **ECHO Leahy Center for Lake Champlain.** Kids and adults can explore the geology and ecology of the Lake Champlain region through the center's more than 100 interactive exhibits, including the newest additions at the Action Lab. The lab's 3D Water Projection Sandbox manages to make learning about watersheds exciting. You can also get an up-close look at 70 species of indigenous animals. ⊠ *1 College St.* ☏ *802/864–1848* ⊕ *www.echovermont.org* ☑ *$13.50.*

Green Mountain Audubon Nature Center. This is a wonderful place to discover Vermont's outdoor wonders. The center's 255 acres of diverse habitats are a sanctuary for all things wild, and the 5 miles of trails provide an opportunity to explore the workings of differing natural communities. Events include bird-monitoring walks, wildflower rambles, nature workshops, and educational activities for children and adults. ✉ *255 Sherman Hollow Rd., 18 miles southeast of Burlington, Huntington* ☎ *802/434–3068* ⊕ *vt.audubon.org* ✉ *Donations accepted.*

Magic Hat Brewing Company. You can take a self-guided tour of the brewery, which puts out hundreds of bottles per minute. Head up the ramp past paintings by local artists and look down on the factory floor. When you're finished, try free beer samples and hang out at the Growler Bar, which has eight or more beers on tap. ✉ *5 Bartlett Bay Rd., South Burlington* ☎ *802/658–2739* ⊕ *www.magichat.net* ✉ *Free.*

University of Vermont. Crowning the hilltop above Burlington is the University of Vermont, known as UVM for the abbreviation of its Latin name, Universitas Viridis Montis, meaning the University of the Green Mountains. With more than 10,000 students, this is the state's principal institution of higher learning. The most architecturally impressive buildings face the green and have gorgeous lake views, as does the statue of founder Ira Allen, Ethan's brother. ✉ *85 S. Prospect St.* ☎ *802/656–3131* ⊕ *www.uvm.edu.*

WHERE TO EAT

$$
PIZZA
Fodor's Choice
★

✕ **American Flatbread Burlington.** It might be worth going to college in Burlington just to be able to gather with friends at this wildly popular organic pizza place. Seating is first-come, first-served, and the scene is bustling with locals and visitors sipping house-made brews. The wood-fired clay dome is where the cooks create delicious pies like the Punctuated Equilibrium, which has kalamata olives, roasted red peppers, goat cheese, fresh rosemary, red onions, mozzarella, and garlic. Fresh salads topped with locally made cheese are also popular. Here's to the college life! ⑤ *Average main: $20* ✉ *115 St. Paul St.* ☎ *802/861–2999* ⊕ *www.americanflatbread.com* ⬧ *Reservations not accepted.*

$$
AMERICAN
Fodor's Choice
★

✕ **Farmhouse Tap and Grill.** This is one of the most popular restaurants in town, so don't be put off by the line on a typical weekend night. Known for using only local beef, cheese, and produce, this farm-to-table enterprise is laid-back in style but provides one of the finest meals in the area. Specialties include burgers, chicken and biscuits, and local cheese and charcuterie plates, and there's a great wine and craft-beer selection. ■ TIP→ Put your name on the list and have a drink at the downstairs Tap Room or the outdoor beer garden while you wait. If the wait feels too long, try El Cortijo, the same owners' small taqueria down the street, for locally raised beef or chicken tacos and terrific margaritas. ⑤ *Average main: $18* ✉ *160 Bank St.* ☎ *802/859–0888* ⊕ *www.farmhousetg.com.*

$$$$
STEAKHOUSE

✕ **Guild Tavern.** Vermont's best steak can be found roasting over hardwood coals in the tavern's open kitchens. All meat is sourced from local farms, dry-aged a minimum of 21 days, and cooked to absolute perfection. The space itself is also a treat, with antique chicken feeders serving as light fixtures and a soapstone-topped bar in the center. Lighter fare is available, but make sure at least one person in your party orders the

CLOSE UP

Vermont by Bike

Vermont has more than 14,000 miles of roads, and almost 80% of them are town roads that see little high-speed traffic, making them ideal for scenic bike rides. More than half are dirt roads, which means they're especially suitable for mountain biking. Although mountain-bike trails and old farm and logging roads wind through the Green Mountain State, most are on private property and therefore uncharted. Several mountain-biking centers around the state have extensive trail networks (and maps) that will keep avid fat-tire fans happy for a few hours or a few days. To road bike in Vermont, you'll want a map and preferably a bicycle with at least 10 gears. The only roads that prohibit cycling are four-lane highways and U.S. 7 and U.S. 4 in Rutland.

TOP ROAD BIKING ROUTES:
For a relatively easy 16-mile loop, begin at the blinker on U.S. 7 in **Shelburne** and follow Mt. Philo Road south to Hinesburg Road, then west

to Charlotte. Lake Road and Orchard Road go past orchards and berry fields; Bostwick Road will take you back to U.S. 7.

In the heart of the central Green Mountains is a moderate 18-mile loop on U.S. 4, Route 100, and Route 100A that passes Calvin Coolidge's home in **Plymouth Notch.**

West of **Rutland** is a beautiful 27-mile ride on Routes 140, 30, and 133 that passes swimming holes, then hugs the shore of Lake St. Catherine. Start in Middletown Springs.

A scenic 43-mile ride in the **Northeast Kingdom** passes through pleasant Peacham and the birches and maples of Groton State Forest. Start in Danville and follow Peacham Road, then Routes 302 and 232, and U.S. 2.

For a real test, try the 48-mile ride over **Middlebury and Brandon Gaps** on Routes 125 and 73, which connect via Routes 153 and 100.

3

---

rib eye. $ *Average main: $45* ⊠ *1633 Williston Rd.* ☎ *802/497–1207* ⊕ *www.guildtavern.com* ☾ *No lunch.*

$$$

MODERN

AMERICAN

Fodor's Choice

★

✗ **Hen of the Wood Burlington.** Arguably Vermont's best restaurant, Hen of the Wood has acquiesced to the desires of its ravenous fans and opened a branch in Burlington. With a more urban feel than that of the original location in Waterbury, the restaurant serves the same inventive yet down-to-earth cuisine that sets diners' hearts aflutter and tongues wagging. Drop your finger anywhere on the menu and you can't go wrong, especially with dishes like brown butter crêpes stuffed with chanterelles, and smoked bluefish toast in buttermilk. If you ever need to say "I love you," this is the place to do it. $ *Average main: $27* ⊠ *55 Cherry St.* ☎ *802/540–0534* ⊕ *www.henofthewood.com* ☾ *No lunch.*

$$$

MODERN

AMERICAN

✗ **Juniper.** The Hotel Vermont has generated excitement not only for its new-school accommodations, but also its ground-floor restaurant and bar. Juniper's delightful design—a perfect blend of boutique chic and real Vermont, with reclaimed antique red-oak floors, black granite walls, and a free-flowing layout—is only part of the fun. The rest is in the inventive menu, which dazzles with items such as juniper-roasted quail and applewood-smoked pickled eggs. The cocktails lineup is among the best in town. Weather permitting, you can stay toasty on the outdoor patio with its central fire pit. $ *Average main: $29* ⊠ *41 Cherry St.* ☎ *802/651–5027* ⊕ *www.hotelvt.com/dining-drinking.*

$$$
CAFÉ

✗**Leunig's Bistro and Cafe.** This popular café delivers alfresco bistro cuisine, a friendly European-style bar, and live jazz. Favorite entrées include salade niçoise, *soupe au pistou* (vegetable and white bean soup with Asiago and pesto), and beef bourguignon. Fans of crème brûlée: this place makes the best in town. A prix-fixe dinner for two goes for $35: it's one of the city's best bargains. An expanded upstairs lounge offers cocktails, a smart wine selection, and local cheese plates and other light fare. This is a great spot for weekend brunch. $ *Average main: $28* ⊠ *115 Church St.* ☎ *802/863–3759* ⊕ *www.leunigsbistro.com.*

$
AMERICAN
FAMILY

✗**Penny Cluse Cafe.** This popular breakfast and brunch spot is often buzzing with activity. Weekend lines can be long, but locals think it's worth the wait for the famous gingerbread-blueberry pancakes, warm biscuits with herb gravy, huevos rancheros, and homemade banana bread. $ *Average main: $10* ⊠ *169 Cherry St.* ☎ *802/651–8834* ⊕ *www.pennycluse.com* ☾ *No dinner.*

$$
CHINESE

✗**A Single Pebble.** The creative, authentic Chinese fare served on the first floor of this residential row house includes traditional clay-pot dishes as well as wok specialties like beef with baby bok choy and chicken with peanuts and chili peppers. The dry-fried green beans, sautéed with flecks of pork, black beans, preserved vegetables, and garlic, are a house specialty, as is the "mock eel" (braised shiitake mushrooms) served in a crispy ginger sauce. Any dish can be made without meat. ■TIP→ **Try the dim sum on Sunday 11:30–1:45.** $ *Average main: $22* ⊠ *133 Bank St.* ☎ *802/865–5200* ⊕ *www.asinglepebble.com* ⚄ *Reservations essential.*

$$$
ITALIAN

✗**Trattoria Delia.** If you didn't make that trip to Umbria this year, the next best thing is this Italian country eatery around the corner from City Hall Park. Seafood, beef, and fresh produce are the stars; go for the braised or wood-grilled items on the menu. In winter, try to reserve a table near the fire. The husband-and-wife owners also run an adjoining wine bar called Sotto. $ *Average main: $25* ⊠ *152 St. Paul St.* ☎ *802/864–5253* ⊕ *www.trattoriadelia.com* ☾ *No lunch* ⚄ *Reservations essential.*

$$
AMERICAN

✗**Waterworks Food + Drink.** The converted Champlain Mill houses one of the most popular restaurants in Winooski, Burlington's hip, more diverse neighbor to the north. Come for the expansive bar and dining room, with its lofty wood-beam ceilings and exposed brick, and be wowed by the river views—pure drama in winter. Dishes can be pricey, but there's a good burger with garlicky fries, and you can order flatbread topped with eclectic ingredients that include duck confit, lobster, and sweet corn. Waterworks hosts live music on many weekend nights, brunch on Sunday, and upstairs you can visit the Winooski Historical Society Museum. $ *Average main: $20* ⊠ *20 Winooski Falls Way, Winooski* ☎ *802/497–3525* ⊕ *www.waterworksvt.com.*

$
AMERICAN

✗**Zabby and Elf's Stone Soup.** A perfect place to stop for a delicious and healthful lunch or early dinner, Stone Soup offers all-local produce and organic ingredients showcased in fresh sandwiches, wonderful soups, homemade breads, and a wide array of baked goods. There are many veggie and vegan options, as well as popular daily specials and a small salad bar. $ *Average main: $12* ✉ *211 College St.* ☎ *802/862–7616* ⊕ *www.stonesoupvt.com* ⊘ *Closed Sun.*

WHERE TO STAY

$$$
HOTEL
Fodor's Choice
★

⊡ **Hotel Vermont.** Ever since the Hotel Vermont opened its doors in 2013, guests have been stepping inside with acute curiosity and walking out with effusive praise. **Pros:** destination restaurant; gorgeous rooms; unbelievable service. **Cons:** luxury doesn't come cheap. $ *Rooms from: $309* ✉ *41 Cherry St.* ☎ *802/651–0080* ⊕ *www.hotelvt.com* ⟲ *120 rooms, 5 suites* ⦿ *No meals.*

$$
B&B/INN

⊡ **The Lang House on Main Street.** Within walking distance of downtown in the historic hill section of town, this grand 1881 Victorian home charms completely with its period furnishings, fine woodwork, plaster detailing, and stained-glass windows. **Pros:** family-friendly vibe; interesting location; well run. **Cons:** no elevator. $ *Rooms from: $209* ✉ *360 Main St.* ☎ *802/652–2500, 877/919–9799* ⊕ *www.langhouse.com* ⟲ *11 rooms* ⦿ *Breakfast.*

$
B&B/INN

⊡ **Willard Street Inn.** High in the historic hill section of Burlington, this ivy-covered house with an exterior marble staircase and English gardens incorporates elements of Queen Anne and Georgian Revival styles. **Pros:** innkeepers passionate about their job; lots of friendly attention. **Cons:** a tad old-fashioned; walk to downtown can be a drag in winter. $ *Rooms from: $150* ✉ *349 S. Willard St.* ☎ *802/651–8710, 800/577–8712* ⊕ *www.willardstreetinn.com* ⟲ *14 rooms* ⦿ *Breakfast.*

NIGHTLIFE AND PERFORMING ARTS

NIGHTLIFE

Higher Ground. When you feel like shaking it up to live music, come to Higher Ground—it gets the lion's share of local and national musicians. ✉ *1214 Williston Rd., South Burlington* ☎ *802/652–0777* ⊕ *www.highergroundmusic.com.*

Nectar's. Jam band Phish got its start at Nectar's, which is always jumping to the sounds of local bands and never charges a cover. Don't leave without a helping of the bar's famous fries and gravy. ✉ *188 Main St.* ☎ *802/658–4771* ⊕ *www.liveatnectars.com.*

Radio Bean. For some true local flavor, head to this funky place for nightly live music, an artsy vibe, and a cocktail. Tuesday is the most fun, as the house band Honkey Tonk blazes through covers of Gram Parsons, Wilco, and the like—all of which goes down especially well with chicken and waffles. ✉ *8 N. Winooski Ave.* ☎ *802/660–9346* ⊕ *www.radiobean.com.*

Vermont Pub & Brewery. Vermont's first brewpub still makes its own beer and remains a popular spot—especially in warm weather, when locals head to the outdoor patio. Folk musicians play here regularly. ✉ *144 College St.* ☎ *802/865–0500* ⊕ *www.vermontbrewery.com.*

PERFORMING ARTS

Fodor's Choice
★

Flynn Center for the Performing Arts. A grandiose art-deco gem, the Flynn Theatre is the cultural heart of Burlington. In addition to being home to Vermont's largest musical theater company, it hosts the Vermont

Burlington's pedestrian-only Church Street Marketplace and the nearby shores of Lake Champlain are great for exploring.

Symphony Orchestra, as well as big-name acts like Neko Case and Elvis Costello. The adjacent Flynn Space is a coveted spot for more offbeat, experimental performances. ⊠ *153 Main St.* ☎ *802/863–5966* ⊕ *www.flynncenter.org.*

SPORTS AND THE OUTDOORS

BEACHES

FAMILY **North Beach.** Along Burlington's "new" North End a long line of beaches stretches to the Winooski River delta, beginning with North Beach, which has a grassy picnic area, a snack bar, and boat rentals. Neighboring Leddy Park offers a more secluded beach. **Amenities:** food and drink; lifeguards; parking (fee); showers; toilets. **Best for:** partiers; swimming; walking; windsurfing. ⊠ *North Beach Park, 52 Institute Rd., off North Ave.* ☎ *802/865–7247* ⊕ *www.enjoyburlington.com/venue/north-beach* 🅿 *Parking $8 (May–Oct.).*

BIKING

FAMILY **Burlington Bike Path.** Anyone who's put the rubber to the road on the
Fodor's Choice 7½-mile Burlington Bike Path and its almost equally long northern
★ extension on the Island Line Trail sings its praises. Along the way there are endless postcard views of Lake Champlain and the Adirondack Mountains. The northern end of the trail is slightly more rugged and windswept, so dress accordingly. ⊠ *Burlington* ☎ *802/864–0123* ⊕ *www.enjoyburlington.com/venue/burlington-bike-path.*

North Star Sports. In addition to stocking an extensive supply of sports apparel and accessories, this family-owned shop rents bikes and provides cycling maps. ⊠ *100 Main St.* ☎ *802/863–3832* ⊕ *www.northstarsportsvt.com.*

Ski Rack. Burlington's one-stop shop for winter sports equipment, the Ski Rack also rents bikes and sells running gear throughout the year. ⊠ *85 Main St.* ☎ *802/658–3313, 800/882–4530* ⊕ *www.skirack.com.*

3

BOATING

Burlington Community Boathouse. This boathouse administers the city's marina as well as a summertime watering hole called Splash, one of the best places to watch the sun set over the lake. ⊠ *Burlington Harbor, College St.* ☎ *802/865–3377* ⊕ *www.enjoyburlington.com/venue/community-boathouse-marina.*

FAMILY **Community Sailing Center.** Dinghies, keelboats, and kayaks are available for rent here, and the center offers classes for all experience levels. ⊠ *1 Lake St.* ☎ *802/864–2499* ⊕ *www.communitysailingcenter.org* ⊙ *Closed mid-Oct.–mid-May.*

Lake Champlain Shoreline Cruises. The trilevel *Spirit of Ethan Allen III,* a 363-passenger vessel, offers narrated cruises, theme dinners, and sunset sails with breathtaking Adirondacks and Green Mountains views. The standard 1½-hour cruise runs four times a day; evening cruises leave at 6:30. ⊠ *Burlington Boat House, 1 College St.* ☎ *802/862–8300* ⊕ *www.soea.com* 🎫 *$16.*

True North Kayak Tours. This company conducts two- and five-hour guided kayak tours of Lake Champlain that include talks about the region's natural history. It also offers customized lessons and runs a kayak camp for kids. ⊠ *25 Nash Pl.* ☎ *802/238–7695* ⊕ *www.vermontkayak.com.*

SKI AREA

Bolton Valley Resort. About 25 miles from Burlington, this ski area is a family favorite. In addition to downhill trails—more than half rated for intermediate and beginner skiers—Bolton offers 62 miles of cross-country and snowshoe trails, night skiing, and a sports center. **Facilities.** 71 trails; 300 acres; 1,704-foot vertical drop; 5 lifts. ⊠ *4302 Bolton Valley Access Rd., north off U.S. 2, Bolton* ☎ *802/434–3444, 877/926–5866* ⊕ *www.boltonvalley.com* 🎫 *Lift ticket: $59.*

SHOPPING

With each passing year, Burlington's industrial South End attracts ever greater numbers of artists and craftspeople, who set up studios, shops, and galleries in former factories and warehouses along Pine Street. The district's annual "Art Hop" is the city's largest arts celebration—and a roaring good time.

CLOTHING

April Cornell. The Vermont designer's flagship store stocks her distinctive floral-print dresses and linens. ⊠ *131 Battery St.* ☎ *802/863–0060* ⊕ *www.aprilcornell.com.*

CRAFTS

Bennington Potters North. Along with the popular pottery line, this store stocks interesting kitchen items. ✉ *127 College St.* ☎ *802/863–2221* ⊕ *www.benningtonpotters.com.*

Frog Hollow. This nonprofit collective and gallery sells contemporary and traditional crafts, paintings, and photographs by more than 200 Vermont artists and artisans. ✉ *85 Church St.* ☎ *802/863–6458* ⊕ *www.froghollow.org.*

FOOD

Lake Champlain Chocolates. This chocolatier makes sensational truffles, caramels, candies, fudge, and hot chocolate. The chocolates are all-natural, made in Vermont, and make a great edible souvenir. ✉ *750 Pine St.* ☎ *800/465–5909* ⊕ *www.lakechamplainchocolates.com.*

SPORTING GOODS

Burton. The folks who helped start snowboarding—a quintessential Vermont company—sell equipment and clothing at their flagship store. ✉ *80 Industrial Pkwy.* ☎ *802/660–3200* ⊕ *www.burton.com.*

SHELBURNE

5 miles south of Burlington.

A few miles south of Burlington, the Champlain Valley gives way to fertile farmland, affording views of the rugged Adirondacks across the lake. In the middle of this farmland is the village of Shelburne (and just farther south, beautiful and more rural Charlotte), chartered in the mid-18th century and partly a bedroom community for Burlington. Shelburne Farms is worth at least a few hours of exploring, as are Shelburne Orchards in fall, when you can pick your own apples and drink fresh cider while admiring breathtaking views of the lake and mountains beyond.

GETTING HERE AND AROUND

Shelburne is south of Burlington after the town of South Burlington, which is notable for its very un-Vermont traffic congestion and a commercial and fast food–laden stretch of U.S. 7. It's easy to confuse Shelburne Farms (2 miles west of town on the lake) with Shelburne Museum, which is right on U.S. 7 just south of town, but you'll want to make time for both.

EXPLORING

Fiddlehead Brewing Company. There isn't much to the tasting room here, but there doesn't need to be: Fiddlehead only occasionally cans its celebrated beer, making this the best place outside of a restaurant to sample it on tap (and for free). Decide which one you like best and buy a growler to go—or, better yet, take it to Folino's Pizza next door. The pizzeria may be short on atmosphere, but the pies are mighty fine. ✉ *6305 Shelburne Rd.* ☎ *802/399–2994* ⊕ *www.fiddleheadbrewing.com* ⊠ *Free.*

FAMILY
Fodor's Choice
★

Shelburne Farms. Founded in the 1880s as a private estate for two very rich New Yorkers, this 1,400-acre farm is much more than an exquisite landscape: it's an educational and cultural resource center with a working dairy farm, an award winning cheese producer, an organic market garden, and a bakery whose aroma of fresh bread and pastries is an olfactory treat. It's a brilliant place for parents to expose their kids to the dignity of farmwork and the joys of compassionate animal husbandry—indeed, children and adults alike will get a kick out of hunting for eggs in the oversize coop, milking a cow, and watching the chicken parade. There are activities every half hour 10–4, and a lunch cart serves up fresh-from-the-farm soups, salads, and sandwiches. Frederick Law Olmsted, the co-creator of New York City's Central Park, designed the magnificent grounds overlooking Lake Champlain; walk to Lone Tree Hill for a splendid view. If you fall in love with the scenery, arrange a romantic dinner at the lakefront mansion, or spend the night. ⊠ *1611 Harbor Rd., west of U.S. 7* ☎ *802/985–8498* ⊕ *www. shelburnefarms.org* ⊑ *$8.*

FAMILY
Fodor'sChoice
★

Shelburne Museum. You can trace much of New England's history simply by wandering through the 45 acres and 38 buildings of this museum. Some 25 buildings were relocated here, including an old-fashioned jail, an 1871 lighthouse, and a 220-foot steamboat, the *Ticonderoga*. The outstanding 150,000-object collection of art, design, and Americana consists of antique furniture, fine and folk art, quilts, trade signs, and weather vanes; there are also more than 200 carriages and sleighs. The Pizzagalli Center for Art and Education is open year-round with changing exhibitions and programs for kids and adults. ⊠ *6000 Shelburne Rd.* ☎ *802/985–3346* ⊕ *www.shelburnemuseum.org* ⊑ *$22.*

Shelburne Vineyard. From U.S. 7, you'll see rows and rows of organically grown vines. Visit the attractive tasting room and learn how wine is made. ⊠ *6308 Shelburne Rd.* ☎ *802/985–8222* ⊕ *www.shelburnevineyard.com* ⊑ *Tasting $7, tour free.*

FAMILY

Vermont Teddy Bear Company. On the 30-minute tour of this fun-filled factory you'll hear more puns than you ever thought possible, while learning how a few homemade bears sold from a cart on Church Street have turned into a multimillion-dollar business. Patrons and children can relax, eat, and play under a large canvas tent in summer, or wander the beautiful 57-acre property. ⊠ *6655 Shelburne Rd.* ☎ *802/985–3001* ⊕ *www.vermontteddybear.com* ⊑ *Tour $4.*

WHERE TO EAT

$$
ECLECTIC

✕ **The Bearded Frog.** This is the top restaurant in the Shelburne area, perfect for a casual dinner in the bar or a more sophisticated experience in the attractive dining room. At the bar, try the soups, burgers, and terrific cocktails; the dining room serves fresh salads, seared seafood, roasted poultry, grilled steaks, and decadent desserts. ⑤ *Average main: $20* ⊠ *5247 Shelburne Rd.* ☎ *802/985–9877* ⊕ *www.thebeardedfrog. com* ⊙ *No lunch.*

$$$
AMERICAN
Fodor'sChoice
★

✕ **The Dining Room at the Inn at Shelburne Farms.** Dinner here will make you dream of F. Scott Fitzgerald. Piano music wafts in from the library as you carry a drink through the rooms of this 1880s mansion, gazing across a long lawn and formal gardens on the shore of dark Lake Champlain—you'll swear Jay Gatsby is about to come down the stairs. Count on just-grown ingredients that come from market gardens, as well as flavorful locally grown venison, beef, pork, and chicken. On weekends a spread of produce is set up next to a cocktail bar with fresh specialties, and Sunday brunch is the area's best. The dining room overlooks the lake. $ *Average main: $32 ⊠ Inn at Shelburne Farms, 1611 Harbor Rd.* ☎ *802/985–8498* ⊕ *www.shelburnefarms.org* ⊙ *Closed mid-Oct.–mid-May.*

$$
AMERICAN
✕ **Rustic Roots.** Wednesday through Sunday, this downtown restaurant inside a converted farmhouse serves a hearty brunch. Scuffed wood floors and chunky country tables bring the "rustic," but not too much so: an intimate bar and maroon walls adorned with woodcrafts and art add a touch of elegance, and the food is carefully prepared. If your dish doesn't come with the coffee-maple sausage or popovers, order them on the side. There are only seven tables, so reservations are essential for the French-inspired dinners, served on weekend nights only. $ *Average main: $19 ⊠ 195 Falls Rd.* ☎ *802/985–9511* ⊕ *www.rusticrootsvt.com* ⊙ *Closed Mon. and Tues. No dinner Wed., Thurs., and Sun.* ⌂ *Reservations essential.*

WHERE TO STAY

$$
B&B/INN
⌂ **Heart of the Village Inn.** Each of the elegantly furnished rooms at this bed-and-breakfast in an 1886 Queen Anne Victorian provides coziness and tastefully integrated modern conveniences. **Pros:** adorable village inn; elegant; well run; easy walk to shops and restaurants. **Cons:** near to but not within Shelburne Farms. $ *Rooms from: $200 ⊠ 5347 Shelburne Rd.* ☎ *802/985–9060* ⊕ *www.heartofthevillage.com* ↝ *7 rooms, 2 suites* ¶○¶ *Breakfast.*

$
B&B/INN
Fodor's Choice
★
⌂ **The Inn at Shelburne Farms.** It's hard not to feel like an aristocrat at this exquisite turn-of-the-20th-century Tudor-style inn, one of the most memorable properties in the country. **Pros:** stately lakefront setting in a fantastic historic mansion; great service; wonderful value; romantic restaurant. **Cons:** lowest-priced rooms have shared baths; closed in winter; must book far in advance. $ *Rooms from: $170 ⊠ 1611 Harbor Rd.* ☎ *802/985–8498* ⊕ *www.shelburnefarms.org* ⊙ *Closed mid-Oct.–mid-May* ↝ *24 rooms (17 with bath), 2 cottages, 2 houses* ¶○¶ *No meals.*

$$
B&B/INN
Fodor's Choice
★
⌂ **Mt. Philo Inn.** If you've grown tired of the floral wallpaper of so many traditional New England inns, Jane and Dave Garbose's Mt. Philo Inn may be for you. **Pros:** space, and lots of it; elegant rooms; great art collection. **Cons:** a bit remote. $ *Rooms from: $280 ⊠ 27 Inn Rd., Charlotte* ☎ *802/425–3335* ⊕ *www.mtphiloinn.com* ↝ *4 suites* ¶○¶ *No meals.*

SHOPPING

The Flying Pig Bookstore. It should come as no surprise that this bookstore is notable for its whimsy and carefully curated children's section: one of the owners is a stand-up comedian, and the other is a picture-book author. ⊠ *5247 Shelburne Rd.* ☎ *802/985–3999* ⊕ *www. flyingpigbooks.com.*

The Shelburne Country Store. As you enter this store, you'll feel as though you've stepped back in time. Walk past the potbelly stove and take in the aroma emanating from the fudge neatly piled behind huge antique glass cases, alongside a vast selection of penny candies and chocolates. There are creemees, of course, but here the specialties are candles, weather vanes, glassware, and local foods. ⊠ *29 Falls Rd., off U.S. 7* ☎ *800/660–3657* ⊕ *www.shelburnecountrystore.com.*

Shelburne Museum's many attractions include the *Ticonderoga* steamship and other pieces from New England's past.

VERGENNES

12 miles south of Shelburne.

Vermont's oldest city, founded in 1788, has a compact downtown area of restored Victorian homes and public buildings, with a few good eateries sprinkled throughout. Main Street slopes down to Otter Creek Falls, where cannonballs were made during the War of 1812. The statue of Thomas Macdonough on the green immortalizes the victor of the Battle of Plattsburgh (1814).

ESSENTIALS

Visitor Information Addison County Chamber of Commerce. ⊠ *93 Court St., Middlebury* ☎ *802/388-7951* ⊕ *www.addisoncounty.com.*

EXPLORING

OFF THE BEATEN PATH

Lake Champlain Maritime Museum. This museum documents centuries of activity on the historically significant lake. Climb aboard a replica of Benedict Arnold's Revolutionary War gunboat moored in the lake, learn about shipwrecks, watch craftsmen work at traditional boatbuilding and blacksmithing, or take a course—for an hour or all day—in boatbuilding, rowing, blacksmithing, or other endeavors. ⊠ *4472 Basin Harbor Rd., 7 miles west of Vergennes* ☎ *802/475-2022* ⊕ *www.lcmm.org* 🖃 *$12.*

Rokeby Museum. A Quaker family farm for nearly two centuries, this National Historic Landmark served as a safe haven for runaway slaves during the days of the Underground Railroad. Join one of the guided house tours, explore the grounds and the historic farm buildings, or set off on the 50 acres of hiking trails. ⊠ *4334 U.S. 7, Ferrisburgh* ☎ *802/877-3406* ⊕ *www.rokeby.org* 🖃 *$10.*

WHERE TO EAT AND STAY

$$$ ✕**Starry Night Café.** This chic restaurant is one of the hottest spots
ECLECTIC around. The proprietors serve seasonal, farm-to-table cuisine, like
grilled organic pork loin and fennel-pollen-scented seared salmon,
among handcrafted tableware and furniture. A rotating display of
works by local artists graces the walls, and the fireside porch, with
its views of gardens and trees, is open at least three seasons of the
year. $ *Average main: $28* ⊠ *5371 U.S. 7, 5 miles north of Vergennes,
Ferrisburgh* ☎ *802/877–6316* ⊕ *www.starrynightcafe.com* ⊘ *Closed
Mon. and Tues. No lunch* ⚲ *Reservations essential.*

$ ✕**Vergennes Laundry.** Though its decor is minimalist, this bakery is
BAKERY full of delights. The morning buns and cardamom buns are worth a
stop alone, but there's so much more—including a rotating selection
of delicious breads, pastries, and cookies, along with sandwiches
on fresh baguettes, artisanal cheeses, gazpacho, and raw oysters.
Pair whatever you order with a fresh-squeezed juice or espresso,
and you'll be more than satisfied. $ *Average main: $8* ⊠ *247 Main
St.* ☎ *802/870–7157* ⊕ *vergenneslaundry.squarespace.com* ⊘ *Closed
Mon.–Wed., and Sept.*

$$ ⊡**Basin Harbor Club.** Set amid 700 acres overlooking Lake Champlain,
RESORT this ultimate family resort provides luxurious accommodations and
FAMILY a full roster of amenities, including an 18-hole golf course, various
Fodor's Choice boating options, and morning and evening children's programs. **Pros:**
★ gorgeous lakeside property; activities galore; wonderful for families.
Cons: open only half the year; pricey; often booked by corporate
groups. $ *Rooms from: $270* ⊠ *4800 Basin Harbor Rd.* ☎ *802/475–
2311, 800/622–4000* ⊕ *www.basinharbor.com* ⊘ *Closed mid-Oct.–
mid-May* ⇱ *47 rooms, 73 cottages* ⊚⊙ *Breakfast.*

SHOPPING

Dakin Farm. Cob-smoked ham, aged cheddar cheese, maple syrup made
on-site, and other well-crafted specialty foods can be sampled here.
You can also visit the smokehouse and watch the waxing and sealing
of cheeses. ⊠ *5797 U.S. 7, 5 miles north of Vergennes* ☎ *800/993–2546*
⊕ *www.dakinfarm.com.*

LAKE CHAMPLAIN ISLANDS

Lake Champlain stretches more than 100 miles south from the Canadian border and forms the northern part of the boundary between New
York and Vermont. Within it is an elongated archipelago comprising
several islands—Isle La Motte, North Hero, Grand Isle, and South
Hero—and the Alburg Peninsula. Enjoying a temperate climate, the
islands hold several apple orchards and are a center of water recreation
in summer and ice fishing in winter. A scenic drive through the islands
on U.S. 2 begins at Interstate 89 and travels north to Alburg Center;
Route 78 takes you back to the mainland.

ESSENTIALS

Visitor Information Lake Champlain Islands Chamber of Commerce. ⊠ *3501 U.S. 2, Suite 100, North Hero* ☎ *802/372-8400, 800/262-5226* ⊕ *www.champlainislands.com.* **Lake Champlain Regional Chamber of Commerce.** ⊠ *60 Main St., Suite 100, Burlington* ☎ *802/863-3489, 877/686-5253* ⊕ *www.vermont.org.*

EXPLORING

Allenholm Farm. The pick-your-own apples at this farm are amazingly tasty—if you're here at harvesttime, don't miss out. The farm also has a petting area with donkeys, miniature horses, sheep, goats, and other animals. At the store, you can buy cheeses, dried fruit, homemade pies, and maple syrup creemees. ⊠ *111 South St., South Hero* ☎ *802/372-5566* ⊕ *www.allenholm.com* 🆓 *Free.*

Snow Farm Vineyard and Winery. Vermont's first vineyard was started here in 1996; today, the winery specializes in nontraditional botanical hybrid grapes designed to withstand the local climate. Take a self-guided tour and sip some samples in the tasting room—dessert wines are their strong suit. On Thursday evening, mid-June–early September, you can picnic and enjoy the free concerts on the lawn. ⊠ *190 W. Shore Rd., South Hero* ☎ *802/372-9463* ⊕ *www.snowfarm.com* 🆓 *Free.*

St. Anne's Shrine. This spot marks the site where, in 1665, French soldiers and Jesuits put ashore and built a fort, creating Vermont's first European settlement. Vermont's first Roman Catholic Mass was celebrated here on July 26, 1666. ⊠ *92 St. Anne's Rd., Isle La Motte* ☎ *802/928-3362* ⊕ *www.saintannesshrine.org* 🆓 *Free.*

WHERE TO STAY

$

B&B/INN

FAMILY

North Hero House Inn and Restaurant. This inn has four buildings right on Lake Champlain, among them the 1891 Colonial Revival main house with nine guest rooms, a restaurant, a pub room, a library, and a sitting room. **Pros:** relaxed complex; superb lakefront setting. **Cons:** closed in winter. ⑤ *Rooms from: $140* ⊠ *3643 U.S. Rural Rte. 2, North Hero* ☎ *802/372-4732, 888/525-3644* ⊕ *www.northherohouse.com* ☉ *Closed Nov.–Mar.* ⌛ *23 rooms, 3 suites* ⦿ *Breakfast.*

$

HOTEL

Ruthcliffe Lodge & Restaurant. Good food and splendid scenery make this off-the-beaten-path motel directly on Lake Champlain a great value. **Pros:** inexpensive rates; serene setting; laid-back vibe. **Cons:** rooms simple, not luxurious. ⑤ *Rooms from: $142* ⊠ *1002 Quarry Rd., Isle La Motte* ☎ *802/928-3200* ⊕ *www.ruthcliffe.com* ☉ *Closed mid-Oct.–mid-May* ⌛ *7 rooms* ⦿ *Breakfast.*

SPORTS AND THE OUTDOORS

Alburg Dunes State Park. This park has one of the longest sandy beaches on Lake Champlain and some fine examples of rare flora and fauna along the hiking trails. ⊠ *151 Coon Point Rd., off U.S. 2, Alburg* ☎ *802/796-4170* ⊕ *www.vtstateparks.com/htm/alburg.htm* 🆓 *$4.*

Apple Island Resort. The resort's marina rents pontoon boats, rowboats, canoes, kayaks, and pedal boats. ⊠ *71 U.S. 2, South Hero* ☎ *802/372-3922* ⊕ *www.appleislandresort.com.*

Grand Isle State Park. You'll find hiking trails, boat rentals, and shore fishing at Grand Isle. ⊠ *36 E. Shore S, off U.S. 2, Grand Isle* ☎ *802/372–4300* ⊕ *www.vtstateparks.com/htm/grandisle.htm* 🖙 *$4.*

Hero's Welcome. This general store rents bikes, canoes, kayaks, and paddleboards; come winter, they switch to ice skates, cross-country skis, and snowshoes. ⊠ *3643 U.S. 2, North Hero* ☎ *802/372–4161, 800/372–4376* ⊕ *www.heroswelcome.com.*

Missisquoi National Wildlife Refuge. Located on the mainland east of the Alburg Peninsula, the refuge consists of 6,729 acres of federally protected wetlands, meadows, and woods. It's a beautiful area for birdwatching, canoeing, and walking nature trails. ⊠ *29 Tabor Rd., 36 miles north of Burlington, Swanton* ☎ *802/868–4781* ⊕ *www.fws.gov/refuge/missisquoi.*

North Hero State Park. The 399-acre North Hero has a swimming beach and nature trails. It's open to rowboats, kayaks, and canoes. ⊠ *3803 Lakeview Dr., North Hero* ☎ *802/372–8727* ⊕ *www.vtstateparks.com/htm/northhero.htm* 🖙 *$4.*

Sand Bar State Park. One of Vermont's best swimming beaches is at Sand Bar State Park, along with a snack bar, a changing room, and boat rentals. ⊠ *1215 U.S. 2, South Hero* ☎ *802/893–2825* ⊕ *www.vtstateparks.com/htm/sandbar.htm* 🖙 *$4.*

MONTGOMERY AND JAY

51 miles northeast of Burlington.

Montgomery is a small village near the Jay Peak ski resort and the Canadian border. Amid the surrounding countryside are seven covered bridges.

GETTING HERE AND AROUND

Montgomery lies at the junction of Routes 58, 118, and 242. From Burlington, take Interstate 89 north to Routes 105 and 118 east. Route 242 connects Montgomery and, to the northeast, the Jay Peak Resort.

EXPLORING

OFF THE BEATEN PATH

Lake Memphremagog. Vermont's second-largest body of water, Lake Memphremagog extends 33 miles north from Newport into Canada. Prouty Beach in Newport has tennis courts, boat rentals, and a nine-hole disc-golf course. Watch the sunset from the deck of the East Side Restaurant, which serves excellent burgers and prime rib. ⊠ *242 Prouty Beach Rd., Newport* ☎ *802/334–6345* ⊕ *www.newportrecreation.org.*

WHERE TO STAY

$$
B&B/INN
Fodor'sChoice
★

The INN. Innkeepers Nick Barletta and Scott Pasfield have transformed this older property into a smart chalet-style lodging with tons of character. **Pros:** Trout River views from back rooms; within walking distance of shops and supplies. **Cons:** noise from bar can seep into nearby rooms. ⑤ *Rooms from: $209* ⊠ *241 Main St.* ☎ *802/326–4391* ⊕ *www.theinn.us* 🛏 *11 rooms* ⦿ *Breakfast.*

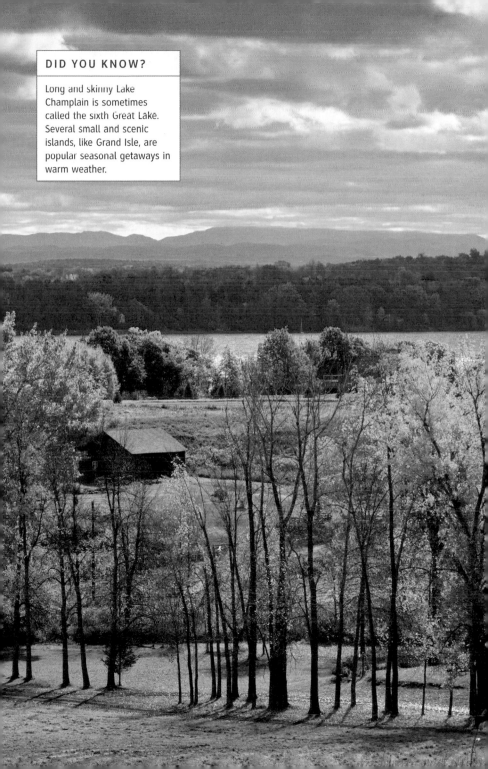

DID YOU KNOW?

Long and skinny Lake Champlain is sometimes called the sixth Great Lake. Several small and scenic islands, like Grand Isle, are popular seasonal getaways in warm weather.

$$ 🏨 **Jay Peak Resort.** Accommodations at Jay Peak include standard hotel
HOTEL   rooms, suites, condominiums, town houses, and new cottage and club-
FAMILY   house suites near the golf course. **Pros:** great for skiers; wide range of
accommodations; kids 14 and under stay and eat free. **Cons:** can get
noisy; not very intimate; service isn't always helpful. $ *Rooms from:*
$264 ⊠ 4850 Rte. 242 ☎ 802/988–2611 ⊕ www.jaypeakresort.com
➯ 321 rooms, studios, and suites; 94 condominiums; 100 cottage suites
❍⎮ Some meals.

$ 🏨 **Phineas Swann Bed & Breakfast Inn.** The top-hatted bulldog on the
B&B/INN   sign of this 1880 farmhouse isn't just a mascot: it reflects the hotel's
welcoming attitude to pet owners. **Pros:** walking distance from shops
and supplies; lots of dogs. **Cons:** decor is a tad old-fashioned; lots of
dogs. $ *Rooms from: $189 ⊠ 195 Main St. ☎ 802/326–4306 ⊕ www.*
phineasswann.com ➯ 3 rooms, 6 suites ❍⎮ Breakfast.

SPORTS AND THE OUTDOORS
ICE-SKATING
FAMILY   **Ice Haus Arena.** The sprawling arena contains a professional-size hockey
rink and seating for 400 spectators. You can practice your stick-han-
dling, and the rink is open to the public for skating several times a week.
There are tournaments throughout the year. ⊠ *830 Jay Peak Rd., Jay*
☎ *802/988–2611 ⊕ www.jaypeakresort.com ⛸ $6.*

SKI AREAS
Hazen's Notch Cross Country Ski Center and B&B. Delightfully remote at
any time of the year, this center has 40 miles of marked and groomed
trails and rents equipment and snowshoes. ⊠ *1419 Hazen's Notch Rd.*
☎ *802/326–4799 ⊕ www.hazensnotch.org ⛸ Trail pass: $12.*

Jay Peak. Sticking up out of the flat farmland, Jay Peak averages 380
inches of snow per year—more than any other Vermont ski area—and
it's renowned for its glade skiing and powder. There are two intercon-
nected mountains, the highest reaching nearly 4,000 feet. The smaller
mountain has straight-fall-line, expert terrain that eases mid-mountain
into an intermediate pitch. Beginners should stay near the bottom on
trails off the Metro quad lift. There are also four terrain parks, snow-
shoeing, telemark skiing, and a state-of-the art ice arena for hockey,
figure skating, and curling. The Pump House, an indoor water park
with pools and slides, is open year-round. **Facilities:** 78 trails; 385 acres;
2,153-foot vertical drop; 9 lifts. ⊠ *830 Jay Peak Rd., Jay ☎ 802/988–*
2611 ⊕ www.jaypeakresort.com ⛸ Lift ticket: $79.

▌ **EN ROUTE**   **Northeast Kingdom.** Routes 14, 5, 58, and 100 make for a scenic drive
around the Northeast Kingdom, so named for the remoteness and stal-
wart independence that have helped preserve its rural nature. You can
extend the loop and head east on Route 105 to the city of Newport on
Lake Memphremagog. Some of the most unspoiled areas in all Vermont
are on the drive south from Newport on either U.S. 5 or Interstate 91
(the latter is faster, but the former is prettier). ⊠ *Montgomery.*

LAKE WILLOUGHBY

30 miles southeast of Montgomery (summer route; 50 miles by winter route), 28 miles north of St. Johnsbury.

The jewel of the Northeast Kingdom is clear, deep, and chilly Lake Willoughby, edged by sheer cliffs and surrounded by state forest. The only town on its shores is tiny Westmore, which has a beach and a few shops that cater to campers and seasonal residents.

EXPLORING

FAMILY **Bread and Puppet Museum.** This ramshackle barn houses a surrealistic collection of props used by the world-renowned Bread and Puppet Theater. The troupe has been performing social and political commentary with the towering (they're supported by people on stilts) and eerily expressive puppets for 50 years. In July and August, there are performances on Saturday night and Sunday afternoon, with museum tours before Sunday shows. ⊠ *753 Heights Rd., 1 mile east of Rte. 16, Glover* ☎ *802/525-3031* ⊕ *www.breadandpuppet.org* ✉ *Donations accepted.*

OFF THE
BEATEN
PATH

Hill Farmstead Brewery. Recognized as one of the country's leading craft-beer producers, Shaun Hill runs his brewery out of a bucolic Greensboro farm. Though it's off the beaten path down a relatively empty dirt road, beer lovers find their way here to sample and buy whatever is available. Area restaurants serve some of Hill's offerings, but this is the only place to buy bottles of the coveted brews. The selections change regularly—check the website for details—and Hill loves trying out new recipes, so you'll always find something interesting and different. This one's a must for microbrew aficionados. ⊠ *403 Hill Rd., 21 miles southwest of Lake Willoughby, off Rte. 16, Greensboro* ✛ *From Rte. 16 take Taylor Rd. northwest to Jaffin Flat north to Hill Rd. west* ☎ *802/533-7450* ⊕ *www.hillfarmstead. com* ✉ *Tasting $5.*

Lake Willoughby. The cliffs of Mt. Pisgah and Mt. Hor drop to the edge of Lake Willoughby on opposite shores, giving this beautiful, deep, glacially carved lake a striking resemblance to a Norwegian fjord. The trails to the top of Mt. Pisgah reward hikers with glorious views. Take note: the beach on the southern end is Vermont's most famous nude beach. ⊠ *Westmore.*

EAST BURKE

17 miles south of Lake Willoughby.

Once a sleepy village, East Burke is now the Northeast Kingdom's outdoor-activity hub. The Kingdom Trails attract thousands of mountain bikers in summer and fall; many of them are groomed for cross-country skiing in winter.

GETTING HERE AND AROUND

From U.S. 5 in Lyndon, take Route 114 northeast 4¾ miles to get to East Burke. (Lyndon is 2 miles southeast of Interstate 91 on Route 122, which becomes Route 114.)

WHERE TO STAY

$$ **Inn at Mountain View Farm.** Animal lovers will jump at the chance to
B&B/INN   stay at this 440-acre estate, home to a farm animal sanctuary. **Pros:**
family friendly; incredible scenery and setting. **Cons:** no dinner; fills
up with weddings. *$ Rooms from: $215 ⊠1 E. Darling Hill Rd.*
☎ 802/626–9924, 800/572–4509 ⊕ www.innmtnview.com ⊗ Closed
Nov.–mid-May ➔9 rooms, 5 suites ⎹⊘⎸Breakfast.

SPORTS AND THE OUTDOORS

BIKING

East Burke Sports. This shop rents, sells, and repairs mountain bikes,
kayaks, skis, snowboards, and snowshoes. The owners are among the
key developers of Kingdom Trails. ⊠ *439 Rte. 114 ☎ 802/626–3215*
⊕ *www.eastburkesports.com.*

Kingdom Trails. Locals maintain this 110-mile network of trails for moun-
tain biking and hiking in the summer, 37 miles of which are groomed
for snowshoeing and cross-country skiing in the winter. ⊠ *478 Rte. 114*
☎ *802/626–0737 ⊕ www.kingdomtrails.com.*

Village Sport Shop. This shop rents bikes, canoes, kayaks, paddleboats,
skis, and snowshoes. There's a satellite store on Darling Hill Road.
⊠ *511 Broad St., Lyndonville ☎ 802/626–8448 ⊕ www.villages-*
portshop.com.

SKI AREA

Q Burke Mountain. About an hour's drive from Montpelier, Q Burke is
a quiet playground compared to the big resorts of the north. A lower
slope of beginner trails is served by separate lifts; the upper slope has
exclusively intermediate and expert runs. In the summer, you can moun-
tain bike down from the summit. A new hotel and convention center
welcomes guests at the base. **Facilities:** 52 trails; 270 acres; 2,111-foot
vertical drop; 6 lifts. ⊠ *1 Mountain Rd. ☎ 802/626–7300 ⊕ www.ski-*
burke.com ➔Lift ticket: $64.

ST. JOHNSBURY

16 miles south of East Burke, 39 miles northeast of Montpelier.

St. Johnsbury, the southern gateway to the Northeast Kingdom, was
chartered as early as 1786, but really only came into its own after 1830,
when Thaddeus Fairbanks invented the platform scale, a device that
revolutionized weighing methods. The Fairbanks family's subsequent
philanthropic efforts left the city with a strong cultural and architec-
tural imprint. Today "St. J," as locals call it, is the friendly, adventure
sports–happy hub of the Northeast Kingdom.

EXPLORING

TOP ATTRACTIONS

FAMILY   **Dog Mountain.** The late Stephen Huneck, an artist and the creator of
Fodor's Choice   Dog Mountain, was famous for his colorful folk art sculptures and
★   paintings of dogs. Much more than an art gallery–gift shop, this
deeply moving spot even has a chapel, where animal lovers can reflect
on their beloved pets. With hiking trails and a swimming pond, this is,

Catch a show and some social commentary at the Bread and Puppet Theater in summer, or visit the museum year-round.

first and foremost, a place to spend time with your dog. ✉ *143 Parks Rd., off Spaulding Rd.* ☎ *800/449–2580* ⊕ *www.dogmt.com* ✉ *Free.*

FAMILY
Fodor's Choice
★

Fairbanks Museum and Planetarium. This odd and deeply thrilling museum displays the eccentric collection of Franklin Fairbanks, who surely had one of the most inquisitive minds in American history. He built this magnificent barrel-vaulted gallery in 1889 to house the specimens of plants, animals, birds, and reptiles, and the collections of folk art and dolls—and a seemingly unending variety of beautifully mounted curios—he picked up around the world. The museum showcases over 175,000 items, but it's surprisingly easy to feast your eyes on everything here without getting a museum headache. The popular 45-seat planetarium is Vermont's only public planetarium, and there's also the Eye on the Sky Weather Gallery, home to live NPR weather broadcasts. ✉ *1302 Main St.* ☎ *802/748–2372* ⊕ *www.fairbanksmuseum. org* ✉ *Museum $8, planetarium $3–$5.*

WORTH NOTING

Catamount Arts. At the Northeast Kingdom's art hub you can catch a movie, check out an art exhibit, attend a concert, or take a class. Catamount also stages performances at larger regional venues. ✉ *115 Eastern Ave.* ☎ *802/748–2600* ⊕ *www.catamountarts.org.*

Peacham. Tiny Peacham, 10 miles southwest of St. Johnsbury, is on almost every tour group's list of "must-sees." With views extending to the White Mountains of New Hampshire and a white-steeple church, Peacham is perhaps the most photographed town in New England. The movie adaptation of *Ethan Frome,* starring Liam Neeson, was filmed here. The soups and stews are especially tasty at **Peacham Café,** which serves breakfast and lunch. Next door, the **Peacham Corner Guild** sells local handicrafts. ⊠ *Peacham* ⊕ *www.peacham.net.*

St. Johnsbury Athenaeum. With its polished Victorian woodwork, dramatic paneling, and ornate circular staircases, this building is both the town library—one of the nicest you're likely to ever come across—and one of the oldest art galleries in the country, housing more than 100 original works, mainly from the Hudson River school. Albert Bierstadt's enormous *Domes of Yosemite* dominates the beautiful painting gallery. ⊠ *1171 Main St.* ☎ *802/748–8291* ⊕ *www.stjathenaeum.org* ⊠ *Free.*

WHERE TO EAT AND STAY

$

AMERICAN

✕ **Dylan's Café.** Inside St. Johnsbury's redbrick former post office, this sparsely decorated gallery space and restaurant offers a reliable lineup of fresh soups, salads, and sandwiches for lunch. Heartier fare is served for dinner, like the mahimahi tacos and grilled short ribs—the cheddar-bacon burger is popular. So is brunch, where you can get fine eggs Benedict or huevos rancheros. There are also baked goods and daily specials, and in good weather you can sit outside. $ *Average main: $15* ⊠ *139 Eastern Ave.* ☎ *802/748–6748* ⊙ *No dinner Sun.–Tues.*

$

B&B/INN

▦ **Emergo Farm.** Bebo and Lori Webster rent out three guest rooms and a suite in their 1890 farmhouse on a 240-acre working dairy farm that has been in their family for six generations (counting their son Justin, who works on the farm). **Pros:** simple but clean; peaceful setting. **Cons:** very remote; only open seasonally. $ *Rooms from: $120* ⊠ *261 Webster Hill Rd., 8 miles west of St. Johnsbury, Danville* ☎ *802/684–2215, 888/383–1185* ⊕ *www.emergofarm.com* ⊙ *Closed Nov.–Apr.* ➴ *3 rooms, 1 suite* ▯⊙▯ *Breakfast.*

$$

B&B/INN

▦ **Rabbit Hill Inn.** Few inns in New England garner the word-of-mouth buzz that Rabbit Hill seems to from its satisfied guests. **Pros:** attractive, spacious rooms; romantic; gardens and trails; good food. **Cons:** might be too quiet a setting for some. $ *Rooms from: $215* ⊠ *48 Lower Waterford Rd., 11 miles south of St. Johnsbury, Lower Waterford* ⊕ *www.rabbithillinn.com* ⊙ *Closed Apr. and 1st 2 wks of Nov.* ➴ *18 rooms, 1 suite* ▯⊙▯ *Breakfast.*

NEW HAMPSHIRE

WELCOME TO NEW HAMPSHIRE

TOP REASONS TO GO

★ **The White Mountains:** Great for hiking and skiing, these dramatic peaks and notches are unforgettable.

★ **Lake Winnipesaukee:** Water parks, arcades, boat cruises, and classic summer camps fuel a whole season of family fun.

★ **Fall Foliage:** Head to the Kancamagus Highway in autumn for one of America's best drives, or seek out a less-trafficked route that's equally stunning.

★ **Portsmouth:** Less than an hour's drive from Boston, this great American city has coastline allure, colorful Colonial architecture, romantic dining, and fine arts and crafts.

★ **Pristine Towns:** Jaffrey Center, Walpole, Tamworth, Center Sandwich, and Jackson are among the most charming tiny villages in New England.

1 **The Seacoast.** You can find historic sites, hopping bars, beaches, and both whale-watching and deep-sea fishing opportunities along New Hampshire's 18 miles of coastline. Hampton Beach is the center of summertime activities, while Portsmouth is a hub of nightlife, dining, art, and Colonial history.

2 **Lakes Region.** Throughout central New Hampshire are lakes and more lakes. The largest, Lake Winnipesaukee, has 240 miles of coastline and attracts all sorts of water-sports enthusiasts, but there are many quiet, secluded lakes with enchanting B&Bs where relaxation is the main activity.

3 **The White Mountains.** Skiing, snowshoeing, and snowboarding in the winter; hiking, biking, and riding scenic railways in the summer: the Whites, as locals call their mountains, have plenty of natural wonders—some just a stone's throw from the road, others a lung-busting hike through the backcountry. Mt. Washington, the tallest mountain in the Northeast, can be conquered by trail, train, or car.

4 **Lake Sunapee.** Quiet villages can be found throughout the Lake Sunapee region. Many seem barely removed from Colonial times, and others thrive as centers of arts and education, filled with quaint shops. Hanover, home to Dartmouth College (founded 1769), retains that true New England college-town feel, with ivy-draped buildings and cobblestone walkways. Lake Sunapee itself is a wonderful place to swim, fish, or enjoy a cruise.

5 **The Monadnocks and Merrimack Valley.** New and old coexist in the Granite State's southwestern region, where high-tech firms have helped reshape the cities of Manchester and Nashua while small towns in the hills surrounding Mt. Monadnock celebrate tradition and history.

GETTING ORIENTED

Although New Hampshire has three interstates (I–95, I–93, and I–89), most of its regions are accessible only by smaller, rural roads. From Boston or Portland, Maine, Interstate 95 provides access to Portsmouth and beaches, though many people like the drive along Route 1A, which runs parallel to the coast. North of Portsmouth, Route 16 leads to the White Mountains and the lakes region, home to Lake Winnipesaukee. From there, Interstate 93 cuts north toward Franconia and Littleton and south into Concord, Manchester, and Nashua. State roads east and north of Interstate 93 lead to Dixville Notch and the Connecticut Lakes. Following the Connecticut River takes you to Hanover, Claremont, Charleston, Walpole, and Keene. From Concord, travelers head west to reach the Monadnock Region.

Updated by
Debbie Hagan

New Hampshire's mountain peaks, clear air, and sparkling lakes have attracted trailblazers and artists (and untold numbers of tourists) for centuries. The state's varied geography—not to mention the range of outdoor activities its mountains, lakes, and forests support—is part of the attraction, but hospitality and friendliness are major factors, too: visitors tend to feel quickly at home in this place of beauty and history. Whether you're an outdoors enthusiast seeking adventure or just want to enjoy a good book on the porch swing of a century-old inn, you'll find plenty of opportunities to fulfill your heart's desire.

Ralph Waldo Emerson, Henry David Thoreau, Nathaniel Hawthorne, and Louisa May Alcott all visited and wrote about the state, sparking a fervent literary tradition that continues today. It also has a strong political history: this was the first colony to declare independence from Great Britain, the first to adopt a state constitution, and the first to require its constitution be referred to the people for approval.

The state's diverse terrain makes it popular with everyone from avid adventurers to young families looking for easy access to nature. You can hike, climb, ski, snowboard, snowshoe, and fish, as well as explore on snowmobiles, sailboats, and mountain bikes. New Hampshirites have no objection to others enjoying the beauty here as long as they leave a few dollars behind: the state has long resisted both sales and income taxes, so tourism brings in much-needed revenue.

With a number of cities consistently rated among the most livable in the nation, New Hampshire has seen considerable growth over the past decade. Longtime residents worry that the state will soon develop two distinct personalities: one characterized by rapid urbanization in the southeast and the other by quiet village life in the west and north. Although newcomers have brought change, the free-spirited sensibility of the Granite State remains intact, as does its natural splendor.

PLANNING

WHEN TO GO

Summer and fall are the best times to visit most of New Hampshire. Winter is a great time to travel to the White Mountains, but most other tourist sights in the state, including museums in Portsmouth and many attractions in the Lakes Region, are closed due to snow and cold weather. In summer people flock to beaches, mountain trails, and lakeside boat launches; in the cities, festivals showcase music, theater, and crafts. Fall brings leaf peepers, especially to the White Mountains and along the Kancamagus Highway (Route 112). Skiers and snowboarders take to the slopes in winter, when Christmas lights and carnivals brighten the long, dark nights. Spring's unpredictable weather—along with April's mud and late May's black flies—tends to deter visitors. Still, the season has its joys, not the least of which is the appearance, mid-May–early June, of the state flower, the purple lilac, soon followed by the blooming of colorful rhododendrons.

PLANNING YOUR TIME

Some people come to New Hampshire to hike or ski the mountains, fish and sail the lakes, or cycle along backcountry roads. Others prefer to drive through scenic towns, stopping at museums and shops along the way. Although New Hampshire is a small state, roads curve around lakes and mountains, making distances longer than they appear on a map. You can get a taste of the coast, lake, and mountain areas in three to five days; eight days will give you time to make a more complete loop.

AIR TRAVEL

Manchester Boston Regional Airport, the state's largest airport, has nonstop service from more than a dozen cities. The drive from Boston's Logan Airport to most places in New Hampshire takes one–three hours; the same is true for Bradley International Airport in Hartford, Connecticut.

BIKE TRAVEL

A safe, scenic route along New Hampshire's seacoast is the bike path along Route 1A, where you can park at Odiorne Point and follow the road 14 miles south to Seabrook. Another pretty route runs from Newington Town Hall to the Great Bay Estuary. White Mountains routes are detailed in the *White Mountain Ride Guide,* which is sold at area sporting-goods stores and bookshops and online at Amazon.com. There's also a bike path in Franconia Notch State Park, and a mountain-biking center, Great Glen Trails, at the base of Mt. Washington. Many ski areas offer lift services to mountain bikers in summer.

Maps, Routes, Tours, Information Bike New England. ⊕ *www.bikenewengland.com.*

CAR TRAVEL

New Hampshire is an easy drive north from Boston and serves as a good base for exploring Northern New England. Many destinations are near major highways, so getting around by car is a great way to travel. Interstate 93 stretches from Boston to Littleton and on into neighboring Vermont. Interstate 89 will get you from Concord to Hanover and eventually to Burlington, Vermont. To the east, Interstate 95 (a toll road) passes through southern New Hampshire's coastal area on its way from Massachusetts to Maine. Throughout the state are quiet backcountry lanes and winding roads that might take a little longer but can make for some of the best parts of the journey.

The speed limit on interstate and limited-access highways is usually 65 mph, except in heavily settled areas, where 55 mph is the norm. On state and U.S. routes, speed limits vary considerably. On any given stretch, the limit may be anywhere from 25 mph to 55 mph, so watch the signs carefully. Right turns on red lights are permitted unless otherwise indicated. The website of the **New Hampshire Department of Transportation** (⊕ *hb.511nh. com*) has up-to-the-minute information about traffic and road conditions.

TRAIN TRAVEL

Amtrak's *Downeaster* passenger train operates between Boston and Portland, Maine, with New Hampshire stops in Exeter, Durham, and Dover.

Amtrak. ☎ *800/872–7245* ⊕ *www.amtrakdowneaster.com.*

RESTAURANTS

New Hampshire prides itself on its seafood: not only lobster, but also salmon pie, steamed mussels, fried clams, and seared tuna. Across the state you'll find country taverns with upscale Continental and American menus, many of them emphasizing regional ingredients. Alongside a growing number of contemporary restaurants are such state traditions as greasy-spoon diners, pizzerias, and pubs that serve hearty comfort fare. No matter where you go, reservations are seldom required, and dress is casual. *Restaurant prices are the average cost of a main course at dinner or, if dinner is not served, at lunch.*

HOTELS

In the mid-19th century, wealthy Bostonians retreated to imposing New Hampshire country homes in the summer. Grand hotels were built across the state, especially in the White Mountains, which at that time competed with Saratoga Springs, Newport, and Bar Harbor to draw the nation's elite vacationers. A handful of these hotel-resorts survive, with their large kitchen staffs and their tradition of top-notch service. And many of those country houses have since been converted into inns. The smallest have only a couple of rooms and are typically done in period style; the largest contain 30 or more rooms and suites and have in-room fireplaces and even hot tubs. You'll also find a great many well-kept, often family-owned motor lodges, particularly in the White Mountains and Lakes regions. In ski areas, expect the usual ski condos and lodges. In the Merrimack River valley, as well as along major highways, chain hotels and motels predominate. The state's numerous campgrounds accommodate RVers and tent campers alike. The White Mountains provide an excellent base for camping and hiking.

OUTDOOR ACTIVITIES

Skiing: Ski areas abound in New Hampshire, among them Bretton Woods, Mt. Sunapee, Waterville Valley, and Cannon Mountain. For cross-country skiing, nothing beats Gunstock Mountain Resort, with 32 miles of trails, also open for snowshoeing. Or visit Franconia Village, which has 37 miles of cross-country trails.

Biking: Many ski resorts in the White Mountains offer mountain-biking opportunities, providing chairlift rides to the mountaintop and trails for all skill levels at the bottom. Some of the state's best road biking can be found along the Kancamagus Highway and around Lake Sunapee.

Hiking: For the adventurous, hiking the White Mountains or along the Appalachian Trail is the reason for visiting. For those interested in less arduous treks, there are plenty of day hikes in the White Mountain National Forest and in state parks like Pisgah in Cheshire County, the Crawford Notch and Franconia Notch state parks in the Whites, and Mt. Monadnock.

Hotel prices are the lowest cost of a standard double room in high season. Some inns add a 15%–18% service charge. Hotel reviews have been shortened. For full information, visit Fodors.com.

WHAT IT COSTS			
	$	**$$**	**$$$**	**$$$$**
Restaurants	under $18	$18–$24	$25–$35	over $35
Hotels	under $200	$200–$299	$300–$399	over $399

VISITOR INFORMATION

Contacts New Hampshire State Parks. ☎ 603/271-3556 ⊕ www.nhstate-parks.org. **Visit New Hampshire.** ☎ 603/271-2665, 800/386-4664 *for vacation kit (also available via website)* ⊕ www.visitnh.gov.

THE SEACOAST

New Hampshire's 18-mile stretch of coastline packs in a wealth of scenery and diversions. The honky-tonk of Hampton Beach gets plenty of attention—good and bad—but first-timers are often surprised by the significant portion of the shoreline that remains pristine, especially through the town of Rye. This section begins in the regional hub, Portsmouth; cuts down the coast to the beaches; branches inland to the prep-school town of Exeter; and runs back up north through Dover, Durham (home to the University of New Hampshire), and Rochester; from here it's a short drive to the Lakes Region.

ESSENTIALS
Visitor Information Seacoast New Hampshire & South Coast Maine.
☎ *603/427–2020* ⊕ *www.seacoastnh.com.*

PORTSMOUTH

47 miles southeast of Concord; 50 miles southwest of Portland, Maine; 56 miles north of Boston.

Fodor's Choice
★

More than a quaint harbor town with a long, colorful history, Portsmouth is an upscale community with trendy farm-to-table restaurants, contemporary art galleries, and cultural venues that host nationally recognized speakers and performers. Swank cocktail bars, jumping live music, and late-night eateries create a convivial evening buzz in downtown's Market Square. Settled in 1623 as Strawbery Banke, Portsmouth grew into a prosperous port before the Revolutionary War, during which it harbored many Tory sympathizers. These days, this city of 22,000 has many grand residences from the 18th to the early 20th century; some of them can be found among the restored buildings that make up the Strawbery Banke Museum.

GETTING HERE AND AROUND
Both Interstate 95 and Route 1 run through Portsmouth. From the west, take Route 101 and from the north take Route 16. Amtrak runs through Durham, which is a short drive from the coast. Downtown Portsmouth is walkable, though you'll need a car for attractions farther afield.

ESSENTIALS
Bus and Trolley COAST Bus. ☎ *603/743–5777* ⊕ *www.coastbus.org.*

Taxi Anchor Taxi. ☎ *603/436–1888* ⊕ *www.anchortaxicab.com.* **Annie's Taxi.**
☎ *603/531–9955* ⊕ *www.anniestaxi.com.*

Visitor Information Greater Portsmouth Chamber of Commerce. ⊠ *500 Market St.* ☎ *603/610–5510* ⊕ *www.portsmouthchamber.org.*

FESTIVALS
FAMILY   **Prescott Park Arts Festival.** This outdoor festival presents theater, dance, and music events June–August. ⊠ *105 Marcy St.* ☎ *603/436–2848* ⊕ *www.prescottpark.org.*

BOAT TOURS
FAMILY   **Gundalow Company.** Sail the Piscataqua River in a flat-bottom gundalow (a type of barge) built at Strawbery Banke. Help the crew set sail, steer the vessel, and trawl for plankton while learning about the region's history from an onboard educator. Passengers are welcome to bring food and beverages on the boat. ⊠ *60 Marcy St.* ☎ *603/433–9505* ⊕ *www. gundalow.org* ☎ *From $20* ◷ *Closed Nov.–late May.*

FAMILY   **Isles of Shoals Steamship Company.** This company runs cruises aboard the *Thomas Laighton,* a replica of a Victorian steamship. Cruises take you to the Isles of Shoals, Portsmouth Harbor, or the nearby lighthouses. Lunches and light snacks are available on board, or you can bring your own. ⊠ *Barker Wharf, 315 Market St.* ☎ *603/431–5500, 800/441–4620* ⊕ *www.islesofshoals.com* ☎ *From $24* ◷ *Closed Nov.–Apr.*

Portsmouth Harbor Cruises. Tours of Portsmouth Harbor and the Isles of Shoals, inland-river foliage trips, and sunset cruises are all in this company's repertoire. ⊠ *64 Ceres St.* ☎ *603/436–8084, 800/776–0915* ⊕ *www.portsmouthharbor.com* ✉ *From $18* ⊙ *Closed Nov.–Apr.*

FAMILY **Portsmouth Kayak Adventures.** Explore the Piscataqua River Basin and the New Hampshire coastline on a guided kayak or stand-up paddleboard tour. Beginners are welcome (instruction included). ⊠ *185 Wentworth Rd.* ☎ *603/559–1000* ⊕ *www.portsmouthkayak.com* ✉ *From $45* ⊙ *Closed mid-Oct.–May.*

WALKING TOURS

FAMILY **Discover Portsmouth.** The Portsmouth Historical Society operates this combination visitor center–museum, where you can pick up maps, get the scoop on what's happening while you're in town, and view cultural and historical exhibits. Discover Portsmouth is also the place to learn about self-guided historical tours and to sign up for guided ones. ⊠ *10 Middle St.* ☎ *603/436–8433* ⊕ *www.portsmouthhistory.org* ✉ *Tours from $12.*

FAMILY **Portsmouth Black Heritage Trail.** Important local sites in African American history can be seen on the 90-minute guided Sankofa Tour. Included are the African Burying Ground and historic homes of local slave traders and abolitionists. Tours, which begin at Strawbery Banke, are conducted on Saturday throughout the summer. ⊠ *Discover Portsmouth, 10 Middle St.* ☎ *603/380–1231* ⊕ *www.portsmouthhistory.org* ✉ *$15.*

EXPLORING
TOP ATTRACTIONS

Albacore Park. Built in Portsmouth in 1953, the USS *Albacore* is the centerpiece of Albacore Park. You can board this prototype submarine, which served as a floating laboratory to test an innovative hull design, dive brakes, and sonar systems for the Navy. The visitor center exhibits *Albacore* artifacts, and the nearby Memorial Garden is dedicated to those who have lost their lives in submarine service. ⊠ *600 Market St.* ☎ *603/436–3680* ⊕ *www.ussalbacore.org* ✉ *$7.*

FAMILY **Great Bay Estuarine National Research Reserve.** Just inland from Portsmouth is one of southeastern New Hampshire's most precious assets. In this 10,235 acres of open and tidal waters, you can spot blue herons, ospreys, and snowy egrets, particularly during the spring and fall migrations. The Great Bay Discovery Center has indoor and outdoor exhibits, a library and bookshop, and a 1,700-foot boardwalk, as well as other trails, which wind through mudflats and upland forest. ⊠ *89 Depot Rd., Greenland* ☎ *603/778–0015* ⊕ *www.greatbay.org* ✉ *Free.*

FAMILY **John Paul Jones House.** Revolutionary War hero John Paul Jones lived at this boardinghouse while he supervised construction of the USS *America* for the Continental Navy. The 1758 hip-roof building displays furniture, costumes, glass, guns, portraits, and documents from the late 18th century. The collection's specialty is textiles, among them some extraordinary early-19th-century embroidery samplers. ⊠ *43 Middle St.* ☎ *603/436–8420* ⊕ *www.portsmouthhistory.org* ✉ *$6.*

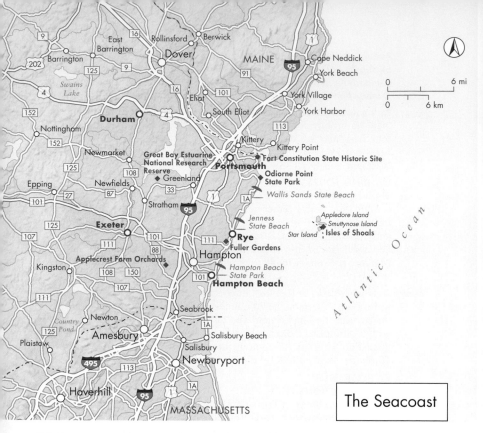

The Seacoast

QUICK
BITES

Breaking New Grounds. If you're going out to dinner, consider skipping the coffee and dessert and instead head here for a hot beverage and a pastry, gelato, or other sweet treat. In nice weather, sit outside and soak up the street entertainment. ⊠ *14 Market Sq.* ☎ *603/436-9555* ⊕ *www.bngcoffee.com.*

Redhook Ale Brewery. Guided tours of this brewery take just under an hour and end with a beer tasting; participants receive a souvenir tasting glass. You can also stop at the Cataqua Public House for a mug of ale and a bite to eat. The grounds host many summer events, including August's outdoor multiband concert, Hookfest. ⊠ *Pease International Tradeport, 1 Redhook Way* ☎ *603/430-8600* ⊕ *www. redhook.com* ✉ *$5.*

FAMILY
Fodor's Choice
★

Strawbery Banke Museum. The first English settlers named the area around today's Portsmouth for the wild strawberries along the shores of the Piscataqua River. The name survives in this 10-acre outdoor history museum, one of the largest in New England. The compound has 38 homes and other structures dating from 1695 to 1820, some restored and furnished to a particular period, others used for historical exhibits. Half of the interior of the Shapley-Drisco House (built in 1795) depicts its use as a dry-goods store in Colonial times; its living room and kitchen are decorated as they were in the 1950s, showing how buildings were adapted over time. The Shapiro House has been restored to reflect the life of the Russian-Jewish immigrant family who lived there in the early 1900s. Perhaps the most opulent house, done in decadent Victorian style, is the 1860 Goodwin Mansion, former home of Governor Ichabod Goodwin. ⊠ *14 Hancock St.* ☎ *603/433–1100* ⊕ *www.strawberybanke.org* 🎫 *$20.*

WORTH NOTING

FAMILY **Fort Constitution State Historic Site.** The original military outpost on the island of New Castle was built on this site in 1631 and rebuilt in 1666 as Fort William and Mary, a British stronghold overlooking Portsmouth Harbor. The fort earned its fame in 1774, when patriots raided it in one of Revolutionary America's first overtly defiant acts against King George III. Munitions captured here were used against the British at the Battle of Bunker Hill. The structure was renamed Fort Constitution in 1791; the current ruins date to 1808. The fort commands a great view of nearby Portsmouth Lighthouse. ⊠ *25 Wentworth Rd., off Rte. 1B* ✛ *Park at Battery Farnsworth and walk into Coast Guard Station* ☎ *603/436–1552* ⊕ *www.nhstateparks.org* 🎫 *Free.*

FAMILY **Moffatt-Ladd House and Garden.** The period interior of this 1763 home tells the story of Portsmouth's merchant class through portraits, letters, and furnishings. The Colonial Revival garden includes a horse chestnut tree planted by General William Whipple when he returned home after signing the Declaration of Independence in 1776. ⊠ *154 Market St.* ☎ *603/436–8221* ⊕ *www.moffattladd.org* 🎫 *$7 garden and house, $2 garden only.*

QUICK BITES **Annabelle's Natural Ice Cream.** Drop by Annabelle's for a dish of maple-walnut ice cream or rich French vanilla, made with golden egg yolks. ⊠ *49 Ceres St.* ☎ *603/436–3400* ⊕ *www.annabellesicecream.com.*

Warner House. The highlight of this circa 1716 gem is the curious folk-art murals lining the hall staircase, which may be the oldest-known murals in the United States still gracing their original structure. The house, a notable example of Georgian architecture, contains original art, furnishings, and extraordinary examples of area craftsmanship. The west-wall lightning rod is believed to have been installed in 1762 under the supervision of Benjamin Franklin. ⊠ *150 Daniel St.* ☎ *603/436–5909* ⊕ *www.warnerhouse.org* 🎫 *$7.*

FAMILY **Wentworth-Coolidge Mansion Historic Site.** A National Historic Landmark now part of Little Harbor State Park, this was originally the residence of Benning Wentworth, New Hampshire's first royal governor (1741–67). Notable among its period furnishings is the carved pine mantelpiece in the council chamber. Wentworth's imported lilac trees bloom each May. Call ahead for house tours, offered on the hour until 3. Also worth a look is the Drift Gallery, which exhibits contemporary art in the adjacent visitor center. ⊠ *375 Little Harbor Rd., near South Street Cemetery* ☎ *603/436–6607* ⊕ *www.nhstateparks.org* 🎫 *$5.*

Strawbery Banke Museum includes period gardens and 38 historic buildings.

OFF THE BEATEN PATH

Isles of Shoals. Four of the nine, small rocky Isles of Shoals belong to New Hampshire (the other five belong to Maine), many of them still known by the earthy names—Hog and Smuttynose, to cite but two—17th-century fishermen bestowed on them. A history of piracy, murder, and ghosts suffuses the archipelago, long populated by an independent lot who, according to one writer, hadn't the sense to winter on the mainland. Celia Thaxter, a native islander, romanticized these islands with her poetry in *Among the Isles of Shoals* (1873). In the late 19th century, **Appledore Island** became an offshore retreat for Thaxter's coterie of writers, musicians, and artists. **Star Island** contains a small museum, the Rutledge Marine Lab, with interactive family exhibits. From May to late October you can take a narrated history cruise of the Isles of Shoals, a day trip to Star Island, or a walking tour of Star Island with Isles of Shoals Steamship Company. ⊠ *315 Market St.* ☎ *800/441–4620* ⊕ *www.islesofshoals.com* 🚢 *4-hr trip $42, 1-hr guided walk $35.*

OFF THE BEATEN PATH

Prescott Park. Picnicking is popular at this waterfront park, whose large formal garden with fountains is perfect for whiling away an afternoon. The park contains Point of Graves, Portsmouth's oldest burial ground, and two 17th-century warehouses. The summerlong Prescott Park Arts Festival features concerts, outdoor movies, and food-related events. ⊠ *105 Marcy St.* ☎ *603/436–2848* ⊕ *www.prescottpark.org.*

WHERE TO EAT

$$$
INTERNATIONAL
Fodor's Choice
★

✕ **Black Trumpet Bistro.** Award-winning chef Evan Mallett brings the bold flavors of Latin America, North Africa, Turkey, and Mexico to bear on the eclectic fare of this romantic harbor-view restaurant. The menu is constantly changing, offering such delights as roasted allium soup, rabbit-and-mushroom enchiladas, and potato and cheese pierogi with smoked-corn bisque and a salad with sautéed kale and blueberries. Mallett belongs to the Heirloom Harvest Project and brings unusual vegetables—sometimes in surprising colors—to the table. Vegetarians will always find out-of-the-ordinary entrées. On busy nights, walk-ins might find a table in the upstairs wine bar. $ *Average main: $25* ✉ *29 Ceres St.* ☎ *603/431–0887* ⊕ *www.blacktrumpetbistro.com* ☾ *No lunch.*

$$ **✕ Blue Mermaid Island Grill.** This fun, colorful place is good for seafood,
CARIBBEAN sandwiches, and quesadillas. Specialties include plantain-encrusted cod
FAMILY topped with a grilled mango vinaigrette and served with grilled banana–sweet potato hash, and short ribs braised in a guava-soy reduction and accompanied by garlic–green onion mashed potatoes. In summer you can eat on a deck that overlooks adorable Colonial homes. There's live music on most nights of the week. $ *Average main: $20* ✉ *409 The Hill* ☎ *603/427–2583* ⊕ *www.bluemermaid.com.*

$ **✕ The Friendly Toast.** In this 1950s-era throwback, furnished with chrome
AMERICAN dinette sets and adorned with atomic-age memorabilia, you might expect
FAMILY molded Jell-O salad on the menu—but you'd be wrong. Instead, you'll find the biggest and best breakfasts featuring hefty omelets, Coconut Cakes (buttermilk pancakes made with chocolate chips, coconut, and cashews), and Drunkard French toast (with a Grand Marnier–raspberry sauce). The homemade breads and muffins are worth trying, too, and the cheese fries—topped with blue cheese and served with a raspberry-habanero dipping sauce—are completely addictive. This is also a great stop for lunch, dinner, or a quick snack. $ *Average main: $13* ✉ *113 Congress St.* ☎ *603/430–2154* ⊕ *www.thefriendlytoast.net.*

$$$ **✕ Jumpin' Jay's Fish Cafe.** A wildly popular downtown spot, this offbeat,
SEAFOOD dimly lighted eatery has a changing menu of fresh seafood from as far away as Iceland and Costa Rica. Try the steamed Prince Edward Island mussels with jalapeños, spicy ginger, and saffron sauce, or the haddock with lemon, white wine, and capers. Or go with one of the fresh catches, topped with one of seven different sauces. Singles like to gather at the central bar for dinner and furtive glances. $ *Average main: $25* ✉ *150 Congress St.* ☎ *603/766–3474* ⊕ *www.jumpinjays.com.*

$$$ **✕ Library Restaurant.** Bibliophiles may find themselves fully enraptured
STEAKHOUSE while dining in this historic library whose hand-carved ceiling was constructed by the Pullman Car woodworkers in 1889. The paneling is Spanish mahogany, and the original lighting fixtures are by Shreve, Crump & Low of Boston. Although the kitchen offers light dishes, such as jumbo crab cakes and crispy fried shrimp served with a sweet chili sauce, the mainstays are thick-cut, juicy steaks and chops. (The crushed-peppercorn steak is meat heaven.) Choose from six different rich, creamy sauces, including hollandaise and Gorgonzola, plus an array of fresh vegetables. The English-style pub serves nearly 100 martinis made from more than 250 brands of international vodkas. Sunday brunch is popular here. $ *Average main: $34* ✉ *401 State St.* ☎ *603/431–5202* ⊕ *www.libraryrestaurant.com.*

$ **✕ Poco's Bow Street Cantina.** This casual but contemporary eatery turns
LATIN AMERICAN out exceptional Southwestern and Latin American cuisine. Cajun red snapper tacos, fried calamari, and lobster quesadillas are among the best

choices. Most tables have views of the Piscataqua River. The downstairs bar and spacious outdoor deck are local hangouts—try one of the craft cocktails, perhaps a cucumber martini. $ *Average main: $14* ⊠ *37 Bow St.* ☎ *603/431–5967* ⊕ *www.pocosbowstreetcantina.com* ⚱ *Reservations not accepted.*

WHERE TO STAY

$
HOTEL
⊞ **Ale House Inn.** Talk about prime location: this urban-style hotel is steps from the city's historic houses, boutiques, and restaurants. **Pros:** welcome beers from local breweries upon arrival; complimentary tickets to local theater; bicycles for local jaunts. **Cons:** no breakfast; 12 steps to enter hotel. $ *Rooms from: $199* ⊠ *121 Bow St.* ☎ *603/431–7760* ⊕ *www.alehouseinn.com* ⇗ *10 rooms* ⟡ *No meals.*

$$
HOTEL
⊞ **Hotel Portsmouth.** John E. Sise, a wealthy ship merchant, built this downtown hotel's main Queen Anne Victorian structure in 1881, and it retains its original architectural beauty and charm. **Pros:** downtown location near most attractions; free parking; lounge serving wine, beer, and small bites. **Cons:** light Continental breakfast; no desks in guest rooms. $ *Rooms from: $249* ⊠ *40 Court St.* ☎ *603/433–1200* ⊕ *www. thehotelportsmouth.com* ⇗ *28 rooms, 4 suites* ⟡ *Breakfast.*

$
B&B/INN
⊞ **Martin Hill Inn.** You may fall in love with this yellow 1815 house surrounded by flower-filled gardens, a 10- to 15-minute walk from the historic district and the waterfront. **Pros:** refrigerators in rooms; central location; furnished with antiques; off-street parking. **Cons:** not in historic district. $ *Rooms from: $190* ⊠ *404 Islington St.* ☎ *603/436–2287* ⊕ *www.martinhillinn.com* ⇗ *7 rooms* ⟡ *Breakfast.*

$$$
RESORT
Fodor'sChoice
★
⊞ **Wentworth by the Sea.** What's not to love about this white colossus overlooking the sea on New Castle Island? Built in 1874 as a summer resort and popular with East Coast socialites, wealthy patrons, and former presidents, the hotel, run by Marriott, retains its grand feel. **Pros:** great spa; spectacular Sunday brunch; new tennis court (rackets and balls available); marina with charters for harbor cruises and deep-sea fishing. **Cons:** not in downtown Portsmouth. $ *Rooms from: $339* ⊠ *588 Wentworth Rd., New Castle* ☎ *603/422–7322, 866/384–0709* ⊕ *www.wentworth.com* ⛳ *18-hole championship course* ⇗ *161 rooms, 31 suites* ⟡ *Some meals.*

NIGHTLIFE AND PERFORMING ARTS
NIGHTLIFE

BARS
Two Ceres Street. This artsy bar serves original martinis, like the Lumberjack (Maker's Mark and maple syrup) and the Hammer and Sickle (Grey Goose vodka, peperoncini, and olive juice), plus small plates. ⊠ *2 Ceres St.* ☎ *603/433–2373* ⊕ *www.twocerestreet.com.*

MUSIC
Portsmouth Gas Light Co. This brick-oven pizzeria hosts local rock bands in its lounge, courtyard, and slick upstairs space. ⊠ *64 Market St.* ☎ *603/430–9122* ⊕ *www.portsmouthgaslight.com.*

The Press Room. People come from Boston and Portland just to hang out at the Press Room, which showcases folk, jazz, blues, and bluegrass performers nightly. ⊠ *77 Daniel St.* ☎ *603/431–5186* ⊕ *www. pressroomnh.com.*

Four of the nine rocky Isles of Shoals belong to New Hampshire; the other five belong to Maine.

The Red Door Lounge. Discover the local music scene at the Red Door. Indie music fans shouldn't miss Monday night's Hush Hush Sweet Harlot live music series. ✉ *107 State St.* ⊕ *www.reddoorportsmouth.com.*

PERFORMING ARTS

FAMILY **Music Hall.** Beloved for its acoustics, the 1878 hall presents top-drawer music concerts, from pop to classical, along with dance and theater. The more intimate Music Hall Loft, around the corner, screens art films and hosts lectures by leading writers and artists. ✉ *28 Chestnut St.* ☎ *603/436–2400* ⊕ *www.themusichall.org.*

SHOPPING

Market Square, in the center of town, has gift and clothing boutiques, book and gourmet food shops, and exquisite crafts stores.

Byrne & Carlson. Watch elegant chocolates being made in the European tradition at this small shop. ✉ *121 State St.* ☎ *888/559–9778* ⊕ *www. byrneandcarlson.com.*

Nahcotta. Stylish ceramics, jewelry, glassware, and art fill this contemporary design boutique. ✉ *110 Congress St.* ☎ *603/433–1705* ⊕ *www. nahcotta.com.*

N.W. Barrett Gallery. Marine paintings and handmade jewelry, pottery, and glass are featured in this gallery. You'll also find one-of-a-kind lamps and rocking chairs. ✉ *53 Market St.* ☎ *603/431–4262* ⊕ *www. nwbarrett.com.*

Piscataqua Fine Arts. This gallery mainly shows works by master wood-cutter Don Gorvett, who creates spellbinding scenes of New England's coast, particularly the Portsmouth area. There are also works by some of New England's finest printmakers, including Sidney Hurwitz, Alex deConstant, and Sean Hurley. ⊠ *123 Market St.* ☏ *603/436–7278* ⊕ *www.dongorvettgallery.com.*

RYE

8 miles south of Portsmouth.

On Route 1A, as it winds south through Rye, you'll pass a group of late-19th- and early-20th-century mansions known as **Millionaires' Row.** Because of the way the road curves, the drive south along this route is breathtaking. In 1623 the English established a settlement at Odiorne Point in what is now the largely undeveloped and picturesque town of Rye, making it the birthplace of New Hampshire. Today, the area's main draws include a lovely state park, beaches, and the views from Route 1A. Strict town laws have prohibited commercial development in Rye, creating a dramatic contrast with its frenetic neighbor, Hampton Beach.

GETTING HERE AND AROUND
Interstate 95 and U.S. 1, both west of town, provide the easiest access, but Rye shows its best face from Route 1A, which leads north from Hampton Beach and south from Portsmouth along the coast.

EXPLORING

FAMILY
Fodor'sChoice
★

Odiorne Point State Park. These 135 acres of protected seaside land are where David Thompson established the first permanent English settlement in what is now New Hampshire. Several nature trails from which you can enjoy vistas of the nearby Isles of Shoals have informative panels describing the park's military history. The rocky shore's tidal pools shelter crabs, periwinkles, and sea anemones. Throughout the year, the **Seacoast Science Center** hosts exhibits on the area's natural history. Its tidal-pool touch tank and 1,000-gallon Gulf of Maine deepwater aquarium are popular with kids. There are also guided nature walks. ⊠ *570 Ocean Blvd.* ☏ *603/436–8043* ⊕ *www.seacoastsciencecenter.org* ⊠ *$10.*

BEACHES

Jenness State Beach. Good for swimming and sunbathing, this long, sandy beach is a favorite among locals who enjoy its light crowds and nice waves for bodysurfing. Wide and shallow, Jenness Beach is a great place for kids to run and build sand castles. **Amenities:** lifeguards; parking (fee); showers; toilets. **Best for:** surfing; swimming; walking. ⊠ *2280 Ocean Blvd.* ☏ *603/436–1552* ⊕ *www.nhstateparks.org* ⊠ *Parking $2/ hr May–Sept.*

FAMILY
Wallis Sands State Beach. This family-friendly swimmers' beach has bright white sand, a picnic area, a store, and beautiful views of the Isles of Shoals. **Amenities:** food and drink; lifeguards; parking (no fee); showers; toilets. **Best for:** swimming; walking. ⊠ *1050 Ocean Blvd.* ☏ *603/436– 9404* ⊕ *www.nhstateparks.org* ⊠ *$15 per car.*

WHERE TO EAT

$$$
AMERICAN
✕ **The Carriage House.** Across from Jenness Beach, this elegant cottage serves innovative dishes with a Continental flair. Standouts include creative curries, penne chock-full of fresh seafood, and steak with peppercorns. Savor a hot-fudge ice-cream croissant for dessert. Upstairs is a wood-panel tavern with ocean views. $ *Average main: $28* ✉ *2263 Ocean Blvd.* ☎ *603/964–8251* ⊕ *www.carriagehouserye. com* ⊙ *No lunch.*

SPORTS AND THE OUTDOORS

FISHING AND WHALE-WATCHING

FAMILY **Atlantic Whale Watch.** Captain Brad Cook takes the *Atlantic Queen II* out on half-day whale-watching trips and helms the vessel on fishing excursions. ✉ *1870 Ocean Blvd.* ☎ *603/964–5220, 800/942–5364* ⊕ *www. atlanticwhalewatch.com* ✉ *$36* ⊙ *Closed mid-Oct.–mid-May.*

FAMILY **Granite State Whale Watch.** This outfit conducts naturalist-led whale-watching tours aboard the 100-passenger *Granite State.* ✉ *Rye Harbor State Marina, 1860 Ocean Blvd.* ☎ *603/964–5545, 800/964–5545* ⊕ *www.granitestatewhalewatch.com* ✉ *$36* ⊙ *Closed mid-Oct.–mid-May.*

HAMPTON BEACH

8 miles south of Rye.

This is an authentic seaside amusement center, the domain of fried-dough stands, loud music, arcade games, palm readers, parasailing, and bronzed bodies. The 3-mile-long boardwalk, where kids play games and watch saltwater taffy being made, looks like a relic of the 1940s—indeed, the whole community remains remarkably free of modern franchises. Free outdoor concerts are held on many a summer evening, and once a week there's a fireworks display. An estimated 150,000 people visit the town and its free public beach on the 4th of July, and it draws plenty of people through late September, when its season ends.

GETTING HERE AND AROUND

Interstate 95 is the fastest way to get to Hampton, but the town is best seen by driving along Route 1A, which follows the coast and passes several beaches. Once here, you'll find that Route 1 is the quickest way to get around, but be prepared for strip malls and stoplights.

ESSENTIALS

Visitor Information Hampton Area Chamber of Commerce. ✉ *160 Ocean Blvd.* ☎ *603/926–8718* ⊕ *www.hamptonchamber.com.*

EXPLORING

Fuller Gardens. Arthur Shurtleff, a noted landscape architect from Boston, designed this late-1920s estate garden in the Colonial Revival style. Away from the beach crowds, it encompasses 1,700 rosebushes, hosta and Japanese gardens, and a tropical conservatory. ✉ *10 Willow Ave., North Hampton* ☎ *603/964–5414* ⊕ *www.fullergardens.org* ✉ *$9.*

BEACHES

FAMILY   **Hampton Beach State Park.** A long, sandy strand at the mouth of the Hampton River, this beach has a boardwalk edged by restaurants, attractions, and hotels. There's a visitor center (open year-round), along with multiple picnic areas and a store (seasonal). **Amenities:** food and drink; lifeguards; parking (fee); showers; toilets. **Best for:** swimming. ⊠ *160 Ocean Blvd.* ☎ *603/227–8722* ⊕ *www.nhstateparks.org* ⌨ *Parking $15.*

WHERE TO EAT AND STAY

$$$ ✕ **Ron's Landing.** Diners enjoy sweeping ocean views from many tables

AMERICAN   at this casually elegant restaurant. The seared ahi tuna with a citrus, chili, and soy glaze is a tasty starter. Outstanding entrées include the oven-roasted salmon with cream sauce, slivered almonds, and sliced apples. Another winner is the baked haddock stuffed with scallops and lobster. Sunday brunch (November–April) is popular here. ⑤ *Average main: $30* ⊠ *379 Ocean Blvd.* ☎ *603/929–2122* ⊕ *www.ronslanding. com* ⊘ *Closed Mon., and Tues. early Sept.–late May. No lunch Mon.– Sat., no lunch Sun. May–Oct.*

$ ⊞ **Ashworth by the Sea.** Even though this hotel across from the beach

HOTEL   has been around for a century, you'll be surprised how contemporary it feels. **Pros:** center-of-town location; comfortable rooftop bar; open year-round. **Cons:** breakfast not included; very busy. ⑤ *Rooms from: $139* ⊠ *295 Ocean Blvd.* ☎ *603/926–6762, 800/345–6736* ⊕ *www. ashworthhotel.com* ⌁ *98 rooms, 7 suites* ◎ *No meals.*

NIGHTLIFE

Hampton Beach Casino Ballroom. Despite its name, the ballroom isn't a gambling establishment but rather an 1,800-seat late-19th-century auditorium that has hosted top performers, from the likes of Duke Ellington and Janis Joplin to Trace Adkins and Dweezil Zappa. ⊠ *169 Ocean Blvd.* ☎ *603/929–4100* ⊕ *www.casinoballroom.com* ⊘ *Closed Dec.–Mar.*

SPORTS AND THE OUTDOORS

FISHING AND WHALE-WATCHING

Several companies conduct whale-watching excursions as well as half-day, full-day, and nighttime cruises. Most leave from the Hampton State Pier on Route 1A.

FAMILY   **Al Gauron Deep Sea Fishing.** This company maintains a fleet of three boats for whale-watching cruises and fishing charters. ⊠ *State Pier, 1 Ocean Blvd.* ☎ *603/926–2469, 800/905–7820* ⊕ *www.algauron.com* ⌨ *From $33.*

FAMILY   **Eastman's Docks.** This company offers whale-watching excursions and fishing charters. ⊠ *River St., Seabrook* ☎ *603/474–3461* ⊕ *www.east-mansdocks.com* ⌨ *From $33.*

FAMILY   **Smith & Gilmore.** Enjoy half-day and full-day deep-sea fishing expeditions with Smith & Gilmore. ⊠ *State Pier, Ocean Blvd.* ☎ *603/926–3503, 877/272–4005* ⊕ *www.smithandgilmore.com* ⌨ *From $33.*

EN ROUTE

Applecrest Farm Orchards. At this 400-acre farm, you can pick your own apples and berries or buy freshly baked fruit pies and cookies, homemade ice cream, and many other treats. Fall brings cider pressing, hayrides, pumpkins, and music on weekends. Author John Irving worked here as a teenager, and his experiences inspired the book *The Cider House Rules*. ⊠ *133 Exeter Rd., Hampton Falls* ☎ *603/926–3721* ⊕ *www.applecrest.com.*

EXETER

9 miles northwest of Hampton, 52 miles north of Boston, 47 miles southeast of Concord.

Fodor's Choice
★

During the Revolutionary War, Exeter was the state capital, and it was here amid intense patriotic fervor that the first state constitution and the first Colonial Declaration of Independence from Great Britain were put to paper. These days Exeter shares more in appearance and personality with Boston's blue-blooded satellite communities than the rest of New Hampshire—indeed, plenty of locals commute to Beantown. Cheerful cafés, coffeehouses, and shops with artisanal wares make up this bustling town center.

GETTING HERE AND AROUND

Amtrak's *Downeaster* service stops here between Boston and Portland, Maine. On the road, Exeter is 9 miles northwest of Hampton on Route 111. Route 101 is also a good way to get to Exeter from the east or west. The town itself is easy to walk around.

ESSENTIALS

Visitor Information Exeter Area Chamber of Commerce. ⊠ *24 Front St., Suite 101* ☎ *603/772–2411* ⊕ *www.exeterarea.org.*

EXPLORING

American Independence Museum. This museum celebrates the birth of the nation. The story unfolds over the course of a guided tour, which focuses on the Gilman family, who lived in the house during the Revolutionary War era. See drafts of the U.S. Constitution and the first Purple Heart, as well as letters and documents written by George Washington and the household furnishings of John Taylor Gilman, one of New Hampshire's early governors. In July, the museum hosts the American Independence Festival. ⊠ *Ladd-Gilman House, 1 Governor's La.* ☎ *603/772–2622* ⊕ *www.independencemuseum.org* ⌑ *$6.*

Phillips Exeter Academy. The 1,000-plus students of this elite high school give Exeter a certain youthful energy. The grounds, open to the public, resemble an Ivy League university campus. The school's library is one of the masterworks of modernist architect Louis I. Kahn. The Lamont Gallery, in the Frederick R. Mayer Art Center, mounts free contemporary art exhibitions. ⊠ *20 Main St.* ☎ *603/772–4311* ⊕ *www.exeter.edu.*

WHERE TO EAT

$ ✕ **The Green Bean.** All the soups at this self-serve restaurant are made fresh daily, and the sandwiches are perfect for dunking. Soups commonly include curried butternut squash, spicy corn chowder, and tarragon potato with peas; often on the sandwich menu are vegetables

AMERICAN

and walnut pesto and turkey with cranberry and stuffing. Salads with an array of toppings are another lunch option. Breakfast burritos star in the early morning along with French toast and ham and eggs. The Green Bean is a popular spot for those on the go, but if you have the time, sit in the little courtyard for a quiet view of the town. ⑤ *Average main: $7* ⊠ *33 Water St.* ☎ *603/778–7585* ⊕ *www.nhgreenbean.com* ⊗ *No dinner.*

$$$
AMERICAN

✕ **The Tavern At River's Edge.** A convivial downtown gathering spot on the Exeter River, this downstairs tavern pulls in college students, suburbanites, and parents of prep-school kids. The place may be informal, but the kitchen turns out sophisticated meals. Start with sautéed ragout of mushrooms stewed in a marsala cream sauce with sun-dried tomatoes, roasted shallots, garlic, and Asiago cheese, then move on to Moroccan salmon marinated in yogurt and fresh herbs. The bar serves lighter fare. ⑤ *Average main: $25* ⊠ *163 Water St.* ☎ *603/772–7393* ⊕ *www. tavernatriversedge.com.*

WHERE TO STAY

$
HOTEL

🏨 **The Exeter Inn.** This elegant, Georgian-style red-brick inn on the Phillips Exeter campus has been the choice of visiting parents since it opened in the 1930s. **Pros:** well-designed rooms; elegant feel; near the center of town. **Cons:** some distance to shops. ⑤ *Rooms from: $139* ⊠ *90 Front St.* ☎ *603/772–5901,* ⊕ *www.theexeterinn.com* ⤵ *46 rooms, 3 suites* ⑩ *Breakfast.*

$
B&B/INN
Fodor's Choice
★

🏨 **Inn by the Bandstand.** This bed-and-breakfast in the heart of town exudes character and comfort. **Pros:** in-town location; bikes available; friendly staff. **Cons:** no lunch or dinner. ⑤ *Rooms from: $189* ⊠ *6 Front St.* ☎ *603/772–6352, 877/239–3837* ⊕ *www.innbythebandstand.com* ⤵ *9 rooms, 4 suites* ⑩ *Breakfast.*

SHOPPING

Exeter Fine Crafts. Fine creations by more than 300 of Northern New England's top pottery, painting, jewelry, textile, glassware, and other artisans are on display and available for sale here. ⊠ *61 Water St.* ☎ *603/778–8282* ⊕ *www.exeterfinecrafts.com.*

A Picture's Worth a Thousand Words. A destination for bibliophiles, this shop sells rare books, town histories, old maps, and antique and contemporary prints. ⊠ *65 Water St.* ☎ *603/778–1991* ⊕ *www.apwatw. com.*

Willow. This creative shop stocks finely stitched linens, handcrafted jewelry, woven throws, organic teas, gardening accessories, and gorgeous bags. ⊠ *183 Water St.* ☎ *603/773–9666.*

DURHAM

12 miles north of Exeter, 11 miles northwest of Portsmouth.

Settled in 1635 and later the home of General John Sullivan, a Revolutionary War hero and three-time New Hampshire governor, Durham was where Sullivan and his band of rebel patriots stored the gunpowder they captured from Fort William and Mary in New Castle. Easy access to Great Bay via the Oyster River made Durham a maritime hub in the 19th century. Among its lures today are the water, nearby farms that welcome visitors, and the University of New Hampshire, which occupies much of the town's center.

GETTING HERE AND AROUND

By car, Durham can be reached on Route 108 from the north or south and Route 4 from Portsmouth in the east or Concord in the west. The *Downeaster* Amtrak train stops here between Boston and Portland, Maine.

ESSENTIALS

Visitor Information University of New Hampshire ☎ 603/862-1234 ⊕ *www.unh.edu.*

EXPLORING

Museum of Art. Notable items in this gallery's collection include 19th-century Japanese wood-block prints, Boston expressionist works, and art of New England. ⊠ *Paul Creative Arts Center, University of New Hampshire, 30 College Rd.* ☎ *603/862-3712* ⊕ *www.unh.edu/moa* ⚑ *Free.*

WHERE TO EAT AND STAY

$$$
AMERICAN
FAMILY

✕ **ffrost Sawyer Tavern.** That's not a typo, but an attempt to duplicate the quirky, obsolete rendering of the name of a former owner of this hilltop house. The eccentric stone basement tavern has its original wooden beams, from which hang collections of mugs, hats, and—no way around it—bedpans. Choose from fine dinner fare, such as grilled rib eye steak with cippolini onions or potato-encrusted haddock. Lunch standards include burgers, pizza, and fish-and-chips. There's a terrific old bar. ⑤ *Average main: $25* ⊠ *Three Chimneys Inn, 17 Newmarket Rd.* ☎ *603/868-7800* ⊕ *www.threechimneysinn.com.*

$
B&B/INN

⌸ **Three Chimneys Inn.** This stately yellow structure has graced a hill overlooking the Oyster River since 1649. **Pros:** intimate inn experience; room rate includes breakfast. **Cons:** have to walk or drive into town. ⑤ *Rooms from: $189* ⊠ *17 Newmarket Rd.* ☎ *603/868-7800, 888/399-9777* ⊕ *www.threechimneysinn.com* ↬ *23 rooms* ⦿| *Some meals.*

NIGHTLIFE

Stone Church. Music aficionados head to the Stone Church—an 1835 former Methodist church—for its craft beers, pub grub, and live rock, jazz, blues, reggae, soul, and folk music. ⊠ *5 Granite St., Newmarket* ☎ *603/659-7700* ⊕ *www.stonechurchrocks.com.*

SPORTS AND THE OUTDOORS

FAMILY

Wagon Hill Farm. You can hike several trails and picnic at this 130-acre farm that overlooks the Oyster River. The old farm wagon on the top of a hill is one of the most photographed sights in New England. Park next to the farmhouse and follow walking trails to the wagon and through the woods to the picnic area by the water. Sledding and cross-country skiing are winter activities. ⊠ *U.S. 4, across from Emery Farm.*

SHOPPING

FAMILY

Emery Farm. In the same family for 11 generations, Emery Farm sells produce in summer (including pick-your-own blueberries), pumpkins in fall, and Christmas trees in winter. The farm shop carries breads, pies, and local crafts. Pumpkin-patch hayrides take place on some weekends in September and October, and May–October children can visit the petting barn. ✉ *135 Piscataqua Rd.* ☏ *603/742–8495* ⊕ *www.emeryfarm.com.*

LAKES REGION

Lake Winnipesaukee, a Native American name for "smile of the great spirit," is the largest of the dozens of lakes scattered across the eastern half of central New Hampshire. With about 240 miles of shoreline dotted with inlets and coves, it's the state's largest lake. Some claim Winnipesaukee has an island for each day of the year—the total, though impressive, falls short: 274.

In contrast to Winnipesaukee, which bustles all summer long, stands the more secluded Squam Lake. Its tranquillity is no doubt what attracted the producers of *On Golden Pond*: several scenes of the Academy Award–winning film were shot here. Nearby Lake Wentworth is named for the state's first royal governor, who, in building his country manor here, established North America's first summer resort.

Well-preserved Colonial and 19th-century villages are among the region's many landmarks, and you'll find hiking trails, good antiques shops, and myriad water-oriented activities. This section begins at Wolfeboro and more or less circles Lake Winnipesaukee clockwise, with several possible side trips.

ESSENTIALS

Visitor Information Lakes Region Association. ✉ *Behind Tilt'n Diner, 61 Laconia Rd., Tilton* ☏ *603/286–8008, 800/605–2537* ⊕ *www.lakesregion.org.*

WOLFEBORO

40 miles northeast of Concord, 49 miles northwest of Portsmouth.

Quietly upscale and decidedly preppy Wolfeboro has been a resort since Royal Governor John Wentworth built his summer home on the shore of the lake in 1768. The town bills itself as the oldest summer resort in the country, and its center, bursting with tony boutiques, fringes Lake Winnipesaukee and sees a major population increase each summer. The century-old, white clapboard buildings of the Brewster Academy prep school bracket the town's southern end. Wolfeboro marches to a steady, relaxed beat, comfortable for all ages.

GETTING HERE AND AROUND

Enter on the west side of Lake Winnipesaukee on Route 28. Be prepared for lots of traffic in the summertime.

ESSENTIALS

Visitor Information Wolfeboro Area Chamber of Commerce. ✉ *32 Central Ave.* ☏ *603/569–2200* ⊕ *www.wolfeborochamber.com.*

EXPLORING

FAMILY **New Hampshire Boat Museum.** Two miles northeast of the town center, this museum celebrates New Hampshire's maritime legacy with displays of vintage wooden boats, models, antique engines, racing photography,

Lakes Region

MAINE

trophies, and vintage marina signs. You can also take a 45-minute narrated ride on the lake in a reproduction of a 1928 triple-cockpit HackerCraft (call for details). ⊠ *399 Center St.* ☎ *603/569–4554* ⊕ *www. nhbm.org* ⌷ *$7.*

FAMILY **Wright Museum.** Uniforms, vehicles, and other artifacts at this museum illustrate the contributions of those on the home front to the U.S. World War II effort. ⊠ *77 Center St.* ☎ *603/569–1212* ⊕ *www.wrightmuseum. org* ⌷ *$10.*

QUICK BITES

Kelly's Yum Yum Shop. Picking up freshly baked breads, pastries, cookies, and other sweets at Kelly's has been a tradition since 1948. The buttercrunch cookies are highly addictive. ⊠ *16 N. Main St.* ☎ *603/569–1919* ⊕ *www.yumyumshop.net* ⊘ *Closed mid-Oct.–Apr.*

BEACHES

FAMILY **Wentworth State Beach.** Away from the hustle and bustle of Wolfeboro, this no-frills park features a quiet beach with good fishing, picnic tables and grills, and ballfields. **Amenities:** parking (no fee); showers; toilets. **Best for:** swimming; walking. ⊠ *297 Governor Wentworth Hwy.* ☎ *603/569–3699* ⊕ *www.nhstateparks.org* ⌷ *$4.*

With 240 miles of shoreline, Lake Winnipesaukee has something for everyone.

WHERE TO EAT AND STAY

$$
PHILIPPINE
FAMILY
×**East of Suez.** In a countrified lodge on the south side of town, this friendly restaurant serves creative Asian cuisine, with an emphasis on Philippine fare, such as *lumpia* (pork-and-shrimp spring rolls with a sweet-and-sour fruit sauce) and *pancit canton* (panfried egg noodles with sautéed shrimp and pork and Asian vegetables with a sweet oyster sauce). You can also sample Thai red curries, Japanese tempura, and Korean-style flank steak. Gluten-free and vegan options are available. ⑤ *Average main: $19* ✉ *775 S. Main St.* ☎ *603/569–1648* ⊕ *www.east-ofsuez.com* ⊗ *Closed early Sept.–late May.*

$
B&B/INN
⊡ **Topsides Bed & Breakfast.** Each of the rooms at this stylish retreat captures the allure of a particular region, from Martha's Vineyard to coastal France to British fox-hunting country. **Pros:** close to downtown; appealing rooms; great service. **Cons:** some rooms are upstairs. ⑤ *Rooms from: $185* ✉ *209 S. Main St.* ☎ *603/569–3834* ⊕ *www.topsidesbb.com* ⇘ *5 rooms* ⦿*Breakfast.*

$$
B&B/INN
⊡ **The Wolfeboro Inn.** This 1812 inn with a commanding lakefront location is a perennial favorite for Lake Winnipesaukee visitors. **Pros:** lakefront setting; interesting pub. **Cons:** breakfast not included. ⑤ *Rooms from: $279* ✉ *90 N. Main St.* ☎ *603/569–3016* ⊕ *www.wolfeboroinn.com* ⇘ *41 rooms, 3 suites* ⦿*Breakfast.*

SPORTS AND THE OUTDOORS
HIKING

FAMILY **Abenaki Tower.** A quarter-mile hike to the 100-foot post-and-beam Abenaki Tower, followed by a more rigorous climb to the top, rewards you with a view of Lake Winnipesaukee and the Ossipee mountain range. The setting is particularly photogenic at sunset. ✉ *Trailhead on Rte. 109, Tuftonboro.*

WATER SPORTS

Scuba divers can explore *The Lady,* a 125-foot-long cruise ship that sank in 30 feet of water off Glendale in 1895.

Dive Winnipesaukee Corp. This corporation runs charters out to wrecks, rents boats, and offers scuba equipment rentals, repairs, and sales. ✉ *Wolfeboro Bay, 4 N. Main St.* ☎ *603/569–8080* ⊕ *www.divewinnipesaukee.com.*

SHOPPING

FAMILY **The Country Bookseller.** You'll find an excellent regional-history section and plenty of children's titles at this independent bookstore, where you can do a little reading in the small café. ✉ *23A N. Main St.* ☎ *603/569–6030* ⊕ *www.thecountrybookseller.com.*

Hampshire Pewter. The artisans at Hampshire Pewter use 16th-century techniques to make pewter tableware, accessories, and gifts. ✉ *9 Railroad Ave.* ☎ *603/569–4944* ⊕ *www.hampshirepewter.com.*

ALTON BAY

10 miles south of Wolfeboro.

Lake Winnipesaukee's southern shore is alive with visitors from the moment the first flower blooms until the last maple sheds its leaves. Two mountain ridges hold 7 miles of the shoreline in Alton Bay, which is the name of both the inlet and the town at its tip. Cruise boats dock here, and small planes land year-round on the water and the ice. There's a dance pavilion, along with miniature golf, a public beach, and a Victorian-style bandstand.

GETTING HERE AND AROUND

To get to Alton Bay from Wolfeboro, head south on Route 28, also signed as Wolfeboro Highway, departing at Route 28A, which winds along the bays eastern shoreline. Head briefly west at Route 11 to the dock and small business district.

EXPLORING

FAMILY **Mt. Major.** About 5 miles north of Alton Bay, Mt. Major has a 3-mile trail up a series of challenging cliffs. At the top you'll find a four-sided stone shelter built in 1925, but the real reward is the spectacular view of Lake Winnipesaukee. ✉ *Rte. 11.*

WHERE TO EAT

$$$$ ✕ **The Crystal Quail.** With just four tables tucked inside an 18th-cen-
AMERICAN tury farmhouse, this restaurant is worth the drive for its sumptuous
Fodor'sChoice meals. Longtime proprietors Harold and Cynthia Huckaby use free-
★ range meats and mostly organic produce and herbs in their cooking. Their prix-fixe menu changes daily but may include saffron-garlic soup, a house pâté, mushroom and herb quail, or goose confit with apples and onions. Credit cards are not accepted. ⑤ *Average main: $75* ✉ *202 Pitman Rd., 12 miles south of Alton Bay, Center Barnstead*

☎ *603/269–4151* ⊕ *www.crystalquail.com* ▤ *No credit cards* ⊗ *Closed Mon. and Tues. No lunch* ⬥ *Reservations essential* ☞ *BYOB.*

WEIRS BEACH

17 miles northwest of Alton Bay.

Weirs Beach is Lake Winnipesaukee's center for summertime arcade activity, with souvenir shops, fireworks, waterslides, and hordes of children—there's even a drive-in theater. Cruise boats also depart from here.

GETTING HERE AND AROUND

Weirs Beach is just north of Laconia and south of Meredith on U.S. 3.

EXPLORING

FAMILY **Funspot.** The mothership of Lake Winnipesaukee's family-oriented amusement parks, Funspot claims that its more than 500 video games make it the world's largest arcade. You can also work your way through a miniature golf course, a driving range, an indoor golf simulator, and 20 lanes of bowling. Some outdoor attractions are closed in winter. ⊠ *579 Endicott St. N* ☎ *603/366–4377* ⊕ *www.funspotnh.com.*

FAMILY
Fodor'sChoice
★

M/S Mount Washington. The 230-foot M/S *Mount Washington* offers 2½-hour scenic cruises of Lake Winnipesaukee, departing Weirs Beach with stops at Wolfeboro, Alton Bay, Center Harbor, and Meredith depending on the day. Sunset cruises include live music and a buffet dinner, and the Sunday Champagne brunch cruise includes plenty of bubbly. The same company operates the *Sophie C.* ($27), which has been the area's floating post office for more than a century. The boat departs from Weirs Beach with mail and passengers, passing through parts of the lake not accessible to larger ships. The M/V *Doris E.* ($19) has one- and two-hour scenic cruises into Meredith Bay throughout the summer. ⊠ *211 Lakeside Ave., Laconia* ☎ *603/366–5531, 888/843–6686* ⊕ *www.cruisenh.com* ▣ *$30.*

FAMILY **Winnipesaukee Scenic Railroad.** You can board this scenic railroad's restored cars at Weirs Beach or Meredith for one- or two-hour rides along the shoreline. Special excursions include fall foliage and the Santa train. ⊠ *154 Main St., Meredith* ☎ *603/745–2135* ⊕ *www.hoborr.com* ▣ *$16.*

BEACHES

FAMILY **Ellacoya State Beach.** Families enjoy this secluded 600-foot sandy beach and park on the southwestern shore of Lake Winnipesaukee. Ellacoya, with views of the Sandwich and Ossipee mountains, is never crowded, and its shallow beach is safe for small children. It has sheltered picnic tables and a small campground. **Amenities:** parking (no fee); toilets. **Best for:** solitude; swimming. ⊠ *266 Scenic Rd., Gilford* ☎ *603/293–7821* ⊕ *www.nhstateparks.org* ▣ *$5.*

NIGHTLIFE AND PERFORMING ARTS

New Hampshire Music Festival. From early July to early August, this festival presents chamber music on Tuesday and classical orchestra on Thursday. ⊠ *Hanaway Theater, Silver Center for the Arts, 7 Main St., Plymouth* ☎ *603/535–2787 for box office* ⊕ *www.nhmf.org.*

SPORTS AND THE OUTDOORS

BOATING

Thurston's Marina. This marina rents boats and equipment and has a gas dock. ⊠ *18 Endicott St. N* ☎ *603/366–4811* ⊕ *www.thurstonsmarina.com.*

GOLF

Pheasant Ridge Golf Club. In a bucolic setting frequented by amazing waterfowl, the course here offers great farm and mountain views. ⊠ *140 Country Club Rd., Gilford* ☎ *603/524–7808* ⊕ *www.playgolfne.com* ⊠ *$30–$44* ⅃. *18 holes, 6044 yards, par 71.*

SKI AREA

FAMILY **Gunstock Mountain Resort.** High above Lake Winnipesaukee, this ski resort has invested millions to increase its snowmaking capacity, introduce more options for beginners, and add slope-side dining. Thrill Hill, a snow-tubing park, has five runs, a lift service, and 21 acres of terrain park. The ski area has 55 trails (24 of them open for night skiing) and 32 miles of cross-country and snowshoeing trails. In summer, the Mountain Adventure Park offers an adrenaline rush with 22 zip lines—the longest at 3,981 feet—an aerial obstacle course, and scenic chairlift rides. There are also mountain-bike trails, Segway tours, and paddleboats. **Facilities:** 55 trails; 2,200 acres; 1,400-foot vertical drop; 8 lifts. ⊠ *719 Cherry Valley Rd., Gilford* ☎ *603/293–4341* ⊕ *www.gunstock. com* ⊠ *Lift ticket $70.*

SHOPPING

FAMILY **Pepi Herrmann Crystal.** Watch artists at work crafting hand-cut crystal glasses, as well as contemporary tableware, ornaments, and jewelry. ⊠ *3 Waterford Pl., Gilford* ☎ *603/528–1020* ⊕ *www.handcut.com* ⊘ *Closed Sun. and Mon.*

LACONIA

4 miles west of Gilford, 27 miles north of Concord.

The arrival of the railroad in 1848 turned the sleepy hamlet of Laconia—then called Meredith Bridge—into the Lakes Region's chief manufacturing hub. Even today it acts as the area's supply depot, a perfect role given its accessibility to both Winnisquam and Winnipesaukee lakes, as well as to Interstate 93. In June the town draws bikers from around the world for Laconia Motorcycle Week.

GETTING HERE AND AROUND

The best way to Laconia is on Route 3 or Route 11. Scenic rides from the south include Route 106 and Route 107.

EXPLORING

FAMILY **Belknap Mill.** Inside this 1823 textile mill, you can see how cloth and clothing were made almost two centuries ago. Belknap Mill contains operational knitting machines, a 1918 hydroelectric power system, and changing exhibits. ⊠ *Mill Plaza, 25 Beacon St. E* ☎ *603/524–8813* ⊕ *www.belknapmill.org* ⊠ *Free.*

OFF THE
BEATEN
PATH

Canterbury Shaker Village. Established in 1792, this village flourished in the 1800s and practiced equality of the sexes and races, common ownership, celibacy, and pacifism. The last member of the religious community passed away in 1992. Shakers invented such household items as the clothespin and the flat broom and were known for the simplicity and integrity of their designs. Engaging tours pass through some of the 694-acre property's more than 25 restored buildings, many of them with original furnishings. Crafts demonstrations take place daily. Ask the admissions desk for a map of the many nature trails. The Shaker Box Lunch and Farm Stand offers salads, soups, and baked goods, and sells seasonal vegetables and locally produced maple syrup. A shop sells handcrafted items. ⊠ *288 Shaker Rd., 15 miles south of Laconia via Rte. 106, Canterbury* ☎ *603/783–9511* ⊕ *www.shakers.org* ⌂ *$17.*

BEACHES

FAMILY **Bartlett Beach.** On Lake Winnisquam, this small but pleasant city-run park has a 600-foot-long sand beach. Picnic tables and a playground make Bartlett Beach ideal for families, particularly those with small children. **Amenities:** lifeguards; parking (no fee); toilets. **Best for:** swimming. ⊠ *99 Winnisquam Ave.* ⌂ *Free.*

FAMILY **Opechee Park.** Nestled in a quiet cove, this medium-size, family-friendly beach has a playground, a baseball field, tennis courts, and picnic areas. **Amenities:** parking (no fee); toilets. **Best for:** swimming. ⊠ *N. Main St.* ⌂ *Free.*

WHERE TO EAT AND STAY

$ ✕ **Tilt'n Diner.** Lakes Region travelers have long been familiar with the flashy pink exterior and neon signage of this convivial 1950s-style restaurant. Specialties include omelets served every possible way, Reuben sandwiches, shepherd's pie, and Southern breakfasts (sausage gravy, biscuits, and baked beans with two eggs). Breakfast is served all day, and there's free Wi-Fi. ⑤ *Average main: $11* ⊠ *61 Laconia Rd., Tilton* ☎ *603/286–2204* ⊕ *www.thecman.com.*

AMERICAN
FAMILY

$ ⬚ **The Lake House at Ferry Point.** Four miles southwest of Laconia, this home across the street from Lake Winnisquam is a quiet retreat with a dock and a small beach. **Pros:** affordable; lovely setting. **Cons:** away from main attractions. ⑤ *Rooms from: $185* ⊠ *100 Lower Bay Rd., Sanbornton* ☎ *603/637–1758* ⊕ *www.lakehouseatferrypoint.com* ⌿ *8 rooms, 1 suite* ⌢ *Breakfast.*

B&B/INN

MEREDITH

11 miles north of Laconia.

Meredith is a favored spot for water-sports enthusiasts and anglers. For a true taste of Meredith, take a walk down Main Street (just one block from busy Route 3), which is dotted with intimate coffee shops, salons and barber shops, family restaurants, redbrick buildings, and antiques stores. You can pick up area information at a kiosk across from the town docks. One caveat: on busy weekends getting into town from the west can mean sitting in traffic for 30 minutes or more.

What's your vessel of choice for exploring New Hampshire's Lakes Region: kayak, canoe, powerboat, or sailboat?

ESSENTIALS

Visitor Information Meredith Area Chamber of Commerce. ☎ 877/279–6121 ⊕ www.meredithareachamber.com.

WHERE TO EAT AND STAY

$$$
AMERICAN

✕ **Lakehouse Grille.** Come to this upscale lodge for some of the best lake views of any restaurant in the region. The chef hand-selects steaks from Creekstone Farm and serves them with applewood bacon and cheddar potato cakes. There's a fine assortment of seafood dishes, and the house specialties include duck, roasted chicken, and gnocchi. Breakfast is served daily, with brunch on Sunday. ⑤ *Average main: $25* ⊠ *Church Landing, 281 Daniel Webster Hwy.* ☎ *603/279–5221* ⊕ *www.thecman.com.*

$
HOTEL
Fodor's Choice
★

👣 **Mill Falls at the Lake.** You have your choice of four lodgings here: relaxing Church Landing and Bay Point are both on the shore of Lake Winnipesaukee; convivial Mill Falls, across the street, has a swimming pool and a 19th-century mill that now houses more than a dozen unique shops; and Chase House, also across the street, has 21 rooms, all with fireplaces and lake views. **Pros:** many lodging choices and prices; lakefront rooms; fun environment. **Cons:** rooms with views are expensive; two buildings are not on the lake. ⑤ *Rooms from: $185* ⊠ *312 Daniel Webster Hwy., at Rte. 25* ☎ *603/279–7006, 800/622–6455* ⊕ *www.millfalls.com* 🛏 *172 rooms, 15 suites* ⑩ *Breakfast.*

PERFORMING ARTS

FAMILY

Interlakes Summer Theatre. During its 10-week season of summer stock, the theater presents Broadway musicals like *42nd Street, Godspell,* and *West Side Story.* ⊠ *Interlakes Auditorium, 1 Laker La., off Rte. 25* ☎ *603/707–6035* ⊕ *www.interlakestheatre.com.*

SPORTS AND THE OUTDOORS

BOATING

Meredith is near the quaint village of Center Harbor, another boating hub that's in the middle of three bays at the northern end of Lake Winnipesaukee.

FAMILY **Meredith Marina.** Between May and October, you can rent powerboats and other vessels at this marina. ⊠ *2 Bayshore Dr.* ☎ *603/279-7921* ⊕ *www.meredithmarina.com.*

FAMILY **Wild Meadow Canoes & Kayaks.** Canoes and kayaks are available here. ⊠ *6 Whittier Hwy., Center Harbor* ☎ *603/253-7536, 800/427-7536* ⊕ *www.wildmeadowcanoes.com.*

HIKING

FAMILY **Red Hill.** Off Route 25, Red Hill really does turn red in autumn. The reward at the end of this hiking trail is a fire tower and a view of Squam Lake and the mountains. ⊠ *Trailhead on Old Red Hill Rd., 9 miles northeast of Meredith, Moultonborough.*

SHOPPING

Home Comfort. The owners of Lavinia's Relaxed Dining next door operate this three-floor showroom of designer furnishings, antiques, and accessories. ⊠ *Senters Market, Rte. 25B, Center Harbor* ☎ *603/253-6660* ⊕ *www.homecomfortnh.com.*

Keepsake Quilting. Reputedly America's largest quilting shop, this store contains 5,000 bolts of fabric, hundreds of quilting books, and plenty of supplies. There are also gorgeous handmade quilts. ⊠ *Senters Market, 12 Main St., Center Harbor* ☎ *603/253-4026, 800/525-8086* ⊕ *www. keepsakequilting.com.*

League of New Hampshire Craftsmen. Here you'll find works by more than 250 area artisans who regularly demonstrate their skills. There are other branches in Littleton, Hanover, North Conway, and Concord. ⊠ *279 U.S. 3, next to the Inn at Church Landing* ☎ *603/279-7920* ⊕ *www. nhcrafts.org/meredith.*

Old Print Barn. This shop carries rare prints—Currier & Ives, antique botanicals, and more—from around the world. ⊠ *343 Winona Rd., New Hampton* ☎ *603/279-6479.*

HOLDERNESS

8 miles northwest of Meredith.

The prim small town of Holderness sits between Squam and Little Squam lakes. *On Golden Pond,* starring Katharine Hepburn and Henry Fonda, was filmed on Squam, whose quiet beauty attracts nature lovers.

GETTING HERE AND AROUND

Routes 25B and 25 lead to Holderness.

EXPLORING

FAMILY

Fodor'sChoice

★

Squam Lakes Natural Science Center. This 230-acre property includes a ¾-mile nature trail that passes by trailside exhibits of black bears, bobcats, otters, mountain lions, red and gray fox, and other native wildlife. A pontoon boat cruise, one of the center's main attractions, is the best way to tour the waterfront. Naturalists talk about the animals that make their home here, and give fascinating facts about the loon. Children's activities include learning about bugs and wilderness survival skills. ⊠ *23 Science Center Rd.* ☎ *603/968–7194* ⊕ *www.nhnature.org* ⬚ *Trail $17, lake cruise $25.*

WHERE TO EAT

$$$
AMERICAN
✕ **Manor on Golden Pond Restaurant.** Leaded-glass panes and wood paneling set a decidedly romantic tone at this wonderful inn overlooking Squam Lake. The main dining room is in the manor's original billiards room and retains woodwork from 1904. Two others have very different looks: one has white linens, fresh flowers, and candlelight; the other is in the style of a Parisian bistro. The menu changes weekly, but might include lobster risotto, filet mignon, quail, or monkfish. Ask about the fabulous seven-course tasting menu. Breakfast is also served. ⑤ *Average main: $35* ⊠ *31 Manor Dr., at U.S. 3 and Shepard Dr.* ☎ *603/968–3348* ⊕ *www.manorongoldenpond.com* ⬚ *Reservations essential.*

$$
AMERICAN
✕ **Walter's Basin.** A former bowling alley in the heart of Holderness makes an unlikely but charming setting for meals overlooking Little Squam Lake—local boaters dock right beneath the dining room. Among the specialties on the seafood-intensive menu are toasted orzo with panfried rainbow trout and lobster macaroni and cheese. Sandwiches and salads are good choices for those looking for lighter fare. ⑤ *Average main: $22* ⊠ *859 U.S. 3* ☎ *603/968–4412* ⊕ *www.waltersbasin.com.*

WHERE TO STAY

$
B&B/INN
⛫ **Glynn House.** Pam, Ingrid, and Glenn Heidenreich operate this beautifully restored 1890s Queen Anne–style Victorian and, next door, a handsome 1920s carriage house. **Pros:** luxurious rooms; complimentary afternoon hors d'oeuvres; social atmosphere. **Cons:** not much to do in town. ⑤ *Rooms from: $179* ⊠ *59 Highland St., Ashland* ☎ *603/968–3775* ⊕ *www.glynnhouse.com* ⬚ *6 rooms, 6 suites* ⦿⊙ *Breakfast.*

$
B&B/INN
FAMILY
⛫ **Inn on Golden Pond.** Sweet-as-pie Bill and Bonnie Webb run this comfortable and informal bed-and-breakfast a short distance from Squam Lake, to which they provide hiking trail maps. **Pros:** friendly innkeepers; comfortable rooms and common spaces. **Cons:** not directly on the lake; not luxurious. ⑤ *Rooms from: $160* ⊠ *1080 U.S. 3* ☎ *603/968–7269* ⊕ *www.innongoldenpond.com* ⬚ *6 rooms, 2 suites* ⦿⊙ *Breakfast.*

$$$
B&B/INN
Fodor'sChoice
★
⛫ **The Manor on Golden Pond.** A name like this is a lot to live up to, but the Manor succeeds: it's the Lakes Region's most charming inn. **Pros:** wood fireplaces; comfortable sitting rooms; great food; welcoming hosts. **Cons:** expensive. ⑤ *Rooms from: $310* ⊠ *31 Manor Rd., off Shepard Hill Rd.* ☎ *603/968–3348, 800/545–2141* ⊕ *www.manorongoldenpond.com* ⬚ *22 rooms, 2 suites* ⦿⊙ *Breakfast.*

$
B&B/INN
⛫ **Squam Lake Inn.** Graceful Victorian furnishings fill the nine stylish rooms at this peaceful farmhouse inn a short stroll from Squam Lake. **Pros:** quiet setting; comfortable beds; big breakfasts. **Cons:** short walk to lake. ⑤ *Rooms from: $159* ⊠ *28 Shepard Hill Rd.* ☎ *603/968–4417, 800/839–6205* ⊕ *www.squamlakeinn.com* ⊙ *Closed late Oct.–May* ⬚ *9 rooms* ⦿⊙ *Breakfast.*

View simple yet functional furniture, architecture, and crafts at Canterbury Shaker Village.

CENTER SANDWICH

12 miles northeast of Holderness.

With Squam Lake to the west and the Sandwich Mountains to the north, Center Sandwich claims one of the prettiest settings of any Lakes Region community. So appealing are the town and its views that John Greenleaf Whittier used the Bearcamp River as the inspiration for his poem "Sunset on the Bearcamp." The town attracts artisans—crafts shops abound among its clutch of charming 18th- and 19th-century buildings.

ESSENTIALS

Visitor Information Squam Lake Area Chamber of Commerce. ☎ *603/968–4494* ⊕ *www.visitsquam.com.* **Sandwich Historical Society.** ⊠ *4 Maple St.* ☎ *603/284–6269* ⊕ *www.sandwichhistorical.org.*

EXPLORING

FAMILY **Castle in the Clouds.** Looking for all the world like a fairy-tale castle, this wonderful mountaintop estate was finished in 1914. The elaborate mansion has 16 rooms, eight bathrooms, and doors made of lead. Owner Thomas Gustave Plant spent $7 million—the bulk of his fortune—on this project and died penniless in 1941. A tour includes the mansion and the Castle Springs water facility on this high Ossipee Mountain Range property overlooking Lake Winnipesaukee; hiking and pony and horse rides also take place here. ⊠ *455 Old Mountain Rd., Moultonborough* ☎ *603/476–5900* ⊕ *www.castleintheclouds.org* ☞ *$16.*

FAMILY **Loon Center.** Recognizable for its eerie calls and striking black-and-white coloring, the loon resides on many New Hampshire lakes but is threatened by the gradual loss of its habitat. Two trails wind through the 200-acre

Loon Center; vantage points on the Loon Nest Trail overlook the spot resident loons sometimes occupy in late spring and summer. ☒ *183 Lee's Mills Rd., Moultonborough* ☏ *603/476–5666* ⊕ *www.loon.org* ▣ *Free.*

WHERE TO EAT

$$ ✗ **Corner House Inn.** In a converted barn adorned with paintings by local
AMERICAN artists, this restaurant dishes up classic American fare. Salads made with local greens are a house specialty, but don't overlook the chef's lobster-and-mushroom bisque or the shellfish sauté. Storytelling often takes place on Thursday evening, on Friday night there's live music, and brunch is served on Sunday. ⑤ *Average main: $21* ☒ *22 Main St.* ☏ *603/476–3060* ⊕ *www.cornerhouseinn.com* ⊘ *Closed Tues. No lunch Mon., and Wed.–Sun. mid-Oct.–June.*

$$$ ✗ **Lavinia's Relaxed Dining.** Talk about relaxing: that's exactly what you'll
AMERICAN want to do in this splendidly restored mansion, built in 1820 by John Coe for his bride, Lavinia. Enjoy a glass of wine on the veranda, then sink into a plush chair in the dining room, where the original French wallpaper depicts the Seven Wonders of the World. The chef offers new twists on New England comfort foods with such dishes as pumpkin-and-mascarpone ravioli and Gorgonzola-stuffed artichoke hearts. Two good entrées are the lobster potpie and the grilled red snapper with pineapple pico de gallo. Lighter fare can be ordered in the upstairs lounge. For an unforgettable romantic evening, reserve the cupola—it seats only two. ⑤ *Average main: $26* ☒ *18 Main St., Center Harbor* ☏ *603/253–8617* ⊕ *www.laviniasdining.com* ⊘ *No lunch.*

SHOPPING

FAMILY **Old Country Store and Museum.** The store has been selling maple syrup, aged cheeses, jams, molasses, penny candy, and other items since 1781. Much of the equipment used in the store is antique, and the free museum displays old farming and forging tools. ☒ *1011 Whittier Hwy.* ☏ *603/476–5750* ⊕ *www.nhcountrystore.com.*

TAMWORTH

13 miles east of Center Sandwich, 20 miles southwest of North Conway.

President Grover Cleveland summered in what remains a place of almost unreal quaintness: Tamworth is equally photogenic in verdant summer, during the fall foliage season, or under a blanket of winter snow. Cleveland's son, Francis, returned and founded the acclaimed Barnstormers Theatre in 1931. One of America's first summer theaters, it continues to this day. Tamworth has a clutch of villages within its borders. At one of them—Chocorua—the view through the birches of Chocorua Lake has been so often photographed that you may experience déjà vu. Rising above the lake is Mt. Chocorua (3,490 feet), which has many good hiking trails.

GETTING HERE AND AROUND

The five villages of Tamworth boast six churches, which are worth a half-day's casual drive to admire their white clapboard elegance. Downtown Tamworth is tiny and can be strolled in a few minutes, but you might linger in the hope of meeting one of the town's many resident poets and artists.

EXPLORING

FAMILY **Remick Country Doctor Museum and Farm.** For 99 years (1894–1993) Dr. Edwin Crafts Remick and his father provided medical services to the Tamworth area and operated a family farm. After the younger Remick died, these two houses were turned into the Remick Country Doctor Museum and Farm. The second floor of the house has been kept as it was when Remick passed away; it's a great way to see the life of a country doctor. Each season, the still-working farm features a special activity such as maple-syrup making. The farm also has hiking trails and picnicking areas. ⊠ *58 Cleveland Hill Rd.* ☎ *603/323–7591, 800/686–6117* ⊕ *www.remickmuseum.org* ▣ *$5.*

WHERE TO EAT

$ ✕ **Jake's Seafood and Grill.** Oars and other nautical trappings adorn the

SEAFOOD   wood-panel walls at this stop between West and Center Ossipee, about

FAMILY   8 miles southeast of Tamworth. The kitchen serves some of eastern New Hampshire's freshest and tastiest seafood, notably lobster pie, fried clams, and seafood casserole. Other choices include steak, ribs, and chicken dishes. Ⓢ *Average main: $17* ⊠ *2055 Rte. 16, West Ossipee* ☎ *603/539–2805* ⊕ *www.jakesseafoodco.com* ☾ *Closed Apr. and Nov.*

$$ ✕ **Yankee Smokehouse.** This down-home barbecue joint's logo depicting a

BARBECUE   happy pig foreshadows the gleeful enthusiasm with which patrons dive

FAMILY   into the hefty sandwiches of sliced pork and smoked chicken and the immense platters of baby back ribs and smoked sliced beef. Ample sides of slaw, beans, fries, and garlic toast complement the hearty fare. Even Southerners have come away impressed. The restaurant serves gluten-free items, too. Ⓢ *Average main: $20* ⊠ *Rtes. 16 and 25, about 5 miles southeast of Tamworth* ☎ *603/539–7427* ⊕ *www.yankeesmokehouse.com.*

PERFORMING ARTS

FAMILY **Arts Council of Tamworth.** The council sponsors artist residencies and children's programs, hosts lectures, presents dancers, storytellers, musicians of various genres, and other performers, and produces an art show and sale in late July. ⊠ *77 Main St.* ☎ *603/323–0104* ⊕ *www. artstamworth.org.*

FAMILY **Barnstormers Theatre.** Founded in 1931, this theater company presents dramas and comedies June–August. ⊠ *104 Main St.* ☎ *603/323–8500* ⊕ *www.barnstormerstheatre.org.*

SPORTS AND THE OUTDOORS

FAMILY **White Lake State Park.** The 72-acre stand of native pitch pine here is a National Natural Landmark. The park has a picnic area and a sandy beach, trails you can hike, trout you can fish for, and canoes you can rent. ⊠ *98 State Park Rd.* ☎ *603/323–7350* ⊕ *www.nhstateparks.org* ▣ *$5.*

THE WHITE MOUNTAINS

Sailors approaching East Coast harbors frequently mistake the pale peaks of the White Mountains—the highest range in the northeastern United States—for clouds. It was 1642 when explorer Darby Field could no longer contain his curiosity about one mountain in particular. He set off from his Exeter homestead and became the first European to climb what would later be called Mt. Washington. The 6,288-foot peak must have presented Field with formidable obstacles—its summit claims the highest wind velocity in the world ever recorded (231 mph in 1934) and can see snow every month of the year.

Today an auto road and a cog railway lead to the top of Mt. Washington, and people come by the tens of thousands to hike and climb, photograph the vistas, and ski. The peak is part of the Presidential Range, whose peaks are named after early presidents, and part of the White Mountain National Forest, which has roughly 770,000 acres that extend from northern New Hampshire into southwestern Maine. Among the forest's scenic notches (deep mountain passes) are Pinkham, Kinsman, Franconia, and Crawford. In these notches, you'll find trail heads for short hikes and multiday adventures; they are also excellent spots for photographing the majestic White Mountains.

This section of the guide begins in Waterville Valley, off Interstate 93, and continues to North Woodstock. It then follows portions of the White Mountains Trail, a 100-mile loop designated as a National Scenic and Cultural Byway.

ESSENTIALS

Visitor Information Bike the Whites. ☎ 603/356–9025 ⊕ www.bikethewhites. com. **Ski New Hampshire.** ☎ 603/745–9396 ⊕ www.skinh.com. **White Mountain National Forest.** ✉ 71 White Mountain Dr., Campton ☎ 603/536–6100 ⊕ www. fs.fed.us. **White Mountains Visitors Bureau.** ✉ 200 Kancamagus Hwy., off I–93, North Woodstock ☎ 603/745–8720 ⊕ www.visitwhitemountains.com.

WATERVILLE VALLEY

60 miles north of Concord.

Visitors began to arrive in Waterville Valley as early as 1835. A 10-mile cul-de-sac follows the Mad River, surrounded by mountains. The valley was first a summer resort and then became more of a ski area. Although it's now a year-round getaway, it still has a small-town charm. There are inns, condos, restaurants, shops, conference facilities, a grocery store, and a post office.

GETTING HERE AND AROUND

Depot Camp is a great starting point for hiking, snowshoeing, and cross-country skiing. In town, the Schuss bus has regular stops at the shops in Village Square, the lodges and condos, the Waterville Valley Conference Center, and the ski area. There's enough to do in this small village to keep outdoors enthusiasts busy for several days.

WHERE TO STAY

$$
RENTAL
🖼 **Black Bear Lodge.** This family-friendly property has one-bedroom suites that sleep up to six people. **Pros:** affordable rates; perfect for families. **Cons:** basic in decor and services. ⓢ *Rooms from: $200* ✉ *3 Village Rd.* ☎ *603/236–4501, 800/349–2327* ⊕ *www.blackbearlodgenh.com* ⊅ *10/ suites* ⦿ *No meals.*

$
HOTEL
FAMILY
🖼 **Golden Eagle Lodge.** Waterville's premier condominium property, its steep roof punctuated by dozens of gabled dormers, recalls the grand hotels of an earlier era. **Pros:** plenty of elbow room; kitchens. **Cons:**

unremarkable architecture and decor. [$] *Rooms from: $129* ⊠ *28 Packard's Rd.* ☎ *888/703–2453* ⊕ *www.goldeneaglelodge.com* ⇨ *139 condos* ⫿⨀ *No meals.*

$

HOTEL

⊞ **Snowy Owl Inn & Resort.** On weekends, visitors are treated to afternoon wine and cheese in this hotel's atrium lobby, which has a three-story fieldstone fireplace and wonderful watercolors of its namesake raptor. **Pros:** affordable; rate includes Continental breakfast. **Cons:** guests must pay for access to nearby gym. [$] *Rooms from: $104* ⊠ *41 Village Rd.* ☎ *603/236–8383, 800/766–9969* ⊕ *www.snowyowlinn.com* ⇨ *85 rooms* ⫿⨀ *Breakfast.*

SPORTS AND THE OUTDOORS

FAMILY

Waterville Valley Resort. Tom Corcoran, a former U.S. ski-team star, designed this family-oriented resort. The lodgings and various amenities are about a mile from the slopes, but a shuttle renders a car unnecessary. This ski area has hosted more World Cup races than any other in the East, so most advanced skiers can look forward to a challenge. Most of the 50 trails are intermediate: straight down the fall line, wide, and agreeably long. About 20 acres of tree-skiing add heart-pounding stimulus. Complete snowmaking coverage ensures good skiing even when nature doesn't cooperate. The Waterville Valley cross-country network, with the ski center in the town square, provides over 43 miles of groomed trails. **Facilities:** 50 trails; 500 acres; 2,020-foot vertical drop; 11 lifts. ⊠ *1 Ski Area Rd.* ☎ *603/236–8311, 800/468–2553 for snow conditions, 800/468–2553 for lodging* ⊕ *www.waterville.com* 🎫*Lift ticket $77.*

LINCOLN AND NORTH WOODSTOCK

64 miles north of Concord.

These neighboring towns at the southwestern end of the White Mountains National Forest and one end of the Kancamagus Highway (Route 112) form a lively resort area, especially for Bostonian families who can make an easy day trip straight up Interstate 93 to Exit 32. Festivals such as the New Hampshire Scottish Highland Games in mid-September keep Lincoln swarming with people year-round. The town itself is not much of an attraction. Tiny North Woodstock maintains more of a village feel.

GETTING HERE AND AROUND

Lincoln and North Woodstock are places to spend a day shopping in their quaint shops, which are within easy walking distance of each other. It's a pleasant 1-mile stroll between the two towns. On Route 112, which connects the two villages, there is a state visitor center.

ESSENTIALS

Visitor Information Lincoln–Woodstock Chamber of Commerce. ⊠ *126 Main St., North Woodstock* ☎ *603/745–6621* ⊕ *www.lincolnwoodstock.com.*

TOURS

FAMILY   **Hobo Railroad.** Restored vintage train cars take you along the scenic shores of the Pemigewassett River. Tours take 80 minutes. The Santa Express runs late November–late December. ⊠ *64 Railroad St., off Kancamagus Hwy., Lincoln* ☎ *603/745–2135* ⊕ *www.hoborr.com* ☜ *$16.*

EXPLORING

FAMILY   **Clark's Trading Post.** Chock-full of hokum, this old-time amusement park is a favorite with families. There are half-hour train rides over a 1904 covered bridge, a museum of Americana inside an 1880s firehouse, a restored gas station filled with antique cars, circus performers, and an Old Man of the Mountain rock-climbing tower—there's even a mining sluice where you can pan for gems. Tour guides tell tall tales, and vendors sell popcorn, ice cream, and pizza. The ensemble also includes a mammoth gift shop and a penny-candy store. ⊠ *110 Daniel Webster Hwy., off I–93, Lincoln* ☎ *603/745–8913* ⊕ *www.clarkstradingpost. com* ☜ *$20.*

FAMILY   **Lost River Gorge in Kinsman Notch.** Parents can enjoy the looks of wonder on their children's faces as they negotiate wooden boardwalks and stairs leading through a granite gorge formed by the roaring waters of the Lost River. One of the 10 caves they can explore is called the Lemon Squeezer (and it's a tight fit). Kids can also pan for gems and search for fossils, while grown-ups might prefer the attractions in the snack bar, gift shop, and nature garden. The park offers weekend lantern tours. ⊠ *1712 Lost River Rd., North Woodstock* ☎ *603/745–8720, 800/346–3687* ⊕ *www. lostrivergorge.com* ☜ *$18.*

FAMILY   **Whale's Tale Waterpark.** You can float on an inner tube along a gentle river, plunge down one of five waterslides, or bodysurf in the large wave pool at Whale's Tale. There's plenty here for toddlers and small children. ⊠ *491 Daniel Webster Hwy., off I–93, Lincoln* ☎ *603/745–8810* ⊕ *www.whalestalewaterpark.net* ☜ *$35.*

WHERE TO EAT AND STAY

$
AMERICAN
FAMILY
✕ Sunny Day Diner. Up in the skiing and hiking haven of Lincoln, this cozy, handsomely restored late-1950s diner is a popular stop for breakfast or coffee and dessert. The banana-bread French toast and cherry pie à la mode are two local favorites. ⑤ *Average main: $9* ⊠ *90 U.S. 3, off I–93, Lincoln* ☎ *603/745–4833* ⊟ *No credit cards.*

$$
AMERICAN
FAMILY
✕ Woodstock Inn, Station & Brewery. If you like restaurants loaded with character, don't miss this one inside North Woodstock's late-1800s train station. The walls are decorated with old maps, historic photographs, and local memorabilia; there are also fun curiosities, such as an old phone booth. The menu offers gluten-free items as well as standard pub fare: pizza, burgers, steaks, and seafood. Gourmet breakfasts are served daily. The on-site brewery makes 17 different kinds of beer; ask your server which are on tap. Kids will find a small game room. ⑤ *Average main: $20* ⊠ *135 Main St., off I–93, North Woodstock* ☎ *603/745–3951* ⊕ *www.woodstockinnnh.com.*

$
RESORT
FAMILY
☷ Indian Head Resort. The resort's inexpensive and spacious rooms make this a good choice for families on a budget. **Pros:** great prices; fun for the whole family; near kid-friendly attractions. **Cons:** can be crowded;

Continued on page 186

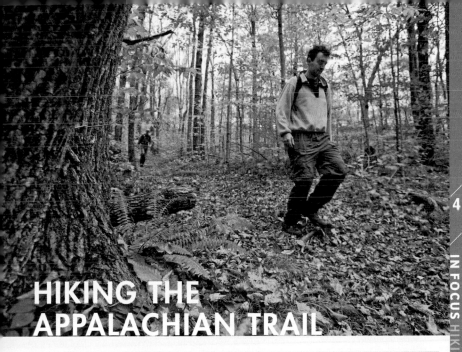

HIKING THE APPALACHIAN TRAIL

Tucked inside the nation's most densely populated corridor, a simple footpath in the wilderness stretches more than 2,100 miles, from Georgia to Maine. The Appalachian Trail passes through some of New England's most spectacular regions, and daytrippers can experience the area's beauty on a multitude of accessible, rewarding hikes. *By Melissa Kim*

Running along the spine of the Appalachian Mountains, the trail was fully blazed in 1937 and designed to connect anyone and everyone with nature. Within a day's drive of two-thirds of the U.S. population, it draws an estimated two to three million people every year. Through-hikers complete the whole trail in one daunting six-month season, but all ages and abilities can find renewal and perspective here in just a few hours. One-third of the AT passes through New England, and it's safe to say that the farther north you go, the harder the trail gets. New Hampshire and Maine challenge experienced hikers with windy, cold, and isolated peaks.

Top, hiking in New Hampshire's White Mountains. Above, autumn view of Profile Lake, Pemigewasset, NH.

ON THE TRAIL

New England's prime hiking season is in late summer and early fall, when the blaze of foliage viewed from a high peak is unparalleled. Popular trails see high crowds; if you seek solitude, try hiking at sunrise, a peaceful time that's good for wildlife viewing. You'll have to curb your enthusiasm in spring and early summer to avoid mud season in late April and black flies in May and June.

With the right gear, attitude, and preparation, winter can also offer fine opportunities for hiking, snowshoeing, and cross-country skiing.

FOLLOW THE TRAIL

Most hiking trails are marked with blazes, blocks of colored paint on a tree or rock. The AT, and only the AT, is marked by vertical, rectangular 2- by 6-inch white blazes. Two blazes mark route changes; turn in the direction of the top blaze. At higher elevations, you might also see cairns, small piles of rocks carefully placed by trail rangers to show the way when a blaze might be obscured by snow or fog.

Scenic U.S. 302—and the AT—pass through Crawford Notch, a spectacular valley in New Hampshire's White Mountains.

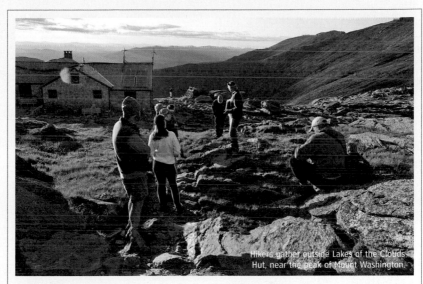

Hikers gather outside Lakes of the Clouds Hut, near the peak of Mount Washington.

TRIP TIPS

WHAT TO WEAR: For clothes, layer with a breathable fabric like polypropylene, starting with a shirt, a fleece, and a wind- or water-resistant shell. Bring gloves, a hat, and a change of socks.

WHAT TO BRING: Carry plenty of water and lightweight high-energy food. Don't forget sunscreen and insect repellent. Bring a map and compass. Just in case: a basic first-aid kit, a flashlight or headlamp, whistle, multi-tool, and matches.

PLAN AHEAD: In your car, leave a change of clothing, especially dry socks and shoes, as well as extra water and food.

PLAY IT SAFE: Tell someone your hiking plan and take a hiking partner. Carry a rescue card with emergency contact information and allergy details.

BE PREPARED: Plan your route and check the weather forecast in advance.

REMEMBER YOUR BEGINNINGS: Look back at the trail especially at the trailhead and at tricky junctions. If you've got a digital camera, photograph trail maps posted at the trailhead or natural landmarks to help you find your way.

WHERE TO STAY

Day hikers looking to extend the adventure can also make the experience as hard or as soft as they choose. Through-hikers combine camping with overnight stays in primitive shelters, mountain huts, comfortable lodges, and resorts just off the trail.

Rustic cabins and lean-tos provide basic shelter in Maine's Baxter State Park. In Maine and New Hampshire, the Appalachian Mountain Club runs four-season lodges as well as a network of mountain huts for backcountry hikers. A hiker code of camaraderie and conviviality prevails in these huts. Experience a night and you might just find yourself dreaming of a through-hike.

FOR MORE INFORMATION

Appalachian Trail Conservancy
(⊕ www.appalachiantrail.org)

Appalachian National Scenic Trail
(⊕ www.nps.gov/appa)

Appalachian Mountain Club
(⊕ www.outdoors.org)

ANIMALS ALONG THE TRAIL

❶ Black bear

Black bears are the most common—and smallest—bear in North America. Clever and adaptable, these adroit mammals will eat whatever they can (though they are primarily vegetarian, favoring berries, grasses, roots, blossoms, and nuts). Not naturally aggressive, black bears usually make themselves scarce when they hear hikers. The largest New England populations are in New Hampshire and Maine.

❷ Moose

Spotting a moose in the wild is unforgettable: their massive size and serene gaze are truly humbling. Treasure the moment, then slowly back away. At more than six feet tall, weighing 750 to 1,000 pounds, a moose is not to be trifled with, particularly during rutting and calving seasons (fall and spring, respectively). Dusk and dawn are the best times to spot the iconic animal; you're most likely to see one in Maine, especially in and around ponds.

⚠ Black flies

Especially fierce in May and June, these pesky flies can upset the tranquility of a hike in the woods as they swarm your face and bite your neck. To ward them off, cover any exposed skin and wear light colors. You'll get some relief on a mountain peak; cold weather and high winds also keep them at bay.

❸ Bald eagles

Countless bird species can be seen and heard along the AT, but what could be more exciting than to catch a glimpse of our national bird as it bounces back from near extinction? Now it's not uncommon to see the majestic bald eagle with its tremendous wing span, white head feathers, and curved yellow beak. The white head and tail distinguish the bald from the golden eagle, a bit less rare but just as thrilling to see. Most of New England's bald eagles are in Maine, but they are now present—albeit in small numbers—in all six states.

WILDFLOWERS ALONG THE TRAIL

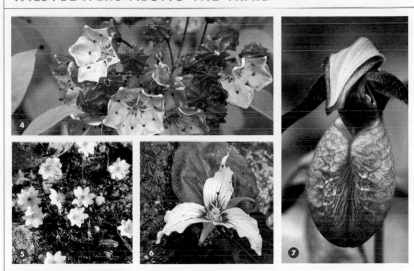

❹ Mountain laurel

The clusters of pink and white blooms of the mountain laurel look like bursts of fireworks. Up close, each one has the delicate detail of a lady's parasol. Blooms vary in color, from pure white to darker pink, and have different amounts of red markings. Connecticut's state flower, mountain laurel flourishes in rocky woods, blooming in May and June. Look for the shrub in southern New England; it's rare along the Appalachian trail in Vermont and Maine.

❺ Mountain avens

A member of the rose family, these showy yellow flowers abound in New Hampshire's White Mountains. You can't miss the large buttercup-like blooms on long green stems when they are in bloom from June through August. So common here, yet extremely rare: the only other place in the whole world where you can find mountain avens is on an island off the coast of Nova Scotia.

❻ Painted trillium

You might smell a trillium before you see it; these flowers have an unpleasant odor that may attract the flies that pollinate it. To identify this impressive flower, look for sets of three: three large pointed blue-green leaves, three sepals (small leaves beneath the petals), and three white petals with a brilliant magenta center. It can take four or five years for a trillium to produce one flower, which blooms in May and June in wet woodlands.

❼ Pink lady slippers

These delicate orchids can grow from 6 to 15 inches high and favor specific wet wooded areas in dappled sunlight. The slender stalk rises from a pair of green leaves, then bends a graceful neck to suspend the paper-thin pale pink closed flower. The slow-growing plant needs help from fungus and bees to survive and can live to be 20 years old. New Hampshire's state wildflower, the pink lady slipper blooms in June throughout New England.

● = Somewhat Common   ● = Rare

4

IN FOCUS HIKING THE APPALACHIAN TRAIL

CHOOSE YOUR DAY HIKE

MAINE

GULF HAGAS, Greenville

Difficult, 8-plus miles round-trip, 6–7 hours

This National Natural Landmark in the North Maine Woods is a spectacular sight for the adventurous day hiker. It involves a long drive on logging roads east from Greenville (see Inland Maine section) to a remote spot and a slippery, sometimes treacherous 8-mile hike around the rim of what's been dubbed Maine's Grand Canyon. Swimming in one of the sparkling pools under a 30-foot-high waterfall and admiring the views of cliffs, cascades, gorges, and chasms in this slate canyon, otherwise unthinkable in New England, will take your breath away.

TABLE ROCK, Bethel

Medium, 2.4 miles round-trip, 2 hours

Maine's Mahoosuc Range is thought to be one of the most difficult stretches of the entire AT, but north of Bethel at Grafton Notch State Park, day hikes range from easy walks in to cascading waterfalls to strenuous climbs up Old Speck's craggy peak. The Table Rock trail offers interesting sights—great views of the notch from the immense slab of granite that gives this trail its name, as well as one of the state's largest system of slab caves—narrow with tall openings unlike underground caves.

NEW HAMPSHIRE

ZEALAND TRAIL, Berlin

Easy, 5.6 miles round-trip, 3.5–4 hours

New Hampshire's Presidential range gets so much attention and traffic that sometimes the equally spectacular Pemigewasset Wilderness, just to its west, gets overlooked. Follow State Route 302 to the trailhead on Zealand Rd. near Bretton Woods. For an easy day hike to one of the Appalachian Mountain Club's excellent overnight huts, take the mostly flat Zealand Trail over bridges and past a beaver swamp to Zealand Pond. The last tenth of a mile is a steep ascent to the mountain retreat, where you might spot an AT through-hiker taking a well-deserved rest. (Most north-bound through-hikers reach this section around July or August.) In winter, you can get here by a lovely cross-country ski trip.

TRAIL NAMES

For through-hikers, doing the AT can be a life-altering experience. One of the trail's most respected traditions is taking an alter ego: a trail name. Lightning Bolt: fast hiker. Pine Knot: tough as one. Bluebearee: because a bear got all her food on her very first night on the trail.

VERMONT

HARMON HILL, Bennington

Medium to difficult, 3.6 miles round-trip, 3–4 hours

This rugged hike in the Green Mountains goes south along the AT where it coincides with the Long Trail, Vermont's century-old "footpath in the wilderness." From the trailhead on Route 9 just east of Bennington, the first half mile or so is strenuous, with some rock and log staircases and hairpins. The payback is the sweeping view from the top; you'll see Mount Anthony, Bennington and its iconic war monument, and the rolling green hills of the Taconics to the west.

STRATTON MOUNTAIN, Stratton

Difficult, 6.6 miles round-trip, 5–6 hours

A steep and steady climb from the trailhead on Kelly Stand Rd. (between West Wardsboro and Arlington) up the 3,936-foot-high Stratton Mountain follows the AT and Long Trail through mixed forests. It's said that this peak is where Benton MacKaye conceived of the idea for the Appalachian Trail in 1921. An observation tower at the summit gives you a great 360-degree view of the Green Mountains. From July to October, you can park at Stratton resort and ride the gondola up (or down) and follow the .75-mile Fire Tower Trail to the southern true peak.

MASSACHUSETTS

MOUNT GREYLOCK, North Adams

Easy to difficult, 2 miles round-trip, less than 1 hour

There are many ways to experience Massachusetts's highest peak. From North Adams, follow Route 2 to the Notch Rd. trailheads. For a warm-up, try the Rounds Rock trail (Easy, 0.7 mi) for some spectacular views. Or drive up the 8-mile-long summit road and hike down the Robinson's Point trail (Difficult, 0.8 miles) for the best view of the Hopper, a glacial cirque that's home to an old-growth red spruce forest. At the summit, the impressive **Bascom Lodge**, built in the 1930s by the Civilian Conservation Corps, provides delicious meals and overnight stays (⊕ www. bascomlodge.net).

CONNECTICUT

LION'S HEAD, Salisbury

Medium, 4.6 miles round-trip, 3.5–4 hours

The AT's 52 miles in Connecticut take hikers up some modest mountains, including Lion's Head in Salisbury. From the trailhead on State Route 41, follow the white blazes of the AT for two easy miles, then take the blue-blazed Lion's Head Trail for a short, steep push over open ledges to the 1,738-foot summit with its commanding views of pastoral southern New England. Try this in summer when the mountain laurels—Connecticut's state flower—are in bloom.

EXPERIENCE MOUNT WASHINGTON

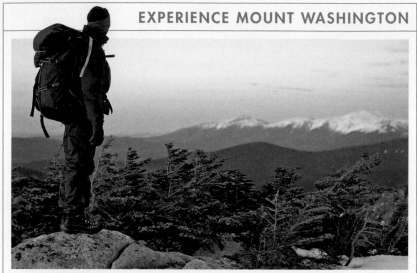

Looking at Mt. Washington from Mt. Bond in the Pemigewasset Wilderness Area, New Hampshire.

Mount Washington is the Northeast's peak of superlatives: worst weather in the world, highest spot in the northeast, windiest place on Earth. It snows in the summer, there are avalanches in winter, and it's foggy 60 percent of the time. Strong 35-mile-per-hour winds are the average, and extreme winds of 100 miles per hour with higher gusts blow year-round. Here, you can literally get blown away.

Explorers, scientists, artists, and botanists have been coming to the mountain for hundreds of years, drawn by its unique geologic features, unusual plants, and exceptional climate.

WHY SO WINDY? The 6,288-foot-high treeless peak is the highest point for miles around, so nothing dampens the force of the wind. Also, the sharp vertical rise causes wind to accelerate. Dramatic changes in air pressure also cause strong, high winds. Add to that the fact that three major storm tracks converge here, and you've got a mountain that has claimed more than 135 lives in the past 150 years.

GOING UP THE MOUNTAIN

An ascent up Mount Washington is for experienced hikers who are prepared for severe, unpredictable weather. Even in summer, cold, wet, foggy, windy conditions prevail. The most popular route to the top is on the eastern face up the Tuckerman Ravine Trail. But countless trails offer plenty of moderate day hikes, like the Alpine Garden Trail, as an alternative to a summit attempt. Start at the Pinkham Notch Visitor Center on Route 16 to review your options.

BACKPACKING ON THE MOUNTAIN

Lakes of the Clouds Hut perches 5,050 feet up the southern shoulder, providing bunkrooms and meals in summer; reservations are required. On the eastern face, the **Hermit Lake Shelter Area** has shelters and tent platforms; to camp here you'll need a first-come, first-served permit from the Visitors Center. Both are operated by the **AMC** (☎ 603/466-2727; ⊕ www.outdoors.org).

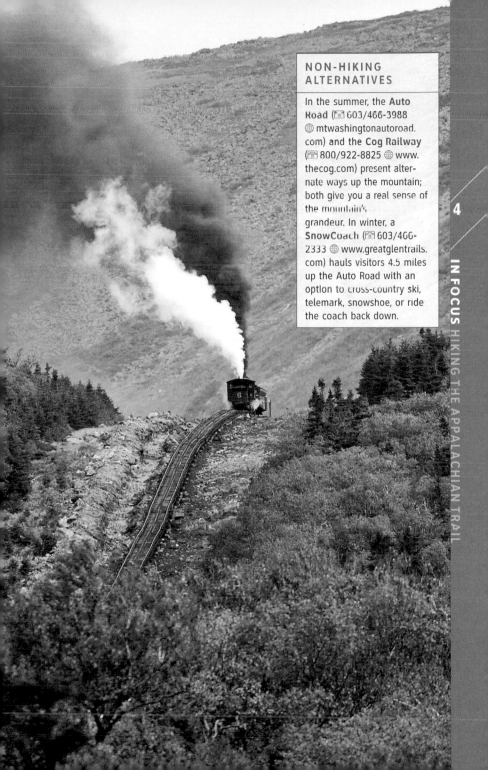

NON-HIKING ALTERNATIVES

In the summer, the **Auto Road** (☎ 603/466-3988 ⊕ mtwashingtonautoroad. com) and the **Cog Railway** (☎ 800/922-8825 ⊕ www. thecog.com) present alternate ways up the mountain; both give you a real sense of the mountain's grandeur. In winter, a **SnowCoach** (☎ 603/466-2333 ⊕ www.greatglentrails. com) hauls visitors 4.5 miles up the Auto Road with an option to cross-country ski, telemark, snowshoe, or ride the coach back down.

sometimes hard to get a reservation. $ *Rooms from: $169* ⌧ *664 U.S. 3, 5 miles north of North Woodstock, Lincoln* ☎ *603/745–8000, 800/343–8000* ⊕ *www.indianheadresort.com* ⤵ *98 rooms, 40 cottages* ❍ *Some meals.*

$$
RESORT
FAMILY
▥ **Mountain Club on Loon.** If you want a ski-in, ski-out stay on Loon Mountain, this lodge centered around a lobby with a large stone fireplace is your only option. **Pros:** within walking distance of the lifts; full-service spa; close to the national forest. **Cons:** very busy in winter. $ *Rooms from: $237* ⌧ *90 Loon Mountain, off Kancamagus Hwy., Lincoln* ☎ *603/745–2244, 800/229–7829* ⊕ *www.mtnclub.com* ⤵ *117 rooms, 117 suites* ❍ *No meals.*

NIGHTLIFE AND PERFORMING ARTS

NIGHTLIFE

Black Diamond Pub. For après-ski socializing, skiers head to this often bustling ski-resort hangout. ⌧ *Mountain Club on Loon, 90 Loon Mountain Rd., Lincoln* ☎ *603/745–2244* ⊕ *www.mtnclub.com.*

FAMILY **Thunderbird Lounge.** Live music, a large dance floor, and great lake views make this a year-round hot spot. ⌧ *Indian Head Resort, 664 U.S. 3, Lincoln* ☎ *603/745–8000* ⊕ *www.indianheadresort.com.*

PERFORMING ARTS

FAMILY **Jean's Playhouse.** The area's year-round stage for comedy, theater, music, and other performances is a popular venue. ⌧ *34 Papermill Dr., Lincoln* ☎ *603/745–2141* ⊕ *www.jeans-playhouse.com.*

SPORTS AND THE OUTDOORS

FAMILY **Loon Mountain.** Wide, straight, and consistent intermediate ski trails prevail at Loon, a modern resort on the western edge of the Pemigewasset River. The most advanced runs are grouped on the North Peak section, with 2,100 feet of vertical skiing. Beginner trails are set apart. There's snow tubing on the lower slopes, and eight terrain parks suitable for all ages and ability levels. In the base lodge are the usual dining and lounging facilities. There are 13 miles of cross-country trails, ice-skating on an outdoor rink, snowshoeing and snowshoeing tours, and a rock-climbing wall. **Facilities:** 61 trails; 370 acres; 2,100-foot vertical drop; 12 lifts. ⌧ *60 Loon Mountain Rd., off the Kancamagus Hwy., Lincoln* ☎ *603/745–8111* ⊕ *www.loonmtn.com* ▱ *Lift ticket $85.*

FAMILY **Pemi Valley Moose Tours.** If you're eager to see a mighty moose, embark on a moose-watching bus tour into the northernmost White Mountains. The three-hour trips depart at 8:30 pm May to mid-October for the best wildlife-sighting opportunities. ⌧ *136 Main St., off I–93, Lincoln* ☎ *603/745–2744* ⊕ *www.moosetoursnh.com* ▱ *$30.*

FRANCONIA

16 miles northwest of Lincoln/North Woodstock.

Travelers have long passed through the White Mountains via the spectacular Franconia Notch, and in the late 18th century a town evolved just to the north. It and the region's jagged rock formations and heavy coat of evergreens stirred the imaginations of Washington Irving, Henry Wadsworth Longfellow, and Nathaniel Hawthorne, who penned a short story about the craggy cliff known as the Old Man of the Mountain. There is almost no town proper to speak of here, just a handful of stores near Interstate 93, aka the Franconia Notch Parkway.

Four miles west of Franconia, Sugar Hill is a town of about 500 people. It's famous for its spectacular sunsets and views of the Franconia Mountains, best seen from Sunset Hill, where a row of grand hotels and mansions once stood.

GETTING HERE AND AROUND

Franconia is a small town with not much to offer tourists, but it is an access point for many ski areas and the villages of Sugar Hill, Easton, Bethlehem, Bretton Woods, Littleton, Lincoln, and North Woodstock—towns replete with general stores, country inns, picturesque farms, and churches with white steeples.

ESSENTIALS

Visitor Information Franconia Notch Chamber of Commerce. ☎ *603/823–5661* ⊕ *www.franconianotch.org.*

EXPLORING

FAMILY **Flume Gorge.** This 800-foot-long chasm has narrow walls that cause an eerie echo from the gorge's running water. A long wooden boardwalk and a series of stairways lead to the top of the falls that thunder down the gorge. The 2-mile loop takes about an hour to complete. The boardwalk begins at the visitor center, which also has a gift shop, a cafeteria, and a small museum. ⊠ *Franconia Notch State Park, 852 Daniel Webster Hwy.* ☎ *603/745–8391* ⊕ *www.nhstateparks.org* ⌕ *$16.*

The Frost Place Museum. Robert Frost's year-round home from 1915 to 1920, this is where the poet soaked up the New England life. The place is imbued with the spirit of his work, down to the rusted mailbox in front that's painted "R. Frost" in simple lettering. Two rooms contain memorabilia and signed editions of his books. Out back, you can follow short trails marked with lines from his poetry. This place will slow you down and remind you of the intense beauty of the surrounding countryside. Poetry readings are scheduled on many summer evenings. ⊠ *158 Ridge Rd.* ☎ *603/823–5510* ⊕ *www.frostplace.org* ⌕ *$5.*

FAMILY **New England Ski Museum.** This small museum lets you travel back in time to see how skiing began as a sport, particularly in New England. Here you can examine artifacts, clothing, and equipment, as well as Bode Miller's five Olympic medals. For lifelong ski enthusiasts, the trip down memory lane will likely evoke warm smiles. ⊠ *Franconia Notch State Park, 135 Tramway Dr., next to Cannon Mountain Tramway* ⊕ *www.skimuseum.org* ⌕ *Free.*

FAMILY **Old Man of the Mountain.** This somber profile in the rock high above Franconia Notch crumbled somewhat unexpectedly in 2003. The iconic image had defined New Hampshire, and the Old Man's "death" stunned and saddened residents. You can see photographs and learn about the history of the Old Man at the visitor center at Flume Gorge. Better yet, follow signs to a small Old Man of the Mountain Park. There you can view the mountain face through newly installed steel rods that seem to literally put the beloved visage back on the mountain. ⊠ *Franconia Notch State Park, U.S. 3* ⊕ *www.oldmannh.org* ⊠ *Free.*

WHERE TO EAT AND STAY

$ ✕ **Polly's Pancake Parlor.** In the Dexter family for three generations,
AMERICAN Polly's has been serving up pancakes and waffles (from its own origi-
FAMILY nal recipe) since the 1930s. Smoked bacon and ham, sandwiches on homemade bread, delicious baked beans, and, more recently, gluten-free items have since been added to the menu. Desserts include raspberry pie. Much of the food is made from grains ground on-site. The gift shop sells maple products. In 2015, a new dining room was built, though all the antiques and country charm remain. ⑤ *Average main: $10* ⊠ *672 Rte. 117* ☎ *603/823–5575* ⊕ *www.pollyspancakeparlor.com* ۞ *Closed Mon.–Wed. Nov.–early Mar.*

$$$$ ✕ **Sugar Hill Inn.** Inside this romantic 1789 farmhouse you'll find a very
AMERICAN elegant dining room where memorable prix-fixe meals ($68) are pre-
Fodor's Choice pared by chef Val Fortin. Start with a trio of his favorite soups or a
★ butternut squash risotto, followed by a beet-and-anise garden salad. Entrées may include peppercorn-crusted sirloin steak with grilled mush-rooms and truffle oil, or free-range duck served three ways: breast with a bittersweet chocolate sauce, braised leg, and foie-gras ravioli. The apple dumpling with pumpkin ice cream and the goat cheese crème brûlée with fruit are among the creative homemade desserts. ⑤ *Average main: $68* ⊠ *116 Rte. 117* ☎ *603/823–5621* ⊕ *www.sugarhillinn.com* ۞ *Closed Wed. No lunch* ⚬ *Reservations essential.*

$ 🏨 **Franconia Inn.** At this 100-acre family-friendly resort, you can play
RESORT tennis on four clay courts, soak in the outdoor heated pool or hot tub,
FAMILY hop on a mountain bike, or soar in a glider. **Pros:** good for kids; amaz-ing views; outdoor heated pool. **Cons:** may be too remote for some. ⑤ *Rooms from: $149* ⊠ *1172 Easton Rd.* ☎ *603/823–5542, 800/473–5299* ⊕ *www.franconiainn.com* ۞ *Closed Apr.–mid-May* ⤴ *34 rooms, 3 suites, 1 cottage with 2 units with kitchens* ⏀ *Some meals.*

SPORTS AND THE OUTDOORS

SKI AREAS

FAMILY **Cannon Mountain.** The first aerial tramway in North America was built here in 1938, and the view from the top of the 4,080-foot summit is spectacular on a clear day. The ride is free with a ski lift ticket; other-wise it's $17. In winter, you'll find classic New England ski terrain that runs the gamut from steep pitches off the peak to gentle blue cruisers. Beginners may want to head over to the separate Tuckerbrook family area, which offers 13 trails and four lifts. Adventurous types will want to try out the Mittersill area, which has 86 acres of lift-accessed "side country" trails and glades where the snow is au naturel. **Facilities:** 81 trails; 282 acres; 2,180-foot vertical drop; 10 lifts. ⊠ *9 Franconia Notch State Park, off U.S. 3* ☎ *603/823–8800, 603/823–7771 for snow condi-tions* ⊕ *www.cannonmt.com* ⊠ *Lift ticket $75.*

FAMILY **Franconia Village Cross-Country Ski Center.** The cross-country ski center at the Franconia Inn has more than 40 miles of groomed and backcountry trails and rents skis, boots, and poles. One popular route leads to Bridal Veil Falls, a great spot for a picnic lunch. You can also enjoy horse-drawn sleigh rides, snowshoeing, snow tubing, and ice-skating on a lighted rink. ✉ *Franconia Inn, 1172 Easton Rd.* ☎ *603/823–5542, 800/473–5299* ⊕ *www.franconiainn.com/cross_country_ski_center.php* 🍴 *$12.*

SHOPPING

FAMILY **Sugar Hill Sampler.** In this 1815 barn set high on a hill, you'll find an old-fashioned general store filled with quilts, lamps, candles, ornaments, and other crafts, along with gourmet jams, sauces, and condiments. In the back, owner Barbara Serafini has set up a folksy museum with local photos, newspaper clippings, and curiosities—Bette Davis's will among them. ✉ *22 Sunset Rd., Sugar Hill* ☎ *603/823–8478* ⊕ *www. sugarhillsampler.com.*

LITTLETON

7 miles north of Franconia, 86 miles north of Concord.

One of northern New Hampshire's largest towns (this isn't saying much, mind you) is on a granite shelf along the Ammonoosuc River, whose swift current and drop of 235 feet enabled the community to flourish as a mill center in its early days. The railroad came through some time later, and Littleton grew into the region's commercial hub. In the minds of many, it's more a place to stock up on supplies than a real destination itself, but few communities have worked harder at revitalization. Intriguing shops and eateries line Main Street, whose tidy 19th- and early-20th-century buildings suggest a set in a Jimmy Stewart movie.

GETTING HERE AND AROUND

Littleton sits just off Interstate 95. Take Exit 41 and follow Cottage Street north to Main Street, portions of which are also signed as Route 116, Route 18, and U.S. 302.

EXPLORING

FAMILY **The Rocks Estate.** The estate of John Jacob Glessner (1843–1936), one of the founders of International Harvester, now serves as the 1,400-acre North Country Conservation and Education Center for the Forest Society. Some of the most striking restored buildings here are in the Shingle style. The property is named for the many surface boulders on the estate when Glessner bought it—some were used to erect its rambling rock walls. Open year-round, the Rocks presents natural-history programs and has self-guided tours and hiking trails with excellent views of the Presidential Range. Come winter, cross-country ski trails and a select-your-own-Christmas-tree farm open up. In spring, watch syrup being made in the New Hampshire Maple Experience Museum. ✉ *4 Christmas Tree La., Bethlehem* ☎ *603/444–6228* ⊕ *www.therocks.org.*

QUICK
BITES

Miller's Cafe & Bakery. Next to the Riverwalk Covered Bridge, this great stop for breakfast or lunch serves salads, sandwiches, and fabulous baked goods like the chocolate-pecan pie. On a nice day, enjoy the Ammonoosuc River views from the deck. If staying in the area, order a meal to go or have it delivered. ✉ *16 Mill St.* ☎ *603/444–2146* ⊕ *www.millerscafeandbakery. com* ⊘ *No dinner.*

4

FAMILY　**Thayers Inn.** A former grande-dame hotel and still a working inn, Thayers also functions as an informal museum. Many of the rooms have been recently renovated with new paint, linens, and furniture, but enough antiques remain to lend it yesteryear charm. In the lobby and lining the hall are photos and memorabilia from movie star Bette Davis's huge birthday bash and artifacts of other illustrious guests, including Ulysses S. Grant, Henry Ford, P. T. Barnum, and Richard Nixon. Request a key to climb up to the cupola for a 360-degree view of the town. Two rooms are open to the public: one set up as a guest room from the 1840s, and the other a scene from *Pollyanna*, written by Littleton native Eleanor Hodgman Porter (born 1868). ⊠ *111 Main St.* ☏ *603/444–6469* ⊕ *www.thayersinn.com.*

OFF THE BEATEN PATH　**Whitefield.** About 11 miles northeast of Littleton, the small village of Whitefield became a prominent summer resort in the late 19th century, when wealthy industrialists flocked to this rolling valley to play golf and hobnob with each other. The yellow clapboard Mountain View Grand Hotel, which first opened in 1865, is once again one of New England's grandest resorts. It's worth driving through the courtly Colonial center of town and up Route 116 just beyond to see this magnificent structure atop a bluff overlooking the Presidentials. ⊠ *Whitefield* ⊕ *www.whitefieldnh.org.*

WHERE TO EAT AND STAY

$$$
AMERICAN
✕ **Tim-bir Alley.** Here's a rare find in New Hampshire: an independent restaurant in a contemporary setting that's been serving customers for decades yet still takes its food seriously. If you're in town, don't miss it. Tim Carr's menu changes weekly and uses regional American ingredients in creative ways. Entrées may include an eggplant pâté with feta cheese, red pepper, and a tomato-herb marmalade, or basil-and-olive-oil salmon with a spinach-Brie-pecan pesto. Save room for white chocolate–coconut cheesecake and other desserts. ⑤ *Average main: $25* ⊠ *7 Main St.* ☏ *603/444–6142* ▭ *No credit cards* ⊙ *Closed Jan.–Apr., and Mon. and Tues. No lunch.*

$$
B&B/INN
Fodor's Choice
★
⌂ **Adair Country Inn and Restaurant.** An air of yesteryear refinement suffuses Adair, a three-story Georgian Revival home that attorney Frank Hogan built as a wedding present for his daughter in 1927. **Pros:** refined, book-filled spaces; rates include a gourmet breakfast; cross-country skiing. **Cons:** removed from town. ⑤ *Rooms from: $229* ⊠ *80 Guider La., off I–93, Bethlehem* ☏ *603/444–2600, 888/444–2600* ⊕ *www.adairinn. com* ⊙ *Closed mid-Nov. and Apr.* ⬳ *11 rooms* ⦿| *Some meals.*

SHOPPING

FAMILY　**Little Village Toy and Book Stop.** If you're looking for hiking maps or good books about the history of the area, you'll find them here, along with unusual children's toys and many adult fiction and nonfiction titles. On the lower level is the League of New Hampshire Craftsmen's shop, featuring glass, prints, ceramics, fiber, and more. ⊠ *81 Main St.* ☏ *603/444–5263.*

Potato Barn Antiques Center. Ten dealers operating out of an old potato-storage barn sell antique lamps, vintage clothing and hats, costume jewelry, books, railroad lanterns, signs, and old tools. ⊠ *960 Lancaster Rd., 6 miles north of Lancaster, Northumberland* ☏ *603/636–2611* ⊕ *www.potatobarnantiques.com.*

BRETTON WOODS

14 miles southeast of Bethlehem; 28 miles northeast of Lincoln/ Woodstock.

In the early 1900s private railcars brought the elite from New York and Philadelphia to the Omni Mount Washington Hotel, the jewel of the White Mountains. A visit to the hotel, which was the site of the 1944 United Nations conference that created the International Monetary Fund and the International Bank for Reconstruction and Development (and the birth of many conspiracy theories), is not to be missed. The area is also known for its cog railway and the Bretton Woods ski resort.

GETTING HERE AND AROUND

Bretton Woods is in the heart of the White Mountains on U.S. 302. A free shuttle makes it easy to get around the resort's various facilities. Helpful advice on how to enjoy your stay can be found at the concierge and activities desk in the main lobby of the Omni Mount Washington Hotel.

EXPLORING

FAMILY

Fodor's Choice

★

Mount Washington Cog Railway. In 1858, Sylvester Marsh petitioned the state legislature for permission to build a steam railway up Mt. Washington. One politico retorted that Marsh would have better luck building a railroad to the moon, but 11 years later the Mount Washington Cog Railway chugged its way up to the summit along a 3-mile track on the mountain's west side. Today it's one of the state's most beloved attractions—a thrill in either direction. A small museum at the base has exhibits about the cog rail. The full trip takes three hours including an hour spent at the summit. ⊠ *3168 Base Station Rd., 6 miles northeast of Bretton Woods* ☎ *603/278-5404, 800/922-8825* ⊕ *www.thecog. com* ⊠ *$68.*

WHERE TO EAT

$$$

AMERICAN

✕ Bretton Arms Dining Room. You're likely to have the best meal in the area at this intimate restaurant. Though the same chef oversees the Omni Mount Washington Hotel's Main Dining Room, the latter is vast, and the Bretton Arms much cozier. The menu is seasonal and might include Georges Bank scallops with pureed celery root, baby bok choy, and cippolini onions. Locally sourced food features prominently in all dishes. ⑤ *Average main: $30* ⊠ *310 Mt. Washington Rd.* ☎ *603/278–1000* ⊕ *www.omnihotels.com/hotels/bretton-woods-bretton-arms/dining* ⊙ *No lunch.*

$$

AMERICAN

FAMILY

✕ Fabyan's Station. A model train circles the dining room, a nod to the late 19th century, when 60 trains stopped at this former railroad station every day. If you're looking for an easygoing meal, Fabyan's cooks up delicious clam chowder in a bread bowl and house-smoked ribs with coleslaw. There's a kids' menu, too. ⑤ *Average main: $20* ⊠ *U.S. 302, 1 mile north of ski area* ☎ *603/278–2222* ⊕ *www.brettonwoods.com* ⚐ *Reservations not accepted.*

$$$$

AMERICAN

✕ Main Dining Room. You'd be hard-pressed to find a larger or grander space in New Hampshire than the Omni Mount Washington Hotel's enormous octagonal Main Dining Room, which has massive windows that open onto spectacular views of the Presidential Range. Subtle renovations have brought the place, built in 1902, into the 21st century.

Seasonal classics with a twist use ingredients sourced from local New Hampshire farms and suppliers. On the constantly changing menu you may find wild salmon wrapped in buttery pastry served over lobster succotash or a rosemary-scented rack of lamb with candied beets. ■TIP➔ Appropriate evening wear is expected, meaning no shorts or sneakers. $ *Average main: $36* ✉ *Omni Mount Washington Hotel, 310 Mt. Washington Rd.* ☎ *603/278–1000* ⊕ *www.mountwashingtonresort.com* ☾ *No lunch* ♤ *Reservations essential* 🏛 *Jacket required.*

WHERE TO STAY

$ 🔲 **The Lodge.** Rooms at this inexpensive roadside motel have private
HOTEL balconies that overlook the Presidential Range. **Pros:** inexpensive; access to many amenities; free ski shuttle. **Cons:** across street from resort amenities; Continental breakfast only. $ *Rooms from: $159* ✉ *99 Ski Area Rd.* ☎ *603/278–1000, 800/680–6600* ⊕ *www.brettonwoods.com* ⇨ *50 rooms* ⦿ *Breakfast.*

$$ 🔲 **The Notchland Inn.** Built in 1862 by Sam Bemis, America's grandfather
B&B/INN of landscape photography, the house conveys mountain charm on a
Fodor'sChoice scale unmatched in New England. **Pros:** middle-of-the-forest setting;
★ marvelous house and common rooms; good dinners. **Cons:** may seem too isolated for some. $ *Rooms from: $295* ✉ *2 Morey Rd., Hart's Location* ☎ *603/374–6131* ⊕ *www.notchland.com* ⇨ *8 rooms, 5 suites, 2 cottages* ⦿ *Breakfast.*

$$$ 🔲 **Omni Mount Washington Hotel.** The two most memorable sights in the
RESORT White Mountains would have to be Mt. Washington and the Omni
FAMILY Mount Washington Hotel. **Pros:** beautiful resort; loads of activities; free
Fodor'sChoice shuttle to skiing and activities. **Cons:** kids love to run around the hotel.
★ $ *Rooms from: $395* ✉ *310 Mt. Washington Hotel Rd., off U.S. 302* ☎ *603/278–1000* ⊕ *www.mountwashingtonresort.com* ⇨ *175 rooms, 25 suites* ⦿ *Some meals.*

SPORTS AND THE OUTDOORS
SKI AREA

FAMILY **Bretton Woods.** New Hampshire's largest ski area is also one of the coun-
Fodor'sChoice try's best family ski resorts. The views of Mt. Washington alone are
★ worth the visit, and the scenery is especially beautiful from the Latitude 44 restaurant, open during ski season.

The resort has something for everyone. Steeper pitches, near the top of the 1,500-foot vertical, and glades will keep experts busy, and snowboarders will enjoy the three terrain parks. The Nordic trail system has 62 miles of cross-country ski trails. Both night skiing and snowboarding are available on weekends and holidays. Bretton Woods is also a great place to learn to ski. Trails appeal mostly to novice and intermediate skiers, including two magic carpet lifts for beginners. The Hobbit Ski and Snowplay program, for ages 3–5, is an introduction to skiing, and the Hobbit Ski and Snowboard School, for ages 4–12, has full- and half-day lessons. The complimentary Kinderwoods Winter Playground has a sled carousel, igloos, and a zip line. A snowmobile park at the base area is fun for kids ages 4–13. Parents can purchase interchangeable family tickets that allow them to take turns skiing while the other watches the kids—both passes come for the price of one. The ski area also offers an adaptive program for anyone with disabilities.

One recent addition is the year-round Canopy Tour ($110), which has nine zip lines, two sky bridges, and three rappelling stations. Small groups are led by experienced guides. The tour is an exhilarating introduction to flora and fauna of the White Mountains. **Facilities:** 62 trails; 464 acres, 1,500-foot vertical drop; 10 lifts. ⊠ *99 Ski Area Rd.* ☎ *603/278–3320, 603/278–1000 for weather conditions* ⊕ *www.brettonwoods.com* ✉ *Lift ticket $89.*

EN
ROUTE

Crawford Notch State Park. Scenic U.S. 302 winds southeast of Bretton Woods through the steep, wooded mountains on either side of spectacular Crawford Notch, passing through Crawford Notch State Park, where you can picnic and take a short hike to Arethusa Falls, the longest drop in New England, or to the Silver and Flume cascades. The 5,775-acre park has a number of roadside photo opportunities. Its visitor center has a gift shop, a snack bar, and a picnic area. ⊠ *1464 U.S. 302, Hart's Location* ☎ *603/374–2272* ⊕ *www.nhstateparks.org.*

4

BARTLETT

18 miles southeast of Bretton Woods.

With Bear Mountain to its south; Mt. Parker to its north; Mt. Cardigan to its west; and the Saco River to its east; Bartlett, incorporated in 1790, has an unforgettable setting. Lovely Bear Notch Road (closed in winter) has the only midpoint access to the Kancamagus Highway. There isn't much town to speak of: the dining options listed are actually in Glen. It's best known for the Attitash Ski Resort, within walking distance.

GETTING HERE AND AROUND

U.S. 302 passes though Bartlett, southeast from Bretton Woods and west from Glen. Attitash Ski Resort is south of U.S. 302 in Bartlett, signed in town as Crawford Notch Road.

WHERE TO EAT

$$

SOUTHWESTERN
FAMILY

✕ **Margarita Grill.** Après-ski types like to congregate on the Margarita Grill's enclosed heated patio and unwind with a margarita. Tex-Mex and Southwestern specialties served here include homemade salsas, wood-fired steaks, ribs, chicken, and burgers. All ingredients are local and fresh, this being a New Hampshire farm-to-table-certified restaurant. ⑤ *Average main: $22* ⊠ *78 U.S. 302, Glen* ☎ *603/383–6556* ⊕ *www.margaritagrillnh.com* ⊗ *No lunch weekdays.*

$$

AMERICAN
FAMILY

✕ **Red Parka Steakhouse & Pub.** This downtown pub has been an institution for nearly 40 years. Highlights of the family-oriented menu include hand-cut steaks and barbecue ribs, and there's a locally sourced all you-can-eat salad bar. The barbecue sauce is made on-site, and beer is served in mason jars. Plan to spend some time reading the dozens and dozens of license plates that adorn the walls of the downstairs pub. Open-mike night takes place on Monday, live entertainment on Friday and Saturday. ⑤ *Average main: $24* ⊠ *3 Station St., off U.S. 302, Glen* ☎ *603/383–4344* ⊕ *www.redparkapub.com* ⊗ *No lunch* ⋖ *Reservations not accepted.*

WHERE TO STAY

$$ ⌨ **Attitash Grand Summit Hotel & Conference Center.** If ski-in, ski-out con-
HOTEL   venience at Attitash is a must, book your stay at the resort's hotel at
FAMILY   the base of Bear Peak. **Pros:** great location; outdoor pool and hot tubs;
ski-package discounts; kitchenettes in all rooms. **Cons:** generally bland
accommodations; facility could use sprucing up. ⑤ *Rooms from: $259*
✉ *104 Grand Summit Rd.* ☎ *603/374–1900, 888/554–1900* ⊕ *www.
attitash.com* ⇌ *143 rooms* ⊖ *No meals.*

$ ⌨ **Attitash Mountain Village Resort.** Hidden in a cluster of pine trees across
HOTEL   from the ski area is a resort with guest rooms—a few of them actu-
FAMILY   ally slope-side—that crest the top of this mountain. **Pros:** simple fam-
ily place; fitness room; nice pools. **Cons:** more functional than posh.
⑤ *Rooms from: $159* ✉ *784 U.S. 302* ☎ *603/374–6501, 800/862–1600*
⊕ *www.attitashmtvillage.com/lodging* ⇌ *350 units* ⊖ *No meals.*

SPORTS AND THE OUTDOORS

SKI AREA

FAMILY   **Attitash Ski Resort.** With a vertical drop of 1,750 feet, Attitash Mountain
has dozens of trails to explore, and there are more on the adjacent Atti-
tash Bear Peak (vertical drop 1,450 feet). You'll find traditional New
England ski runs and challenging terrain alongside wide-open cruisers
that suit all skill levels. There are acres of glades, plus a progressive free-
style terrain park. The Attitash Adventure Center has a rental shop, and
also offers lessons and children's programs. **Facilities:** 68 trails; 311 acres;
1,750-foot vertical drop; 11 lifts. ✉ *775 U.S. 302* ☎ *800/223–7669*
⊕ *www.attitash.com* ⌁ *Lift ticket $75 weekdays, $79 weekends.*

JACKSON

7 miles northeast of Bartlett.

Fodor's Choice   Just off Route 16 via a red covered bridge, Jackson has retained its
★   storybook New England character. Art and antiques shopping, tennis,
golf, fishing, and hiking to waterfalls are among the draws. When the
snow falls, Jackson becomes the state's cross-country skiing capital, and
there are also four downhill ski areas nearby—hotels and inns provide
ski shuttles. Visit Jackson Falls for a wonderful photo opportunity.

ESSENTIALS

Visitor Information Jackson Area Chamber of Commerce. ☎ *603/383–9356*
⊕ *www.jacksonnh.com.*

EXPLORING

FAMILY   **Story Land.** This theme park with life-size storybook and nursery-rhyme
characters is geared to kids (ages 2–12). The 23 rides include a flumer,
a river raft, and the Roar-O-Saurus and Polar Coaster roller coasters.
Play areas and magic shows provide additional entertainment. ✉ *850
Rte. 16, Glen* ☎ *603/383–4186* ⊕ *www.storylandnh.com* ⌁ *$33.*

WHERE TO EAT

$$ ✕ **Red Fox Bar & Grille.** Some say this big family restaurant overlooking
AMERICAN   the Wentworth Golf Club gets its name from a wily fox with a pen-
FAMILY   chant for stealing golf balls off the nearby fairway. Burgers, barbecue
ribs, and wood-fired pizzas are on the dinner menu, along with more

refined dishes such as seared sea scallops and bourbon steak tips. Lunch is served on Saturday, and there's a popular Sunday breakfast buffet. Younger kids will enjoy the playroom, especially if there's a wait for a table. $ *Average main: $20* ✉ *49 Rte. 16* ☎ *603/383–4949* ⊕ *www. redfoxbarandgrille.com* ⊘ *No lunch weekdays.*

$$$
AMERICAN
Fodor's Choice
★

✕ **Thorn Hill.** This famous inn serves up memorable meals in a romantic atmosphere, with dim lighting and piano music trickling in from the lounge. Many people enjoy dining on the heated porch, which has views of the Presidential Range. The flavorful dishes include pan-seared trout, Peking duck on a scallion pancake with sesame bok choy, and New York sirloin in a blue cheese demi-glace. $ *Average main: $26* ✉ *42 Thorn Hill Rd.* ☎ *603/383–4242, 800/289–8990* ⊕ *www.innatthornhill.com* ⊘ *No lunch.*

WHERE TO STAY

$
B&B/INN
FAMILY

🖼 **Christmas Farm Inn and Spa.** Despite its wintery name, this 1778 inn is an all-season retreat. **Pros:** kids are welcome; indoor and outdoor pools; very close to ski area; room rate includes a full breakfast. **Cons:** can get busy with kids. $ *Rooms from: $169* ✉ *3 Blitzen Way, off Rte. 16B* ☎ *603/383–4313, 800/443–5837* ⊕ *www.christmasfarminn.com* ⇆ *18 rooms, 16 suites, 7 cottages* ❏ *Breakfast.*

$
B&B/INN
Fodor's Choice
★

🖼 **Inn at Jackson.** This bright bed-and-breakfast is impeccably maintained and charmingly furnished. **Pros:** exceptional rooms; peaceful setting; wonderful breakfasts. **Cons:** top-floor rooms lack fireplaces. $ *Rooms from: $189* ✉ *Thorn Hill Rd. and Main St.* ☎ *603/383–4321, 800/289–8600* ⊕ *www.innatjackson.com* ⇆ *14 rooms* ❏ *Breakfast.*

$$
B&B/INN
Fodor's Choice
★

🖼 **The Inn at Thorn Hill & Spa.** With a large reception room and sweeping staircase, this inn—modeled after an 1891 Victorian designed by Stanford White—is breathtaking throughout. **Pros:** romantic setting; soothing spa; full breakfast included; relaxed elegance. **Cons:** Wi-Fi works on main floor, but not in the rooms. $ *Rooms from: $219* ✉ *42 Thorn Hill Rd.* ☎ *800/289–8990, 800/289–8990* ⊕ *www.innatthornhill.com* ⇆ *17 rooms, 5 suites, 3 cottages* ❏ *Some meals.*

SPORTS AND THE OUTDOORS
SKI AREAS

FAMILY

Black Mountain. Friendly, informal Black Mountain has a warming southern exposure. The Family Passport allows two adults and two kids to ski at highly discounted rates both during the week ($129) and on weekends ($159)—a great deal, even with regular rates considered among the lowest in the Mt. Washington Valley. The trails and glades on the 3,303-foot mountain (highest skiable elevation 2,350 feet) are evenly divided among beginner, intermediate, and expert ability levels. There's a nursery for kids over six months old. Enjoy guided horseback riding from spring through fall. **Facilities:** 45 trails; 143 acres; 1,100-foot vertical drop; 4 lifts. ✉ *373 Black Mountain Rd.* ☎ *603/383–4490, 800/475–4669 for snow conditions* ⊕ *www.blackmt.com* ⊿ *Lift ticket $40 weekdays, $55 weekends and holidays.*

FAMILY
Fodor's Choice
★

Jackson Ski Touring Foundation. Experts rate this the best-run cross-country ski operation in the country. That's due to the great advice you get from the attentive staff, and to the 60 miles of groomed trails for skiing, skate skiing, and snowshoeing. The varied terrain offers something for all abilities. Jackson Ski Touring's 80 trails wind through covered bridges and into the picturesque village of Jackson, where you can warm up in cozy trailside restaurants. Lessons and rentals are available. ⊠ *153 Main St.* ☏ *603/383–9355* ⊕ *www.jacksonxc.org.*

MT. WASHINGTON

20 miles northwest of Jackson.

At 6,288 feet, Mt. Washington is the highest peak in the northeastern United States. The world's highest winds, 231 mph, were recorded here in 1934. You can take a guided bus tour, a drive, or a hike to the summit. A number of trails circle the mountain and the other peaks in the Presidential Range, but all of them are strenuous. It gets cold up here: even in the summer, you'll want a jacket.

GETTING HERE AND AROUND
Mt. Washington Road heads west from Route 16 about 2 miles north of Wildcat Mountain ski resort and 8 miles south of Gorham.

EXPLORING
FAMILY **Mt. Washington Auto Road.** The drive to the top of the imposing Mt.
Fodor's Choice Washington is among the most memorable White Mountains experi-
★ ences. Your route: the narrow, curving Mt. Washington Auto Road, which climbs 4,600 feet in a little more than 7 miles. Upon admission to this private road, drivers receive a CD with a narrated tour, along with a bumper sticker that reads, "This car climbed Mt. Washington." The narration is fascinating, and the views are breathtaking. Once at the top, check out **Extreme Mount Washington,** an interactive museum dedicated to science and weather. ⊠ *1 Mt. Washington Auto Rd., at Rte. 16, Pinkham Notch* ☏ *603/356–2137* ⊕ *www.mountwashington. org* ⊠ *Car and driver $28, plus $8 per additional adult; museum $5 (free with auto tour).*

SPORTS AND THE OUTDOORS
All trails to Mt. Washington's peak are rough and take considerable time. Perhaps the most famous is the **Tuckerman Ravine Trail,** the path used by extreme skiers who risk life and limb to fly down the face of the steep ravine. The hike to the top can easily take five–nine hours round-trip. Because the weather here is so erratic, it's critical to check weather conditions, to be prepared, and to keep in mind that Mt. Washington's summit is much colder than its base. The average year-round temperature is below freezing, and the average wind velocity is 35 mph.

FAMILY **Great Glen Trails Outdoor Center.** This outdoor center at the foot of Mt. Washington is the base for year-around outdoor activities. Renowned for its dramatic 25-mile cross-country trail system, Great Glen provides access to more than 1,100 acres of backcountry. Trees shelter most of the trails, so Mt. Washington's infamous weather isn't such a concern. You can travel to the mountain's upper reaches in a Mt. Washington SnowCoach, a nine-passenger van refitted with triangular snowmobile-like treads. You have the option of skiing or snowshoeing down or just enjoying the magnificent winter view. The center has a huge ski and sports shop, a food court, a climbing wall, and an observation deck. In summer it's the base for hiking and biking and has programs in canoeing, kayaking, and fly-fishing. ⊠ *1 Mt. Washington Auto Rd., at Rte. 16, Pinkham Notch* ☎ *603/466–2333* ⊕ *www.greatglentrails.com* ⊠ *Trail pass $20, SnowCoach $49.*

Pinkham Notch. Although not a town per se, scenic Pinkham Notch covers Mt. Washington's eastern side and has several ravines, including the famous Tuckerman Ravine. The Appalachian Mountain Club operates a visitor center that provides year-around trail information to hikers. Guided hikes leave from the center, and you can take outdoor skills workshops there. On-site are an outdoors shop and a cafeteria. ⊠ *Visitor Center, 361 Rte. 16, Pinkham Notch* ☎ *603/466–2721* ⊕ *www.pinkhamnotchnh.com.*

FAMILY **Wildcat Mountain.** Glade skiers will love Wildcat and its 28 acres of designated tree skiing. Runs include some stunning double-black diamond trails; experts can really zip down the Lynx. Skiers who can hold a wedge should check out the 2½-mile-long Polecat, which offers excellent views of the Presidential Range. The trails are classic New England—narrow and winding—and the views are stunning. Beginners will find gentle terrain and a broad teaching slope. For an adrenaline rush, there's a terrain park. In summer you can dart to the top on the four-passenger gondola, hike the many well-kept trails, and fish in the crystal clear streams. **Facilities:** 48 trails; 225 acres; 2,112-foot vertical drop; 5 lifts. ⊠ *Rte. 16, Pinkham Notch* ☎ *603/466–3326, 888/754–9453 for snow conditions* ⊕ *www.skiwildcat.com* ⊠ *Lift ticket $75 weekdays, $79 weekends.*

DIXVILLE NOTCH

63 miles north of Mt. Washington, 66 miles northeast of Littleton, 149 miles north of Concord.

Just 12 miles from the Canadian border, this tiny community is known for the fact that it and another New Hampshire community, Hart's Location, are the first election districts in the nation to vote in presidential general elections.

GETTING HERE AND AROUND
Dixville Notch is along Route 26, 12 miles west of Route 16 and 11 miles east of U.S. 3.

EXPLORING
FAMILY **Poore Farm Historic Homestead.** Maybe you've visited farm museums before, but certainly not one like this. Established in 1825, this farm has survived almost perfectly intact because the Poore family never installed electricity or other modern conveniences. They lived here for a century and a half, and apparently saved everything. The house, barn, outbuildings, and gardens provide a rare opportunity to see how rural New Englanders actually lived, dressed, ate, farmed, and socialized. It's the perfect backdrop for farming demonstrations, music festivals, and discussions about farm life. ⊠ *629 Hollow Rd., 7 miles north of Colebrook, Stewartstown* ⊕ *www.poorefarm.org* ⊠ *$10.*

The highest peak in New England, Mt. Washington rewards those who drive or hike to the top with spectacular views.

OFF THE BEATEN PATH

Pittsburg. In the Great North Woods, Pittsburg contains the springs that form the Connecticut River. The state's northern tip—a chunk of about 250 square miles—lies within the town's borders. Remote though it is, this frontier town teems with hunters, boaters, fishermen, hikers, and photographers from early summer through winter. Moose sightings are common, especially in the colder months. The town has more than a dozen lodges and several informal eateries. It's about a 90-minute drive from Littleton and 40 minutes from Dixville Notch. ⊠ *U.S. 3 and Rte. 145* ✢ *From Dixville Notch take Rte. 26 west 11 miles and Rte. 145 north 13 miles.*

WHERE TO EAT AND STAY

$ ✕ **Le Rendez Vous.** You might not expect to find an authentic French pas-

FRENCH
Fodor's Choice
★

try shop in the workaday village of Colebrook, 11 miles west of Dixville Notch, but Le Rendez Vous serves fabulous tarts and treats—understandably, with Parisian owners. Drop in to this quaint café, furnished with several tables and armchairs, for hand-dipped Belgian chocolates, buttery croissants, freshly baked breads, and gourmet food items. ⑤ *Average main: $5* ⊠ *121 Main St., Colebrook* ☎ *603/237–5150* ⊕ *www. lerendezvousbakerynh.com* ⊗ *Closed Sun. and Mon.*

$$ ✕ **Rainbow Grille.** Everyone loves the Rainbow Grille for one reason or

AMERICAN
FAMILY

another: the moose antlers hanging on the pine paneling, the sunset views over Black Lake, or the lumberjack-size meals. The restaurant is known for its trout and salmon dishes and mesquite-grilled prime rib. The perfect finish to any meal is a slice of bread pudding. Plan ahead to visit this out-of-the-way place worth checking out; some patrons reserve months in advance. ⑤ *Average main: $24* ⊠ *Tall Timbers Lodge,*

609 Beach Rd., Pittsburg ☎ *603/538–9556, 800/563–5633* ⊕ *www. rainbowgrille.com* ⊘ *Closed 1st 2 wks in Dec.* ⌔ *Reservations essential.*

$ 🛏 **Cabins at Lopstick.** In business since 1929, the Cabins at Lopstick
HOTEL have long appealed to outdoors enthusiasts. **Pros:** great views of First
FAMILY Connecticut Lake; full kitchens; good summer and winter sports. **Cons:**
no on-site restaurants; some older cabins are more rustic than homey.
$ *Rooms from: $115* ✉ *45 Stewart Young Rd., Pittsburg* ☎ *800/538–6659* ⊕ *www.cabinsatlopstick.com* ⬭ *53 cabins* 🍽 *No meals.*

SPORTS AND THE OUTDOORS

Dixville Notch State Park. In the northernmost notch of the White Mountains, the park has a waterfall, two mountain brooks, hiking trails, picnic areas, and restrooms. ✉ *1212 W. Rte. 26* ☎ *603/538–6707* ⊕ *www. nhstateparks.org.*

NORTH CONWAY

76 miles south of Dixville Notch; 7 miles south of Glen; 41 miles east of Lincoln/North Woodstock.

Before the arrival of outlet stores, this town drew visitors for its inspiring scenery, ski resorts, and access to White Mountain National Forest.
Today, however, the feeling of natural splendor is gone. Shopping is the
big sport, and businesses line Route 16 for several miles. You'll get a
close look at them as traffic slows to a crawl here. Take the scenic West
Side Road from Conway to Intervale to circumvent the traffic and take
in splendid views.

GETTING HERE AND AROUND

Park near the fire station on Main Street and spend half a day visiting
the unique shops and restaurants in this part of town. Taxis can get you
around between Conway, North Conway, and Jackson.

ESSENTIALS

Visitor Information North Country Chamber of Commerce. ☎ *603/237–8939* ⊕ *www.northcountrychamber.org.*

EXPLORING

FAMILY **Conway Scenic Railroad.** Departing from historic North Conway Station,
the railroad operates various trips aboard vintage trains. The Notch
Train to Crawford Depot (5 hours round-trip) or to Fabyan Station
(5½ hours) travels through rugged territory yielding wonderful views.
The First Class package includes a three-course lunch in the dining
car. The Valley Train overlooks Mt. Washington during a 55-minute
round-trip journey to Conway or a 1¾-hour excursion to Bartlett. The
1874 station displays lanterns, old tickets and timetables, and other
artifacts. Reserve your spot early during foliage season. ✉ *38 Nor-
cross Cir.* ☎ *603/356–5251, 800/232–5251* ⊕ *www.conwayscenic.com* 🎫 *$16.50–$115.*

FAMILY **Hartmann Model Railroad Museum.** All aboard! You can ride a miniature
outdoor train at this museum, which also has 10 operating train layouts
in scales from G to Z. A hobby shop and a snack bar are also on the

premises. ⊠ *15 Town Hall Rd., at Rte. 16, Intervale* ☎ *603/356–9922* ⊕ *www.hartmannrr.com* ⊠ *$6.*

FAMILY **Weather Discovery Center.** Ever wonder what it's like to be in a cabin at the summit of Mt. Washington while 200 mph winds shake the rafters? Find out at this fun, interactive museum, where you can experience simulations of different weather conditions and learn about how weather affects our lives. There's a twice-daily video link with scientists hard at work at Mount Washington Observatory. ⊠ *2779 Main St.* ☎ *603/356–2137* ⊕ *www.mountwashington.org* ⊠ *$2.*

WHERE TO EAT

$$ ✕ **Delaney's Hole in the Wall.** This casual tavern has a real fondness for
AMERICAN ski history, displaying early photos of local ski areas, old signs and
FAMILY placards, and odd bits of lift equipment. Entrées range from fajitas that come sizzling out of the kitchen to mussels and scallops sautéed with spiced sausage and Louisiana seasonings. There's an entirely separate menu devoted to sushi. ⑤ *Average main: $20* ⊠ *2966 White Mountain Hwy., ¼ mile north of North Conway Village* ☎ *603/356–7776* ⊕ *www.delaneys.com.*

$ ✕ **Muddy Moose Restaurant & Pub.** This family restaurant buzzes with
AMERICAN the sound of happy kids. The mac 'n' cheese, blueberry-glazed ribs,
FAMILY and hearty burgers are all hits with the young ones, though grown-ups may prefer the pasta and seafood dishes. One unique carrot side has a pleasantly surprising hint of maple syrup. The Muddy Moose Pie, made of ice cream, fudge, and crumbled Oreos, can feed a family of four. ⑤ *Average main: $17* ⊠ *2344 White Mountain Hwy.* ☎ *603/356–7696* ⊕ *www.muddymoose.com* ⊠ *Reservations not accepted.*

WHERE TO STAY

$ ⚇ **The Buttonwood Inn.** A tranquil oasis in a busy resort area, the Button-
B&B/INN wood sits on Mt. Surprise, 2 miles northeast of North Conway Village. **Pros:** good bedding and amenities; tranquil setting; six acres of grounds. **Cons:** unexciting for those not wanting a remote getaway. ⑤ *Rooms from: $169* ⊠ *64 Mt. Surprise Rd.* ☎ *603/356–2625, 800/258–2625* ⊕ *www.buttonwoodinn.com* ⥽ *10 rooms* ⅋ *Breakfast.*

$ ⚇ **Darby Field Inn.** Most rooms in this unpretentious 1826 farmhouse at
B&B/INN the entrance to White Mountain National Park have stunning views, and several also have fireplaces. **Pros:** romantic setting; away-from-it-all feel. **Cons:** better for couples than families. ⑤ *Rooms from: $165* ⊠ *185 Chase Hill, Albany* ☎ *603/447–2181, 800/426–4147* ⊕ *www.darbyfield.com* ⥽ *13 rooms* ⅋ *Breakfast.*

$ ⚇ **Snowville Inn.** The finest room in the Snowville's main gambrel-roof
B&B/INN house (built in 1916) has 12 windows that look out over the Presidential Range, and many guest rooms have fireplaces. **Pros:** spectacular views; fine dining; full breakfast. **Cons:** off the beaten path. ⑤ *Rooms from: $179* ⊠ *136 Stewart Rd., 6 miles southeast of Conway, Eaton Center* ☎ *603/447–2818* ⊕ *www.snowvilleinn.com* ⥽ *16 rooms, 1 suite* ⅋ *Breakfast.*

$ ⚇ **White Mountain Hotel and Resort.** Rooms in this hotel at the base of
RESORT Whitehorse Ledge have splendid mountain views, and the proximity
FAMILY to White Mountain National Forest and Echo Lake State Park makes

you feel farther away from the outlet malls than you actually are. **Pros:** scenic setting close to shopping; free fitness center and spa. **Cons:** two-night minimum on summer weekends. $ *Rooms from: $189* ✉ *2560 West Side Rd.* ☎ *800/533–6301, 603/356–7100* ⊕ *www.whitemountainhotel.com* 🛏 *69 rooms, 11 suites* ⦿ *Some meals.*

SPORTS AND THE OUTDOORS

CANOEING AND KAYAKING

FAMILY **Outdoors Saco Bound.** This outfitter rents stand-up paddleboards, canoes, and kayaks and will even provide transportation for you and your inner tubes for gentle floats down the Saco River. ✉ *2561 E. Main St., Center Conway* ☎ *888/447–2177* ⊕ *www.sacobound.com.*

FISHING

North Country Angler. One of the best tackle shops in the state, North Country offers casting clinics and guided fly-fishing trips throughout the region. ✉ *2888 White Mountain Hwy.* ☎ *603/356–6000* ⊕ *www.northcountryangler.com.*

PARK

FAMILY **Echo Lake State Park.** You don't have to be a rock climber to enjoy the views from the 700-foot White Horse and Cathedral ledges. From the top, you'll see the entire valley, including Echo Lake, which offers fishing, swimming, boating, and, on quiet days, an excellent opportunity to shout for echoes. ✉ *68 Echo Lake Rd., off U.S 302, Conway* ☎ *603/356–2672* ⊕ *www.nhstateparks.org* 🎟 *$4.*

SKI AREAS

FAMILY **Cranmore Mountain Adventure Park.** This fun-to-ski area has been a favorite with families since it opened in 1938. Most runs are naturally formed intermediates that weave in and out of glades. Beginners have several slopes and routes from the summit; experts must be content with a few short, steep pitches. Snowboarders can explore five different terrain parks. Snow tubing, a mountain coaster, a giant swing, and a zip line provide additional entertainment. Twilight skiing is offered on Saturday and holidays. **Facilities:** 56 trails; 170 acres; 1,200-foot vertical drop; 9 lifts. ✉ *1 Skimobile Rd.* ☎⊕ *www.cranmore.com* 🎟 *Lift ticket $70.*

FAMILY **King Pine Ski Area at Purity Spring Resort.** About 9 miles south of Conway, this family-run ski area has been going strong since 1962. King Pine's gentle trails are ideal for beginner and intermediate skiers; experts won't be challenged except for a brief section of the Pitch Pine trail. There are nine miles of cross country ski trails. Indoors, you can enjoy a pool and fitness complex and go ice-skating. In summer the resort has every outdoor activity imaginable, including archery, waterskiing, kayaking, loon-watching, tennis, hiking, mountain biking, and fishing. **Facilities:** 17 trails; 48 acres; 350-foot vertical drop; 6 lifts. ✉ *1251 Eaton Rd. (Rte. 153), East Madison* ☎ *603/367–8896* ⊕ *www.kingpine.com* 🎟 *Lift ticket $52.*

Mt. Washington Valley Ski Touring and Snowshoe Foundation. Nearly 30 miles of groomed cross-country trails weave through the North Conway countryside, maintained by this foundation. Membership to the Mt. Washington Valley Ski Touring Club is required; it can be purchased by the day or

Sit back and enjoy the view on the Conway Scenic Railroad.

year. Equipment rentals are available. ⊠ *279 Rte. 16/U.S. 302, Intervale* ☏ *603/356–9920* ⊕ *www.mwvskitouring.org* ⛷ *$10 half day, $15 full day.*

SHOPPING

ANTIQUES

Richard M. Plusch Antiques. This shop deals in period furniture and accessories, including glass, sterling silver, Oriental porcelains, rugs, and paintings. ⊠ *2584 White Mountain Hwy.* ☏ *603/356–3333* ⊕ *www. conwayantiquesandappraisals.com.*

CLOTHING

Joe Jones' Sun & Ski Sports. You'll find outdoor clothing and gear here, as well as that bathing suit you forgot to pack for the hot tub. Joe Jones' also rents gear and clothing. ⊠ *2709 White Mountain Hwy.* ☏ *603/356–9411* ⊕ *www.joejonessports.com.*

CRAFTS

Handcrafters Barn. This place stocks the work of 150 area artists and artisans. ⊠ *2473 White Mountain Hwy.* ☏ *603/356–8996* ⊕ *www. handcraftersbarn.com.*

FAMILY **Zeb's General Store.** This old-fashioned country store sells specialty foods, crafts, and clothing, as well as a range of products made in New England. ⊠ *2675 Main St.* ☏ *800/676–9294* ⊕ *www.zebs.com.*

EN ROUTE One great place to settle into the White Mountains, take in one of the greatest panoramic views of the mountains, and get visitor info is at the **Intervale Scenic Vista.** The stop, off Route 16 a few miles north of North Conway, has a helpful volunteer staff, features a wonderful large topographical map, and has terrific bathrooms.

KANCAMAGUS HIGHWAY

36 miles between Conway and Lincoln/North Woodstock.

In 1937, two old town roads were connected to create this remarkable 35-mile stretch of roadway, winding through some of the state's most unspoiled mountain scenery. Kancamagus (pronounced kank-ah-MAH-gus) was one of the first roads in the nation to be designated a National Scenic Byway. No gas stations, hotels, gift shops, or billboards mar the vistas. You'll see one great view after another: the White Mountains, the Swift River, Sabbaday Falls, Lower Falls, and Rocky Gorge. The highest point is just under 3,000 feet, on the flank of Mt. Kancamagus, near Lincoln.

EXPLORING

Fodor's Choice
★
Kancamagus Highway. Interstate 93 is the fastest way to the White Mountains, but it's hardly the most appealing. The section of Route 112 known as the Kancamagus Highway passes through some of the state's most unspoiled mountain scenery—it was one of the first roads in the nation to be designated a National Scenic Byway. The Kanc, as it's called by locals, is punctuated by overlooks and picnic areas, and erupts into fiery color each fall, when photo-snapping drivers really slow things down. In bad weather, check with the White Mountains Visitors Bureau for road conditions. ⊕ *www.kancamagushighway.com.*

SPORTS AND THE OUTDOORS

FAMILY **Lincoln Woods Trail.** This hiking trail off the Kancamagus Highway greatly rewards relatively little effort. Find the trailhead in the large parking lot of the Lincoln Woods Visitor Center, 5 miles east of Lincoln. On-site or online you can purchase a parking pass ($5 per week) for White Mountain National Forest lots and overlooks. (Stopping briefly to take photos or to use the restrooms at the visitor center is permitted without a pass.) The trail crosses a suspension bridge over the Pemigewasset River and follows an old railroad bed for 3 miles along the river. ⊠ *Trailhead on Kancamagus Hwy., 5 miles east of I-93, Exit 32* ☎ *603/530-5190* ⊕ *www.fs.usda.gov/whitemountain.*

FAMILY **Sabbaday Falls.** The parking and picnic area for Sabbaday Falls, about 15 miles west of Conway, is the trailhead for an easy ½-mile route to this multilevel cascade that plunges through two potholes and a flume. Swimming is not allowed. There are restrooms on-site. ⊠ *Trailhead on Kancamagus Hwy., 20 miles east of Lincoln, 16 miles west of Conway* ⊕ *www.kancamagushighway.com.*

LAKE SUNAPEE

In the west-central part of the state, the towns around prestigious Dartmouth College and rippling Lake Sunapee vary from sleepy, old-fashioned outposts that haven't changed much in decades to bustling, sophisticated towns filled with cafés, art galleries, and boutiques. Among the latter, Hanover and New London are the area's main hubs, both of them increasingly popular vacation destinations. Although distinctly removed from the Lakes Region, greater Lake Sunapee quite

4

resembles a miniature Lake Winnipesaukee, albeit with far less commercial development. This part of the state, along with the even quieter Monadnock area to the south, has long been an informal artists' colony where people come to write, paint, and weave in solitude.

For a great drive, follow the Lake Sunapee Scenic and Cultural Byway, which runs about 25 miles from Georges Mills (a bit northwest of New London) down into Warner, tracing much of the Lake Sunapee shoreline.

ESSENTIALS

Visitor Information Lake Sunapee Region Chamber of Commerce.
☎ *603/526–6575, 877/526–6575* ⊕ *www.lakesunapeenh.org.*

NEW LONDON

16 miles northwest of Warner, 25 miles west of Tilton.

New London, the home of Colby-Sawyer College (1837), is a good base for exploring the Lake Sunapee region. A campus of stately Colonial-style buildings abuts the vibrant commercial district, where you'll find several cafés and boutiques.

GETTING HERE AND AROUND

From the south, take Interstate 93's Exit 11 to Crockett Corner and then head north on Route 114. From the north, take Exit 12 and travel south on Route 114. Mount Sunapee Ski Area offers a ski shuttle to and from many area hotels and inns.

WHERE TO EAT AND STAY

$$

AMERICAN

✕ **Flying Goose Brew Pub & Grille.** Offering a regular menu of 11 hand-crafted beers—as well as a few seasonal varieties—made with hops grown on-site, this restaurant, pub, and solar-powered brewery is a hit with beer connoisseurs. Diners go for the juicy ribs, paper-thin onion rings, fresh-cut steaks, and the burger topped with blue cheese and bacon. Enjoy live music on Thursday evening. ⑤ *Average main: $20* ✉ *40 Andover Rd., at Rtes. 11 and 114* ☎ *603/526–6899* ⊕ *www.flyinggoose.com.*

$

B&B/INN

⌂ **Follansbee Inn.** Built in 1840, this country inn on the shore of Kezar Lake is the kind of place that almost automatically turns strangers into fast friends. **Pros:** relaxed lakefront setting; free use of canoes, kayaks, sailboats, rowboats, and bicycles; nice breakfast. **Cons:** not all rooms have lake views; some Wi-Fi dead zones. ⑤ *Rooms from: $170* ✉ *2 Keyser St., North Sutton* ☎ *603/927–4221, 800/626–4221* ⊕ *www.follansbeeinn.com* ⤳ *18 rooms* ⏍ *Breakfast.*

$

B&B/INN

⌂ **The Inn at Pleasant Lake.** Across Pleasant Lake from majestic Mt. Kearsarge, this 1790s inn has spacious rooms filled with country antiques. **Pros:** lakefront with a small beach; kayaks and stand-up paddleboards available; room rate includes a full breakfast and afternoon tea. **Cons:** away from town; no mobile phone reception. ⑤ *Rooms from: $139* ✉ *853 Pleasant St.* ☎ *603/526–6271, 800/626–4907* ⊕ *www.innatpleasantlake.com* ⤳ *10 rooms* ⏍ *Breakfast.*

SPORTS AND THE OUTDOORS

FAMILY

Rollins State Park. A 3½-mile scenic auto route through Rollins State Park snakes up the southern slope of Mt. Kearsarge, where you can hike a ½-mile trail to the summit. The road often closes in winter due to hazardous conditions. ✉ *1066 Kearsarge Rd., off Rte. 103, Warner* ☎ *603/456–3808* ⊕ *www.nhstateparks.org* ⛴ *$4.*

NEWBURY

8 miles southwest of New London.

Newbury is on the edge of Mt. Sunapee State Park. The sparkling lake and the mountain, which rises to an elevation of nearly 3,000 feet, serve as the region's outdoor recreation centers. The popular League of New Hampshire Craftsmen's Fair, the oldest crafts fair in the nation, is held at the base of Mt. Sunapee each August.

GETTING HERE AND AROUND

From New London, take Route 114 West to Route 103A South, which follows the eastern coast of Lake Sunapee to Newbury.

EXPLORING

The Fells Historic Estate & Gardens. John M. Hay, who served as private secretary to Abraham Lincoln, built the Fells on Lake Sunapee as a summer home in 1890. House tours offer a glimpse of early-20th-century life on a New Hampshire estate. The grounds, a gardener's delight, include a 100-foot-long perennial garden and a rock garden with a brook flowing through it. Miles of hiking trails can also be accessed from the estate. The 40-minute guided house and garden tour costs an additional $6. ⊠ *456 Rte. 103A* 🕾 *603/763–4789* ⊕ *www.thefells.org* ⊠ *Apr.–Nov., $10 when house open, $8 when house closed; Dec.–Mar., $5 per household.*

FAMILY **Sunapee Harbor.** On the west side of Lake Sunapee, this old-fashioned summer resort community has a large marina, a handful of restaurants and shops on the water, a tidy village green with a gazebo, and a small museum. A plaque on Main Street outside the Wild Goose Country Store details some of Lake Sunapee's attributes: it's one of the highest lakes in New Hampshire, for example, and one of the cleanest. Lake Sunapee is home to brook and lake trout, salmon, smallmouth bass, perch, and pickerel. ⊠ *Sunapee* ⊕ *www.sunapeevacations.com.*

BEACHES

FAMILY **Mt. Sunapee State Park Beach.** A great family spot, this beach has picnic areas, fishing, and a bathhouse. You can also rent canoes and kayaks, and there's a campground on-site. **Amenities:** lifeguards; parking (fee); showers; toilets. **Best for:** swimming; walking. ⊠ *86 Beach Access Rd.* 🕾 *603/763–5561* ⊕ *www.nhstateparks.org* ⊠ *$5.*

WHERE TO EAT AND STAY

$ ✕ **Anchorage at Sunapee Harbor.** Fans of this long, gray restaurant with
AMERICAN a sprawling deck overlooking Sunapee Harbor's marina come as much
FAMILY for the great views as for the dependable—and occasionally creative—American chow. It's as likely a place for a burger or a fried seafood platter as for homemade lobster spring rolls. There's live entertainment Friday–Sunday. This is where the founding members of Aerosmith first met back in the early 1970s. ⑤ *Average main: $18* ⊠ *71 Main St., Sunapee Harbor* 🕾 *603/763–3334* ⊕ *www.theanchorageatsunapeeharbor. com* ☽ *Closed Oct.–mid-May.*

$$ ⊡ **Sunapee Harbor Cottages.** The six charming cottages here are within
RENTAL a stone's throw of Sunapee Harbor. **Pros:** spacious units; free beach passes. **Cons:** no maid service; little clothes storage. ⑤ *Rooms from: $225* ⊠ *4 Lake Ave., Sunapee Harbor* 🕾 *603/763–5052, 888/763–5052* ⊕ *www.sunapeeharborcottages.com* ⊅ *6 cottages* ⍾ *No meals.*

SPORTS AND THE OUTDOORS
BOAT TOURS

Sunapee Cruises. This company operates afternoon and dinner cruises of Lake Sunapee narrated by the captains from June to mid-October. Ninety-minute afternoon cruises on the M/V *Mt. Sunapee* focus on Lake Sunapee's history and the mountain scenery. A buffet dinner is included on the two-hour sunset cruises aboard the M/V *Kearsarge*. The boats operate daily in summer and on weekends in late spring and early fall. ⊠ *Town Dock, 81 Main St., Sunapee Harbor* 🕾 *603/938–6465* ⊕ *www. sunapeecruises.com* ⊠ *$20–$40.*

SKI AREA

FAMILY **Mount Sunapee.** This family-friendly resort is one of New England's best-kept secrets. The owners have spent millions upgrading their snow machines and grooming equipment and turning this into a four-season resort. Mount Sunapee offers over 1,500 vertical feet of downhill excitement, 11 lifts (including three quads), and 66 trails and slopes for all abilities. There are four terrain parks and nine glade trails. In summer, the adventure park features a canopy zip-line tour, an aerial challenge course, an 18-hole disc-golf course, miniature golf, and numerous hiking trails. **Facilities:** 66 trails; 233 acres; 1,500-foot vertical drop; 11 lifts. ⊠ *1398 Rte. 103* ☎ *603/763–3500* ⊕ *www.mtsunapee.com* ⌂ *Lift ticket $72 midweek, $82 weekends and holidays.*

4

HANOVER

12 miles northwest of Enfield; 62 miles northwest of Concord.

Eleazar Wheelock founded Hanover's Dartmouth College in 1769 to educate the Abenaki "and other youth." When he arrived, the town consisted of about 20 families. Over time the college and the town grew symbiotically, with Dartmouth eventually becoming the northernmost Ivy League school. Hanover is still synonymous with Dartmouth, but it's also a respected medical and cultural center for the upper Connecticut River Valley.

Plan on spending a day visiting Hanover and to see all the sights on the Dartmouth campus. Shops, mostly of the independent variety but with a few upscale chains sprinkled in, line Hanover's main street. The commercial district blends almost imperceptibly with the Dartmouth campus. West Lebanon, south of Hanover on the Vermont border, has many more shops.

GETTING HERE AND AROUND

Lebanon Municipal Airport, near Dartmouth College, is served by Cape Air. By car, Interstate 91 North and Interstate 89 are the best ways to get to Lebanon, Hanover, and the surrounding area.

ESSENTIALS

Airport Lebanon Municipal Airport. ⊠ *5 Airpark Rd., West Lebanon* ☎ *603/298–8878* ⊕ *www.flyleb.com.*

Visitor Information Hanover Area Chamber of Commerce. ⊠ *Nugget Arcade Bldg., 53 S. Main St., Suite 208* ☎ *603/643–3115* ⊕ *www.hanoverchamber.org.*

EXPLORING

Dartmouth College. The poet Robert Frost spent part of a brooding freshman semester at this Ivy League school before giving up college altogether, but the school counts politician Nelson Rockefeller, actor Mindy Kaling, and author Theodor ("Dr.") Seuss Geisel among its many illustrious grads. The buildings clustered around the green include the **Baker Memorial Library,** which houses such literary treasures as 17th-century editions of William Shakespeare's works. The library is also well-known for Mexican artist José Clemente Orozco's 3,000-square-foot murals that depict the story of civilization in the Americas. Free campus tours are available on request. ⊠ *N. Main and Wentworth Sts.* ☎ *603/646–1110* ⊕ *www.dartmouth.edu.*

QUICK
BITES

Dirt Cowboy Cafe. Take a respite from museum-hopping with a cup of espresso, a ham-and-cheese scone, or a freshly baked brownie at this café across from the green next to a used-book store. ⊠ *7 S. Main St.* ☎ *603/643–1323* ⊕ *www.dirtcowboycafe.com.*

FAMILY **Enfield Shaker Museum.** In 1782, two Shaker brothers from Mount Lebanon, New York, arrived on Lake Mascoma's northeastern side, about 12 miles southeast of Hanover. Eventually, they formed Enfield, the ninth of 18 Shaker communities in the United States, and moved it to the lake's southern shore, where they erected more than 200 buildings. The Enfield Shaker Museum preserves the legacy of the Shakers, who numbered 330 members at the village's peak. By 1923, interest in the society had waned, and the last 10 members joined the Canterbury community, south of Laconia. A self-guided walking tour takes you through 13 of the remaining buildings, among them an 1849 stone mill. Demonstrations of Shaker crafts techniques and numerous special events take place year-round. ⊠ *447 Rte. 4A, Enfield* ☎ *603/632–4346* ⊕ *www.shakermuseum.org* ⊠ *$12.*

FAMILY **Hood Museum of Art.** Dartmouth's art museum owns Picasso's *Guitar on a Table*, silver by Paul Revere, a set of Assyrian reliefs from the 9th century BC, along with other noteworthy examples of African, Peruvian, Oceanic, Asian, European, and American art. The range of contemporary works—including pieces by John Sloan, William Glackens, Mark Rothko, Fernand Léger, and Joan Miró—is particularly notable. Rivaling the collection is the museum's architecture: a series of austere, copper-roof, redbrick buildings arranged around a courtyard. ⊠ *Dartmouth College, Wheelock St.* ☎ *603/646–2808* ⊕ *hoodmuseum. dartmouth.edu.*

Hopkins Center for the Arts. If the towering arcade at the entrance to the center appears familiar, it's probably because it resembles the project that architect Wallace K. Harrison completed just after designing it: New York City's Metropolitan Opera House at Lincoln Center. The complex includes a 900-seat theater for concerts and film screenings, a 480-seat theater for plays, and a black-box theater for new plays. This is the home of the Dartmouth Symphony Orchestra. ⊠ *Dartmouth College, 2 E. Wheelock St.* ☎ *603/646–2422 for box office* ⊕ *hop.dartmouth.edu.*

OFF THE
BEATEN
PATH

Upper Valley. From Hanover, you can make the 60-mile drive up Route 10 all the way to Littleton for a highly scenic tour of the upper Connecticut River valley. You'll have views of the river and Vermont's Green Mountains from many points along the way. The road passes through groves of evergreens, over leafy ridges, and through delightful hamlets. Grab gourmet picnic provisions at the general store on Lyme's village common and stop at the bluff-top village green in historic Haverhill (28 miles north of Hanover) for a picnic amid the panorama of classic Georgian- and Federal-style mansions and faraway farmsteads. ⊠ *Hanover* ⊕ *www.uppervalleychamber.com.*

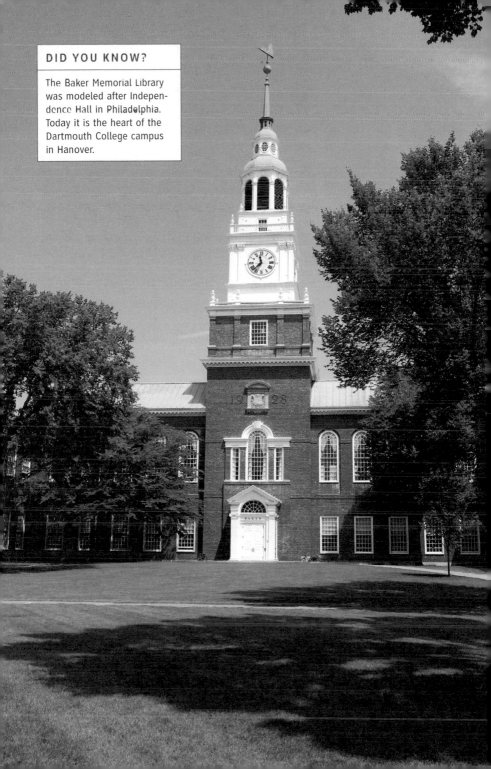

WHERE TO EAT

$$
AMERICAN

✕ **Canoe Club.** Bedecked with canoes, paddles, and classic Dartmouth paraphernalia, this festive spot presents live jazz and folk music on most nights. The mood may be casual, but the kitchen offers imaginative preparations, including memorable starters like a roasted beet medley with a spiced chocolate sauce and an orange glaze, and steamed mussels in a delectable garlic-and-herb sauce. Among the main courses, the Malay curry shrimp with cucumbers, peanuts, and coconut curry is a favorite. There's also a lighter, late-night menu. ⑤ *Average main: $19* ✉ *27 S. Main St.* ☏ *603/643–9660* ⊕ *www.canoeclub.us.*

$
AMERICAN
FAMILY

✕ **Lou's Restaurant.** A Hanover tradition since 1948, this diner-cum-café-cum-bakery serves possibly the best breakfast in the valley. The blueberry-cranberry buttermilk pancakes really satisfy, and a plate of *migas* (eggs, cheddar, salsa, and guacamole mixed with tortilla chips) can fill you up for the better part of the day. Or just grab a seat at the old-fashioned soda fountain for an ice-cream sundae. Lou's can accommodate diners on gluten-free diets, too. One of the few spots in town where students and locals really mix, this place is hard to resist. ⑤ *Average main: $9* ✉ *30 S. Main St.* ☏ *603/643–3321* ⊕ *www.lousrestaurant. net* ☉ *No dinner.*

$$
ITALIAN
FAMILY

✕ **Lui Lui.** The creatively topped thin-crust pizzas and huge portions of pasta are only part of the draw at this chatter-filled eatery; the other is its dramatic setting inside a former power station on the Mascoma River. Pizza picks include the Zeppo (pepperoni, mozzarella, tomato sauce) and di Carni, with house-made meatballs. Pasta fans should dive into a bowl of linguine with homemade clam sauce. ⑤ *Average main: $18* ✉ *8 Glen Rd., West Lebanon* ☏ *603/298–7070* ⊕ *www.luilui.com.*

$$
ECLECTIC

✕ **Murphy's On the Green.** Students, visiting alums, and locals regularly descend on this wildly popular pub, which has walls lined with shelves of old books. The varied menu features burgers and salads as well as meat loaf, crusted lamb sirloin, and vegetarian dishes like eggplant stuffed with tofu. Check out the extensive beer list. ⑤ *Average main: $20* ✉ *5 Main St.* ☏ *603/643–7777* ⊕ *www.murphysonthegreen.com.*

WHERE TO STAY

$$$
HOTEL
FAMILY

🏨 **The Hanover Inn.** If you're in town for a Dartmouth event, you'll want to stay on the college's—and the town's—main square, above which this sprawling Georgian-style brick structure rises five white-trimmed stories. **Pros:** center of campus and town; great service; handy fitness center. **Cons:** rates do not include breakfast; pricey. ⑤ *Rooms from: $319* ✉ *The Green, 2 E. Wheelock St.* ☏ *603/643–4300, 800/443–7024* ⊕ *www.hanoverinn.com* ⇆ *93 rooms, 15 suites* ⑪ *No meals.*

$$
B&B/INN

🏨 **Trumbull House.** The rooms at this white Colonial-style house on 16 acres on Hanover's outskirts have king- and queen-size beds, feather pillows, writing desks, and other comfortable touches, as well as Wi-Fi access. **Pros:** many activities on-site; lovely home; big breakfast. **Cons:** 3 miles east of town. ⑤ *Rooms from: $230* ✉ *40 Etna Rd.* ☏ *603/643–2370, 800/651–5141* ⊕ *www.trumbullhouse.com* ⇆ *4 rooms, 1 suite, 1 cottage* ⑪ *Breakfast.*

The Cornish–Windsor Bridge is the second-longest covered bridge in the United States, at 460 feet.

SPORTS AND THE OUTDOORS

FAMILY **Ledyard Canoe Club.** On the banks of the Connecticut River, the Ledyard Canoe Club of Dartmouth rents canoes, kayaks, and stand-up paddleboats by the hour. The club also rents rustic cabins. ⊠ *9 Boathouse Rd., below Ledyard Bridge ✢ East side of Connecticut River; parking lot past pillars* ☎ *603/643–6709* ⊕ *www.ledyardcanoeclub.org.*

CORNISH

22 miles south of Hanover.

Today Cornish is best known for its covered bridges and for being the home of the late reclusive author J. D. Salinger, but at the turn of the 20th century the village was known primarily as the home of the country's then-most-popular novelist, Winston Churchill (no relation to the British prime minister). His novel *Richard Carvel* sold more than a million copies. Churchill was such a celebrity that he hosted Theodore Roosevelt during the president's 1902 visit. At that time Cornish was an artistic enclave: painter Maxfield Parrish lived and worked here, and sculptor Augustus Saint-Gaudens set up his studio here, where he created the heroic bronzes for which he is known.

GETTING HERE AND AROUND

About 5 miles west of town on Route 44, the Cornish–Windsor Bridge crosses the Connecticut River between New Hampshire and Vermont. The Blacksmith Shop covered bridge is 2 miles east of Route 12A on Town House Road, and the Dingleton Hill covered bridge is 1 mile east of Route 12A on Root Hill Road. Cornish itself is small enough to see in one morning.

EXPLORING

FAMILY **Cornish-Windsor Bridge.** This 460-foot bridge, 1½ miles south of the Saint-Gaudens National Historic Site, connects New Hampshire to Vermont across the Connecticut River. Erected in 1866, it is the longest covered wooden bridge in the United States. The notice on the bridge reads, "Walk your horses or pay two dollar fine." ⊠ *Bridge St.* ⊕ *www. nh.gov/nhdhr/bridges/p39.html.*

FAMILY **Saint-Gaudens National Historic Site.** Just south of Plainfield, a small road
Fodor's Choice leads to this historic site that celebrates the life and artistry of Augustus
★ Saint-Gaudens, a leading 19th-century sculptor with major works on Boston Common and in Manhattan's Central Park. You can tour his house (with original furnishings), studio, and gallery, as well as 150 acres of grounds and gardens, scattered throughout which are casts of his works. The property has two hiking trails, the longer of which is the Blow-Me-Down Trail. Concerts are held at 2 pm on Sunday in July and August. ⊠ *139 Saint-Gaudens Rd., off Rte. 12A* ☎ *603/675–2175* ⊕ *www.nps.gov/saga* ⊡ *$7.*

THE MONADNOCKS AND MERRIMACK VALLEY

Southwestern and south-central New Hampshire mix village charm with city hustle and bustle across two distinct regions. The Merrimack River Valley has the state's largest and fastest-growing cities: Nashua, Manchester, and Concord. To the west, in the state's sleepy southwestern corner, is the Monadnock region, one of New Hampshire's least developed and most naturally stunning parts. Here you'll find plenty of hiking trails, as well as peaceful hilltop hamlets that appear to have barely changed in the past two centuries. Mt. Monadnock, southern New Hampshire's largest peak, stands guard over the region, which has more than 200 lakes and ponds. Rainbow trout, smallmouth and largemouth bass, and some northern pike swim in Chesterfield's Spofford Lake. Goose Pond, just north of Keene, holds smallmouth bass and white perch.

NASHUA

98 miles south of Lincoln/North Woodstock; 48 miles northwest of Boston; 36 miles south of Concord; 50 miles southeast of Keene.

Once a prosperous manufacturing town that drew thousands of immigrant workers in the late 1800s and early 1900s, Nashua fell into decline following World War II, as many factories shut down or moved in search of cheaper labor. Since the 1970s, however, the metro area has jumped in population, developing into a charming community. In its low-key downtown area, classic redbrick buildings line the Nashua River, a tributary of the Merrimack. Though not as popular with tourists as other communities in the region, Nashua (population 90,000) has some good restaurants and a few major shopping centers.

GETTING HERE AND AROUND

A good place to start exploring Nashua is at Main and High streets, where a number of fine restaurants and shops are located. Downtown Nashua has free Wi-Fi.

ESSENTIALS

Taxi SK Taxi. ☎ 603/882–5155 ⊕ www.sktaxi.com.

EXPLORING

Florence Hyde Speare Memorial Museum. The city's impressive industrial history is retold here, the home of the Nashua Historical Society. In this two-story museum, you'll find artifacts, early furnishings, photos, a vintage printing press, and a research library. Adjacent to the museum is the Federal-style **Abbot-Spalding House**, furnished with 18th- and 19th-century antiques, art, and household items. ⊠ 5 Abbott St. ☎ 603/883–0015 ⊕ www.nashuahistoricalsociety.org/spearemuseum ☕ Free (donations accepted).

WHERE TO EAT

$$$
BISTRO
Fodor'sChoice
★

✕ **MT's Local Kitchen and Wine Bar.** Part hip bistro, part jazzy wine bar, MT's is so popular that foodies from across the state make a beeline for this hot spot. The regularly changing menu highlights local products and might include pork scaloppine with a cognac-soaked raisin sauce or wood-grilled Vermont chicken with marinated mushrooms. The pesto fries are legendary. Wood-fired pizzas are also a specialty—try the one topped with Green Mountain smoked pepperoni and MT's own pickled jalapeños. ⑤ Average main: $27 ⊠ 212 Main St. ☎ 603/595–9334 ⊕ www.mtslocal.com.

MANCHESTER

18 miles north of Nashua, 53 miles north of Boston.

With 108,000-plus residents, Manchester is New Hampshire's largest city. The town grew up around the Amoskeag Falls on the Merrimack River, which drove small textile mills through the 1700s. By 1828 Boston investors had bought the rights to the Merrimack's water power and built the Amoskeag Mills, which became a testament to New England's manufacturing capabilities. In 1906 the mills employed 17,000 people and churned out more than 4 million yards of cloth weekly. This vast enterprise served as Manchester's entire economic base; when it closed in 1936, the town was devastated.

Today Manchester is mainly a banking and business center. The old mill buildings have been converted into warehouses, classrooms, restaurants, museums, and office space. The city has the state's major airport, as well as the Verizon Wireless Arena, which hosts minor-league hockey matches, concerts, and conventions.

GETTING HERE AND AROUND

Manchester Airport, the state's largest airport, is a cost-effective, hassle-free alternative to Boston's Logan Airport, with nonstop service from 16 cities. Manchester can be hard to get around, but there are several taxi companies.

The Monadnocks and Merrimack Valley

ESSENTIALS

Airport Manchester-Boston Regional Airport. ⊠ *1 Airport Rd.* ☎ *603/624–6539* ⊕ *www.flymanchester.com.*

Taxi Manchester Taxi. ☎ *603/623–2222.* **Queen City Taxi.** ☎ *603/622–0008.*

Visitor Information Greater Manchester Welcome Center. ⊠ *Elm St. and Merrimack St., northwest corner Veterans Memorial Park* ☎ *603/666–6600* ⊕ *www.manchester-chamber.org.*

EXPLORING

FAMILY **Amoskeag Fishways.** From May to mid-June, salmon, shad, and river herring "climb" the 54-step fish ladder at this spot near the Amoskeag Dam. The visitor center has an underwater viewing window, and there are interactive exhibits and programs about the aquatic wildlife of the Merrimack River. ⊠ *4 Fletcher St., off I–293/Rte. 3A* ☎ *603/626–3474* ⊕ *www.amoskeagfishways.org* ⬚ *Free ($2 suggested donation).*

Fodor's Choice **Currier Museum of Art.** The Currier maintains an astounding permanent
★ collection of works by European and American masters, among them Claude Monet, Edward Hopper, Winslow Homer, John Marin, Andrew Wyeth, and Childe Hassam, and it presents changing exhibits of contemporary art. The museum also arranges guided tours of the nearby Zimmerman House. Completed in 1950, it's New England's only Frank

Lloyd Wright–designed residence open to the public. Wright called this sparse, utterly functional living space "Usonian," an invented term used to describe several dozen similar homes based on his vision of distinctly American architecture. ⊠ *150 Ash St.* ☎ *603/669–6144, 603/669–6144 ext. 108 for house tours* ⊕ *www.currier.org* ⊠ *$12; $20 with Zimmerman House.*

Millyard Museum. In the Amoskeag Mills building, state-of-the-art exhibits depict the region's history from when Native Americans lived here and fished the Merrimack River to when the machines of Amoskeag Mills wove cloth. The museum also offers lectures and walking tours, and has a Discovery Gallery and a gift shop. ⊠ *200 Bedford St.* ☎ *603/622–7531* ⊕ *www.manchesterhistoric.org* ⊠ *$8.*

FAMILY
Fodor's Choice
★
SEE Science Center. The world's largest permanent LEGO installation at minifigure scale, depicting Amoskeag Millyard and Manchester as they were a century ago, is the star attraction at this hands-on science lab and children's museum. The mind-blowing exhibit, covering 2,000 square feet, is made up of about 3 million LEGO bricks. It conveys the massive size and importance of the mills, which ran a mile on each side of the Merrimack. The museum also offers daily science demonstrations, as well as changing exhibits. ⊠ *200 Bedford St.* ☎ *603/669–0400* ⊕ *www. see-sciencecenter.org* ⊠ *$8.*

WHERE TO EAT

$$
AMERICAN
✕ **Cotton.** Mod lighting and furnishings lend this restaurant inside an old Amoskeag Mills building a swanky atmosphere. For warm weather there's also a patio set in an arbor. Chef Jeffrey Paige, a leader in the farm to-table movement, puts a winning new spin on comfort food. Start with pan-seared crab cakes or a kale and blueberry salad. The menu changes four times a year but might include an all-natural Delmonico steak or wood-grilled scallops with sweet-potato corn hash. The martinis here have won awards for good reason. ⑤ *Average main: $24* ⊠ *75 Arms St.* ☎ *603/622–5488* ⊕ *www.cottonfood.com* ☼ *No lunch weekends.*

$
AMERICAN
Fodor's Choice
★
✕ **Red Arrow Diner.** Once listed among the country's "top 10 diners," this bustling downtown diner caters to politicians, students, artists, and everyone in between. The 1922 restaurant, open around the clock, is a friendly place with fresh daily specials sized for the famished. Menu classics include kielbasa and cheese omelets and triple-bun Dinahmoe burgers. Order a house-brewed root beer or cream soda to round out the nostalgic dining experience. ⑤ *Average main: $9* ⊠ *61 Lowell St.* ☎ *603/626–1118* ⊕ *www.redarrowdiner.com.*

WHERE TO STAY

$
B&B/INN
⛺ **Ash Street Inn.** This five-room bed-and-breakfast is one of many striking Victorian homes in its residential neighborhood. **Pros:** nicely decorated rooms; within walking distance of Currier Museum. **Cons:** not a full-service hotel. ⑤ *Rooms from: $189* ⊠ *118 Ash St.* ☎ *603/668–9908* ⊕ *www.ashstreetinn.com* ⊃ *5 rooms* ⦿*|Breakfast.*

$$$
B&B/INN
⛺ **Bedford Village Inn.** If you've decided to sacrifice downtown conveniences and venture a few miles southwest of Manchester to this lovely manor, you'll be rewarded by comfort and beauty. **Pros:** tuck down

At the Currier Museum of Art, you can enjoy European and American classics, or visit a nearby Frank Lloyd Wright house.

with homemade cookies; exceptional grounds; great restaurant. **Cons:** outside town. ⑤ *Rooms from: $319* ✉ *2 Olde Bedford Way, Bedford* ☎ *603/472–2001, 800/852–1166* ⊕ *www.bedfordvillageinn.com* ↪ *12 suites, 2 apartments, 1 cottage* ⦿ *Some meals.*

$ **HOTEL** 🖵 **Radisson Hotel Manchester Downtown.** Of Manchester's many chain properties, the 12-story Radisson has the most central location: a short walk from Amoskeag Mills and the great dining along Elm Street. **Pros:** downtown location; free airport shuttle; pets welcome. **Cons:** fee for parking; unexciting decor. ⑤ *Rooms from: $159* ✉ *700 Elm St.* ☎ *603/625–1000, 800/333–3333* ⊕ *www.radisson.com/manchester-hotel-nh-03101/nhmanch* ↪ *244 rooms, 6 suites* ⦿ *No meals.*

NIGHTLIFE AND PERFORMING ARTS

PERFORMING ARTS

The Palace Theatre. The century-old Palace, a former vaudeville house, presents musicals and plays, comedy, and concerts throughout the year. ✉ *80 Hanover St.* ☎ *603/668–5588* ⊕ *www.palacetheatre.org.*

NIGHTLIFE

Midnight Rodeo Bar. On Saturday night, country-music lovers swarm to the bar at the Yard Restaurant for line-dancing lessons, followed by live music and mechanical-bull riding. ✉ *1211 S. Mammoth Rd.* ☎ *603/623–3545* ⊕ *www.midnightrodeobar.com* 🎟 *$10.*

SHOPPING

FAMILY **Bedford Farmers' Market.** Just outside Manchester, this market hosts a rich mix of local growers and food purveyors selling seasonal jams, pasture-raised lamb and chicken, homemade treats for dogs and cats, goats' milk soaps and balms, and even New Hampshire wines. There's usually live music, along with activities for children. ✉ *St. Elizabeth Seton Parish parking lot, 190 Meetinghouse Rd., 5 miles south of downtown Manchester off I–293, Bedford* ☎ *603/203–8440* ⊕ *www.bedfordfarmersmarket.org* ☉ *June–Oct., Tues. 3–6.*

CONCORD

20 miles northwest of Manchester, 67 miles northwest of Boston, 46 miles northwest of Portsmouth.

New Hampshire's capital (population 42,000) is a quiet town that tends to state business and little else—the sidewalks roll up promptly at 6. Stop in town to get a glimpse of New Hampshire's State House, which is crowned by a gleaming, eagle-topped gold dome.

4

GETTING HERE AND AROUND
Interstate 93 bisects Concord north–south. Coming from the west, reach the city by Interstate 89; from the east use U.S. 202, which becomes Interstate 393 near the city line. Taxis can help get you around town, though Main Street near the State House is walkable.

ESSENTIALS
Taxi Concord Cab. ☎ *603/225–4222.*

Visitor Information Greater Concord Chamber of Commerce. ✉ *49 S. Main St.* ☎ *603/224–2508* ⊕ *www.concordnhchamber.com.*

TOURS
FAMILY **Concord on Foot.** This walking trail winds past 62 points of interest throughout the historic district. Download the map online for free or pick up a printed copy ($2) at the chamber of commerce or at stores along the trail. ✉ *Greater Concord Chamber of Commerce, 49 S. Main St.* ⊕ *www.concordnhchamber.com/visitor_info.html.*

EXPLORING
FAMILY **McAuliffe-Shepard Discovery Center.** New England's only air-and-space center offers a full day of activities focused mostly on the heavens. See yourself in infrared light, learn about lunar spacecraft, examine a replica of the Mercury-Redstone rocket, or experience what it's like to travel in space—you can even try your hand at being a television weather announcer. There's also a café and a gift shop. ✉ *2 Institute Dr.* ☎ *603/271–7827* ⊕ *www.starhop.com* 🎫 *$10.*

New Hampshire Historical Society. Steps from the state capitol, this museum is a great place to learn about the Concord coach, a popular mode of transportation before railroads. Temporary exhibitions might include locally made quilts or historical portraits of residents. ✉ *6 Eagle Sq.* ☎ *603/228–6688* ⊕ *www.nhhistory.org* 🎫 *$7.*

Pierce Manse. Franklin Pierce lived in this Greek Revival home before he moved to Washington to become the 14th U.S. president. He's buried nearby. A guided tour covers his life in mid-19th-century historical context. ✉ *14 Horseshoe Pond La.* ☎ *603/225–4555* ⊕ *www.pierce-manse.org* 🎫 *$7.*

FAMILY
Fodor'sChoice
★

State House. The gilded-dome state house, built in 1819, is the nation's oldest capitol building in which the legislature still uses the original chambers. From January through June, you can watch the two branches in action. The Senate has 24 members, and the House house has 400—a ratio of 1 representative per 3,500 residents (a world record). The visitor center coordinates guided and self-guided tours, bookable online or on-site. The center also has history exhibits and paraphernalia from presidential primaries. ⊠ *Visitor center, 107 N. Main St.* ☎ *603/271–2154* ⊕ *www.gencourt.state.nh.us/nh_visitorcenter/default.htm* ▨ *Free.*

WHERE TO EAT AND STAY

$
AMERICAN
FAMILY

✕ **Arnie's Place.** If you need a reason to make the 1½-mile detour from Interstate 93, the selection of more than 50 kinds of homemade ice cream at Arnie's should do it: try the raspberry, vanilla, or toasted coconut. Chocoholics will love the shakes, and the lemon freeze will give you a headache in no time (it's worth it). A small dining room serves hamburgers, hot dogs, and a barbecue platter, but the five walk-up windows are the way to go: grab some grub and head to one of the picnic tables. $ *Average main: $12* ⊠ *164 Loudon Rd., off I–93, Concord Heights* ☎ *603/228–3225* ⊕ *www.arniesplace.com* ☉ *Closed mid-Oct.–late Feb.*

$$
ECLECTIC

✕ **Barley House.** A lively, old-fashioned tavern with Irish overtones, the Barley House is often abuzz with a mix of politicos, businesspeople, and tourists. The impressive melting pot of a menu includes chorizo-topped pizzas, burgers smothered with a peppercorn-whiskey sauce, chicken potpies, beer-braised bratwurst, and Mediterranean chicken salad—all reliably prepared. The bar serves dozens of interesting beers, on tap and by the bottle, and the wine list is decent. On Tuesday night, musicians play traditional Irish tunes. $ *Average main: $20* ⊠ *132 N. Main St.* ☎ *603/228–6363* ⊕ *www.thebarleyhouse.com* ☉ *Closed Sun.* ⌲ *Reservations not accepted.*

$
HOTEL

▥ **The Centennial.** The most modern hotel in New Hampshire, the Centennial is fittingly home to Granite, the state's most contemporary restaurant and bar, making it a draw for politicians and those doing business here. **Pros:** sleek redesign of historic structure; very comfortable and clean rooms; great bar and restaurant. **Cons:** busy. $ *Rooms from: $199* ⊠ *96 Pleasant St.* ☎ *603/227–9000* ⊕ *www.thecentennial-hotel.com* ⌂ *27 rooms, 5 suites* ⍥ *Some meals.*

$
THAI
FAMILY

✕ **Siam Orchid Thai Bistro.** This Thai restaurant recently moved closer to the capitol building and now has outdoor seating in the summer. It's known for serving spicy and reasonably authentic dishes prepared with flair, and attracts a stately weekday lunch crowd. $ *Average main: $16* ⊠ *12 N. Main St.* ☎ *603/228–3633* ⊕ *www.siamorchid.net.*

NIGHTLIFE AND PERFORMING ARTS

FAMILY

Capitol Center for the Arts. The Egyptian-motif artwork, part of the original 1927 decor, has been restored in the former Capitol Theatre. Now the Capitol Center for the Arts, it hosts touring Broadway shows, dance companies, and musical acts. ⊠ *44 S. Main St.* ☎ *603/225–1111* ⊕ *www.ccanh.com.*

SHOPPING

Capitol Craftsman Jewelers. Fine jewelry, pottery, hand-painted glassware, and hand-tooled leather goods are among the specialties here. ✉ *16 N. Main St.* ☎ *603/224–6166* ⊕ *www.capitolcraftsman.com.*

Mark Knipe Goldsmiths. The designers at this shop near the capitol create highly original rings, pendants, earrings, bracelets, and other jewelry. ✉ *2 Capitol Plaza, Main St.* ☎ *603/224–2920* ⊕ *www.knipegold.com.*

CHARLESTOWN

70 miles northwest of Concord.

Charlestown boasts the state's largest historic district, with about 60 homes—all handsome examples of Federal, Greek Revival, and Gothic Revival architecture (and 10 built before 1800)—clustered about the town center. Several merchants on the main street distribute brochures that describe an interesting walking tour of the district.

GETTING HERE AND AROUND

You can reach Charlestown from Interstate 91, but it's best to follow Route 12 North from Keene for the gorgeous scenery. Walking downtown Charlestown should take only 15 minutes of your day, but it's worth admiring the buildings in the town center. The Fort at No. 4 is less than 2 miles out of town, north on Route 11.

EXPLORING

FAMILY **Fort at No. 4.** In 1747, this fort 1½ miles north of downtown Charlestown was an outpost on the periphery of Colonial civilization. That year fewer than 50 militiamen at the fort withstood an attack by 400 French soldiers, ensuring that Northern New England remained under British rule. Today, costumed interpreters at this living-history museum cook dinner over an open hearth and demonstrate weaving, gardening, and candle making. Each year the museum holds reenactments of militia musters and the battles of the French and Indian War. ✉ *267 Springfield Rd. (Rte. 11), off Rte. 12A* ☎ *603/826–5700* ⊕ *www.fortat4.com* 🎟 *$10.*

SPORTS AND THE OUTDOORS

FAMILY **Morningside Flight Park.** Here's a place for the adrenaline junkie: laser tag, zip-lining, paragliding, and hang gliding are all on the menu at Morningside Flight Park, where lessons are also available for the uninitiated. Morningside is considered among the best flying areas in the country, so even if you have a fear of flying, stop and watch the bright colors of the gliders as they take off from the 450-foot peak. ✉ *357 Morningside La., off Rte. 12* ☎ *603/542–4416* ⊕ *flymorningside.kittyhawk.com.*

WALPOLE

13 miles south of Charlestown.

Walpole possesses one of the state's most perfect town greens. Bordered by Elm and Washington streets, it's surrounded by homes dating to 1790 or so, when the townsfolk constructed a canal around the Great Falls of the Connecticut River, bringing commerce and wealth to the area. The town now has 3,200 inhabitants, more than a dozen of whom are millionaires. Walpole is also home to Florentine Films, documentarian Ken Burns's production company.

GETTING HERE AND AROUND

Walpole is a short jaunt off Route 12, north of Keene. The small downtown area is especially photogenic.

WHERE TO EAT

$ ✕ **The Restaurant at L. A. Burdick Handmade Chocolates.** Famous candy-man
FRENCH Larry Burdick, who sells his hand-filled, hand-cut chocolates to top
Fodor's Choice restaurants around the Northeast, is a Walpole resident. The restaurant
★ next door to his shop has the easygoing sophistication of a Parisian café and may tempt you to linger over an incredibly rich hot chocolate. The French-inspired menu utilizes fresh, often local, ingredients and changes daily. For dinner, you might start with a selection of grilled octopus, followed by the house beef stew or honey-roasted duck breast. Naturally, dessert is a big treat here, and features Burdick's own chocolates and pastries. $ *Average main: $17* ✉ *47 Main St.* ☎ *603/756–9058* ⊕ *www. burdickchocolate.com.*

SHOPPING

FAMILY **Boggy Meadow Farm.** At this farm, you can watch the cheese-making process unfold, from the 200 cows being milked to the finer process of cheese making. Boggy Meadow cheeses can be sampled in the store and are available for purchase, as are cheese boards, cider doughnuts, and root vegetables. It's worth the trip just to see the beautiful 400-acre farm. ✉ *13 Boggy Meadow La.* ☎ *603/756–3300, 877/541–3953* ⊕ *www.boggymeadowfarm.com.*

KEENE

17 miles southeast of Walpole; 20 miles northeast of Brattleboro, Vermont; 56 miles southwest of Manchester.

Keene is the largest city in the state's southwestern corner. Its gentrified main street, with several engaging boutiques and cafés, is America's widest (132 feet); you can spend a fun few hours strolling along it. Even though settlers first arrived as far back as 1735, the city's atmosphere remains youthful, with its funky crafts stores and eclectic entertainment, like the Monadnock International Film Festival, held in April.

ESSENTIALS

Visitor Information Greater Keene Chamber of Commerce. ✉ *48 Central Sq.* ☎ *603/352–1303* ⊕ *www.keenechamber.com.* **Monadnock Travel Council.** ⊕ *www.monadnocktravel.com.*

EXPLORING

FAMILY **Keene State College.** The hub of the local arts community is this bustling college. The permanent collection of the Thorne-Sagendorph Art Gallery includes works by Richard Sumner Meryman, Abbott Handerson Thayer, and Robert Mapplethorpe. ✉ *Thorne-Sagendorph Art Gallery, 229 Main St.* ☎ *603/358–2720* ⊕ *www.keene.edu.*

QUICK BITES

Prime Roast Coffee Company. Serving fine coffee and pastries alongside fine art (covering the walls and tables), Prime Roast is a sensory experience; the beans are roasted and ground on-site, so the air is filled with the scent of delicious coffee. The café is two blocks from Keene State College. ⊠ *16 Main St.* ☎ *603/352-7874* ⊕ *www.primeroastcoffee.com.*

OFF THE BEATEN PATH

Chesterfield's Route 63. If you're in the mood for a country drive, head west from Keene along Route 9 to Route 63 (about 11 miles) and turn left toward the hilltop town of Chesterfield. This is an especially rewarding journey at sunset: from many points along the road you can see west out over the Connecticut River valley and into Vermont. The village center itself consists of little more than a handful of dignified granite buildings and a small general store. ⊠ *Chesterfield.*

4

WHERE TO EAT AND STAY

$$
MEDITERRANEAN
Fodor's Choice
★

✕ **Luca's Mediterranean Café.** A deceptively simple storefront bistro overlooking Keene's graceful town square, Luca's dazzles with epicurean creations influenced by Italy, France, Greece, Spain, and North Africa. Enjoy sautéed shrimp with cilantro pesto and plum tomatoes, three-cheese ravioli with artichoke hearts, or grilled salmon marinated in cumin and coriander. Don't forget to order the locally made gelato or sorbet for dessert. Luca's Market, next door, offers many of the same flavors in wraps, salads, and panini. ⑤ *Average main: $23* ⊠ *10 Central Sq.* ☎ *603/358-3335* ⊕ *www.lucascafe.com.*

$
B&B/INN

⊡ **Chesterfield Inn.** With views of the hill in the distance, the Chesterfield Inn is nestled on a 10-acre farm. **Pros:** attractive gardens; close to Connecticut River; room rate includes full breakfast. **Cons:** no dinner on Sunday. ⑤ *Rooms from: $149* ⊠ *20 Cross Rd., West Chesterfield* ☎ *603/256-3211, 800/365-5515* ⊕ *www.chesterfieldinn.com* ⊅ *13 rooms, 2 suites* ⦿I *Breakfast.*

$
HOTEL

⊡ **Fairfield Inn and Suites Keene Downtown.** You get a rare urban touch in the sleepy Monadnocks at this upscale property in the middle of Main Street. **Pros:** spacious and comfortable rooms; center of town. **Cons:** no pool. ⑤ *Rooms from: $199* ⊠ *30 Main St.* ☎ *603/357-7070, 888/300-5056* ⊕ *www.fairfieldinnkeene.com* ⊅ *33 rooms, 7 suites* ⦿I *Breakfast.*

$
RESORT
FAMILY

⊡ **The Inn at East Hill Farm.** For those with kids who like animals, East Hill Farm is heaven: a family resort with daylong children's programs on a 160-acre farm overlooking Mt. Monadnock. **Pros:** rare agritourism and family resort; activities galore; beautiful setting; no TVs. **Cons:** remote location; noisy mess-hall dining. ⑤ *Rooms from: $135* ⊠ *460 Monadnock St., 10 miles southeast of Keene, Troy* ☎ *603/242-6495, 800/242-6495 for reservations* ⊕ *www.east-hill-farm.com* ⊅ *65 rooms* ⦿I *All meals.*

NIGHTLIFE AND PERFORMING ARTS
ARTS VENUES

Colonial Theatre. This renovated 1924 vaudeville theater now shows art-house movies on the largest screen in town, and also hosts comedy, music, and dance performances. ⊠ *95 Main St.* ☎ *603/352-2033* ⊕ *www.thecolonial.org.*

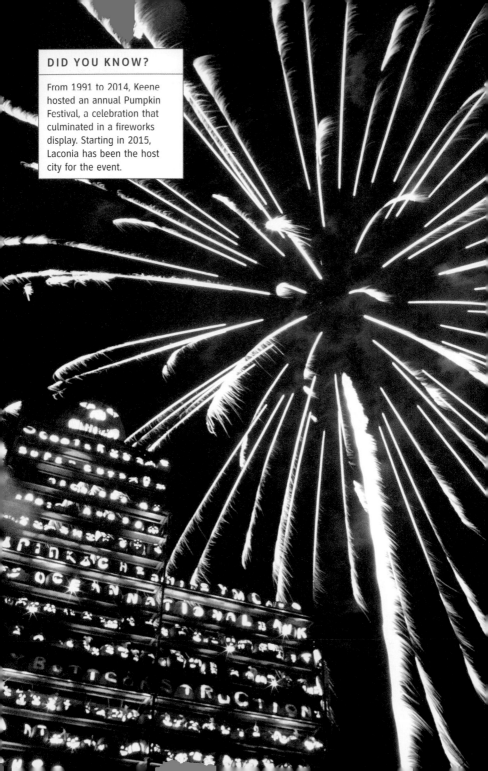

BREWPUB

FAMILY **Elm City Restaurant & Brewery.** This microbrewery is an affordable hangout for everyone from college students to families. Burgers, steaks, and seafood are all on the menu. The beers range from light golden ales to dark and heavy porters and stouts. ☒ *Colony Mill, 222 West St.* ☎ *603/355–3335* ⊕ *www.elmcitybrewing.com.*

SHOPPING

Fairgrounds Antiques. If you're not afraid of a little dust, there's no telling what kind of treasure you'll find at this longtime collection of several dozen dealers. Vintage furniture, prints and paintings, collectibles, ephemera, and much more are for sale. ☒ *Cheshire Fairgrounds, 249 Monadnock Hwy., 3 miles southeast of downtown, East Swanzey* ☎ *603/352–4420.*

JAFFREY CENTER

16 miles southeast of Keene.

Novelist Willa Cather came to Jaffrey Center in 1919 and stayed in the Shattuck Inn, which is now the Shattuck Golf Club. Not far from here, she pitched the tent in which she wrote several chapters of *My Ántonia*. She returned nearly every summer thereafter until her death and was buried in the Old Burying Ground, also the resting place of Amos Fortune, a former slave who bought his freedom in 1863 and moved to town when he was 71. Fortune, who was a tanner, also bought the freedom of his two wives.

GETTING HERE AND AROUND

Jaffrey Center's historic district is on Route 124 and is home to a number of brick buildings. It should take less than an hour to view it in its entirety. The Old Burying Ground is 2 miles east of town on Route 124, behind the Old Meeting House.

ESSENTIALS

Visitor Information Jaffrey Chamber of Commerce. ☎ *603/532–4549* ⊕ *www.jaffreychamber.com.*

EXPLORING

FAMILY **Cathedral of the Pines.** This outdoor memorial pays tribute to Americans who have sacrificed their lives in service to their country. There's an inspiring view of Mt. Monadnock and Mt. Kearsarge from the Altar of the Nation, which is composed of rock from every U.S. state and territory. All faiths are welcome; organ music for meditation is played at midday Tuesday–Thursday in July and August. The Memorial Bell Tower, with a carillon of bells from around the world, is built of native stone. Norman Rockwell designed the bronze tablets over the four arches. Flower gardens, an indoor chapel, and a museum of military memorabilia share the hilltop. ☒ *10 Hale Hill Rd., off Rte. 119, 8 miles southeast of Jaffrey Center, Rindge* ☎ *603/899–3300* ⊕ *www.cathedralofthepines.org.*

WHERE TO EAT AND STAY

$ ⛺ **Benjamin Prescott Inn.** Thanks to the dairy farm surrounding this 1853
B&B/INN   Colonial house—with its stenciling and wide pine floors—you'll feel as
though you're miles out in the country rather than just minutes from Jaffrey Center. **Pros:** inexpensive; homey and comfortable. **Cons:** not many
amenities. ⑤ *Rooms from: $129* ✉ *433 Turnpike Rd.* ☎ *603/532–6637*
⊕ *www.benjaminprescottinn.com* ⟿ *7 rooms, 3 suites* ⦿ *Breakfast.*

$ ⛺ **The Fitzwilliam Inn.** Once a stagecoach stop, the Fitzwilliam Inn has
B&B/INN   graced this picturesque town green since 1786. **Pros:** affordable; friendly
staff; full country breakfast. **Cons:** stair access issues. ⑤ *Rooms from:
$127* ✉ *Town Common, 62 Rte. 119 W, Fitzwilliam* ☎ *603/585–9000*
⊕ *www.fitzwilliaminn.com* ⟿ *10 rooms* ⦿ *Breakfast.*

$ ⛺ **The Monadnock Inn.** Rooms in this 1830s home are painted in lively
B&B/INN   lavenders, yellows, and peaches, lending it a cheery air in the heart of
pristine Jaffrey Center—a perfect place to get away from it all. **Pros:**
well-lit rooms with lacy curtains; feels cozy, like grandma's house. **Cons:**
limited amenities. ⑤ *Rooms from: $110* ✉ *379 Main St.* ☎ *603/532–
7800* ⊕ *www.monadnockinn.com* ⟿ *11 rooms, 2 suites* ⦿ *Some meals.*

$ ⛺ **Woodbound Inn.** A favorite of families and outdoors enthusiasts,
B&B/INN   this 1819 farmhouse became an inn in 1892. **Pros:** scenic lakefront
FAMILY   location; focus on food; private beach. **Cons:** older property; simple
furnishings. ⑤ *Rooms from: $159* ✉ *247 Woodbound Rd., Rindge*
☎ *603/532–8341, 855/966–3268* ⊕ *www.woodboundinn.com* ⟿ *44
rooms, 11 cabins* ⦿ *Breakfast.*

SPORTS AND THE OUTDOORS

FAMILY   **Monadnock State Park.** The oft-quoted statistic about Mt. Monadnock
is that it is America's most-climbed mountain—third in the world after
Japan's Mt. Fuji and China's Mt. Tai. Whether this is true or not, locals
agree that it's never lonely at the top: some days, more than 400 people
crowd its bald peak. However, when the parking lot fills up, rangers close
the park. Thus, an early morning start, especially during fall foliage, is
recommended. Monadnock rises to 3,165 feet, and on a clear day the
hazy Boston skyline is visible. Five trailheads branch out into more than
two dozen trails of varying difficulty (though all rigorous) that wend
their way to the top. Allow three–four hours for any round-trip hike.
The visitor center has free trail maps as well as exhibits documenting the
mountain's history. In winter, you can cross-country ski along roughly
12 miles of groomed trails on the lower elevations. ✉ *116 Poole Rd., off
Rte. 124* ☎ *603/532–8862* ⊕ *www.nhstateparks.org* ▣ *$5* ⟿ *No pets.*

SHOPPING

Bloomin' Antiques. Fine art and unusual antiques abound in this quaint
shop overlooking the town green. ✉ *3 Templeton Pike, Village Green,
Fitzwilliam* ☎ *603/585–6688.*

Charming Peterborough was the inspiration for the fictional Grover's Corners in Thornton Wilder's *Our Town*.

PETERBOROUGH

9 miles northeast of Jaffrey Center, 30 miles northwest of Nashua.

Thornton Wilder's play *Our Town* was based on Peterborough. The nation's first free public library opened here in 1833. The town, which was the first in the region to be incorporated (1760), is still a commercial and cultural hub.

GETTING HERE AND AROUND

Parking can be found just off Main Street, with shopping, coffee, and food all close by. Stand on the bridge and watch the roiling waters of the Nubanusit River at the north end of Main Street.

ESSENTIALS

Visitor Information Greater Peterborough Chamber of Commerce.
☎ *603/924–7234* ⊕ *www.peterboroughchamber.com.*

EXPLORING

FAMILY **Mariposa Museum.** You can play instruments or try on costumes from around the world and indulge your cultural curiosity at this nonprofit museum dedicated to hands-on exploration of international folk art. The three floor museum is housed inside a historic Baptist church, across from the Universalist church in the heart of town. The museum hosts workshops and presentations on dance and arts and crafts. ✉ *26 Main St.* ☎ *603/924–4555* ⊕ *www.mariposamuseum.org* ✆ *$6.*

WHERE TO STAY

$ ☷ **Birchwood Inn.** Henry David Thoreau slept here, probably on his way
B&B/INN to climb Monadnock or to visit Jaffrey or Peterborough. **Pros:** nice tavern; pleasant rooms; inexpensive. **Cons:** remote small town. Ⓢ *Rooms from: $109* ✉ *340 Rte. 45, Temple* ☎ *603/878–3285* ⊕ *www.thebirchwoodinn.com* ⬎ *3 rooms, 3 suites* ⦿ *Breakfast.*

$$ ☷ **The Hancock Inn.** This Federal-style 1789 inn is the real deal—the
B&B/INN oldest in the state and the pride of this idyllic town 8 miles north of Peterborough. **Pros:** quintessential Colonial inn in a perfect New England town; cozy rooms. **Cons:** remote. Ⓢ *Rooms from: $209* ✉ *33 Main St., Hancock* ☎ *603/525–3318* ⊕ *www.hancockinn.com* ⬎ *13 rooms* ⦿ *Breakfast.*

PERFORMING ARTS

Monadnock Music. From early July to late August, Monadnock Music sponsors a series of solo recitals, chamber music concerts, and orchestra and opera performances by renowned musicians. Events take place throughout the area Wednesday–Saturday evening and on Sunday afternoon. Many of the offerings are free. ✉ *2A Concord St.* ☎ *603/924–7610* ⊕ *www.monadnockmusic.org.*

Peterborough Folk Music Society. The Music Society presents folk concerts by artists such as John Gorka, Greg Brown, and Cheryl Wheeler. Concerts are held in the Peterborough Players Theatre, a fantastic repurposed old barn. ✉ *55 Hadley Rd., off Middle Hancock Rd.* ☎ *603/827–2905* ⊕ *www.pfmsconcerts.org.*

FAMILY **Peterborough Players.** This theater troupe has been performing since 1933, these days presenting seven main-stage productions in a converted 18th-century barn throughout the summer. The Players also present children's shows in July and August. ✉ *55 Hadley Rd., off Middle Hancock Rd.* ☎ *603/924–7585* ⊕ *www.peterboroughplayers. org* ⊘ *Closed mid-Sept.–late June.*

SPORTS AND THE OUTDOORS

GOLF

Crotched Mountain Golf Club. Donald Ross, one of golf's earliest stars of course architecture, designed this club's hilly, rolling 18-hole layout here. The course has a nice view of the Monadnocks. ✉ *740 Francestown Rd., Francestown* ☎ *603/588–2923* ⊕ *www.crotchedmountaingolfclub.com* ▧ *$39 weekdays, $49 weekends* ⚐ *18 holes, 6111 yards, par 71.*

SKI AREA

FAMILY **Crotched Mountain.** New Hampshire's southernmost skiing and snowboarding facility has 25 trails, almost half of them intermediate, and the rest divided pretty evenly between beginner and expert. There are four glade areas. Ample snowmaking capacity ensures good skiing all winter long. Crotched Mountain is famous for its night skiing: if you can stay up, you will save on a lift ticket and maybe hear a few good bands, too. Other facilities include a 40,000-square-foot lodge with a couple of restaurants, a ski school, and a snow camp for youngsters. **Facilities:** 25 trails; 100 acres; 1,000-foot vertical drop; 5 lifts. ✉ *615 Francestown Rd., Bennington* ☎ *603/588–3668* ⊕ *www.crotchedmountain.com* ▧ *Lift ticket $52 midweek, $64 weekends and holidays.*

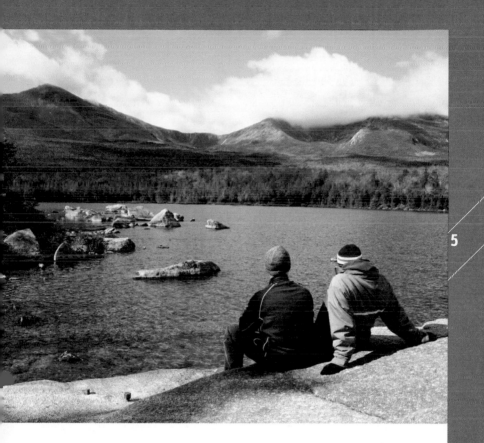

INLAND MAINE

WELCOME TO INLAND MAINE

TOP REASONS TO GO

★ **Baxter State Park:** Mt. Katahdin, the state's highest peak, stands sentry over Baxter's forestland in its "natural wild state."

★ **Moosehead Lake:** Surrounded by mountains, Maine's largest lake—dotted with islands and chiseled with inlets and coves—retains the rugged beauty that so captivated author Henry David Thoreau in the mid-1800s.

★ **Water Sports:** It's easy to get out on the water on scheduled cruises of large inland lakes; guided or self-guided boating, canoeing, and kayaking trips; and white-water rafting excursions on several rivers.

★ **Winter Pastimes:** Downhill skiing, snowmobiling, snowshoeing, cross-country skiing, and dogsledding are all popular winter sports.

★ **Foliage Drives:** Maine's best fall foliage is inland, where hardwoods outnumber spruce, fir, and pine trees in many areas.

1 Western Lakes and Mountains. Lakes both quiet and busy, classic New England villages, and ski resorts fit perfectly into the forested landscape. Snowmobiling and snowshoeing are popular in winter, while the woods and water draw summer vacationers for a cool escape. Spectacular fall foliage invites exploration of the region's national forest, state parks, and scenic byways. Crowds are thinner in spring, but fishermen, white-water rafters, kayakers, and canoeists still find their way here.

2 The North Woods. Much of the North Woods is best experienced by canoeing or kayaking, fishing, hiking, snowshoeing, or snowmobiling. Baxter State Park and Allagash Wilderness Waterway are premier wilderness destinations, and commercial forestland is open for public recreation. The woodsy town of Greenville, on Moosehead Lake, is a good base for day trips—take a drive (go slow!) down a "moose alley."

GETTING ORIENTED

Though Maine is well known for its miles of craggy coastline, the inland part of the state is surprisingly vast and far less populated. Not one hour's drive from the bays and ocean, huge swaths of forestland are punctuated by lakes (sometimes called ponds, despite their size). Summer camps, ski areas, and small villages populate the mountainous western part of the state, which stretches north along the New Hampshire border to Québec. In the remote North Woods, wilderness areas beckon outdoors lovers.

5

Updated by
Mary Ruoff

Unlike the state's higher-profile coastline, inland Maine is a four-season destination. Natural beauty is abundant here, in the form of mountains, lakes, rivers, and hilly pastoral stretches, and there's an ample supply of classic New England villages. Spring is the slow season, to be sure, though canoeists, kayakers, fishermen, and white-water rafters all venture inland at this time of year.

Sebago and Long lakes, north of Portland and the gateway to the Western Lakes and Mountains region, hum with boaters and watercraft in the summer. Mt. Katahdin, Maine's highest peak and the terminus of the Appalachian Trail, rises in 210,000-acre Baxter State Park, outside Millinocket in the North Woods.

Come winter, ski resorts—including Maine's largest, Sugarloaf and Sunday River, both in the state's western section—wait for large snowfalls (and make it themselves in between). Maine often receives snow when the rest of New England doesn't and vice versa, so track the weather if you're coming for winter sports or to bask in the serenity of a good snowfall.

Rangeley, in western Maine, has been a haven for anglers since the 19th century, but these days this lakes-strewn area is also known for hiking and winter sports. Remote forestland lines most of Moosehead Lake, the biggest natural lake east of the Mississippi River within a single state. Greenville, at its southern end, is a hub for visitors who come to enjoy the lake and explore nearby wilderness locales.

Wealthy urban "rusticators" began flocking to inland Maine on vacation in the mid-1800s. The legacy of the rusticators and the locals who catered to them lives on at sporting camps still found—albeit in smaller numbers than in days past—on remote lakes and rivers, and through Maine's unique system of licensed outdoor guides. Known as Registered Maine Guides, these well-qualified practitioners lead excursions that might involve kayaking, white-water rafting, hiking, fishing, hunting, canoeing, and moose spotting.

PLANNING

WHEN TO GO

As a rule, inland Maine's most popular hiking trails and lakeside beaches get busier when the weather gets warmer, but if splendid isolation is what you crave, you can still find it. Summertime is when lodging rates peak and traffic picks up—though rarely jams, outside of a few spots—but the weather makes it a beautiful time of year to visit. Inland Maine gets hotter than the coast in July and August; lakes and higher elevations are naturally cooler. September is a good bet: the weather is more moderate, and the crowds thinner.

Western Maine is the state's premier destination for leaf peepers—hardwoods are more abundant here than on the coast. Peak foliage season runs late September–mid-October.

Maine's largest ski areas can make their own snow—at least one of them opens its doors in mid-November and remains open until May. Inland Maine typically has snow cover by Christmas, so cross-country skiing, snowshoeing, and snowmobiling are in full swing by the end of the year. In ski towns, lodging rates peak in winter.

Early spring snowmelt ushers in mud season, which leads to black fly season mid-May–mid-June. The flies are especially pesky in the woods but less bothersome in town. Spring is prime time for canoeing and fishing.

PLANNING YOUR TIME

Visitors to inland Maine often spend their entire vacation in the region. That's certainly true of those who come to ski at a resort, fish at a remote sporting camp, or just relax at a lakeside cabin. After a day hike on a mountain trail reached by driving gravel-logging roads, visitors are unlikely to hurry along to another town. Vacation rental homes and cottages often require a week's stay, minimum, as do lakeside cottage resorts. And generally speaking, the farther inland you go, the farther it is between destinations.

GETTING HERE AND AROUND

AIR TRAVEL

Two primary airports serve Maine: Portland International (PWM) and Bangor International (BGR). Portland is closer to the Western Lakes and Mountains area; Bangor is more convenient to the North Woods. Regional flying services, operating from regional and municipal airports, provide access to remote lakes and wilderness areas and offer scenic flights.

CAR TRAVEL

Because Maine is large and rural, a car is essential. U.S. 2 is the major east–west thoroughfare in Western Maine, winding from Bangor to New Hampshire. Interstate 95 is a departure point for many visitors to inland Maine, especially the North Woods. The highway heads inland at Brunswick and becomes a toll road (the Maine Turnpike) from the New Hampshire border to Augusta. Because of the hilly terrain and abundant lakes and rivers, inland Maine can get curvy. Traffic rarely gets heavy, though highways often pass right through instead of around the larger towns, which can slow your trip a bit.

There are few public roads in Maine's North Woods, but private logging roads there are often open to the public (sometimes by permit and fee). When driving these roads, always give lumber company trucks the right-of-way; loggers must drive in the middle of the road and often can't move over or slow down for cars. Be sure to have a full tank of gas before heading onto private roads in the region.

RESTAURANTS

Fear not, lobster lovers: this succulent, emblematic Maine food is on the menu at many inland restaurants, from fancier establishments to roadside places. Dishes containing lobster are more common than boiled lobster dinners, but look for daily specials. Shrimp, scallops, and other seafood are also menu mainstays, and you may find surprises like bison burgers or steaks from a nearby farm. Organic growers and natural foods producers do business throughout the state and often sell their products to inland restaurants. Pumpkins, blackberries, strawberries, and other seasonal foods make their way into homemade desserts, as do Maine's famed blueberries. Many lakeside resorts and sporting camps have a reputation for good food—some of the latter will even cook the fish you catch. *Prices in the reviews are the average cost of a main course at dinner or, if dinner is not served, at lunch.*

HOTELS

Well-run inns, bed-and-breakfasts, and motels can be found throughout inland Maine, including some more sophisticated lodgings. At places near ski resorts, peak-season rates may apply in winter and summer. Both hotel rooms and condo units are among the options at the two largest ski resorts, Sunday River and Sugarloaf. Greenville has the largest selection of lodgings in the North Woods region, with elaborate and homey accommodations alike. Lakeside sporting camps, from the primitive to the upscale, are popular around Rangeley and the North Woods; many have cozy cabins heated with wood stoves and serve three hearty meals a day. Conservation organizations also operate wilderness retreats. In Maine's mountains, as on its coast, many small inns don't have air-conditioning. *Prices in the reviews are the lowest cost of a standard double room in high season. Hotel reviews have been shortened. For full reviews visit Fodors.com.*

Maine Campground Owners Association. The association's helpful membership directory is available by mail and on its website, which also has an interactive campground map. Many campgrounds have RV spaces and cabin rentals. ☎ *207/782–5874 ⊕ www.campmaine.com.*

Maine State Parks Campsite Reservations Service. You can get information about and make reservations for 12 state park campgrounds through this service. Note: reservations for Baxter State Park, which is administered separately, are not handled by the service. ☎ *207/624–9950, 800/332–1501 in Maine ⊕ www.campwithme.com.*

WHAT IT COSTS			
$	$$	$$$	$$$$
Restaurants under $18	$18–$24	$25–$35	over $35
Hotels under $200	$200–$299	$300–$399	over $399

VISITOR INFORMATION

Maine Office of Tourism. ☎ 888/624–6345 ⊕ *www.visitmaine.com.*
Maine Tourism Association. ☎ *207/623–0363, 800/767–8709* ⊕ *www. mainetourism.com.*

WESTERN LAKES AND MOUNTAINS

From Sebago Lake, less than 20 miles northwest of Portland, the sparsely populated Western Lakes and Mountains region stretches north and west, bordered by New Hampshire and Québec. Each season offers different outdoor highlights: you can choose from snow sports, hiking, mountain biking, leaf peeping, fishing, swimming, and paddling. The Sebago Lake area bustles with activity in summer. Bridgton is a classic New England town, as is Bethel, in the valley of the Androscoggin River. Sunday River, a major ski resort nearby, also offers a host of summer activities. The more rural Rangeley Lakes area contains long stretches of pine, beech, spruce, and sky, and more classic inns. Just north of Kingfield is Sugarloaf Mountain Resort, Maine's other big ski resort, which has plenty to offer year-round.

SEBAGO LAKE AREA

20 miles northwest of Portland.

The shores of sprawling Sebago Lake and fingerlike Long Lake are popular with water-sports enthusiasts, as are Brandy Pond and many other bodies of water in the area. Several rivers flow into Sebago Lake, linking nearby lakes and ponds to form a 43-mile waterway. Naples, on the causeway separating Long Lake from Brandy Pond, pulses with activity in the summer, when the area swells with seasonal residents and weekend visitors. Open-air cafés overflow with patrons, boats buzz along the water, and families parade along the sidewalk edging Long Lake. On clear days the view includes snowcapped Mt. Washington.

GETTING HERE AND AROUND

Sebago Lake, gateway to Maine's Western Lakes and Mountains, is less than 20 miles from Portland on U.S. 302.

ESSENTIALS

Vacation Rentals Krainin Real Estate. ✉ 1539 Roosevelt Tr., Raymond ☎ 207/655–3811 ⊕ www.krainin.com.

Visitor Information Sebago Lakes Region Chamber of Commerce. ✉ 747 Roosevelt Tr., Windham ☎ 207/892–8265 ⊕ www.sebagolakeschamber.com.

CLOSE UP

Inland Maine Outdoor Activities

People visit inland Maine year-round for hiking, biking, camping, fishing, canoeing, kayaking, downhill and cross-country skiing, snowshoeing, and snowmobiling. During the summer, mountain biking is big at some ski resorts.

The Kennebec and Dead rivers, which converge at The Forks in Western Maine, and the West Branch of the Penobscot River, near Millinocket in the North Woods, provide thrilling white-water rafting. Boating, canoeing, and kayaking are popular on inland Maine's many lakes and rivers.

BICYCLING

Bicycle Coalition of Maine. The coalition provides information about biking in the state. ☎ 207/623–4511 ⊕ www.bikemaine.org.

FISHING

Maine Department of Inland Fisheries and Wildlife. You can get information about and purchase fishing and hunting licenses by phone and online through this state agency. ☎ 207/287–8000 ⊕ www.mefishwildlife.com.

HIKING

Maine Appalachian Trail Club. The club publishes seven Appalachian Trail maps ($8), all of which are bound together in its Maine trail guide ($30).

Its interactive online map divides the AT in Maine into 30-plus sections, with photos and information on each. ⊕ www.matc.org.

Maine Trail Finder. Visitors can find Maine trails to hike, mountain bike, paddle, snowshoe, and cross-county ski on this website, which includes trail descriptions, photos, user comments, directions, links to maps, weather conditions, and more. ⊕ www.mainetrailfinder.com.

RAFTING

Maine Professional Guides Association. The association can help you find a state-licensed guide to lead a fishing, kayaking, canoeing, white-water rafting, or wildlife-watching trip. ⊕ www.maineguides.org.

SKIING

Ski Maine. For alpine and cross-country skiing information, contact Ski Maine. ☎ 207/773–7669 ⊕ www.skimaine.com.

SNOWMOBILING

Maine Snowmobile Association. The association's excellent statewide map of about 3,500 miles of interconnected trails is available online and by mail. Their website also has contacts and links for 11,000 miles of local and regional trails. ☎ 207/622–6983 ⊕ www.mesnow.com.

EXPLORING

Sebago Lake. Year-round and seasonal dwellings, from simple camps to sprawling showplaces, line the shores of Maine's second-largest lake, the source of Greater Portland's drinking water. ⊠ *Windham* ☎ *207/892–8265* ⊕ *www.sebagolakeschamber.com.*

FAMILY **Sebago Lake State Park.** This 1,400-acre expanse on the north shore of Sebago Lake is a great spot for swimming, boating, and fishing for both salmon and togue. Its 250-site campground is the largest of any of the Maine state parks. Songo Lock State Historic Site, an operational lock along the twisting, narrow Songo River, is a pleasant picnic area.

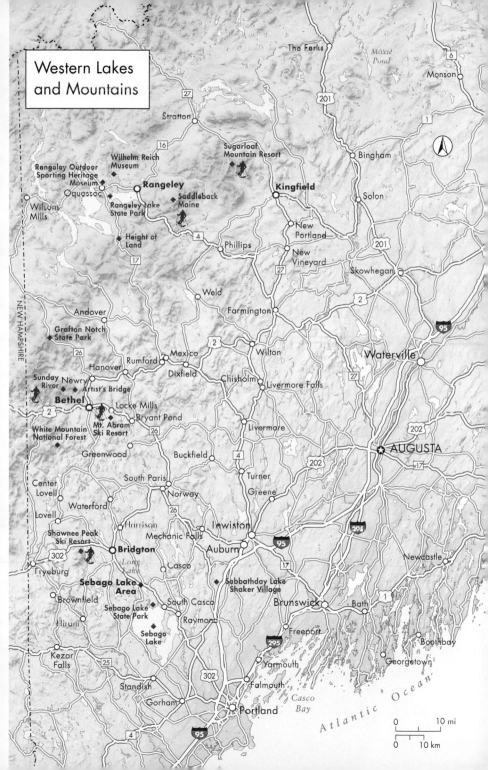

Western Lakes and Mountains

The Forks

Moxie Pond

Monson

Stratton

Sugarloaf Mountain Resort

Wilhelm Reich Museum

Bingham

Rangeley Outdoor Sporting Heritage Museum

Oquossoc

Rangeley

Kingfield

Solon

Rangeley Lake State Park

Saddleback Maine

Wilsons Mills

Height of Land

New Portland

Phillips

New Vineyard

Skowhegan

Weld

Farmington

Andover

Grafton Notch State Park

Rumford

Mexico

Wilton

Waterville

Hanover

Dixfield

Chisholm

Livermore Falls

Sunday River

Newry

Artist's Bridge

Bethel

Locke Mills

Bryant Pond

Livermore

Mt. Abram Ski Resort

White Mountain National Forest

Greenwood

Buckfield

AUGUSTA

South Paris

Turner

Center Lovell

Norway

Greene

Waterford

Lewiston

Lovell

Harrison

Mechanic Falls

Auburn

Shawnee Peak Ski Resort

Bridgton

Casco

Newcastle

Fryeburg

Long Lake

Sabbathday Lake Shaker Village

Brownfield

Sebago Lake Area

South Casco

Brunswick

Bath

Sebago Lake State Park

Raymond

Hiram

Sebago Lake

Freeport

Boothbay

Kezar Falls

Georgetown

Standish

Yarmouth

Gorham

Falmouth

Portland

Casco Bay

Atlantic Ocean

NEW HAMPSHIRE

0   10 mi

0   10 km

Bicycling along the park's roads is a popular pastime in warm weather. Come winter, the 6 miles of hiking trails here are groomed for cross-country skiing. ⊠ *11 Park Access Rd., Casco* ☎ *207/693–6231* ⊕ *www. maine.gov/sebagolake* ⊠ *$6.50.*

OFF THE BEATEN PATH **Sabbathday Lake Shaker Village.** Established in the late 18th century, this is the last active Shaker community in the world. Several buildings with Shaker furniture, folk art, tools, farm implements, and crafts from the 18th to the early 20th century are open for guided hour-long tours. The structures include the 1794 Meetinghouse, the 1839 Ministry's Shop, where the elders and eldresses lived until the early 1900s, and the 1821 Sister's Shop, where household goods and candies were made. The 1850 Boys' Shop has a free exhibit about Shaker childhood. A changing exhibit in the 1816 Granary is included with the tour, but tickets are also sold separately. The same is true for the herb garden tours on Tuesday and Thursday afternoons July–early September. The Shaker Store sells community-produced foods and goods as well as handicrafts by area artisans. If you're visiting the village in late August, don't miss the popular Maine Native American Summer Market and Demonstration. ⊠ *707 Shaker Rd., near Rte. 26, New Gloucester* ☎ *207/926–4597* ⊕ *www.maineshakers.com* ⊠ *Tour $10, granary exhibit $7, herb garden tour $7.*

WHERE TO STAY

$$$$ RESORT FAMILY
⌶ Migis Lodge. Scattered under a canopy of trees along Sebago Lake, the classy pine-panel cottages at this 125-acre resort have fieldstone fireplaces and are furnished with colorful rugs and handmade quilts. **Pros:** many water sports included; picnicking on resort's private island; evening cocktail hour. **Cons:** pricey; credit cards not accepted. ⑤ *Rooms from: $688* ⊠ *30 Migis Lodge Rd., off U.S. 302, South Casco* ☎ *207/655–4524* ⊕ *www.migis.com* ⊟ *No credit cards* ⊗ *Closed mid-Oct.–mid-June* ⤳ *35 cottages, 6 rooms* ⌾ *All meals.*

SPORTS AND THE OUTDOORS

Sebago and Long lakes are popular areas for sailing, fishing, and motorboating. As U.S. 302 cuts through the center of Naples, at the Naples causeway you'll find rental craft for fishing or cruising.

FAMILY
Songo River Queen II. Departing from the Naples causeway, the *Songo River Queen II,* a 93-foot stern-wheeler, takes passengers on one- and two-hour cruises on Long Lake. ⊠ *841 Roosevelt Tr., Naples* ☎ *207/693–6861* ⊕ *www.songoriverqueen.net* ⊠ *$15–$25.*

BRIDGTON

8 miles north of Naples, 30 miles south of Bethel.

U.S. 302 becomes Main Street in picturesque Bridgton, whose 10 lakes are popular for boating and fishing. Steps from the tree-lined downtown with its restaurants, galleries, and shops, a covered pedestrian bridge leads to 66-acre Pondicherry Park, a nature preserve with wooded trails and two streams. On hot summer days, kids dive off the dock at the town's Highland Lake Beach, just north of Main Street at the lake's southern end. Come winter, visitors hit the slopes at Shawnee Peak.

The surrounding countryside is a good choice for leaf peepers and outdoors lovers. A few miles north, Harrison anchors the northern end of Long Lake. In fall, Fryeburg, 15 miles west on the New Hampshire border, is home to the Fryeburg Fair (⊕ *www.fryeburgfair.org*), the region's largest agricultural fair.

GETTING HERE AND AROUND

From Portland, U.S. 302 runs northwest to Bridgton along the east side of Sebago Lake and the west side of Long Lake. From there it continues west to Fryeburg, where you can take Route 5 north to Center Lovell.

ESSENTIALS

Vacation Rentals Maine Lakeside Getaways. ⊠ *1 Mountain Rd., Suite 1* 🖾 *207/647-4000, 866/647-8557* ⊕ *www.mainelakesidegetaways.com.*

Visitor Information Greater Bridgton Lakes Region Chamber of Commerce. ⊠ *101 Portland Rd.* 🖾 *207/647-3472* ⊕ *www.mainelakeschamber.com.*

EXPLORING

Rufus Porter Museum. Local youth Rufus Porter became a leading folk artist in the early 1800s, painting landscape and harbor murals on the walls of New England homes, like this museum's red Cape Cod–style house, which bears unsigned murals by Porter (or one of his apprentices). Also an inventor, Porter founded *Scientific American* magazine. Early issues are on display, as are some of his inventions and miniature portraits. By 2016, the museum plans to include an 1840s-era house at 121 Main Street. ⊠ *67 N. High St.* 🖾 *207/647-2828* ⊕ *www.rufus-portermuseum.org* 🎟 *$8.*

WHERE TO STAY

$ 🛏 **Noble House Inn.** On a quiet road, this 1903 estate above Highland
B&B/INN   Lake offers a convenient location, plenty of creature comforts, and a relaxing atmosphere. **Pros:** bottomless cookie jar; skiing and golfing packages; distinctive suites. **Cons:** limited lake views; only suites have TVs. $ *Rooms from: $175* ⊠ *81 Highland Rd.* 🖾 *207/647-3733, 888/237-4880* ⊕ *www.noblehouseinn.com* ⇆ *4 rooms, 4 suites* ⦿ *Breakfast.*

SPORTS AND THE OUTDOORS

FAMILY **Shawnee Peak.** Just a few miles from Bridgton, Shawnee Peak appeals to families and to those who enjoy nighttime skiing—trails are lighted most evenings. Three terrain parks and seven glade areas offer alternatives to trails and downhill runs. The main base lodge has a restaurant with an expansive deck; the smaller East Lodge has a second-floor bunkhouse. Lodging choices also include Shawnee Peak House, slopeside condos, and a mountaintop yurt and cabin. Summer visitors can hike and pick blueberries. **Facilities:** 41 trails; 249 acres; 1,300-foot vertical drop; 5 lifts. ⊠ *119 Mountain Rd., off U.S. 302* 🖾 *207/647-8444* ⊕ *www.shawneepeak.com* 🎟 *Lift ticket $63.*

BETHEL

27 miles north of Bridgton; 65 miles north of Portland.

Bethel is pure New England: a town with white clapboard houses, white-steeple churches, and a mountain vista at the end of every street. The campus of Gould Academy, a college prep school founded in 1836, anchors the east side of downtown. In winter, this is ski country—Sunday River, one of Maine's big ski resorts, is only a few miles north in Newry. On the third weekend in July, MollyOckett Day, which includes a parade, fireworks, and a frog-jumping contest, honors a Pequawket Indian renowned for her medicinal cures in the early days of white settlement.

GETTING HERE AND AROUND

From the south, both Routes 35 and 5 lead to Bethel, overlapping several miles south of town. Route 5 from Bethel to Fryeburg is especially pretty come fall, with long stretches of overhanging trees. Kezar Lake can be glimpsed as the road passes through tiny Center Lovell. If you're coming to Bethel from the west on U.S. 2, you'll pass White Mountain National Forest.

ESSENTIALS

Vacation Rentals Four Seasons Realty & Rentals. ⊠ *32 Parkway Plaza, Suite 1* ☏ *207/824–3776* ⊕ *www.fourseasonsrealtymaine.com.*

Visitor Information Bethel Area Chamber of Commerce. ⊠ *8 Station Pl., off Cross St.* ☏ *207/824–2282, 800/442–5826* ⊕ *www.bethelmaine.com.*

EXPLORING

FAMILY **Grafton Notch State Park.** Route 26 runs through Grafton Notch, a favorite destination for viewing fall foliage that stretches along the Bear River Valley 14 miles north of Bethel. It's an easy walk from roadside parking areas to Mother Walker Falls, Moose Cave, and spectacular Screw Auger Falls. The Table Rock Loop Trail (about 2 miles roundtrip) rewards hikers with views of the mountainous terrain. For more of a challenge, make the 7.6-mile round-trip trek along the Appalachian Trail to the viewing platform atop Old Speck Mountain, the state's third-highest peak. The AT also traverses the 9,993-acre Mahoosuc Public Reserved Land—its two tracts sandwich the park—whose trails offer stunning, if strenuous, backcountry hiking (there are backcountry campsites). In winter, a popular snowmobile trail follows the river through the park. ⊠ *1941 Bear River Rd., Newry* ☏ *207/824–2912 Mid-May–mid-Oct. only, 207/624–6080* ⊕ *www.maine.gov/grafton-notch* ⊠ *$3.*

Museums of the Bethel Historical Society. Start your stroll in Bethel here, across from the Village Common. The center's campus comprises two buildings: the 1821 O'Neil Robinson House and the 1813 Dr. Moses Mason House, both listed on the National Register of Historic Places. The O'Neil Robinson House has changing and permanent exhibits pertaining to the region's history. One parlor room serves as a gift shop with a nice book selection. The Moses Mason House has nine period rooms, and the front hall and stairway are decorated with Rufus Porter School folk art murals. The barn gallery has changing and traveling exhibits. ✉ *10 Broad St.* ☎ *207/824-2908, 800/824-2910* ⊕ *www.bethelhistorical.org* ⬚ *O'Neil Robinson free, Moses Mason $3.*

FAMILY **White Mountain National Forest.** This forest straddles New Hampshire and Maine, with the highest peaks on the New Hampshire side. The Maine section, though smaller, has magnificent rugged terrain. Hikers can enjoy everything from hour-long nature loops to a day hike up Speckled Mountain. The mountain is part of the 11,000-acre Caribou-Speckled Mountain Wilderness Area, one of several in the forest, but the only one entirely contained within Maine. The most popular Maine access to the national forest is via Route 113, which runs south from its terminus at U.S. 2 in Gilead, 10 miles from downtown Bethel. Most of the highway is the Pequawket Trail Maine Scenic Byway, and the section through the forest is spectacular come fall. This stretch is closed in winter but is used by snowmobilers and cross-country skiers. Two of the forest's campgrounds are in Maine; backcountry camping is allowed. ✉ *Rte. 113, off U.S. 2, Gilead* ☎ *603/466-2713* ⊕ *www.fs.usda.gov/whitemountain* ⬚ *Day pass $3 per car, weekly $7.*

WHERE TO STAY

$ ⛺ **Holidae House.** New owners took over this affordable downtown
B&B/INN bed-and-breakfast in 2015, and they have embraced the welcoming hospitality that keeps guests returning year after year. **Pros:** courtesy cordials in parlor; fresh-baked treats in afternoon; blow-up mattresses available. **Cons:** little outdoor space. ⑤ *Rooms from: $139* ✉ *85 Main St.* ☎ *207/824-3400, 877/224-3400* ⊕ *www.holidaehouse.com* ⤳ *7 rooms* ⦿ *Breakfast.*

Artist's Bridge. The most painted and photographed of Maine's nine cov-
EN ered bridges can be found on a detour from Newry. Head south on U.S.
ROUTE 2 and then northwest on Sunday River Road (stay to the right at "Y" intersections). ✉ *Sunday River Rd., 4 miles northwest of U.S. 2, Newry.*

Height of Land. The most direct route from Bethel to Rangeley is a stunning 67-mile drive, much of it along Rangeley Lakes National Scenic Byway. Take U.S. 2 east toward Mexico and head north on Route 17, which winds through the Swift River Valley before ascending to Height of Land, with unforgettable views of mountains and lakes. In Oquossoc, continue on Route 4 to Rangeley ✉ *Rte. 17, Rangeley.*

SPORTS AND THE OUTDOORS

CANOEING AND KAYAKING

FAMILY **Bethel Outdoor Adventure.** On the Androscoggin River, this outfitter rents canoes, kayaks, tubes, paddleboards, and drift boats; leads guided fishing and boating trips; and operates a shuttle service and campground. Maine Mineralogy Expeditions is based here, with an open-air facility where you can sluice for precious gems. ✉ *121 Mayville Rd.* ☎ *207/824-4224* ⊕ *www.betheloutdooradventure.com.*

DOGSLEDDING

Mahoosuc Guide Service. This acclaimed guide company leads dogsledding expeditions in the Umbagog National Wildlife Refuge on the Maine–New Hampshire border and in northern Maine and Canada. Canoe trips in the refuge and elsewhere in Maine take place in the summer. The company

One of the Rangeley Lakes, Mooselookmeguntic is said to mean "portage to the moose feeding place" in the Abenaki language.

has lodging for customers and groups. ✉ *1513 Bear River Rd., Newry* ☎ *207/824–2073* ⊕ *www.mahoosuc.com* ✉ *From $280.*

SKI AREAS

FAMILY **Carter's Cross-Country Ski Center.** This cross-country ski center offers about 30 miles of trails for all levels of skiers. Snowshoes, skis, and sleds to pull children are all available for rental. The place also rents lodge rooms and ski-in cabins. Carter's has another ski center in Oxford. ✉ *786 Intervale Rd.* ☎ *207/824–3880, 207/539–4848* ⊕ *www.cartersx-cski.com* ✉ *$15.*

FAMILY **Mt. Abram.** Family-friendly and affordable, Mt. Abram is open Thursday–Sunday during ski season, with night skiing on Saturday. It allows off-trail "boundary-to-boundary" skiing, and has a tubing area and two terrain parks. Westside, the popular lift-served beginner area, has its own base lodge. The main lodge is home to the Loose Boots Lounge, which features live music on Saturday night. **Facilities:** 51 trails; 250 acres; 1,150-foot vertical drop; 5 lifts. ✉ *308 Howe Hill Rd., off Rte. 26, Greenwood* ☎ *207/875–5000* ⊕ *www.skimtabram.com* ✉ *Lift ticket $55.*

FAMILY **Sunday River.** Once-sleepy Sunday River has evolved into a sprawling
Fodor's Choice resort that attracts skiers from around the world. Stretching for 3 miles,
★ it encompasses eight trail-connected peaks, six terrain parks, a superpipe, and multiple glade areas. There's night skiing on midwinter weekends. Sunday River has three base areas and several lodging choices, including condos and two slope-side hotels: the family-friendly Grand Summit, at one of the mountain bases, and the more upscale Jordan

CLOSE UP

Whoopie Pies

When a bill aiming to make the whoopie pie Maine's official dessert was debated in state legislature, some lawmakers countered that the blueberry pie (made with Maine wild blueberries, of course) should have the honor. The blueberry pie won out, but what might have erupted into civil war instead ended civilly, with whoopie pies designated the official state "treat." Spend a few days anywhere in Maine and you'll notice just how popular it really is.

The name is misleading: it's a "pie" only in the sense of a having a filling between two "crusts"—namely, a thick layer of sugary frosting sandwiched between two saucers of rich cake, usually chocolate. It may have acquired its distinctive moniker from the jubilant "yelp" farmers emitted after discovering it in their lunchboxes. The whoopie pie is said to have Pennsylvania Dutch roots, but many Mainers insist that it originated here. Typically, the filling is made with butter or shortening; some recipes add Marshmallow Fluff. Many bakers have indulged the temptation to experiment with flavors and ingredients, particularly in the filling but also in the cake, offering pumpkin, raspberry, oatmeal cream, red velvet, peanut butter, and more.

Grand, near a summit at the resort's western end. (It's really up there, several miles by vehicle from the base areas, but during ski season there's a shuttle, or you can ski over for lunch.) From the less costly Snow Cap Inn, it's a short walk to the slopes. Maine Adaptive Sports & Recreation, which serves skiers with disabilities, is at the resort, whose summer hub, the main South Ridge Base Lodge, hosts activities that include zip-lining and mountain biking. **Facilities:** 135 trails; 870 acres; 2,340-foot vertical drop; 15 lifts. ⊠ *15 S. Ridge Rd., off U.S. 2, Newry* 🕾 *207/824–3000, 207/824–5200 for snow conditions, 800/543–2754 for reservations* ⊕ *www.sundayriver.com* 🎟 *Lift ticket $89.*

RANGELEY

66 miles north of Bethel.

Situated on the north side of Rangeley Lake along Route 4, Rangeley has long attracted anglers and winter-sports enthusiasts. The vastly forested Rangeley Lakes region has 100-plus lakes and ponds linked by rivers and streams. Right behind Main Street, Lakeside Park ("Town Park" to locals) has a large swimming area, a playground, and a boat launch. Equally popular in summer and winter, Rangeley has a rough, wilderness feel. In late January, the Rangeley Lakes Snowmobile Club's Snodeo offers thrilling snowmobile acrobatics, fireworks, a parade, and a cook-off for which area restaurants enter their chilies and chowders. Family-friendly Saddleback ski resort is several miles from town on its namesake mountain.

GETTING HERE AND AROUND

To reach Rangeley on a scenic drive through Western Maine, take Route 17 north from U.S. 2 in Mexico to Route 4 in Oquossoc, then head east into town. Route 16 soon joins the highway and from Rangeley continues east to Sugarloaf ski resort and Kingfield.

ESSENTIALS

Vacation Rentals Morton and Furbish Vacation Rentals. ✉ *2478 Main St.* ☎ *207/864–9065, 888/218–4882* ⊕ *www.rangeleyrentals.com.*

Visitor Information Rangeley Lakes Chamber of Commerce. ✉ *6 Park Rd., off Main St.* ☎ *207/864–5364, 800/685–2537* ⊕ *www.rangeleymaine.com.*

EXPLORING

FAMILY **Rangeley Lake State Park.** On the south shore of Rangeley Lake, this 869-acre park has superb lakeside scenery, swimming, picnic tables, a playground, a few short hiking trails, a boat ramp, and a campground. ✉ *S. Shore Dr., off Rte. 17 or Rte. 4* ☎ *207/864–3858 May–mid-Oct. only, 207/624–6080 for regional state parks office* ⊕ *www.maine.gov/rangeleylake* ✉ *$4.50.*

FAMILY **Rangeley Outdoor Sporting Heritage Museum.** Spruce railings and siding on the museum's facade replicate a local taxidermy shop from about 1900. The welcome center inside is an authentic log-built sporting camp from the same period, when grand hotels and full-service sporting lodges drew well-to-do rusticators on long stays. One of the big draws is the exhibit on local flytier Carrie Stevens, whose famed streamer flies increased the region's fly-fishing fame in the 1920s. Displays also include vintage watercraft and Native American birch-bark canoes. ✉ *8 Rumford Rd., Oquossoc* ☎ *207/864–3091* ⊕ *www.rangeleyoutdoormuseum.org* ✉ *$5.*

FAMILY **Wilhelm Reich Museum.** The museum showcases the life and work of the Austrian physician, scientist, and writer Wilhelm Reich (1897–1957), who believed that all living matter and the atmosphere contained a force called orgone energy. The hilltop Orgone Energy Observatory exhibits biographical materials, inventions, and equipment used in his experiments, whose results were disputed by the Food and Drug Administration and other government agencies. The observatory deck has magnificent countryside views. In July and August, the museum presents engaging nature programs; trails lace the largely forested 175-acre property, which has two vacation rental cottages. Reich's tomb sits next to one of his inventions. ✉ *19 Orgonon Cir., off Rte. 4* ☎ *207/864–3443* ⊕ *www.wilhelmreichtrust.org* ✉ *Museum $8, grounds free.*

WHERE TO EAT AND STAY

$$ ✕ **Gingerbread House Restaurant.** With a fieldstone fireplace in the main
AMERICAN dining room, tables scattered around the deck, and an antique marble soda fountain, there are lots of reasons to stop at what really does look like a giant gingerbread house at the edge of the woods. Sandwiches and burgers at lunch give way at dinnertime to crab cake appetizers big enough for a meal and entrées that include lobster mac 'n' cheese and barbecued ribs with a blueberry-chipotle sauce. Locals also come for the baked goods and the ice cream. ⑤ *Average main: $22* ✉ *55 Carry*

Rd., Oquossoc ☎ *207/864 3602* ⊕ *www.gingorbroadhouserestaurant net* ⊗ *Closed late Oct.–Nov. and Apr.; Mon.–Thurs. Dec.–Mar.; Mon. and Tues. May–late June; and Mon. early Sept.–late Oct.*

$ 🖼 **Country Club Inn.** Built in 1920 as the country club for the adjacent

D&D/INN Mingo Springs Golf Course, this hilltop retreat has sweeping mountain

FAMILY and lake views and plenty of charm. **Pros:** super-helpful staff; discount coupons for neighboring golf course; pool and sledding hill. **Cons:** rooms in main building are smaller; no TV in rooms. ⓢ *Rooms from: $169* ⊠ *56 Country Club Rd., off Rte. 4* ☎ *207/864–3831* ⊕ *www. countryclubinnrangeley.com* ⊗ *Closed Nov.–late Dec. and mid-Apr.– mid-May* ⏎ *19 rooms* 🍴 *Some meals.*

$ 🖼 **The Rangeley Inn.** Painted eggshell blue, this historic downtown hotel

HOTEL was built around 1900 for wealthy urbanites on vacation. **Pros:** Continental breakfast in elegant original dining room; impressive baths (some with claw-foot tubs); canoeing and kayaking on Hayley Pond. **Cons:** no elevator; restaurant open only for dinner. ⓢ *Rooms from: $145* ⊠ *2443 Main St.* ☎ *207/864–3341* ⊕ *www.therangeleyinn.com* ⊗ *Closed Nov. and late Apr.* ⏎ *41 rooms, 4 suites* 🍴 *Breakfast.*

SPORTS AND THE OUTDOORS

BOATING AND FISHING

Rangeley and Mooselookmeguntic lakes are good for canoeing, kayaking, sailing, fishing, and motorboating. Several outfits rent equipment and provide guide service if needed. Lake fishing for brook trout and landlocked salmon is at its best in May, June, and September. The Rangeley area's rivers and streams are especially popular with fly-fishers, who enjoy the sport May–October.

GOLF

Mingo Springs Golf Course. This popular course is known for its mountain and water views. The course is short but challenging, with very angled drives. The front nine holes are the hilliest; the back nine holes are the longest. You can also take in the views and spot wildlife on the Mingo Springs Trail & Bird Walk, an easy 3-mile loop trail through the woods along the course. ⊠ *43 Country Club Rd.* ⊹ *From Rte. 4 head south on Proctor Rd.* ☎ *207/864–5021* ⊕ *www.mingosprings.com* ⛳ *$32 for 9 holes, $44 for 18 holes* 🏌 *18 holes, 6024 yards, par 71.*

SEAPLANES

Fodor's Choice   **Acadian Seaplanes.** In addition to 15- to 90-minute scenic flights high

★   above the mountains by seaplane or helicopter, this operator offers enticing "fly-in" excursions. You can travel by seaplane to wilderness locales to fish, dine at a sporting camp, spot moose in their natural habitat, observe nature, or go white-water rafting on the remote Rapid River. Arcadian also provides charter service between Rangeley and Portland, Boston, and New York. ⊠ *2640 Main St.* ☎ *207/864–5307* ⊕ *www.acadianseaplanes.com* ⛟ *From $99.*

SKI AREAS

Rangeley Lakes Trails Center. About 35 miles of groomed cross-country and snowshoe trails stretch along the side of Saddleback Mountain. The trail network is largely wooded and leads to Saddleback Lake. A yurt lodge has ski and snowshoe rentals and a snack bar known for tasty soups. In warmer weather, the trails are popular with mountain bikers, hikers, and runners. ⊠ *524 Saddleback Mountain Rd., off Rte. 4, Dallas* ☎ *207/864–4309* ⊕ *www.rangeleylakestrailscenter.com* ⊑ *$19 ($9 for snowshoe).*

FAMILY **Saddleback Maine.** A family atmosphere prevails at this resort that entices many return visitors with its relatively thin crowds, affordable prices, and spectacular valley views. The beginner ski area is one of New England's best, partly because it is *below* the base lodge. At the other end of the spectrum, it's black diamonds all the way down at Kennebago Steeps!, touted as the East's largest steep-skiing area. Saddleback also has several glade areas and three terrain parks. A fieldstone fireplace keeps things warm in the post-and-beam base lodge, which has a second-story pub with views of Saddleback Lake. Lodging choices include ski-in, ski-out homes and trailside condos. Summer guests enjoy hiking. At the time of this writing a sale of the property was being negotiated, with the prospective new owners likely to initiate major upgrades. **Facilities:** 66 trails; 220 acres; 2,000-foot vertical drop; 5 lifts. ⊠ *976 Saddleback Mountain Rd., off Rte. 4, Dallas* ☎ *207/864–5671, 866/918–2225* ⊕ *www.saddlebackmaine.com* ⊑ *Lift ticket $69.*

KINGFIELD

38 miles east of Rangeley.

In the shadows of Mt. Abraham ("Mt. Abram" to locals) and Sugarloaf Mountain, home to the eponymous ski resort, Kingfield has everything a "real" New England town should have: a general store, historic inns, and white clapboard churches.

ESSENTIALS

Visitor Information Franklin County Chamber of Commerce. ⊠ *615 Wilton Rd., Farmington* ☎ *207/778–4215* ⊕ *www.franklincountymaine.org.*

EXPLORING

Stanley Museum. Original Stanley Steamer cars built by twin brothers Francis and Freelan Stanley—Kingfield's most famous natives—are the main draw at this museum inside a 1903 Georgian-style former school. Also worth a look are the exhibits about the glass-negative photography business the twins sold to Eastman Kodak, and the well-composed photographs, taken by their sister, Chansonetta Stanley Emmons, of everyday country life at the turn of the 20th century. ⊠ *40 School St.* ☎ *207/265–2729* ⊕ *www.stanleymuseum.org* ⊑ *$4.*

SPORTS AND THE OUTDOORS

SKI AREAS

FAMILY **Sugarloaf Mountain Resort.** An eye-catching setting, abundant natural snow, and the only above-the-tree line lift-service skiing in the East have made Sugarloaf one of Maine's best-known ski resorts. Glade areas, three terrain parks, a border-cross track, and a super pipe amp up the skiing options. There are two slope-side hotels and hundreds of slope-side condos with ski-in, ski-out access. Sugarloaf Mountain Hotel is in the ski village; the smaller, more affordable Sugarloaf Inn is a bit down the mountain. The Outdoor Center has more than 90 miles of

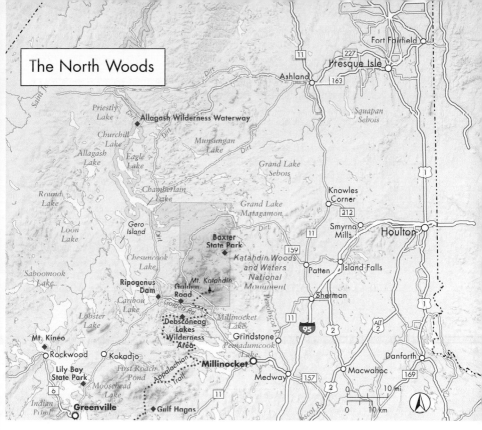

cross-country ski trails, and you can snowshoe and ice-skate. Indoor skateboarding and trampolining are among the many kids-oriented activities. Once at Sugarloaf, you'll find a car unnecessary—a shuttle connects all mountain operations. The ski season runs November–May. Summer is much quieter, but you can mountain bike, hike, zip-line, take a moose safari, or play a round of golf. **Facilities:** 122 trails; 1,240 acres; 2,820-foot vertical drop; 14 lifts. ☒ *5092 Access Rd., Carrabassett Valley* ☎ *207/237-2000, 800/843-5623 for reservations* ⊕ *www.sugarloaf.com* ☒ *Lift ticket $86.*

THE NORTH WOODS

Moosehead Lake, Baxter State Park, the Allagash Wilderness Waterway, and the four-season resort town of Greenville are dispersed within Maine's remote North Woods. This vast area in the state's north-central section is best experienced by canoe, kayak, or white-water raft; along the hiking, snowshoeing, cross-country-skiing, or snowmobiling trails; or on a fishing trip. As Maine's largest lake, Moosehead supplies more in the way of rustic camps, guides, and outfitters than any other northern locale. Its 400-plus miles of shorefront, three-quarters of which is owned by lumber companies or the state, are virtually uninhabited.

Rafting in the North Woods

Virtually all of Maine's white-water rafting takes place between the dam-controlled Kennebec and Dead rivers, which meet at The Forks in Western Maine, and on the West Branch of the Penobscot River, near Millinocket in the North Woods. Guided single- or multiday excursions run rain or shine daily from spring (late April on the Kennebec, early May on the Dead, and mid-May on the Penobscot) to mid-October.

Maine is New England's premier destination for the sport, which is why thousands of people come here every year to ride the waves. The Kennebec is known for abundant big waves and splashes; the Dead has New England's longest stretch of continuous white water, some 16 miles. The most challenging rapids are on the West Branch of the Penobscot River, a Class V river on the southern border of Baxter State Park outside Millinocket.

Many rafting outfitters operate resort facilities in their base towns. It's not uncommon for outfitters to run trips in both the Millinocket region and The Forks. On family-friendly rafting trips you can explore some of the gentler stretches of these mighty rivers. North Country Rivers, based south of The Forks in Bingham, and New England Outdoor Center, outside Millinocket, are leading white-water-rafting outfitters. The website of **Raft Maine** (⊕ *www.raftmaine.com*), an association of licensed outfitters, has answers to basic questions about everything from what happens on white-water trips to what to wear and when to go. Many companies offer packages that include lodging.

GREENVILLE

155 miles northeast of Portland; 70 miles northwest of Bangor.

Greenville, tucked at the southern end of island-dotted, mostly forest-lined Moosehead Lake, is an outdoors lover's paradise. Boating, fishing, and hiking are popular in summer, ice fishing and snowmobiling in winter. The town has the best selection of shops, restaurants, and inns in the North Woods region. Restaurants and lodgings are also clustered 20 miles north in Rockwood, where the Moose River flows through the village and—across from Mt. Kineo's majestic cliff face—into the lake.

GETTING HERE AND AROUND

To reach Greenville from Interstate 95, get off at Exit 157 in Newport and head north, successively, on Routes 7, 23, and 15.

ESSENTIALS

Vacation Rentals Northwoods Camp Rentals. ⊠ *14 Lakeview St.* ☎ *800/251–8042, 207/695–4300* ⊕ *www.mooseheadrentals.com.*

Visitor Information Moosehead Lake Region Chamber of Commerce. ⊠ *480 Moosehead Lake Rd.* ☎ *207/695–2702* ⊕ *www.mooseheadlake.org.*

EXPLORING

FAMILY **Lily Bay State Park.** Nine miles northeast of Greenville on Moosehead Lake, this park has good lakefront swimming, a 1.6-mile walking trail with water views, two boat-launching ramps, a playground, and two campgrounds with a total of 90 sites. In winter, the entrance road is plowed to access the groomed cross-country ski trails and the lake for ice fishing and snowmobiling. ☒ *State Park Rd. and Lily Bay Rd., Beaver Cove* ☎ *207/695–2700 mid-May–mid-Oct. only, 207/941–4014 for regional parks bureau office* ⊕ *www.maine.gov/lilybay* ⌇ *$4.50.*

FAMILY

Fodor'sChoice

★

Moosehead Historical Society & Museums. Guides in period costume lead tours of the Eveleth-Crafts-Sheridan House, a late-19th-century Victorian mansion filled with antiques, most of them original to the home. The Lumberman's Museum, with exhibits about the region's logging history, is in the carriage house, and the barn next door houses a recreation of a one-room schoolhouse and a general-store display. You can savor lunch and the architecture of these meticulously maintained buildings from the art-accented Sunken Garden. A mile away in downtown Greenville, the former Universalist Church houses the Center for Moosehead History and Moosehead Lake Aviation Museum. The former has a fine exhibit of Native American artifacts from the Moosehead Lake region, dating from 9,000 BC to the 1700s. The latter focuses on the impact of aviation on the area, from early bush pilots to Greenville's annual International Seaplane Fly-in. ☒ *444 Pritham Ave., Greenville Junction* ☎ *207/695–2909* ⊕ *www.mooseheadhistory.org* ⌇ *Eveleth-Crafts-Sheridan House $5, other museums free.*

OFF THE
BEATEN
PATH

Mt. Kineo. Accessible primarily by steamship, Mt. Kineo House was a thriving upscale summer resort set below its namesake's 700-foot cliff on an islandlike peninsula jutting into Moosehead Lake. The last of three successive hotels with this name was built in 1884 and became America's largest inland waterfront hotel. It was torn down in 1938, but Kineo remains a pleasant day trip. Mt. Kineo State Park occupies most of the 1,200-acre peninsula, with trails to the summit of the spectacular landmark. You can also play a round on Mt. Kineo Golf Course, one of the oldest courses in New England. There is no road access, but you can take a 15-minute boat trip from Rockwood on the golf course's seasonal shuttle. ☒ *Kineo Dock, Village Rd., Rockwood* ☎ *207/534–9012 for golf course and shuttle, 207/941–4014 for park regional office* ⊕ *www.maine.gov/mountkineo* ⌇ *$3.*

WHERE TO STAY

$$$

RESORT

FAMILY

Fodor'sChoice

★

Appalachian Mountain Club Maine Wilderness Lodges. When you want to get away from it all, head to the Appalachian Mountain Club's 70,000 acres in Maine's 100-Mile Wilderness, where you can choose between two historic sporting-camp retreats: Gorman Chairback and Little Lyford. **Pros:** great for outdoors lovers; sauna; made-to-order trail lunch. **Cons:** winter access only by cross-country skis or snowmobile transport (fee). ⑤ *Rooms from: $374* ☒ *Off Katahdin Iron Works Rd.* ☎ *603/466–2727* ⊕ *www.outdoors.org/lodging/mainelodges* ☽ *Closed mid-Mar.–mid-May and late Oct.–late Dec.* ⌁ *Gorman Chairback: 12 cabins, 1 bunkhouse (sleeps 10); Little Lyford: 10 cabins, 1 bunkhouse (sleeps 12)* ⑩ *All meals.*

$$$

B&B/INN

Fodor'sChoice

★

Blair Hill Inn. Beautiful gardens and a hilltop location with marvelous views over the lake distinguish this 1891 country estate, one of New England's top inns. **Pros:** free concierge plans outdoor excursions; amazing restaurant; 15-acre property with stone paths, wooded picnic area, and trout pond; lake-view views from all but one room. **Cons:** pricey; no direct lake access. $ *Rooms from: $399* ⊠ *351 Lily Bay Rd.* ☎ *207/695–0224* ⊕ *www.blairhill.com* ⊗ *Closed mid-Oct.–Apr.* ⇋ *8 rooms, 1 suite* ⦿ *Breakfast.*

SPORTS AND THE OUTDOORS

Togue (lake trout), landlocked salmon, smallmouth bass, and brook trout attract anglers to the region from ice-out in mid-May until September; the hardiest return in winter to ice fish.

MULTI-SPORT OUTFITTERS

Moose Country Safaris & Eco Tours. This outfit leads moose-spotting and bird-watching excursions; snowshoe, hiking, and canoe trips; and tours highlighting waterfalls, late-summer meteor showers, and an ice cave near Baxter State Park. ⊠ *191 N. Dexter Rd., Sangerville* ☎ *207/876–4907* ⊕ *www.moosecountrysafaris.com* ⊡ *From $88.*

Northwoods Outfitters. You can rent canoes, kayaks, camping equipment, ATVs, bikes, snowmobiles, snowshoes, skates, ski equipment, snowboards, and winter clothing here. Northwoods organizes a host of outdoor trips, including fishing and moose-watching (by land or water), and operates a shuttle to remote areas. At the base in downtown Greenville, you can pick up sporting goods, get trail advice, or kick back in the Internet café. ⊠ *5 Lily Bay Rd.* ☎ *207/695–3288, 866/223–1380* ⊕ *www.maineoutfitter.com.*

BOATING

Allagash Canoe Trips. Run by a husband and wife, both championship paddlers and Registered Maine Guides, Allagash offers single-day, overnight, and weeklong canoe trips on the Allagash Wilderness Waterway, the Moose and St. John rivers, and the East and West branches of the Penobscot River. White-water canoe and kayak trips are run on the Kennebec and Dead rivers. The company also conducts clinics on white-water paddling and kayaking and canoe poling. ⊠ *156 Scammon Rd.* ☎ *207/280–1551, 207/280–0191* ⊕ *www.allagashcanoetrips.com* ⊡ *From $225.*

SEAPLANES

Currier's Flying Service. You can take sightseeing flights over the Moosehead Lake region with Currier's from ice-out until mid-October. ⊠ *447 Pritham Ave., Greenville Junction* ☎ *207/695–2778* ⊕ *www.curriersflyingservice.com* ⊡ *From $40.*

TOURS

Katahdin Cruises. The Moosehead Marine Museum runs 3- and 4½-hour afternoon trips on Moosehead Lake aboard the *Katahdin*, a 115-foot 1914 steamship converted to diesel. (The longer trip skirts Mt. Kineo's cliffs.) Also called the *Kate*, this ship carried resort guests to Mt. Kineo until 1938; the logging industry then used it until 1975. The boat and the free shore-side museum have displays about these steamships, which transported people and cargo on Moosehead Lake for a century starting in the 1830s. ⊠ *12 Lily Bay Rd.* ☎ *207/695–2716* ⊕ *www.katahdin-cruises.com* ⊡ *From $33.*

OFF THE
BEATEN
PATH

Gulf Hagas. Called the "Grand Canyon of the East," this National Natural Landmark has chasms, cliffs, four major waterfalls, pools, exotic flora, and intriguing rock formations. Part of the Appalachian Trail Corridor, the slate-walled gorge east of Greenville is located in a remote, privately owned commercial forest, KI Jo-Mary, which allows access to it via gravel logging roads (always yield to trucks). A fee is usually charged at forest checkpoints, where you can also get trail maps and hiking information.

From either parking area you can hike to one of the showcase falls and mostly avoid the difficult rim trail. Start at Head of Gulf parking area for a 3½-mile round-trip hike, a good choice for families with young children, to Stair Falls on the gorge's western end. From the Gulf Hagas parking area, a 3-mile round-trip hike takes you to spectacular Screw Auger Falls on the gulf's eastern end. Gulf hikers who start from this parking area must ford the Pleasant River—easily done in summer, but dangerous in high water—and pass through the Hermitage, a stand of old pines and hemlock. A loop route that follows the rim and the less difficult Pleasant River Tote Trail is an 8- to 9-mile trek; there are shorter loops as well. Slippery rocks and rugged terrain make for challenging progress along the rim trail. ✉ *Greenville ✛ From Greenville, travel 11 miles east via Pleasant St., which eventually becomes Katahdin Iron Works Rd., to the Hedgehog checkpoint. Follow signs to the parking areas: Head of Gulf, 2½ miles; Gulf Hagas, 6½ miles ⊕ www.northmainewoods.org.*

MILLINOCKET

67 miles north of Bangor, 88 miles northwest of Greenville.

Millinocket, a former paper-mill town with a population of about 4,000, is a gateway to Baxter State Park and Maine's North Woods. Millinocket is the place to stock up on supplies, fill your gas tank, and grab a hot meal or shower before heading into the wilderness. Numerous rafting and canoeing outfitters and guides are based in the region.

GETTING HERE AND AROUND

From Interstate 95, take Route 157 (Exit 244) west to Millinocket. From here follow signs to Baxter State Park (Millinocket Lake Road becomes Baxter Park State Road), 18 miles from town.

ESSENTIALS

Visitor Information Katahdin Area Chamber of Commerce. ✉ *1029 Central St.* ☎ *207/723–4443* ⊕ *www.katahdinmaine.com.*

EXPLORING

Allagash Wilderness Waterway. A spectacular 92-mile corridor of lakes, ponds, streams, and rivers, the waterway park cuts through vast commercial forests, beginning near the northwestern corner of Baxter State Park and running north to the town of Allagash, 10 miles from the Canadian border. From May to mid-October, the Allagash is prime canoeing and camping country. The Maine Bureau of Parks and Lands has campsites along the waterway, most not accessible by vehicle. The complete 92-mile course, part of the 740-mile Northern Forest Canoe

Trail, which runs from New York to Maine, requires 7–10 days to canoe. Novices may want to hire a guide, as there are many areas with strong rapids. A good outfitter can help plan your route and provide equipment and transportation. ⊠ *Millinocket* ☎ *207/941–4014 for regional parks bureau office* ⊕ *www.maine.gov/allagash.*

FAMILY

Fodor's Choice

★

Baxter State Park. A gift from Governor Percival Baxter, this is the jewel in the crown of northern Maine: a 210,000-acre wilderness area that surrounds **Mt. Katahdin,** Maine's highest mountain and the terminus of the Appalachian Trail. Every year, the 5,267-foot Katahdin draws thousands of hikers to make the daylong summit, rewarding them with stunning views of forests, mountains, and lakes. There are three parking-lot trailheads for Katahdin, including the one for Abol Trail (closed since 2014 because of landslide activity but likely to reopen in 2016). Depart from the Roaring Branch trailhead for a route that includes the hair-raising Knife Edge Ridge. ■**TIP→** Reserve a day-use parking space at the trailheads May 15–October 15.

The crowds climbing Katahdin can be formidable on clear summer days and fall weekends, so if it's solitude you crave, tackle one of the park's many other mountains. All are accessible from the extensive trail network, and 14 peaks exceed an elevation of 3,000 feet. The Brothers and Doubletop Mountain are challenging daylong hikes; the Owl takes about six hours; and South Turner can be climbed in a morning—its summit has a great view across the valley. A trek around Daicey Pond, or from the pond to Big and Little Niagara Falls, are good options for families with young kids. Another option if you only have a couple of hours is renting a canoe at Daicey or Togue ponds. Park roads are unpaved, narrow, and winding, and there are no pay phones, gas stations, or stores. Camping is primitive and reservations are required; there are 10 campgrounds plus backcountry sites. ⊠ *Baxter State Park Rd.* ⊕ *Togue Pond Gate (park's southern entrance) is 18 miles northwest of Millinocket; follow signs from Rte. 157* ☎ *207/723–5140, 207/723–4636 for hiking hotline* ⊕ *www.baxterstateparkauthority. com* ⊠ *$14 per vehicle.*

Debsconeag Lakes Wilderness Area. Bordering the south side of the Golden Road below Baxter State Park, the Nature Conservancy's 46,271-acre Debsconeag Lakes Wilderness Area is renowned for its rare ice cave, old forests, abundant pristine ponds, and views of Mt. Katahdin. The access road for the Ice Cave Trail (2 miles round-trip) and Hurd Pond is 17 miles northwest of Millinocket, just west of the Golden Road's Abol Bridge. Near here the Appalachian Trail exits the conservancy land, crossing the bridge en route to Baxter. Before hiking, paddling, fishing, or camping in the remote preserve (no fees or reservations required) visit the conservancy's website for directions and other information. The Golden Road accesses are marked, but the signs aren't large. There are trail kiosks and marked trailheads within the preserve. ⊠ *Golden Rd.* ⊕ *www.nature.org/maine.*

Golden Road. For a scenic North Woods drive, set off on the roughly 20-mile stretch of this private east–west logging road near Baxter State Park northwest of Millinocket. Have patience with ruts and bumps, and yield to logging trucks (keep right!). From Millinocket follow the signs for Baxter State Park from Route 157. This scenic drive begins about 9 miles from town, at the crossover from Millinocket Lake Road to the Golden Road, the latter named for the huge sum a paper company paid to build it.

The North Woods Trading Post, a great stop for takeout and souvenirs and the last place to gas up before Baxter, is at this junction, across from Ambajejus Lake. From here it's about 9 miles on the Golden Road to one-lane Abol Bridge, which has parking areas on both sides. Take photos of Baxter's Mt. Katahdin from the footbridge alongside the bridge: this view is famous. Abol Bridge Campground, with a restaurant and store, is right before the bridge. Just beyond it is an access road for Debsconeag Lakes Wilderness Area. From here the road flows alongside the West Branch of the Penobscot River.

At the western end of the drive, the river drops 70-plus feet per mile through Ripogenus Gorge, giving white-water rafters a thrilling ride during scheduled releases from Ripogenus Dam. The Crib Works Rapid (Class V) overlook is off the Golden Road about 10 miles from Abol Bridge. (Turn right on Telos Road; parking is on the right after the bridge.) To drive across the dam on Ripogenus Lake and view the gorge, return to the Golden Road and continue west to Rip Dam Road, which veers right about a mile after Telos Road. Returning to the crossover at the North Woods Trading Post, turn left for Baxter or right for Millinocket. ⊠ *Golden Rd.*

Katahdin Woods and Waters National Monument. The day before the National Parks Service Centennial, President Obama named 87,500 acres of Maine's North Woods east of Baxter State Park a national monument. The land was donated by Burt's Bees co-founder Roxanne Quimby's foundation, Elliotsville Plantation. The foundation also donated millions to fund infrastructure and future support of the monument. Currently there is no visitor's center or services and the only access points are from gravel roads. From Sherman, take Route 11 to Swift Brook Road. From there, you can access the park's 14-mile Katahdin Loop Road to visit the southern portion of the monument. The road has various scenic viewpoints as well as trailheads to short hikes. The land is home to animals such as moose, bald eagles, salmon, and bobcats; and the rivers provide opportunities for paddling and fishing. There are also views of Mount Katahdin, in nearby Baxter State Park. ⊠ *Millinocket* ✛ *Take Route 11 (Katahdin Woods and Waters Scenic Byway) north to Swift Brook Road* ☎ *207/456–6001* ⊕ *www.nps.gov/kaww.*

SPORTS AND THE OUTDOORS
MULTI-SPORT OUTFITTERS

Katahdin Outfitters. This company provides gear and shuttles for over-night canoe and kayak expeditions on the Allagash Wilderness Water-way, the West Branch of the Penobscot River, and the St. John River. They also rent canoes and kayaks from their location just outside Mil-linocket at the base of Wilderness Edge Campground. ⌗ *Millinocket* ☎ *207/723–5700* ⊕ *www.katahdinoutfitters.com* ✉ *Call for prices.*

FAMILY
Fodor'sChoice
★

New England Outdoor Center (*NEOC*). With Baxter State Park's Mt. Katahdin rising above the shore opposite both its locations, this busi-ness helps visitors enjoy the North Woods. Its year-round home base, NEOC/Twin Pines on Millinocket Lake, 8 miles from the park's south-ern entrance, has rental cabins and a restaurant and conducts many guided trips, some within the park. Older log cabins (and a few newer ones) sit beneath tall pines on a grassy nub of land that juts into Mil-linocket Lake; upscale "green" units (spacious lodges and cozy cabins) are tucked among trees on a cove. Amenities include kayaks and canoes for use on the lake and a recreation center with a sauna.

At the deservedly popular **River Driver's Restaurant,** wood for the trim, wainscoting, bar, and floors was milled from old logs salvaged from local waters. Diners enjoy views of Katahdin from behind rows of windows or from the patio, and your dish may feature farm-to-table fare from the center's own gardens.

In addition to offering a full slate of guided snowmobiling, fishing, canoe, kayak, hiking, and moose-spotting trips, NEOC rents canoes, kayaks, and paddleboards, gives paddling lessons, and rents snowmo-biles. Trails for hiking, cross-country skiing (11 miles, groomed), and mountain biking are right on the 1,400-acre property. About 2 miles from Baxter, the seasonal Penobscot Outdoor Center is the base for white-water rafting trips on the West Branch of the Penobscot River. The center also has a wooded campground on Pockwockamus Pond. There are tent sites as well as canvas tents and simple wood-frame cab-ins with cots or bunks. A circular fireplace anchors the open-plan base lodge, which has a snack bar, a pub area, a hot tub, pool tables, and a communal outdoor fire pit. A towering window wall reveals glimpses of water through trees, and there are campsites near the water with Katahdin views. ■TIP➜ Nonguests can use showers for $2 after hiking or camping at Baxter. ⌗ *30 Twin Pines Rd.* ✦ *From Millinocket Lake Rd., take Black Cat Rd. east 1 mile* ☎ *207/723–5438, 800/766–7238* ⊕ *www.neoc.com.*

North Country Rivers. From spring to fall, North Country Rivers runs white-water rafting trips on the Dead and Kennebec rivers in The Forks in Western Maine, and on the West Branch of Penobscot River outside Millinocket in the North Woods. North Country's 55-acre resort south of The Forks in Bingham has cabin and cottage rentals, a restaurant, pub, and store; its Millinocket base is the Big Moose Inn. The outfitter also offers moose and wildlife safaris and rents snowmobiles, mountain and trail bikes, and kayaks. ⌗ *36 Main St., Bingham* ☎ *207/672–4814, 800/348–8871* ⊕ *www.northcountryrivers.com.*

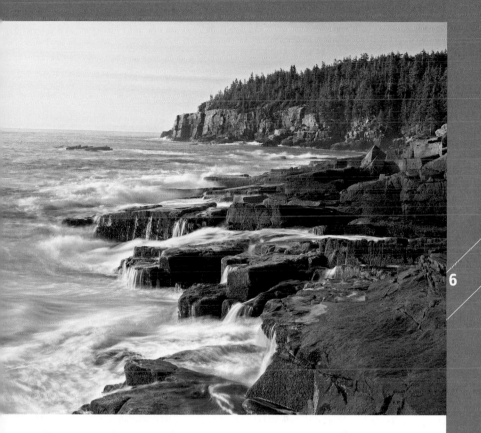

6

MAINE COAST

Visit Fodors.com for advice, updates, and bookings

WELCOME TO THE MAINE COAST

TOP REASONS TO GO

★ **Lobster and Wild Maine Blueberries:** It's not a Maine vacation unless you don a bib and dig into a steamed lobster with drawn butter, and finish with a wild blueberry pie for dessert.

★ **Boating:** The coastline of Maine was made for boaters: whether it's your own boat, a friend's, or a charter, make sure you get out on the water.

★ **Hiking the Bold Coast:** Miles of unspoiled coastal and forest paths Down East make for a hiker's (and a bird-watcher's) dream.

★ **Cadillac Mountain:** Drive a winding 3½ miles to the 1,530-foot summit in Acadia National Park for the sunrise.

★ **Dining in Portland:** With over 250 restaurants and counting, Forest City is a foodie haven with one of the highest per-capita restaurant densities in the U.S.

1 The Southern Coast. Stretching north from Kittery to just outside Portland, this is Maine's most visited region; miles of sandy expanses and shore towns cater to summer visitors. Kittery, the Yorks, Wells, and the Kennebunks offer low-key getaways, while Biddeford—a stone's throw from Portland—is on the rise, with charming boutiques and top-notch restaurants.

2 Portland. Maine's largest and most cosmopolitan city, Portland balances its historic role as a working harbor with its newer identity as a foodie mecca and the center of a thriving arts community.

3 The Mid-Coast Region. North of Portland, from Brunswick to Monhegan Island, the craggy coastline winds its way around pastoral peninsulas. Its villages boast maritime museums, innovative restaurants, antiques shops, and beautiful architecture.

6

GETTING ORIENTED

Much of the appeal of the Maine Coast lies in geographical contrasts— from its long stretches of swimming and walking beaches in the south to the rugged, rocky cliffs in the north. As the shoreline physically evolves, each town along the way reveals a distinct character.

4 **Penobscot Bay.** This region's dramatic natural scenery highlights its lively coastal towns, and Camden is one of Maine's most picture-perfect, with pointed church steeples, historic homes, a cozy harbor, and celebrated windjammer fleet.

5 **The Blue Hill Peninsula.** Art galleries are plentiful here, and the entire region is ideal for biking, hiking, kayaking, and boating. For many, the peninsula epitomizes the silent beauty of the Maine Coast.

6 **Acadia National Park and Mount Desert Island.** Millions come to enjoy Acadia National Park's stunning peaks and vistas. Bar Harbor is fun to explore, with its many gift shops and restaurants, while Southwest Harbor and Bass Harbor offer quieter retreats.

7 **Way Down East.** The "real Maine," as some call it, unfurls in thousands of acres of wild blueberry barrens, congestion-free coastlines, vast wilderness preserves, and a tangible sense of rugged endurance.

Updated by
Grace-Yvette
Gemmell

As you drive across the border into Maine, a sign reads, "The way life should be." It's a slogan that's hard to argue with once you've spent some time in the Pine Tree State. Here, time stays in step with you, and Mainers take their play just as seriously as their work.

Romantics thrill at the wind and salt spray in their faces on a historic windjammer. Birders fill their notebooks to the brim with new field notes. Families love the unspoiled beaches and sheltered inlets dotting the shoreline—not to mention the numerous homemade-ice-cream stands. Foodies revel in greater Portland's booming restaurant scene, while artists and art lovers find inspiration both on and off the canvas amid art galleries and museums or along the craggy seaboard. Adventure-seekers find many opportunities to kayak and cycle at the Bold Coast and Acadia National Park, whose trails invigorate hikers with their natural beauty. At night, the sky is dark enough to spot rare constellations and experience the magic of auroras.

The Maine Coast is several places in one. Classic New England town-scapes with picturesque downtowns mingle with rocky shorelines punctuated by sandy beaches and secluded coves with sweeping views of lighthouses, forested islands, and the wide-open sea. So, no matter what strikes your fancy—a spontaneous picnic on the beach or a sunset cruise with a bottle of local wine, an afternoon exploring hidden tide pools or a dose of culture followed by shopping and dining in town—there's something to suit every disposition.

Counting all its nooks, crannies, and crags, Maine's coast would stretch thousands of miles if you could pull it straight, which means there's always some new, undiscovered territory awaiting you. Stretching north from Kittery to just outside Portland, the Southern Coast is the most popular area, with many top-notch restaurants, museums, and wineries. Don't let that stop you from heading further Down East (Maine-speak for "way up the coast"), where you'll be rewarded with the majestic mountains and rugged coastline of Acadia National Park, as well as the unspoiled, dramatic scenery of the Bold Coast.

PLANNING

WHEN TO GO

Maine's dramatic coastline and pure natural beauty welcome visitors year-round, but note that many smaller museums and attractions are open only in high season (Memorial Day–mid-October), as are many waterside attractions and eateries.

Summer begins in earnest on July 4th, and you'll find that many smaller inns, B&Bs, and hotels from Kittery on up to Bar Harbor are booked a month or two in advance for dates through August. That's also the case come fall, when the fiery foliage draws leaf peepers. After Halloween, hotel rates drop significantly until ski season begins around Thanksgiving. Bed-and-breakfasts that stay open year-round but are not near ski slopes will often rent rooms at far lower prices than in summer.

In spring, the fourth Sunday in March is designated as Maine Maple Sunday, and farms throughout the state open their doors to visitors not only to watch sap turn into golden syrup but to sample the sweet results.

PLANNING YOUR TIME

You could easily spend a lifetime's worth of vacations along the Maine Coast and never truly see it all. But if you are determined to travel the coast end-to-end, allot at least two weeks at a comfortable pace. Count on longer transit time getting from place to place in summer, as traffic along Route 1 can be agonizing in high season, especially in the areas around Wiscasset and Acadia National Park.

6

DRIVING IN COASTAL MAINE		
	Miles	Time
Boston–Portland	112	2 hours
Kittery–Portland	50	50 minutes
Portland–Freeport	18	20 minutes
Portland–Camden	80	2 hours
Portland–Bar Harbor	175	3 hours 20 minutes

GETTING HERE AND AROUND

AIR TRAVEL

Maine has two major international airports, Portland International Jetport and Bangor International Airport, to get you to or close to your coastal destination. Manchester–Boston Regional Airport in New Hampshire is about 45 minutes away from the southern end of the Maine coastline. Boston's Logan Airport is the only truly international airport in the region; it's about 90 minutes south of the Maine border.

CAR TRAVEL

Once you are here the best way to experience the winding back roads of the craggy Maine Coast is in a car. There are miles and miles of roads far from the larger towns that have no bus service, and you won't want to miss the chance to discover your own favorite ocean vista while on a scenic drive.

BUS TRAVEL

The Shoreline Explorer links seasonal trolleys in southern Maine beach towns from the Yorks to the Kennebunks, allowing you to travel between towns without a car. Concord Coach Lines has express service between Portland and Boston's Logan Airport and South Station. Concord operates out of the Portland Transportation Center (✉ *100 Thompson's Point Rd.*).

FAMILY **Shoreline Explorer.** Running late June–Labor Day, the Shoreline Explorer offers seasonal trolley and shuttle service along the southern Maine coast. With links to private trolley operators in Kennebunkport, Ogunquit, and York, the service also provides access to the Amtrak Downeaster at Wells, as well as to the Sanford Regional Airport. Many lines have bicycle racks and wheelchair lifts, as well as stops close to trailheads for hiking. The Shoreline Explorer's Orange Line 5 offers year-round shuttle service with a bike rack from Sanford to Wells. A Day Pass or Multipass can be purchased from the driver. ☎ *207/459-2932* ⊕ *www.shorelineexplorer.com.*

TRAIN TRAVEL

Amtrak offers regional service from Boston to Portland via its Downeaster line, which originates at Boston's North Station and makes six stops in Maine: Wells, Saco, Old Orchard Beach (seasonal), Portland, Freeport, and Brunswick.

RESTAURANTS

Many breakfast spots along the coast open as early as 6 am to serve the working crowd, and as early as 4 am for fishermen. Lunch generally runs 11–2:30; dinner is usually served 5–9. Only in larger cities will you find full dinners offered much later than 9, although in larger towns you can usually find a bar or bistro with a limited menu available late into the evening.

Many restaurants in Maine are closed Monday. Resort areas take exception to this in high season, but these eateries often shut down altogether in the off-season. *Unless otherwise noted in reviews, restaurants are open daily for lunch and dinner.*

Credit cards are generally accepted at restaurants throughout Maine, even in more modest establishments, but it's still a good idea to have cash on hand wherever you go, just in case.

The one signature meal on the Maine Coast is, of course, the lobster dinner. It typically includes a whole boiled lobster with drawn butter for dipping, a clam or seafood chowder, corn on the cob, coleslaw, and a bib. Lobster prices vary from day to day, but generally a full lobster dinner should cost around $25–$30, or about $18–$20 without all the extras. *Prices in the reviews are the average cost of a main course at dinner or, if dinner is not served, at lunch.*

HOTELS

Beachfront and roadside motels, historic-home B&Bs and inns, as well as a handful of newer boutique hotels, make up the majority of lodging along the Maine Coast. There are a few larger luxury resorts, such as the Samoset Resort in Rockport or the Bar Harbor Inn in Bar Harbor, but most accommodations are simple, comfortable, and relatively inexpensive. You will find some chain hotels in larger cities and towns, including major tourist destinations like Portland, Freeport, and Bar Harbor. Many properties close during the off-season (mid-October–mid-May); those that stay open year-round often drop their rates dramatically after high season. (It is often possible to negotiate a nightly rate with smaller establishments during low season.) There is a 9% state hospitality tax on all room rates. *Prices in the reviews are the lowest cost of a standard double room in high season. Hotel reviews have been shortened. For full reviews visit Fodors.com.*

WHAT IT COSTS				
	$	$$	$$$	$$$$
Restaurants	under $18	$18–$24	$25–$35	over $35
Hotels	under $200	$200–$299	$300–$399	over $399

OUTDOOR ADVENTURES

No visit to the Maine Coast is complete without some outdoor activity—on two wheels, two feet, two paddles, or pulling a bag full of clubs.

BICYCLING

Both the Bicycle Coalition of Maine and Explore Maine by Bike are excellent resources for trail maps and other riding information.

FAMILY **Bicycle Coalition of Maine.** The well-regarded Bicycle Coalition of Maine provides cyclists with essential touring information like cycling routes, safety tips, where to rent and repair bikes, and annual events. ⊠ *34 Preble St., Portland* ☎ *207/623–4511* ⊕ *www.bikemaine.org.*

Explore Maine by Bike. Run by the Maine Department of Transportation, this helpful website includes an exhaustive list of the state's most popular bike routes, as well as other valuable cycling resources. ☎ *207/624–3300* ⊕ *www.exploremaine.org/bike.*

HIKING

Exploring the Maine Coast on foot is a quick way to acclimate yourself to the relaxed pace of life here—and sometimes the only way to access some of the best coastal spots. Many privately owned lands are accessible to hikers, especially way Down East. Inquire at a local establishment about hikes that may not appear on a map.

Healthy Maine Walks. The Healthy Maine Walks website has comprehensive listings and a searchable database for statewide walks that can be done in an hour or less, from park paths to routes that follow roads and streets. ⊕ *www.healthymainewalks.com.*

KAYAKING

Nothing gets you literally off the beaten path like plying the salt waters in a graceful sea kayak.

Maine Association of Sea Kayaking Guides and Instructors. This association lists state-licensed guides and offers information about instructional classes, guided tours, and trip planning. ⊕ *www.mainepaddlesports.org.*

6

Maine Island Trail Association. Seasoned paddlers can join the Maine Island Trail Association ($45 individual, $65 family) for a map of and full access to Maine's famous sea trail: more than 200 islands and mainland sites—most privately owned but open to members—on a 375-mile path from the southernmost coast to the Canadian Maritimes. Member benefits include discounts at outfitters and retailers. ⊠ *58 Fore St., Suite 30-3, Portland* ☎ *207/761–8225* ⊕ *www.mita.org.*

THE SOUTHERN COAST

The Maine Coast's southernmost stretch—including Kittery, the Yorks, Ogunquit, the Kennebunks, and Biddeford—features miles and miles of inviting sandy beaches and beautifully preserved historic towns and charming lighthouses. There is something for everyone here, whether you seek solitude in a kayak or the infectious conviviality of locals and fellow vacationers alike.

North of Kittery, long stretches of hard-packed white-sand beach are closely crowded by nearly unbroken ranks of beach cottages, motels, and oceanfront restaurants. The summer colonies of York Beach and Wells brim with family crowds, T-shirt and gift shops, and shorefront development; nearby wildlife refuges and land preserves promise an easy quiet escape. York Village's acclaimed historic district evokes the New England of yesteryear, while Ogunquit attracts visitors with its array of boutiques and art galleries and its paved cliff-side walk.

More than any other region south of Portland, the Kennebunks—and especially Kennebunkport—provide the complete Maine Coast experience: classic townscapes where white-clapboard houses rise from manicured lawns and gardens; rocky shorelines punctuated by sandy beaches; quaint downtown districts packed with gift shops, ice cream stands, and spas; harbors with lobster boats bobbing alongside stately yachts; and both five-star restaurants and rustic, picnic-table eateries serving fresh lobster and fried seafood.

KITTERY

65 miles north of Boston; 3 miles north of Portsmouth, New Hampshire.

Known as the "Gateway to Maine," Kittery has become primarily a major shopping destination thanks to its massive complex of factory outlets. Flanking both sides of U.S. 1 are more than 120 stores, which attract serious shoppers year-round. But Kittery has more to offer than just retail therapy: head east on Route 103 to the area around **Kittery Point** to experience the great outdoors. Here you'll find hiking and biking trails, as well as fantastic views of Portsmouth, New Hampshire, Whaleback Ledge Lighthouse, and the nearby Isles of Shoals. The isles and the light, along with two others, can be seen from two forts near this winding stretch of Route 103: Fort McClary State Historic Site and Fort Foster, a town park (both closed to vehicles off-season).

DID YOU KNOW?

Maine may not have many
sandy beaches or warm
water, but the rocky shoreline, dramatic tides, and
contrasting evergreens have
inspired photographers and
artists for years.

GETTING HERE AND AROUND

Three bridges—on U.S. 1, U.S. 1 Bypass, and Interstate 95—cross the Piscataqua River from Portsmouth, New Hampshire to Kittery. Interstate 95 has three Kittery exits. Route 103 is a scenic coastal drive through Kittery Point to York.

ESSENTIALS

VISITOR INFORMATION **Greater York Region Chamber of Commerce.** This is a good resource for exploring all that the region has to offer, including York Village, York Harbor, York Beach, Cape Neddick, Kittery, Eliot, and South Berwick. ✉ *1 Stonewall La., off U.S. 1, York* ☎ *207/363–4422* ⊕ *www.gateway-tomaine.org.*

Kittery Visitor Information Center. The Kittery Visitor Information Center is an excellent place to get information for mapping out your tour of Maine (and for a quick photo op with Smokey the Bear). Sometimes local organizations are on hand selling delicious homemade goodies for the road. ✉ *U.S. 1 and I–95* ☎ *800/767–8709* ⊕ *www.mainetourism.com.*

WHERE TO EAT

$$ SEAFOOD FAMILY ✗ **Chauncey Creek Lobster Pier.** From the road you can barely see the red roof hovering below the trees, but chances are you can see the line of cars parked at this popular outdoor restaurant that has been serving up fresh lobster for over 70 years. Brightly colored picnic tables fill the deck and enclosed eating areas atop the high banks of the tidal river, beside a working pier. The menu has lots of fresh lobster choices, as well as a raw bar. Bring your own beer or wine, if you like; you can pick up a growler of local, handcrafted suds at the Tributary Brewing Company just around the corner on Shapleigh Road off Highway 103. You can also bring sides and desserts that aren't on the menu. ⑤ *Average main: $22* ✉ *16 Chauncey Creek Rd.* ☎ *207/439–1030* ⊕ *www.chaunceycreek.com* ☾ *Closed Columbus Day–mid-May, and Mon. Labor Day–Columbus Day.*

$ ASIAN FUSION ✗ **Anju Noodle Bar.** With a cozy, open-plan dining area and a laid-back atmosphere, Anju Noodle Bar serves up free-style Asian dishes such as house-made shredded pork buns packed with hoisin, cucumbers, kimchi mayo and pickled red onion, spicy miso ramen, and inspired local seafood dishes. This is one of the few places in the Pine Tree State outside Portland where you'll find fresh and innovative Asian-inspired cuisine done really well. You'll likely be eating lobster and fried seafood for every meal the farther north you go in Maine, so it's well worth stopping here en route Down East, or on the ride home, for a (delicious) palate cleanser. ⑤ *Average main: $14* ✉ *7 Wallingford Sq., Unit 102* ☎ *207/703-4298* ⊕ *www.anjunoodlebar.com* ☾ *Closed Mon.*

SPORTS AND THE OUTDOORS

HIKING AND WALKING

Cutts Island Trail. For a peek into the Rachel Carson National Wildlife Refuge, this scenic 1.8-mile upland trail leads into the 800-acre Brave Boat Harbor Division and is a prime bird-watching area. There's a restroom and an information kiosk at the trailhead. The trail is open dawn–dusk year-round; dogs are not allowed. ✉ *Seapoint Rd.* ☎ *207/646–9226* ⊕ *www.fws.gov/refuge/rachel_carson.*

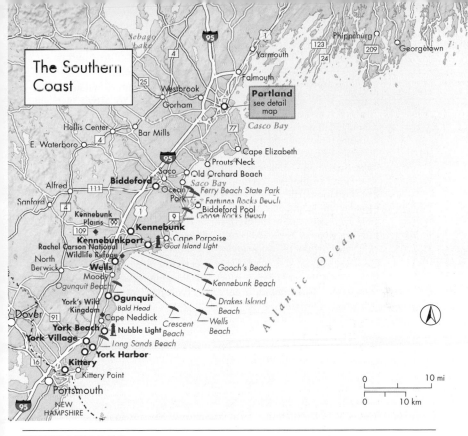

The Southern Coast

YORK VILLAGE

8 miles north of Kittery via I–95, U.S. 1, and U.S. 1A.

Spending an afternoon in York village is like going back in time—and you really only need a couple of hours here to roam the historic streets of this pint-size but worthwhile town. One of the first permanent settlements in Maine, the village museums detail its rich history. York is also home to the flagship store of Stonewall Kitchen, one of Maine's signature gourmet-food purveyors; the store has a café and a cooking school. There's also a cluster of vibrant contemporary-art galleries.

GETTING HERE AND AROUND

York is Exit 7 off Interstate 95; follow signs to U.S. 1, the modern commercial strip. From here, U.S. 1A will take you to the village center and on to York Harbor and York Beach before looping back up to U.S. 1 in Cape Neddick.

EXPLORING

George Marshall Store Gallery. The storefront windows and beadboard trim at the George Marshall Store Gallery (built in 1867) pay homage to its past as a general store, but the focus here is on the present. Changing exhibits, installations, and educational programs focus on prominent and up-and-coming regional artists. ⌧ *140 Lindsay Rd.* ☎ *207/351–1083* ⊕ *www.georgemarshallstoregallery.com.*

Museums of Old York. Nine historic 18th- and 19th-century buildings, clustered on York Street and along Lindsay Road and the York River, highlight York's rich history, which dates back to early Colonial times. The Old York Gaol (1719) was once the King's Prison for the Province of Maine; inside are dungeons, cells, and the jailer's quarters. The many period rooms in the Emerson-Wilcox House, the main part of which was built in 1742, display items from daily life here in centuries past, including furniture from the 1600s and an impressive ceramic dishware collection. The 1731 Elizabeth Perkins House reflects the Victorian style of its last occupants, the prominent Perkins family. Start your visit at the museum's Visitor Center, located at 3 Lindsay Road in the Remick Barn at the corner of Route 1A and Lindsay Road in York. ⌧ *Visitor Center, 3 Lindsay Rd.* ☎ *207/363–4974* ⊕ *www.oldyork.org* ⌧ *$5 single-museum entry, $12 for all.*

Stonewall Kitchen. You've probably seen the kitchen's smartly labeled jars of gourmet chutneys, jams, jellies, salsas, and sauces in specialty stores back home. This complex houses the expansive flagship company store, which has a viewing area of the bottling process and stunning gardens. Sample all the mustards, salsas, and dressings you can stand, or have lunch at the café and take-out restaurant. The campus also houses a cooking school where you can join in evening or daytime courses. Reservations are required; most classes are shorter than two hours and cost $45–$80. ⌧ *2 Stonewall La., off U.S. 1* ☎ *207/351–2712* ⊕ *www.stonewallkitchen.com/yorkstore.html.*

SHOPPING

Gateway Farmers' Market. Bring your own bag for morning shopping at the Gateway Farmers' Market, held in the back lot at the Greater York Region Chamber of Commerce in summer, and in the First Parish Church Fellowship Hall (180 York Street) in winter. You'll find fresh local produce, lots of baked goods and artisanal breads, local seafood and meat, fresh flowers, and handcrafted items like soaps and candles. It's a good place to gather the makings for a beach picnic or to stock up on holiday gifts. The summer market is open on Saturday 9–1, June–October, as well as on Thursday 9–1, July and August; the winter market is open on Saturday 9–1, November–April. ⌧ *1 Stonewall La., off U.S. 1, York* ☎ *207/363–4422* ⊕ *www.gatewayfarmersmarket.com.*

Ocean Fire Pottery. This artist-owned and -operated studio and gallery features unique wheel-thrown stoneware. Live demonstrations are available daily; call ahead to make sure the studio is open during the off-season. ⌧ *23 Woodbridge Rd.* ☎ *207/361–3131* ⊕ *www.oceanfirepottery.com.*

YORK HARBOR

1 mile from York Village via U.S. 1A.

A short distance from the village proper, York Harbor opens to the water and offers many places to linger and explore. The harbor itself is busy with boats of all kinds, while the sandy harbor beach is good for swimming. Much quieter and more formal than York Beach to the north, this area has a somewhat exclusive air. Perched along the cliffs on the north side of the harbor are huge "cottages" built by wealthy summer residents in the late 1800s, when the area became a premier seaside resort destination with several grand hotels.

GETTING HERE AND AROUND

After passing through York Village to York Harbor (originally called Lower Town), U.S. 1A winds around and heads north to York Beach's village center, a 4-mile trip.

EXPLORING

Sayward-Wheeler House. Built in 1718, the waterfront home was remodeled in the 1760s by Jonathan Sayward, a local merchant who had prospered in the West Indies trade. By 1860 his descendants had opened the house to the public to share the story of their Colonial ancestors. Accessible only by guided tour, the house reveals the decor of a prosperous New England family at the outset of the Revolutionary War. The parlor—considered one of the country's best preserved Colonial interiors, with a tall clock and mahogany Chippendale-style chairs—looks pretty much as it did when Sayward lived here. ⊠ *9 Barrell La. Ext.* ☎ *207/384–2454* ⊕ *www.historicnewengland.org* ⊠ *$5.*

WHERE TO EAT

$$$ ╳ **Dockside Restaurant.** On an island-like peninsula overlooking York
SEAFOOD Harbor, this restaurant has plenty of seafood on the menu. Popular dishes include haddock stuffed with Maine shrimp, and "drunken" lobster (sautéed lobster, scallops, shallots, and herbs in an Irish-whiskey cream), as well as beef tenderloin, slow-roasted duckling, seafood chowder, or cakes of native crab and wild mushrooms. Lighter fare is served in the cozy mahogany bar. Floor-to-ceiling windows in the stepped modern dining space transport diners to the water beyond—every seat has a water view. The Dockside Restaurant is part of a 7-acre property with guest rooms and suites in several buildings, from a grand 1895 summer home to condo-style quarters. $ *Average main: $25* ⊠ *22 Harris Island Rd., off Rte. 103* ☎ *207/363–2722* ⊕ *www.dockside-restaurant.com* ☉ *Closed late Oct.–late May, and Tues. in June and Sept.*

$$$ ╳ **Foster's Downeast Clambake.** Save your appetite for this one. Special-
SEAFOOD izing in the traditional Maine clambake—a feast consisting of rich clam chowder, a pile of mussels and steamers, Maine lobster with drawn butter for dipping, corn on the cob, roasted potatoes and onions, and Maine blueberry crumb cake (phew!) this massive complex provides musical entertainment to go with its belly-busting meals. There are also several barbecue offerings. $ *Average main: $28* ⊠ *5 Axholme Rd., at U.S. 1A* ☎ *207/363–3255, 800/552–0242* ⊕ *www.fostersclambake. com* ☉ *Closed early Sept.–late May, and weekdays late May–mid-June.*

WHERE TO STAY

$ ⌂ **Inn at Tanglewood Hall.** The inn's artfully painted floors, lush wall-
B&B/INN paper, and meticulous attention to detail are the fruits of a former designation as a designers' showcase home. **Pros:** authentic historic lodging; short walk to beaches. **Cons:** no water views. $ *Rooms from: $185* ⊠ *611 York St., York* ☎ *207/351–1075* ⊕ *www.tanglewoodhall. com* ⋨ *4 rooms, 2 suites* ⦿ *Breakfast.*

6

$$$ **Stage Neck Inn.** Built in the 1970s, this 58-room resort hotel takes
B&B/INN full advantage of its harborside location, with chaise lounges and a
fire pit on the surrounding lawns, water views from most guest rooms,
floor-to-ceiling windows in the Harbor Porches and Sandpiper Grille
restaurants, and outdoor dining in season. **Pros:** elaborate full-breakfast
buffet with scrumptious baked goods; poolside service and snack bar in
season; rooms have balconies or deck areas and most have water views.
Cons: no suites. $ *Rooms from: $345* ✉ *8 Stage Neck Rd., off U.S. 1A*
☎ *800/340–1130, 207/363–3850* ⊕ *www.stageneck.com* ☿ *Closed 1st
2 wks in Jan.* ⤏ *58 rooms* ⦿ *Breakfast.*

$ **York Harbor Inn.** A mid-17th-century fishing cabin with dark timbers
B&B/INN and a fieldstone fireplace forms the heart of this historic inn, which
now includes several neighboring buildings. **Pros:** many rooms have
harbor views; close to beaches, scenic walking trails. **Cons:** rooms
vary greatly in style, size, and appeal. $ *Rooms from: $189* ✉ *480
York St.* ☎ *207/363–5119* ⊕ *www.yorkharborinn.com* ⤏ *61 rooms*
⦿ *Breakfast.*

SPORTS AND THE OUTDOORS

BIKING
Berger's Bike Shop. This former auto garage and full-service bike shop
rents hybrid bikes for local excursions and sells bikes of all kinds. ✉ *241
York St., York* ☎ *207/363–4070* ⊕ *www.bergersbikeshop.com.*

FISHING
For a list of fishing charters, check the directory on the Maine Fishing
Guides website (⊕ *www.maineguides.com/activity/fishing-guides*).

Shearwater Charters. Shearwater Charters offers light tackle and fly-
fishing charters in the York River and along the shoreline from Kittery
to Ogunquit. Bait-fishing trips are also available. Departures are from
Town Dock #2 in York Harbor. ✉ *Town Dock #2, 20 Harris Island
Rd., York* ☎ *207/363–5324* ⊕ *www.mainestripers.net.*

HIKING AND WALKING
Cliff Walk and Fisherman's Walk. Two walking trails begin near Harbor
Beach. Starting in a small nearby park, the Cliff Walk ascends its granite
namesake and passes the summer "cottages" at the harbor entrance.
There are some steps, but, as signs caution, tread carefully because of
erosion. Fisherman's Walk, on the other hand, is an easy stroll. Starting
across Stage Neck Road from the beach, it passes waterfront businesses,
historic homes, and rocky harbor beaches on the way to York's beloved
Wiggly Bridge. This pedestrian suspension bridge alongside Route 103
(there is minimal parking here) leads to Steedman Woods, a public pre-
serve with a shaded loop trail along the York River estuary's ambling
waters. You can also enter the preserve near the George Marshall Store
in York Village ✉ *Stage Neck Rd., off U.S. 1A, York.*

YORK BEACH

6 miles north of York Harbor via U.S. 1A.

Like many shorefront towns in Maine, York Beach has a long history entertaining summer visitors. It's easy to imagine tourists adorned in the full-length bathing garb of the late 19th century. Visitors still come here to eat ice cream, enjoy carnival-like novelties, and indulge in the sun and salty sea air.

York Beach is a real family destination, devoid of all things staid and stuffy—children are meant to be both seen and heard here. Just beyond the sands of Short Sands Beach are a host of amusements, from bowling to indoor minigolf and the Fun-O-Rama arcade. Nubble Light is at the tip of the peninsula separating Long Sands and Short Sands beaches. The latter is mostly lined with unpretentious seasonal homes, with motels and restaurants mixed in.

GETTING HERE AND AROUND

It's a scenic 6 miles to York Beach via the loop road, U.S. 1A, from its southern intersection with U.S. 1. Although 2 miles longer, it's generally faster to continue north on U.S. 1A to Cape Neddick and then U.S 1A south to the village center, home to Short Sands Beach. Here U.S. 1A is known as Ocean Avenue as it heads north from York Harbor along Long Sands Beach en route to York Beach village and Short Sands Beach. A trolley along U.S. 1 links the beaches in summer. You can also get from beach to beach on a series of residential streets that wind around Nubble Point between these beaches.

York Trolley Co. From late June through Labor Day, these bright-red trolleys link Short Sands Beach in York Beach village and nearby Long Sands Beach, running along U.S. 1A, making a number of stops. Maps can be picked up throughout York; fares are $2 one way, $4 round-trip, cash only (payable to driver upon boarding). You can also connect with a shuttle service to Ogunquit. ⊠ *York* ☎ *207/363–9600* ⊕ *www.yorktrolley.com.*

EXPLORING

Fodor's Choice ★ **Nubble Light.** On a small island just off the tip of the cape jutting dramatically into the Atlantic Ocean between Long Sands Beach and Short Sands Beach, Nubble Light is one of the most photographed lighthouses on the globe. Direct access is prohibited, but the small Sohier Park right across from the light has parking, historical placards, benches, and a seasonal information center that shares the 1879 light's history. ⊠ *End of Nubble Rd., off U.S. 1A, York* ☎ *207/363–3569 (Memorial Day weekend–Labor Day)* ⊕ *www.nubblelight.org.*

FAMILY **York's Wild Kingdom.** Surrounded by forest, this popular zoo has an impressive variety of exotic animals and is home to the state's only white Bengal tiger. There's a nostalgic charm to the amusement park, which offers discounts for kids under 13—the target market, as there are no large thrill rides. Many York Beach visitors come just to enjoy the ocean views from the Ferris wheel and share what's advertised as the "seaboard's largest fried dough." ⊠ *1 Animal Park Rd., off U.S. 1* ☎ *207/363–4911* ⊕ *www. yorkzoo.com* ⊠ *Zoo $14.74, zoo and rides $22.25.*

WHERE TO EAT AND STAY

$ ✕ **The Goldenrod.** People line the windows to watch Goldenrod Kisses
AMERICAN being made the same way they have since 1896—and some 50 tons
FAMILY are made every year. Aside from the famous taffy (there's penny candy, too), this eatery is family oriented, very reasonably priced, and a great place to get ice cream from the old-fashioned soda fountain. Breakfast is served all day, while the simple lunch menu of sandwiches and burgers does just as well for dinner, with the addition of a handful of entrées, like baked haddock and meat loaf. ⑤ *Average main: $10 ⊠ 2 Railroad Ave.* ☎ *207/363-2621* ⊕ *www.thegoldenrod.com* ☼ *Closed mid-Oct.–mid-May.*

$$ ⊡ **Atlantic House Inn.** In a nicely renovated 1888 beauty, this inn's stan-
B&B/INN dard guest rooms feel fresh with designer fabrics, gas fireplaces, and
FAMILY whirlpool tubs. **Pros:** lots of amenities; walk to beach, shops; suites are a good choice for weekly stay; some ocean views. **Cons:** not on beach; lacks public spaces; some rooms have a two-night minimum. ⑤ *Rooms from: $269 ⊠ 2 Beach St.* ☎ *207/361-6677* ⊕ *www.atlantichouseinn. com* ☼ *Closed Nov.–Apr.* ⌁ *7 rooms, 9 suites* ⑩ *No meals.*

$$ ⊡ **Union Bluff Hotel.** This massive, turreted structure still looks much
HOTEL the same as it did when it opened in the mid-19th century. **Pros:** many spectacular ocean views; in the middle of the action. **Cons:** rooms lack any charm or character befitting of inn's origins; not for those looking for a quiet getaway. ⑤ *Rooms from: $229 ⊠ 8 Beach St.* ☎ *207/363-1333, 800/833-0721* ⊕ *www.unionbluff.com* ⌁ *65 rooms, 6 suites* ⑩ *No meals.*

NIGHTLIFE

Inn on the Blues. This hopping music club attracts nationally known bands playing funk, jazz, and reggae, as well as blues. It's open April–December and weekends only in the shoulder seasons. ⊠ *7 Ocean Ave., York* ☎ *207/351-3221* ⊕ *www.in3ontheblues.com.*

OGUNQUIT

8 miles north of the Yorks via U.S. 1.

A resort village since the late 19th century, Ogunquit made a name for itself as an artists' colony. Today it has become a mini Provincetown, with a gay population that swells in summer, and many inns and small clubs cater to a primarily gay and lesbian clientele. The nightlife in Ogunquit revolves around the precincts of Ogunquit Square and Perkins Cove, where people stroll, often enjoying an after-dinner ice cream cone or espresso. For a scenic drive, take Shore Road from downtown to the 175-foot Bald Head Cliff; you'll be treated to views up and down the coast. On a stormy day the surf can be quite wild here.

GETTING HERE AND AROUND

Parking in the village and at the beach is costly and limited, so leave your car at the hotel or in a public parking space and hop the trolley. It costs $1.50 per trip and runs Memorial Day weekend–Columbus Day, with weekend-only service during the first few weeks. From Perkins Cove, the trolley runs through town along Shore Road and then down to Ogunquit Beach; it also stops along U.S. 1.

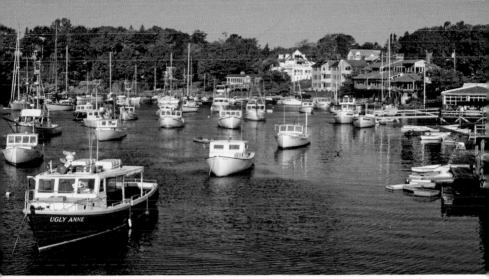

Ogunquit's Perkins Cove is a pleasant place to admire the boats (and wonder at the origin of their names).

ESSENTIALS

Transportation Information Ogunquit Trolley. ☎ 207/646–1411 ⊕ www.ogunquittrolley.com.

Visitor Information Ogunquit Chamber of Commerce. ⊠ 36 Main St. ☎ 207/646–2939 ⊕ www.ogunquit.org.

EXPLORING

Perkins Cove. This neck of land off Shore Road in the lower part of Ogunquit village has a jumble of sea-weathered fish houses and buildings that were part of an art school. These have largely been transformed by the tide of tourism into shops and restaurants. When you've had your fill of browsing, stroll out along **Marginal Way,** a mile-long, paved footpath that hugs the shore of a rocky promontory known as Israel's Head. Benches allow you to appreciate the open sea vistas. Expect heavy foot traffic along the path, even in the off-season. ⊠ Perkins Cove Rd., off Shore Rd.

WHERE TO EAT

$ ╳ **Amore Breakfast.** You could hardly find a more satisfying, heartier
AMERICAN breakfast than at this smart and busy joint just shy of the entrance to Perkins Cove. A lighthearted mix of retro advertising signs adorns the walls of this bright, open, and bustling dining room. You won't find tired standards here—the only pancakes are German potato, and the Oscar Madison omelet combines crabmeat with asparagus and Swiss, topped with a béarnaise sauce. For a really decadent start, opt for the Banana Foster: pecan-coated, cream cheese–stuffed French toast with a side of sautéed bananas in rum syrup. Next door, at the Cafe

Amore, you can pick up sandwiches and other light fare. $ *Average main: $10* ✉ *309 Shore Rd.* ☎ *207/646–6661* ⊕ *www.amorebreakfast. com* ⊘ *Closed mid-Dec.–early Apr. No dinner.*

$$ ✕**The Velveteen Habit.** With an on-site microgarden, which supplies most
AMERICAN of the ingredients used in the restaurant's dishes, The Velveteen Habit takes farm-to-table to a new level. House-cured meats and pickled veggies are served alongside fresh and smoked seafood and craft cocktails in a cozy, refurbished farmhouse with tables looking out over the kitchen garden. $ *Average main: $20* ✉ *37 Ogunquit Rd., 3 miles outside Ogunquit, Cape Neddick* ☎ *207/216–9884* ⊕ *www.thevelveteenhabit.com* ⊟ *No credit cards.*

WELLS

5 miles north of Ogunquit via U.S. 1.

Lacking any kind of discernible village center, Wells could be easily overlooked as nothing more than a commercial stretch of U.S. 1 between Ogunquit and the Kennebunks. But look more closely: this is a place where people come to enjoy some of the best beaches on the coast. Until 1980 the town of Wells incorporated Ogunquit, and today this family-oriented beach community has 7 miles of densely populated shoreline, along with nature preserves, where you can explore salt marshes and tidal pools.

GETTING HERE AND AROUND

Just $2 per trip, the seasonal Shoreline Trolley serves Wells Beach and Crescent Beach and has many stops along U.S. 1 at motels, campgrounds, restaurants, and so on. You can also catch it at the Wells Transportation Center when Amtrak's *Downeaster* pulls in.

ESSENTIALS

Transportation Information Shoreline Trolley. ☎ *207/324–5762* ⊕ *www. shorelineexplorer.com.*

Visitor Information Wells Chamber of Commerce. ✉ *136 Post Rd.* ☎ *207/646–2451* ⊕ *www.wellschamber.org.*

EXPLORING

FAMILY **Rachel Carson National Wildlife Refuge.** At the headquarters of the Rachel Carson National Wildlife Refuge, which has 11 divisions from Kittery to Cape Elizabeth, is the Carson Trail, a 1-mile loop. The trail traverses a salt marsh and a white-pine forest where migrating birds and waterfowl of many varieties are regularly spotted, and it borders Branch Brook and the Merriland River. ✉ *321 Port Rd.* ☎ *207/646–9226* ⊕ *www.fws.gov/northeast/rachelcarson.*

QUICK BITES

Congdon's Doughnuts. These superior doughnuts have been made by the same family since 1945. Congdon's has about 40 different varieties, though the plain variety really gives you an idea of just how good these doughnuts are: it's the biggest seller, along with the honey dipped and black raspberry jelly. You're welcome to sit inside for breakfast or lunch, but waits can be long in summer. There are also drive-through and take-out windows. ✉ *1090 Post Rd.* ☎ *207/646–4219* ⊕ *www.congdons.com* ⊘ *Closed Mon.–Wed. No dinner.*

BEACHES

With its thousands of acres of marsh and preserved land, Wells is a great place to spend time outdoors. Nearly 7 miles of sand stretch along the boundaries of Wells, making beachgoing a prime occupation. Tidal pools sheltered by rocks are filled with all manner of creatures awaiting discovery. During the summer season a pay-and-display parking system (no quarters, receipt goes on dashboard) is in place at the public beaches.

A summer trolley serves **Crescent Beach,** along Webhannet Drive, and **Wells Beach,** at the end of Mile Road off U.S. 1. There is another parking lot, but no trolley stop, at the north end of Atlantic Avenue, which runs north along the shore from the end of Mile Road. Stretching north from the jetty at Wells Harbor is **Drakes Island Beach** (end of Drakes Island Road off U.S. 1). Lifeguards are on hand at all beaches, and all have public restrooms.

FAMILY **Crescent Beach.** Lined with summer homes, this sandy strand is busy in the summer, but the beach and the water are surprisingly clean, considering all the traffic. The swimming's good, and beachgoers can also explore tidal pools and look for seals on the sea rocks nearby. **Amenities:** food and drink; lifeguards; parking (fee); toilets. **Best for:** swimming. ⊠ *Webhannet Dr., south of Mile Rd.* ☎ *207/646–5113.*

FAMILY **Drakes Island Beach.** Smaller and quieter than the other two beaches in Wells, Drakes Island Beach is also a little more natural, with rolling sand dunes and access to salt-marsh walking trails at an adjacent estuary. The ice-cream truck swings by regularly in the summer. **Amenities:** lifeguards; parking (fee); toilets. **Best for:** walking. ⊠ *Island Beach Rd., 1 mile southwest of U.S. 1* ☎ *207/646–5113.*

FAMILY **Wells Beach.** The northern end of a 2-mile stretch of golden sand, Wells Beach is popular with families and surfers, who line up in the swells and preen on the boardwalk near the arcade and snack shop. The beach's northern tip is a bit quieter, with a long rock jetty perfect for strolling. **Amenities:** food and drink; lifeguards; parking (fee); toilets. **Best for:** surfing; walking. ⊠ *Atlantic Ave., north of Mile Rd.* ☎ *207/646–5113.*

Wheels and Waves. Rent bikes, surfboards, wet suits, boogie boards, kayaks, and all sorts of outdoor gear at Wheels and Waves. ⊠ *365 Post Rd., Rte. 1* ☎ *207/646–5774* ⊕ *www.wheelsnwaves.com.*

WHERE TO EAT AND STAY

$ ✕ **Billy's Chowder House.** Locals and vacationers head to this classic road-
SEAFOOD side seafood restaurant in the midst of a salt marsh en route to Wells Beach. They come for the generous lobster rolls, haddock sandwiches, and chowders, but there are plenty of non-seafood choices, too. Big windows in the bright dining rooms overlook the marsh, part of the Rachel Carson National Wildlife Refuge. ⑤ *Average main: $15* ⊠ *216 Mile Rd.* ☎ *207/646–7558* ⊕ *www.billyschowderhouse.com* ⊘ *Closed mid-Dec.–mid-Jan.*

$ ✕ **Maine Diner.** One look at the 1953 exterior, and you'll start craving
DINER diner food. Here, you'll get a little more than you bargained for: after all, how many greasy spoons make an award-winning lobster pie? It's a house favorite, along with a heavenly seafood chowder. There's plenty

of fried seafood in addition to the usual diner fare, and breakfast is served all day. Check out the adjacent gift shop, Remember the Maine. ⑤ *Average main: $15* ✉ *2265 Post Rd.* ☎ *207/646–4441* ⊕ *www.main-ediner.com* ☉ *Closed at least 1 wk in Jan.*

$$
B&B/INN
Fodor'sChoice
★

📷 **Haven by the Sea.** Once the summer mission of St. Martha's Church in Kennebunkport, this exquisite inn has retained many original details from its former life as a seaside church, including cathedral ceilings and stained-glass windows. **Pros:** unusual structure with elegant appointments; tucked-away massage room. **Cons:** not an in-town location. ⑤ *Rooms from: $250* ✉ *59 Church St.* ☎ *207/646–4194* ⊕ *www.havenbythesea.com* ↗ *7 rooms, 2 suites, 1 apartment* ⦿ *Breakfast.*

KENNEBUNK AND KENNEBUNKPORT

5 miles north of Wells via U.S. 1.

The town centers of Kennebunk and Kennebunkport are separated by 5 miles and two rivers, but united by a common history and a laid-back seaside vibe. Perhaps best described as the Hamptons of the Pine Tree State, Kennebunkport has been a resort area since the 19th century. Its most recent residents have made it even more famous: the dynastic Bush family is often in residence on its immense estate here, which sits dramatically out on Walker's Point on Cape Arundel. Newer homes have sprung up alongside the old, and a great way to take them all in is with a slow drive out Ocean Avenue along the cape.

Sometimes bypassed on the way to its sister town, Kennebunk has its own appeal. Once a major shipbuilding center, Kennebunk today retains the feel of a classic New England small town, with an inviting shopping district, steepled churches, and fine examples of 18th- and 19th-century brick and clapboard homes. There are also plenty of natural spaces for walking, swimming, birding, and biking, and the Kennebunks' major beaches are here.

GETTING HERE AND AROUND

Kennebunk's main village sits along U.S. 1, extending west from the Mousam River. The Lower Village is along Routes 9 and 35, 4 miles down Route 35 from the main village, and the drive between the two keeps visitors agog with the splendor of the area's mansions, spread out on both sides of Route 35. To get to the grand and gentle beaches of Kennebunk, continue straight (the road becomes Beach Avenue) at the intersection with Route 9. If you turn left instead, Route 9 will take you across the Kennebunk River, into Kennebunkport's touristy downtown, called Dock Square (or sometimes just "the Port"), a commercial area with restaurants, shops, boat cruises, and galleries. Here you'll find the most activity (and crowds) in the Kennebunks.

Take the Intown Trolley for narrated 45-minute jaunts that run daily from Memorial Day weekend through Columbus Day. The $16 fare is valid for the day, so you can hop on and off—or start your journey—at any of the stops. The route includes Kennebunk's beaches and Lower Village as well as neighboring Kennebunkport's scenery and sights. The main stop is at 21 Ocean Avenue in Kennebunkport, around the corner from Dock Square.

ESSENTIALS

Visitor Information Intown Trolley. ☎ *207/967–3686* ⊕ *www.intowntrolley. com.* **Kennebunk-Kennebunkport Chamber of Commerce.** ✉ *16 Water St.* ☎ *207/967–0857* ⊕ *www.gokennebunks.com.*

WALKING TOURS

To take a little walking tour of Kennebunk's most notable structures, begin at the Federal-style Brick Store Museum at 117 Main Street. Head south on Main Street (turn left out of the museum) to see several extraordinary 18th- and early-19th-century homes, including the **Lexington Elms** at No. 99 (1799), the **Horace Porter House** at No. 92 (1848), and the **Benjamin Brown House** at No. 85 (1788).

When you've had your fill of historic homes, head back up toward the museum, pass the 1773 **First Parish Unitarian Church** (its Asher Benjamin–style steeple contains an original Paul Revere bell), and turn right onto **Summer Street.** This street is an architectural showcase, revealing an array of styles from Colonial to Federal. Walking past these grand beauties will give you a real sense of the economic prowess and glamour of the long-gone shipbuilding industry.

For a guided 90-minute architectural walking tour of Summer Street, contact the museum at ☎ *207/985–4802.* You can also purchase a $4.95 map that marks historic buildings or a $15.95 guidebook, *Windows on the Past.*

For a dramatic walk along Kennebunkport's rocky coastline and beneath the views of Ocean Avenue's grand mansions, head out on the **Parson's Way Shore Walk,** a paved 4.8 mile round-trip. Begin at Dock Square and follow Ocean Avenue along the river, passing the Colony Hotel and St. Ann's Church, all the way to Walker's Point. Simply turn back from here.

EXPLORING

FAMILY **Brick Store Museum.** The cornerstone of this block-long preservation of early-19th-century commercial and residential buildings is William Lord's Brick Store. Built as a dry-goods store in 1825 in the Federal style, the building has an openwork balustrade across the roofline, granite lintels over the windows, and paired chimneys. Exhibits chronicle the Kennebunk area's history and Early American decorative and fine arts. Museum staff lead architectural walking tours of Kennebunk's National Historic District by appointment late May–September. ✉ *117 Main St., Kennebunk* ☎ *207/985–4802* ⊕ *www.brickstoremuseum.org* ⌦ *$7.50.*

Dock Square. Clothing boutiques, T-shirt shops, art galleries, and restaurants line this bustling square, spreading out along the nearby streets and alleys. Walk onto the drawbridge to admire the tidal Kennebunk River; cross to the other side and you are in the Lower Village of neighboring Kennebunk. ✉ *Dock Sq., Kennebunkport.*

FAMILY **First Families Kennebunkport Museum.** Also known as White Columns, the imposing Greek Revival mansion with Doric columns is furnished with the belongings of four generations of the Perkins-Nott family. From mid-July through mid-October, the 1853 house is open for guided tours and also serves as a gathering place for village walking tours. It is owned by the Kennebunkport Historical Society, which has several other historical buildings a mile away at 125–135 North Street, including an old jail and schoolhouse. ⊠ *8 Maine St., Kennebunkport* ☎ *207/967–2751* ⊕ *www.kporthistory.org* ⊜ *$10.*

FAMILY **First Parish of Kennebunk Unitarian Universalist Church.** Built in 1773, just before the American Revolution, this stunning church is a marvel. The 1804 Asher Benjamin–style steeple stands proudly atop the village, and the sounds of the original Paul Revere bell can be heard for miles. The church holds Sunday service at 9:30 am in the summer (at 10:30 the rest of the year). ⊠ *114 Main St., Kennebunk* ☎ *207/985–3700* ⊕ *www. uukennebunk.org.*

FAMILY **Kennebunk Plains.** For an unusual experience, visit this 135-acre grasslands habitat that is home to several rare and endangered species. Locals call it Blueberry Plains, and a good portion of the area is abloom with the hues of ripening wild blueberries in late July; after August 1, you are welcome to pick and eat all the berries you can find. The area is maintained by the Nature Conservancy. ⊠ *Webber Hill Rd., 4½ miles northwest of town, Kennebunk* ☎ *207/729–5181* ⊕ *www.nature.org.*

FAMILY **Seashore Trolley Museum.** Streetcars were built here from 1872 to 1972, including trolleys for major metropolitan areas—from Boston to Budapest, New York to Nagasaki, and San Francisco to Sydney. Many of them are beautifully restored and displayed. Best of all, you can take a nearly 4-mile ride on the tracks of the former Atlantic Shoreline trolley line, with a stop along the way at the museum restoration shop, where trolleys are transformed from junk into gems. The outdoor museum is self-guided. ⊠ *195 Log Cabin Rd., Kennebunkport* ☎ *207/967–2712* ⊕ *www.trolleymuseum.org* ⊜ *$10.*

BEACHES

FAMILY **Gooch's Beach.** Kennebunk has three beaches, one after another, along Beach Avenue, which is lined with cottages and old Victorians. The most northerly, and the closest to downtown Kennebunkport, is Gooch's Beach, the main swimming beach. Next is stony Kennebunk Beach, followed by Mother's Beach, which is popular with families. There's a small playground and tidal puddles for splashing; rock outcroppings lessen the waves. **Amenities:** lifeguards; parking (fee); toilets. **Best for:** walking; swimming. ⊠ *Beach Ave., south of Hwy. 9, Kennebunk.*

Goose Rocks Beach. Three-mile-long Goose Rocks, a 10-minute drive north of town, has a good long stretch of smooth sand and plenty of shallow pools for exploring. It's a favorite of families with small children. Pick up a $15 daily permit at the Kennebunkport Town Hall. Dogs are allowed, but only before 8 am and after 6 pm. No facilities are available at the beach. **Amenities:** parking (fee). **Best for:** walking. ⊠ *Dyke Rd., off Rte. 9, Kennebunkport* ⊕ *www.visitmaine.com.*

WHERE TO EAT

The Kennebunks are chock-full of restaurants and cafés vying for attention. Service and food can be hit-or-miss in this area; often the best meals are those that you pack yourself into a picnic basket to enjoy on one of the area's many sandy beaches.

$ ✕ **Duffy's Tavern & Grill.** Every small town needs its own lively and friendly
AMERICAN tavern, and this bustling spot is Kennebunk's favorite, housed in a former shoe factory, with exposed brick, soaring ceilings, and hardwood
floors. Right outside are the tumbling waters of the Mousam River as
it flows from the dam. There's a large bar with overhead televisions and
plenty of seating in the main room, plus a less captivating rear section.
You'll find lots of comfortable standards, like burgers, pizza, and the
popular fish 'n' chips. The tasty onion rings are hand dipped. ⑤ *Average main: $16* ✉ *4 Main St., Kennebunk* ☎ *207/985–0050* ⊕ *www.
duffyskennebunk.com.*

$ ✕ **Federal Jack's.** Run by the Kennebunkport Brewing Company, this
AMERICAN two-story complex is near the bridge from Lower Village into Ken-
nebunkport. All beers are handcrafted on-site, including the Blue Fin
Stout and Goat Island Light—try the sampler if you can't decide. In
the upstairs restaurant, an American pub-style menu includes plenty of
seafood; the clam chowder is rich and satisfying. The restaurant has two
dining rooms and a huge deck that packs in the crowds in the summer.
There's a brunch buffet on Sunday, and live entertainment Thursday–
Saturday (Sunday, too, in summer). ⑤ *Average main: $14* ✉ *8 Western
Ave., Kennebunk* ☎ *207/967–4322* ⊕ *www.federaljacks.com.*

$$$ ✕ **Mabel's Lobster Claw.** Since the 1950s, Mabel's has been serving lob-
SEAFOOD sters, homemade pies, and lots of seafood for lunch and dinner in this
FAMILY tiny dwelling out on Ocean Avenue. The decor includes paneled walls,
wooden booths, and autographed photos of various TV stars (and
members of the Bush family). There's outside seating, and paper place
mats with illustrated instructions on how to eat a Maine lobster. The
house favorite is the Lobster Savannah: split and filled with scallops,
shrimp, and mushrooms, and baked in a Newburg sauce. Save room
for the peanut-butter ice-cream pie. There's also a take-out window
where you can order ice cream and food. ⑤ *Average main: $25* ✉ *124
Ocean Ave., Kennebunkport* ☎ *207/967–2562* ⊕ *www.mabelslobster.
com* ♡ *Closed Nov.–early Apr.*

$$$ ✕ **Pier 77 Restaurant.** The view takes center stage at this restaurant and
AMERICAN bar. Located on the ground level, the restaurant, Pier 77, serves sophis-
ticated fare with an emphasis on meats and seafood. There are large
windows overlooking the harbor, and every seat has a nice view. The
place is vibrant, with live music in summer—a great place for cocktails
on the water. Tucked down below, the tiny but oh-so-funky-and-fun
Ramp Bar & Grill pays homage to a really good burger, fried seafood,
and other pub-style classics. ⑤ *Average main: $25* ✉ *77 Pier Rd., Cape
Porpoise* ☎ *207/967–8500* ⊕ *www.pier77restaurant.com.*

WHERE TO STAY

$ ▦ **Bufflehead Cove Inn.** On the Kennebunk River, this gray-shingled
B&B/INN B&B sits at the end of a winding dirt road amid fields and apple trees.
Pros: pastoral setting; riverfront location; perfect for a serene getaway.
Cons: two-night minimum stay on weekends. ⑤ *Rooms from: $190*
✉ *18 Bufflehead Cove Rd., Kennebunk* ☎ *207/967–3879* ⊕ *www.
buffleheadcove.com* ♡ *Closed mid-Nov.–Apr.* ⤳ *4 rooms, 1 suite, 1
cottage* ⦿️ *Breakfast.*

6

$$ | ▣ **Cape Arundel Inn.** This shingle-style 19th-century mansion, originally
B&B/INN | one of the area's many summer "cottages," commands a magnificent
ocean view that takes in the Bush estate at Walker's Point. **Pros:** extraordinary views from most rooms; across the road from rockbound coast. **Cons:** not for the budget-minded. ⑤ *Rooms from: $294* ✉ *208 Ocean Ave., Kennebunkport* ☎ *855/346–5700* ⊕ *www.capearundelinn.com* ☉ *Closed late Dec.–late Feb.* ↩ *14 rooms, 1 suite* �‖ *Breakfast.*

$$$ | ▣ **Captain Fairfield Inn.** With its inviting common spaces, tastefully
B&B/INN | designed rooms, central location, and delicious, healthy breakfast,
Fodor's Choice | this boutique inn makes for an excellent stay. **Pros:** wide selection of
★ | rooms, all well-appointed with modern updates; fireplaces in many rooms and communal spaces; friendly, generous service. **Cons:** short walk to the water. ⑤ *Rooms from: $339* ✉ *8 Pleasant St., Kennebunkport* ☎ *207/967–4454* ⊕ *www.captainfairfield.com* ↩ *7 rooms, 2 suites* �‖ *Breakfast.*

$$$ | ▣ **The Captain Lord Mansion.** Of all the mansions in Kennebunkport's
B&B/INN | historic district that have been converted to inns, the 1814 Captain
Fodor's Choice | Lord Mansion is the stateliest and most sumptuously appointed. **Pros:**
★ | beautiful landscaped grounds; bikes for guests; putting green. **Cons:** not a beachfront location. ⑤ *Rooms from: $329* ✉ *6 Pleasant St., Kennebunkport* ☎ *207/967–3141, 800/522–3141* ⊕ *www.captainlord.com* ↩ *18 rooms, 2 suites* �‖ *Breakfast.*

$$ | ▣ **The Colony Hotel.** You can't miss this place: it's grand, white, and
RESORT | incredibly large, set majestically atop a rise overlooking the ocean.
FAMILY | **Pros:** private beach; heated saltwater swimming pool; activities and
Fodor's Choice | entertainment for all ages. **Cons:** not intimate. ⑤ *Rooms from: $245*
★ | ✉ *140 Ocean Ave., Kennebunkport* ☎ *207/967–3331, 800/552–2363* ⊕ *www.colonymaine.com* ☉ *Closed Nov.–mid-May* ↩ *112 rooms, 11 suites, 2 cottages* �‖ *Breakfast.*

$$ | ▣ **The Seaside.** This handsome seaside property has been in the hands of
HOTEL | the Severance family since 1667. **Pros:** great ocean views from upper-
FAMILY | floor rooms; tasty breakfast; rates drop significantly in winter. **Cons:** motel-style rooms; not an in-town location. ⑤ *Rooms from: $259* ✉ *80 Beach Ave., Kennebunk* ☎ *207/967–4461, 800/967–4461* ⊕ *www.kennebunkbeachmaine.com* ↩ *22 rooms* �‖ *Breakfast.*

$ | ▣ **Waldo Emerson Inn.** The home itself is a historical gold mine, made
B&B/INN | grand with unusual maritime architectural touches by a shipbuilder in
1784. **Pros:** good base for exploring Kennebunk and Kennebunkport; authentic historic lodging; complimentary afternoon tea. **Cons:** some steep stairs; no water views or beachfront; not in town. ⑤ *Rooms from: $175* ✉ *108 Summer St., Kennebunk* ☎ *207/985–4250, 877/521–8776* ⊕ *www.waldoemersoninn.com* ↩ *6 rooms* �‖ *Breakfast.*

$$$ | ▣ **White Barn Inn.** For a romantic, indulgent overnight stay, look no
B&B/INN | further than the exclusive White Barn Inn, known for its attentive, old-school service and intimate atmosphere. **Pros:** 10-minute walk to the beach; elegant spa offers it all; over-the-top service. **Cons:** prices are steep. ⑤ *Rooms from: $340* ✉ *37 Beach Ave., Kennebunk* ☎ *207/967–2321* ⊕ *www.whitebarninn.com* ↩ *13 rooms, 9 suites, 5 cottages* �‖ *Breakfast.*

Kennebunk is a classic New England town, while Kennebunkport (pictured) has more upscale inns and shopping.

SPORTS AND THE OUTDOORS

FISHING

FAMILY **Cast-Away Fishing Charters.** Find and catch fish with Cast-Away Fishing Charters. The captain also offers a lobstering trip that's fun for kids, who can help haul in the traps. ⊠ *Performance Marine, 4-A Western Ave., Kennebunk* ☎ *207/284–1740* ⊕ *www.castawayfishingcharters.com.*

FAMILY *Rugosa.* Lobster-trap hauling trips aboard the *Rugosa* in the scenic waters off the Kennebunks run daily, Memorial Day weekend–early October. ⊠ *Nonantum Resort, 95 Ocean Ave., Kennebunkport* ☎ *207/468–4095* ⊕ *www.rugosalobstertours.com.*

WHALE-WATCHING

FAMILY **First Chance.** This company leads whale-watching cruises on 85-foot *Nick's Chance.* If you don't see a whale, you get a ticket for a free trip. Scenic lobster cruises are also offered aboard 65-foot *Kylie's Chance.* Trips run daily in summer and on weekends in the shoulder season. ⊠ *Performance Marine, 4-A Western Ave., Kennebunk* ☎ *207/967–5507* ⊕ *www.firstchancewhalewatch.com.*

SHOPPING

Abacus. This shop sells eclectic crafts, jewelry, and furniture. It's a good place to pick up gifts. ⊠ *2 Ocean Ave., at Dock Sq., Kennebunkport* ☎ *800/206–2166* ⊕ *www.abacusgallery.com.*

Fodor'sChoice **Daytrip Society.** The impossibly hip and well-selected array of goods
★ that this modern-design shop stocks makes it an excellent place for both window-shopping and finding gifts for just about anyone on your list (including yourself). A refreshing departure from the rest of the somewhat stodgy gift shops in the village, this boutique is chock-full

of eye candy, most of which is also very functional. There are many locally sourced and decidedly contemporary products, from hats and jewelry to novelty books, home decor, and scents. Check out Daytrip Jr., their equally hip children's store around the corner. ⊠ *4 Dock Sq., Kennebunkport* ☎ *207/967–4440* ⊕ *www.daytripsociety.com.*

Maine Art. Showcasing works by artists from Maine and New England, Maine Art has a two-story gallery with a sculpture garden. There's another gallery space on Western Avenue. ⊠ *14 Western Ave., Kennebunk* ☎ *207/967–2803* ⊕ *www.maine-art.com.*

Mast Cove Galleries. Since 1979, Mast Cove Galleries has been selling paintings and sculpture by artists from New England and beyond. It occupies the barn and first floor of the owner's 1851 village home, which has a sculpture garden. The gallery hosts indoor jazz and blues concerts year-round. ⊠ *2 Mast Cove La., at Main St., Kennebunkport* ☎ *207/967–3453* ⊕ *www.mastcove.com.*

EN ROUTE   For a rewarding drive that goes into the reaches of the coastline on the way to Old Orchard Beach, head out of Kennebunkport on Route 9. You'll soon come to the fishing village of Cape Porpoise, where the pier has wondrous views. Continuing on Route 9, plan to do some beach walking at Goose Rocks Beach or Fortunes Rocks Beach, both ideal for stretching your legs or for just looking for shells or critters in the tide pools. (Pick up a parking permit first.) Route 9 winds through wooded areas, then heads past the charming resort villages of Camp Ellis and Ocean Park. You could pack a picnic and spend some time at Ferry Beach State Park. The varied landscapes here include forested sections, swamp, beach, a rare stand of tupelo (black gum) trees, and lots of dunes. There are a few miles of marked trails to hike.

BIDDEFORD

11 miles north of Kennebunkport; 18 miles south of Portland.

Biddeford is waking from a deep sleep, having devolved into something of a ghost town for a good deal of the past half century. It's a ghost town no more, thanks to chefs and small-business owners who have relocated from Portland; they are giving Biddeford's beautiful old-mill-town architecture a new lease on life. Developers have taken note as well, revamping many of the mill district's historic buildings, including the town's imposing 233,000-square-foot Lincoln Mill. Today, Biddeford is filled with art galleries and quirky boutiques, a distillery, an art school, and top-notch restaurants.

GETTING HERE AND AROUND

From Interstate 95, get off at Exit 2A. U.S. 1 runs right through town.

ESSENTIALS   **Visitor Information Biddeford-Saco Chamber of Commerce.** ⊠ *28 Water St., Biddeford* ☎ *207/282–1567* ⊕ *www.biddefordsacochamber.org.*

EXPLORING

Round Turn Distilling. There's a reason why all the good craft cocktail bars in Maine stock Bimini Gin, the flagship spirit of this distillery, located in a 150-year-old textile mill on the Saco River. Learn more about the best small-batch gin in the Pine Tree State, and be sure to take a peek at the production area; the distillery uses steam to power its modern steel-and-copper still. The Tasting Room is open Friday 4–9, Saturday 2–8, and otherwise by appointment. ⊠ *32 Maine St., Bldg. 13 W, Suite 103, Biddeford* ☎ *207/370–9446* ⊕ *www.roundturndistilling.com.*

EN ROUTE **Ocean Park.** Ten miles east of Biddeford lies Ocean Park, a vacation community founded in 1881 by Free Will Baptist leaders as a summer assembly with both religious and educational purposes, following the example of Chautauqua, New York. The 1881 Temple, in an unusual octagon shape, is on the National Register of Historic Places. Today the community hosts an impressive variety of cultural events, from concerts to sand-sculpture contests. There's even a public shuffleboard area for vacationers not interested in the neon carnival attractions in Old Orchard Beach just up the road. Get an old-fashioned raspberry-lime rickey at the Ocean Park Soda Fountain, at Furber Park. ⊠ *14 Temple Ave., Ocean Park* ☎ *207/934–9068* ⊕ *www.oceanpark.org.*

WHERE TO EAT

$ ✕ **Custom Deluxe.** In a cozy space with exposed-brick walls and high
AMERICAN   pressed-tin ceilings that can only accommodate 28 diners, Custom Deluxe serves unassuming but creative bistro dishes, like rich mushroom soup topped with toasted benne seeds, roasted chicken on rye bread with jardiniere relish and miso mayo, or crispy fries with garlic oil and black pepper. And desserts don't disappoint either—with treats like a perfectly divine fresh-yeast doughnut with maple-smoked cheddar and maple mousse, you'll be tempted to eat dessert first. Ⓢ *Average main: $12* ⊠ *140 Main St., Biddeford* ☎ *207/494–7110* ☉ *Closed Sun. and Mon.*

$ ✕ **Elements: Books, Coffee, Beer.** You could easily while away an entire
CAFÉ   day at this cozy spot that's part café, part bookstore, and part pub, starting with coffee in the morning to fuel an afternoon of reading, followed by a satisfying brew in the early evening. Pop by for any combination of the three, plus the occasional poetry reading or evening of live local music. Ⓢ *Average main: $10* ⊠ *265 Main St., Biddeford* ☎ *207/710–2011* ⊕ *www.elementsbookscoffeebeer.com.*

$ ✕ **Palace Diner.** Located in an old-fashioned train car just off of Main
AMERICAN   Street, everything about this diner is retro except the food. Hop on a
Fodor's Choice   stool at the counter (that's all there is), enjoy the Motown tunes, and
★   tuck into one of their deluxe sandwiches with applewood bacon, egg, jalapeño, and cheddar, or the challah French toast with Maine maple syrup, with a side of caramelized grapefruit for breakfast. At lunch you'll do well to order the delicious fried-chicken sandwich with cabbage slaw and french fries. Ⓢ *Average main: $10* ⊠ *18 Franklin St., Biddeford* ☎ *207/284–0015* ⊕ *www.palacedinerme.com* ▭ *No credit cards.*

SHOPPING

Farrell & Co. At Farrell & Co. you can find fine, hand-dyed leather goods, such as wallets, purses, and belts. Everything is individually handcrafted by owner Meg Farrell. ⊠ *22 Pearl St., Biddeford* ☎ *No phone* ⊕ *www. farrellandcompany.com.*

6

Fodor's Choice
★

Rabelais Books. Recently relocated from their longtime Portland location, Rabelais Books, whose cheeky slogan is "Thought for Food," is an ode to the art of cooking, drinking, and eating (and writing about it). Get lost in one of the many recipe reference tomes, many of which are very rare, or pick up a book or two for your favorite foodie. Rabelais is located in the massive North Dam Mill complex, which houses a bevy of unique local shops, many featuring products made by local artisans. ⊠ *North Dam Mill Building 18, 2 Main St., Biddeford* ☏ *207/602–6246* ⊕ *www.rabelaisbooks.com.*

PORTLAND

28 miles from Kennebunk via I–95 and I–295.

Fodor's Choice
★

Maine's largest city may be considered small by national standards—its population is just 66,000—but its character, spirit, and appeal make it feel much larger. It's well worth at least a day or two of exploration, even if all you do is spend the entire time eating and drinking at the many phenomenal restaurants, bakeries and specialty dessert shops, craft cocktail bars, and microbreweries scattered across the city. Work up your appetite roaming the working waterfront and strolling the Eastern Promenade, shopping in the boutiques lined up along the brick streets of the Old Port, or sauntering through the galleries of its top-notch art museum.

A city of many names throughout its history, including Casco and Falmouth, Portland has survived many dramatic transformations, the most recent of which is the massive influx of hipsters and foodies who have opened up artisanal bars and quirky boutiques that are rapidly changing the city's character. Sheltered by the nearby Casco Bay Islands and blessed with a deep port, Portland was a significant settlement right from its start in the early 17th century. Settlers thrived on fishing and lumbering, repeatedly building up the area while the British, French, and Native Americans continually sacked it. Many considered the region a somewhat dangerous frontier, but its potential for prosperity was so apparent that settlers came anyway to tap its rich natural resources.

In 1632 Portland's first home was built on the Portland Peninsula in the area now known as Munjoy Hill. The British burned the city in 1775, when residents refused to surrender arms, but it was rebuilt and became a major trading center. Much of Portland was destroyed again in the Great Fire on July 4, 1866, when a flicked ash or perhaps a celebratory firecracker started a fire in a boatyard that grew into conflagration; 1,500 buildings burned to the ground.

GETTING HERE AND AROUND

From Interstate 95, take Interstate 295 to get to the Portland Peninsula and downtown. Commercial Street runs along the harbor, Fore Street is in one block up in the heart of the Old Port, and the Arts District stretches along diagonal Congress Street. Munjoy Hill is on the eastern end of the peninsula and the West End on the opposite side.

Portland's busy harbor is full of working boats, pleasure craft, and ferries headed to the Casco Bay Islands.

ESSENTIALS

Contacts Downtown Portland. ✉ *549 Congress St.* ☎ *207/772–6828* ⊕ *www. portlandmaine.com.* **Greater Portland Convention and Visitors Bureau.** ✉ *Visitor Information Center, 14 Ocean Gateway Pier* ☎ *207/772–5800* ⊕ *www. visitportland.com.*

TOURS

BUS TOURS

Portland Discovery Land & Sea Tours. The informative trolley tours of Portland Discovery detail the city's historical and architectural highlights, Memorial Day–October. Options include combining a city tour with a bay or lighthouse cruise. ✉ *Long Wharf, 170 Commercial St.* ☎ *207/774–0808* ⊕ *www.portlanddiscovery.com* 🎫 *From $14.*

WALKING TOURS

Greater Portland Landmarks. Take 1½-hour walking tours of Portland's historic West End on Friday, July–September, with Greater Portland Landmarks. Tours past the neighborhood's Greek Revival mansions and grand Federal-style homes begin at the group's headquarters and cost $10. You can also pick up maps for self-guided tours of the Old Port or the Western Promenade. ✉ *93 High St.* ☎ *207/774–5561* ⊕ *www. portlandlandmarks.org* 🎫 *From $10.*

Maine Foodie Tours. Learn about Portland's culinary history and sample local delights like lobster hors d'oeuvres, organic cheese, and the famous Maine whoopie pie. The culinary foot tours include stops at fishmongers, bakeries, and cheese shops that provide products to Portland's famed restaurants. From summer into early fall, you can also take a chocolate tour, a bike-and-brewery tour, or a trolley tour with a stop at a microbrewery. Tours begin at various locales in the Old Port. ☎ 207/233–7485 ⊕ *www.mainefoodietours.com* ✉ *From $55.*

Portland Freedom Trail. The Portland Freedom Trail offers a self-guided tour of sites associated with the Underground Railroad and the antislavery movement. ✉ *Portland* ☎ *207/591–9980* ⊕ *www.portlandfreedomtrail.org* ✉ *Free.*

THE OLD PORT

Fodor'sChoice
★

A major international port and a working harbor since the early 17th century, the Old Port bridges the gap between the city's historic commercial activities and those of today. It is home to fishing boats docked alongside whale-watching charters, luxury yachts, cruise ships, and oil tankers from around the globe. Commercial Street parallels the water and is lined with brick buildings and warehouses that were built following the Great Fire of 1866. In the 19th century, candle makers and sail stitchers plied their trades here; today specialty shops, art galleries, and restaurants have taken up residence.

As with much of the city, it's best to park your car and explore the Old Port on foot. You can park at the city garage on Fore Street (between Exchange and Union streets) or opposite the U.S. Custom House at the corner of Fore and Pearl streets. A helpful hint: look for the "Park & Shop" sign on garages and parking lots, and get one hour of free parking for each stamp collected at participating shops. Allow a couple of hours to wander at leisure on Market, Exchange, Middle, and Fore streets. The city is very pedestrian-friendly. Maine state law requires vehicles to stop for pedestrians in crosswalks.

Harbor Fish Market. A Portland favorite since 1968, this freshest-of-the-fresh seafood market ships lobsters and other Maine delectables almost anywhere in the country. A bright-red facade on a working wharf opens into a bustling space with bubbling lobster tanks and fish, clams, and other shellfish on ice; employees are as skilled with a fillet knife as sushi chefs. There is also a small retail store. ✉ *9 Custom House Wharf* ☎ *207/775–0251* ⊕ *www.harborfish.com* ✉ *Free.*

FAMILY **Maine Narrow Gauge Railroad Museum.** Whether you're crazy about old trains or just want to see the sights from a different perspective, the railroad museum has an extensive collection of locomotives and rail coaches, and offers scenic tours on narrow-gauge railcars. The 3-mile jaunts run on the hour and take you along Casco Bay, at the foot of the Eastern Promenade. The operating season caps off with a fall harvest ride (complete with cider), and during the Christmas season there are special Polar Express rides, based on the popular children's book. ✉ *58 Fore St.* ☎ *207/828–0814* ⊕ *www.mainenarrowgauge.org* ✉ *Museum $3, train rides $10.*

■ NEED A
BREAK

Two Fat Cats Bakery. This bakery's whoopie pies are delicately proportioned, with a smooth and light marshmallow-cream filling, and a conservative selection of flavors (no mint-chocolate-chip pies to be found here). ✉ *47 India St.* ☎ *207/347–5144* ⊕ *www.twofatcatsbakery.com.*

Portland

WEST END

TO PORTLAND AIRPORT

Casco Bay

Back Cove

Fore River

TO FEAKS ISLAND

Portland Harbor

Fish Point

Eastern Promenade

ARTS DISTRICT

OLD PORT

Visitor Information Center

Ocean Gateway Terminal

Maine State Pier

Portland Pier

Portland Fish Pier

Deering Oaks Park

Western Cemetery

500 yards
500 meters

6

KEY

 Ferry Lines

Children's Museum &
Theatre of Maine **3**

Eastern Promenade **8**

Harbor Fish Market **10**

Longfellow House
and Garden **7**

Maine Narrow Gauge
Railroad Museum **11**

Neal Dow Memorial **2**

Portland Fish Exchange ... **5**

Portland Museum of Ar... **4**

Portland Observatory **9**

Tate House Museum **12**

Victoria Mansion **6**

Western Promenade **1**

Portland Fish Exchange. You may want to hold your nose as you take a dip into the Old Port's active fish business at the 20,000-square-foot Portland Fish Exchange. Peek inside coolers teeming with cod, flounder, and monkfish, and watch fishermen repairing nets outside. ⊠ *6 Portland Fish Pier* ☎ *207/773–0017* ⊕ *www.pfex.org* ✉ *Free.*

THE ARTS DISTRICT

This district starts at the top of Exchange Street, near the upper end of the Old Port, and extends west past the Portland Museum of Art. The district's central artery is Congress Street, which is lined with art galleries, specialty stores, and a score of restaurants and cafés. Parking is tricky; two-hour meters dot the sidewalks, but there are several garages nearby.

TOP ATTRACTIONS

FAMILY **Children's Museum & Theatre of Maine.** Kids can pretend they are lobstermen, veterinarians, shopkeepers, or actors in a play at Portland's small but fun Children's Museum. Most exhibits, many of which have a Maine theme, are hands-on and best for kids 10 and younger. Have a Ball! teaches about the science of motion, letting kids build ramps that make balls speed up, slow down, and leap across tracks. Don't miss the life-size inflatable humpback whale rising to the ceiling at the whale exhibit. The outdoor pirate-ship play area is a great place for a picnic lunch. Camera Obscura, an exhibit about optics, provides fascinating panoramic views of the city; it's aimed at adults and older children, and admission is therefore separate. ⊠ *142 Free St.* ☎ *207/828–1234* ⊕ *www.kitetails.org* ✉ *Museum $10, Camera Obscura $4 ($2 on 1st Fri. of the month).*

Longfellow House and Garden. The boyhood home of the famous American poet was the first brick house in Portland and the oldest building on the peninsula. It's particularly interesting, because most of the furnishings, including the young Longfellow's writing desk, are original. Wallpaper, window coverings, and a vibrant painted carpet are period reproductions. Built in 1785, the large dwelling (a third floor was added in 1815) sits back from the street and has a small portico over its entrance and four chimneys surmounting the roof. It's part of the Maine Historical Society, which includes an adjacent research library and a museum with exhibits about Maine life. After your guided tour, stay for a picnic in the Longfellow Garden; it's open to the public during museum hours. ⊠ *489 Congress St.* ☎ *207/774–1822* ⊕ *www.mainehistory.org* ✉ *House and museum $15, gardens free.*

Fodor's Choice **Portland Museum of Art.** Maine's largest public art institution's collection
★ includes fine seascapes and landscapes by Winslow Homer, John Marin, Andrew Wyeth, Edward Hopper, Marsden Hartley, and other American painters. Homer's *Weatherbeaten,* a quintessential Maine Coast image, is here, and the museum owns and displays, on a rotating basis, 16 more of his paintings, plus more than 400 of his illustrations. The museum has works by Monet and Picasso, as well as Degas, Renoir, and Chagall. I. M. Pei designed the strikingly modern Charles Shipman Payson building, which fittingly displays modern art. The nearby L. D.

M. Sweat Galleries showcase the collection of 19th-century American art. Special events are held in the gorgeous Federal-style 1801 McLellan House. ⊠ *7 Congress Sq.* ☎ *207/775–6148* ⊕ *www.portlandmuseum. org* ⊠ *$12 (free Fri. 5–9).*

Victoria Mansion. Built between 1858 and 1860, this Italianate mansion is widely regarded as the most sumptuously ornamented dwelling of its period remaining in the country. Architect Henry Austin designed the house for hotelier Ruggles Morse and his wife, Olive. The interior design—everything from the plasterwork to the furniture (much of it original)—is the only surviving commission of New York designer Gustave Herter. Behind the elegant brownstone exterior of this National Historic Landmark are colorful frescoed walls and ceilings, ornate marble mantelpieces, gilded gas chandeliers, a magnificent 6-foot-by-25 foot stained-glass ceiling window, and a freestanding mahogany staircase. A guided tour runs about 45 minutes and covers all the architectural highlights. Victorian era–themed gifts and art are sold in the museum shop, and the museum often has special themed events. ⊠ *109 Danforth St.* ☎ *207/772–4841* ⊕ *www.victoriamansion.org* ⊠ *$15.*

WORTH NOTING

FAMILY **Eastern Promenade.** Between the city's two promenades, this one, often overlooked by tourists, has by far the best view. Gracious Victorian homes, many now converted to condos and apartments, border one side of the street. On the other is 68 acres of hillside parkland that includes Ft. Allen Park and, at the base of the hill, the Eastern Prom Trail and tiny East End Beach and Boat Launch. On a sunny day the Eastern Prom is a lovely spot for picnicking and people-watching. ⊠ *Washington Ave. to Fore St.*

Neal Dow Memorial. The mansion, once a stop on the Underground Railroad, was the home of Civil War general Neal Dow, who became known as the "Father of Prohibition." He was responsible for Maine's adoption of the anti-alcohol bill in 1851, which spurred a nationwide temperance movement. Now a museum, this majestic 1829 Federal-style home is open for guided tours that start on the hour. ⊠ *714 Congress St.* ☎ *207/773–7773* ⊠ *$5.*

FAMILY **Portland Observatory.** This octagonal observatory on Munjoy Hill was built in 1807 by Captain Lemuel Moody, a retired sea captain, as a maritime signal tower. Moody used a telescope to identify incoming ships, and flags to signal to merchants where to unload their cargo. Held in place by 122 tons of ballast, it's the last remaining historic maritime signal station in the country. The guided tour leads all the way to the dome, where you can step out on the deck and take in views of Portland, the islands, and inland toward the White Mountains. ⊠ *138 Congress St.* ☎ *207/774–5561* ⊕ *www.portlandlandmarks.org* ⊠ *$9.*

OFF THE BEATEN PATH

Tate House Museum. Built astride rose-granite steps and a period herb garden overlooking the Stroudwater River on the outskirts of Portland, this magnificent 1755 house was built by Captain George Tate. Tate had been commissioned by the English Crown to organize "the King's Broad Arrow"—the marking and cutting down of gigantic trees, which were shipped to England to be fashioned as masts for the British Royal Navy.

The house has several period rooms, including a sitting room with some fine English Restoration chairs. With its clapboard siding still gloriously unpainted, its impressive Palladian doorway, dogleg stairway, unusual clerestory, and gambrel roof, this house will delight all lovers of Early American decorative arts. ⊠ *1267 Westbrook St.* ☎ *207/774–6177* ⊕ *www.tatehouse.org* ⊠ *$12.*

THE WEST END

A leisurely walk through Portland's West End, beginning at the top of the Arts District, offers a real treat to historic-architecture buffs. The quiet and stately neighborhood, on the National Register of Historic Places, presents an extraordinary display of architectural splendor, from High Victorian Gothic to lush Italianate, Queen Anne, and Colonial Revival.

Western Promenade. A good place to start is at the head of the Western Promenade, which has benches and a nice view. From the Old Port, take Danforth Street all the way up to Vaughn Street; take a right on Vaughn and then an immediate left onto Western Promenade. Pass by the Western Cemetery, Portland's second official burial ground, laid out in 1829—inside is the ancestral plot of poet Henry Wadsworth Longfellow—and look for street parking. ⊠ *Danforth St. to Bramhall St.*

WHERE TO EAT

America's "Foodiest Small Town" is how one magazine described Portland, which is practically bursting at the seams with fabulous restaurants to rival those of a major metropolis. It's worth it to splurge and try as many as possible while visiting. Fresh seafood, including the famous Maine lobster, is still popular and prevalent, but it is being served up in unexpected ways that are a far cry from the usual bib and butter. There is a broad spectrum of cuisines to be enjoyed, and many chefs are pushing the envelope in their reinventions of traditional culinary idioms. More and more restaurants are using local meats, seafood, and organic produce as much as possible; changing menus reflect what is available in the region at the moment. Even the many excellent food trucks that have popped up across the city—several of which remain open in the off-season—reflect this trend. As sophisticated as many of these establishments have become in the way of food and service, the atmosphere is generally laid-back; with a few exceptions, you can leave your jacket and tie at home—just not your appetite.

Smoking is banned in all restaurants, taverns, and bars in Maine.

$ ✕ **BaoBao Dumpling House.** Situated in a historic town house with tradi-
ASIAN   tional Asian decor in Portland's quaint West End, this dumpling house
FAMILY   serves deeply satisfying Asian-inspired comfort food in an intimate set-
ting. Start with their crispy braised chicken skin with ponzu, cucumber, scallion, and *togarashi* chili, then move on to one of their satisfying dumpling dishes with fillings like lamb, black-bean chili, and peanuts, or thread-cut hake with burdock. ⑤ *Average main: $10* ⊠ *133 Spring*

For the full Maine experience, try a classic lobster dinner.

St., at Park St. in Portland's West End ☎ *207/772–8400* ⊕ *www.bao-baodumplinghouse.com* ⊘ *Closed Mon. and Tues.*

$ ✕ **Becky's Diner.** You won't find a more local or unfussy place—or one
DINER more abuzz with conversation at 4 am—than this waterfront institu
FAMILY tion way down on the end of Commercial Street. The food is cheap,
generous in proportion, and has that satisfying, old-time-diner quality.
Sitting next to you at the counter or in a neighboring booth could be
rubber-booted fishermen back from sea, college students soothing a
hangover, or suited business folks with BlackBerrys. From the upstairs
deck you can watch the working waterfront in action. $ *Average main:*
$14 ⊠ *390 Commercial St.* ☎ *207/773–7070* ⊕ *www.beckysdiner.com.*

$ ✕ **Duckfat.** Even in midafternoon, this small, hip sandwich shop in the
MODERN Old Port is packed. The focus here is everyday farm-to-table fare: the
AMERICAN signature Belgian fries are made with Maine potatoes cooked, yes, in
duck fat and served in paper cones. Sandwiches are made with panini
bread; choices like tuna melt with Thai chili mayo change seasonally,
but the meat loaf and B.G.T. (bacon, goat cheese, tomato) are standards.
Drink choices include gelato milk shakes, French-press coffee, lime-mint
fountain sodas, beer, and wine. $ *Average main: $12* ⊠ *43 Middle St.*
☎ *207/774–8080* ⊕ *www.duckfat.com* ⬈ *Reservations not accepted.*

$$ ✕ **East Ender.** It doesn't get much better than the Maine lobster melt with
AMERICAN bacon jam and peppadew relish served at this pint-size restaurant; once
FAMILY you've had it, you may find it hard to go back to lobster merely dressed
Fodor's Choice in mayo on buttery bread. You'd also do well to try dishes like grilled
★ escarole and radicchio with poached egg and Parmesan, fried brus-
sels sprouts and chili-lime vinaigrette, or pork-belly chili-cheese fries,
washed down with a delicious craft cocktail. The emphasis is on the

CLOSE UP

Lobster Shacks

If it's your first time to the Maine Coast, it won't be long before you stumble upon that famous and quintessentially Maine seaside eatery: the lobster shack. Also known as a lobster "pound" (especially elsewhere in New England), lobster shacks are essentially wooden huts with picnic tables set around the waterfront. The menu is simplicity itself: steamed lobster or clams by the pound, or a lobster roll; sides may include potato chips, coleslaw, or corn on the cob. Some pounds are even BYOB—no, not "bring your own bib" (those are usually provided)—but "bring your own beer" or refreshments.

One signature item at a lobster shack is the lobster dinner. Although it can vary from pound to pound, generally this means the works: a whole steamed lobster, steamed clams, corn on the cob, and potato chips. If the lobster dinner sounds like a bit much, then go for the classic lobster roll, a buttered New England–style hot-dog roll filled with chunks of lobster meat and a bit of mayo. Some pounds will serve it with lemon, some will serve it with butter, and some with even a touch of lettuce or herbs. Purists will serve no toppings at all—and why bother, when the unadulterated taste of fresh, sweet lobster meat can't be beat. Most shacks will even have a tank with live lobsters; a few will let you pick your own.

We can say this much: the best place to get a lobster dinner or lobster roll is at a shack, and the only authentic pounds are the simplest: a wooden shack, right on the water, with wooden picnic tables and—perhaps most important of all—a beautiful unobstructed view of working lobster boats in a scenic Maine harbor.

Maine Lobster Marketing Collaborative. You can find out more about Maine lobster from the Maine Lobster Marketing Collaborative. ⊠ *2 Union St., Suite 204* ☎ *207/541–9310* ⊕ *www. lobsterfrommaine.com.*

food rather than the atmosphere, which isn't surprising, given that the owners formerly served their tasty fare from a truck. Ⓢ *Average main: $24* ⊠ *47 Middle St.* ☎ *207/879–7669* ⊕ *www.eastenderportland.com.*

$ **✕ El Rayo Taqueria.** For some of the best Mexican food in town, head to
MEXICAN this hip spot housed in a former gas station. The flavors are as vibrant as the turquoise, yellow, and fuchsia decor. The guacamole and salsas are made fresh daily. Pull up a stool at the counter, or grab a bright oilcloth-covered picnic table out front. Wash down achiote-seasoned fish tacos or a citrus-and-cumin-marinated chicken burrito with a lemon-hibiscus *refresca* (cold drink) or a house margarita. Ⓢ *Average main: $10* ⊠ *101 York St., at High St.* ☎ *207/780–8226* ⊕ *www.elrayotaqueria.com.*

$ **✕ Elevation Burger.** There's nothing like tucking into a nice, juicy burger;
BURGER it's even better when you can do so with a clear conscience. Elevation Burger serves up simple, delicious fare made from high-quality ingredients, most of which are sustainably sourced, like their organic, grass-fed, free-range beef. The crispy french fries here are cooked in 100% olive oil and a tasty organic veggie burger means that grass-fed visitors don't have to miss out on the fun. Ⓢ *Average main: $10* ⊠ *205 Commercial St.* ☎ *207/775–6800* ⊕ *www.elevationburger.com.*

$
SEAFOOD
Fodor's Choice
★

✕ **Eventide Oyster Co.** Eventide is not just any old oyster bar. Not only do they have fresh and tasty oysters artfully prepared with novel accoutrements like kimchi and ginger ices and cucumber-champagne mignonette, they also serve a delicious scallop crudo with blood orange and chili miso, and smoked arctic char with cucumber and Pernod. If seafood isn't exactly your cup of tea, they also have good alternatives like house-cured corned beef and a fried-chicken sandwich with pickled watermelon. The menu constantly changes, depending on what's in season, so it's best to order a handful of small plates, a glass of bubbly, or one of their signature tiki-style cocktails, and, of course, a dozen oysters. $ *Average main: $15* ✉ *86 Middle St.* ☎ *207/774-8538* ⊕ *www. eventideoysterco.com.*

$$$
MODERN
AMERICAN

✕ **Five Fifty-Five.** Classic dishes are cleverly updated at this classy and very popular Congress Street spot. The menu changes seasonally to reflect ingredients available from local waters, organic farms, and food purveyors, but seared local diver scallops, served in a buttery carrot-vanilla emulsion, are an exquisite mainstay. So is the mac 'n' cheese, which boasts artisanal cheeses and shaved black truffles. You may also find dishes such as milk-braised rabbit with Himalayan red rice and lemon-dressed local greens. Try the tasting menus, which start at $70, or come for Sunday brunch. The space, with exposed brick and copper accents, is a former 19th-century firehouse. A sister restaurant, Petite Jacqueline bistro in Longfellow Square, has also earned accolades and fans. $ *Average main: $30* ✉ *555 Congress St.* ☎ *207/761-0555* ⊕ *www.fivefifty-five.com* ⊘ *No lunch.*

$
PIZZA
FAMILY

✕ **Flatbread.** Families, students, and bohemian types gather at this popular New England chain flatbread-pizza place. Two massive wood-fire ovens are the heart of the soaring, warehouse-like space; in summer, you can escape the heat by dining on the deck overlooking the harbor. The menu has eight signature pizzas made with fresh, local ingredients, plus weekly veggie and meat specials; everything is homemade, organic, and nitrate-free. Be sure to order the delicious house salad with toasted sesame seeds, seaweed, blue or goat cheese, and ginger-tamarind vinaigrette, and don't neglect to gulp down one of the delicious microbrews on tap. ■**TIP→** Waits can be long on weekends and in summer, but you can call a half-hour ahead to put your name on the list, or grab a drink from the bar and wait outside with a view of the harbor. $ *Average main: $15* ✉ *72 Commercial St.* ☎ *207/772-8777* ⊕ *www.flatbread-company.com.*

$$$
MODERN
AMERICAN
Fodor's Choice
★

✕ **Fore Street.** One of Maine's best chefs, Sam Hayward, opened this restaurant in a renovated warehouse on the edge of the Old Port in 1996. The menu changes daily to reflect the freshest ingredients from Maine's farms and waters, as well as the tremendous creativity of the staff. Every copper-top table in the main dining room has a view of the enormous brick oven and soapstone hearth that anchor the open kitchen, where sous-chefs seem to dance as they create such dishes as turnspit-roasted dry-rubbed pork loin, wood-grilled Maine-island lamb chop with sunchoke purée, and Maine mussels oven roasted in garlic and almond butter. Desserts include artisanal cheeses, homemade chocolate truffles, and pastries. In July or August, book two months in

6

advance; otherwise, a week is usually fine. ■TIP→ Last-minute planners take heart: a third of the tables are reserved for walk-ins. ⑤ *Average main: $30* ✉ *288 Fore St.* ☎ *207/775–2717* ⊕ *www.forestreet.biz* ◔ *No lunch* ⚷ *Reservations essential.*

$

CAFÉ

FAMILY

Fodor'sChoice

★

✕ **Gelato Fiasco.** Proper Italian gelato and sorbetto here come in traditional flavors, as well as more offbeat varieties like molasses peppermint stick, Wild Turkey bourbon, Girl Scout cookie, Vietnamese coffee, and spiked eggnog. There are new flavors every day, along with espresso and other hot drinks. If you can't make a decision from the impossible selection, they also sell mystery pints that make that selection for you. ⑤ *Average main: $5* ✉ *425 Fore St.* ☎ *207/699–4314* ⊕ *www.gelato-fiasco.com.*

$$

SEAFOOD

FAMILY

✕ **Gilbert's Chowder House.** This is the real deal, as quintessential as Maine dining can be. Clam rakes and nautical charts hang from the walls of this unpretentious waterfront diner. The flavors are from the depths of the North Atlantic, prepared and presented simply: fried shrimp, haddock, clam strips, extraordinary clam cakes, and fish, clam, and seafood chowders (corn, too). A chalkboard of daily specials often features fish 'n' chips. Don't miss out on the lobster roll: a toasted hot-dog bun bursting with claw and tail meat lightly dressed with mayo but otherwise unadulterated. It's classic Maine, fuss-free, and presented on a paper plate. ⑤ *Average main: $19* ✉ *92 Commercial St.* ☎ *207/871–5636* ⊕ *www.gilbertschowderhouse.com.*

$

CAFÉ

FAMILY

✕ **The Holy Donut.** Even if you're a health freak, you'll love the doughnuts at this place. Sweet and savory all-natural, potato-based doughnuts are glazed in flavors such as dark chocolate sea salt, maple, pomegranate, coffee brandy, and chai, or stuffed with delicious fillings like Maine wild blueberries, bacon cheddar, or ricotta. And if those aren't adventurous enough for you, they're always coming up with new inventions, like the preposterously wonderful lobster-stuffed doughnut. Many vegan and gluten-free options are available regularly, and the shop closes once all the doughnuts are sold for the day. ⑤ *Average main: $5* ✉ *7 Exchange St.* ☎ *207/874–7774* ⊕ *www.theholydonut.com.*

$

DELI

✕ **Home Catering Company.** Nestled in a former grocer's shop in Portland's West End, this deli has all the fixings you need for an impromptu picnic, a cozy night in, or just chowing down on the bench outside. Order a delicious sandwich with their famous candied bacon, or try one of their decadent French onion grilled cheeses. You can also grab a bottle of good wine, craft beer, or an artisanal soft drink from their coolers, as well as a bag of specialty chips and maybe a dessert (or two). ⑤ *Average main: $10* ✉ *129 Spring St.* ☎ *207/536–0260* ⊕ *www.homecateringcompany.com* ◔ *Closed Sun.*

$

ASIAN FUSION

✕ **The Honey Paw.** Come for the salty wontons, piping-hot broths, and wok-fried noodles; stay for the turntable music, the well-stocked cocktail bar, and the soft-serve ice cream that comes in flavors like honeycomb, magic shell, or caramelized honey. If you order one thing here, make it the lobster tartine, topped with a cilantro emulsion, radish, and hijiki. Slurp down some oysters and bubbly next door at their sister restaurant, Eventide Oyster Co., and then skip over here for something more substantial. ⑤ *Average main: $15* ✉ *7 Middle St.* ☎ *207/774–8538* ⊕ *www.thehoneypaw.com* ☉ *Closed Tues.*

$$$$ ✕ **Hugo's.** Serving the freshest local organic foods is a high priority at
ECLECTIC Hugo's, and your server is sure to know everything about their various purveyors. Updated daily, the menu at this stylish eatery is made up of smartly prepared, seasonally inspired dishes like crispy-skin pork belly and crêpe-wrapped arctic char. You can choose five courses for $90, or go light with two courses for $45. A 2013 renovation added an open kitchen, a handsome curved bar, and an airy, open-concept dining room. ⑤ *Average main: $45* ✉ *88 Middle St.* ☎ *207/774–8538* ⊕ *www.hugos. net* ☉ *Closed Sun. No lunch.*

$$ ✕ **Local 188.** There's an infectious vibe at this eclectic, Spanish-inspired
SPANISH Arts District eatery, a foodie hot spot as well as a longtime local favor-
Fodor's Choice ite. The 2,000-square-foot space has lofty tin ceilings and worn maple
★ floors; mismatched chandeliers dangle over the dining area, and a pair of antlers crowns the open kitchen. Regulars chat with servers about which just-caught seafood will decorate the paella or which organic veggies will star in the tortillas, one of several tapas choices. You'll find entrées like Casco Bay hake with herb salsa verde, poached purple potatoes, smoked aioli, and beets. Many of the 10 or so draft brews are Maine crafted; there are some 150 wines (mostly European). Reservations aren't taken for the large bar area. ⑤ *Average main: $23* ✉ *685 Congress St.* ☎ *207/761–7909* ⊕ *www.local188.com* ☉ *No lunch.*

$$$ ✕ **Lolita.** Perched on Munjoy Hill near the Portland Observatory, Lolita
TAPAS has a sophisticated bodega vibe, where wood-fired dishes like scallops with hazelnuts and roasted clams are offered alongside charcuterie and cheese boards and plenty of robust wine—the intimate setting makes for a great date night. Or come for a midday snack alone or with a group of friends and pass around a bevy of the many small, tapas-style dishes. ⑤ *Average main: $30* ✉ *90 Congress St.* ☎ *207/775–5652* ⊕ *www.lolita-portland.com.*

$ ✕ **Portland Pâtisserie and Grand Café.** This is the perfect spot for a quick,
FRENCH delicious bite any time of day, but early risers will be rewarded with
FAMILY a wider selection of pastries at this chic patisserie, with floor-to-ceil-
Fodor's Choice ing picture windows that allow for superb people-watching. Whether
★ you're in the mood for a frothy café au lait and a macaron, or a deca-dent duck-confit-and-Gruyère-filled crêpe, Portland Pâtisserie does not disappoint. Don't shy away from sharing a couple of different desserts, or taking some for the road. ⑤ *Average main: $10* ✉ *46 Market St.* ☎ *207/553–2555* ⊕ *www.portlandpatisserie.com.*

$$$$ ✕ **Tempo Dulu.** Probably the only place in Maine that focuses exclu-
ASIAN FUSION sively on top-notch Southeast Asian cuisine, Tempo Dulu offers both three-course and tasting menus with outstanding service. This tastefully appointed restaurant and bar has refined decor that includes special touches like a hollowed-out lamp-shade topiary, a bevy of giant golden eggs, and shimmering chandeliers. The exceptional cocktail bar serves drinks concocted with exotic ingredients like smoked Chinese spices, absinthe mist, jasmine-infused Plymouth gin, and rose air. Splurge and try the lobster tasting menu, or order the Indonesian *rijsttafel*, with many small dishes that are well suited to both a family-style meal and

a more adventurous palate. $ *Average main: $67* ⊠ *Danforth Inn, 163 Danforth St.* ☎ *207/879–8755* ⊕ *www.tempodulu.restaurant.*

$$$
AMERICAN
FAMILY

✕**Union.** Located in the newly minted Press Hotel, Union Restaurant has a sophisticated (but not stuffy) air that is reflected in its menu, which focuses on local ingredients, many of which are foraged and fished. Most dishes are modern comfort food, like the local venison carpaccio with toasted hazelnuts, juniper, spruce-bud oil, and endive drizzled with white-truffle emulsion, or the caramelized brussels sprouts with orange aioli and smoked almonds. Breakfast is also a treat: you'll find maple *pain perdu* served alongside smoked-salmon tartines and classic dishes like eggs Benedict. $ *Average main: $30* ⊠ *Press Hotel, 390 Congress St.* ☎ *207/808–8700* ⊕ *www.unionportland.com.*

$$$
ECLECTIC

✕**Walter's.** A fixture in the Old Port since the late 1980s, this relaxed, busy place with a chic modern interior is popular with suits and tourists alike. The seasonal menu nicely balances local seafood and meats with Asian and other international flavors. You'll find appetizers like calamari dressed with lemon-and-cherry-pepper aioli and such entrées as crispy duck breast served with spaetzle, baby bok choy, and plum sauce. An inviting bar has a lighter menu; try the mussels or the Greek lamb sliders. $ *Average main: $28* ⊠ *2 Portland Sq.* ☎ *207/871–9258* ⊕ *www.waltersportland.com* ☽ *Closed Sun. No lunch Sat.*

WHERE TO STAY

As Portland's popularity as a vacation destination has increased, so have its options for overnight visitors. Though several large hotels—geared toward high-tech, amenity-obsessed guests—have been built in the Old Port, they have in no way diminished the success of smaller, more intimate lodgings. Inns and B&Bs have taken up residence throughout the West End, often giving new life to the grand mansions of Portland's wealthy 19th-century merchants. For the least expensive accommodations, you'll find chain hotels near the interstate and the airport.

Expect to pay at least $150 or so per night for a pleasant room (often with complimentary breakfast) within walking distance of the Old Port during high season, and more than $400 for the most luxurious of suites. At the height of summer, many places are booked; make reservations well in advance, and ask about off-season specials.

$$
B&B/INN

▥ **The Danforth.** A stunning showpiece, this stylish inn was one of Portland's grandest Federal-style dwellings when it was built in 1823. **Pros:** gorgeous rooms; basement billiards room; city views from cupola. **Cons:** small windows in some third-floor rooms. $ *Rooms from: $298* ⊠ *163 Danforth St.* ☎ *207/879–8755, 800/879–8755* ⊕ *www.danforthinn.com* ⇲ *9 rooms* ⦿❘ *Breakfast.*

$
B&B/INN
FAMILY

▥ **Inn on Carleton.** This 1869 Victorian has a curved mahogany staircase to the third floor, a bay window overlooking the street from the front parlor, and gleaming pumpkin-pine floors. **Pros:** most rooms have electric fireplaces; English garden with fountain; attentive resident innkeeper. **Cons:** no elevator. $ *Rooms from: $195* ⊠ *46 Carleton St.* ☎ *207/775–1910, 800/639–1779* ⊕ *www.innoncarleton.com* ⇲ *6 rooms* ⦿❘ *Breakfast.*

$ **Morrill Mansion.** This 19th-century town house has tastefully
B&B/INN appointed rooms with well-executed color schemes—blue is a favorite
FAMILY hue here. **Pros:** close to arts district; parlors on each floor for relaxing.
Cons: not on a grand block. $ *Rooms from: $169* ⊠ *249 Vaughan
St.* ☎ *207/771-6900, 888/566-7745* ⊕ *www.morrillmansion.com* ➳ *6
rooms, 2 suites* ⦿ *Breakfast.*

$$ **Pomegranate Inn.** The classic facade of this handsome 1884 Italianate
B&B/INN in the architecturally rich Western Promenade area gives no hint of the
Fodor's Choice splashy, modern, but cozy surprises within. **Pros:** funky, modern decor;
★ many rooms have gas fireplaces; close to Western Promenade. **Cons:**
15- to 20-minute walk to the Old Port. $ *Rooms from: $299* ⊠ *49 Neal
St.* ☎ *207/772-1006, 800/356-0408* ⊕ *www.pomegranateinn.com* ➳ *7
rooms, 1 suite* ⦿ *Breakfast.*

$$ **The Portland Regency Hotel & Spa.** Not part of a chain despite the
HOTEL "Regency" name, this brick building in the center of the Old Port
served as Portland's armory in the late 19th century. **Pros:** easy walk to
sites; lots of room variety for a hotel. **Cons:** lower-than-standard ceilings in many rooms. $ *Rooms from: $284* ⊠ *20 Milk St.* ☎ *207/774–
4200, 800/727–3436* ⊕ *www.theregency.com* ➳ *95 rooms, 10 suites*
⦿ *No meals.*

$$$ **The Press Hotel.** Housed in a former newspaper building, this boutique
HOTEL hotel is part of the Marriott group—though you'd never guess it. **Pros:**
FAMILY excellent views of the water from the top two floors; sparkling-clean
Fodor's Choice rooms with a modern-design feel; art gallery and excellent public spaces
★ with tasteful furnishings; Frette bed linens and Maine-made Cuddle-
down comforters and bed throws. **Cons:** right next to the fire depart-
ment. $ *Rooms from: $332* ⊠ *119 Exchange St.* ☎ *877/890–5641*
⊕ *www.thepresshotel.com* ➳ *110 rooms* ⦿ *No meals.*

$ **West End Inn.** Set among the glorious homes of the Western Prom-
B&B/INN enade, this 1871 Georgian displays much of the era's grandeur, with
FAMILY high pressed-tin ceilings, intricate moldings, ceiling medallions, and
a dramatic ruby-red foyer. **Pros:** fireplace library is a cozy place to
relax; just heading out for the paper is a historical walking tour. **Cons:**
15-to 20-minute walk downtown. $ *Rooms from: $189* ⊠ *146 Pine
St.* ☎ *800/338–1377* ⊕ *www.westendbb.com* ➳ *6 rooms* ⦿ *Breakfast.*

NIGHTLIFE AND PERFORMING ARTS

NIGHTLIFE

Portland's nightlife scene is largely centered on the bustling Old Port
and a few smaller, artsy spots on Congress Street. There's a great empha-
sis on live music from local bands and pubs serving award-winning
local microbrews. Several hip bars have cropped up, serving appetizers
along with a full array of specialty wines and serious craft cocktails.
Portland is a fairly sleepy city after midnight, but you can usually find
a couple of bars and restaurants open, even after the clock strikes 12.

The Bearded Lady's Jewelbox. This hip, craft cocktail–centric hole-in-the-
wall has tons of charm and a speakeasy vibe (indeed, there's no sign on
the door). Sip a dainty glass of potent French absinthe, or one of the
many creative concoctions on the ever-changing cocktail list. Rotating

WHAT'S ON TAP: MICROBREWERIES

One of the nation's craft-beer hotbeds, Maine is home to around 40 breweries, and several of the larger ones—Allagash, Geary's, and Shipyard—are in and around Portland. These breweries are open for tours and tastings, but beer lovers may prefer the smaller brewpubs that make their own beer and serve it fresh from their own taps in neighborhood taverns. In the Old Port you'll find Gritty McDuff's, Sebago Brewing Company, and Liquid Riot Bottling Company. In Bayside there's Rising Tide and Bunker Brewing Company. Sign up for one of the excellent sudsy tours offered by Maine Beer Tours (⊕ www.mainebeertours.com), and if you're in town in November, check out the Maine Brewer's Festival (⊕ www.mainebrewersfestival. com). Or pick up a Maine Beer Trail map from the Maine Brewers' Guild (⊕ www.mainebrewersguild.org).

bar snacks include things like house meatballs, turmeric pickles, and candied popcorn with bacon butter and cayenne pepper. Check out the massive, hand-painted mural on the wall that depicts—you guessed it—some elegant bearded ladies. ⊠ *644 Congress St.* ☎ *207/747–5384* ⊕ *www.thebeardedladysjewelbox.com.*

Bull Feeney's. For nightly specials, plenty of Guinness, and live entertainment, head to Bull Feeney's, a lively two-story Irish pub and restaurant. ⊠ *375 Fore St.* ☎ *207/773–7210.*

Gritty McDuff's Portland Brew Pub. Maine's original brewpub serves fine ales, British pub fare, and seafood dishes. There are between six and eight rotating ales on tap, and there's always a seasonal offering. Come on Tuesday, Saturday, and Sunday nights for live music. ⊠ *396 Fore St.* ☎ *207/772–2739* ⊕ *www.grittys.com.*

Fodor'sChoice ★ **Novare Res Bier Café.** At tucked-away Novare Res Bier Café, choose from some three dozen rotating drafts and more than 300 bottled brews. Relax on an expansive deck, munch on antipasti, or share a meat-and-cheese plate. Maine craft beers occupy at least eight of the taps at any given time, and the rest span the globe, with an emphasis on Belgian and Trappist ales. ⊠ *4 Canal Plaza, off Exchange St.* ☎ *207/761–2437* ⊕ *www.novareresbiercafe.com.*

Fodor'sChoice ★ **Portland Hunt and Alpine Club.** Scandinavian-inspired small bites and serious craft cocktails drive this hip new locale that includes delicious negronis on tap and excellent charcuterie and seafood boards in an intimate Alpine-style hut. Go for the excellent happy hour, on Monday 3–6 or on Friday 1–6. ⊠ *75 Market St.* ☎ *207/747–4754* ⊕ *www. huntandalpineclub.com.*

Rí Rá. This happening Irish pub has live music Thursday–Saturday nights and a pub quiz on Tuesday. For a more mellow experience, settle into a couch at the upstairs bar. ⊠ *72 Commercial St.* ☎ *207/761–4446* ⊕ *www.rira.com.*

Sonny's. In a Victorian-era bank building with arched windows overlooking an Old Port square, this stylish bar and lounge packs in the late-night crowd. It has quite a list of cocktails, many of which use house-infused liquors—try the chili tequila. Bluegrass and funk bands play on Thursday, and there's a DJ on Saturday. Their Latin American cuisine is a winner, too; at night you can order lighter fare like a poblano cheeseburger with yam fries, as well as entrées like the braised brisket enchilada. On weekends, brunch is served 10–3, and the kitchen stays open until 10:30 pm. ⊠ *83 Exchange St.* ☎ *207/772–7774* ⊕ *www. sonnysportland.com.*

Fodor's Choice ★ **Vena's Fizz House.** The old-fashioned soda fountain gets a modern update at Vena's Fizz House, where flavors like raspberry mint, chocolate-covered cherry cordial, and frothy blood orange go into delicious, fizzy "mocktails," while their cocktails feature artisanal ingredients such as peppercorn-bacon bitters, saffron, and ghost pepper. ⊠ *345 Fore St.* ☎ *207/747–4901* ⊕ *www.venasfizzhouse.com.*

PERFORMING ARTS

Art galleries and studios have spread throughout the city, infusing many abandoned, yet beautiful, old buildings and shops with new life. Many are concentrated along the Congress Street downtown corridor; others are hidden amid the boutiques and restaurants of the Old Port and the East End. A great way to get acquainted with the city's artists is to participate in the First Friday Art Walk, a free self-guided tour of galleries, museums, and alternative-art venues that happens—you guessed it— on the first Friday of each month.

FAMILY **Mayo Street Arts.** An alternative arts venue for the innovative and up-and-coming, Mayo Street Arts often features intimate concerts, contemporary exhibitions, and offbeat puppet shows in a repurposed church. ⊠ *10 Mayo St.* ☎ *207/879–4629* ⊕ *www.mayostreetarts.org.*

FAMILY **Merrill Auditorium.** This soaring concert hall hosts numerous theatrical and musical events, including performances by the Portland Symphony Orchestra and the Portland Opera Repertory Theatre. Ask about organ recitals on the auditorium's huge 1912 Kotzschmar Memorial Organ. ⊠ *20 Myrtle St.* ☎ *207/842–0800* ⊕ *www.merrillauditorium.net.*

FAMILY **Portland Stage.** This company mounts theatrical productions on its two stages September–May. ⊠ *25-A Forest Ave.* ☎ *207/774–0465* ⊕ *www. portlandstage.org.*

FAMILY **Space Gallery.** Space Gallery sparkles as a contemporary art gallery and alternative arts venue, opening its doors to everything from poetry readings and art fairs to live music to documentary films. The gallery is open Wednesday–Saturday. ⊠ *538 Congress St.* ☎ *207/828–5600* ⊕ *www. space538.org.*

SPORTS AND THE OUTDOORS

When the weather's good, everyone in Portland heads outside, whether for boating on the water, lounging on a beach, or walking and biking the promenades. There are also many green spaces nearby Portland, including Crescent Beach State Park, Two Lights State Park, and Fort Williams Park, home to Portland Head Light. All are on the coast south of the city in suburban Cape Elizabeth and offer walking trails, picnic facilities, and water access. Bradbury Mountain State Park, in Pownal, has incredible vistas from its easily climbed peak. In Freeport is Wolfe's Neck Woods State Park, where you can take a guided nature walk and see nesting ospreys. Both are north of Portland.

BICYCLING

FAMILY **Bicycle Coalition of Maine.** For state bike trail maps, club and tour listings, or hints on safety, contact the Bicycle Coalition of Maine. Maps are available at the group's headquarters in the Arts District. ⊠ *34 Preble St.* ☎ *207/623–4511* ⊕ *www.bikemaine.org.*

FAMILY **Cycle Mania.** Rent bikes downtown at Cycle Mania. The $25 per day rate includes a helmet and lock. ⊠ *65 Cove St.* ☎ *207/774–2933* ⊕ *www.cyclemania1.com.*

FAMILY **Gorham Bike and Ski.** You can rent several types of bikes, including hybrid and tandem models, starting at $35 per day. ⊠ *693 Congress St.* ☎ *207/773–1700* ⊕ *www.gorhambike.com.*

FAMILY **Portland Trails.** For local biking and hiking information, contact Portland Trails. The staff can tell you about designated paved and unpaved routes that wind along the water, through parks, and beyond. ⊠ *305 Commercial St.* ☎ *207/775–2411* ⊕ *www.trails.org.*

BOATING

Various Portland-based skippers offer whale-, dolphin-, and seal-watching cruises; excursions to lighthouses and islands; and fishing and lobstering trips. Board the ferry to see nearby islands. Self-navigators can rent kayaks or canoes.

FAMILY **Casco Bay Lines.** Casco Bay Lines operates ferry service to the seven bay islands with year-round populations. Summer offerings include music cruises, lighthouse excursions, and a trip to Bailey Island with a stopover for lunch. ⊠ *Maine State Pier, 56 Commercial St.* ☎ *207/774–7871* ⊕ *www.cascobaylines.com.*

FAMILY **Lucky Catch Cruises.** Set sail in a real lobster boat: this company gives you the genuine experience, which includes hauling traps and the chance to purchase the catch. ⊠ *Long Wharf, 170 Commercial St.* ☎ *207/761–0941* ⊕ *www.luckycatch.com.*

FAMILY **Odyssey Whale Watch.** From mid-May to mid-October, Odyssey Whale Watch leads whale-watching and deep-sea-fishing excursions. ⊠ *Long Wharf, 170 Commercial St.* ☎ *207/775–0727* ⊕ *www.odysseywhalewatch.com.*

FAMILY **Portland Discovery Land & Sea Tours.** For tours of the harbor and Casco Bay in a boat or on a trolley, including an up-close look at several lighthouses, try Portland Discovery Land & Sea Tours. ⊠ *Long Wharf, 170 Commercial St.* ☎ *207/774–0808* ⊕ *www.portlanddiscovery.com.*

The Eastern Prom Trail

To experience the city's busy shoreline and take in the grand views of Casco Bay, walkers, runners, and cyclists head out on the 2.1-mile Eastern Prom Trail.

Beginning at the intersection of Commercial and India streets, this paved trail runs along the water at the bottom of the Eastern Promenade, following an old rail bed alongside the still-used railroad tracks of the Maine Narrow Gauge Railroad Co. & Museum. There are plenty of places with benches and tables for a picnic break along the way. From the trailhead, it's about 1 mile to the small East End Beach.

Continuing along the trail, you'll pass underneath busy Interstate 295, and emerge at the Back Cove Trail, a popular 3½-mile loop you can connect with for a long trek. To return to the Old Port, backtrack along the trail or head up the steep path to the top of the promenade. Here you can continue along the promenade sidewalk or take the trails through this 68-acre stretch of parkland to the lovely picnic area and playground.

Continuing along the sidewalk toward the Old Port, a gazebo and several old cannons to your left indicate you're at the small Fort Allen Park. Use one of the coin operated viewing scopes to view Civil War–era Fort Gorges, which never saw action.

Where the Eastern Prom becomes Fore Street, continue on for a few blocks to India Street and take a left, which will bring you back to where you started. Or, continue into the Old Port.

Plan at least an hour to walk the trail with brief stops, or two if you continue along the Back Cove Trail. But if you can, make time for the Prom—it's truly an urban jewel.

FAMILY **Portland Paddle.** Run by a pair of Registered Maine Guides, Portland Paddle leads introductory sea kayaking clinics along with guided trips between the Casco Bay islands June through September. Two-hour sunset paddles ($38) are a fave, but the most unique offering involves a four-hour paddle to the abandoned island military installation of Fort Gorges ($65), where you'll enjoy a short acoustic concert before heading back. Kayak and paddleboard rentals are available. ⊠ *Eastern Promenade, East End Beach, off Cutter St.* ☎ *207/370–9730* ⊕ *www. portlandpaddle.net* ☉ *Closed Nov.–May. Oct. by appt. only.*

FAMILY **Portland Schooner Co.** May through October this company offers daily windjammer cruises aboard the vintage schooners *Bagheera* and *Wendameen.* You can also arrange overnight trips. ⊠ *Maine State Pier, 56 Commercial St.* ☎ *207/766–2500* ⊕ *www.portlandschooner.com.*

HOT-AIR BALLOON RIDES

FAMILY **Hot Fun First Class Balloon Flights.** Hot Fun First Class Balloon Flights flies mainly sunrise trips and can accommodate two people. The price of $325 per person includes a postflight champagne toast, snacks, and shuttle to the liftoff site. Additional passengers can sometimes be accommodated, especially children. ⊠ *Portland* ☎ *207/799–0193* ⊕ *www.hotfunballoons.com.*

SHOPPING

Exchange Street is great for arts and crafts and boutique browsing, while Commercial Street caters to the souvenir hound—gift shops are packed with nautical items, and lobster and moose emblems are emblazoned on everything from T-shirts to shot glasses.

ART AND ANTIQUES

Abacus. This appealing crafts gallery has gift items in glass, wood, and textiles, as well as fine modern jewelry. ⊠ *44 Exchange St.* ☎ *207/772–4880* ⊕ *www.abacusgallery.com.*

Greenhut Galleries. The contemporary art at this gallery changes with the seasons. Artists represented include David Driskell, an artist and leading art scholar. ⊠ *146 Middle St.* ☎ *207/772–2693, 207/772–2693* ⊕ *www.greenhutgalleries.me.*

Portland Architectural Salvage. A fixer-upper's dream, Portland Architectural Salvage has four floors of unusual finds from old buildings, including fixtures, hardware, and stained-glass windows, as well as assorted antiques. ⊠ *131 Preble St.* ☎ *207/780–0634* ⊕ *www.portlandsalvage.com.*

FAMILY **Portland Flea-for-All.** Friday through Sunday, head to the city's Bayside neighborhood for the Portland Flea-for-All, where you'll find all sorts of vintage eye candy from an-ever rotating array of antiques and artisan vendors—a fun excursion, whether or not you actually buy anything. ⊠ *125 Kennebec St.* ☎ *207/370–7570* ⊕ *www.portlandfleaforall.com.*

BOOKS

Longfellow Books. This shop is known for its good service, author readings, and excellent selection of new and used books and magazines. Even if you go in looking for something specific, you'll almost certainly stumble on something even better you didn't know about before. ⊠ *1 Monument Way* ☎ *207/772–4045* ⊕ *www.longfellowbooks.com.*

Fodor's Choice **Sherman's Books and Stationery.** Open since 1886, Sherman's is Maine's ★ oldest bookstore chain. The Portland store has an impressive stock of well-selected books interspersed with excellent gift choices, such as stationery, candles, and holiday decor, as well as a fun array of toys. It's a good place to spend a cold or rainy day perusing the selection. ⊠ *49 Exchange St.* ☎ *207/773–4100* ⊕ *www.shermans.com.*

CLOTHING

Bliss. Hip boutique Bliss stocks clothing and accessories by cutting-edge designers, plus jeans by big names like J Brand and Mother. There's also a great selection of Frye boots. ⊠ *58 Exchange St.* ☎ *207/879–7129* ⊕ *www.blissboutiques.com.*

Fodor's Choice **Judith.** Owned and operated by a former fashion designer, this stunning, ★ well-curated concept boutique features women's apparel, shoes, accessories, and contemporary housewares. ⊠ *3 Market St.* ☎ *207/747–4778* ⊕ *www.shopjudith.com* ☉ *Closed Tues.*

Sea Bags. At Sea Bags, totes made from recycled sailcloth and decorated with bright, graphic patterns are sewn right in the store. ⊠ *25 Custom House Wharf* ☎ *207/780–0744* ⊕ *www.seabags.com.*

HOUSEHOLD ITEMS/FURNITURE

Angela Adams. Maine islander Angela Adams specializes in simple but bold geometric motifs parlayed into dramatic rugs (custom, too), canvas totes, bedding, and other home accessories. The shop also carries sleek wood furniture from her husband's wood shop. ⊠ *131 Middle St.* ⊕ *www.angelaadams.com.*

Asia West. For reproduction and antique furnishings with a Far East feel, head to this stylish showroom on the waterfront. ⊠ *219 Commercial St.* ☎ *207/775–0066* ⊕ *www.asiawest.net.*

Fodor'sChoice ★ **More & Co.** Each month this peppy design store stocks a new collection centered on a certain theme, featuring a wide selection of well-designed and charming items that range from unique ceramics and glassware to children's clothing. It's excellent for gift shopping and window-shopping alike. ⊠ *112 High St.* ☎ *207/747–4730* ⊕ *www.alittlemorelikethis.com.*

TOYS

FAMILY
Fodor'sChoice ★ **Treehouse Toys.** An instant mood-lifter, this shop is chock-full of offbeat toys and novelty items that are certain to delight children of all ages. ⊠ *47 Exchange St.* ☎ *207/775–6133* ⊕ *www.treehousetoys.us.*

SIDE TRIPS FROM PORTLAND

CASCO BAY ISLANDS

The islands of Casco Bay are also known as the Calendar Islands, because an early explorer mistakenly thought there was one for each day of the year (in reality there are only 140 or so). These islands range from ledges visible only at low tide to populous Peaks Island, a suburb of Portland. Some are uninhabited; others support year-round communities, as well as stores and restaurants. Fort Gorges commands Hog Island Ledge, and Eagle Island is the site of Arctic explorer Admiral Robert Peary's home. The brightly painted ferries of Casco Bay Lines are the islands' lifeline. There is frequent service to the most populated ones, including Peaks, Long, Little Diamond, and Great Diamond.

There is little in the way of overnight lodging on the islands—the population swells during the warmer months due to summer residents—and there are few restaurants or organized attractions other than the natural beauty of the islands themselves. Meandering about by bike or on foot is a good way to explore on a day trip.

Casco Bay Lines provides ferry service from Portland to the islands of Casco Bay.

Transportation Information Casco Bay Lines. ⊠ *56 Commercial St., Portland* ☎ *207/774–7871* ⊕ *www.cascobaylines.com.*

CAPE ELIZABETH

Winslow Homer painted many of his famous oceanscapes from a tiny studio on the rocky peninsula known as Prout's Neck, 12 miles south of Portland. Visitors today navigate a neighborhood of summer homes and a sprawling country-club property for a glimpse of the same dramatic coastline. Follow Highway 77 through South Portland (sometimes called "SoPo"), stopping off for bagels and coffee in its hipper residential neighborhoods. In the affluent bedroom community of Cape Elizabeth, a detour along the two-lane Shore Road shows off the famed Portland Head Light and quite a few stunning oceanfront homes.

EXPLORING

FAMILY **Cape Elizabeth Light.** This was the first twin lighthouse erected on the Maine coast in 1828—and locals still call it Two Lights—but half of the Cape Elizabeth Light was dismantled in 1924 and converted into a private residence. The other half still operates, and you can get a great photo of it from the end of Two Lights Road in the surrounding state park of the same name. The lighthouse itself is closed to the public, but you can explore the tidal pools at its base for small, edible snails known as periwinkles, or just "wrinkles," as they're sometimes referred to in Maine. Picnic tables are also available. ⊠ *7 Tower Dr.* ☎ *207/799–5871* ⊕ *www.maine.gov/twolights* ⊠ *$4.50.*

FAMILY

Fodor's Choice

★

Portland Head Light. Familiar to many from photographs and the Edward Hopper painting *Portland Head-Light* (1927), this lighthouse was commissioned by George Washington in 1790. The towering, white-stone structure stands over the keeper's quarters, a white home with a blazing red roof, today the Museum at Portland Head Light. The lighthouse is in 90-acre Fort Williams Park, a sprawling green space with walking paths, picnic facilities, a beach and—you guessed it—a cool old fort. ⊠ *Museum, 1000 Shore Rd.* ☎ *207/799–2661* ⊕ *www.portlandheadlight.com* ⊠ *$2.*

FAMILY **Scarborough Marsh Audubon Center.** You can explore this Maine Audubon Society–run nature center by foot or canoe, on your own or by signing up for a guided walk or paddle. Canoes and kayaks are available to rent and come with a life jacket and map. The salt marsh is Maine's largest and is an excellent place for bird-watching and peaceful paddling along its winding ways. The center has a discovery room for kids, programs for all ages ranging from basket making to astronomy, and a good gift shop. Tours include birding walks. ⊠ *Pine Point Rd., Scarborough* ☎ *207/883–5100 (May–Sept.), 207/781–2330 (Oct.–Apr.)* ⊕ *www.maineaudubon.org* ⊠ *Free, guided tours from $5.*

FAMILY **Winslow Homer Studio.** The great American landscape painter created many of his best-known works in this seaside home between 1883 until his death in 1910. It's easy to see how this rocky, jagged peninsula might have been inspiring. The only way to get a look is on a tour with the Portland Museum of Art, which leads 2½-hour strolls through the historic property. ⊠ *5 Winslow Homer Rd., Scarborough* ☎ *207/775–6148* ⊕ *www.portlandmuseum.org* ⊠ *$55.*

WHERE TO EAT AND STAY

$$

SEAFOOD

FAMILY

✕ **The Lobster Shack at Two Lights.** You can't beat the location—right on the water, below the lighthouse pair that gives Two Lights State Park its name—and the food's not bad either. Enjoy fresh lobster whole or piled into a hot-dog bun with a dollop of mayo. Other menu musts include chowder, fried clams, and fish 'n' chips. It's been a classic spot since the 1920s. Eat inside or out. ⑤ *Average main: $18* ⊠ *225 Two Lights Rd.* ☎ *207/799–1677* ⊕ *www.lobstershacktwolights.com* ⊗ *Closed late Oct.–late Mar.*

$$$$ **Black Point Inn.** Toward the tip of the peninsula that juts into the ocean
RESORT   at Prout's Neck stands this stylish, tastefully updated 1878 resort inn
FAMILY   with spectacular views up and down the coast. **Pros:** dramatic setting;
geothermally heated pool; discounts in shoulder seasons. **Cons:**"guest
service charge" is tacked onto room rate. *⑤ Rooms from: $500 ⊠ 510
Black Point Rd., Scarborough ☎ 207/883–2500 ⊕ www.blackpointinn.
com ⊙ Closed late Oct.–early May ⇆ 20 rooms, 5 suites ⑩ Some meals.*

FREEPORT
17 miles north of Portland via I–295.

Those who flock straight to L.L. Bean and see nothing else of Freeport
are missing out. The city's charming backstreets are lined with historic
buildings and old clapboard houses, and there's a pretty little harbor on
the south side of the Harraseeket River. It's true that many who come to
the area do so simply to shop: L.L. Bean is the store that put Freeport
on the map, and plenty of outlets and some specialty stores have settled
here. Still, if you choose, you can stay a while and experience more than
fabulous bargains; beyond the shops are bucolic nature preserves with
miles of walking trails and plenty of places for leisurely ambling that
don't require the overuse of your credit cards.

Interstate 295 has three Freeport exits and passes by on the edge of the
downtown area. U.S. 1 is Main Street here.

EXPLORING

FAMILY **Freeport Historical Society.** Pick up a village walking map and check out the historical exhibits at the Freeport Historical Society, located in Harrington House, a hybrid Federal- and Greek Revival–style home built in the 1830s. Always call ahead when planning a visit. ⊠ *45 Main St.* 🕾 *207/865–3170* ⊕ *www.freeporthistoricalsociety.org.*

Pettengill Farm. The grounds of the Freeport Historical Society's saltwater Pettengill Farm—140 beautifully tended acres along an estuary of the Harraseeket River—are open to the public. It's about a 15-minute walk from the parking area down a farm road to the circa-1800 saltbox farmhouse, which is open by appointment. Little has changed since it was built, and it has rare etchings (called sgraffitti) of ships and sea monsters on three bedroom walls. ⊠ *Pettengill Rd.* 🕾 *207/865–3170* ⊕ *www.freeporthistoricalsociety.org* 🖼 *Free (donations appreciated).*

WHERE TO EAT AND STAY

$$ ✕**Harraseeket Lunch & Lobster Co.** Seafood baskets and lobster dinners
SEAFOOD   are the focus at this popular, bare-bones place beside the town landing
FAMILY   in South Freeport. Order at the counter, find a seat inside or out, and expect long lines in summer. ⑤ *Average main: $18* ⊠ *36 S. Main St., South Freeport* 🕾 *207/865–4888* ⊕ *www.harraseeketlunchandlobster. com* ▭ *No credit cards* ☾ *Closed mid-Oct.–Apr.* ⌖ *Reservations not accepted.*

$$ 🛏**Harraseeket Inn.** Despite some modern appointments, this large
HOTEL   hotel has a country-inn ambience throughout. **Pros:** full breakfast and
FAMILY   afternoon tea; elevators and other modern touches; walk to shopping
Fodor'sChoice   district. **Cons:** additions have diminished some authenticity. ⑤ *Rooms*
★   *from: $235* ⊠ *162 Main St.* 🕾 *207/865–9377, 800/342–6423* ⊕ *www. harraseeketinn.com* ⤳ *82 rooms, 2 suites, 9 town houses* ⫯⊙⫯ *Breakfast.*

PERFORMING ARTS

FAMILY **L.L. Bean Summer Concert Series.** Throughout the summer, L.L.Bean hosts free activities, including concerts, at the L.L. Bean Discovery Park. It's set back from Main Street, along a side street the runs between the company's flagship and home furnishings stores. ⊠ *L.L. Bean Discovery Park, 95 Main St.* 🕾 *877/755–2326* ⊕ *www.llbean.com.*

SPORTS AND THE OUTDOORS

FAMILY **L.L. Bean Outdoor Discovery Schools.** It shouldn't come as a surprise that one of the world's largest outdoor outfitters also provides its customers with instructional adventures to go with its products. L.L. Bean's year-round Outdoor Discovery Schools offer courses in canoeing, biking, kayaking, fly-fishing, snowshoeing, cross-country skiing, and other outdoor sports. ⊠ *95 Main St.* 🕾 *888/552–3261* ⊕ *www.llbean.com/ods.*

SHOPPING

The *Freeport Visitors Guide* lists the more than 200 stores on Main Street, Bow Street, and elsewhere, including Coach, Brooks Brothers, Banana Republic, J. Crew, and Cole Haan. You can pick it up around town.

Edgecomb Potters. Nationally known Edgecomb Potters produces vibrantly colored, hand-thrown porcelain tableware finished with an unusual crystalline glaze. It also sells jewelry, glassware, glass sculptures, and gifts for the home, almost all made by American artisans. ⊠ *8 School St.* ☏ *207/865–1705* ⊕ *www.edgecombpotters.com.*

FAMILY

Fodor'sChoice

★

L.L. Bean. Founded in 1912 as a mail-order merchandiser after its namesake invented a hunting boot, L.L. Bean's giant flagship store attracts more than 3 million shoppers annually and is open 365 days a year in the heart of Freeport's outlet shopping district. You can still find the original hunting boots, along with cotton and wool sweaters; outerwear of all kinds; casual clothing, boots, and shoes for men, women, and kids; and camping equipment. Nearby are the company's home furnishings store; bike, boat, and ski store; and outlet. ⊠ *95 Main St.* ☏ *877/755–2326* ⊕ *www.llbean.com.*

R. D. Allen Freeport Jewelers. This shop specializes in brightly colored tourmaline and other gemstones mined in Maine. Most of the pieces are the work of Maine artisans. Watermelon tourmaline is a specialty. ⊠ *13 Middle St., Suite 1* ☏ *207/865–1818, 877/837–3835* ⊕ *www.rdallen.com.*

Thos. Moser Cabinetmakers. Famed local furniture company Thos. Moser Cabinetmakers sells artful, handmade wood pieces with clean, classic lines. The store has information on tours at the workshop 30 minutes away in Auburn (by appointment only). ⊠ *149 Main St.* ☏ *207/865–4519* ⊕ *www.thosmoser.com.*

THE MID-COAST REGION

Lighthouses dot the headlands of Maine's Mid-Coast region, where thousands of miles of coastline wait to be explored. Defined by chiseled peninsulas stretching south from U.S. 1, this area has everything from the sandy beaches and sandbars of Popham Beach to the jutting cliffs of Monhegan Island. If you are intent on hooking a trophy-size fish or catching a glimpse of a whale, there are plenty of opportunities. If you want to explore deserted beaches and secluded coves, kayaks are your best bet; put in at the Harpswells, or on the Cushing and Saint George peninsulas, or simply paddle among the lobster boats and other vessels that ply the waters here.

Tall ships often visit Maine, sometimes sailing up the Kennebec River for a stopover at Bath's Maine Maritime Museum, on the site of the old Percy & Small Shipyard. Next door to the museum, the Bath Iron Works still builds the U.S. Navy's Aegis-class destroyers.

Along U.S. 1, charming towns, each unique, have an array of attractions. Brunswick, while a bigger, more commercial city, has rows of historic brick and clapboard homes and is home to Bowdoin College. Bath is known for its maritime heritage. Wiscasset has arguably the best antiques shopping in the state. On its waterfront you can choose from a variety of seafood shacks competing for the best lobster rolls. Damariscotta, too, is worth a stop for its good seafood restaurants, and you'd be hard-pressed to find better-tasting oysters than those from the Damariscotta River.

South along the peninsulas, the scenery opens to glorious vistas of working lobster harbors and marinas. It's here you find the authentic lobster pounds, where you can watch your lunch come right out of the traps. Boothbay Harbor and Camden are two of the quaintest towns in the Mid-Coast—and busy tourist destinations come summer, with lots of little stores that are perfect for window-shopping. Boothbay Harbor is one of three towns from which you can take a ferry to Monhegan Island, which seems to be inhabited exclusively by painters at their easels, intent on capturing the windswept cliffs and weathered homes with colorful gardens.

ESSENTIALS

Visitor Information Southern Midcoast Maine Chamber. ⊠ *Maine Technology Institute Bldg., 8 Venture Ave., Brunswick* ☎ *207/725–8797* ⊕ *www. midcoastmaine.com.* **State of Maine Visitor Information Center.** ⊠ *1100 U.S. 1, off I–295 (Exit 17), Yarmouth* ☎ *207/846–0833, 888/624–6345 for Maine Office of Tourism* ⊕ *www.mainetourism.com.*

BRUNSWICK

10 miles north of Freeport via U.S. 1.

Lovely brick and clapboard buildings are the highlight of Brunswick's Federal Street Historic District, which includes Federal Street and Park Row and the stately campus of Bowdoin College. From the intersection of Pleasant and Maine streets, in the center of town, you can walk in any direction and discover an impressive array of restaurants, as well as bookstores, gift shops, boutiques, and jewelers.

Below Brunswick are Harpswell Neck and the more than 40 islands that make up the town of Harpswell, known collectively as the Harpswells. Route 123 runs down Harpswell Neck, where small coves shelter lobster boats, and summer cottages are tucked away among birch and spruce trees. On your way down from Cook's Corner to Land's End at the end of Route 24, you cross Sebascodegan Island. Heading east here leads to East Harpswell and Cundy's Harbor. Continuing straight south down Route 24 leads to Orr's Island. Stop at Mackerel Cove to see a real fishing harbor; there are a few parking spaces, where you can stop to picnic and look for beach glass or put in your kayaks. Inhale the salt breeze as you cross the world's only cribstone bridge (designed so that water flows freely through gaps between the granite blocks) on your way to Bailey Island, home to a lobster pound made famous thanks in part to a Visa commercial.

GETTING HERE AND AROUND

From Interstate 295 take the Coastal Connector to U.S. 1 in Brunswick. From here Route 24 runs to Bailey Island and Route 123 down Harpswell Neck.

EXPLORING

FAMILY
Fodor'sChoice
★

Bowdoin College Museum of Art. This small museum housed in a stately building on Bowdoin's main quad features one of the oldest permanent collections of art in the United States, comprising paintings, sculpture, decorative arts, and works on paper. The museum often mounts well-curated, rotating exhibitions and has stellar programs for getting children excited about art. ⊠ *245 Maine St.* ☎ *207/725–3275* ⊕ *www. bowdoin.edu/art-museum* ⊠ *Free.*

WHERE TO EAT

$$
SEAFOOD
FAMILY
Fodor's Choice
★

✕ **Cook's Lobster House.** What began as a lobster shack on Bailey's Island in 1955 has grown into a huge, internationally famous family-style restaurant with a small gift shop. The restaurant still catches its own seafood, so you can count on the lobster casserole and the haddock sandwich to be delectable. A shore dinner will still set you back close to $50, but you won't leave hungry after a 1¼-pound lobster with coleslaw, potato, chowder, and mussels or clams. Whether you choose indoor or deck seating, you can watch the activity on the water as people check lobster pots and kayakers fan across the bay. $ *Average main: $24* ⊠ *68 Garrison Cove Rd., Bailey Island* ☎ *207/833-2818* ⊕ *www.cookslobster.com* ☉ *Closed early Jan.–mid-Feb.*

SPORTS AND THE OUTDOORS

H2Outfitters. The coast near Brunswick is full of hidden nooks and crannies waiting to be explored by kayak. H2Outfitters, at the southern end of Orr's Island just before the cribstone bridge, is the place in Harpswell to get on the water. It provides top-notch kayaking instruction and also offers half-day, full-day, bed-and-breakfast, and camping trips in the waters off its home base and elsewhere in Maine. ⊠ *1894 Harpswell Island Rd., Orrs Island* ☎ *207/833-5257, 800/205-2925* ⊕ *www.h2outfitters.com.*

BATH

11 miles north of Brunswick via U.S. 1.

Bath has been a shipbuilding center since 1607. The result of its prosperity can be seen in its handsome mix of Federal, Greek Revival, and Italianate homes along Front, Centre, and Washington streets. In the heart of Bath's historic district are some charming 19th-century homes, including the 1820 Federal-style home at 360 Front Street; the 1810 Greek Revival mansion at 969 Washington Street, covered with gleaming white clapboards; and the Victorian gem at 1009 Washington Street, painted a distinctive shade of raspberry. All three operate as inns. One easily overlooked site is the town's City Hall; the bell in its tower was cast by Paul Revere in 1805.

The venerable Bath Iron Works completed its first passenger ship in 1890. During World War II, BIW (as it's locally known) launched a new ship every 17 days. Not only is it still in production today, BIW is one of the state's largest employers, with about 5,600 workers, who turn out destroyers for the U.S. Navy. (It's a good idea to avoid U.S. 1 on weekdays 3:15–4:30 pm, when a major shift change takes place.) You can tour BIW through the Maine Maritime Museum.

GETTING HERE AND AROUND

U.S. 1 passes through downtown and across the Kennebec River at Bath. Downtown is on the north side of the highway along the river.

EXPLORING

FAMILY
Fodor's Choice
★

Maine Maritime Museum. No trip to Bath is complete without a visit to this cluster of buildings that once made up the historic Percy & Small Shipyard. Plan to spend at least half a day here. In fact, admission tickets are

Low tide is the perfect time to explore tidal flats, tide pools, or fish from the shore at Popham Beach State Park.

good for two days; there's just that much to see at this museum, which examines the world of shipbuilding and which is the only way to tour Bath Iron Works (June–mid-Oct.) From mid-June through Columbus Day, five nature and lighthouse boat tours cruise the scenic Kennebec River—one takes in 10 lights. The 142-foot Grand Banks fishing schooner *Sherman Zwicker* docks here during the same period. Hour-long tours of the shipyard show how these massive wooden ships were built. In the boat shop, you can watch boatbuilders wield their tools. Inside the main museum building, exhibits use ship models, paintings, photographs, and historic artifacts to tell the maritime history of the region. A separate historic building houses a fascinating lobstering exhibit; it's worth coming here just to watch the 18-minute video on lobstering written and narrated by E. B. White. A gift shop and bookstore are on the premises, and you can grab a bite to eat in the café or bring a picnic to eat on the grounds. ■ TIP→ **Kids ages six and younger get in free.** ⊠ *243 Washington St.* ☎ *207/443–1316* ⊕ *www.mainemaritime-museum.org* ✉ *$15, good for 2 days within 7-day period.*

OFF THE BEATEN PATH

Popham Beach State Park. This park has bathhouses and picnic tables. At low tide you can walk several miles of tidal flats and also out to a nearby island, where you can explore tide pools or fish off the ledges. It's on a peninsula facing the open Atlantic, between the mouths of the Kennebec and Morse rivers. About a mile from Popham Beach State Park, the road ends at the Civil War–era Fort Popham State Historic Site, an unfinished semicircular granite fort on the sea. Enjoy the beach views at nearby Spinney's Restaurant, or grab a quick bite next door at Percy's Store, which has picnic tables and a path to the beach. **Amenities:**

food and drink; lifeguards; parking (no fee); showers; toilets. **Best for:** swimming; walking. ⊠ *10 Perkins Farm La., off Rte. 209, Phippsburg* ☎ *207/389–1335* ⊕ *www.maine.gov/pophambeach* ⊠ *$6.*

WHERE TO EAT AND STAY

$ ✕ **Beale Street Barbecue.** Ribs are the thing at one of Maine's oldest
BARBECUE barbecue joints, opened in 1996. Hearty eaters should ask for one of the platters piled high with pulled pork, pulled chicken, or shredded beef. Fried calamari with habanero mayo served with corn bread is a popular appetizer. Enjoy a Maine microbrew at the bar while you wait for your table. ⑤ *Average main: $15* ⊠ *215 Water St.* ☎ *207/442–9514* ⊕ *www.mainebbq.com.*

$$ 🏨 **Sebasco Harbor Resort.** A family-friendly resort spread over 575 acres
RESORT on the water near the foot of the Phippsburg Peninsula, this place has a
FAMILY golf course, tennis courts, and even a lawn-bowling green and a cricket
Fodor's Choice pitch, among a host of other amenities. **Pros:** good choice for families;
★ perfect location; children's activities; wonderful array of lawn games. **Cons:** no sand beach. ⑤ *Rooms from: $289* ⊠ *29 Kenyon Rd., off Rte. 217, Phippsburg* ☎ *207/389–1161, 877/389–1161* ⊕ *www.sebasco. com* ⊗ *Closed late Oct.–mid-May* ⇆ *107 rooms, 8 suites, 23 cottages* ⑩ *Some meals.*

WISCASSET

10 miles north of Bath via U.S. 1.

Settled in 1663, Wiscasset sits on the banks of the Sheepscot River. It bills itself "Maine's Prettiest Village," and it's easy to see why: it has graceful churches, old cemeteries, and elegant sea captains' homes (many converted into antiques shops or galleries).

There's also a good wine and specialty foods shop called Treats (stock up here if you're heading north). Pack a picnic and take it down to the dock on Water Street, where you can watch the fishing boats, or grab a lobster roll from Red's Eats or the lobster shack nearby. Wiscasset has expanded its wharf, and this is a great place to catch a breeze on a hot day.

GETTING HERE AND AROUND

U.S. 1 becomes Main Street, and traffic often slows to a crawl come summer. You'll likely have success parking on Water Street rather than Main. It's a good idea to do your driving around Wiscasset very early in the morning and after 7 in the evening when traffic eases a bit. The best way to get around here is on foot.

WHERE TO EAT

$ ✕ **Red's Eats.** It's hard to miss the long line of hungry customers outside
FAST FOOD this little red shack on the Wiscasset side of the bridge. Red's is a local
FAMILY landmark famous for its hamburgers, hot dogs, lobster and crab rolls, and crispy onion rings and clams fried in their own house-made batters. Maine-made Round Top ice cream is also sold (try blueberry or black raspberry). Enjoy views of the tidal Sheepscot River from picnic tables on the bi-level deck or down on the grass by the water. ⑤ *Average main:*

6

Continued on page 315

MAINE'S LIGHTHOUSES
GUARDIANS OF THE COAST By John Blodgett

Perched high on rocky ledges, on the tips of wayward
islands, and sometimes seemingly on the ocean itself are
the more than five dozen lighthouses standing watch along
Maine's craggy and ship-busting coastline.

Marshall Point Light

LIGHTING THE WAY: A BIT OF HISTORY

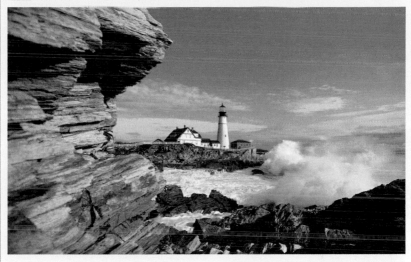

Portland Head Light

Most lighthouses were built in the first half of the 19th century to protect vessels from running aground at night or when the shoreline was shrouded in fog. Along with the mournful siren of the foghorn and maritime lore, these practical structures have come to symbolize Maine throughout the world.

SHIPWRECKS AND SAFETY

These alluring sentinels of the eastern seaboard today have more form than function, but that certainly was not always the case. Safety was a strong motivating factor in the erection of the lighthouses. Commerce also played a critical role. For example, in 1791 Portland Head light was completed, partially as a response to local merchants' concerns about the rocky entrance to Portland Harbor and the varying depths of the shipping channel, but approval wasn't given until a terrible accident in 1787 in which a 90-ton sloop wrecked. In 1789, the federal government created the U.S. Lighthouse Establishment (later the U.S. Lighthouse Service) to manage them. In 1939 the U.S. Coast Guard took on the job.

Some lighthouses in Maine were built in a much-needed venue, but the points and islands upon which they sat were prone to storm damage. Along with poor construction, this meant that over the years many lighthouses had to be rebuilt or replaced.

LIGHTHOUSES TODAY

In modern times, many of the structures still serve a purpose. Technological advances, such as GPS and radar, are mainly used to navigate through the choppy waters, but a lighthouse or its foghorns are helpful secondary aids, and sometimes the only ones used by recreational boaters. The numerous channel-marking buoys still in existence also are testament to the old tried-and-true methods.

Of the 66 lighthouses along this far northeastern state, 55 are still working, alerting ships (and even small aircraft) of the shoreline's rocky edge. Government agencies, historic preservation organizations, and mostly private individuals own the decommissioned lights.

KEEPERS OF THE LIGHT

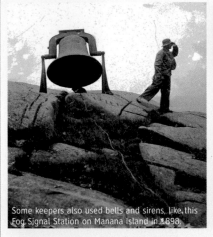

Some keepers also used bells and sirens, like this Fog Signal Station on Manana Island in 1898.

Pemaquid Point's fourth-order Fresnel lens

LIFE OF A LIGHTKEEPER

One thing that has changed with the modern era is the disappearance of the lighthouse keeper. In the early 20th century, lighthouses began the conversion from oil-based lighting to electricity. A few decades later, the U.S. Coast Guard switched to automation, phasing out the need for an on-site keeper.

While the keepers of tradition were no longer needed, the traditions of these stalwart, 24/7 employees live on through museum exhibits and retellings of Maine's maritime history, legends, and lore. The tales of a lighthouse keeper's life are the stuff romance novels are made of: adventure, rugged but lonely men, and a beautiful setting along an unpredictable coastline.

The lighthouse keepers of yesterday probably didn't see their own lives so romantically. Their daily narrative was one of hard work and, in some cases, exceptional solitude. A keeper's primary job was to ensure that the lamp was illuminated all day, every day. This meant that oil (whale or coal oil and later kerosene) had to be carried about and wicks trimmed on a regular basis. When fog shrouded the coast, they sounded the solemn horn to pierce through the damp darkness that hid their light. Their quarters were generally small and often attached to the light tower itself. The remote locations of the lights added to the isolation a keeper felt, especially before the advent of radio and telephone, let alone the Internet. Though some brought families with them, the keepers tended to be men who lived alone.

THE LIGHTS 101

Over the years, Fresnel (fray-NELL) lenses were developed in different shapes and sizes so that ship captains could distinguish one lighthouse from another. Invented by Frenchman Augustin Fresnel in the early 19th century, the lens design allows for a greater transmission of light perfectly suited for lighthouse use. Knowing which lighthouse they were near helped captains know which danger was present, such as a submerged ledge or shallow channel. Some lights, such as those at Seguin Island Light, are fixed and don't flash. Other lights are colored red.

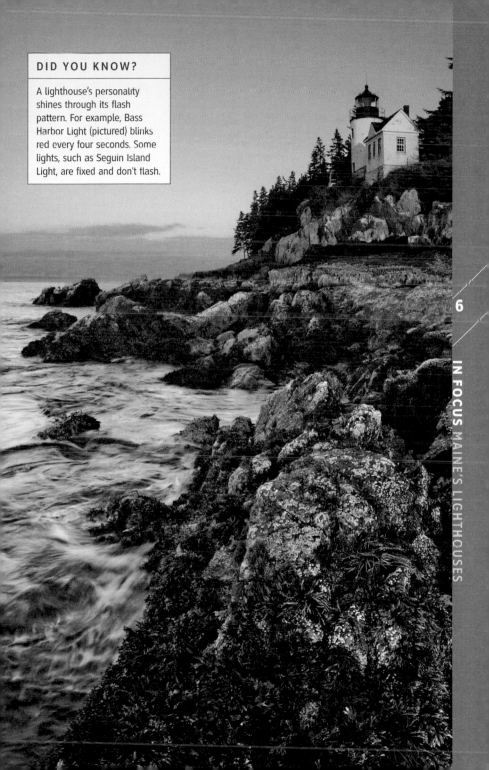

DID YOU KNOW?

A lighthouse's personality shines through its flash pattern. For example, Bass Harbor Light (pictured) blinks red every four seconds. Some lights, such as Seguin Island Light, are fixed and don't flash.

LIGHTHOUSE FINDER

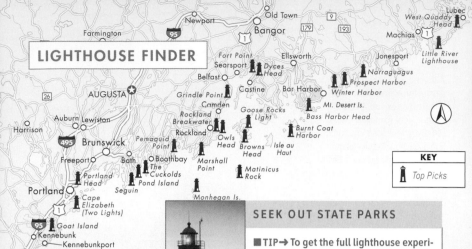

West Quoddy Head

SEEK OUT STATE PARKS

■ TIP→ To get the full lighthouse experience your best bet is to visit one that is part of a state or local park. These are generally well kept and tend to allow up-close approach, though typically only outside. While you're at the parks you can picnic or stroll on the trails. Wildlife is often abundant in and near the water; you might spot sea birds and even whales in certain locations (try West Quoddy Head, Portland Head, or Two Lights).

VISITING MAINE'S LIGHTHOUSES

As you travel along the Maine Coast, you won't see lighthouses by watching your odometer—there were no rules about the spacing of lighthouses. The decision as to where to place a lighthouse was a balance between a region's geography and its commercial prosperity and maritime traffic.

Lighthouses dot the shore from as far south as York to the country's easternmost tip at Lubec. Accessibility varies according to location and other factors. A handful are so remote as to be outright impossible to reach (except perhaps by kayaking and rock climbing). Some don't allow visitors according to Coast Guard policies, though you can enjoy them through the zoom lens of a camera. Others you can walk right up to and, occasionally, even climb to the top. Lighthouse enthusiasts and preservation groups restore and maintain many of them. All told, approximately 30 lighthouses allow some sort of public access.

MUSEUMS, TOURS, AND MORE

Most keeper's quarters are closed to the public, but some of the homes have been converted to museums, full of intriguing exhibits on lighthouses, the famous Fresnel lenses used in them, and artifacts of Maine maritime life in general. Talk to the librarians at the **Maine Maritime Museum** in Bath (⊕ *www.mainemaritimemuseum.org*) or sign up for one of the museum's daily lighthouse cruises to pass by no fewer than ten on the Lighthouse Lovers Cruise. In Rockland, the **Maine Lighthouse Museum** (⊕ *www.mainelighthousemuseum.org*) has the country's largest display of Fresnel lenses. The museum also displays keepers' memorabilia, foghorns, brassware, and more. Maine Open Lighthouse Day is the second Saturday after Labor Day; you can tour and even climb lights usually closed to the public.

For more information, check out the lighthouse page at Maine's official tourism site: ⊕ *visitmaine.com.*

SLEEPING LIGHT: STAYING OVERNIGHT

Goose Rocks, where you can play lighthouse keeper for a week.

Want to stay overnight in a lighthouse? There are several options to do so. ■TIP→ Book lighthouse lodgings as far in advance as possible, up to one year ahead.

Our top pick is **Pemaquid Point Light** (*Newcastle Square Vacation Rentals* ☎ *207/563–6500* ⊕ *www.mainecoast-cottages.com*) because it has one of the most dramatic settings on the Maine coast. Two miles south of **New Harbor**, the second floor of the lighthouse keeper's house is rented out on a weekly basis early May through mid-November to support upkeep of the grounds. When you aren't enjoying the interior, head outdoors: the covered front porch has a rocking-chair view of the ocean. The one-bedroom, one-bath rental sleeps up to a family of four.

Situated smack dab in the middle of a major maritime thoroughfare between two Penobscot Bay islands, **Goose Rocks Light** (☎ *203/400–9565* ⊕ *www.beacon-preservation.org*) offers lodging for the adventuresome—the 51-foot "spark plug" lighthouse is completely surrounded by water. Getting there requires

a ferry ride from Rockland to nearby **North Haven**, a 5- to 10-minute ride by motorboat, and then a climb up an iron-rung ladder from the pitching boat—all based on high tide and winds, of course. There's room for up to eight people. It's a bit more cushy experience than it was for the original keepers: there's a flat-screen TV with DVD player and a selection of music and videos for entertainment. In addition, a hammock hangs on the small deck that encircles the operational light; it's a great place from which to watch the majestic windjammers and the fishing fleet pass by.

Little River Lighthouse (☎ *877/276–4682* ⊕ *www.littleriverlight.org*), along the far northeastern reaches of the coast in **Cutler**, has three rooms available for rent in July and August. You're responsible for food and beverages, linens, towels, and other personal items (don't forget the bug spray), but kitchen and other basics are provided. The lighthouse operators will provide a boat ride to the island upon which the lighthouse sits.

TOP LIGHTHOUSES TO VISIT

BASS HARBOR LIGHT
Familiar to many as the subject of countless photographs is Bass Harbor Light, at the southern end of **Mount Desert Island**. It is within Acadia National Park and 17 miles from the town of Bar Harbor. The station grounds are open year-round.

CAPE ELIZABETH LIGHT
Two Lights State Park is so-named because it's next to two lighthouses. Both of these **Cape Elizabeth** structures were built in 1828. The western light was converted into a private residence in 1924; the eastern light, Cape Elizabeth Light, still projects its automated cylinder of light. The grounds surrounding the building and the lighthouse itself are closed to the public, but the structure is easily viewed and photographed from nearby at the end of Two Lights Road.

CAPE NEDDICK LIGHT
More commonly known as Nubble Light for the smallish offshore expanse of rock it rests upon, Cape Neddick Light sits a few hundred feet off a rock point in **York Beach**. With such a precarious location, its grounds are inaccessible to visitors, but close enough to be exceptionally photogenic, especially during the Christmas season.

MONHEGAN ISLAND LIGHT
Only the adventuresome and the artistic see this light, because **Monhegan Island** is accessible by an approximately one-hour ferry ride. To reach the lighthouse, you have an additional half-mile walk uphill from the ferry dock. The former keeper's quarters is home to the Monhegan Museum, which has exhibits about the island. The tower itself is closed to the public.

PORTLAND HEAD LIGHT
One of Maine's most photographed lighthouses (and its oldest), the famous Portland Head Light was completed in January 1791. At the edge of Fort Williams Park, in **Cape Elizabeth**, the towering white stone lighthouse stands 101 feet above the sea. The Coast Guard operates it and it is not open for tours. However the adjacent keeper's dwelling is now a museum.

WEST QUODDY HEAD LIGHT
Originally built in 1808 by mandate of President Thomas Jefferson, West Quoddy Head Light sits in **Lubec** on the easternmost tip of land in the mainland United States. The 49-foot-high lighthouse with distinctive red and white stripes, is part of Quoddy Head State Park.

Cape Neddick

Portland Head

West Quoddy Head

$12 ⊠ 41 Water St. ☎ 207/882–6128 ⚏ No credit cards ☺ Closed mid-Oct.–mid-Apr. ⚐ Reservations not accepted.

SHOPPING

Edgecomb Potters. Edgecomb Potters is not to be missed: they make vibrantly colored, exquisitely glazed porcelain known all around the country. The store also carries jewelry, glassware, and glass sculptures. ⊠ *727 Boothbay Rd., Edgecomb* ☎ *207/882–9493* ⊕ *www.edgecombpotters.com.*

In the Clover. There's something charmingly old-school about this pretty boutique with its warm and friendly service and fine displays of women's clothing, accessories, and beauty products. Geared towards elegant but no-fuss women of every age, the shop stocks clothing items such as fine cashmere shawls; pretty but not froufrou lingerie; and sophisticated loungewear as well as a good selection of natural beauty products and fragrances, unique jewelry, and inspiring books. ⊠ *85 Main St.* ☎ *207/882–9435* ⊕ *inthecloverbeauty.blogspot.com.*

Fodor's Choice
★ **Rock Paper Scissors.** Not your run-of-the-mill gift shop, this well-curated boutique stocks offbeat cards and letterpress stationary, local handcrafted goods such as blankets, purses, and ceramics, and beautiful, one-of-a-kind objects for the home and kitchen. Stocked to the brim with charming goodies for anyone on your list (including yourself), this shop is decidedly contemporary, with a Scandinavian bent, and is well worth a stop, if only to peruse the gorgeously arranged array of products on display. ⊠ *68 Main St.* ☎ *207/882–9930.*

Sheepscot River Pottery. This shop boasts beautifully glazed kitchen tiles, as well as kitchenware and home accessories, including sinks. Jewelry and other items by local artisans are also on sale. ⊠ *34 U.S. 1, Edgecomb* ☎ *207/882–9410* ⊕ *www.sheepscot.com.*

BOOTHBAY

10 miles south of Wiscasset via Rte. 27.

The shoreline of the Boothbay Peninsula is a craggy stretch of inlets, where pleasure craft anchor alongside trawlers and lobster boats. The town of Boothbay comprises the village center, Boothbay Harbor, as well as East Boothbay. The harbor is like a smaller version of Bar Harbor—touristy, but friendly and fun—with pretty, winding streets and lots to explore. Commercial Street, Wharf Street, Townsend Avenue, and the By-Way are lined with shops and ice-cream parlors. One of the biggest draws here is the stunning Coastal Maine Botanical Gardens, with its beautiful café and gift shop, as well as its famous children's garden.

GETTING HERE AND AROUND

In season, boat trips to Monhegan Island leave from the piers off Commercial Street. Drive out to Ocean Point in East Boothbay for some incredible scenery. Boothbay is 13 miles south of Wiscasset via U.S. 1 and Route 27.

EXPLORING

FAMILY
Fodor's Choice
★

Coastal Maine Botanical Garden. Set aside a couple of hours to stroll among the roses, lupines, and rhododendrons at the 250-acre Coastal Maine Botanical Garden. In the summer, free docent-led tours leave from the visitor center at 11 and 1 on Thursday and Saturday. The "children's garden" is a wonderland of stone sculptures, rope bridges, small teahouse-like structures with grass roofs, and even a hedge maze. Children and adults alike adore the separate woodland fairy area. The on-site restaurant and café, as well as the bookshop and resource library, are also delightful. It's easy to spend an entire day here and not see everything—be sure to wear comfortable walking shoes. For those less inclined to go by foot, the gardens offer free shuttle service to most spots on the property. ⊠ *132 Botanical Gardens Dr., off Rte. 27* ☎ *207/633–8000* ⊕ *www.mainegardens.org* ⊠ *$16.*

WHERE TO EAT AND STAY

$$
TAPAS

✕ **Boat House Bistro.** The multitier rooftop terrace (complete with an outdoor bar) stays crowded all summer at the Boat House Bistro. Austrian-born chef Karin Guerin dishes up tapas-style small plates ranging from mango empanadas to sweet-potato latkes. For those seeking the full-on Maine experience, there are plenty of seafood options, too, including a different paella each day. The waitstaff are young, friendly, and just as diverse as the menu. ⑤ *Average main: $21* ⊠ *12 By-Way, Boothbay Harbor* ☎ *207/633–0400* ⊕ *www.theboathousebistro.com* ۞ *Closed mid-Oct.–mid-Apr.*

$$$
B&B/INN

▨ **Topside Inn.** The Adirondack chairs on the immense lawn of this historic hilltop B&B have what is probably the best bay view in town. **Pros:** knockout views; plenty of green space for croquet; easy walk downtown. **Cons:** walls are a bit thin in the annexes. ⑤ *Rooms from: $300* ⊠ *60 McKown St., Boothbay Harbor* ☎ *207/633–5404* ⊕ *www.top-sideinn.com* ۞ *Closed mid-Oct.–mid-May* ⤴ *25 rooms* ▥ *Breakfast.*

DAMARISCOTTA

8 miles north of Wiscasset via U.S. 1.

The Damariscotta region comprises several communities along the rocky coast. The town itself sits on the water, a lively place filled with attractive shops and restaurants, as well as some of the best oysters around.

Just across the bridge over the Damariscotta River is the town of Newcastle, between the Sheepscot and Damariscotta rivers. Newcastle was settled in the early 1600s. The earliest inhabitants planted apple trees, but the town later became an industrial center, home to several shipyards and a couple of mills. The oldest Catholic church in New England, St. Patrick's, is here, and it still rings its original Paul Revere bell.

Bremen, which encompasses more than a dozen islands and countless rocky outcrops, has many seasonal homes along the water, and the main industries in the small community are fishing and clamming. Nobleboro, a bit north of here on U.S. 1, was settled in the 1720s by Colonel David Dunbar, sent by the British to rebuild the fort at Pemaquid. Neighboring Waldoboro is situated on the Medomak River and was settled largely by Germans in the mid-1700s. You can still visit the old German Meeting House, built in 1772. The Pemaquid Peninsula stretches south from Damariscotta to include Bristol, South Bristol, Round Pond, New Harbor, and Pemaquid.

NEED A BREAK

✕ **Moody's Diner.** This famous diner makes pies of considerable size— prized for their filling above all—and there's no better place to chat with locals. There is a beloved gift shop on site and they also have cabins and simple motel rooms to rent. ✉ *1885 Atlantic Hwy., Waldoboro* ☎ *207/832– 7785* ⊕ *www.moodysdiner.com.*

GETTING HERE AND AROUND

In Newcastle, U.S. 1B runs from U.S. 1 across the Damariscotta River to Damariscotta. From this road take Route 129 south to South Bristol and Route 130 south to Bristol and New Harbor. From here you can return to U.S. 1 heading north on Route 32 through Round Pond and Bremen. In Waldoboro, turn off U.S. 1 on Jefferson Street to see the historic village center.

6

ESSENTIALS

Visitor Information Damariscotta Region Chamber of Commerce. ✉ *67-A Main St.* ☎ *207/563–8340* ⊕ *www.damariscottaregion.com.*

WHERE TO EAT AND STAY

$$
AMERICAN
FAMILY

✕ **King Eider's Pub & Restaurant.** This classic pub with a super-cozy atmosphere right downtown bills itself as having the finest crab cakes in New England. Start with the fresh local oysters that the Damariscotta region is known for, then move on to entrées like steak-and-ale pie, sea-scallop Florentine, or sautéed haddock with chips. With exposed-brick walls and low wooden beams, it's a cozy place to enjoy your favorite ale. Stop by on Thursday night for live music. $ *Average main: $18* ✉ *2 Elm St.* ☎ *207/563–6008* ⊕ *www.kingeiderspub.com.*

$$
AMERICAN
FAMILY
Fodor's Choice
★

✕ **Publick House.** Located in a historic building that has been handsomely renovated, Publick House serves delicious comfort food, including fresh oysters, creative flatbreads, and local craft beers, as well as one of the best French onion soups around. There is often live music, making it a great place for a night out on a date or with the entire family. $ *Average main: $20* ✉ *52 Main St., Newcastle* ☎ *207/563–3434* ⊕ *www. newcastlepublickhouse.com.*

$$
AMERICAN

✕ **Van Lloyd's Bistro.** Packed with funky decor culled from the owners' travels and local antiquing trips, this lively new restaurant serves an eclectic mix of dishes that lean towards a Mediterranean style. Pop in for the excellent happy hour and stay for dishes like pork-belly tortillas, Welsh rarebit, and Angus beef–stuffed grape leaves, or the fantastic Hunter's Plate, which includes a tasty rabbit porchetta. $ *Average main: $20* ✉ *85 Parking Lot La.* ☎ *207/563–5005* ⊕ *www.vanlloydsbistro. com* ▭ *No credit cards.*

Lobster trap buoys are popular decorations in Maine; the markings represent a particular lobsterman's claim.

$
B&B/INN
FAMILY

🏨 **Newcastle Inn.** A riverside location, tasteful decor, and lots of common areas (inside and out) make this a relaxing country inn. **Pros:** guests can order beer or wine; one suite-like room and two suites with sitting areas. **Cons:** short walk into the village. ⑤ *Rooms from: $180* ⊠ *60 River Rd., Newcastle* ☎ *207/563–5685* ⊕ *www.newcastleinn.com* ⇨ *12 rooms, 2 suites* ⦿ *Breakfast.*

PEMAQUID POINT

10 miles south of Damariscotta via U.S. 1, U.S. 1B, and Rte. 130.

Pemaquid Point is the tip of the Pemaquid Peninsula, bordered by Muscongus and Johns bays. It's home to the famous lighthouse of the same name and its attendant fog bell and tiny museum. Also at the bottom of the peninsula, along the Muscongus Bay, is the Nature Conservancy's Rachel Carson Salt Pond Preserve.

GETTING HERE AND AROUND

From U.S. 1, take U.S. 1B into Damariscotta and head south on Route 130 to Pemaquid Point.

EXPLORING

FAMILY
Fodor's Choice
★

Pemaquid Point Light. At the end of Route 130, this lighthouse at the tip of the Pemaquid Peninsula looks as though it sprouted from the ragged, tilted chunk of granite it commands. Most days in the summer you can climb the tower to the light. The former keeper's cottage is now the Fishermen's Museum, which displays historic photographs, scale models, and artifacts that explore commercial fishing in Maine. Also here are the original fog bell and bell house. The on-site Pemaquid Art Gallery mounts exhibitions by area artists in the summer. There are restrooms and picnic tables. ⊠ *3115 Bristol Rd., Pemaquid* ☎ *207/677 2492* ⊕ *www.pemaquidpoint.org* ⊠ *$2.*

WHERE TO EAT AND STAY

$$ ✕ **Moscungus Bay Lobster Co.** The food here is practically guaranteed to be fresh: lobsters come in off the boat at one end of the pier, and the restaurant is at the other. Grab a picnic table and be careful not to hit your head on the colorful, dangling wooden buoys. It's fun to watch the lobstermen unload their catch over lunch. ⑤ *Average main: $18* ⊠ *28 Landing Rd., Round Pond* ☎ *207/529–2251* ⊕ *www.mainefreshlobster. com* ⊗ *Closed mid-May–mid-Oct.*

SEAFOOD
FAMILY

$$ ✕ **Round Pond Fisherman's Coop.** Sheltered Moscungus Bay is where you'll find this down-home lobster shack, right on the pier with pleasant views of the water. Competition with the neighboring Moscungus Bay Lobster Co. keeps the prices low for fresh-off-the-boat lobster and steamers. ⑤ *Average main: $18* ⊠ *25 Town Landing Rd., Round Pond* ☎ *207/529–5725* ⊗ *Closed Labor Day–mid-May.*

SEAFOOD

$ 🏠 **Christmas Cove Inn.** If you're traveling with a dog, you'll find few more accommodating spots in Maine than this out-of-the-way place on Rutherford Island. **Pros:** great if you're traveling with dogs; great views from lookout. **Cons:** dogs on premises. ⑤ *Rooms from: $150* ⊠ *53 Coveside Rd., South Bristol* ☎ *207/644–1502, 866/644–1502* ⊕ *www. christmascoveinn.com* ⊰ *7 rooms* ⑪ *No meals.*

B&B/INN
FAMILY

6

SPORTS AND THE OUTDOORS

FAMILY **Hardy Boat Cruises.** Mid-May through mid-October, you can take a cruise to Monhegan with Hardy Boat Cruises. The company also offers seal- and puffin-watching trips and lighthouse and fall coastal cruises. Dogs are welcome on the boat for $5. ⊠ *Shaw's Wharf, 132 State Rte. 32, New Harbor* ☎ *207/677–2026, 800/278–3346* ⊕ *www.hardyboat.com.*

THOMASTON

10 miles northeast of Waldoboro, 72 miles northeast of Portland.

Thomaston is a delightful town, full of beautiful sea captains' homes and dotted with antiques and specialty shops. A National Historic District encompasses parts of High, Main, and Knox streets. The town is the gateway to the two peninsulas; you'll see water on both sides as you arrive.

GETTING HERE AND AROUND

U.S. 1 is Main Street through Thomaston. Route 131 runs down the St. George Peninsula from here and Route 97 leads down the Cushing Peninsula and to Friendship.

WHERE TO EAT

$$$ ✕ **Thomaston Cafe.** This is a great pit stop on the long, slow drive up U.S. 1. Works by local artists adorn the walls of this small downtown café, which uses local ingredients as much as possible. It serves an excellent breakfast, including homemade corned beef hash. For lunch there's scrumptious haddock chowder and delicious sandwiches. Try the sandwich with panfried haddock lightly breaded with panko bread crumbs,

AMERICAN

or a salad and crab cakes (sold at breakfast, too). Entrées include lobster ravioli and filet mignon with béarnaise sauce. Sunday brunch is popular. $ *Average main: $30* ✉ *154 Main St.* ☎ *207/354–8589* ⊕ *www.thomastoncafe.com* ☽ *Closed Mon.–Wed. No dinner Sun.*

$$
SEAFOOD
FAMILY

✕ **Waterman's Beach Lobster.** This place in South Thomaston is authentic, inexpensive, and scenic, overlooking islands in the Atlantic. You can eat lunch or dinner under the pavilions right next to the beach and pier, or get closer to the water at picnic tables. In addition to seafood favorites, Waterman's also sells freshly baked pies and locally made ice cream. It's strictly BYOB. $ *Average main: $18* ✉ *343 Waterman's Beach Rd., South Thomaston* ☎ *207/596–7819, 207/594–7518* ⊕ *www.watermansbeachlobster.com* ☽ *Closed Oct.–mid-June.*

PORT CLYDE

5 miles south of Tenants Harbor via Rte. 131.

Sitting at the end of the St. George Peninsula, the sleepy fishing village of Port Clyde is a haven for artists, with a number of galleries and a sweeping vista of the ocean that can't be beat. It's also a good spot to spend time nursing a beer or a coffee while waiting for your boat out to Monhegan. Like many places in Maine, lobster fishing is an economic mainstay here. Marshall Point Lighthouse, right in the harbor, has a small museum.

EXPLORING

FAMILY
Fodor's Choice
★

Marshall Point Lighthouse. This 31-foot lighthouse, which has been in operation since it was erected in 1858, is perhaps best known as the spot where Forrest Gump concluded his very long cross-country run in the 1994 film adaptation of the book by the same name. Be prepared for sweeping views of the ocean and a resounding "Run, Forrest, run!" coming from visitors taking full advantage of an exceptional photo op. The site also has a small museum and a gift shop, housed in the old lightkeepers' house. ✉ *Marshall Point Rd.* ☎ *207/372–6450* ⊕ *www.marshallpoint.org.*

MONHEGAN ISLAND

East of Pemaquid Peninsula, 10 miles south of Port Clyde.

If you love rocky cliffs, this is your place. And if you happen to be an artist you might never leave; studios and galleries are all over the island. The village bustles with activity in summer, when many artists open their studios. Several shops are available for browsers. You can escape the crowds on the island's 17 miles of hiking trails, which lead to the lighthouse and to the cliffs. Bring your camera!

GETTING HERE AND AROUND

Three excursion boats dock here. The boat trip out to Monhegan is almost as exhilarating as exploring the island itself. You'll likely pass by the Marshall Point Lighthouse; be sure to be on the lookout for porpoises, seals, puffins, and small whales en route to the island.

FAMILY
Monhegan Boat Line. The Port Clyde boat landing is home to the *Elizabeth Ann* and the *Laura B*, the mail boats that serve Monhegan Island,

about 10 miles offshore. There are three round-trips daily Memorial Day weekend–Columbus Day; one daily in late fall and early spring; and three weekly in the winter. ✉ *880 Port Clyde Rd., Port Clyde* ☎ *207/372–8848* ⊕ *www.monheganboat.com.*

EXPLORING

FAMILY **Monhegan Island Light.** Getting a look at this squat stone lighthouse—from land, anyway—requires a slightly steep half-mile walk uphill from the island's ferry dock. The lighthouse was automated in 1959, and the former keeper's quarters became the Monhegan Museum shortly thereafter. Exhibits at the museum have as much to do with life on the island as they do with the lighthouse itself. The tower is open sporadically throughout the summer for short tours. ✉ *Lighthouse Hill Rd., ½ mile east of dock, Monhegan* ☎ *207/596–7003.*

WHERE TO EAT AND STAY

$$ ✗ **Fish House Market.** The menu here is focused on fresh, local seafood
SEAFOOD prepared simply. Order inside the little hut by the water, and when your meal is ready, eat outside at a table inches from the shoreline, lapping up the view of the bay and the lobster boats moored there. Bring your own wine or beer and savor the outstanding fish chowder or a steamed lobster. ⑤ *Average main: $18* ✉ *98 Fish Beach La., Monhegan* ▭ *No credit cards.*

$ ☷ **Island Inn.** This three-story inn, which dates to 1907, has a command-
B&B/INN ing presence on Monhegan Island's harbor. **Pros:** great food; great view. **Cons:** pricey; no a/c. ⑤ *Rooms from: $185* ✉ *1 Ocean Ave., Monhegan* ☎ *207/596–0371* ⊕ *www.islandinnmonhegan.com* ☾ *Closed Columbus Day–Memorial Day* ⚑ *28 rooms (20 with bath), 4 suites* ⦿ *No meals* ▭ *No credit cards.*

PENOBSCOT BAY

Few could deny that Penobscot Bay is one of Maine's most dramatically beautiful regions. Its more than 1,000 miles of coastline is made up of rocky granite boulders, often undeveloped shores, a sprinkling of colorful towns and quaint villages, and views of the sea and islands that are a photographer's (and painter's) dream.

Penobscot Bay stretches 37 miles from Port Clyde in the south to Stonington, the little fishing village at the tip of Deer Isle, in the north. The bay begins near Stockton Springs, where the Penobscot River, New England's second-largest river system, ends, and terminates in the Gulf of Maine, where it is 47 miles wide. It covers an estimated 1,070 square miles and is home to more than 1,800 islands.

Initially, shipbuilding was the primary moneymaker here. In the 1800s, during the days of the great tall ships (or Down Easters, as they were often called), more wooden ships were built in Maine than in any other state in the country, and many were constructed along Penobscot Bay. This golden age of billowing sails and wooden sailing ships came to an end with the development of the steam engine, and by 1900, sailing ships were no longer a viable commercial venture in Maine. However, as you will see when traveling the coast, the tall ships have not entirely disappeared—some, albeit tiny in number compared to their 1800s heyday, have been revived as recreational boats known as windjammers. Today, once again, there are more tall ships along Penobscot Bay than anywhere else in the country.

ROCKLAND

3 miles north of Thomaston via U.S. 1.

This town is considered the gateway to Penobscot Bay and is the first stop on U.S. 1 offering a glimpse of the often-sparkling and island-dotted blue bay. Though once merely a place to pass through on the way to tonier ports like Camden, Rockland now gets attention on its own, thanks to a trio of attractions: the renowned Farnsworth Art Museum, the increasingly popular summer Lobster Festival, and the lively North Atlantic Blues Festival. Specialty shops and galleries line the main street, and one of the restaurants, Primo (between Camden and the little village of Owls Head), has become nationally famous. The town is still a large fishing port and the commercial hub of this coastal area.

Rockland Harbor bests Camden (by one) as home to the largest fleet of Maine windjammers. The best place in Rockland to view these handsome vessels as they sail in and out of the harbor is the mile-long granite breakwater, which bisects the outer portion of Rockland Harbor. To get there, from U.S. 1, head east on Waldo Avenue and then right on Samoset Road; follow this short road to its end.

GETTING HERE AND AROUND

U.S. 1 runs along Main Street here, while U.S. 1A curves through the residential neighborhood west of the business district, offering a faster route if you are passing through.

FESTIVALS

FAMILY **Maine Lobster Festival.** Rockland's annual Maine Lobster Festival, held in early August, is the region's largest annual event. About 10 tons of lobsters are steamed in a huge lobster cooker—you have to see it to believe it. The festival, held in Harbor Park, includes a parade, live entertainment, food booths, and, of course, the crowning of the Maine Sea Goddess. ⊠ *Harbor Park, Main St., south of Rte. 1* ☎ *800/576–7512* ⊕ *www.mainelobsterfestival.com.*

FAMILY **North Atlantic Blues Festival.** About a dozen well-known musicians gather for the North Atlantic Blues Festival, a two-day affair held the first full weekend after July 4th. The show officially takes place at the public landing on Rockland Harbor Park, but it also includes a "club crawl" through downtown Rockland on Saturday night. Admission to the festival is $30 in advance, $40 at the gate. ⊠ *Harbor Park, Main St.* ☎ *207/691–2248* ⊕ *www.northatlanticbluesfestival.com.*

Visitor Information Penobscot Bay Regional Chamber of Commerce. ⊠ *Visitor Center, 1 Park Dr.* ☎ *207/596–0376, 800/562–2529* ⊕ *www.therealmaine.com.*

EXPLORING

FAMILY **Farnsworth Art Museum.** One of the most important small museums in the
Fodor's Choice country, much of the Farnsworth's collection is devoted to Maine-related
★ works of the famous Wyeth family: N. C. Wyeth, an accomplished

Windjammer Excursions

Nothing defines the Maine coastal experience better than a sailing trip on a windjammer. These vessels were built all along the East Coast in the 19th and early 20th centuries. Designed primarily to carry cargo, these beauties (most are wood hulled) have a rich past: the *Schooner Ladona* served in World War II, while others plied the waters in the lumbering, granite, fishing, and oystering trades or served as pilot boats. They vary in size but can be as small as 46 feet, holding six passengers (plus a couple of crew members), or more than 130 feet, holding 40 passengers and 10 crew members. During a windjammer excursion, passengers are usually able to participate in the navigation, be it hoisting a sail or playing captain at the wheel.

During the Camden Windjammer Festival, held Labor Day weekend, crowds gather to watch the region's fleet sail into the harbor, and most boats are open for tours. The schooner-crew talent show later in the weekend is a bit more irreverent than the majestic arrival ceremony.

A windjammer cruise gives you a chance to admire Maine's dramatic coast from the water. They can run anywhere from one to eight days, and day trips usually involve a tour of the harbor and some lighthouse sightseeing. The price—ranging $230–$1,100, depending on length of trip—includes all meals. Trips leave from Camden, Rockland, and Rockport. You can get information on the fleets by contacting one of two windjammer organizations:

Maine Windjammer Association. ☎ *800/807–9463* ⊕ *www.sailmaine-coast.com.*

Maine Windjammer Cruises. A fleet of three handsome vessels offer a variety of cruises. ☎ *207/236–2938, 800/736–7981* ⊕ *www.mainewind-jammercruises.com.*

illustrator whose works were featured in many turn-of-the-20th-century books; his late son Andrew, one of the country's best-known painters; and Andrew's son James, also an accomplished painter, who like his elders before him summers nearby. Galleries in the main building always display some of Andrew Wyeth's works, such as *The Patriot, Witch-craft,* and *Turkey Pond*. The **Wyeth Center,** a former church, shows art by his father and son. The museum's collection also includes works by Fitz Henry Lane, George Bellows, Frank W. Benson, Edward Hopper (as watercolors, they may be "resting"), Louise Nevelson, and Fairfield Porter. Changing exhibits are shown in the **Jamien Morehouse Wing.** The **Farnsworth Homestead,** a handsome circa-1850 Greek Revival dwelling that's part of the museum, retains its original lavish Victorian furnishings and is open late June–mid-October.

In Cushing, a tiny town about 10 miles south of Thomaston on the St. George River, the museum operates the **Olson House,** which is depicted in Andrew Wyeth's famous painting *Christina's World,* as well as in other works by the artist. It's accessible by guided tour only. ✉ *16 Museum St.* ☎ *207/596–6457* ⊕ *www.farnsworthmuseum.org* 🎟 *$12 (July–Sept., free Wed. 5–8).*

FAMILY **Maine Lighthouse Museum.** The lighthouse museum has more than 25 Fresnel lighthouse lenses, as well as a collection of lighthouse artifacts and Coast Guard memorabilia. Permanent exhibits spotlight topics like lighthouse heroines—women who manned the lights when the keepers couldn't—and lightships. ⊠ *1 Park Dr.* ☎ *207/594-3301* ⊕ *www. mainelighthousemuseum.org* ⊠ *$8.*

WHERE TO EAT

$$$$
MEDITERRANEAN
Fodor's Choice
★

✕ **Primo.** Award-winning chef Melissa Kelly and her world-class restaurant have been written up in *Gourmet, Bon Appétit,* and O magazines. In this restored Victorian home, upstairs seating has a funky vibe; downstairs is fancier. No matter where you sit, it's farm-to-table here: the restaurant raises its own chickens and pigs, cures its own meats, produces its own eggs, and grows its own fruits and vegetables. Combining fresh Maine ingredients with Mediterranean influences, the daily menu includes dishes like kale salad with creamy garlic dressing, house-made pasta with local squid, and duck with sweet-and-sour rhubarb chutney. Pastry chef Price Kushner creates delectable desserts like cannoli featuring crushed pistachios and amarena cherries. ⑤ *Average main: $40* ⊠ *2 N. Main St.* ☎ *207/596-0770* ⊕ *www.primorestaurant. com* ☾ *No lunch.*

$
DINER
FAMILY

✕ **Rockland Cafe.** It may not look like much from the outside, but the Rockland Cafe is one of the most popular eateries in town. It's famous for the size of its breakfasts—don't pass up the fish-cake Benedict. If you're a late riser, don't worry: breakfast is served until noon (until 4 November–April). At dinner, the seafood combo of shrimp, scallops, clams, and haddock is excellent, or there's also classic liver and onions. ⑤ *Average main: $15* ⊠ *441 Main St.* ☎ *207/596-7556* ⊕ *www.rocklandcafe.com.*

WHERE TO STAY

$
B&B/INN

▦ **Berry Manor Inn.** Originally the residence of Rockland merchant Charles H. Berry, this 1898 shingle-style B&B sits in Rockland's National Historic District. **Pros:** quiet neighborhood; within walking distance of downtown and the harbor; rooms have TVs. **Cons:** not much of a view. ⑤ *Rooms from: $185* ⊠ *81 Talbot Ave.* ☎ *207/596-7696, 800/774-5692* ⊕ *www.berrymanorinn.com* ⇨ *12 rooms* ⦿ *Breakfast.*

$
B&B/INN

▦ **LimeRock Inn.** In the center of town in Rockland's National Historic District, the LimeRock Inn puts you within easy walking distance of the Farnsworth Museum and many restaurants. **Pros:** all rooms have TVs and DVD players; large in-town lot with gazebo. **Cons:** not on the water. ⑤ *Rooms from: $169* ⊠ *96 Limerock St.* ☎ *207/594-2257, 800/546-3762* ⊕ *www.limerockinn.com* ⇨ *8 rooms* ⦿ *Breakfast.*

$$$
RESORT
FAMILY
Fodor's Choice
★

▦ **Samoset Resort.** Occupying 230 waterfront acres on the Rockland–Rockport town line, this all-encompassing resort offers luxurious rooms and suites with private balconies overlooking the water or the grounds. **Pros:** full-service spa; children's programs; activities from basketball to croquet. **Cons:** no beach. ⑤ *Rooms from: $339* ⊠ *220 Warrenton St., Rockport* ☎ *207/594-2511, 800/341-1650* ⊕ *www.samoset.com* ⇨ *160 rooms, 18 suites, 4 cottages, 72 condos* ⦿ *Breakfast.*

6

WALK FROM ROCKPORT TO CAMDEN

For a stunning walk or drive, take the two-lane paved road that winds up and down on its way out of Rockport, with occasional views of the ocean and the village, en route to Camden. Begin at the intersection of U.S. 1 and Pascal Avenue in Rockport. Take a right off U.S. 1 toward Rockport Harbor, then cross the bridge and go up the hill to Central Street. One block later, bear right on Russell Avenue, which becomes Chestnut Street at the Camden town line; take this all the way to downtown Camden.

Lining the way are some of the most beautiful homes in Maine,

surrounded by an abundance of flora and fauna. Keep an eye out for views of the sparkling ocean, as well as for Aldermere Farm and its Belted Galloway cows. (These rare cows get their name from the foot-wide white "belt" around their middles.) The walk or drive is beautiful at any time of the year, but in fall it's breathtaking. Like the rest of New England, the coast of Maine gets a large number of fall-foliage "leaf peepers," and the reds and golds of the chestnut, birch, and elm trees along this winding route are especially beautiful.

SPORTS AND THE OUTDOORS

Schooner Ladona. A handsome racing yacht built in 1922 (and rebuilt in 1971), recently restored from nose to tail, the *Schooner Ladona* leads chartered trips lasting from a single afternoon up to six days. All trips include breakfast and lunch, including a traditional Downeast lobster bake and beach barbecue, as well as a selection of wines and ports every evening. ⊠ *Rockland* ☎ *800/999–7352, 207/594–4723* ⊕ *www. schoonerladona.com.*

FAMILY **Schooner Heritage.** The newest windjammer in Maine's fleet offers three- to six-day cruises. Captain Doug Lee is a storyteller and author of nautical histories. ⊠ *North End Shipyard, 11 Front St.* ☎ *207/594–8007, 800/648–4544* ⊕ *www.schoonerheritage.com.*

CAMDEN

8 miles north of Rockland.

More than any other town along Penobscot Bay, Camden is the perfect picture-postcard of a Maine coastal village. It is one of the most popular destinations on the Maine Coast, and June–September the town is crowded with visitors—but don't let that scare you away: Camden is worth it. Just come prepared for busy traffic on the town's Main Street, and make reservations for lodging and restaurants well in advance.

Camden is famous not only for its geography, but also for its large fleet of windjammers—relics and replicas from the age of sailing—with their romantic histories and great billowing sails. At just about any hour during warm months you're likely to see at least one windjammer tied up in the harbor. Excursions, whether for an afternoon or a week, are best June–September.

The town's compact size makes it perfect for exploring on foot: shops, restaurants, and galleries line Main Street, as well as the side streets and alleys around the harbor. But be sure to include Camden's residential area on your walking tour. It is quite charming and filled with many fascinating old period houses from the time when Federal, Greek Revival, and Victorian architectural styles were the rage among the wealthy, and many of them are now B&Bs. The Chamber of Commerce, at the Public Landing, can provide you with a walking map. Humped on the north side of town are the Camden Hills; drive or hike to the summit at the state park to enjoy mesmerizing views of the town, harbor, and island-dotted bay.

WORD OF MOUTH

"Camden is an absolute must to visit. A writer for *Yankee* magazine famously declared that the two-plus mile walk between Camden and Rockport is "the most beautiful in the world." Decided to find out for myself, and it is indeed well worth doing."

—bachslunch

GETTING HERE AND AROUND

U.S. 1 becomes Camden's Main Street. Take Route 90 west from U.S. 1 and rejoin it in Warren to bypass Rockland—this is the quickest route south.

ESSENTIALS

Visitor Information Penobscot Bay Regional Chamber of Commerce. ⊠ *Visitor Center, 2 Public Landing* ☎ *207/236–4404, 800/562–2529* ⊕ *www. mainedreamvacation.com.*

FESTIVALS

FAMILY **Windjammer Weekend.** One of the biggest and most colorful events of the year is the Camden Windjammer Festival, which takes place over Labor Day weekend. The harbor is packed with historic vessels, and there are lots of good eats. Visitors can tour the ships. ⊠ *Camden* ☎ *800/223–5459* ⊕ *www.camdenwindjammerfestival.org.*

WHERE TO EAT

$ ✕ **Boynton-McKay Food Co.** At Camden's longtime go-to breakfast and
AMERICAN lunch spot, Boynton-McKay's new owners have updated the tried-and-
FAMILY true menu with foodie touches, while staying true to cherished staples.
Fodor's Choice Order one of their ever-changing breakfast skillets, with eggs perched
★ atop veggies and chorizo, say, or a breakfast salad with poached duck egg, bacon, avocado, and hot-sauce vinaigrette. Pop by for lunch to grab a slow-cooked brisket sandwich with a side of quinoa salad and avocado. Try the house-made kombucha or one of their rotating desserts with a cup of coffee made from locally roasted beans. The walls are covered in local historic documents and objects, and this spot has a retro feel to it, having once been a drugstore and soda fountain. ⑤ *Average main: $10* ⊠ *30 Main St.* ☎ *207/236–2465* ⊕ *www.boynton-mckay. com* ⊗ *Closed Mon.*

The view from Camden Hills is a great way to see Penobscot Bay and the town of Camden.

$ **✕ The Drouthy Bear.** The Drouthy ("thirsty" in old Scots) Bear serves
BRITISH up excellent pub food in an intimate, authentic setting. Tuck into the
FAMILY bangers and mash, or a traditional ploughman's lunch with a Branston
Fodor'sChoice pickle, or pop in for full afternoon tea, complete with a selection of
★ sandwiches, scones, and of course, a pot of hot tea. ⑤ *Average main:*
$10 ✉ *50 Elm St.* ☎ *207/236–2327* ⊕ *www.drouthybear.com.*

$ **✕ Long Grain.** It doesn't look like much from the outside, but don't let
ASIAN FUSION that deter you from this cozy Asian-fusion eatery with an emphasis on
Thai curries and house-made noodles. Chef Ravin Nakjaroen was a
James Beard semifinalist for the Best Northeast Chef Award in 2015.
A very popular restaurant with locals and visitors alike, reservations
are essential, though you might be able to squeeze in at the tiny bar
without one if you're dining solo and don't mind a little chaos. ⑤ *Aver-*
age main: $12 ✉ *13 Elm St.* ☎ *207/236–9001* ⊘ *Closed Sun. and Mon.*
⚠ *Reservations essential.*

$$$$ **✕ Natalie's Restaurant.** One of the most sought-after dining spots in Cam-
MODERN den, Natalie's is the creation of Dutch owners Raymond Brunyanszki
AMERICAN and Oscar Verest, who brought in chefs to create splurge-worthy dishes
Fodor'sChoice in an intimate setting. Located in the cozy and elegant Camden Harbour
★ Inn, the restaurant is fine dining with a distinctly Maine flair, and seasonal ingredients set the tone. Choose from two prix-fixe menus (three
courses for $76 or a seven-course chef's tasting menu for $102), which
may feature cabbage-wrapped Maine monkfish or local lamb with root
veggies. There's also a five-course lobster tasting menu ($109) that may
include lobster with peaches and wasabi cream, or Maine lobster salad
with sunchoke, caviar, and foie gras. The service is phenomenal. In the
lounge, you can order small tapas-style dishes or enjoy a pre-dinner

cocktail in front of the big fireplace. ⑤ *Average main: $76* ✉ *Camden Harbour Inn, 83 Bay View St.* ☎ *207/236–7008* ⊕ *www.nataliesrestaurant.com* ◷ *Closed Sun. Nov.–May. No lunch* ⚏ *Reservations essential.*

WHERE TO STAY

$

B&B/INN

🏨 **Camden Hartstone Inn.** This 1835 mansard-roofed Victorian home has been turned into a plush, sophisticated retreat and a fine culinary destination. **Pros:** luxury in the heart of town; extravagant breakfasts; some private entrances. **Cons:** not on water. ⑤ *Rooms from: $199* ✉ *41 Elm St.* ☎ *207/236–4259* ⊕ *www.hartstoneinn.com* ⇆ *11 rooms, 11 suites* ⏐◉⏐ *Breakfast.*

$$

B&B/INN

FAMILY

🏨 **Lord Camden Inn.** If you want to be in the center of town and near the harbor, look for this handsome brick building with the bright blue-and-white awnings. **Pros:** large Continental breakfast; suitelike "premier" rooms have balconies and sitting areas. **Cons:** traffic noise in front rooms. ⑤ *Rooms from: $259* ✉ *24 Main St.* ☎ *207/236–4325, 800/336–4325* ⊕ *www.lordcamdeninn.com* ⇆ *36 rooms and suites* ⏐◉⏐ *Breakfast.*

$$

B&B/INN

Fodor'sChoice

★

🏨 **Norumbega Inn.** This welcoming B&B is one of the most photographed pieces of real estate in Maine, and once you get a look at its castle-like facade, you'll understand why. **Pros:** eye-popping architecture; beautiful views, close to town. **Cons:** stairs to climb. ⑤ *Rooms from: $269* ✉ *63 High St.* ☎ *207/236–4646, 877/363–4646* ⊕ *www.norumbegainn.com* ⇆ *9 rooms, 2 suites (including 1 penthouse)* ⏐◉⏐ *Breakfast.*

$

B&B/INN

FAMILY

Fodor'sChoice

★

🏨 **Whitehall.** Although the oldest part of the Whitehall is an 1834 white-clapboard sea captain's home, the bright and cheery design characteristic of the Lark Hotel group that recently redesigned and renovated the hotel is decidedly contemporary with nostalgic touches here and there. **Pros:** short walk to downtown and harbor; breakfast entrée choices; beautifully renovated with a design focus. **Cons:** no good water views. ⑤ *Rooms from: $189* ✉ *52 High St.* ☎ *207/236–3391, 800/789–6565* ⊕ *www.whitehall-inn.com* ◷ *Closed mid-Oct.–mid-May* ⇆ *37 rooms, 4 suites* ⏐◉⏐ *Breakfast.*

SPORTS AND THE OUTDOORS

FAMILY

Angelique. Captain Mike and Lynne McHenry have more than three decades' experience on the high seas. Three- to six-day cruise options aboard the *Angelique* include photography workshops and meteor-watching trips, as well as yoga and wellness excursions. ✉ *Camden Harbor* ☎ *800/282–9899* ⊕ *www.sailangelique.com.*

FAMILY

Heron. This schooner, which had a cameo in the movie *The Rum Diary*, offers lunchtime sails, wildlife-watching trips, and sunset cruises. ✉ *Rockport Marine Park, Pascal Ave., Rockport* ☎ *207/236–8605, 800/599–8605* ⊕ *www.sailheron.com.*

FAMILY

Fodor'sChoice

★

Mary Day. Sailing for more than 50 years, the *Mary Day* is the first schooner in Maine built specifically for vacation excursions. Meals are cooked on an antique wood-fired stove. ✉ *Camden Harbor, Atlantic Ave.* ☎ *800/992–2218* ⊕ *www.schoonermaryday.com.*

Olad. Captain Aaron Lincoln runs two-hour trips on both the *Olad* and a smaller sailing vessel, spotting lighthouses, coastal mansions, the occasional seal, and the red-footed puffin cousins known as guillemots.

6

Either boat can also be chartered for longer trips. ⊠ *Camden Harbor, Bay View St.* ☎ *207/236–2323* ⊕ *www.maineschooners.com.*

SHOPPING

Camden's downtown area makes for excellent window-shopping, with lots of adorable and sophisticated boutiques stocking a curated assortment of local products. Most shops and galleries are along Camden's main drag. From the harbor, turn right on Bay View, and walk to Main/High Street. U.S. 1 has lots of names as it runs through Maine. Three are within Camden's town limits—it starts as Elm Street, changes to Main Street, then becomes High Street.

Lily, Lupine & Fern. This full-service florist offers a wonderful array of gourmet foods, chocolates, wines, imported beers, high-quality olive oils, and cheeses. There's a small deck where you can enjoy harbor views and a cup of coffee. ⊠ *11 Main St.* ☎ *207/236–9600* ⊕ *www. lilylupine.com* ☺ *Sun.*

FAMILY
Fodor's Choice
★
Owl and Turtle Bookshop and Cafe. This pint-size but well-stocked independent bookstore has been serving Camden for over 45 years, and has recently added a cozy café. It also hosts author events. It's closed on Monday. ⊠ *33 Bay View St.* ☎ *207/230–7335* ⊕ *www.owlandturtle.com.*

Planet. In this storefront shop you'll find unique clothing, lots of books, and quality toys, many of them made in Maine. ⊠ *10 Main St.* ☎ *207/236–4410.*

Fodor's Choice
★
Swans Island. For gorgeous, handmade blankets, throws, and pillows, as well as wraps and scarves, look no further. All products are made in Maine using natural, heirloom-quality yarns—the expert craftsmanship explains the hefty price tag. ⊠ *2 Bayview St.* ☎ *207/706–7926* ⊕ *www. swansislandcompany.com.*

LINCOLNVILLE

6 miles north of Camden via U.S. 1.

Lincolnville's area of most interest is Lincolnville Beach, where you'll find a few restaurants, the ferry to Islesboro, and a swimming beach that attracts folks from neighboring Camden and Belfast. The village is tiny: you could go through it in less than a minute. Still, it has a history going back to the Revolution, and you can see a small cannon on the beach here (never fired), intended to repel the British in the War of 1812.

GETTING HERE AND AROUND

Lincolnville Beach is on U.S. 1, and the town of Lincolnville Center is inland on Route 173.

WHERE TO EAT

$$
SEAFOOD
FAMILY
✗**Lobster Pound Restaurant.** If you're looking for an authentic place to enjoy a Maine lobster dinner, this is it. This large restaurant has rustic wooden picnic tables outside, an enclosed patio, and two dining rooms with a gift shop in between. Hundreds of live lobsters swim in tanks out back, so feel free to pick your own. There's a full bar, and the wine list includes some local labels. The classic "shore dinner deluxe" consists of lobster stew or fish chowder, steamed clams or mussels, fried clams,

and a 1½-pound lobster, along with sides and dessert. Because this is such a big place, you won't have to wait long, even if it's busy. Right on U.S. 1, next to a small beach, the restaurant has beautiful views. $ *Average main: $22* ⌧ *2521 Atlantic Hwy.* ☎ *207/789 5550* ⊕ *www. lobsterpoundmaine.com* ☉ *Closed Nov.–mid-Apr.*

BELFAST

13 miles north of Lincolnville via U.S. 1.

Lots of Maine coastal towns like to think of themselves as the prettiest little town in the state, and any judge would be spoiled for choice. Charming Belfast (originally to be named Londonderry) is a strong contender, with a beautiful waterfront; an old and interesting main street rising from the harbor; a delightful array of B&Bs, restaurants, and shops; and friendly townsfolk. The downtown even has old-fashioned street lamps, which set the streets aglow at night.

GETTING HERE AND AROUND

U.S. 1 runs through Belfast as it travels up the coast. From Interstate 95, take U.S. 3 in Augusta to get here. The highways meet in Belfast, heading north. The information center has a large array of magazines, guidebooks, maps, and brochures that cover the entire Mid-Coast. It also can provide you with a free walking-tour brochure that describes the various historic buildings.

ESSENTIALS

Visitor Information Belfast Area Chamber of Commerce. ⌧ *93 Main St.* ☎ *207/338–1975* ⊕ *www.belfastmaine.org.*

EXPLORING

Belfast is a funky coastal town, where the streets are lined with eclectic boutiques and a decidedly laissez-faire attitude presides. There is still evidence of the wealth of the mid-1800s, when Belfast was home to a number of business magnates, shipbuilders, ship captains, and so on. Their mansions still stand along High Street and in the residential area above it, offering excellent examples of Greek Revival and Federal-style architecture. In fact, the town has one of the best showcases of Greek Revival homes in the state. Don't miss the "White House," where High and Church streets merge several blocks south of downtown.

WHERE TO EAT

$$
AMERICAN
FAMILY

✕ **Darby's Restaurant and Pub.** This charming, old-fashioned restaurant and bar is very popular with locals. With pressed-tin ceilings, it has been a bar or a restaurant since it was built in the 1890s. On the walls are works for sale by local artists and old murals of Belfast scenes. Pad thai and chicken with chili and cashews are signature dishes. The menu also has hearty homemade soups and sandwiches and classic fish 'n' chips. $ *Average main: $23* ⌧ *155 High St.* ☎ *207/338–2339* ⊕ *www. darbysrestaurant.com.*

6

$$$
SEAFOOD
FAMILY
Fodor's Choice
★

✗**Young's Lobster Pound.** The corrugated-steel building looks more like a fish cannery than a restaurant, but it's one of the best places for an authentic Maine lobster dinner. It sits right on the water's edge, across the harbor from downtown Belfast. When you first walk in, you'll see numerous tanks of live lobsters of varying size. The traditional meal here is the "shore dinner," consisting of clam chowder or lobster stew, steamed clams or mussels, a 1½-pound boiled lobster, corn on the cob, and chips. Surf-and-turf dinners and hot dogs are popular, too. It's BYOB. Order your dinner at the counter, then find a table inside or on the deck. Don't leave your outdoor table unattended—seagulls *love* lobster. $ *Average main: $25* ✉ *2 Fairview St., off U.S. 1* ☎ *207/338–1160* ⊕ *youngslobsterpound.webs.com* ⊗ *Takeout only Jan.–Mar.*

NIGHTLIFE

FAMILY **Rollie's Bar & Grill.** Up a bit from the harbor, Rollie's Bar & Grill has been in business since 1972. The vintage bar is from a 19th-century sailing ship. Rollie's is the town's most popular watering hole, especially among sports fans who come to watch the big game. It just may serve the best hamburgers in the state, and you'll see families crop up around dinnertime. Food is served until midnight on Friday and Saturday and there's an excellent happy hour weekdays 3–6. ✉ *37 Main St.* ☎ *207/338–4502* ⊕ *www.rollies.me.*

SEARSPORT

6 miles north of Belfast via U.S. 1.

Searsport is well-known as the antiques and flea-market capital of Maine, and with good reason: the Antique Mall alone, on U.S. 1 just north of town, is home to some 60 dealers, and flea markets during the visitor season line both sides of U.S. 1.

Searsport also has a rich history of shipbuilding and seafaring. In the early to mid-1800s there were 10 shipbuilding facilities in Searsport, and the population of the town was about 1,000 people more than it is today, and jobs were plentiful. By the mid-1800s Searsport was home to more than 200 sailing-ship captains.

GETTING HERE AND AROUND

Downtown Searsport is right along U.S. 1, as is much of the town, which doesn't have lots of side streets. Just north of here in Stockton Springs, U.S. 1A leads to Bangor.

EXPLORING

FAMILY **Penobscot Marine Museum.** Just off Main Street, this downtown museum
Fodor's Choice explores the maritime culture of the Penobscot Bay region. Exhibits of
★ artifacts and paintings are spread throughout six nearby buildings, most dating to the first half of the 19th century, and one of the former sea captain's homes has period rooms. Outstanding marine art includes a notable collection of works by Thomas and James Buttersworth. There are photos of local sea captains, model ships, lots of scrimshaw, navigational instruments, and tools from the area's history of logging, granite mining, and ice cutting. There are also exhibits just for kids. ✉ *2 Church St.* ☎ *207/548–2529* ⊕ *www.penobscotmarinemuseum.org* ✉ *$12.*

SHOPPING

Searsport Antique Mall. The area's biggest collection of antiques is in the Searsport Antique Mall, which has more than 60 dealers. ✉ *149 E. Main St.* ☎ *207/548-2610.*

BUCKSPORT

9 miles north of Searsport via U.S. 1.

The stunning Penobscot Narrows Bridge, spanning the Penobscot River, makes Bucksport, a town founded in 1763, well worth a visit, even if you only stop while passing through to points north. Fort Knox, Maine's largest historic fort, overlooks the town from across the river. There are magnificent views of the imposing granite structure from the pleasant riverfront walkway downtown.

GETTING HERE AND AROUND

After you pass over the spectacular Penobscot Narrows Bridge onto Verona Island driving north on U.S. 1, you cross another bridge into Bucksport; turn left for downtown and right to continue on the highway. Route 15 heads north to Bangor from here.

EXPLORING

FAMILY **Penobscot Narrows Bridge & Observatory Tower/Fort Knox Historic Site.**
Fodor's Choice An "engineering marvel" is how experts describe the 2,120-foot-long
★ Penobscot Narrows Bridge, which opened in 2006 and which is taller than the Statue of Liberty. It's certainly beautiful to look at—from the surrounding countryside it pops up on the horizon like the towers of a fairy-tale castle. Spanning the Penobscot River across from Bucksport, the bridge's 437-foot observation tower is the tallest in the world; an elevator shoots you to the top. Don't miss it—the panoramic views, which take in the hilly countryside and the river as it widens into Penobscot Bay, are breathtaking. In summer, the observatory often offers moonrise viewings.

Also here is Fort Knox, the largest historic fort in Maine. It was built between 1844 and 1869, when, despite a treaty with Britain settling boundary disputes, invasion was still a concern—after all, the British controlled this region during both the Revolutionary War and the War of 1812. The fort never saw any real action, but it was used for troop training and as a garrison during the Civil War and the Spanish-American War. Visitors are welcome to explore the many rooms and passageways. Guided tours are given daily during the summer and several days a week in the shoulder seasons. ✉ *711 Ft. Knox Rd., off U.S. 1, Prospect* ☎ *207/469-6553* ⊕ *www.fortknox.maineguide.com* ✉ *Fort $4.50, fort and observatory $7.*

BANGOR

122 miles north of Portland via I-95, 19 miles north of Bucksport via Rte. 15.

The state's second-largest metropolitan area (Portland is the largest), Bangor is about 20 miles from the coast and is the unofficial capital of northern Maine. Back in the 19th century, the most important product and export of the "Queen City" was lumber from the state's vast North Woods. Now, because of its airport, Bangor has become a gateway to Mount Desert Island, Bar Harbor, and Acadia National Park. Along the revitalized waterfront, the American Folk Festival draws big crowds on the last full weekend in August, and an outdoor stage attracts top bands and musicians throughout the summer.

GETTING HERE AND AROUND

Interstate 95 has five Bangor exits: 45–49. U.S. 1A loops up to Bangor from Stockton Springs and Ellsworth, near Bar Harbor, and connects with Interstate 395 on the western side of the Bangor area.

ESSENTIALS

Visitor Information Greater Bangor Convention & Visitors Bureau. ✉ *33 Harlow St.* ☎ *207/947–5205, 800/916–6673* ⊕ *www.bangorcvb.org.*

EXPLORING

FAMILY **Maine Discovery Museum.** Three floors with more than 60 interactive exhibits let kids explore the state's ecosystem in Nature Trails, learn about other cultures in TradeWinds, step into classic children's books like *Charlotte's Web*—all written by Maine authors—in Booktown, and unearth dinosaur "bones" in DINO DIG. There's also drop-in art studio and daily programs on art and other topics. ■**TIP**➔ **Visitors to Acadia National Park often head here on a rainy day.** ✉ *74 Main St.* ☎ *207/262–7200* ⊕ *www.mainediscoverymuseum.org* ⌂ *$7.50.*

▮ NEED A BREAK

Friars' Bakehouse. Locals say this place has the best whoopie pies in the Bangor area, and its yeasty breads are equally prized. The bakery and restaurant are run by three Franciscan friars, one of whom spent time in various highly regarded culinary programs. ✉ *21 Central St.* ☎ *207/947–3770.*

Governor's Restaurant & Bakery. This old family-friendly standby, with six locations including Bangor, is famed for its peanut-butter whoopie pies as well as the classic black-and-white, and can grant any special flavor combinations by request with 24-hour notice. ✉ *643 Broadway* ☎ *207/947–3113* ⊕ *www.governorsrestaurant.com.*

WHERE TO STAY

$ ⊞ **Lucerne Inn.** Nestled in the mountains, the Lucerne Inn overlooks
HOTEL beautiful Phillips Lake. **Pros:** golf course across the road; lake views. **Cons:** most rooms are dated. ⑤ *Rooms from: $109* ✉ *2517 Main Rd., Dedham* ☎ *207/843–5123, 800/325–5123* ⊕ *www.lucerneinn.com* ⤹ *21 rooms, 10 suites* ⑩ *Breakfast.*

SHOPPING

Fodor's Choice **The Rock and Art Shop.** With things like taxidermied bats and terraria
★ filled with tropical plants mixed in among books, stationery, jewelry, and natural history objects this is no ordinary store: it's a veritable cabinet of curiosities, and a delight for the serious shopper and the window-shopper alike. The store has rotating exhibitions of local art that is also for sale. You'll find their other outposts in Bar Harbor,

Ellsworth, and just outside Ellsworth off Route 1A. ✉ *36 Central St.*
☎ *207/947–2205* ⊕ *www.therockandartshop.com.*

THE BLUE HILL PENINSULA

If you want to see unspoiled Down East Maine landscapes, explore art
galleries, savor exquisite meals, or simply enjoy life at an unhurried
pace, you should be quite content on the Blue Hill Peninsula.

The large peninsula juts south into Penobscot Bay. Not far from the
mainland are the islands of Little Deer Isle, Deer Isle, and, at the latter's
tip, the picturesque fishing town of Stonington. A twisting labyrinth of
roads winds through blueberry barrens and around picturesque coves,
linking the towns of Blue Hill, Brooksville, Sedgwick, and Brooklin.
Blue Hill and Castine are the area's primary business hubs. Painters,
photographers, sculptors, and other artists are drawn to the peninsula;
you can find more than 20 galleries on Deer Isle and in Stonington and
at least half as many on the mainland. With its small inns, charming
B&Bs, and outstanding restaurants scattered across the area, the Blue
Hill Peninsula may just persuade you to leave the rest of the coastline
to the tourists.

VISITOR INFORMATION

Contacts Blue Hill Peninsula Chamber of Commerce. ✉ *16 South St., Suite
B, Blue Hill* ☎ *207/374–3242* ⊕ *www.bluehillpeninsula.org.* **Deer Isle–Stonington Chamber of Commerce.** ✉ *Main St., and Rte. 15, Deer Isle* ☎ *207/348–
6124* ⊕ *www.deerisle.com.*

CASTINE

18 miles north of Bucksport via U.S. 1 and Rtes. 175 and 166.

A summer destination for more than 100 years, Castine is a well-preserved seaside village that serves as an excellent base for exploring the
Blue Hill area and Mount Desert Island.

GETTING HERE AND AROUND

From U.S. 1 in Orland, near Bucksport, Route 175 heads south along
the Penobscot River toward Castine. Continue on Route 166 at the
crossroads of West Penobscot, and after a bit you have the option
of taking Route 166A into the village. Routes 166 and 166A form a
loop—taking either will get you to Castine—but the latter is especially
scenic, passing expansive Wadsworth Cove at the mouth of the river as
it enters its namesake bay.

EXPLORING

Federal- and Greek Revival–style architecture, rich history, and spectacular views of Penobscot Bay make Castine an ideal spot to spend
a day or two. Explore its lively harbor front, two small museums (the
Wilson Museum and the Castine Historical Society), and the ruins of
a British fort. You can't miss the oversize historical signs throughout
the village.

An excellent self-guided walking tour is available at local businesses and the historical society. For a nice stroll, park your car at the landing and walk up Main Street toward the white Trinitarian Congregational Church. Turn right on Court Street and go one block to the town common. Among the white-clapboard buildings ringing this green space are the Ives House (once the summer home of poet Robert Lowell), the Adams School, the former Abbott School (home to the historical society), and the Unitarian Church, capped by a whimsical belfry. From lower Main Street, head out Perkins Street on foot or by bike or car. You'll pass summer "cottage" mansions and the Wilson Museum on the way to Dyces Head Lighthouse (private), where a path leads to cliffs (careful here) fronting Penobscot Bay, site of a major Revolutionary War battle. You can return on Battle Avenue to make a loop.

WHERE TO EAT

$$

AMERICAN

FAMILY

✕ **Dennett's Wharf.** Originally built as a sail-rigging loft in the early 1800s, this longtime favorite is a good place for oysters and fresh seafood of all kinds. The waterfront restaurant also serves burgers, sandwiches, and light fare. There are over 20 microbrews on tap, including Dennett's tasty Wharf Rat Ale. Eat in the dining room or outside on the deck: there are covered and open sections, another bar, and Adirondack chairs if you just stop by for a brew. ⑤ *Average main: $18* ⊠ *15 Sea St.* ☎ *207/326–9045* ⊕ *www.dennettswharf.net.*

SPORTS AND THE OUTDOORS

Castine Kayak International Adventures. At Eaton's Wharf, Castine Kayak Adventures operates tours run by owner Karen Francoeur, a Registered Maine Guide. Sign up for a half day of kayaking along the shore, a full day of kayaking in Penobscot Bay, or for nighttime trips—paddling stirs up a type of bioluminescent phytoplankton, causing them to light up like fireflies as they shoot through the water. The company also offers overnight kayak camping trips and rents mountain bikes and kayaks. ⊠ *Eaton's Wharf, 17 Sea St.* ☎ *207/866–3506* ⊕ *www.castinekayak.com.*

BLUE HILL

20 miles east of Castine via Rtes. 166, 175, and 176.

Nestled snugly between 943-foot Blue Hill Mountain and Blue Hill Bay, the village of Blue Hill sits right beside its harbor. About 30 miles from Acadia National Park, Blue Hill makes for a more laid-back base for exploring the Mount Desert Island area, but bear in mind that 30 miles can take at least twice as long to travel with heavy traffic in summertime. Originally known for its granite quarries, copper mines, and shipbuilding, today the town is known for its pottery and galleries, bookstores, antiques shops, and studios that line its streets. The Blue Hill Fair (⊕ *www.bluehillfair.com*), held Labor Day weekend, is a tradition in these parts, with agricultural exhibits, food, rides, and entertainment. A charming little park with a great playground is tucked away near the harbor downtown.

GETTING HERE AND AROUND

From U.S. 1 in Orland, Route 15 heads south to Blue Hill. To continue north on the highway, take Route 172 north to Ellsworth.

WHERE TO EAT AND STAY

$$$
MODERN
AMERICAN
Fodor's Choice
★

✕ **Arborvine.** Glowing gas fireplaces, period antiques, exposed beams, and hardwood floors covered with Oriental rugs distinguish the four candlelit dining areas in this renovated Cape Cod–style house. Begin with a salad of mixed greens, sliced beets, and pears with blue cheese crumbled on top. For your entrée, choose from seasonal dishes such as crispy duck with rhubarb and lime glaze, or roasted rack of lamb with a basil-and-pine-nut crust—fresh fish dishes are also superb. Save room for dessert; the ice cream is homemade. Return when you're in a more casual mood: like the restaurant, the adjacent nautical-theme DeepWater Brew Pub serves dishes made with organic ingredients to go with its own beer. It's housed in an inviting, historic barn that opens to lawn seating come summer. $ *Average main: $31* ✉ *33 Tenney Hill* ☎ *207/374–2119* ⊕ *www.arborvine.com* ⊙ *No lunch.*

$$
B&B/INN

⊡ **Blue Hill Inn.** One side of this Federal-style inn was built as a home in 1835, but it soon became lodging, adding a wing with a matching facade in the 1850s. **Pros:** plenty of charm; modern suites with kitchens in separate building; 30 miles from Acadia National Park. **Cons:** some narrow stairs and thin walls consistent with historic property. $ *Rooms from: $225* ✉ *40 Union St.* ☎ *207/374–2844* ⊕ *www.bluehillinn.com* ⊙ *Closed Nov.–mid-May, except for the Cape House Suite and the Studio* ⊃ *10 rooms, 3 suites* ⦿ *Breakfast.*

SHOPPING

ART GALLERIES

Blue Hill Bay Gallery. This gallery sells oil and watercolor landscapes and seascapes of Maine and New England from the 19th through the 21st century. It also carries the proprietor's own photography. Call ahead in the off-season. ✉ *11 Tenney Hill* ☎ *207/374–5773* ⊕ *www. bluehillbaygallery.com.*

POTTERY

Rackliffe Pottery. In business since 1969, this shop sells colorful pottery made with lead-free glazes. You can choose between water pitchers, serving platters, tea-and-coffee sets, and sets of canisters, among other lovely items. ✉ *132 Ellsworth Rd.* ☎ *888/631–3321, 207/374–2297* ⊕ *www.rackliffepottery.com.*

WINE

Blue Hill Wine Shop. In a restored barn at the rear of one of Blue Hill's earliest houses, the Blue Hill Wine Shop carries more than 1,200 carefully selected wines. Coffee, tea, cheeses, and prewrapped sandwiches are also available. ✉ *138 Main St.* ☎ *207/374–2161* ⊕ *www.bluehillwineshop.com.*

6

DEER ISLE VILLAGE

16 miles south of Blue Hill via Rtes. 176 and 15.

Around Deer Isle Village, thick woods give way to tidal coves. Stacks of lobster traps populate the backyards of shingled houses, and dirt roads lead to secluded summer cottages. This region is prized by artists, and studios and galleries are plentiful.

GETTING HERE AND AROUND

From Sedgwick, Route 15 crosses a 1930s suspension bridge onto Little Deer Isle and continues on to the larger Deer Isle.

EXPLORING

Edgar M. Tennis Preserve. Enjoy several miles of woodland and shore trails at the Edgar M. Tennis Preserve. Look for hawks, eagles, and ospreys and wander among old apple trees, fields of wildflowers, and ocean-polished rocks. ⊠ *Tennis Rd., Deer Isle* ☎ *207/348–2455* ⊕ *www. islandheritagetrust.org* ⌲ *Free.*

Haystack Mountain School of Crafts. Want to learn a new craft? This school 6 miles from Deer Isle Village offers one- and two-week courses for people of all skill levels in crafts such as blacksmithing, basketry, print-making, and weaving. Artisans from around the world present free evening lectures throughout summer. Tours of the school and studios are available on Wednesday. ⊠ *89 Haystack School Dr., off Rte. 15, Deer Isle* ☎ *207/348–2306* ⊕ *www.haystack-mtn.org* ⌲ *Tours $5.*

SHOPPING

Nervous Nellie's Jams and Jellies. Jams and jellies are made right on the property at Nervous Nellie's. There is a tearoom with homemade goodies, and also a fanciful sculpture garden with everything from knights to witches to a lobster and a flamingo. They are the works of sculptor Peter Beerits, who operates Nervous Nellie's with his wife. ⊠ *598 Sunshine Rd., off Rte. 15, Deer Isle* ☎ *207/348–6182, 800/777–6845* ⊕ *www. nervousnellies.com.*

STONINGTON

6 miles south of Deer Isle.

Stonington is at the southern end of Route 15, which has helped it to retain its small-town flavor. The boutiques and galleries lining Main Street cater mostly to out-of-towners, but the village remains a fishing and lobstering community at heart. The principal activity is at the waterfront, where you can watch boats arrive with the day's catch. The sloped island that rises to the south is Isle au Haut, which contains a remote section of Acadia National Park.

GETTING HERE AND AROUND

From Deer Isle village, Route 15 runs all the way to Stonington at the tip of the island. There is a ferry from here to Isle au Haut.

EXPLORING

Deer Isle Granite Museum. This tiny museum documents Stonington's quarrying tradition. The museum's centerpiece is a working model of quarrying operations on Crotch Island and the town of Stonington at the turn of the last century. Granite was quarried here for Rockefeller Plaza in New York City and for the John F. Kennedy Memorial in Arlington National Cemetery, among other well-known structures. ⊠ *51 Main St.* ☎ *207/367–6331* *July and Aug. only* ⊕ *deerislegranitemuseum.wordpress.com* ⛶ *Free.*

SPORTS AND THE OUTDOORS

Old Quarry Ocean Adventures. Departing Webb Cove and passing Stonington Harbor en route to the outer islands, Captain Bill Baker's refurbished lobster boat takes visitors on puffin-watching, whale-watching, sunset, and lighthouse trips. There's also a three-hour Sightseeing and Natural History Eco-Cruise that goes by Crotch Island, which has one of the area's two active stone quarries, and stops at Green Island, where you can take a dip in a water-filled quarry. There are also day trips for biking or kayaking on nearby islands, including Isle au Haut. ⊠ *130 Settlement Rd.* ☎ *207/367–8977* ⊕ *www.oldquarry.com.*

ISLE AU HAUT

6 miles south of Stonington via ferry.

Isle au Haut thrusts its steeply ridged back out of the sea south of Stonington. French explorer Samuel D. Champlain discovered Isle au Haut—or "High Island"—in 1604, but heaps of shells suggest that native populations lived on or visited the island prior to his arrival. The island is accessible only by mail boat, but the 45-minute journey is well worth the effort. Acadia National Park extends to cover part of the island, with miles of trails, and the boat will drop visitors off there in peak season. The island has some seasonal rentals but no inns. With only three stores, you wouldn't think folks would come here to shop, but some do, as the island is home to Black Dinah Chocolatiers (☎ *207/335–5010* ⊕ *www.blackdinahchocolatiers.com*), which makes artful high-end chocolates and has a small café.

GETTING HERE AND AROUND

There's one main road here: it circles the island and goes through the Acadia National Park section. Locals have different names for sections of the road.

Isle au Haut Boat Services (☎ *207/367–5193* ⊕ *www.isleauhaut.com*) operates daily mail-boat ferry service out of Stonington. During the summer season, trips increase from two to five Monday–Saturday and from one to two on Sunday. From mid-June until late September, the boat also stops at Duck Harbor, in the island section of Acadia National Park (it will not unload bicycles, kayaks, or canoes). Ferry service is scaled back in the fall, then returns to the regular or "winter" schedule.

QUICK BITES

Maine Lobster Lady. Come summer, this former island innkeeper sells yummy and quick eats, many of them made with fish from local waters and her own organic garden produce. Her "food truck" (actually a tow trailer) is parked near the ranger's station at the Acadia National Park section on Isle au Haut. She sells lobster rolls, naturally, but you might try her shrimp-salad sandwich with paprika-dill mayo on a homemade roll, or shrimp puffs served in a paper cone. ⊠ *Off Main Rd., Isle Au Haut* ☎ *207/335–5141 in summer, 207/669–2751* ⊕ *www.mainelobsterlady.com.*

6

ACADIA NATIONAL PARK AND MOUNT DESERT ISLAND

With some of the most dramatic and varied scenery on the Maine Coast—and home to Maine's only national park—Mount Desert Island (pronounced "dessert" by locals) is Maine's most popular tourist destination, attracting well over 2 million visitors a year. Much of the approximately 12-by-15-mile island belongs to Acadia National Park. You can take a scenic drive along the island's rocky coastline, whose stark cliffs rise from the ocean. A network of old carriage roads lets you explore Acadia's wooded interior, filled with birds and other wildlife, and trails for hikers of all skill levels lead to rounded mountaintops, providing views of Frenchman and Blue Hill bays and beyond. Ponds and lakes beckon you to swim, fish, or boat, and ferries and charter boats provide a different perspective on the island and a chance to explore the outer islands.

Mount Desert Island has four different towns, each with its own personality. The town of Bar Harbor is on the northeastern corner of the island and includes the little villages of Hulls Cove, Salisbury Cove, and Town Hill. Aside from Acadia, Bar Harbor is the major tourist destination here, with plenty of lodging, dining, and shopping. The town of Mount Desert, in the middle of the island, has four main villages: Somesville, Seal Harbor, Otter Creek, and Northeast Harbor, a summer haven for the very wealthy. Southwest Harbor includes the smaller village of Manset south of the village center. Tremont is at the southernmost tip of the island and stretches up the western shore. It includes the villages of Bass Harbor, Bernard, and Seal Cove. Yes, Mount Desert Island is a place with three personalities: the hustling, bustling tourist mecca of Bar Harbor; the "quiet side" on the western half; and the vast natural expanse of Acadia National Park. But though less congested and smaller, Northeast Harbor and Southwest Harbor are home to inns, campgrounds, restaurants, ferries, galleries, and small museums.

ESSENTIALS

VISITOR INFORMATION

Bar Harbor Chamber of Commerce. ✉ *1201 Bar Harbor Rd., Trenton* ☎ *800/345–4617, 207/288–5103* ⊕ *www.barharborinfo.com.*

Mount Desert Chamber of Commerce. ✉ *18 Harbor Dr., Northeast Harbor* ☎ *207/276–5040* ⊕ *www.mountdesertchamber.org.*

Mt. Desert Island Information Center at Thompson Island. Sponsored by several Mount Desert Island communities as well as Acadia National Park, the Mt. Desert Island Information Center is along Route 3 just before it crosses to Mount Desert Island. The center is loaded with pamphlets about island tours, restaurants, inns, and attractions, including Acadia National Park. You can buy park passes here, and the staff includes a park ranger. ✉ *1319 Bar Harbor Rd., Trenton* ☎ *207/288–3411.*

Acadia National Park and Mount Desert Island

Marlboro

Union River Bay

230

3

Lamoine State Park

East Lamoine

Trenton

230

Eastern Bay

Frenchman Bay

Salisbury Cove

3

Hulls Cove Visitor Center

198

Town Hill

3

BAR IS.

○ **Bar Harbor**

233

Park Loop Road

SEASONAL FERRY TO WINTER HARBOR

Western Bay

Somesville

Eagle Lake

Acadia National Park

◆

Abbe Museum

BARTLETT ISLAND

Pretty Marsh

Somes Sound

Echo Lake

Cadillac Mountain ◆

Park Loop Rd.

Bubble Pond

3

198

Jordan Pond

Loop Rd.

3

Sand Beach

Long Pond

Echo Lake Beach

Thunder Hole ◆

102

Seal Cove Pond

Otter Point

102

Seal Cove

Northeast Harbor

BEAR ISLAND

Seal Harbor

3

Southwest Harbor

SUTTON ISLAND

Eastern Way

West Tremont

Manset

Islesford

LITTLE CRANBERRY ISLAND

Bernard

Cranberry Isles

Bass Harbor

BAKER ISLAND

Blue Hill Bay

GREAT CRANBERRY ISLAND

Bass Harbor Head Light

Atlantic Ocean

Atlantic

SWANS ISLAND

FERRY TO FRENCHBORO

0   2 mi

0   2 km

BAR HARBOR

34 miles from Blue Hill via Rte. 172 and U.S. 1.

A resort town since the 19th century, Bar Harbor is the artistic, culinary, and social center of Mount Desert Island, and it serves visitors to Acadia National Park with inns, motels, and restaurants. Around the turn of the last century the island was known as a summer haven for the very rich because of its cool breezes. The wealthy built lavish mansions throughout the island, many of which were destroyed in a huge fire that devastated the island in 1947—a good number of those that survived have been converted into businesses. In Bar Harbor, shops are clustered along Main, Mount Desert, and Cottage streets; take a stroll down West Street, a National Historic District, where you can see some fine old houses.

THE EARLY BIRD GETS THE SUN

During your visit to Mount Desert, pick a day when you are willing to get up very early, around 4:30 or 5 am. Drive with a friend, or a camera with a timer, to the top of Cadillac Mountain in Acadia National Park, and stand on the highest rock you can find and wait for the sun to come up. When it does, have your friend, or your camera, take a photo of you looking at it and label the photo something like, "The first person in the country to see the sun come up today."

The island and the surrounding Gulf of Maine are home to a great variety of wildlife: whales, seals, eagles, falcons, ospreys, and puffins (though not right offshore here), and forest dwellers such as deer, foxes, coyotes, and beavers.

GETTING HERE AND AROUND

In Ellsworth, Route 3 leaves U.S. 1 and heads to Bar Harbor. In season, free Island Explorer buses (☎ 207/667–5796 ⊕ *www.exploreacadia. com*) take visitors to Acadia National Park and other island towns. There is also a passenger ferry to Winter Harbor across Frenchman Bay.

EXPLORING

FAMILY **Abbe Museum.** This small museum dedicated to Maine's indigenous tribes—collectively known as the Wabanaki—is the state's only Smithsonian-affiliated facility. The year-round archaeology exhibit displays spear points, bone tools, and other artifacts found around Mount Desert Island. Rotating exhibits often feature contemporary Native American art, and there are frequent demonstrations of everything from boatbuilding to basket weaving. Call on rainy days for impromptu children's activities. A second location, inside the park at Sieur de Monts Spring, open only during the summer, features artifacts from the earliest digs around the island. ⊠ *26 Mount Desert St.* ☎ *207/288–3519* ⊕ *www. abbemuseum.org* ⊠ *$8.*

Long ramps on Maine's many docks make it easier to access boats at either high or low tide.

WHERE TO EAT

$$$ ✕**Burning Tree.** One of the top restaurants in Maine, this easy-to-miss
SEAFOOD gem with a festive dining room is on Route 3 between Bar Harbor and
Fodor's Choice Otter Creek. The seasonal menu emphasizes freshly caught seafood, and
★ seven species of fish are offered virtually every day—all from the Gulf
of Maine. Monkfish is always on the menu: you may find it sautéed,
glazed with sweet chili sauce, and served with Thai-flavored eggplant
and coconut rice. Oven-poached cod and stuffed gray sole are two
other signature dishes. There are always two or three vegetarian options
using organic produce, much of it from the owners' garden. ⑤ *Average
main: $25* ✉ *69 Otter Creek Dr., 5 miles from Bar Harbor, 7 miles
from Northeast Harbor, Otter Creek* ☎ *207/288–9331* ⊙ *Closed mid-
Oct.–mid-June. No lunch* ⌕ *Reservations essential.*

$$ ✕**Havana.** A lively yet intimate spot, Havana serves Latin-inspired
CUBAN dishes paired with robust wines right in the middle of downtown Bar
Fodor's Choice Harbor. In the summer, have a bite on their patio; during winter months,
★ dine in a pleasant indoor space with a modern aesthetic, featuring clean
lines and cheery colors. Don't miss the Spanish tortilla, served with
a dollop of garlic aioli and chili oil, as well as the excellent seafood
paella, which includes lobster, mussels, mahogany clams, shrimp, scallops, chorizo, tomatoes, peppers, and smoked chicken, piled in with
fragrant saffron rice. You'd do well to finish off your meal with a serving of affogato made with MDI vanilla-bean ice cream and a side of
dulce de leche. ⑤ *Average main: $24* ✉ *318 Main St.* ☎ *207/288–2822*
⊕ *www.havanamaine.com.*

$ ✕ **Lazy Lobster.** This breakfast and lunch spot in the middle of town
SEAFOOD serves some of the freshest lobster around at a reasonable price. The full
FAMILY breakfast here features a fabulous lobster Benedict, as well as lobster
omelets and crêpes. At lunch you can go for a whole lobster or a tasty,
no-fuss lobster roll, or tuck into their classic clam chowder or lobster
bisque. If seafood isn't your thing, they also have nice panini, wraps,
and flatbreads, as well as an impressive selection of craft beers. $ *Aver-
age main: $17* ⊠ *16 Mount Desert St.* ☎ *207/288–1066.*

$$$ ✕ **Mâche Bistro.** This lively restaurant serves eclectic French bistro fare
FRENCH FUSION in a hip space with dim lighting and a modern aesthetic. Share some
tapas-style appetizers, like the black-truffle salami with truffle-whipped
brie, the duck-confit tartine, or the roasted beets with burrata cheese,
or go for something more substantial like steak frites with truffle fries
or seared Atlantic scallops with fennel salad, caper relish, and charred
onion. If you're looking for a spot to have an intimate tête-à-tête this
isn't the place, given the noise level. $ *Average main: $28* ⊠ *321 Main
St.* ☎ *207/288–0447* ⊕ *www.machebistro.com* ☾ *No lunch.*

WHERE TO STAY

$$ ▦ **Bar Harbor Grand Hotel.** Taking one of the well-appointed, modern
HOTEL rooms in this renovated historic building puts you right in the middle
of Bar Harbor, just a stone's throw from lively restaurants, cafés, and
gift shops. **Pros:** excellent center-of-town location; breakfast included;
good value. **Cons:** street noise; decor could use updates. $ *Rooms from:
$245* ⊠ *269 Main St.* ☎ *207/288–5226* ⊕ *www.barharborgrand.com*
☾ *Closed mid-Nov.–Mar.* ⤳ *71 rooms* ⦿ *Breakfast.*

$$ ▦ **Bar Harbor Inn & Spa.** Originally established in the late 1800s as a
HOTEL men's social club, this waterfront inn has rooms spread among three
Fodor's Choice buildings on well-landscaped grounds. **Pros:** views of the beach and
★ harbor; some two-level suites. **Cons:** dated room decor and bathrooms;
views often include cruise ships in port; service can be hit or miss.
$ *Rooms from: $229* ⊠ *1 Newport Dr.* ☎ *207/288–3351, 800/248–
3351* ⊕ *www.barharborinn.com* ☾ *Closed late Nov.–mid-Mar.* ⤳ *138
rooms, 15 suites* ⦿ *Breakfast.*

$ ▦ **The Colony Cottages on Frenchman's Bay.** These clean, old-fashioned cot-
HOTEL tages are situated on a sweeping lawn that overlooks Frenchman's Bay.
FAMILY Just a five-minute drive or bus ride away from Bar Harbor and Acadia
National Park, this is an ideal base for exploring Mount Desert Island.
Pros: views of Frenchman's Bay; private beach access; good value. **Cons:**
five-minute drive to center of town and Acadia. $ *Rooms from: $150*
⊠ *20 Rte. 3, Hulls Cove* ☎ *207/288–3383* ⊕ *www.colonyathullscove.
com* ⤳ *31 cottages* ⦿ *No meals.*

$ ▦ **Primrose Place.** Recently renovated guest rooms at Primrose Place
HOTEL have retained their quaint local charm. **Pros:** centrally located. **Cons:**
two-night minimum in high season; basic rooms; renovated motel-style
lodgings are not for everyone. $ *Rooms from: $175* ⊠ *51 Holland Ave.*
☎ *207/288–3771* ⊕ *www.primroseplacebarharbor.com* ⤳ *10 rooms*
⦿ *No meals.*

$$
B&B/INN
FAMILY
Fodor'sChoice
★

Ullikana Inn. Nestled in a quiet spot secluded from the chaos of Bar Harbor proper, this quaint inn has elegant but cozy guest rooms, many of which have fireplaces, snug and sophisticated sitting areas, as well as private balconies overlooking the water. **Pros:** generous gourmet breakfast included; outdoor patio with landscaped gardens; intimate atmosphere; water views; quiet central location. **Cons:** no pool. $ *Rooms from: $205* ✉ *16 The Field* ☎ *207/288 9552* ⊕ *www.ullikana.com* ⊃ *10 rooms* ⦿ *Breakfast.*

$
HOTEL

Wonder View Inn. Situated on 14 sweeping acres just a stone's throw from downtown Bar Harbor and Acadia National Park, the Wonder View Inn is one of the most pet-friendly properties in town. **Pros:** pet-friendly. **Cons:** basic rooms; dated interiors; older hotel. $ *Rooms from: $150* ✉ *50 Eden St.* ☎ *207/288–3358* ⊕ *www.wonderviewinn. com* ⊗ *Closed Nov.–Apr.* ⊃ *15 rooms* ⦿ *No meals.*

SPORTS AND THE OUTDOORS

AIR TOURS

Acadia Air Tours. This outfit runs sightseeing flights over Bar Harbor and Acadia National Park. Most tours run 15 minutes to an hour and range $150–$450 for two people. The sunset tour is $50 extra. ✉ *968 Bar Harbor Rd., Trenton* ☎ *207/667–7627* ⊕ *www.acadiaairtours.com.*

BICYCLING

Acadia Bike. Rent mountain bikes and hybrids at Acadia Bike, both good models for negotiating the carriage roads in Acadia National Park. ✉ *48 Cottage St.* ☎ *207/288–9605, 800/526–8615* ⊕ *www.acadiabike.com.*

Bar Harbor Bicycle Shop. Rent bikes for anywhere from four hours to a full day at the Bar Harbor Bicycle Shop. ✉ *141 Cottage St.* ☎ *207/288–3886, 800/824–2453* ⊕ *www.barharborbike.com.*

BOATING

Coastal Kayaking Tours. This outfitter has been leading trips in the scenic waters off Mount Desert Island since 1982. Rentals are provided through its sister business, Acadia Outfitters, on the same downtown street. Trips are limited to no more than 12 people. The season is May–October. ✉ *48 Cottage St.* ☎ *207/288–9605, 800/526–8615* ⊕ *www. acadiafun.com.*

Downeast Sailing Adventures. Take two-hour sailing trips and sunset cruises for $35 per person with six passengers ($50 per person with fewer), or hire a private charter starting at $100 per hour. Boats depart the Upper Town Dock in Southwest Harbor and several other locations. ✉ *Upper Town Dock, Clark Point Rd., Southwest Harbor* ☎ *207/288–2216* ⊕ *www.downeastsail.com.*

FAMILY

Margaret Todd. The 151-foot four-masted schooner *Margaret Todd* operates 1½- to 2-hour trips three times daily among the islands of Frenchman's Bay. The sunset sail has live music, and the 2 pm trip is sometimes narrated by an Acadia National Park ranger. Trips are $39.50 and depart mid-May–mid-October. ✉ *Bar Harbor Inn pier, Newport Dr.* ☎ *207/288–4585* ⊕ *www.downeastwindjammer.com.*

6

WHALE-WATCHING

FAMILY **Bar Harbor Whale Watch Co.** This company has four boats, one of them a 140-foot jet-propelled double-hulled catamaran with spacious decks. It's one of two large catamarans used for whale-watching trips, some of which depart at sunset or include a side trip to see puffins. The company also offers lighthouse, lobstering, and seal-watching cruises, as well as a trip to Acadia National Park's Baker Island. ⊠ *1 West St.* ☎ *207/288–2386, 800/942–5374* ⊕ *www.barharborwhales.com.*

SHOPPING

ART

Alone Moose Fine Crafts. The oldest made-in-Maine gallery in Bar Harbor, Alone Moose Fine Crafts offers bronze wildlife sculptures, jewelry, pottery, photography, and watercolors. ⊠ *78 West St.* ☎ *207/288–4229 Mid-May–Oct., 207/288–9428* ⊕ *www.finemainecrafts.com.*

Eclipse Gallery. Eclipse Gallery carries handblown glass, ceramics, wood and metal furniture, and home decor items like mirrors and lamps. The gallery is open mid-May–October. ⊠ *12 Mount Desert St., Suite B* ☎ *207/288–9088, 207/610–2862 off-season* ⊕ *www.eclipsegallery.us.*

Island Artisans. This shop sells basketry, pottery, fiber work, and jewelry created by about 150 Maine artisans. It's open May–December. ⊠ *99 Main St.* ☎ *207/288–4214* ⊕ *www.islandartisans.com.*

Native Arts Gallery. Silver and gold Southwest Indian jewelry is a specialty at Native Arts Gallery, open May–October. ⊠ *99 Main St.* ☎ *207/288–4474* ⊕ *www.nativeartsgallery.com.*

Fodor's Choice **The Rock and Art Shop.** As advertised, there are both "rocks" and "art"
★ for sale at this eclectic family-owned store. There are also taxidermied animals, fossils, home decor and plants, interesting jewelry, and bath products. There are other locations in Bangor, Ellsworth, and just outside Ellsworth off Route 1A; here, they're open May–November. ⊠ *13 Cottage St.* ☎ *207/288–4800* ⊕ *www.therockandartshop.com.*

SPORTING GOODS

Cadillac Mountain Sports. One of the best sporting-goods stores in the state, Cadillac Mountain Sports has developed a following of locals and visitors alike. Here you'll find top-quality climbing, hiking, boating, paddling, and camping equipment, and in winter you can rent cross-country skis, ice skates, and snowshoes. ⊠ *26 Cottage St.* ☎ *207/288–4532* ⊕ *www.cadillacsports.com.*

ACADIA NATIONAL PARK

3 miles from Bar Harbor via U.S. 3.

Fodor's Choice With about 49,000 acres of protected forests, beaches, mountains, and
★ rocky coastline, Acadia National Park is one of the most visited national parks in America. According to the National Park Service, over 2 million people visit Acadia each year, and the number is steadily rising. The park holds some of the most spectacular scenery on the Eastern Seaboard: a rugged coastline of surf-pounded granite and an interior graced by sculpted mountains, quiet ponds, and lush, deciduous forests. Cadillac Mountain (named after a Frenchman who explored here in the

late 1600s and who later founded Detroit)—the highest point of land on the East Coast—dominates the park. Although rugged, the park also has graceful stone bridges, miles of carriage roads (popular with walkers, runners, and bikers as well as horse-drawn carriages), and the Jordan Pond House restaurant (famous for its popovers).

The 27-mile Park Loop Road provides an excellent overview, but to truly appreciate the park you must get off the main road and experi-

BOOK A CARRIAGE RIDE

Riding down one of the park's scenic carriage roads in a horse-drawn carriage is a truly unique way to experience Acadia. You can book a reservation for a ride, late May–mid-October, with Wildwood Stables, located next to Park Loop Road (☎ 877/276–3622). One of the carriages can accommodate wheelchairs.

ence it by walking, hiking, biking, sea kayaking, or taking a carriage ride. Get off the beaten path, and you can find places you'll have practically all to yourself. Mount Desert Island was once a preserve of summer homes for the very rich (and still is for some), and, partly because of this, Acadia is the first national park in the United States largely created by donations of private land. There are two smaller parts of the park: on Isle au Haut, 15 miles away out in the ocean, and on the Schoodic Peninsula, on the mainland across Frenchman Bay from Mt. Desert.

PARK ESSENTIALS
ADMISSION FEE
A user fee is required May–October. The per-vehicle fee is $25 ($20 for motorcycles) for a seven-consecutive-day pass; you can walk or bike in on a $12 individual pass (also good for seven days); or you can use your National Park America the Beautiful Pass, which allows entrance to any national park in the United States. There are also a few fee-free days throughout the year.

ADMISSION HOURS
The park is open 24 hours a day, year-round, but roads are closed December–mid-April, except for the Ocean Drive section of Park Loop Road and a small part of the road with access to Jordan Pond.

PARK CONTACT INFORMATION
Acadia National Park. ✉ *Acadia National Park* ☎ *207/288–3338* ⊕ *www. nps.gov/acad.*

GETTING HERE AND AROUND
Route 3 leads to the island and Bar Harbor from Ellsworth and circles the eastern part of the island. Route 102 is the major road on the west side.

Island Explorer buses, which serve the park and island villages June 23–Columbus Day, offer transportation to and around the park. In addition to regularly scheduled stops, they also pick up and drop off passengers anywhere in the park it is safe to stop.

Fodor's Choice **Island Explorer.** These free buses transport locals and visitors throughout
★ Acadia National Park on clean propane-powered buses. Eight routes connect the campgrounds, including Bar Harbor, Sand Beach, Southwest Harbor, and others. The bus system operates June 23–Columbus

Acadia's Best Campgrounds

Acadia National Park's two main campgrounds, Seawall and Blackwoods, don't have water views, but the price is right and the ocean is just a 10-minute walk from each. The park added a third campground on the Schoodic Peninsula in 2015.

Blackwoods Campground. Located only 5 miles from Bar Harbor, this is Acadia's most popular campground. It is open year-round and well served by the Island Explorer bus system. ⊠ *Rte. 3, 5 miles south of Bar Harbor* ☎ *877/444–6777 for reservations* ⊕ *www.recreation.gov.*

Schoodic Woods Campground. Opened in September 2015, this campground is in the Schoodic Peninsula section of Acadia, meaning you have to take the ferry from Winter Harbor in order to cross over to Mount Desert Island (or drive). It is open May–Columbus Day. ⊠ *Schoodic Loop Road, 1 mile south of Rte. 186, Winter Harbor.*

Seawall Campground. On the quiet western side of the island, Seawall is open late May–September. ⊠ *Rte. 102A, 4 miles south of Southwest Harbor* ☎ *877/444–6777 for reservations* ⊕ *www.recreation.gov.*

Day, and buses are equipped with bicycle racks. ⊠ *Acadia National Park* ☎ *207/667–5796* ⊕ *www.exploreacadia.com.*

EXPLORING

SCENIC DRIVES AND STOPS

FAMILY
Fodor's Choice
★

Cadillac Mountain. At 1,530 feet, this is one of the first places in the United States to see the sun's rays at daybreak. It is the highest mountain on the eastern seaboard north of Brazil. Hundreds of visitors make the trek to see the sunrise or—for those less inclined to get up so early—sunset. From the smooth summit you have a stunning 360-degree view of the jagged coastline that runs around the island. The only structures at the top are restrooms and a small gift shop, which sells coffee and snacks. The road up the mountain is closed December–mid-May. ⊠ *Cadillac Summit Rd.* ⊕ *www.nps.gov/acad/.*

FAMILY
Fodor's Choice
★

Park Loop Road. This 27-mile road provides a perfect introduction to the park. You can drive it in an hour, but allow at least half a day, so that you can explore the many sites along the way. The route is also served by the free Island Explorer buses, which also picks up and drops off passengers anywhere it is safe to stop along the route. Traveling south on Park Loop Road toward Sand Beach, you'll reach a small ticket booth, where, if you haven't already, you will need to pay the park entrance fee (May–October). Traffic is one way from the Route 233 entrance to the Stanley Brook Road entrance south of the Jordan Pond House. The section known as Ocean Drive is open year-round, as is a small section that provides access to Jordan Pond from Seal Harbor. ⊠ *Acadia National Park.*

VISITOR CENTER

FAMILY **Hulls Cove Visitor Center.** This is a great spot to get your bearings. A large 3-D relief map of Mount Desert Island gives you the lay of the land, and a free 15-minute video about everything the park has to offer plays every half hour. You can pick up guidebooks, maps of hiking trails and carriage roads, and recordings for drive-it-yourself tours—don't forget to grab a schedule of ranger-led programs, which includes guided hikes and other interpretive events. Junior-ranger programs for kids, nature hikes, photography walks, tide-pool explorations, and evening talks are all popular. The

CAUTION

Every few years, someone falls off one of the park's trails or cliffs and is swept out to sea. There is a lot of loose, rocky gravel along the shoreline, and sea rocks can often be slippery—so watch your step.

Acadia National Park Headquarters, off Route 233 near the north end of Eagle Lake, serves as the park's visitor center during the off-season. ⊠ *Rte. 3, Hulls Cove* ☎ *207/288–3338* ⊕ *www.nps.gov/acad.*

SPORTS AND THE OUTDOORS

The best way to see Acadia National Park is to get out of your vehicle and explore on foot or by bicycle or boat. There are more than 45 miles of carriage roads that are perfect for walking and biking in the warmer months and for cross-country skiing and snowshoeing in winter. There are 125 miles of trails for hiking, numerous ponds and lakes for canoeing or kayaking, two beaches for swimming, and steep cliffs for rock climbing.

HIKING

Acadia National Park maintains more than 125 miles of hiking trails, from easy strolls around lakes and ponds to rigorous treks with climbs up rock faces and scrambles along cliffs. Although hiking trails are concentrated on the east side of the island, the west side also has some scenic trails. For those wishing for a longer trek, try the trails leading up Cadillac Mountain or Dorr Mountain; you may also try Parkman, Sargeant, and Penobscot mountains. Most hiking is done mid-May–mid-November; snow falls early in Maine, so from as early as late November to the end of March, cross-country skiing and snowshoeing replace hiking. Volunteers groom most of the carriage roads if there's been four inches of snow or more. ■ **TIP→ You can park at one end of any trail and use the free shuttle bus to get back to your starting point.**

Distances for trails are given for round-trips.

Fodor's Choice ★ **Acadia Mountain Trail.** If you're up for a challenge, this is one of the area's best trails. The 2.5-mile round-trip climb up Acadia Mountain is a steep and strenuous 700-foot climb, but the payoff views of Somes Sound are grand. If you want a guided trip, look into ranger-led hikes for this trail. ⊠ *Rte. 102* ☎ *207/288–3338* ⊕ *www.nps.gov/acad.*

Fodor's Choice ★ **Ocean Path Trail.** This easily accessible 4.4-mile round-trip trail runs parallel to the Ocean Drive section of the Park Loop Road from Sand Beach to Otter Point. It has some of the best scenery in Maine: cliffs and boulders of pink granite at the ocean's edge, twisted branches of dwarf jack pines, and ocean views that stretch to the horizon. Be sure to save time to stop at **Thunder Hole,** named for the sound the waves make as they thrash through a narrow opening in the granite cliffs, into a sea cave, and whoosh up and out. Approximately halfway between Sand Beach and Otter Cliff, steps lead down to the water, where you can watch the wave action close-up. Use caution as you descend (access may be limited due to storms), and also if you venture onto the outer cliffs along this walk. ⌧ *Ocean Dr. section of Park Loop Rd.*

SWIMMING

The park has two swimming beaches, Sand Beach and Echo Lake

> **ACADIA LEAF PEEPING**
>
> The fall foliage in Maine can be spectacular. Because of littoral humidity, leaves turn later here—usually around the middle of October—than they do in the interior of the state. The best way to catch the colors along the coast is travel on the Acadia National Park Loop Road. For up-to-date information, go to ⊕ *www.mainefoliage.com.*

Beach. Sand Beach, along Park Loop Road, has changing rooms, restrooms, and a lifeguard on duty Memorial Day–Labor Day. Echo Lake Beach, on the western side of the island just north of Southwest Harbor, has much warmer water, as well as changing rooms, restrooms, and a lifeguard on duty throughout the summer. This beach is particularly well suited for small children, as the water remains relatively shallow fairly far out.

FAMILY **Echo Lake Beach.** A quiet lake surrounded by woods in the shadow of Beech Mountain, Echo Lake draws swimmers to its sandy southern shore. The lake bottom is a bit muckier than the ocean beaches nearby, but the water is considerably warmer. The surrounding trail network skirts the lake and ascends the mountain. The beach is 2 miles north of Southwest Harbor. **Amenities:** lifeguards; toilets. **Best for:** swimming. ⌧ *Echo Lake Beach Rd., off Rte. 102.*

Sand Beach. This pocket beach is hugged by two picturesque rocky outcroppings, and the combination of the crashing waves and the chilly water (peaking at around 55°F) keeps most people on the beach. You'll find some swimmers at the height of summer, but the rest of the year this is a place for strolling and snapping photos. In the shoulder season, you'll have the place to yourself. **Amenities:** lifeguards; parking; toilets. **Best for:** solitude; sunrise; walking. ⌧ *Ocean Dr. section of Park Loop Rd., 3 miles south of Rte. 3.*

NORTHEAST HARBOR

12 miles south of Bar Harbor via Rtes. 3 and 198.

The summer community for some of the nation's wealthiest families, Northeast Harbor has one of the best ports on the coast, which fills with yachts and powerboats during peak season. Some summer residents rebuilt here after the Great Fire of 1947 destroyed their mansions in Bar Harbor. This quiet village has a handful of restaurants, inns, boutiques, and art galleries. It's also a great place to sign up for a cruise around Somes Sound or to the Cranberry Isles.

WHERE TO STAY

$

B&B/INN

FAMILY

Fodor'sChoice

★

Asticou Inn. Overlooking the water in Northeast Harbor, the Asticou Inn is tucked away in a quiet location but still has easy access to Acadia and the Asticou Azalea Garden. **Pros:** near hiking trails; excellent breakfast; manicured grounds with water views; quiet location. **Cons:** located 11 miles southwest of Bar Harbor ⑤ *Rooms from: $150* ✉ *15 Peabody Rd., Bar Harbor* ☎ *207/276-3344* ⊕ *www.asticou.com* ⌐ *48 rooms* ⑩ *Breakfast.*

SOUTHWEST HARBOR

6 miles south of Somesville via Rte. 102.

Across the water from Northeast Harbor, Southwest Harbor sits on the south side of the entrance to Somes Sound, which cuts up the center of the island. The town makes for a mellower Acadia base camp than Bar Harbor, with handsome yachts and towering sailboats lining the waterfront throughout the summer. Just north of town, trailheads at Echo Lake Beach and Fernald Point access some of the park's less explored territory.

6

BASS HARBOR

10 miles south of Somesville via Rtes. 102 and 102A.

Bass Harbor is a tiny lobstering village with a relaxed atmosphere and a few accommodations and restaurants. If you're looking to get away from the crowds, consider using this hardworking community as your base. Although Bass Harbor does not draw as many tourists as other villages, the Bass Harbor Head Light in Acadia National Park is one of the region's most popular attractions and is undoubtedly one of the most photographed lighthouses in Maine. From Bass Harbor, you can hike the Ship Harbor Nature Trail or take a ferry to Frenchboro or Swans Island.

GETTING HERE AND AROUND

From Bass Harbor, the Maine State Ferry Service operates the *Captain Henry Lee,* carrying both passengers and vehicles to Swans Island (40 minutes; $17.50 per person round-trip, $49.50 per car with driver) and Frenchboro (50 minutes; $11.25 per person round-trip, $32.25 per car with driver). The Frenchboro ferry doesn't run daily; a passenger-only ferry on a smaller boat (same price) runs on Fridays, April–November. Round-trip excursions (you don't get off the boat) are $10.

ESSENTIALS

Transportation Information Maine State Ferry Service. ✉ *45 Granville Rd.* ☎ *207/244-3254* ⊕ *www.maine.gov/mdot.*

EXPLORING

Fodor'sChoice

★

Bass Harbor Head Light. Built in 1858, this lighthouse is one of the most photographed lights in Maine. Now automated, it marks the entrance to Bass Harbor and Blue Hill Bay. You can't actually go inside—the

grounds and residence are Coast Guard property—but two trails around the facility have excellent views. It's within Acadia National Park, and there is parking. ■**TIP→** The best place to take a picture is from the rocks below—but watch your step, as they can be slippery. ⊠ *Lighthouse Rd., off Rte. 102A* ☎ *207/244–9753* ☎ *Free.*

WHERE TO EAT

$$ ✕ **Thurston's Lobster Pound.** Right on Bass Harbor, looking across to the
SEAFOOD village, Thurston's is easy to spot because of its bright yellow awning. You can buy fresh lobsters to go, or you can eat at covered outdoor tables. Order everything from a grilled-cheese sandwich, soup, or hamburger to a boiled lobster served with clams or mussels. ⑤ *Average main: $20* ⊠ *Steamboat Wharf, 9 Thurston Rd., Bernard* ☎ *207/244–7600* ⊕ *www.thurstonslobster.com* ⊘ *Closed mid-Oct.–Memorial Day.*

WAY DOWN EAST

Slogans like "The Real Maine" ring true Way Down East, where raw, mostly undeveloped coast dominates the remote region. Even in summer here you're likely to have rocky beaches and shady hiking trails all to yourself. And the slower pace is as calming as a sea breeze.

One innkeeper relates that visitors who plan to stay a few days often opt for a week after learning more about all the region has to offer, including historic sites; museums on local history, culture, and art; national wildlife refuges; state parks and preserves; and increasingly, conservancy-owned public land. Cutler's Bold Coast, with its dramatic granite headlands, is protected from development. Waters near Eastport have some of the world's highest tides. Lakes perfect for canoeing and kayaking are sprinkled inland, and rivers snake through marshland as they near the many bays. Boulders are strewn on blueberry barrens. Rare plants thrive in coastal bogs and heaths, and dark-purple and pink lupines line roads in late June.

VISITOR INFORMATION

Many chambers of commerce in the region distribute free copies of the pamphlet "Maine's Washington County: Just Off the Beaten Path." It's several cuts above the usual tourist promotion booklet, but chatting with locals is often the best way to find out about lesser-known trails and beaches, as well as which restaurants are worth a stop.

Contacts DownEast and Acadia Regional Tourism. ⊠ *87 Milbridge Rd., Cherryfield* ☎ *207/546–3600, 888/665–3278* ⊕ *www.downeastacadia.com.*

SCHOODIC PENINSULA

25 miles east of Ellsworth via U.S. Rte. 1 and Rte. 186.

The landscape of Schoodic Peninsula's craggy coastline, towering evergreens, and views over Frenchman Bay are breathtaking year-round. A drive through the well-to-do summer community of Grindstone Neck shows what Bar Harbor might have been like before so many of its mansions were destroyed in the Great Fire of 1947. Artists and artisans have opened galleries in and around Winter Harbor. Anchored at the foot of the peninsula, Winter Harbor was once part of Gouldsboro, which wraps around it. The southern tip of the peninsula is home to the Schoodic section of Acadia National Park.

GETTING HERE AND AROUND

From U.S. 1, Route 186 loops around the peninsula. Route 195 runs from U.S. 1 to Prospect Harbor and on to its end in Corea.

Island Explorer. The Island Explorer operates on the Schoodic Peninsula, with bus service from Prospect Harbor, Birch Harbor, and Winter Harbor to anywhere in the Schoodic Peninsula section of the park that's safe to stop. The bus also connects with the Winter Harbor ferry terminal, where you can take a ferry back to Bar Harbor. ⊠ *Winter Harbor* ☎ *207/288–2984* ⊕ *www.exploreacadia.com.*

ESSENTIALS

Visitor Information Schoodic Chamber of Commerce. ⊕ *www.acadia-schoodic.org.*

EXPLORING

Within Gouldsboro on the Schoodic Peninsula are several small coastal villages. You drive through Wonsqueak and Birch Harbor after leaving the Schoodic section of Acadia National Park. Near Birch Harbor you can find Prospect Harbor, a small fishing village nearly untouched by tourism. In Corea, there's little to do besides watch fishermen at work, wander along stone beaches, or gaze out at the sea.

Fodor's Choice
★
Acadia National Park. The only section of Maine's national park that sits on the mainland is at the southern end of the Schoodic Peninsula in the town of Winter Harbor. The park has a scenic 6-mile loop that edges along the coast, yielding views of Grindstone Neck, Winter Harbor, Winter Harbor Lighthouse, and, across the water, Cadillac Mountain. At the tip of the point, huge slabs of pink granite lie jumbled along the shore, thrashed unmercifully by the crashing surf, and jack pines cling to life amid the rocks. Fraser Point, at the beginning of the loop, is an ideal place for a picnic. Work off lunch with a hike up Schoodic Head for the panoramic views up and down the coast. During the summer season you can take a passenger ferry ($22 one way, $32 round-trip) to Winter Harbor from Bar Harbor. In Winter Harbor catch the free Island Explorer bus, which stops throughout the park, but you'll need to take the ferry to get back to Bar Harbor. ⊠ *End of Moore Rd., off Rte. 186, Winter Harbor* ☎ *207/288–3338* ⊕ *www.nps.gov/acad.*

Schoodic Education and Research Center. In the Schoodic Peninsula section of Acadia National Park, this center offers lectures, workshops, and kid-friendly events about nature. It's worth a drive-by just to see the Rockefeller Building, a massive 1935 French Eclectic and Renaissance-style structure with a stone-and-half-timber facade that served as naval offices and housing. In 2013, the building reopened as a visitor center after an extensive renovation. ⊠ *9 Atterbury Circle, Winter Harbor* ☎ *207/288–1310* ⊕ *www.schoodicinstitute.org.*

6

Wild for Blueberries

There's no need to inquire about cheesecake topping in August, when the wild blueberry crop comes in: anything else would be unthinkable.

Way Down East, wild blueberries have long been a favorite food and a key ingredient in cultural and economic life. Maine produces about a third of the commercial harvest, which totals about 80 million pounds annually—Canada supplying virtually all the rest. Washington County yields more than half of Maine's total crop, which is why the state's largest blueberry processors are here: Jasper Wyman & Son and the predecessor of what is now Cherryfield Foods were founded shortly after the Civil War.

Wild blueberries, which bear fruit every other year, thrive in the region's cold climate and sandy, acidic soil. Undulating blueberry barrens stretch for miles in Deblois and Cherryfield (the "Blueberry Capital of the World") and are scattered throughout Washington County. Look for tufts among low-lying plants along roadways. In spring, the fields shimmer as the small-leaf plants turn myriad shades of mauve, honey orange, and lemon yellow. White flowers appear in June. Fall transforms the barrens into a sea of otherworldly red.

Amid Cherryfield's barrens, a plaque on a boulder lauds the late J. Burleigh Crane for helping advance an industry that's not as wild as it used to be: fields are irrigated, honeybees have been brought in to supplement native pollinators, and barrens are burned and mowed to rid plants of disease and insects, reducing the need for pesticides. Most of the barrens in and around Cherryfield are owned by large blueberry processors. About 80% of Maine's crop is now harvested with machinery. That requires moving boulders, so the rest continues to be harvested by hand with blueberry rakes, which resemble large forks and pull the berries off their stems. Years ago, year-round residents did the work; today, migrant workers make up 90% of this seasonal labor force.

Blueberries get their dark color from anthocyanin, believed to act as an antioxidant. Wild blueberries have more of these anti-aging, anticancer compounds than their cultivated cousins; they're also smaller and more flavorful, and therefore mainly used in packaged foods. Less than 1% of the state's crop (about 500,000 pints) is consumed fresh, most of it in Maine. Look for fresh berries (sometimes starting in late July and lasting until early September) at roadside stands, farmers' markets, and supermarkets.

Wild Blueberry Land in Columbia Falls sells everything blueberry, from muffins and candy to socks and books. Find farm stores, stands, and markets statewide, many selling blueberries and blueberry jams and syrups, at ⊕ *www.getrealmaine.com*, a Maine Department of Agriculture site that promotes Maine foods.

DID YOU KNOW?

A far cry from the bloated berries at most grocery stores, Maine's small, flavor-packed wild blueberries are a must in-season, late July–early September. Try a handful fresh, in pancakes, or a pie.

WHERE TO EAT AND STAY

$

SEAFOOD

FAMILY

✗ **Chase's Restaurant.** This family restaurant has a reputation for serving good, basic fare—and in this region that means a whole lot of fresh fish. There are large and small fried seafood dinners, as well as several more expensive seafood platters. Try the sweet-potato fries as a side. Lunch fare, sold all day, includes wraps and burgers. It's also open for breakfast. $ *Average main: $10* ⊠ *193 Main St., Winter Harbor* ☎ *207/963–7171.*

$

B&B/INN

FAMILY

▢ **Bluff House Inn.** This cozy, modern inn is on a secluded hillside with expansive views of Frenchman's Bay. You can see its granite shores from the wraparound porches on each floor; the downstairs porch is partially screened. **Pros:** good value; largest room has sitting area with pull-out couch. **Cons:** only two rooms have good water views. $ *Rooms from: $105* ⊠ *57 Bluff House Rd., off Rte. 186, Gouldsboro* ☎ *207/963–7805* ⊕ *www.bluffinn.com* ↝ *9 rooms* ○| *Breakfast.*

$

B&B/INN

FAMILY

Fodor's Choice

★

▢ **Oceanside Meadows Inn.** A must for nature lovers, this lodging sits on a 200-acre preserve dotted with woods, streams, salt marshes, and ponds. **Pros:** one of the region's few sand beaches; staff share info about the area over tea. **Cons:** need to cross road to beach. $ *Rooms from: $179* ⊠ *202 Corea Rd., Prospect Harbor* ☎ *207/963–5557* ⊕ *www.oceaninn. com* ○ *Closed mid-Oct.–late May* ↝ *13 rooms, 2 suites* ○| *Breakfast.*

SPORTS AND THE OUTDOORS
KAYAKING
SeaScape Kayaking. Led by a Registered Maine Guide, SeaScape's morning and afternoon kayak tours include an island stop and a blueberry snack. The company also rents canoes, kayaks, and bikes from its location in Birch Harbor and welcomes handicapped kayakers. ⊠ 8 *Duck Pond Rd., Winter Harbor* ☎ *207/963–5806* ⊕ *www.seascape-kayaking.com.*

SHOPPING
ANTIQUES AND MORE
U.S. Bells. Hand-cast bronze doorbells and wind chimes are among the items sold at U.S. Bells. You can also buy finely crafted quilts and wood fired pottery made by the owner's family. Ask for a tour of the foundry. ⊠ *56 W. Bay Rd., Prospect Harbor* ☎ *207/963–7184* ⊕ *www. usbells.com.*

ART GALLERIES
Lee Fusion Art Glass. Window glass is fused in a kiln to create unusual glass dishware. Colorful enamel accents depict birds, lighthouses, flowers, and designs made from doilies. The store is open June–October. ⊠ *679 S. Gouldsboro Rd., Rte. 186, Gouldsboro* ☎ *207/712–2118* ⊕ *www.leefusionartglass.com.*

LUBEC

28 miles northeast of Machias via U.S. 1 and Rte. 189.

Lubec is one of the first places in the United States to see the sunrise. A popular destination for outdoors enthusiasts, it offers plenty of opportunities for hiking and biking, and the birding is renowned. It's a good base for day trips to New Brunswick's Campobello Island, reached by a bridge—the only one to the island—from downtown Lubec, so don't forget to bring your passport. One of the main attractions there, Roosevelt Campobello International Park, operates a visitor center on the U.S. side of the border, which provides information about the region, generally; it's in a Whiting general store and gas station at the corner of U.S. 1 and Route 189. The village itself is perched at the end of a narrow strip of land at the end of Route 189, so you often see water in three directions in this laid-back, off-the-beaten-path place.

GETTING HERE AND AROUND
From U.S. 1 in Whiting, Route 189 leads to Lubec; it's about 13 miles to the village. You can stock up on groceries in nearby Machias, just before you hit Whiting, en route to Lubec. In summer you can take a water taxi from here to Eastport—about a mile by boat, but 40 miles by the circuitous northerly land route.

EXPLORING
FAMILY
Fodor'sChoice
★

West Quoddy Head Light. The easternmost point of land in the United States is marked by candy-stripe West Quoddy Head Light. In 1806 President Thomas Jefferson signed an order authorizing construction of a lighthouse on this site. You can't climb the tower, but the former lightkeeper's house has a museum with a video with shots of the interior, as well as displays on Lubec's maritime past; a gallery displays works by artists who live or summer in the area. The mystical 2-mile path along the cliffs at Quoddy Head State Park (one of five trails) yields magnificent views of Canada's cliff-clad Grand Manan Island. Whales and seals—as well as the ubiquitous bald eagles—can often be sighted offshore. The 540-acre park has a picnic area with grills, but sometimes the best place to take lunch is perched on a rock overlooking the sea. Don't miss the easy, 0.2-mile bog trail that includes a fascinating array of subarctic vegetation, including carnivorous pitcher plants. ⊠ *973 S. Lubec Rd., off Rte. 189* ☎ *207/733–2180* ⊕ *www. westquoddy.com* ☜ *$3.*

WHERE TO EAT AND STAY

$ ✕**Lubec Brewing Company.** Tucked downtown on Water Street, the
AMERICAN Lubec Brewing Company serves up a rotating array of suds. The pub sometimes hosts impromptu potluck dinners—check their Facebook page—and usually has one or two things to fill you up other than beer. ⑤ *Average main: $8* ⊠ *41 Water St.* ☎ *207/733–4555* ⊘ *Closed Mon.–Wed. No lunch.*

$$ ✕**Water Street Tavern and Inn.** Perched right on the water in downtown
SEAFOOD Lubec, this favorite local restaurant recently spruced up its menu, which
FAMILY includes some of the sweetest scallops you'll ever eat, a very satisfying burger, and a massive chunk of chocolate cake. It's also a great place to grab a drink or a slice of blueberry pie and a coffee while looking out at the water from the deck or through the picture windows. If you want the lowdown on where to go or what to see in Lubec, this is the place to ask. There's often live music by local performers on Thursday. It also offers two cozy suites and three guest rooms, most with good views of the water. ⑤ *Average main: $20* ⊠ *12 Water St.* ☎ *207/733–2477* ⊕ *www.watersttavernandinn.com* ⊘ *Closed late-Oct.–Mar.*

$ ⛺**Peacock House.** Five generations of the Peacock family lived in this
B&B/INN 1860 sea captain's home before it was converted to an inn. **Pros:** piano
Fodor's Choice and fireplace in living room; lovely garden off deck; think-of-every-
★ thing innkeepers direct guests to area's tucked-away spots. **Cons:** not on the water. ⑤ *Rooms from: $105* ⊠ *27 Summer St.* ☎ *207/733–2403, 888/305–0036* ⊕ *www.peacockhouse.com* ⊘ *Closed Nov.–Apr.* ☜ *3 rooms, 4 suites* ⦿ *Breakfast.*

SHOPPING

Monica's Chocolates. Taking in all the appetizing scents in this shop is almost enough, but sinking your teeth into one of Monica's truffles, bonbons, crèmes, or caramels is pure heaven. ⊠ *100 County Rd.* ☎ *207/733–4500* ⊕ *www.monicaschocolates.com.*

CAMPOBELLO ISLAND, CANADA

4 miles northeast of Lubec.

A popular excursion from Lubec, New Brunswick's Campobello Island has two fishing villages, Welshpool and Wilson's Beach. The only land route is the bridge from Lubec, but in summer a car ferry shuttles passengers from Campobello Island to Deer Island, where you can continue on to the Canadian mainland.

GETTING HERE AND AROUND

After coming across the bridge from Lubec, Route 774 runs from one end of the island to the other, taking you through the two villages and to Roosevelt Campobello International Park.

EXPLORING

FAMILY

Fodor's Choice

★

Roosevelt Campobello International Park. President Franklin Roosevelt and his family spent summers at this estate, which is now an international park with neatly manicured lawns that stretch out to the beach. You can take a self-guided tour of the 34-room Roosevelt Cottage that was presented to Eleanor and Franklin as a wedding gift. The wicker-filled structure looks essentially as it did when the family was in residence. A visitor center has displays about the Roosevelts and Canadian-American relations. Eleanor Roosevelt Teas are held at 11 and 3 daily in the neighboring Hubbard Cottage. A joint project of the American and the Canadian governments, this park is crisscrossed with interesting hiking trails. Groomed dirt roads attract bikers. Eagle Hill Bog has a wooden walkway and signs identifying rare plants. ■**TIP→ Note that the Islands are on Atlantic Time, which is an hour later than Eastern Standard Time.** ✉ *459 Rte. 774, Welshpool* ☎ *506/752–2922, 877/851–6663* ⊕ *www. fdr.net* ⌨ *Free.*

WHERE TO EAT

$

SEAFOOD

FAMILY

✕ **Family Fisheries.** Seafood lovers know that fried fish doesn't have to be greasy. That's why people keep heading across the international bridge to eat at this family establishment in Wilson's Beach. The freshest seafood is delivered to the restaurant, where you can bring your own wine (corkage $2). Order fried haddock, scallops, shrimp, or clams, alone or as part of a platter. Eat in the large dining room or near the playground at picnic tables or in a screened room. Lobsters are cooked outside and also sold live or steamed to go. You can buy ice cream at the take-out window, and the restaurant also serves breakfast in July and August. ⑤ *Average main: C$15* ✉ *1977 Rte. 774, Wilsons Beach* ☎ *506/752–2470* ⊕ *www.familyfisheries.com* ⊗ *Closed late Oct.–early Apr.*

$$

CANADIAN

FAMILY

✕ **Fireside Restaurant.** Named after FDR's famous "fireside chats," this cozy lodge-style restaurant serves fresh seafood dishes and comfort food, like grilled cheese sandwiches and jumbo hot dogs. Try and get seated close to one of the enormous fireplaces or picture windows. ⑤ *Average main: C$20* ✉ *610 Rte. 774, Welshpool* ☎ *506/752–6055* ⊕ *www.fdr.net/fireside-restaurant.php.*

EASTPORT

39 miles northeast of Lubec via Rte. 189, U.S. 1, and Rte. 190; 109 miles north of Ellsworth via U.S. 1 and Rte. 190.

Connected by a granite causeway to the mainland at Pleasant Point Reservation, Eastport has wonderful views of the nearby islands, and because the harbor is so deep, you can sometimes spot whales from the waterfront. Known for its diverse architecture, the island city was one of the nation's busiest seaports in the early 1800s.

If you find yourself in town mid- to late summer, you might catch one of a few notable events. For starters, Maine's largest Fourth of July parade takes place in Eastport—be sure to get downtown early to secure a viewing spot. Then, on the weekend of the second Sunday in August, locals celebrate Sipayik Indian Days at the Pleasant Point Reservation; this festival of Passamaquoddy culture includes canoe races, dancing, drumming, children's games, fireworks, and traditional dancing. And on the weekend after Labor Day, the Eastport Pirate Festival brings folks out in pirate attire for a ship race, a parade, fireworks, cutlass "battles" by reenactors, and other events, including a children's breakfast and a schooner ride with pirates.

GETTING HERE AND AROUND

From U.S. 1, Route 190 leads to the Island City. Continue on Washington Street to the water. In the summer, you can also take a water taxi from here to Lubec—a mile or so by boat, but about 40 miles by land.

ESSENTIALS

Visitor Information Eastport Area Chamber of Commerce. ⊠ *64 Water St.* ☎ *207/853–4644* ⊕ *www.eastport.net.*

WHERE TO EAT

$ ✕**Chowder House.** Just north of downtown Eastport, this expansive
SEAFOOD   waterfront eatery sits on the pier next to the ferry dock. Built atop
FAMILY   the foundation of an old cannery, it has original details such as wood beams and a stone wall. Eat in the downstairs pub, in the upstairs dining room, or on the large deck. House specialties include a smoked fish appetizer and seafood pasta in a wine-and-cheese sauce. Lunch, served until 4, includes fried seafood plates, burgers, wraps, and sandwiches. ⑤ *Average main: $17* ⊠ *167 Water St.* ☎ *207/853–4700* ⊕ *www.eastportchowderhouse.org* ⊘ *Closed mid-Oct.–mid-May.*

$ ✕**Dastardly Dick's Wicked Good Coffee.** The coffee isn't the only thing
CAFÉ   that's wicked good at this local café; homemade pastries, rich soups,
FAMILY   and tasty sandwiches are all prepared daily, and the hot chocolate and chai are worth writing home about. ⑤ *Average main: $6* ⊠ *62 Water St.* ☎ *207/853–2090* ⊘ *Closed Mon.*

TRAVEL SMART
MAINE, VERMONT
& NEW HAMPSHIRE

GETTING HERE AND AROUND

Boston, New England's largest and most cosmopolitan city, is also the region's major transportation and cultural center. Portland, Maine, is a secondary hub. Your best bet for exploring widely is to travel by car: flying within the region is expensive, and driving distances between most attractions are short. Within most cities, however, public transportation is a viable—and often preferable—means for getting around. Passenger ferry service is available to outlying islands (some vessels accommodate vehicles).

See the Getting Here and Around section at the beginning of each chapter for more transportation information.

■ AIR TRAVEL

Most travelers visiting New England head for a major gateway, such as Boston, Manchester, or Portland and then rent a car to explore the region. The New England states form a fairly compact region, with few important destinations more than six hours apart by car. It's costly and generally impractical to fly within New England.

Boston's Logan Airport is one of the nation's most important domestic and international airports, with direct flights arriving from all over North America and abroad. New England's other major airports receive few international flights (mostly from Canada) but receive many direct domestic flights from East Coast and Midwest destinations and, to a lesser extent, from the western United States. Some sample flying times to Boston are: 2½ hours from Chicago, 6½ hours from London, and 6 hours from Los Angeles.

AIRPORTS

The main gateway to New England is Boston's Logan International Airport (BOS). Other airports in the region include Manchester Boston Regional Airport (MHT), in New Hampshire and Portland

International Jetport (PWM) in Maine and Burlington International Airport (BTV) in Vermont.

Airport Information Bangor International Airport. ✉ *287 Godfrey Blvd., Bangor* ☎ *207/992-4600* ⊕ *www.flybangor.com.* **Burlington International Airport.** ✉ *1200 Airport Dr., South Burlington* ☎ *802/863-2874* ⊕ *www.btv.aero.* **Logan International Airport.** ✉ *1 Harborside Dr., Boston* ☎ *800/235-6426* ⊕ *www.massport.com/logan-airport* Ⓜ *Blue, Silver.* **Manchester Boston Regional Airport.** ✉ *1 Airport Rd., Manchester* ☎ *603/624-6539* ⊕ *www.flymanchester.com.* **Portland International Jetport.** ✉ *1001 Westbrook St., Portland* ☎ *207/874-8877* ⊕ *www.portland-jetport.org.*

FLIGHTS

Numerous airlines serve airports in Boston, Manchester, and Portland. Discount airlines serving some of these airports and others in New England include JetBlue, and Spirit.

Airline Contacts American Airlines. ☎ *800/433-7300* ⊕ *www.aa.com.* **Delta Airlines.** ☎ *800/221-1212* ⊕ *www.delta.com.* **JetBlue.** ☎ *800/538-2583* ⊕ *www.jetblue. com.* **Southwest Airlines.** ☎ *800/435-9792* ⊕ *www.southwest.com.* **Spirit Airlines.** ☎ *801/401-2222* ⊕ *www.spirit.com.* **United Airlines.** ☎ *800/864-8331* ⊕ *www.united.com.*

■ BOAT TRAVEL

Ferries provide access to many islands off the Maine coast as well as across Lake Champlain between Vermont and Upstate New York. International service between Portland, Yarmouth, and Bar Harbor, Maine, and Nova Scotia, is also available. With the exception of the Lake Champlain ferries—which are first-come, first-served—reservations are advisable for cars.

▌ BUS TRAVEL

Once in New England, regional bus service is relatively extensive. It can be a handy and affordable means of getting around, as buses travel many routes that trains do not. Concord Coach runs buses between Boston and Concord, New Hampshire, Portland, Maine, and Bangor, Maine; the company also operates a route between New York City and Portland. C&J sends buses (with Wi-Fi) up the New Hampshire coast to Dover, Durham, and Portsmouth, and provides service to New York City. Both Concord and C&J leave from Boston's South Station, which is connected to the Amtrak rail station, and Logan Airport.

Information C&J. ☎ 800/258–7111 ⊕ www. ridecj.com. **Concord Coach.** ☎ 800/639–3317 ⊕ www.concordcoachlines.com.

▌ CAR TRAVEL

New England is best explored by car. Inland, especially in Vermont, New Hampshire, and Maine, public transportation options are limited and a car is almost essential. If you rent a car at Logan International Airport, allow plenty of time to return it—as much as an hour to be on the safe side.

GASOLINE

Gas stations are easy to find along major highways and in most communities throughout the region. Prices vary from station to station within any city. The majority are self-serve with pumps that accept credit cards, though you may find a holdout full-service station here and there (tipping is not expected).

PARKING

In Boston and other large cities, finding a parking space on the street can be time-consuming. Your best bet is to park in a garage, but rates in large cities can top $30 a day. In smaller cities, street parking is usually simpler, though parking garages are still convenient and less expensive than their big-city counterparts. Pay attention

to signs: some cities allow only residents to park on certain streets. In most small towns parking is not a problem, though some beach and lake parking areas are reserved for those with resident stickers.

ROAD CONDITIONS

Major state and U.S. routes are generally well maintained, with snowplows at the ready during the winter to salt and plow road surfaces soon after the flakes begin to fall. Traffic is heaviest around Boston, especially during rush hour. Secondary state routes and rural roads can be a mixed bag; Route 1, for example, is well maintained, but traffic is slow and can get tied up in even the smallest coastal towns.

ROADSIDE EMERGENCIES

Throughout New England, call ☎ 911 for any travel emergency, such as an accident or a serious health concern. For breakdowns, dial a towing service.

CAR RENTAL

A car is the most practical way to get around New England. Major airports serving the region all have on-site car-rental agencies. A few train or bus stations have one or two car-rental agencies on-site.

Rates at Boston's Logan Airport begin at around $50 per day and $200 per week for an economy car with air-conditioning, automatic transmission, and unlimited mileage. The same car might go for around $70 per day and $300 per week at a smaller airport, such as Portland's. These rates do not include state tax on car rentals, which varies depending on the airport but generally runs 12%–15%. It usually costs less to rent a car away from an airport, but be sure to consider how easy or difficult it may be to get to that off-airport location with luggage.

Most agencies won't rent to drivers under the age of 21, and several major agencies won't rent to anyone under 25. When picking up a rental car, non-U.S. residents need a voucher for any prepaid reservation made in their home country, a passport, a driver's license, and a travel policy that covers each driver. Logan Airport is spread out and usually congested, so if returning a rental vehicle there, allow plenty of time to do so before heading to your flight.

Major Rental Agencies Alamo. ☎ 877/222–9075 ⊕ www.alamo.com. **Avis.** ☎ 800/331–1212 ⊕ www.avis.com. **Budget.** ☎ 800/527–0700 ⊕ www.budget.com. **Hertz.** ☎ 800/654–3131 ⊕ www.hertz.com. **National Car Rental.** ☎ 877/222–9058 ⊕ www.nationalcar.com.

▮ TRAIN TRAVEL

Amtrak offers frequent daily service along its Northeast Corridor route from Washington, D.C., Philadelphia, and New York to Boston. Amtrak's high-speed Acela trains link Boston and Washington, with stops at New York, Philadelphia, and other cities along the way. The *Downeaster* connects Boston and Portland, Maine, with stops in coastal New Hampshire.

Other Amtrak services include the *Vermonter* between Washington, D.C., and St. Albans, Vermont; the *Ethan Allen Express* between New York and Rutland, Vermont; and the *Lake Shore Limited* between Boston and Chicago, with stops at Pittsfield, Springfield, Worcester, and Framingham, Massachusetts.

Information Amtrak. ☎ 800/872–7245 ⊕ www.amtrak.com.

ESSENTIALS

■ ACCOMODATIONS

In New England you can bed down in a basic chain hotel or a luxurious grande dame, but unless you're staying in a city, this is really bed-and-breakfast land. Charming—and sometimes historic—inns, small hotels, and bed-and-breakfasts dot the region and provide a glimpse of local life.

Hotel prices are the lowest cost of a standard double room in high season.

BED-AND-BREAKFASTS

In many less touristy areas, bed-and-breakfasts offer an affordable, homey alternative to chain properties. In most major towns, expect to pay about the same or more for a historic inn. Many of the region's finest restaurants are attached to country inns, so you often don't have to go far for the best meal in town. Quite a few inns serve substantial breakfasts.

Reservation Services BedandBreakfast. com. ☎ *512/322–2710, 800/462–2632* ⊕ *www.bedandbreakfast.com.* **Bed & Breakfast Inns Online.** ☎ *800/215–7365* ⊕ *www. bbonline.com.* **DnBFinder.com.** ☎ *888/469–6663* ⊕ *www.bnbfinder.com.*

HOUSE AND APARTMENT RENTALS

You are most likely to find a house, apartment, or condo rental in areas of New England in which ownership of second homes is common, such as beach resorts and ski country. Home-exchange directories sometimes list rentals alongside exchanges. Another good bet is to contact real-estate agents in the area in which you are interested.

Contacts Home Away. ☎ *512/782–0805* ⊕ *www.homeaway.com.* **Interhome.** ☎ *800/882–6864* ⊕ *www.interhomeusa. com.* **Villas International.** ☎ *415/499–9490, 800/221–2260* ⊕ *www.villasintl.com.*

HOTELS

Major hotel and motel chains are amply represented in New England. The region is also liberally supplied with small, independent motels. Don't overlook these mom-and-pop operations; they frequently offer cheerful, convenient accommodations at lower rates than the chains.

Reservations are always a good idea, particularly in summer and winter resort areas; at college towns in September and at graduation time in spring; and at areas renowned for autumn foliage. Most hotels and motels will hold your reservation until 6 pm; call ahead if you plan to arrive late. All will hold a late reservation for you if you guarantee it with your credit card.

In Vermont all hotels are no-smoking by state law. All lodgings listed have private baths unless otherwise noted.

Information New England Inns & Resorts Association. ☎ *603/964–6689* ⊕ *www. newenglandinnsandresorts.com.*

■ TRAVELING WITH CHILDREN

Favorite destinations for family vacations in Northern New England include the White Mountains and coastal Maine, but in general, the entire region has plenty to offer families. Throughout Northern New England you'll have no problem finding comparatively inexpensive kid-friendly hotels and family-style restaurants, as well as museums, beaches, parks, planetariums, and lighthouses, though some of the quieter and more rural areas lack child-oriented attractions.

LODGING

New England has many family-oriented resorts with lively children's programs. Farms that accept guests can be great fun for children. Rental houses and apartments abound, particularly around ski areas. In the off-season, these can be economical because most have kitchens, saving you the expense of restaurant dining for some or all meals.

Most hotels in New England allow children under a certain age to stay in their parents' room at no extra charge, but others charge for them as extra adults; find out the cutoff age. Bed-and-breakfasts and historic inns are not always suitable for kids, and many flat-out refuse to accommodate them. In Maine, only hotels and inns with five or fewer rooms can put age restrictions on children.

Most lodgings that welcome infants and small children will provide a crib or cot, but remember to provide notice so that one will be available for you. Many family resorts make special accommodations for small children during meals.

▌ COMMUNICATIONS

INTERNET
Most major chain hotels and many smaller motels throughout New England now offer Wi-Fi. Many have a desktop computer available for guest use; access is often free, but be sure to ask about possible fees when you book. Many coffee shops offer Wi-Fi, as do most libraries.

▌ EATING OUT

Although certain ingredients and preparations are common to the region as a whole, New England's cuisine varies greatly from place to place. Urban centers like Boston and Portland, and upscale resort areas have stellar restaurants, many of them with culinary luminaries at the helm and a reputation for creative—and occasionally daring—menus.

Elsewhere, restaurant food tends more toward the simple, traditional, and conservative. Towns and cities have a variety of international restaurants, especially excellent Italian, French, Japanese, Indian, and Thai eateries. There are also many diners serving burgers and other comfort food—a few serve breakfast all day.

The proximity to the ocean accounts for the abundance of very fresh seafood, and the area's numerous boutique dairy, meat, and vegetable suppliers account for other choice ingredients. Menus in the more upscale and tourism-driven communities often note which Vermont dairy or Berkshires farm a particular goat cheese or heirloom tomato came from.

For information on food-related health issues, see Health below.

MEALS AND MEALTIMES
For an early breakfast, pick places that cater to a working clientele. City, town, and roadside establishments specializing in breakfast for early workers often open their doors at 5 or 6 am. At country inns, breakfast is seldom served before 8 am; if you need to get an earlier start, ask ahead of time. Lunch generally runs 11 am–2:30 pm; dinner is usually served 6–9 pm, with early-bird specials sometimes beginning at 5. Only in larger cities will you find dinner available much later than 9 pm. Many restaurants in New England close Monday and sometimes Sunday or Tuesday, although this is never true in resort areas during high season. However, resort-town eateries often shut down completely in the off-season.

Unless otherwise noted, the restaurants listed are open daily for lunch and dinner.

PAYING
Credit cards are accepted for meals throughout New England in all but the most modest establishments. *Prices in the reviews are the average cost of a main course at dinner or, if dinner is not served, at lunch.*

RESERVATIONS AND DRESS
It's a good idea to make a reservation if you can. We only mention them specifically when reservations are essential—there's no other way you'll ever get a table—or when they are not accepted. For popular restaurants, book as far ahead as you can, and reconfirm as soon as you arrive. Large parties should always call ahead to check the reservations policy. We mention dress

only when men are required to wear a jacket or a jacket and tie.

WINE, BEER, AND SPIRITS

New England is no stranger to microbrews. The granddaddy of New England's independent breweries is the Boston Beer Company, maker of Samuel Adams, Following the Sam Adams lead in offering hearty English-style ales and special seasonal brews are breweries such as Vermont's Long Trail, Maine's Shipyard, and New Hampshire's Smuttynose Brewing Co. Green Mountain Cidery makes Woodchuck hard cider in Middlebury, Vermont.

New England is beginning to earn some respect as a wine-producing region. Vermont is getting into the act with the Snow Farm Vineyard in the Lake Champlain Islands and Boyden Valley Winery in Cambridge.

Although a patchwork of state and local regulations affect the hours and locations of places that sell alcoholic beverages, New England licensing laws are fairly liberal. State-owned or -franchised stores sell hard liquor in New Hampshire, Maine, and Vermont. Many travelers have found that New Hampshire offers the region's lowest prices; look for state-run liquor "supermarkets" on interstates in the southern part of the state.

▌ HEALTH

Lyme disease, so named for its having been first reported in the town of Lyme, Connecticut, is a potentially debilitating disease carried by deer ticks. They thrive in dry, brush covered areas, particularly in coastal areas. Always use insect repellent: the potential for outbreaks of Lyme disease makes it imperative that you protect yourself from ticks from early spring through summer. To prevent bites, wear light-color clothing and tuck pant legs into socks. Look for black ticks about the size of a pinhead around hairlines and the warmest parts of the body. If you have been bitten, consult a physician, especially

if you see the telltale bull's-eye bite pattern. Flu-like symptoms often accompany a Lyme infection. Early treatment is imperative.

New England's two greatest insect pests are black flies and mosquitoes. The former are a phenomenon of late spring and early summer and are generally a problem only in the densely wooded areas of the far north. Mosquitoes, however, are a nuisance just about everywhere. The best protection against both pests is repellent containing DEET; if you're camping in the woods during black fly season, you'll also want to use fine mesh screening in eating and sleeping areas and even wear mesh headgear. One pest particular to coastal areas, especially salt marshes, is the greenhead fly, which has a nasty bite and is hard to kill. It is best repelled by a liberal application of Avon Skin So Soft or a similar product.

Coastal waters attract seafood lovers who enjoy harvesting their own clams, mussels, and even lobsters; permits are required, and casual harvesting of lobsters is strictly forbidden. Amateur clammers should be aware that New England shellfish beds are periodically visited by red tides, during which micro-organisms can render shellfish poisonous. To keep abreast of the situation, inquire when you apply for a license (usually at town halls or police stations) and pay attention to red tide postings as you travel.

▌HOURS OF OPERATION

Hours in New England differ little from those in other parts of the United States. Within the region, shops and other businesses tend to keep slightly later hours in larger cities and along the coast, which is generally more populated than interior New England.

Most major museums and attractions are open daily or six days a week, with Monday being the most likely day of closing. Hours are often shorter on Saturday and especially Sunday, though some prominent museums stay open late one or two nights a week, usually Tuesday, Thursday, or Friday. New England has many small museums—historical societies, art galleries, highly specialized collections—that open only a few days a week and sometimes only by appointment in winter or slow periods.

▌MONEY

It costs a bit more to travel in most of New England than it does in the rest of the country. ATMs are plentiful and larger denomination bills (as well as credit cards) are readily accepted in tourist destinations during the high season.

Prices *throughout this guide* are given for adults. Substantially reduced fees are almost always available for children, students, and senior citizens.

CREDIT CARDS

Major credit cards are readily accepted throughout New England, though in rural areas you may encounter difficulties or the acceptance of only Master-Card or Visa. If you'll be making an excursion into Canada, be aware that many outlets there accept Visa but not MasterCard.

Reporting Lost Cards **American Express.** ☎ 800/528–4800 ⊕ www.americanexpress.com. **Discover.** ☎ 800/347–2683 ⊕ www.discover.com. **MasterCard.** ☎ 800/627–8372 ⊕ www.mastercard.us. **Visa.** ☎ 800/847–2911 ⊕ usa.visa.com.

▌PACKING

The principal rule of weather in New England is that there are no rules. A cold, foggy spring morning often warms to a bright, 60°F afternoon. A summer breeze can suddenly turn chilly, and rain often appears with little warning. Thus, the best advice on how to dress is to layer your clothing; that way, you can peel off or add garments as needed for comfort. Even in summer you should bring long pants, a sweater or two, and a waterproof windbreaker, for evenings are often chilly, and sea spray can make things cool. Showers are frequent, so pack a raincoat and umbrella.

Casual sportswear—walking shoes and jeans or khakis—will take you almost everywhere, but swimsuits and bare feet will not: shirts and shoes are required attire at even the most casual venues. Dress in restaurants is generally casual, except at some of the distinguished restaurants of Boston and Maine coast towns such as Kennebunkport, and a few inns. Upscale resorts, at the very least, will require men to wear collared shirts at dinner, and jeans are often frowned upon.

In summer, bring a hat and sunscreen. Remember also to pack insect repellent: to prevent Lyme disease you'll need to guard against ticks from early spring through summer *(Health)*.

▌SAFETY

Rural New England is one of the country's safest regions, so much so that residents often leave their doors unlocked. In cities—Boston, in particular—observe the usual precautions: avoid out-of-the-way or poorly lighted areas at night; clutch handbags close to your body and don't let them out of your sight; and be on your guard in subways and buses, not only during the deserted wee hours but also during crowded rush hours, when pickpockets are at work. Keep your valuables in hotel safes. Try to use ATMs in busy, well-lighted places such as bank lobbies.

If your vehicle breaks down in a rural area, pull as far off the road as possible, tie a handkerchief to your radio antenna (use flares at night—check if your rental agency can provide them), and stay in your car with the doors locked until help arrives. Don't pick up hitchhikers. If you're planning to leave a car overnight to make use of off-road trails or camping facilities, make arrangements for a supervised parking area if at all possible. Cars left at trailhead parking lots are subject to theft and vandalism.

The universal telephone number for crime and other emergencies throughout New England is 911.

▌ TIPPING

TIPPING GUIDELINES FOR NEW ENGLAND	
Bartender	$1 to $5 per round of drinks, depending on the number of drinks
Bellhop	$1 or $2 per bag, depending on the level of the hotel
Hotel Concierge	$5 or more, if he or she performs a service for you
Hotel Doorman	$1 or $2 if he helps you get a cab
Hotel Maid	$2 to $5 a day depending on the level of the hotel, either daily or at the end of your stay, in cash
Hotel Room-Service Waiter	$2 to $5 per delivery, even if a service charge has been added
Porter at Airport or Train Station	$1 per bag
Skycap at Airport	$2 or $3 per bag checked
Taxi Driver	15% to 20%, but round up the fare to the next dollar amount
Tour Guide	15% of the cost of the tour
Valet Parking Attendant	$3 to $5, but only when you get your car
Waiter	15% to 20%, with 20% being the norm at high-end restaurants; nothing additional if a service charge is added to the bill
Other Attendants	Restroom attendants in expensive restaurants expect some small change or $1. Tip coat-check personnel at least $1 or $2 per item checked unless there is a fee, then nothing.

▌TAXES

Sales taxes in New England are as follows: Maine, 5.5%; Vermont, 6%. No sales tax is charged in New Hampshire. Some states and municipalities levy an additional tax (1%–10%) on lodging or restaurant meals. Alcoholic beverages are sometimes taxed at a higher rate than that applied to food.

▌TIME

New England operates on Eastern Standard Time and follows daylight saving time. When it is noon in Boston, it is 9 am in Los Angeles, 11 am in Chicago, 5 pm in London, and 3 am the following day in Sydney. When taking a ferry to Nova Scotia, remember that the province operates on Atlantic Standard Time and is therefore an hour ahead.

▌TOURS

CULINARY

Creative Culinary Tours. Foodies love exploring a new destination through their stomachs, and this outfit aims to please with three- to seven-day tours all over New England. ☎ 888/889–8681 ⊕ www.creativeculinarytours.com ✉ Call for prices.

GENERAL INTEREST

Contiki Vacations. Specializing in vacations for 18- to 35-year-olds, Contiki conducts tours throughout the Northeast, as well as several in New England specifically. ☎ 866/266–8454 ⊕ www.contiki.com ✉ From $2,255.

Insight Vacations. This company offers fall foliage tours and conducts summer tours that take place in Boston, Newport, and Cape Cod. These luxurious tours are aimed at travelers who want every detail taken care of, so they can simply enjoy the destination. Local expert guides make sure you don't miss a thing. ☎ 888/680–1241 ⊕ www.insightvacations.com/us ✉ From $2,725.

New England Vacation Tours. This versatile company conducts everything from packages that include flights and tours in luxury coaches to ones that involve cruises and sightseeing excursions on land. All transportation is covered, and every detail is attended to. You can also create a completely customized itinerary to take you wherever your heart desires—the people here are very easy to work with. ☎ 800/742–7669 ⊕ www.newenglandvacationtours.com ✉ Call for prices.

Northeast Unlimited Tours. As the name indicates, Northeast Unlimited's range of itineraries includes New England. The eight-day Taste of New England tour, for example, hits all the highlights from Boston to Maine. ☎ 800/759–6820 ⊕ www.newenglandtours.com ✉ From $1,839.

Wolfe Adventures & Tours. Though Wolfe specializes in group tours, a family can be defined as a group. Themed New England tours include Cape Cod, the American Revolution, and the North Shore. ☎ 888/449–6533 ⊕ www.wolfetours.com ✉ Call for prices.

SKIING

New England Action Sports. Through this outfit you can book day trips, midweek overnights, weekend trips, and weeklong visits to popular ski resorts, including Stowe, Okemo, and Killington. ☎ 800/477–7669 ⊕ www.skitrip.net ✉ From $229.

▌VISITOR INFORMATION

Contacts Maine Office of Tourism. ☎ 888/624-6345 ⊕ www.visitmaine.com. **New Hampshire Division of Travel and Tourism Development.** ☎ 603/271-2665 ⊕ www.visitnh.gov. **Vermont Department of Tourism and Marketing.** ☎ 800/837-6668 ⊕ www.vermontvacation.com.

ONLINE RESOURCES

Online Info Visit New England. ⊕ www.visitnewengland.com. **Yankee.** ⊕ www.yankeemagazine.com/travel.

44 4 4 4 4 4 4 4 4 4 4 4 4 4 4 4

4 4 4 4 4 4 4 4 4 4 4 4 4 4 4 4 4 4 4 4 4 4 4 4 4 4 4 4 4 4 4 4 4 4 4 4 4 4 4 4 4 4 4 4 4 4 4 4 4 4 4 4 4 4 4 4 4 4 4 4 4

INDEX

A

Abbe Museum, 342
Abbot-Spalding House, 213
Acadia Mountain Trail, 349
Acadia National Park and Mount Desert Island, 14, 255, 340–354, 355
dining and lodging, 343–345, 348, 354
shopping, 346
sports and outdoor activities, 345–346, 349–350
visitor information, 340, 348–349
Accommodations, 7, 32, 367–368. ⇨ *See also under specific areas*
Adair Country Inn and Restaurant (NH) ✕▥, 190
Adams Family Farm, 59
Air tours, 345
Air travel, 12, 364
Maine, 231, 257
New Hampshire, 143
Vermont, 51
Albacore Park, 147
Allagash Wilderness Waterway, 249–250
Allenholm Farm, 131
Alton Bay (NH), 163–164
American Flatbread Burlington (VT) ✕, 120
American Flatbread Waitsfield (VT) ✕, 98
American Independence Museum, 157
American Museum of Fly Fishing, 66
Amoskeag Fishways, 214
Amusement parks, 164, 172, 176, 194, 219
Antiques, shopping for
Maine Coast, 298, 333, 359
New Hampshire, 190, 202, 223, 224
Vermont, 65, 70, 118
Apartment and house rentals, 367
Appalachian Mountain Club Maine Wilderness Lodges (ME) ▥, 247
Appalachian Trail, 14, 38, 177–184
Applecrest Farm Orchards, 157
Appledore Island, 150
Arborvine (ME) ✕, 337

Arlington (VT), 64–65
Art museums and galleries
Inland Maine, 237, 244
Maine Coast, 263–264, 277–278, 284–285, 295, 298, 300, 302, 304, 322, 324, 334–335, 337, 346, 359
New Hampshire, 159, 208, 212, 214–215, 225
Vermont, 54, 58, 62, 67, 70, 79, 87, 90, 94, 95, 96, 137, 138
Artist's Bridge, 239
Arts District (Portland, ME), 284–286
Asticou Inn (ME) ▥, 351
ATMs, 370
Attitash Ski Resort, 194

B

Backpacking, 184
Baker Memorial Library, 207
Ballooning, 297
Bangor (ME), 333–335
Bar Harbor (ME), 342–346
Bar Harbor Inn & Spa (ME) ▥, 344
Bartlett (NH), 193–194
Basin Harbor Club (VT) ▥, 130
Bass Harbor (ME), 351, 354
Bass Harbor Head Light, 351, 354
Bass Harbor Light, 314
Bath (ME), 305–307
Baxter State Park, 14, 250
Beaches, 20
Maine Coast, 271, 274, 306–307, 350
New Hampshire, 154, 156, 161, 164, 166, 206
Vermont, 124, 131, 132
Bed-and-breakfasts, 367
Belfast (ME), 331–332
Belknap Mill, 165
Ben & Jerry's Ice Cream Factory, 105
Bennington (VT), 61–64
Bennington Battle Monument, 35, 61–62
Bennington Center for the Arts, 62
Bennington College, 62
Bennington Museum, 62
Bethel (ME), 238–241
Bicycling, 20–21

Inland Maine, 234
Maine Coast, 259, 266, 296, 297, 345
tours, 32, 53, 259
New Hampshire, 143, 145
Vermont, 53, 55, 57, 70, 89, 121, 124–125, 136
Biddeford (ME), 277–280
Billboards, 59
Billings Farm and Museum, 84
Bird-watching
Maine Coast, 300, 338, 339
New Hampshire, 170–171
Vermont, 82, 120
Black Mountain (ski area), 195
Black Trumpet Bistro (NH) ✕, 150–151
Blair Hill Inn (ME) ▥, 247
Blue Hill (ME), 336–337
Blue Hill Peninsula (ME), 255, 335–339
dining and lodging, 336, 337, 339
shopping, 337, 338
sports and outdoor activities, 336, 339
visitor information, 335
Blueberries, 274, 356
Blueberry Hill Inn (VT) ▥, 94
Blueberry Lake Cross-Country and Snowshoeing Center, 99
Boat and ferry travel, 51, 364
Boating, 21
Inland Maine, 236, 243, 248
Maine Coast, 296–297, 319, 324, 326, 329–330, 345
New Hampshire, 146–147, 165, 168, 206
Vermont, 60, 91, 125, 131
Bolton Mountain Resort, 125
Books, shopping for
Maine Coast, 280, 298, 330
New Hampshire, 190
Vermont, 58, 71, 128
Boothbay (ME), 315–316
Bowdoin College Museum of Art, 304
Boyden Valley Winery & Spirits, 117
Boynton-McKay Food Co. (ME) ✕, 327
Brandon (VT), 91, 94–95
Brandon Artists Guild, 94
Brandon Museum at the Stephen A. Douglas Birthplace, 94
Brattleboro (VT), 53–58

PHOTO CREDITS

Front cover: E.J. Johnson Photography/iStockphoto. [Description: Twin lobsters]. 1, William Britten/ iStockphoto. 2, Robert Plotz, iStockphoto. 5, Kindra Clineff. **Chapter 1: Experience Northern New England:** 8–9, Kindra Clineff. 14 (left), Ken Canning/iStockphoto. 14 (top right), Kindra Clineff. 14 (bottom right), iStockphoto. 15 (left), drewthehobbit/Shutterstock. 15 (top center), Kindra Clineff. 15 (bottom center), Kindra Clineff. 15 (top right), T. Markley/Shutterstock. 15 (bottom right), Natalia Bratslavsky/iStockphoto. **Chapter 2: Best Fall Foliage Drives & Road Trips:** 25, Aivoges | Dreamstime. com. 26–27, Ken Canning/iStockphoto. 29 (top left), Michael Krakowiak/iStockphoto. 29 (bottom left), Steffen Foerster Photography/Shutterstock. 29 (top center), Lisa Thornberg/iStockphoto. 29 (bottom center), iStockphoto. 29 (top right), Scott Cramer/iStockphoto. 29 (bottom right), Paul Aniszewski/Shutterstock. 30 (top), Denis Jr. Tangney/iStockphoto. 30 (bottom), Kevin Davidson/iStockphoto. 31, Kindra Clineff. 32, Kindra Clineff. 33, Donland | Dreamstime.com. 34, Heeb Christian / age fotostock. 35, Sarah Kennedy/iStockphoto. 36, Denis Tangney Jr./iStockphoto. 37, iStockphoto. 38, Denis Jr. Tangney/iStockphoto. 39, The Wilhelm Reich Infant Trust. **Chapter 3: Vermont:** 48, Marcio Silva/iStockphoto. 50, S. Greg Panosian/iStockphoto. 57, Kindra Clineff. 67, Hildene. 76, Kindra Clineff. 83, Kindra Clineff. 86, Dale Halbur/iStockphoto. 92–93, S. Greg Panosian/iStockphoto. 99, Kindra Clineff. 101, Fraser Hall / age fotostock. 109, Dennis Curran / age fotostock. 110, Skye Chalmers Photography, inc. 111 (left), Henryk T Kaiser / age fotostock. 111 (right), Hubert Schriebl. 112 (left), Marcio Silva/iStockphoto. 112 (right), Hubert Schriebl. 113, SMUGGLERS' NOTCH RESORT/Ski Vermont. 124, Skye Chalmers/State of Vermont. 129, Kindra Clineff. 133, Alan Copson / age fotostock. 137, Jack Sumberg. **Chapter 4: New Hampshire:** 139, Denis Jr. Tangney/iStockphoto. 140, Denis Jr. Tangney/iStockphoto. 142, Sebastien Cote/iStockphoto. 150, Strawbery Banke Museum. 153, Denis Jr. Tangney/iStockphoto. 162, Denis Tangney Jr./iStockphoto. 167, Kindra Clineff. 170, Roy Rainford / age fotostock. 177 (top), Jerry and Marcy Monkman EcoPhotography.com/Alamy 177 (bottom), Liz Van Steenburgh/Shutterstock. 178, Kindra Clineff. 179, Mike Kautz/AMC. 180 (left and bottom right), nialat/Shutterstock. 180 (top right), RestonImages/Shutterstock. 181 (top left), jadimages/Shutterstock. 181 (bottom left), Ansgar Walk/wikipedia.org. 181 (bottom center), J. Carmichael/ wikipedia.org. 181 (right), rebvt/Shutterstock. 183, Matty Symons/Shutterstock. 184, Danita Delimont / Alamy. 185, Frank Siteman / age fotostock. 198, Appalachianviews | Dreamstime.com. 202, Kenneth C. Zirkel/iStockphoto. 209, Luckydoor | Dreamstime.com. 211, Jet Low/Wikimedia Commons. 216, Currier Museum of Art/ 2005 Jose Martinez. 222, Franz Marc Frei / age fotostock. 225, John Greim / age fotostock. **Chapter 5: Inland Maine:** 227, Reddy | Dreamstime.com. 228, Kenneth C. Zirkel/ iStockphoto. 229, Stephen G Page/iStockphoto. 230, BrendanReals/Shutterstock. 240, D A Horchner / age fotostock. **Chapter 6: Maine Coast:** 253, SuperStock/age fotostock. 254, Denis Jr. Tangney/iStockphoto. 255, Andrea Pelletier/iStockphoto. 256, Aimin Tang/iStockphoto. 261, ARCO/L Weyers / age fotostock. 269, Perry B. Johnson / age fotostock. 277, Oleg Albinsky/iStockphoto. 281, SuperStock/age fotostock. 287, Wolfe photo | Dreamstime.com. 306, Jim Kidd/Alamy. 308, Michael Czosnek/iStockphoto. 309, SuperStock / age fotostock. 310 (left), Maine State Museum. 310 (right), David Cannings-Bushell/iStockphoto. 311, Paul D. Lemke/iStockphoto. 312, Michael Rickard/Shutterstock. 313 (left), Dave Johnston. 313 (top right), Robert Campbell. 313 (bottom right), Casey Jordan. 314 (top), Kenneth Keifer/Shutterstock. 314 (center), Doug Lemke/Shutterstock. 314 (bottom), liz west/wikipedia. org. 318, Raymond Forbes / age fotostock. 328, Kindra Clineff. 343, Kindra Clineff. 352–353, Alan Majchrowicz / age fotostock. 357, Kindra Clineff. Back cover, from left to right: S. Greg Panosian/ iStockphoto; Coleong | Dreamstime.com; Kenneth C. Zirkel/iStockphoto. Spine: cdrin/Shutterstock.